Love & Conquest

Love & Conquest

Personal Correspondence of

Catherine the Great and

Prince Grigory Potemkin

Edited and Translated by Douglas Smith

NORTHERN

ILLINOIS

UNIVERSITY

PRESS

DeKalb

© 2004 by Northern Illinois University Press

Published by the Northern Illinois University Press, DeKalb, Illinois   60115

Manufactured in the United States using acid-free paper

All Rights Reserved

Design by Julia Fauci

Library of Congress Cataloging-in-Publication Data

Catherine II, Empress of Russia, 1729–1796.

[Correspondence. English. Selections]

Love and conquest : personal correspondence of Catherine the Great and Prince

Grigory Potemkin / edited and translated by Douglas Smith.— 1st American ed.

   p.   cm.

Translation of and selections from: Ekaterina II i G.A. Potemkin: Lichnaia perepiska,

1769–1791. Moskva : Nauka, 1997.

Includes bibliographical references and index.

ISBN 0-87580-324-5 (cloth : alk. paper)

   1. Catherine II, Empress of Russia, 1729–1796—Correspondence. 2. Potemkin, Grigorii

Aleksandrovich, kniaz', 1739–1791—Correspondence. 3. Empresses—Russia—

Correspondence. 4. Statesmen—Russia—Correspondence. I. Potemkin, Grigorii

Aleksandrovich, kniaz', 1739–1791. II. Smith, Douglas, 1962– III. Title.

DK170 .A2 2004

947'.063'092—dc22

2003027084

To Stephanie

Letters mingle Soules

—*John Donne*

Contents

Acknowledgments

I would like to thank the following individuals for their help and support in preparing this book: Valery Abel, Aleksandr Bobosov, Stephanie Davis, Valentina Fedorova, Michael Henry Heim, Corbin Houchins, Aleksandr Kamensky, Karen Kettering, Andrei Kurilkin, Tyler Lansford, Vicky Lettmann, Ed Marquand, Michelle Marrese, Gordon and Jacquelyn Miller, Bill Nelson, Aleksandr Ospovat, Kirill Ospovat, Liana Paredes, Sean Pollock, Peter Pozefsky, Kristen Regina, the late Hans Rogger, Simon Sebag Montefiore, Daniel Simhon, Theofanis Stavrou, Gerry Stigberg, Willard Sunderland, Kevin Thomas, Elise Wirtschafter, Olga Yeliseeva, and Andrei Zorin. At Northern Illinois University Press, I wish to thank Mary Lincoln, Sarah Atkinson, Susan Bean, Barbara Berg, Julia Fauci, and the rest of the staff for their conscientiousness and professionalism. Sandra Batalden, the book's editor, offered many fine suggestions.

Sofiya Yuzefpolskaya went over every letter in this book—word by word, line by line—checking my translation against the original. Her superb knowledge of Russian and English and great linguistic sensitivity improved these translations immeasurably. I owe her the most profound gratitude. I am also grateful to John T. Alexander, Simon Dixon, Aleksei Kovalchuk, Gary Marker, Ronald Vroon, and Laura Wolfson for reading the translation and offering invaluable comments.

This book would never have been possible without the cooperation of Viacheslav Lopatin, the world's leading authority on Potemkin, whose landmark edition of the correspondence inspired me to undertake this translation. I am most grateful to him and his wife, Natalya, for the enthusiasm with which they greeted me and my idea for such a book. Finally, Stephanie Ellis-Smith has offered many suggestions and constant encouragement during several years' work on this book. It is dedicated to her with love and gratitude.

Introduction

Catherine the Great, Prince Grigory Potemkin,
and Their Correspondence

arly in the evening of 12 October 1791, as Catherine the Great and her court were preparing for that night's ball in the Hermitage, a courier galloped up to St. Petersburg's Winter Palace bearing an urgent letter for the empress. The courier, dressed in black and exhausted after a full week's ride from the Moldavian capital of Jassy, had been sent by Vasily Popov, head of Prince Grigory Potemkin's chancellery, to deliver the dreaded news: "Your Most Gracious Majesty," Popov wrote, "we have been struck a blow. His Highness Prince Grigory Aleksandrovich is no longer among the living."[1]

Word of Potemkin's death devastated the empress. She had been anxiously following his failing condition during the preceding weeks and had tried her best to hold out some hope for recovery. Now he was no more. Catherine broke down in tears. She complained that there was no time to prepare anyone to replace him and that she now had no one she could lean upon. Overcome by grief, she was bled by her doctors and put to bed. She arose in the early hours of the thirteenth to pour out her despair in a letter to her longtime correspondent, Baron Friedrich Melchior Grimm:

> A terrible, crushing blow struck me yesterday. After dinner around six in the evening, a courier brought me the mournful news that my pupil, my friend, one might say my idol, Prince

> Potemkin-Tavrichesky has died after about a month's illness in Moldavia! You have no idea of the extent of my affliction. He combined a sublime understanding and an unusually expansive spirit with a superior heart. His ideas were always grand and lofty. He was extraordinarily benevolent, very knowledgeable, and uniquely kind. New ideas were forever taking shape in his head; no one ever had such a gift for witticism or for saying just the right thing. He displayed staggering military talent in this war—not once did he make a mistake, be it on land or sea. No one led him, but he had a rare ability to lead others. In a word, he was a man of state, who could both advise and execute. He was passionately, fervently devoted to me: he would quarrel and become angry when he felt matters had not been carried out as they ought. . . . He had, however, yet another rare quality that distinguished him from all other men: bravery filled not only his heart, but his mind and soul as well. As a result, we always understood each other and did not pay any attention to the talk of those whose thoughts did not measure up to ours. In my opinion, Potemkin was a great man, who did not carry out even half of what he was capable.[2]

With the death of Potemkin, Catherine lost her closest advisor and Russia, arguably, its greatest statesman. Catherine and Potemkin had known each other for nearly three decades and had ruled Russia together for some seventeen years. Potemkin had been her rescuing knight, her confidant, ablest administrator, and warlord. Catherine had been his beloved sovereign, his protector, and the benefactress from whom all his blessings flowed. They had been lovers and most likely husband and wife. They were one of the most uncommon royal couples in history. To quote Potemkin's biographer, "Their love affair and political alliance was unequalled in history by Antony and Cleopatra, Louis XVI and Marie-Antoinette, Napoleon and Josephine, because it was as remarkable for its achievements as its romance, as endearing for its humanity as for its power."[3]

Catherine and Potemkin's story is told by the remarkable correspondence they shared for twenty-two years, from 1769 until 1791. Their letters are at once an intimate record of their private lives and a chronicle of Russian political, diplomatic, and military history. As a record of their personal affairs, the letters show Catherine and Potemkin at their most unguarded moments. We are privy to their tender expressions of love, their intimate confessions, and their frequent quarrels. In their letters we encounter a moving love story, both timeless and universal. As a historical document, the letters present a unique window onto the conduct of politics in the Russia of Catherine the Great. In their correspondence, Catherine and Potemkin discuss most of the major events of her reign, including the First and Second Russo-Turkish wars, the Pugachev Rebellion, and the annexation of the Crimea, as well as events of broader European and world-historical significance, such as the partitions of Poland, the American War of Independence, and the French Revolution.

Potemkin was at Catherine's side from the beginning of her reign, having participated in the coup d'état that put her on the throne in June 1762. With time she came to learn of this ambitious young officer in her service and raised him from obscurity to the height of great power. He became a field marshal, president of the War College, commander in chief of the Russian armed forces, grand admiral of the Black Sea and Caspian fleets, grand hetman of the Black Sea and Yekaterinoslav Cossacks, prince of the Holy Roman Empire, and chevalier of many Russian and foreign orders. As the governor-general of several provinces—New Russia, Azov, Astrakhan, Saratov, Yekaterinoslav, and Tauride—Potemkin was Catherine's viceroy for all of southern Russia. He was known as "His Most Serene Highness" or "Serenissimus" or simply "The Prince," as if there were only one.[4]

A gigantic figure of immense talent and energy, Potemkin truly was larger than life. He was the sort of man who gives birth to such clichés, to great myths and legends. The Austrian soldier and wit Prince de Ligne, acquainted with several crowned heads including Catherine, Frederick the Great, and later Napoleon, called Potemkin "the most extraordinary man I ever met":

> What is his magic? Genius, and then genius, and again genius; natural intelligence, an excellent memory, elevation of soul, malice without malignity, craft without cunning, a happy mixture of caprices, of which the good when they are uppermost win him all hearts; great generosity, grace, and justice in his rewards, much tact, the talent of divining that which he does not know, and great knowledge of men.[5]

Catherine, too, recognized Potemkin's genius, and it was for this reason that she invested him with so much power and relied so heavily upon him. They formed an effective partnership that brought about some of her reign's greatest achievements. Most significantly, Catherine and Potemkin furthered Russia's ascent to the status of a world power, which Peter the Great had begun in such dramatic fashion at the beginning of the century. Over eight million square miles of new territory were added to the empire in the second half of the century during what has been dubbed Russia's "golden age of imperialism."[6] Much of this expansion came as a result of the annexation of the Crimea and the wars against the Turks in which Potemkin played a defining role. Potemkin was indispensable in extending Russia's southern border to the Black Sea and in projecting Russian influence into the Balkans and the Caucasus. Today he is perhaps best remembered for the so-called Greek Project, the grand scheme to crush the Ottoman Empire, liberate Constantinople from the Muslims, and seat Catherine's grandson Constantine on the throne of a new Christian kingdom, that Potemkin had helped to develop.[7]

◆ ◆ ◆

On 13 September 1739, in the small village of Chizhevo near the town of Smolensk, Daria Potemkina gave birth to her third child, a boy. Shortly before his birth, Daria is said to have had a prophetic dream in which the sun fell from the sky and landed on her belly, a portent of the remarkable son she was about to bring into the world.[8] Potemkin was born into an oppressive, joyless household. His father, Aleksandr, a boorish figure, was a retired veteran of the wars of Peter the Great and came from the middling rungs of the provincial nobility.[9]

There is precious little in Potemkin's heritage or early boyhood to suggest the greatness in store for him. The Potemkin clan was neither rich nor powerful. Occupying the borderlands between Poland and Muscovy, the Potemkins had served at the courts and in the armies of both kingdoms, though without discernible distinction, until the seventeenth century when they began serving Muscovy exclusively. It is interesting to note that to a very large extent the borderlands of the Russian Empire remained Potemkin's home for life: he was born on the western fringes of Russia, won early praise fighting the Turks in the south, made his name and achieved his greatest glory extending her borders and developing her southern regions. It is only fitting that he died and was buried there. The experience of coming from the borderlands shaped his identity in important ways. The mixed Russo-Polish world in which he was born made him sensitive to the question of national identity and allowed him to think of himself as belonging to both groups. Although Potemkin exhibited a strong Russian patriotism, whose fervor was perhaps in part an act of overcompensating for his mixed heritage, he also considered himself a Pole. He was a multiculturalist *avant la lettre,* who not only surrounded himself with representatives of various nationalities and ethnic groups but also borrowed from them.[10]

Young Grigory spent the first five or so years of his life in Chizhevo. His godfather, Grigory Kislovsky, retired president of the College of State Revenues (*Kamer-kollegiia*), took pity on the boy and brought him to live with his own family in Moscow around 1745. Potemkin was initially enrolled in a private school in the German quarter and then transferred to the gymnasium attached to Moscow University. He quickly displayed uncommon intellectual gifts, excelling in Greek, Latin, German, and French, and showing a particularly strong interest in ecclesiastical history and theology. In 1757, Ivan Shuvalov, director of Moscow University and favorite of Empress Elizabeth, selected a dozen of the best pupils to come to St. Petersburg for presentation to the tsaritsa. Potemkin was among them.[11]

This was Potemkin's first trip to the capital, and the glittering splendor of the imperial court made a strong and lasting impression on the young man from the provinces. Until then Potemkin had been thinking of devoting his life to the church, but upon returning to Moscow the previously diligent student began to neglect his studies and skip classes, and in 1760 he was expelled from the university. Potemkin's eyes were set on a military career in the Guards regiments, the elite forces that played a crucial role in the political life of eighteenth-century Russia. Potemkin had been enrolled in the Horse Guards Regiment in 1755 at the age of sixteen, and like other young noblemen at the time was moved up the ranks despite being a full-time student. Shortly after his expulsion from the university, Potemkin borrowed five hundred rubles from a friend to pay for his way to Petersburg and set out for the capital in 1761.[12]

Although Russia was then fighting Prussia in the Seven Years' War (1756–1763), Potemkin did not go to the front but instead joined the staff of Prince Georg-Ludwig of Holstein, uncle of Grand Duke Peter Fyodorovich. On 25 December, not long after Potemkin arrived in the capital, Empress Elizabeth died, and her nephew the grand duke was proclaimed Tsar Peter III. Almost immediately, Peter pulled Russia out of the war against Prussia, thereby saving Frederick the Great from defeat but turning many of the Russian officers against their own tsar. Next, Peter began a series of unpopular and poorly conceived reforms that alienated crucial elements of Russian society—the church, senior officialdom, and, most importantly, the military.[13]

By the spring of 1762, a conspiracy was underway to remove Peter from the throne. The key figure in the plot was the tsar's wife, Grand Duchess Yekaterina Alekseevna, the future Catherine the Great. Catherine had been born Sophia Augusta Fredericka, princess of Anhalt-Zerbst, in Stettin on the Baltic Sea on 21 April (2 May) 1729. In January 1744, Empress Elizabeth invited the young girl to Russia as the prospective bride for Grand Duke Peter. Sophia and the grand duke were second cousins and her uncle, Prince Karl August of Holstein-Gottorp, had been engaged to Elizabeth before dying of smallpox in 1727 prior to their wedding.[14] Sophia arrived in Russia in the winter of 1744. Even as a girl in her early teens, she showed signs of the great political skill that would characterize her life and reign. She made certain to charm the grand duke and Elizabeth, who immediately gave her blessing to the marriage, and set to work learning the language, religion, and customs of her new home. On 28 June, Sophia converted to Orthodoxy and abandoned her given name for Yekaterina (Catherine) Alekseevna. She and Peter wed the following summer.

The two were a poor match, and the initial warmth that existed between Catherine and Peter did not last long. Catherine was repulsed by her husband's childish antics and crude manners, and Peter preferred the company of men to that of his wife. It was during these years that Catherine began a series of love affairs. In 1752, she took as her lover a handsome, young chamberlain named Sergei Saltykov. Her decision was motivated only in part by a personal desire for love: just as important was her need to produce an heir to the throne, which with her cold, sexually stunted husband she had failed to do after seven years of marriage. Finally, in 1754, Catherine gave birth to a healthy son, Grand Duke Paul Petrovich. The question of who was Paul's father—Saltykov or Grand Duke Peter—has been a matter of speculation ever since Paul's birth, although most historians now agree that it was most likely the former.[15] Saltykov was sent abroad after Paul's birth, and the following year Catherine took a new lover, the dashing aristocrat and future king of Poland, Stanislaw Poniatowski, a member of the entourage of the British envoy, Sir Charles Hanbury Williams. Their affair lasted three years until Poniatowski was forced to depart St. Petersburg under a cloud of suspicion during the Seven Years' War in 1758.[16]

Two years later Catherine took a new lover, Grigory Orlov. Endowed with exceptional stature and strength, which he combined with good looks, a cheerful manner, and a reckless love of adventure, Orlov was famous throughout Petersburg for his sexual conquests, and it is not at all surprising that Catherine fell for this bear of a man not long after he was admitted to the young court of the grand duke and duchess. Her actions, however, were driven by more than womanly desire. Orlov was a war hero, a former lieutenant in the elite Izmailovsky Guards Regiment. He and his brothers commanded great respect among their fellow regimental officers in St. Petersburg. Moreover, the Orlov brothers were brave and ambitious. Catherine needed such men behind her since she may have begun to fear for her position after Elizabeth's death. Grand Duke Peter's growing disdain for his wife was no secret, and he had been heard to speak of wanting to lock Catherine up in a convent so that he could marry his mistress, Yelizaveta Vorontsova. After Peter ascended the throne the rumors that he was plotting to have Catherine arrested and sent away to a convent only grew. There was also talk that her son, Grand Duke Paul, was to be disinherited. As her situation became ever more precarious, Catherine, the Orlovs, and a few of their intimates began plotting their own coup.[17]

Early on the morning of 28 June 1762, Catherine was awakened by Aleksei Orlov, Grigory's brother, who had galloped to Peterhof outside the capital to inform her that one of their fellow conspirators had been arrested. After some hesitation, the Orlovs, and then Catherine too, decided it was time to act. Catherine jumped in her carriage and hurried back to St. Petersburg, stopping outside the city at the barracks of the Izmailovsky Guards Regiment. As she alighted, Catherine was surrounded by a mob of cheering soldiers. Minutes later she was proclaimed empress. The armed forces of Petersburg soon followed in expressing their support for Catherine. Peter, who had managed to destroy the foundations of his power in a few short months, fell victim to his own ill-conceived actions. But for his mistress and a small band of supporters, he was abandoned by everyone. The deposed tsar was arrested the next day and held at the nearby estate of Ropsha. He was murdered there on 6 July under what remain to this day mysterious circumstances.[18]

Grigory Potemkin was among the guardsmen who put Catherine on the throne. In a letter to Catherine from Ropsha dated 2 July, Aleksei Orlov makes reference to "a certain Sergeant-Major Potiomkin [*sic*]" as one of the men worthy of reward for his actions during the coup.[19] A month later, Catherine wrote Stanislaw Poniatowski of the recent events and did not fail to mention the "fine judgment, courage and dispatch of a seventeen-year-old petty officer by the name of Potemkin."[20] The list of rewards for the conspirators drawn up shortly thereafter begins with the Orlov brothers and ends with Potemkin. And when his commanders recommended Potemkin for promotion to the rank of cornet, Catherine herself objected, promoting him further up the ranks to that of second-lieutenant.[21] The evidence suggests that Potemkin played a not insignificant role in Catherine's coup. Although he clearly wasn't among the chief conspirators, his actions did single him out from the mass of soldiers who rushed to Catherine's side. Indeed, the fact that despite his modest rank Potemkin managed to distinguish himself suggests something of the ambition, courage, and sense of purpose that would mark him in the coming years.

On 30 November 1762, Potemkin was made a gentleman-of-the-bedchamber and was permitted to join the empress's intimate circle of courtiers. Catherine did not fail to take notice of the new man in her presence. Not unlike Grigory Orlov, Potemkin was tall, broad-shouldered, and powerfully built. His somewhat oblong head bore a long, aquiline nose that ended above a smallish mouth. Bright blue eyes sparkled against his pale complexion. His hair was a thick, luxuriant light brown. He added to this a marvelous sense of humor and considerable learning that appeared all the more profound when viewed alongside Orlov's limited education. The wits of the day called Potemkin "Alcibiades," a reference to the Athenian politician famous for his remarkable looks, talent, and ambition.[22] In 1763, a mysterious illness caused Potemkin to go blind in his right eye, which although it temporarily shattered the cocksure Potemkin did little to mar his beguiling appearance.[23]

Not much is known about Potemkin's relationship with Catherine in the years immediately following her accession to the throne. Sometime in late summer 1762, Potemkin was apparently sent to Sweden to inform Russia's ambassador there of the change of government. In August 1763,

Catherine appointed Potemkin assistant to the chief procurator of the Holy Synod, the state body that administered the Orthodox Church.[24] It was around this time, having been overcome by melancholy over the loss of sight in his right eye, that Potemkin supposedly left court and abandoned society for a year and a half. He lived a recluse, seeing no one, allowing his hair and beard to grow long, studying theology and contemplating becoming a monk. While the story cannot be proven, based on what is known of Potemkin's later life—his crippling depressions, deeply felt religious sensibility, and desire to flee the world when overcome by tragedy—it does ring true.[25] Catherine may well have been the one who called Potemkin back to court. Since being made gentleman-of-the-bedchamber, Potemkin had impressed the empress with his wit, learning, and sense of humor; she was particularly taken by his rare gift for mimicry. Catherine no doubt missed her amusing young courtier, and made certain he returned to her side.

When the Legislative Commission created by Catherine to draft a new Russian law code convened in 1767 in Moscow, Potemkin was present as one of the so-called Guardians of the Tatars and other Exotic Peoples and as a member of the sub-commission on civil and religious matters. In September 1768, Potemkin was promoted to the rank of chamberlain and two months later was permanently removed from the military ranks upon Catherine's order.[26]

Although he had managed to establish a place for himself at court, Potemkin remained committed to the military, which was to be his true home for the rest of his life. Throughout the early 1760s, Potemkin continued to serve in the Horse Guards, eventually reaching the rank of major-general. Not long after the beginning of the First Russo-Turkish War, Potemkin volunteered for active duty. In January 1769, Major-General of the Cavalry Potemkin received the empress's permission to quit the Legislative Commission and leave for the army. Shortly thereafter Potemkin departed St. Petersburg for the front, where he wrote Catherine the first letter in what was to become a life-long correspondence.[27]

◆ ◆ ◆

After Potemkin's death, Catherine wrote Vasily Popov to bundle up the prince's papers and letters and bring them to her in St. Petersburg. Popov arrived in the capital from Jassy on 12 January 1792. Catherine, with tears in her eyes, took the letters from him, locked them up in a special box together with the letters from Potemkin she had received over the years, and hid the key. It is most likely that during her remaining years, Catherine took out the letters on occasion and read them over, possibly destroying those containing secrets she wished to take with her to the grave. Upon her death, all of the documents in her study were gathered and hastily leafed through in the search for anything of importance for the new emperor. Some letters may have been lost or destroyed at this time as well.[28]

For many years thereafter, Russia's tsars kept the correspondence a secret, just as they did Catherine's *Memoirs*. Nevertheless, copies of some of the letters were made (frequently not very accurate) and circulated from hand to hand. In 1834, some of the letters were placed along with other "secret letters" in the State Archive of the Ministry of Foreign Affairs, while the rest remained in the tsars' personal library in the Winter Palace. In 1841, when Nicholas I read Catherine's "Sincere Confession" (Letter 4), he was so shocked he ordered it locked in a secret cabinet where it lay undisturbed for fifty-seven years until a copy was made for inclusion in the publication of Catherine's collected writings.[29]

It was not until the latter decades of the nineteenth century that the letters started to appear in print. Beginning in 1874, academician Yakov Grot published several hundred letters and notes, though none of the intimate letters, in three volumes of the *Collections of the Imperial Russian Historical Society*.[30] And in 1876, the historian and publisher Mikhail Semevsky printed over two hundred letters from the years 1782–1791 in his monthly *Russian Antiquity*.[31] Five years later, Semevsky published ninety-one anonymous love letters under the intentionally misleading title "The Language of Love One Hundred Years Ago. Excerpts from the Letters of an Unknown Lady."[32] In his introduction, Semevsky sought to carry out an overt act of historical obfuscation by implying that the letters belonged to Praskovia Potemkina, Potemkin's onetime mistress and the wife of his second cousin Pavel Potemkin. Six years earlier, Semevsky had published several *billets-doux* from Potemkin to Praskovia, and these intimate scribblings were presented as her responses.[33] Semevsky knew, however, that these letters sprang neither from the pen of Praskovia nor from any mere "unknown lady," but were in fact composed by Catherine the Great herself. His disingenuous presentation of the letters and the artful editing that removed or camouflaged obvious references capable of betraying their true author allowed Semevsky to sneak them past the censors. Russian *dix-huitièmistes*, however, recognized these as Catherine's love letters to Potemkin.[34]

In the closing years of the nineteenth century, scholar Yakov Barskov was asked to catalogue the documents of the Romanovs' palace archive. Barskov was granted access to a great quantity of long-secret papers, including Catherine's correspondence with Potemkin. Although Barskov managed to publish a few of these letters in an edition of Catherine's collected works in 1907, tsarist censorship, even as late as 1917, prohibited a complete, unedited publication of Catherine's love letters.[35] In the early 1930s, Barskov attempted to publish his edition of Catherine's intimate letters in *Literary Heritage*. The letters and Barskov's commentary were accepted for publication and had been set in page proofs when they were rejected at the last moment, apparently in the autumn of 1933. The proofs were then acquired by Vladimir Bonch-Bruevich, Bolshevik revolutionary, comrade of Lenin, and later director of Moscow's Literary Museum. Bonch-Bruevich tried to publish them twice, first in the publication *Links* and later in the Literary Museum's *Annals,* both times without success. They ended up in Bonch-Bruevich's personal archive where they remained unpublished for over fifty years.[36]

Why was Barskov unable to publish Catherine's letters? According to Bonch-Bruevich, the problem lay with Barskov's "apolitical" introduction, which did not adequately reveal "all that vileness and desolation" the good Bolshevik believed characterized the court of "the great fornicatress." He held out hope for publication, but only if the letters were accompanied by the appropriate, political commentary that he himself had intended (in vain) to write one day. As for *Literary Heritage,* according to one of the editors, the letters were dropped from publication because they supposedly lacked any literary or historical significance.[37]

Such opinions reflected the thinking of the Soviet historical profession at the time, which held that the personal documents of Russia's tsars and tsaritsas had value only if they shed light on the life and work of officially approved writers and thinkers (Aleksandr Radishchev or Nikolai Novikov, for example) or if they served to expose the evils of the tsarist state.[38] According to this standard, Catherine's most intimate, personally revealing writings did not warrant publication.

In 1934, however, French journalist and historian Georges Oudard published in Paris an abridged French translation of the letters along with his own introduction. All references to the letters' editorial history were erased, and Oudard made no mention of how he came by them.[39] Writing in the émigré weekly *Illustrated Russia* that same year, Anna Kashina-Yevreinova, the translator of the letters, commented that Oudard had come across the letters during one of his trips to the Soviet Union and brought them back with him to publish in France.[40]

The question of how Oudard came across the letters is an intriguing one that aroused the curiosity of the Soviet authorities. In March 1937, an unsolicited denunciation landed on the desk of comrade Pastukhov of the People's Commissariat for Foreign Affairs. The denunciation, sent by a junior colleague of Pastukhov, one Adamov, contained a report of a recent conversation Adamov had had with a Russian literary scholar in which he learned that about a year and half earlier a journalist from the newspaper *Paris Soir* had visited Leningrad and shortly after his return home had published a French translation of Catherine the Great's intimate letters to Grigory Potemkin. Adamov went on to report that in the translation the scholar Yakov Barskov had recognized his own work, which he had himself been preparing for publication. Moreover, Adamov's source told him that the original letters had reportedly gone missing.

Within days various official agencies—including the NKVD, precursor to the KGB—were involved in the case. A quick search turned up the letters still intact in the State Archive, and a story of how they came to be published in Paris was put together based on the testimony of Ilia Zilbershtein, founder of *Literary Heritage,* and a man by the name of Umansky, a member of the Soviet Literary Agency. According to their testimony, Oudard had traveled to Moscow for the purpose of buying copies of the letters from one comrade Koltsev, and as a result of the sale Barskov's edition of the letters never saw publication. The authorities deemed the sale of the letters to a foreigner to have been "undoubtedly disadvantageous and politically incorrect," and a call went out to punish those responsible. Although no one appears to have suffered as a result of the affair, Koltsev did later wind up in an NKVD torture-chamber, but probably not for his role in the Oudard affair. Barskov's role in the entire business is unclear. It is possible that fearing he might not live to see the letters printed in the Soviet Union, he sold or gave them to Oudard to publish in the West (as the head of the Soviet archival administration suspected), on the provision that his name not be attached to them. The part played by the editors of *Literary Heritage* has also not been fully explained. Perhaps they had intended to publish Barskov's work, until the opportunity to make some easy money off a sale to an interested Oudard unexpectedly presented itself.[41]

It was not until 1989, over half a century after his initial attempt to publish the letters, that Barskov's edition, in modified form, finally appeared in the Soviet Union in the journal *Problems of History.* Some twenty years earlier, the historian Natan Eidelman had been working in the archive of the then Lenin Library in Moscow when he happened across Barskov's page proofs in Bonch-Bruevich's papers. Eidelman hastily made a copy for himself, which he tucked away until the political thaw of the Gorbachev years made publication possible.[42]

Over a decade earlier, in 1978, another Russian scholar, Viacheslav Lopatin, began work on compiling what was to be the most complete collection of Catherine and Potemkin's correspondence. Lopatin spent over a decade combing Russian archives in search of every personal letter the two exchanged. In 1997, almost twenty years after he began his work, Lopatin published his magisterial, densely annotated *Catherine II and G. A. Potemkin. Their Personal Correspondence, 1769–1791,* containing 1,162 notes and letters, hundreds of which had never before been published. As the subtitle states, Lopatin's work contains chiefly the "personal" correspondence—as much as it can be separated from the official communications, of which approximately 60 or 70 percent had already been published.[43] This English edition of the correspondence comprising 464 letters is based directly upon Lopatin's work.

The correspondence can be conceived of as resembling a fifty-pound dumbbell with the bulk of the letters forming two weighty blocks, one from the early years of the relationship during Potemkin's favor (1774–1776) and the other from the final years of Potemkin's life, which coincided with the Second Russo-Turkish War (1787–1791); the intervening eleven years—the dumbbell's handle—between these two periods of intense correspondence produced relatively few letters.[44] The correspondence comprises four distinct periods. The first, and smallest in terms of output, from May 1769 to February 1774, covers the period of Catherine and Potemkin's coming together and consists of no more than a handful of letters, depending on how they are dated. The second, and largest, covers the years of the love affair and break-up (late February 1774–1776) and numbers approximately 470 notes and letters. The overwhelming majority of these (all but approximately thirty-five) belong to Catherine, a regrettable result of the fact that whereas Potemkin saved Catherine's letters, she burned his after having read them. From this period, the letters of Potemkin that have survived are the ones he typically saved after Catherine scrawled her reply on his letters and returned them. The third and sparsest period runs from January 1777 to mid–August 1787, for which 331 letters are extant, an average of about thirty letters a year. Based on information in Catherine's letters from this period, it has been estimated that approximately forty of Potemkin's letters have been lost.[45] The final group (382 letters) begins with the outbreak of the Second Russo-Turkish War in August 1787 and ends with Potemkin's death in October 1791.

Perhaps the greatest challenge in editing the correspondence has to do with the problem of dating. Hundreds of the letters are undated, thus making it difficult—and frequently impossible—to be certain when they were written. The problem has been complicated by the fact that the letters have been repeatedly handled over the past two centuries, apparently with little regard for keeping them in sequence. As a result, any chronological order one gives to the letters and, consequently, any interpretations based on such an order are open to question. The dating of the letters is most problematic for the years of Potemkin's favor. While the letters attest to the passionate, tumultuous nature of Catherine and Potemkin's affair, the lack of precise details surrounding the composition of their letters and the sequence in which they were written makes it impossible to reconstruct with any degree of specificity the course of their love. What remains of their letters presents a static impression of these years more than a clearly unfolding story. Undated letters from later years, on the other hand, which are generally filled with references to specific events, can be dated with much greater confidence, although not in every instance.[46]

The *billets-doux* penned during Catherine and Potemkin's affair were personal in the sense that they chiefly expressed their authors' intimate thoughts and feelings and were private, never intended for anyone's eyes but their own. This explains why so few of Potemkin's letters from these years have survived. Catherine succinctly stated why she chose to destroy correspondence written to her in a note penned to a later favorite, Pyotr Zavadovsky: "I am throwing your letter in the fire to preserve your honor."[47] Catherine apparently burned not only Zavadovsky's and Potemkin's letters, but frequently any letters of her own that were returned to her, as well as letters she received from other correspondents. This penchant for destruction was perhaps a result of lessons learned as grand duchess at the court of Elizabeth when her private mail was routinely opened and read, both with and without her knowledge. Catherine appears not to have destroyed her later correspondence with Potemkin, notably the letters exchanged during the Crimean crisis (1782–1783) and the Second Russo-Turkish War, letters that contained much information on politics and statecraft. It is known that after Catherine read Potemkin's letters from these years, she usually handed them over to Count Aleksandr Bezborodko—one of her closest advisors—for consultation, because they contained considerable information of state importance. This explains why the letters from these periods form a more complete whole.[48]

Unlike the small scraps of paper with their scribbled messages carried back and forth throughout the palace by a valet, the letters Catherine and Potemkin wrote each other during the war against the Ottoman Turks were sent as part of large parcels of written material including various rescripts, reports, communiqués from Russian counsels abroad, copies of letters from foreign crowned heads, and intercepted communications of foreign ambassadors. Potemkin would send these parcels to his steward in St. Petersburg, Mikhail Garnovsky, who together with Potemkin's courier then brought the documents to Count Bezborodko. Bezborodko either handed the documents to Catherine himself or instructed that they be given to Aleksandr Dmitriev-Mamonov, her favorite at the time, for him to present. The privilege of handing the prince's letters to the empress was an important one, for it afforded the opportunity to discuss the letters and learn of their contents and the empress's reaction. When Catherine wrote to Potemkin, both Bezborodko and Mamonov frequently had access to the letters before they were handed over to Garnovsky. Indeed, Catherine often gave her letters to Mamonov before they were sealed and permitted him to read and discuss them with her. On rare occasions, her favorite was even able to influence what she wrote to Potemkin.[49]

The correspondence between Catherine and Potemkin became the focus of considerable attention among the factions at court. The prince's enemies sought to learn what was being communicated in order to undermine Potemkin's authority. If they could glean information on what he was reporting from the front, they could try to refute it or at least subject it to some doubt by supplying contradictory information. The prince's men, on the other hand, sought to ensure the smooth, regular flow of letters between Potemkin and the empress and to block information from outside sources from reaching Catherine. When they sensed tension between Catherine and Potemkin, they would often work to calm the rough waters.

The outbreak of the war with the Porte in late summer 1787 was a difficult time for Catherine. She fretted over Potemkin's poor health and the deep depression that had taken hold of him. In desperation she waited for news from him. Mamonov responded by telling Garnovsky to write to Vasily Popov to request that he write directly to Mamonov of affairs in the south so that Mamonov might keep the empress better informed and, consequently, seek to ease her worries concerning Potemkin. When, on 25 September, Catherine received a letter from Potemkin dated the nineteenth in which he requested permission to give up command and come to St. Petersburg, she became furious and sat down to pen an angry reply. Mamonov realized that such a letter might produce regrettable consequences and tried to calm Catherine. He dissuaded her from her original idea and instead helped her to craft a gentle, encouraging response intended to convince the despondent Potemkin to stay with the army (Letters 322, 325). Mamonov recounted the entire scene to Garnovsky, who wrote Popov to tell Potemkin what had happened. In so doing, Mamonov sought to portray himself as working on the behalf of his patron, Potemkin. His words were carefully chosen to prove to Potemkin his loyalty and the important role he played in defending the prince's place with the empress. His motivation, however, may well have been less noble. According to Count Bezborodko, Mamonov's main goal was to keep Potemkin away from court so as to strengthen his own position.[50]

Catherine would on occasion avail herself of Potemkin's steward as a way of conveying information that she did not wish to write to him directly. On 24 September 1787, a despondent Potemkin wrote to Field Marshal Rumiantsev, then commander of the Ukrainian Army, of his terrible condition and his wish to hand over command to him. Rumiantsev betrayed Potemkin's trust by making a copy of the letter and sending it to Pyotr Zavadovsky, one of the prince's enemies at court, who promptly communicated it to his supporters. The news quickly spread and did considerable damage to Potemkin's reputation back in St. Petersburg. Catherine was upset at the prince's lack of discretion, yet she was hesitant to inform him of this in writing, fearful that the highly sensitive prince might take it as a reprimand. Thus, she told Mamonov of her displeasure and of Potemkin's need for greater caution, and had him convey this to Garnovsky. Potemkin's steward wrote the prince of what Mamonov had told him, and in this way softened Catherine's words and gave them the more palatable appearance of a piece of advice from someone who shared both their confidences.[51]

Until October 1787, Count Bezborodko, whose many titles included director of the postal department and reporter (*dokladchik*) of the College of Foreign Affairs, maintained for himself the privilege of presenting Catherine with Potemkin's letters. Yet when Bezborodko learned that disaster had struck Russia's Black Sea fleet in September, he sensed in the terrible news Potemkin's imminent fall from grace. Seeking to disassociate himself from Potemkin, Bezborodko reported ill on 2 October and ordered that henceforth Mamonov be charged with bringing the prince's mail to the empress. But when news arrived from the south in mid-October of the Russian victory at Kinburn, Bezborodko reversed his decision and tried to win back the privilege he had handed over to Mamonov. A struggle ensued between the count and Mamonov, who did not wish to relinquish the honor bestowed upon him. With the help of Garnovsky, Mamonov eventually won out, and from then on Catherine handed over her letters for Potemkin directly to Mamonov. He would then summon Garnovsky to collect them from his personal chambers in the palace; Mamonov made certain to leave Catherine's letters unsealed so Garnovsky could see that he was fully informed of what was being communicated between Catherine and the prince. He knew, of course, that Garnovsky would pass this information on to Potemkin.[52]

While Mamonov was not above seeking to enhance his own position at the expense of Potemkin's, nevertheless he did not actively seek to harm Potemkin and played a useful role in sharing information about the empress with Garnovsky. It came as a blow therefore when Potemkin learned in May 1789 of Mamonov's dismissal. On 21 June, the same day Garnovsky sent Potemkin a report on Mamonov's fall from grace, Catherine dispatched a special courier, Nikolai Saltykov, with a secret letter about the affair for the prince. The choice of Saltykov was significant for two reasons: first, Saltykov was no friend of Potemkin's, and second, Saltykov happened to be the patron of Platon Zubov, Catherine's latest and final favorite, whom she had chosen to replace Mamonov without bothering to consult Potemkin. The appearance of Zubov meant that groups opposed to Potemkin would now have direct access to his correspondence with the empress and that he could no longer rely on the favorite to pass on information through Garnovsky. Indeed, Catherine intentionally kept Garnovsky in the dark about the letter she sent with Saltykov, and Garnovsky happened to learn of it by chance from one of her valets.[53]

With Mamonov's dismissal, Potemkin's letters were once again delivered to Catherine by Bezborodko, perhaps upon the insistence of both the prince and Garnovsky, who trusted Bezborodko more than the new favorite. As Russia's postmaster general, Bezborodko already possessed excellent means for gathering information, and the return of the privilege of presenting Potemkin's letters strengthened his hand. When a military postal system was established during the war, Bezborodko became less dependent on Potemkin and other military officers in the field for news of the war effort. The postal director's officer intercepted the letters of foreign volunteers, and this gave Bezborodko a very good idea of what was transpiring in Potemkin's army. Potemkin knew of Bezborodko's access to information and wisely duplicated for him much of the material he sent to Catherine in an effort to maintain the count's trust and support. While some of the prince's men at court feared that the information Bezborodko was passing on to Catherine might undermine or contradict that coming from Potemkin, this does not appear to have been the case. In fact, the information Bezborodko was gleaning from his various sources tended to confirm what he was receiving from Potemkin, thus giving it greater currency with Catherine.[54]

Wishing to cultivate warm relations between Zubov and Potemkin, Catherine encouraged her new favorite to write to the prince. She would place her letters to Potemkin inside those from Zubov, just as she had earlier done with Mamonov's letters to Potemkin, and these would then be folded to form an envelope enclosing the two. The letters typically remained with the favorite in his chambers for a few days before Garnovsky was called to fetch them. This allowed Zubov and his supporters the opportunity to acquaint themselves with Catherine's letters to Potemkin. Zubov did not stop there, however, but even tried to flatter his way into Garnovsky's good graces in the hope of extracting from him details of Potemkin's correspondence with other individuals.[55]

Zubov's selection as favorite had a direct bearing on Potemkin's relations with Catherine. With Mamonov gone, Garnovsky found it much more difficult to receive first-hand information about Catherine. His reports to Potemkin on Catherine's moods and her reactions to the prince's letters became less and less detailed as Zubov began to restrict Garnovsky's access to the empress and to withhold information from him. Moreover, Catherine herself began to write to Potemkin less often than in the past. In 1790, she sent him about half the number of letters she had the previous year. Part of this can be explained by the ever changing diplomatic and military scene that had always influenced the frequency of their letters; but also important was Zubov's role in trying to turn Catherine against Potemkin.[56] The prince's position was further compromised by the posting of Zubov's younger brother, Valerian, to Potemkin's army in September 1789. Although with time Potemkin came to develop a genuine respect for the brave Valerian, the lad's presence meant that Potemkin's every word and deed was reported back to the elder brother, who used this information to influence the empress. In 1790, Valerian wrote to his brother from Jassy of how Potemkin had completely given himself over to luxury and decadence and surrounded himself with an entire harem of beauties and a crowd of worthless spongers. Comments such as these could not have been pleasing to Catherine.[57]

The struggle to control the flow of information to and from the empress even extended to the route Potemkin's couriers were permitted to travel. At the outbreak of the war, Catherine granted Garnovsky twelve horses to place at the disposal of Potemkin's couriers. The large number was a sign of the prince's great authority and Catherine's desire to ensure speedy communication between the capital and the army headquarters in Kremenchug. The dozen horses allowed the couriers to switch to a fresh mount at least once a day and ensured that letters leaving Kremenchug would reach St. Petersburg in an average of seven days.[58] There were two main post roads between Potemkin's headquarters and St. Petersburg: the shorter Belorussian route to the west that cut across Polish lands and the longer Moscow route to the east that remained inside the empire's borders. The Belorussian route held two advantages for Potemkin: first, letters could reach the capital approximately two days faster than via the Moscow route, and second, since it crossed through Poland it offered the prince a means for quietly exchanging information with his Polish confederates, of particular importance during this period when he was heavily involved in Polish affairs. The Moscow route, on the other hand, was deemed safer and was favored by Potemkin's foes because it hindered the prince's secret Polish negotiations and slowed the exchange of letters between him and Catherine.[59]

Up until the beginning of the war, Potemkin had been permitted to use the Belorussian highway. Catherine then ordered him to send his couriers by the Moscow route and entrusted the right to use the Belorussian road to Field Marshal Pyotr Rumiantsev, commander of Russia's Ukrainian Army. Catherine's decision was most likely based on her desire to protect the confidentiality of her correspondence with Potemkin at a time of heightened danger. Potemkin's foes supported the decision because it deprived the prince of his prerogative to inform the empress first of news from the front. Since information sent from Rumiantsev would beat that from the prince by several days, Potemkin's foes won valuable time in which to prejudice Catherine's thinking against Potemkin's letters. Moreover, Catherine's move aided Potemkin's enemies seeking to put an end to his Polish machinations. The prince's backers saw the danger of such an arrangement and worked to change the empress's mind. After Mamonov took it upon himself to express his dissatisfaction to Catherine, she agreed to let the prince use either route.[60]

But the contest did not end there and remained a source of contention throughout the war. In October 1787, another attempt was made to impose the Moscow route on Potemkin, and this time Garnovsky spoke up in defense of the prince's need to use the Belorussian road.[61] Potemkin was permitted to use the shorter route until the middle of 1788, when the Russo-Swedish War broke out, and Prussia intensified its meddling in Poland, forcing Catherine to resort to the exclusive use of the Moscow route. In 1790, Potemkin's couriers were once again permitted to use the Belorussian highway for particularly urgent communications. Copies of these documents and highly sensitive letters, however, were still sent via Moscow.[62]

◆ ◆ ◆

Catherine's immense correspondence with Potemkin reflects her graphomaniacal tendencies. Never more at ease than with a pen in her hand, she seems to have spent much of her life at the writing desk and admitted to being forever tempted by "le démon griffonage"—the scribbling demon.[63] Among her voluminous writings, Catherine is today best remembered for her *Memoirs* and for the letters she exchanged with Voltaire and Baron Grimm. Although her love of dissembling has been noted more than once, less appreciated is the fact that Catherine was generally open and frank in her letters to her many correspondents, so much so, in fact, that after their deaths she tried to retrieve her letters and even stopped confiding in Princess Dashkova when the princess threatened to publish Catherine's letters.[64] This readiness to speak candidly in her letters also helps to explain why she burned so much of her personal correspondence and urged her correspondents, Potemkin among them, to guard her letters carefully. Of course, this is not to say that Catherine always presented the same face in her letters. If to Voltaire she sought to convey an image of a *philosophe* on the throne, then to Grimm she tried to present herself as a kind, hardworking lover of the arts, though not without a sense of humor.[65] It would be wrong to put this down merely to Catherine's supposed hypocrisy, however. For according to the century's conventions, the writing of familiar letters was, like the model of polite conversation upon which it was based, a performance that required the careful adjusting of one's self, style, and message to best fit the personality of one's correspondent.[66]

The same practice can be seen in her letters to Potemkin, in which more than one Catherine appears. There is Catherine the all-powerful tsaritsa whose glory is radiated in the reverential gaze of her loyal subject. There is Catherine the doting mother forever worried about her charge's health, passing out advice on how to cure his sniffles and diarrhea and never hesitant to scold him for failing to heed her words. There is Catherine the loving wife, pouring out her heart to her husband and enduring with great patience and humility his wrathful outbursts. This is the Catherine that is most present in the letters she composed during her love affair with Potemkin (1774–1776). These letters convey the honest passion of their affair, yet in ways that reflect some of the specific cultural fashions of the age.

It is well known that Catherine liked to satirize the Russian nobility's Gallomania. She was herself, however, not immune to its influence, and her love letters to Potemkin betray several features common to the jargon of Russia's *petits-maîtres* and *petites-maîtresses*. The most obvious influence is the modish habit of casually inserting the occasional French word or phrase into one's speech. In her letters she also followed the practice of creating new Russian words by adding the Russian suffix -ировать onto French verbs: *embarrasser* becomes *embarrass*ировать, for example, *encourager* becomes *encourag*ировать, etc. Sometimes these neologisms were written as above, half in Latin orthography, half in Cyrillic, and at other times they were written entirely in Cyrillic. Perhaps because Russia's francophiles were forever "exclaiming," Catherine's love notes abound with "Ohs!", "Oohs!", "Ughs!", and "But nos!". Such exclamations expressed the *petits-maîtres'* embrace of hyperbole, especially as it pertained to one's emotions: when Catherine writes to Potemkin of how she is feeling, then it is often "madly," "extraordinarily," "terribly," "extremely." This heightened emotionalism manifested itself, on one end of the spectrum, in references to one's own extreme sensitivity and, on the other, in a fondness for swearing and a certain vulgarity: "morbleau," Catherine cries in frustration (Letter 129), and with a playful wink calls Potemkin an "evil Tatar," a "fool," "Yaik Cossack," and even a "son of a bitch" (Letters 36, 133, 159, 178). The words for various exotic animals (lion, tiger, wolf) and birds (golden pheasant, parrot) that Catherine uses with him come from this court dialect, as does her use of such terms as "doll," "idol," and "Adonis" (Letters 136, 144, 157). According to the *jargon de la galanterie*, love was a state of war, and Catherine's *billets-doux*, chronicling their frequent battles, explosions, and peace negotiations, can be read as despatches from the front.[67]

Although these mannerisms add striking color to Catherine's letters, they are rightly understood as no more than embellishments to what obviously were deeply felt emotions. Unlike her letters to Voltaire, for example, which Catherine wrote and rewrote with great care knowing they would become important for the creation of her public image, Catherine dashed these letters off with little such regard. They represent, rather, the spontaneous display of her thoughts and feelings. As such, these letters provide some of the most honest, revealing glimpses into Catherine's heart and mind. That said, what emerges from these letters is not a never-before-seen Catherine, but one that conforms to what has long been known about her and her character.

The same cannot be said of Potemkin, however. The prevailing view of Potemkin has often been based on what others have written about him, despite the fact that thousands of pages of his letters and papers lie in Russian archives—most of them unpublished and unknown. The image of Potemkin that has traditionally held sway was first crafted by the prince's enemies during his lifetime. They bequeathed to posterity a gross caricature of an evil, vindictive courtier whose greatest talent was his ability to manipulate the empress for his own self-serving ends. This is the Potemkin of the "Potemkin villages," who resorted to artifice to hide his dishonesty and prodigality, robbing the state treasury as he drowned himself in luxury.[68]

As the letters in this volume and as several recent studies attest,[69] the Potemkin of myth bares little resemblance to the Potemkin of history. True, his correspondence does confirm much of what has long been known of his moodiness, his bouts of insecurity and hypochondria. At the same time, however, these letters show a more positive side to his character. Far from being vindictive, Potemkin acted with a profound sense of fairness. He freely acknowledged and praised the deeds of others and never unfairly sullied another's reputation or usurped another's glory. This is perhaps most apparent in the great praise he lavished upon General Aleksandr Suvorov for his actions during the Second Russo-Turkish War. This is not to say, however, that Potemkin could not be critical when necessary: if the men under him failed to execute their duties, he was not loathe to report this to Catherine. Such actions speak to Potemkin's honesty, another often overlooked side to his character.

These letters also attest to Potemkin's unfailing devotion to Catherine and to the Russian Empire. Potemkin worked tirelessly to enhance the glory of both, and was deterred from this only when laid low by illness, both physical and mental, from which he truly did suffer. In his early letters to Catherine, Potemkin cast himself as the valient knight in the Medieval European courtly tradition, striving to win the love of the unattainable lady through heroic deeds.[70] This was the cultural frame though which he viewed his fighting in the First Russo-Turkish War, and although this image of the knight and his lady faded over time as Potemkin and Catherine aged, its faint reflection can still be glimpsed even in the letters from their later years.

• • •

Any discussion of Catherine and Potemkin must address the subject of favoritism. It is a delicate one. To her critics, the seemingly unending procession of males marching through Catherine's boudoir has long provided a handy brush with which to paint her and her reign as licentious and debauched. Catherine has always been a victim of the double standard according to which what is good for the gander is unforgivable in the goose. Others, seeking to adopt a more serious, scholarly approach to Catherine, have been loathe to delve too deeply into the matter out of a misguided sense of decorum: they would have one believe that the handsome adjutant on Catherine's arm is a subject more befitting romance novelists than the sober historian. To ignore her favorites, however, is to overlook one of the defining elements of Catherine's life and reign and to fail to appreciate the intimate nature of power in eighteenth-century Russia. What is more, although favoritism could be found at many European courts, it was at the court of Catherine the Great that it attained its most elaborate development.

The unique form favoritism took under Catherine was a product of her own character and personal history, as well as larger historical factors. It bears noting that the eighteenth century in Russia was an era characterized by powerful favorites. Peter the Great plucked Aleksandr Menshikov from obscurity and made him his most trusted advisor and the most highly decorated man in the empire. Menshikov's favor continued under the reign of Peter's widow, Catherine I (1725–1727) (the former laundress Peter took to his side and eventually crowned), and finally ended in forced exile to Siberia under the new regime of Peter II (1727–1730) following Catherine's death. Peter discarded Menshikov for his own favorite, Prince Ivan Dolgoruky, who was himself arrested after Peter died in 1730 and then banished to the same God-forsaken Siberian hole. Empress Anna Ioannovna (1730–1740) reigned through her favorite Ernst Johann Bühren (Biron), going so far as to set up house with him, his wife, and their children. And Empress Elizabeth (1741–1761) had two longtime favorites, Aleksei Razumovsky and Ivan Shuvalov.

Favorites arose at other European courts during the eighteenth century. Louis XV of France (1710–1774) had his royal mistresses the marquise de Pompadour and Madame du Barry, the latter playing a considerable political role; in Copenhagen, Count Johann Friedrich Struensee (1737–1772) used his position as the king's physician to lay his hands on the reins of power—and on the queen, too—eventually provoking a backlash that led to the count's fall and execution; and in the 1750s, Princess Anne of Hanover ruled over the United Provinces and its colonies from her court at The Hague with the help of various favorites.[71]

Along with these more traditional favorites, the eighteenth century also witnessed the birth of a new type of favorite, what has been called "the first minister," who, though he lacked an explicit title or office, possessed great authority and decision-making power based almost solely on the personal bond he shared with the ruler. These ministers typically began their rise in the sphere of foreign affairs and from there extended their influence to the domestic sphere as well. Thanks to the favor of the ruler, they held sway over their colleagues in the state apparatus and often used their exalted position to enrich themselves and their kinsmen through a robust system of patronage. The first ministers of the eighteenth century can be seen as a rebirth of the minister-favorite of the previous century—men like Count-Duke of Olivares of Spain and Cardinal Richelieu of

France—whose power had been eclipsed during the reign of Louis XIV (1643–1715). The first ministers of the eighteenth century were typically more *minister* than *favorite,* the differentiation between the two having taken place over time. The best examples include Prince Kaunitz in Austria, the marquês de Pombal in Portugal, and Count Heinrich von Brühl in Poland. Potemkin, too, ought to be placed among their ranks. Although he began as a royal favorite, this phase of his career proved to be much shorter and less significant than the many years he spent helping Catherine rule the empire as her chief minister.[72]

The rise of the first minister in eighteenth-century Europe was in part a reflection of the growing range of state activities and the accompanying need rulers felt for help in administering the state. It was also a product of the unique personalities of the European monarchs, some of whom demonstrated little interest in or capacity for rule. Catherine's initial attraction to Potemkin was clearly a combination of the exigencies of rule and her own distinct personality. At the same time as she sought talented men to help her govern, she also sought love. Much has been written of Catherine's amorous nature. She was herself well aware of passion's hold over her and was not afraid to admit this in her writings. In an early letter to Potemkin, for example, she confessed that her "heart is loath to be without love even for a single hour" (Letter 4), and in her *Memoirs* she observed that even though she had committed every moral maxim to heart, she had nevertheless failed to master temptation.[73]

Though lust had its place in Catherine's life and reign, in truth its role was only a supporting one. More important was the direction her life took after arriving in Russia. Grand Duke Peter's sexual inhibition (and possible impotence) forced Catherine to take a lover in order to produce an heir. As a young woman Catherine learned well the intimate connection between sex and power, especially as it related to women. Physical intimacy was not the only thing lacking in Catherine's relations with her husband, however. The absence of genuine warmth, companionship, and mutual understanding caused her even greater anguish. Unable to find happiness in her marriage, Catherine had no choice but to seek it elsewhere and entered into a series of relationships that would continue for the rest of her life.

It is also important to consider the effect that growing up at the court of Elizabeth must have had on Catherine. In the early 1730s, then Grand Duchess Elizabeth took for her lover Aleksei Rozum, a comely Ukrainian singer in the court choir. Upon coming to the throne, she showered her favorite—now known as Razumovsky or "Man of Reason," his name having been upgraded to match his new station—with palaces, estates, and money, eventually making him one of the wealthiest men in Russia. He was made a count of the Holy Roman Empire and a field marshal, though he never would lead any troops. The arc of Razumovsky's fairytale rise from provincial shepherd to mighty aristocrat, an improbable journey made by several other eighteenth-century favorites, is captured by the Russian expression *iz griázi da v kniázi,* "from out of the mud and into the princes." Razumovsky managed to drag several members of his family along with him out of the Ukrainian mud, most notably his brother Kirill, who was appointed president of the Academy of Sciences in 1746 at the age of eighteen after only three years of formal education.[74]

Although dubbed the "Night Emperor," Razumovsky exercised only limited influence over Elizabeth. This was not the case, however, with Ivan Shuvalov, the man who replaced him as official favorite in 1751. As her health deteriorated over the course of the decade, the tsaritsa increasingly relied on Shuvalov to help govern the country. He eventually became her only secretary and advisor and for a while the only one at court with free access to Elizabeth. By the end of her reign, all information to and from the empress had to pass through Shuvalov, and he was openly composing imperial orders in her name. The former page had become a de facto chief minister with the power to subvert officials and institutions whose authority—at least on paper—greatly exceeded his own. With time the entire Shuvalov clan came to dominate political life. At its head was Ivan's cousin Pyotr Shuvalov, whose grand Petersburg residence served as a quasi-state office, crowded from dawn till dusk with high government officials, courtiers, and generals all seeking his advice and approval. Pyotr's authority was nearly limitless: in 1756, he was even granted permission to establish his own private army of some 30,000 soldiers.[75]

This was the world in which Catherine came of age, and it quite naturally left its mark on her. In taking lovers and investing them with considerable power, it is fair to say that Catherine was merely following the example of her predecessors. She surpassed them, however, in the total number of favorites (at least ten beginning with her accession to the throne)[76] and the great prominence accorded them at court. As the historian Kazimierz Waliszewski observed, "Favouritism in Russia is what it is or has been elsewhere, allowing for the difference of scale. It is just this which gives it, under the reign of Catherine, a place apart. She has favourites, . . . but urged by her temperament, her character, her inclination to do things grandly, she gives unparalleled proportions to this usual, traditional order or disorder of things."[77] Catherine took something quite common, both by Russian and broader European standards, and remade it according to her own fashion. Her relationship with Potemkin was of a piece.

When, in 1774, Catherine chose Grigory Potemkin as her new favorite, few could have imagined the incredible future that lay before him. There had never been nor would there ever be a favorite like him in Russian history. By definition, a royal favorite is one who enjoys the greatest physical proximity to the ruler. The favorite's power is based upon intimacy with the sovereign, and this intimacy can be maintained only by constant, unlimited access to her person. The ruler's court is the favorite's native habitat. Potemkin, however, turned all this upside down: he spent much of his life away from court, yet still was able to maintain Catherine's complete trust. It was to him, no matter how far away he was, that she looked for advice and consolation in times of need.

The question of how Catherine and Potemkin shared power has produced wildly divergent answers and is still debated by historians. To her contemporaries, foreign and domestic, Catherine was most often perceived as a puppet in the hands of her favorites, especially Orlov and Potemkin. This is what Louis XVI had in mind when he so famously called Catherine "Madame Potemkin" in a letter to the comte de Vergennes.[78] Exaggerating the power of these favorites was a way to criticize the institution of favoritism and, indirectly, Catherine herself. The critiques of men such as Denis Fonvizin, Prince Mikhail Shcherbatov and Aleksandr Radishchev drew on established European notions of the favorite as an artful sycophant of little merit, blinding the ruler with flattery as he and his kinsmen robbed the treasury and denied the aspirations of all men of true talent.[79] So powerful was this perception that even a former favorite himself, Pyotr Zavadovsky, shared it: "The faintest spark of intelligence in a favorite," he once complained, "is taken for the burning sun."[80] In 1777, a young Aleksei Razumovsky wrote his father Kirill, the former favorite's brother, of the "depraved condition" of the present court at which physical appearance trumped character as the ticket to honor and glory.[81] Inherent in such views was the idea that Catherine, as a woman, was ruled more by passion than reason, held to be a male attribute, and so was particularly vulnerable to flattery. While such criticism reflected a more general bias against women acting in what was considered the rightful sphere of men, Catherine drew particular censure given how she came to the throne, the wrongful fate of Peter III, and the exaggerated form favoritism acquired during her reign.

Some recent observers have argued quite the opposite about Catherine, namely that she guarded her power with great care and shared it with nobody.[82] In an important recent study of the empress and her reign, Aleksandr Kamensky asserts that although Catherine respected Potemkin's advice, she granted him authority only over affairs of minor significance, and then simply so as to flatter his ego, all the while maintaining for herself control over everything of true importance.[83] This view of Catherine corresponds to Diderot's vivid description of her as possessing "the soul of Brutus within the figure of Cleopatra; the firmity of purpose of the one and the seductiveness of the other."[84]

While closer to the truth than the older view, this interpretation errs by underestimating Potemkin's authority. Simon Dixon convincingly shows in an illuminating examination of Catherine's rule the degree to which she adhered to a consensual model of power that granted her advisors considerable freedom of action. This was most apparent with Potemkin, whom Dixon considers to have been a "co-ruler" along with Catherine.[85] The idea of Potemkin as co-ruler is not new, of course, and has been shared by other scholars. Yakov Barskov called Potemkin "a tsar, although without a title or crown," and Marc Raeff has written that "[h]e was a sovereign in fact, if not in name. . . ."[86] Of critical importance in the power-sharing arrangement between Catherine and Potemkin was the role of geography. The vastness of the Russian Empire allowed for its de facto division into northern and southern halves, the latter of which was entrusted to Potemkin.[87] The extent of Potemkin's authority is evident in the free hand he had in administering the southern territories and in the role he had in shaping Russian foreign policy, which according to the latest research, was conducted in the second half of Catherine's reign largely upon plans he drafted.[88] Over time Potemkin managed to acquire both unrivaled official, bureaucratic power connected with the numerous titles and offices he held and the intimate, personal power that came with his singular relationship with Catherine. It was a combination that set him apart from all others in Catherine's Russia and was never repeated after him.[89]

The precise nature of this singular relationship has been the source of considerable speculation. At the heart of this speculation is the question of whether Catherine and Potemkin were more than lovers and co-rulers, but were in fact also secretly husband and wife. While it cannot be conclusively proven that Catherine and Potemkin married, there is considerable evidence to show that they did.[90] Perhaps the best evidence is Catherine's letters to Potemkin in which she refers to him as "cher Epoux" (dear spouse) or simply "husband" and to herself as his "wife" more than a dozen times.[91] One skeptic has argued that Catherine's words should not be taken literally, but that they reflect some sort of epistolary lovers' game.[92] It is an intriguing, though unconvincing, notion. First, there is no known precedent for such role playing among the literary models popular at the time. Second, assuming that it was a lovers' game, why did Catherine play it only with Potemkin? For in the admittedly few extant letters exchanged with her other lovers such words are entirely lacking. Furthermore, what is to be made of Catherine's reference in one letter to the "bonds of Holy Matrimony" that tied her to Potemkin (Letter 184)?

The letters, however, are not the only evidence that suggest a marriage. Equally important is the way Potemkin acted and how he was treated. Unlike all Catherine's other favorites, Potemkin never fell completely out of favor and enjoyed her trust until his death. This is particularly important given that the liberties he took with the empress confounded many

observers.[93] Catherine would have been willing to put up with such behavior from a spouse, but surely not from a mere favorite. Potemkin's ar-
rivals and departures from St. Petersburg were marked by the same ceremony reserved for members of the royal family, an honor not extended to
Catherine's other lovers. Potemkin enjoyed unparalleled access to the state
treasury and had the power to confer ranks (*chiny*) as well as military offices and titles of the highest levels. What is more, Potemkin's behavior,
characterized by supreme self-confidence and a sense of entitlement to all
that he possessed, bespoke that of a monarch, or a monarch's consort at
the very least.[94]

Those who knew them well suspected they had married. Count Louis-
Phillipe Ségur, the French ambassador, wrote Versailles in 1788 that
Potemkin "takes advantage of . . . certain sacred and inviolable rights
which secure the continuance of his privilege. The singular basis of these
rights is a great mystery, which is known only to four people in Russia; a
lucky chance enabled me to discover it, and when I have thoroughly
sounded it, I shall, on the first occasion which presents itself, inform the
King."[95] Years later after Catherine's death, Platon Zubov recalled how
Catherine had always acquiesced to Potemkin's demands and treated him
as if he were her "exacting husband."[96] The choice of words is revealing
and suggests Zubov may have known of the secret bond between Catherine and his rival.

Of the several dates that have been suggested for their marriage, the
most likely is 8 June 1774. Although the following account has never been
proven, and probably never will be, it is believed that late that night
Catherine and her trusted maid Maria Perekusikhina left the Summer
Palace and climbed aboard a waiting launch that took them down the
Fontanka canal to the Neva River. After a short ride, they landed at an isolated corner of the city where a carriage transported them to the Church
of St. Samson. There they met Potemkin, his nephew Aleksandr Samoilov,
and Court Chamberlain Yevgraf Chertkov. Ioann Pamfilov, the empress's
confessor, married the couple in a brief ceremony, after which the witnesses were sworn to secrecy.[97]

Catherine had her reasons for keeping the marriage a secret. Some years
before, after helping to place Catherine on the throne, Grigory Orlov had
expressed a desire to marry Catherine and so solidify his family's position.
Catherine worried that such a marriage would inspire anger and resentment among the other powerful factions at court, particularly that headed
by Nikita Panin. Upon hearing of the idea, Panin, the governor of Catherine's son Paul, is reported to have warned Catherine that "a Mrs. Orlov
would never be Empress of All the Russias." Part of the resistance to the
idea emanated from a concern for what such a marriage would do to the
succession rights of the young Paul, heir to the throne. Word of the pro-

posed marriage incensed many of the guardsmen, and in 1763 a plot was uncovered to unseat Catherine and murder Orlov should the marriage take place.[98] The memory of this episode gave Catherine ample cause to keep her marriage to Potemkin a closely guarded secret. That she was even willing to consider wedding Potemkin in light of the danger such an act presented to them attests not only to the great passion Catherine felt for Potemkin but also to her sense of indebtedness to him.

It should be noted that by marrying Potemkin, Catherine was not acting without precedent. Empress Elizabeth is widely believed to have secretly wed Razumovsky in the early 1740s.[99] And sometime after the death in 1683 of his wife, Marie-Thérèse of Austria, Louis XIV of France married in secret Madame de Maintenon, his confidante and mistress.[100] In December 1785, the Prince Regent (later George IV) of England secretly married a Catholic widow named Maria Anne Fitzherbert.[101] It is striking that all these royal marriages have been more widely accepted by historians as fact than has Catherine's to Potemkin, despite there being considerably greater evidence for hers than for the other three.

Recognizing Catherine and Potemkin's marriage is important not merely for what it adds to the knowledge of their biographies, but also for the light it sheds on Potemkin's unique station in Russian society and how he coped with it. To outsiders, Potemkin was one of Catherine's favorites, and while he and Catherine knew otherwise, neither of them was at liberty to reveal the truth. This situation quite naturally placed a much heavier burden on Potemkin, who had to suffer in silence the aspersions of his enemies. Having to pretend he was something less than he was proved especially trying for a man endowed with so much pride and sense of self-worth. Some of Potemkin's sulky depressions and violent rages, particularly during his years as the official favorite, may well be attributed to the strain produced by the divergence between public appearance and private reality. The awkwardness of his situation is suggested by the Russian word for favorite—*vremenshchik*, the man of the moment (from *vremia*, time). Potemkin's position was anything but momentary, however.

While Potemkin knew his place in Russia was safe as long as the empress was alive, he also knew that his fate would be much less secure in a Russia ruled by her son Paul, who made little attempt to hide his great dislike for his mother's chief minister. Cognizant of the reversal of fortune that had befallen previous favorites following the death of their patrons, Potemkin sought to create a haven outside Russia's borders. Throughout the late 1770s, he unsuccessfully sought the throne of the duchy of Courland. Years later, Potemkin dreamed of founding for himself a kingdom of Dacia in present-day Romania as part of the Greek Project. There were rumors of other such schemes involving eastern Poland—where he owned immense territories—or even two Italian islands, which he was supposedly negotiating to buy from the kingdom of Naples.[102] Fortunately, Potemkin died before Catherine. After ascending the throne, Paul had to content himself with desecrating Potemkin's grave: he ordered the tomb disturbed, the body secretly buried, and the ground smoothed over to hide any trace of Potemkin.[103]

Potemkin's predicament had been shared by other Russian favorites before him. Elizabeth's favorite Ivan Shuvalov purportedly wanted to be made duke of Prussia during the Seven Years' War, and when this failed he quietly began banking money in France as the empress neared death. Under Empress Anna Ioannovna, Ernst Bühren became duke of his native Courland in 1737, as a way of building a foreign power base. And years earlier Prince Menshikov had also sought the crown of Courland.[104] In an age of palace coups and fierce political fighting among the leading families, the favorite's position was extremely vulnerable during the transition from one ruler to the next. An escape plan was always wise, even if not always effective, given that there were no institutional safeguards to protect the favorite. Just as royal favor brought immense power and wealth, royal disfavor often brought banishment and misery.[105]

Excluding the man who replaced him at Catherine's side, Pyotr Zavadovsky, and the last favorite, Platon Zubov, Potemkin guided the selection of all of Catherine's subsequent favorites. The process was not always simple or straightforward. First, Potemkin had to contend with the competing candidates being put forward by rival factions at court. Second, he had to find a young man pleasing to the empress. Not that there was any shortage of candidates. Prospective favorites were typically members of the guards, the sons of minor families of modest means who had served as adjutants to Potemkin. For young men seeking their fortune, nothing could compare with the rewards of being the official favorite. Favoritism was largely responsible for producing the great fortunes of the century. The rewards of favoritism flowed not only to the *amant en titre* but to his entire family and extended clan, who shared in his good fortune through the exercise of patronage and the dispensing of various favors. The massive wealth the favorites and their allies managed to acquire seemingly overnight, particularly in Catherine's reign, surpassed the fortunes that the oldest noble families had patiently accumulated over many years.[106]

As the years passed, and one favorite supplanted the other generally with little interval between them, the office of favorite came to be seen as a court institution. The notion that it would be vacant for long was unimaginable. "A holy place does not remain empty," Zavadovsky remarked regarding the office of favorite after Mamonov's departure.[107] On the rare occasions it did, the wheels of government ground to a halt. On one such occasion the French chargé d'affaires, the chevalier Corberon, wrote to the comte de Vergennes:

We may observe in Russia a sort of interregnum in affairs, caused by the displacement of one favorite and the installation of his successor. This event eclipses everything else. On it hang all the interests of a certain side of things, and even the cabinet ministers, succumbing to the general influence, suspend their operations until the choice has been made, and things fall back into the accustomed groove, and the machine is once more in proper order.[108]

When the favorite Aleksandr Lanskoy died in 1784, Catherine was so overcome by grief that she and thereby the entire court were paralyzed for weeks.[109]

None of the men Potemkin put forward were permitted to play an independent political role. To help ensure this arrangement, Potemkin selected men from insignificant families: lacking any power or prestige of their own, they owed their station and thus their allegiance to Potemkin and were less apt to undermine his status at court. It was understood that they were to defend Potemkin's interests. Those who failed to do so ran into trouble with the prince and Catherine.

The favorites were in a very real sense kept men whose chief duties consisted of offering companionship and affection to the empress. They lived according to Catherine's schedule and enjoyed little freedom or privacy. Zavadovsky likened it to a life spent "under a microscope."[110] Odd as it may appear to modern sensibilities, Catherine, Potemkin, and her favorites constituted a family of sorts. As the two of them aged and the difference in years between them and the favorites grew, Catherine and Potemkin came to adopt the role of surrogate parents. These young men, together with Potemkin's nieces, represented the children they never had.[111] In his letters to Potemkin attached to those from Catherine, Aleksandr Lanskoy addressed his patron as "father" or "dear uncle." Referring to Aleksandr Dmitriev-Mamonov, Catherine wrote Potemkin that "Sasha loves you and regards you like his own father." And when describing the twenty-two-year-old Platon Zubov in 1789, Catherine called him "our child."[112]

Catherine appears to have understood her relationship to these young men more as a nurturing and instructive mother than as a lover. She enjoyed overseeing their education and furthering their knowledge of the arts and culture. Catherine loved beautiful things, and the handsome, statuesque men at her side, so carefully polished by her own hands, added to the splendor of her court and advertised her own exquisite taste. Her role as tutor inverted the more traditional relationship in which the favorite educates the young prince in preparation for the burden of rule, as seen with Olivares and Philip IV of Spain, for example.[113] There were currents of narcissism and insensitivity in Catherine's role as teacher. Following Lanskoy's death, Catherine wrote Baron Grimm that "he had devoted himself to his education with great zeal, had shown success, and had acquired all *my tastes*. He was a young man I was raising, . . . who shared *my sorrows* when they befell me and who rejoiced in *my happiness*"[114] [italics mine]. Before dismissing a distraught Zavadovsky in 1777, she coldly instructed him to translate some Tacitus to help calm his anguished soul.[115]

The family Catherine created for herself included not only the current favorite, but past favorites as well. While it is traditional to think of the favorites as replacing each other—out with the old, in with the new—the situation was in fact a good deal more complex. Several former lovers returned to court, after an appropriate time away, and rejoined Catherine's intimate circle. Orlov left court after his replacement by Vasilchikov and again after the rise of Potemkin, eventually returning to Catherine's side after both episodes. He even participated in Grand Duke Paul's second wedding in September 1776 and acted as a mediator between Catherine and Zavadovsky during their break-up the following year. Ironically, Zavadovsky fulfilled the same role when Aleksandr Yermolov was dismissed as favorite in 1786. When Catherine selected a guardian to look after Aleksei Bobrinsky, her wayward son by Orlov, she chose the steady Zavadovsky.[116] A prime example of Catherinian family life was the celebration of Potemkin's name-day at the Anichkov Palace on 30 September 1777. Guests included Catherine's current lover, Semyon Zorich, and three of her former ones—Orlov, Zavadovsky, and Potemkin.[117]

Also in attendance that day were three pretty young sisters, Aleksandra, Varvara, and Yekaterina Engelhardt, all maids-of-honor at court and nieces of Potemkin. The Engelhardt sisters (there were two others at court as well, Nadezhda and Tatiana) formed part of the core of Catherine and Potemkin's family. Potemkin had brought them to court during his time as favorite and Catherine grew most fond of them. So, too, did Potemkin. It was widely rumored at court and in diplomatic circles that after ceasing to be Catherine's lover Potemkin began a series of incestuous relationships with several of his nieces. The veracity of such claims will never be known for certain; rumors of this nature may well have originated out of a desire to sully Potemkin's reputation. Nevertheless, the surviving letters between Potemkin and Varvara bespeak an intense, burning passion that cannot be explained away as some sort of coquettish epistolary game.[118]

Power being the great universal aphrodisiac, the affections the Engelhardt sisters felt for their uncle were shared by a great many women, and Potemkin had enough mistresses during his lifetime to make even a world-renowned lover such as Catherine look like something of a prude. The archives still contain the trembling *billets-doux* of many of these anonymous lovers: "My darling, my sweetest, my dearest friend, I love you . . . I kiss you a million times . . . "; "I kiss you thirty million times and with a tenderness that grows with each moment . . . "; "Forgive me, my priceless, dearest friend, I love you more than my own life . . . "; "You are so cruel . . . oh, how vexed I am, it is unbearable, at least tell me whether you love me."[119]

Whatever his personal charms, loving Potemkin, just like loving Catherine, brought very practical advantages, and Potemkin spent prodigiously on his mistresses just as Catherine did on her favorites. While the empress had the decency to at least take only single men as her lovers, Potemkin seems to have preferred married women, typically the wives of his officers and even of his close relatives. This was not without its advantages to their cuckolded husbands. In the late 1770s, Potemkin carried on an affair with Countess Sofia Apraksina. When her husband's debts threatened the family with ruin, she was able to turn to Potemkin for help in staving off their creditors.[120] Apraksina's daughter, Vera, later married Pyotr Zavadovsky, thereby adding another thread to the complex web of relations that seems to have linked the entire Russian elite of the era into one large extended family.[121]

♦ ♦ ♦

Writing in the early years of the nineteenth century, Alexander Pushkin damned Catherine by praising her rare talent for finding the weakness in her fellow man and using it to her own advantage. This, he wrote, was the key to her dubious success. By encouraging her own "voluptuousness," Catherine "awoke a vile competition among the highest ranks of society, for one needed neither intelligence nor talent to attain the second place in the government. Many men were called and many were chosen; however, in the long list of her favorites, condemned to disdain by posterity, the name of the bizarre Potemkin will be singled out by the hand of history."[122]

Pushkin's harsh judgement has been shared by others. Much has been written of the purported lascivious ways of Catherine and the evil deeds of her most illustrious favorite. Over two hundred years after their deaths, Catherine and Potemkin have yet to be completely freed from the popular myths that have so thoroughly distorted their lives—she the mariticidal nymphomaniac, he the sybaritic Oriental satrap. To read their letters is to be confronted with individuals who bear little resemblance to such caricatures. If in their admitted weakness to the temptations of wealth, power, and the flesh, Catherine and Potemkin were perhaps no better than other rulers, then in their unshakeable devotion to each other and their shared commitment to serving Russia, they stand alone.

NOTES

1. Simon Sebag Montefiore, *Prince of Princes: The Life of Potemkin* (London, 2000), 9; V. S. Lopatin, *Ekaterina II i G. A. Potemkin. Lichnaia perepiska, 1769–1791* [hereafter cited as *Perepiska*] (Moscow, 1997), 962–63.

2. John T. Alexander, *Catherine the Great: Life and Legend* (New York, 1989), 292; *Pamiatnye zapiski A. V. Khrapovitskogo,* ed. G. N. Gennadi (1862; reprint, Moscow, 1990), 252; *Sbornik imperatorskogo russkogo istoricheskogo obshchestva* [hereafter cited as *SIRIO*] 23 (1878): 561.

3. Montefiore, *Prince of Princes,* 5.

4. A. Loviagin, "Potemkin, Grigorii Aleksandrovich," in *Russkii biograficheskii slovar'* (St. Petersburg, 1905), 14:653, 655; Isabel de Madariaga, *Russia in the Age of Catherine the Great* (New Haven, CT, 1981), 359.

5. *The Prince de Ligne. His Memoirs, Letters, and Miscellaneous Papers,* ed. and trans. Katharine Prescott Wormeley (Boston, 1902), 2:81–82; Montefiore, *Prince of Princes,* 8.

6. William C. Fuller, Jr., *Strategy and Power in Russia, 1600–1914* (New York, 1992), 86–87.

7. For the fullest discussion, see O. I. Eliseeva, *Geopoliticheskie proekty G. A. Potemkina* (Moscow, 2000).

8. Montefiore, *Prince of Princes,* 17; [Elvira Fedorovna Kuznetsova, ed.], *Znamenitye rossiiane XVIII–XIX vekov. Biografii i portrety* (St. Peterburg, 1995), s.v. "Dar'ia Vasil'evna Potemkina."

9. [Kuznetsova], *Znamenitye rossiiane,* s.v. "Dar'ia Vasil'evna Potemkina"; Lopatin, *Perepiska,* 499; Montefiore, *Prince of Princes,* 13–17; K. A. Pisarenko, "Naskol'ko dostoverna romanticheskaia istoriia o svad'be roditelei Potemkina," in O. A. Ivanov, V. S. Lopatin, and K. A. Pisarenko, *Zagadki russkoi istorii. XVIII vek* (Moscow, 2000).

10. Montefiore, *Prince of Princes,* 13–14; Letter 371.

11. Loviagin, "Potemkin," 649–50; Lopatin, *Perepiska,* 499; Montefiore, *Prince of Princes,* 22–28.

12. Montefiore, *Prince of Princes,* 25–29.

13. Loviagin, "Potemkin," 650; Madariaga, *Russia,* 1–26.

14. Alexander, *Catherine the Great,* chap. 2; A. B. Kamenskii, *Zhizn' i sud'ba imperatritsy Ekateriny Velikoi* (Moscow, 1997), 10–14.

15. Alexander, *Catherine the Great,* 43–46; Madariaga, *Russia,* 10–11; *Russkii biograficheskii slovar',* vol. 18, s.v. "Saltykov, Sergei Vasil'evich." Most historians believe Saltykov to have been Paul's father.

16. Alexander, *Catherine the Great,* 46–55; Madariaga, *Russia,* 11–16.

17. Alexander, *Catherine the Great,* 55–60; B. Alekseevskii, "Orlov, kniaz' Grigorii Grigor'evich," in *Russkii biograficheskii slovar'* (St. Petersburg, 1905), vol. 12; [Kuznetsova], *Znamenitye rossiiane,* s.v. "Grigorii Grigor'evich Orlov"; Madariaga, *Russia,* 16–17, 26–29.

18. Alexander, *Catherine the Great,* 3–16; Lopatin, *Perepiska,* 497–98; and O. A. Ivanova, "Zagadki pisem Alekseia Orlova iz Ropshi," *Moskovskii zhurnal* 9, 11, 12 (1995); 1, 2, 3 (1996).

19. *Sochineniia imperatritsy Ekateriny II,* ed. A. N. Pypin (St. Petersburg, 1907), 12:2-oi polutom, 766. Quoted in Lopatin, *Perepiska,* 497.

20. *Sochineniia imperatritsy Ekateriny II,* 12:2-oi polutom, 554. Quoted in Lopatin, *Perepiska,* 497; Loviagin, "Potemkin," 750. Note: Catherine is incorrect: Potemkin was then twenty-two, not seventeen.

21. Lopatin, *Perepiska,* 499; Montefiore, *Prince of Princes,* 51; *SIRIO* 7 (1871):

108–15; 42 (1885): 475–80. Potemkin received 10,000 rubles, 400 serfs, and a silver service for his role in the coup.

22. Montefiore, *Prince of Princes*, 30; A. N. Samoilov, "Zhizn' i deianiia generala-fel'dmarshala kniazia Grigoriia Aleksandrovicha Potemkina-Tavricheskogo," *Russkii arkhiv* 4 (1867): 599 n. 28; 12 (1867): 1561–62.

23. Samoilov, "Zhizn' i deianiia," *Russkii arkhiv* 4 (1867): 598–601. The stories about how Potemkin went blind (from a pair of scissors, from Aleksei Orlov's fist, from a tennis ball, a sword, etc.) are many and form part of the Potemkin mythology. See A. G. Brückner, *Potemkin* (1891; reprint, Moscow, 1996), 22–23; [Jeanne Éleonore de Cérenville], *Memoirs of the Life of Prince Potemkin, Field-Marshal and Commander-in-Chief of the Russian Army, Grand Admiral of the Fleets* . . . (London, 1812), 14.

24. Brückner, *Potemkin*, 24–25; Petr Lebedev, *Grafy Nikita i Petr Paniny* (St. Petersburg, 1863), 105–7; Loviagin, "Potemkin," 650–51; Montefiore, *Prince of Princes*, 69, 70; Russian State Archive of Ancient Acts, Moscow [hereafter cited as RGADA], *fond* 18, *opis'* 1, *delo* 202.

25. Montefiore, *Prince of Princes*, 71–72; Samoilov, "Zhizn' i deianiia," 599–604.

26. Loviagin, "Potemkin," 650–51; Montefiore, *Prince of Princes*, 73–75.

27. Brückner, *Potemkin*, 26–27; Lopatin, *Perepiska*, 500–501; Loviagin, "Potemkin," 651; Montefiore, *Prince of Princes*, 73–77; *SIRIO* 36 (1882): 156.

28. Ia. Barskov, ed., "Pis'ma Ekateriny II k Potemkinu." Manuscript Division, Russian State Library, *fond* 369 (V. D. Bonch-Bruevich), *k.* 375, *n.* 29, *listy* 17–18; *Pamiatnye zapiski Khrapovitskogo*, 259; O. I. Eliseeva, *Perepiska Ekateriny II i G. A. Potemkina perioda vtoroi russko-turetskoi voiny (istochnikovedcheskoe issledovanie)* (Moscow, 1997), 10.

29. P. B. Bartenev, "Dopolnenie k stat'e o brake Ekateriny Velikoi s Potemkinym," *Russkii arkhiv* 2 (1911): 105–8; N. Ia. Eidelman, comp., "Pis'ma Ekateriny II k G. A. Potemkinu," *Voprosy istorii* 7 (1989): 113; Lopatin, *Perepiska*, 486. The "Sincere Confession" was apparently stolen from Aleksandra Branicka, Potemkin's favorite niece, while she was on a trip to Europe in 1819. The theft may have been motivated by the desire to discredit the Romanovs through casting doubt on their legitimacy, for Catherine's letter implies that Sergei Saltykov and not Catherine's husband was the father of the future tsar Paul I. A Russian agent by the name of Butiagin managed to get his hands on the letter ten years later and then returned to St. Petersburg, where he presented it to Constantine, Catherine's grandson.

30. *SIRIO* 13 (1874); 27 (1880); 42 (1885).

31. *Russkaia starina* 16 (May 1876): 33–58 and (June): 239–62; 17 (July 1876): 441–78, (August): 571–90, (September): 21–38, (October): 205–16, (November): 403–26, (December): 635–52. A few letters were earlier published in the journal *Russian Archive* in 1870 and 1879.

32. *Russkaia starina* 32 (July 1881): 498–502, (September): 195–200. The letters are misleadingly numbered up to 111; letters 39 through 52 are missing and some of the letters are printed twice.

33. *Russkaia starina* 13 (June 1875): 163–71.

34. Brückner, *Potemkin*, 253 n. 1; Lopatin, *Perepiska*, 474, 479–80.

35. Eidelman, "Pis'ma," 113.

36. The discussion of Barskov is based on Eidelman, "Pis'ma," 111–15; Lopatin, *Perepiska*, 486–88; State Archive of the Russian Federation, *fond* R-5325, *opis'* 1, *delo*

1219. The extant evidence upon which the story of Barskov's attempts to publish his work is based is scanty, and the precise order of events cannot be reconstructed with complete confidence in its accuracy.

37. Eidelman, "Pis'ma," 111–12. Bonch-Bruevich's comments are attached to Barskov's edition in the archive of the Russian State Library. Quoted from Eidelman, "Pis'ma," 111.

38. Eidelman, "Pis'ma," 112.

39. Georges Oudard, ed., *Lettres d'amour de Catherine II à Potemkine. Correspondence inédite* (Paris, 1934). The letters initially appeared in *Revue de Paris* (June 1934). In his book, Oudard published 357 of Barskov's 419 letters. He left out Barskov's introduction and cut out a good deal of the annotation. This rare book, with its flowery, inaccurate translations, was the only source of Catherine's love letters to Potemkin for western historians for over fifty years.

40. Anna Kashina-Evreinova, "Velikaia v liubvi. Ekaterina II po tol'ko chto opublikovannym pis'mam k kniaziu Potemkinu," *Illiustrirovannaia Rossiia* 40 (29 September 1934): 1–4; 41 (6 October 1934): 2–4; 42 (13 October 1934): 6–7; 43 (20 October 1934): 8–10.

41. This account is based on the file on the Oudard affair in the State Archive of the Russian Federation and Lopatin, *Perepiska*, 487–88.

42. N. Ia. Eidelman, comp., "Pis'ma Ekateriny II k G. A. Potemkinu," *Voprosy istorii* 7 (1989): 111–34; 8: 110–24; 9: 97–111; 10: 102–16; 12: 107–23. Historically significant as this publication was, Eidelman's copy contained many mistakes and inaccuracies that made their way into print, thus undermining its usefulness to historians. See also Marina Vilenovna Babich, ed., "Pis'ma Ekateriny II k G. A. Potemkinu," *Voprosy istorii* 12 (1994): 151–62.

43. Lopatin, *Perepiska*. On the facts of Lopatin's publication and his general comments on the correspondence, see pages 492–93, 541–44. Catherine and Potemkin's official correspondence can be found in: *SIRIO*, vols. 13, 27, 42; *Russkii arkhiv* 2 (1874); and *Sbornik voenno-istoricheskikh materialov* 4, 6–8 (St. Petersburg, 1893–1895). Lopatin states that approximately 320 of the letters in his work are published for the first time or for the first time in their entirety. The figure is actually a bit lower since some previously published letters (e.g., 8 letters from August and September 1787 published by Babich in *Voprosy istorii*) are listed as unpublished by Lopatin.

44. The precise number of letters they exchanged has proven difficult to establish. Lopatin includes 1,162 in his collection and mentions more than 40 as having been lost or destroyed, for a total of over 1,562. Eliseeva, on the other hand, makes reference to at least 1,246 notes and letters having been exchanged, some 118 of which have been lost. Part of the difference in their numbers can be explained by a difference in definition: some of the letters included in Lopatin's count might not be deemed by others to be personal letters. Lopatin wisely points out that more letters may come to light in the future. My discussion is based on Lopatin's collection. Lopatin, *Perepiska*, 493, 541; Eliseeva, *Perepiska*, 4.

45. Eliseeva, *Perepiska*, 7.

46. For further discussion on dating, see the Note on the Translation.

47. Ia. Barskov, ed., "Pis'ma imperatritsy Ekateriny II k gr. P. V. Zavadovskomu. (1775–1777)," *Russkii istoricheskii zhurnal* 5 (1918): 245.

48. Eliseeva, *Perepiska*, 9–10, 12.

49. Ibid., 134–37.

50. Mikhail Garnovskii, "Zapiski Mikhaila Garnovskogo," *Russkaia starina* 15 (1876): 256, 260, 254, 263; 16 (1876): 473–74; *SIRIO* 26 (1879): 405; Eliseeva, *Perepiska*, 43–45.

51. Garnovskii, "Zapiski," 15:476–77; Eliseeva, *Perepiska*, 47–48.

52. Garnovskii, "Zapiski," 15:471, 480, 484; Eliseeva, *Perepiska*, 46–50.

53. Garnovskii, "Zapiski," 16:299–402, 406–13; A. M. Gribovskii, *Zapiski o imperatritse Ekaterine Vtoroi* (1847; reprint, Moscow, 1989), 7; M. I. Semevskii, "Kn. Platon Aleksandrovich Zubov. Biograficheskii ocherk, 1767–1822," *Russkaia starina* 16 (1876): 594; 17 (1876): 50; Eliseeva, *Perepiska*, 83–84.

54. Eliseeva, *Perepiska*, 84–85, 137.

55. Garnovskii, "Zapiski," 16:406–13; Eliseeva, *Perepiska*, 84–85.

56. Eliseeva, *Perepiska*, 107–8.

57. Semevskii, "Kn. Platon Aleksandrovich Zubov," 16:603; Eliseeva, *Perepiska*, 97.

58. Garnovskii, "Zapiski," 15:250; Eliseeva, *Perepiska*, 41.

59. Eliseeva, *Perepiska*, 135.

60. Garnovskii, "Zapiski," 15:259–60; Eliseeva, *Perepiska*, 45, 135.

61. Garnovskii, "Zapiski," 15:475; Eliseeva, *Perepiska*, 50–51.

62. Eliseeva, *Perepiska*, 98, 135.

63. G. P. Gooch, *Catherine the Great, and other Studies* (London, 1954), 80.

64. Simon Dixon, *Catherine the Great* (Harlow, England, 2001), 144.

65. O. I. Eliseeva, "K voprosu o russkom iazyke Ekateriny II v ee perepiske s G. A. Potemkinym," in *Issledovaniia po istochnikovedeniiu istorii Rossii (do 1917). Sbornik statei* (Moscow, 1993), 118; Gooch, *Catherine the Great*, 72, 81–82.

66. See Bruce Redford, *The Converse of the Pen: Acts of Intimacy in the Eighteenth-Century Familiar Letter* (Chicago, 1986); and Howard Anderson and Irvin Ehrenpreis, "The Familiar Letter in the Eighteenth-Century: Some Generalizations," in *The Familiar Letter in the Eighteenth-Century,* ed. Howard Anderson, Philip B. Daghlian, and Irvin Ehrenpreis (Lawrence, KS, 1966).

67. See the discussion in E. E. Birzhakova, "Shchegoli i shchegol'skoi zhargon v russkoi komedii XVIII veka," in *Iazyk russkikh pisatelei XVIII veka,* ed. Iu. S. Sorokin (Leningrad, 1981); and Eliseeva, "K voprosu," 113–17.

68. No one did as much to create the myth of Potemkin as the Saxon diplomat Georg von Helbig in a series of articles in the journal *Minerva* from 1797–1800. Helbig's story of Potemkin's life served as the basis for most subsequent critical treatments.

69. In addition to Lopatin's edition of Catherine and Potemkin's correspondence and Montefiore's biography, mention should also be made of Lopatin's *Potemkin i Suvorov* (Moscow, 1992) as well as O. I. Eliseeva's *Perepiska* and *Geopoliticheskie proekty.*

70. Eliseeva, *Perepiska*, 30–31.

71. Alfred Cobban, *A History of Modern France*, vol. 1: 1715–1799 (New York, 1963); Stefan Winkle, *Johann Friedrich Struensee: Arzt, Aufklärer, Staatsmann: Beitrag zur Kultur-, Medizin-, und Seuchensgeschichte der Aufklärungszeit* (Stuttgart, 1983); Jonathan Israel, "The Courts of the House of Orange, c. 1580–1795," in *The Princely Courts of Europe, 1500–1750,* ed. John Adamson (London, 1999), 138.

72. H. M. Scott, "The Rise of the First Minister in Eighteenth-century Europe," in *History and Biography: Essays in Honour of Derek Beales,* eds. T. C. W. Blanning and David Cannadine (Cambridge, 1996); L. W. B. Brockliss, "Concluding Remarks: The Anatomy of the Minister-Favourite," in J. H. Elliott and L. W. B. Brockliss, eds., *The World of the Favourite,* 301–301.

73. Letter 4; Catherine II, *The Memoirs of Catherine the Great,* ed. Dominique Maroger, with an introduction by G. P. Gooch, tr. Moura Budberg (New York, 1955), 300–301.

74. J. T. Alexander, "Favourites, Favouritism and Female Rule in Russia," in *Russia in the Age of Enlightenment: Essays for Isabel de Madariaga,* eds. Roger Bartlett and Janet M. Hartley (London, 1990): 112–17; Evgenii Anisimov, *Elizaveta Petrovna* (Moscow, 1999), 187–208; idem, *Rossiia v seredine XVIII veka: Bor'ba za nasledie Petra* (Moscow, 1986), 185–86.

75. Alexander, "Favourites," 113–17; Anisimov, *Rossiia,* 186–92, 195–202; Aleksandr B. Kamensky, *The Russian Empire in the Eighteenth Century,* trans. and ed. David Griffiths (Armonk, NY, 1997), 175–79.

76. See the list in M. N. Longinov, "Liubimtsy Ekateriny Vtoroi," *Russkii Arkhiv* 2 (1911): 319. This roster includes twenty names, two of which (Saltykov and Poniatowski) were Catherine's lovers before 1762 and eight that most likely were never intimately involved with her.

77. Kazimierz Waliszewski, *The Romance of an Empress: Catherine II of Russia* (1894; reprint, n.p., 1968), 421.

78. Dixon, *Catherine the Great,* 54.

79. Ibid., 54–56.

80. Waliszewski, *Romance,* 454–55; *Arkhiv kniazia Vorontsova* 12 (1877): 63.

81. A. A. Vasil'chikov, *Semeistvo Razumovskikh,* vol. 2 (St. Petersburg, 1880), 31.

82. Dixon, *Catherine the Great,* 56–57.

83. Aleksandr B. Kamenskii, *Pod seniiu Ekateriny* (St. Petersburg, 1992), 293–94.

84. Diderot, *Correspondance,* eds. G. Roth and J. Varloot (Paris, 1968), 14:12–13. Quoted in Dixon, *Catherine the Great,* 58.

85. Dixon, *Catherine the Great,* 12, 16, 144–47, 167, 180–81.

86. Barskov, "Pis'ma Ekateriny II k Potemkinu," *list* 17; Marc Raeff, "In the Imperial Manner," in *Catherine the Great: A Profile,* ed. Marc Raeff (New York, 1972), 236.

87. Dixon, *Catherine the Great,* 57; Eliseeva, *Perepiska,* 130; Madariaga, *Russia,* 359; Raeff, "In the Imperial Manner," 231–34.

88. Eliseeva, *Geopoliticheskie proekty,* 318.

89. Raeff, "In the Imperial Manner," 246.

90. Most historians now recognize the marriage as fact (Barskov, Eidelman, Lopatin, Eliseeva, Montefiore, N. I. Pavlenko [in *Ekaterina Velikaia* (Moscow, 1999), 367]) or as likely (Madariaga, Alexander).

91. See, for example, Letters 33, 42–44, 47, 56, 67–68, 98–99, 124.

92. Kamenskii, *Pod seniiu Ekateriny,* 295; Eliseeva, *Perepiska,* 29

93. Lopatin, *Perepiska,* 524.

94. Montefiore, *Prince of Princes,* 139; Marc Raeff, "In the Imperial Manner," 233–34, 236.

95. Kazimierz Waliszewski, *The Story of a Throne (Catherine II of Russia)* (1895; reprint, Freeport, NY, 1971), 1:189.

96. Semevskii, "Kn. Platon Aleksandrovich Zubov," 17:43.

97. Lopatin, *Perepiska*, 513–14; Montefiore, *Prince of Princes*, 136–39. On the sources relating to the possible marriage, see Lopatin, *Perepiska*, 479–83.

98. Alexander, *Catherine the Great*, 73–76; David L. Ransel, *The Politics of Catherinian Russia: The Panin Party* (New Haven, CT, 1975), 124–26.

99. Anisimov, 197–99; idem, *Rossiia v seredine XVIII veka*, 186; Tamara Talbot Rice, *Elizabeth, Empress of Russia* (London, 1970), 76–77; Maria Razumovsky, *Die Rasumovskys. Eine Familie am Zarenhof* (Köln, 1998), 6; A. A. Vasil'chikov, *Semeistvo Razumovskikh*, vol. 1 (St. Petersburg, 1880), 19–20.

100. François Bluche, *Louis XIV* (Paris, 1986), 588, 709–15; André Castelot, *Madame de Maintenon. La reine secrète* (Paris, 1996), 133; Louis Hastier, *Louis XIV et Madame de Maintenon* (Paris, 1957), 77–86, 219–23; *Histoire de Mme de Maintenon, fondatrice de Saint-Cyr*, vol. 2 (Paris, 1814), 31; Jean-Christian Petitfils, *Louis XIV* (Paris, 1995), 311–12, 312n1; John B. Wolf, *Louis XIV* (New York, 1968), 332–35.

101. E. A. Smith, *George IV*, Yale English Monarchs (New Haven, CT, 1999), 36–39.

102. Eliseeva, *Geopoliticheskie proekty*, 91–138; Lopatin, *Perepiska*, 655, 694, 698; Montefiore, *Prince of Princes*, 360–62, 242–43, 431.

103. On the truly bizarre fate of Potemkin's corpse, see Montefiore, *Prince of Princes*, 487–502.

104. Alexander, "Favourites," 110–11, 116; Evgenii Viktorovich Anisimov, "Empress Anna Ivanovna, 1730–1740," in *The Emperors and Empresses of Russia: Rediscovering the Romanovs*, ed. Donald J. Raleigh, comp. A. A. Iskenderov (Armonk, NY, 1996); Kamenskii, *Russian Empire*, 132; Lopatin, *Perepiska*, 655.

105. Brenda Meehan-Waters, *Autocracy and Aristocracy: The Russian Service Elite of 1730* (New Brunswick, NJ, 1982), 93, 96.

106. Barskov, "Pis'ma imperatritsy Ekateriny II k gr. P. V. Zavadovskomu. (1775–1777)," 240–41. An accurate assessment of how much Catherine gave to her favorites has yet to be made. See Barskov, p. 240; E. P. Karnovich, *Zamechatel'nye bogatstva chastnykh lits v Rossii* (1885; reprint, Moscow, 1992), chaps. 17, 18, 19; Alexander, *Catherine the Great*, 224.

107. *Arkhiv kniazia Vorontsova* 12 (1877): 63.

108. Quoted in Waliszewski, *Romance*, 428.

109. Alexander, *Catherine the Great*, 216–17; Lopatin, *Perepiska*, 759; Montefiore, *Prince of Princes*, 312–14.

110. *Arkhiv kniazia Vorontsova* 12 (1877): 10.

111. Catherine, of course, had children of her own from her other lovers, but none with Potemkin, although it has been asserted that Catherine gave birth to a daughter, Yelizaveta Grigorevna Tyomkina, in 1775 sired by Potemkin. This is quite unlikely. Tyomkina is never mentioned in their correspondence and Potemkin is not known to have had any children. Tat'iana Vasil'evna Alekseeva, *Vladimir Lukich Borovikovskii i russkaia kul'tura na rubezhe vosemnadtsatogo-deviatnadtsatogo vekov* (Moscow, 1975), 184–90; Lopatin, Perepiska, 521; Montefiore, Prince of Princes, 146. A portrait of Tyomkina hangs in Moscow's Tretiakov Gallery.

112. Lopatin, *Perepiska*, 721; Letters 340, 390; RGADA, *fond* 11, *opis'* 1, *delo* 914, *listy* 1, 6.

113. Elliot and Brockliss, eds., *World of the Favourite*, 33, 113–16.

114. *SIRIO* 23 (1878): 316–17.

115. Montefiore, *Prince of Princes*, 168.

116. Alexander, *Catherine the Great*, 213; Lopatin, *Perepiska*, 666, 669, 673, 766.

117. Lopatin, *Perepiska*, 682.

118. The letters of Varvara (together with some from Potemkin), Aleksandra, Tatiana, and Yekaterina are in RGADA, *fond* 11, *opis'* 1, *dela* 854, 857, 858, 859 respectively. Excerpts from Varvara and Potemkin's correspondence is published in *Russkaia starina* 12 (March 1875): 512–21. For translated excerpts and a discussion of Potemkin's relationship with his nieces, see Montefiore, *Prince of Princes*, 185–95. Lopatin (*Perepiska*, 678 n. 4, and in his *Potemkin i Suvorov*, 38–39) tries to put a more palatable spin on Potemkin's relationship with Varvara.

119. RGADA, *fond* 11, *opis'* 1, *delo* 864, *listy* 3, 8, 14, 15.

120. See her letters to Potemkin in RGADA, *fond* 11, *opis'* 1, *delo* 862, *listy* 1–4.

121. P. Maikov, ed. *Pis'ma grafa P. V. Zavadovskogo k feld'marshalu grafu P. A. Rumiantsevu, 1775–1791 godov* (St. Petersburg, 1901), 8–9.

122. A. S. Pushkin, *Sobranie sochinenii*, ed. D. D. Blagoi (Moscow, 1962), 7:192–93.

Note on the Translation

*T*he translations and annotations in this book are based on the letters and notes published in V. S. Lopatin's *Ekaterina II i G. A. Potemkin. Lichnaia perepiska, 1769-1791* (Moscow, 1997). The result of nineteen years of research and writing, Lopatin's edition of the letters is the most complete and authoritative to date. It is a magisterial work of scholarship, and this English translation would not have been possible without it.

Catherine and Potemkin exchanged thousands of letters, and neither Lopatin's edition of their correspondence nor this one makes any claim to completeness. Although a few official documents have been included in this volume as well as in Lopatin's, both works are almost exclusively devoted to Catherine and Potemkin's personal correspondence, as much as it can be separated from their official communications, a large percentage of which has been published in the *Collections of the Imperial Russian Historical Society* (volumes 13 [1874], 27 [1880], 42 [1885]), in *Russian Antiquity* (volumes 16, 17 [1876]), and in a few other prerevolutionary publications. Of the 1,162 letters and notes published in Lopatin, 464 are included in this volume either in their entirety or in an edited form. In order to be able to include as many letters as possible, material from some of them has been excised. Editorial omissions in the text are marked by ellipses in brackets: [. . .]. Editorial additions are also marked by brackets.

Several criteria dictated the selection of letters for this volume. First, letters that provided the most revealing material on the personalities of Catherine and Potemkin and their relationship were chosen for inclusion. Second, the most important letters dealing with the major events of Catherine's reign (for example, the annexation of the Crimea and the Second Russo-Turkish War) were selected. Third, letters that shed light on other moments of historical significance (the Pugachev Rebellion, the Russo-Austrian Alliance of 1781) and on noteworthy aspects of Potemkin's career (the administration of the southern provinces) or those letters that provide unusual details on life in Catherinian Russia were included. At the same time, every effort has been made to ensure that the letters in this volume accurately reflect both the principal themes of the entire correspondence and their relative significance within it.

Translation not being exegesis, I have sought to render the literal sense of the letters as accurately and faithfully as possible and to resist the temptation to translate what Catherine and Potemkin meant, as opposed to what they wrote. It has been necessary to depart from this servile path on occasion when murky passages demanded concessions to readability. Catherine was reportedly fond of saying that she needed a good laundress to smooth out her rumpled prose, and the same could be said for much of Potemkin's writing. And so, as a favor to the reader I have taken a hot iron to their more wrinkled phrases and sentences. In this same spirit, misspelled names have been silently corrected and abbreviations written out.

These letters present several challenges for the translator. One of them is Catherine's Russian, a rare, if not to say unique, mixture of then antiquated expressions, folk or peasant words and phrases, and the esoteric linguistic mannerisms of the Russian francophile elite. Unfortunately, none of these elements have clear, satisfactory English equivalents, and so to try to reproduce them would result in an awkward, artificial English. As with any translation, this one, too, involves some regrettable loss. A second challenge is the personal pronoun "you." Russian has two forms of the English "you": *ty*, the familiar second person singular, and *vy*, the formal second person and/or plural form. Catherine and Potemkin used both forms of "you" with each other, often in the same sentence. There being no contemporary equivalent in English—by the second half of the eighteenth century, "thou" had largely dropped out of daily use—this distinctive detail is also lost.

Another challenge concerns diminutives and terms of address and endearment. The Russian language is uncommonly rich with such terms and allows for the creation of many diminutive forms from a single word stem. English is poor in this regard: it simply cannot compete with a language that boasts over thirty different endearing forms for "papa." Catherine loved making up all sorts of silly pet names and diminutives for Potemkin, and her letters, chiefly those written during their love affair, are filled with dozens of terms of endearment for which there are no clear

English equivalents. The terms used in this translation (for example, "darling," "dear," "sweetheart") are mere approximations that do not fully reflect the exuberance nor the playfulness of Catherine's vocabulary.

A handful of terms of address lacking any acceptable English equivalents have been left in Russian. The most prevalent of these in the correspondence is *matushka* (with the stress on the first syllable, the "a" in each instance pronounced like the "a" in "father"). It is typically (and unfortunately) translated as "Little Mother," which does not convey in any way the word's richly polysemous quality. While *matushka,* based on *mat'* (Russian for "mother") is an endearing, familiar term for "mother," it has a much broader semantic range and has been used in several other important ways—unique to Russian history and culture—that distinguish it from the English word, including as an affectionate or deferential form of address for any woman, as a term used for one's mistress, or when referring or speaking to either a clergyman's wife or a nun. *Matushka* has also been common as a poetic-folk epithet, usually in combination with other nouns: *matushka Rossiia* (Mother Russia), *matushka Moskva* (Mother Moscow), *matushka zima* (Mother Winter), etc. The Russian tsaritsa, or empress, was addressed as *matushka Gosudarynia* (and the emperor as *tsar'* or *gosudar' batiushka*), which I have translated in Potemkin's letters as "Your Majesty," or "Your Most Gracious Majesty" (for *matushka Vsemilostiveishaia Gosudarynia*), in keeping with general European forms of royal address. When Potemkin uses *matushka* alone, however, this has been left untranslated.

As for Catherine, she favored several endearing terms derived from the Russian word for "father": *baten'ka, batia, bat'ko* (or *bat'ka*). Like *matushka,* the stress falls on the first syllable in all these words and the "a" is pronounced like the "a" in "father." Once again, none of these informal terms of address have any true English equivalents. "Papa" or "pa" hints at their meaning, although both fail to capture the words' peasant origins, and so their highly marked status in Catherine's letters in which the languages of the elite and the lower orders rubbed shoulders; nor do they reflect the way these terms could be used as a casual form of address with men other than one's father (along the lines of "my good man" or "old chap"), just as *matushka* (or *matia, matka*) was used with women besides one's own mother. Catherine's fondness for such words offers insight into that attractive playful side of her character and the nature of her feelings for Potemkin. It also speaks to Catherine's genuine interest in all things Russian and her noted desire to learn the ways of her adopted home.

Although they wrote almost exclusively in Russian, both Catherine and Potemkin liked to sprinkle their letters with bits of French. To preserve this distinctive feature of the correspondence, individual words, phrases, and sentences in French (and the rare Italian) have been left in the text with accompanying English translations in the notes at the end of each letter. In the interest of economy, entire paragraphs and letters in French have been translated directly into English. These sections have been clearly marked in the text. Although gross grammatical and spelling errors in the French have been silently corrected, archaic and idiosyncratic spellings and usage ("-es" for "-ez" in second-person-plural verb conjugations, "tems" for "temps") have been maintained.

A modified Library of Congress system has been used to transliterate Russian names in the text, letters, and annotations. Soft and hard signs have been dropped, and several other modest changes have been made to simplify the spelling of Russian names and to make it more accurately reflect their pronunciation. One important exception is the transliteration of "Potemkin," which according to my system should read "Potyomkin." The former spelling has been chosen due to its traditional and widely accepted usage. Given its familiarity to scholars, the regular Library of Congress system has been used for Russian words translated in the text, for source citations, and for the bibliography. I have kept the Russian form of names except for those individuals already best known by the English equivalent, thus Peter (not Pyotr) the Great and Catherine (not Yekaterina) the Great. The feminized form for Russian surnames has been kept, thus "Countess Vorontsova" not "Vorontsov." Polish and other non-Russian personal names have mostly been spelled according to accepted usage in their respective languages or in their common English equivalents.

With few exceptions (Letters 232–235, 444), this volume follows the chronology established by Lopatin. Unless otherwise noted, all dates are given according to the Old Style (Julian) calendar then in use in Russia that was eleven days behind the New Style (Gregorian) calendar used in the West. Dates given in the Gregorian calendar are designated: (n.s.).

Love & Conquest

I. Ardent Zeal, Sincere Confessions—

1769-1774

*T*n June 1768, Russian Cossacks pursued a group of Polish rebels opposed to King Stanislaw August Poniatowski and his Russian backers into Turkish territory and set to massacring the Jews and Tatars in the village of Balta. The Ottoman Turks, upset at continued Russian meddling in Poland and egged on by the French, responded to this provocation on 25 September by declaring war in the traditional Turkish manner: they promptly seized the Russian envoy, Aleksei Obreskov, and imprisoned him in Constantinople's Seven Towers fortress.

The outbreak of the First Russo-Turkish War (1768–1774) found Potemkin in St. Petersburg serving as a member of the Legislative Commission, which had been moved to the capital from Moscow in early 1768. War with the Turks provided the ambitious Potemkin the opportunity to prove to the empress his valor and devotion on the field of battle. Although he had only recently been removed from the Horse Guards and made court chamberlain, Potemkin requested Catherine's permission to leave St. Petersburg and join the Russian army. The empress acceded to his request, and early in 1769 the twenty-nine-year-old Potemkin rode south from the capital to fight the Turks.

Potemkin immediately reported to the headquarters of Major-General Prince Aleksandr Prozorovsky in the Polish village of Bar. It was from here that Potemkin wrote his first letter to Catherine, a letter overflowing with devotion to her person and the empire, requesting that he be placed in the military roll (Letter 1). Throughout the following months of 1769, Major-General of the Cavalry Potemkin distinguished himself in a series of skirmishes and battles, and word quickly reached Catherine of his exemplary courage. Potemkin's heroics continued in the next year's campaign, and he was awarded the Order of St. Anne, his first decoration, and then the Order of St. George third class, for his role in the defeat of the enemy at the Battle of Larga in July. For this he personally thanked the empress (Letter 2).

As a tribute to his undeniable bravery and military talent, Potemkin was chosen in November 1770 by his commanding officer, General Pyotr Rumiantsev, to deliver to the empress the news of Russia's successes against the Turks. Potemkin returned to the capital a war hero and remained there for several months during which time he dined with Catherine on numerous occasions. Potemkin's stay in Petersburg marked an important if mysterious phase in their warming relationship. While Potemkin was undeniably growing in the empress's estimation, historians do not have any clear idea of what transpired between them during his visit, although it seems safe to assume that inklings of what lay ahead were first felt by both of them at this time. Potemkin returned to the army in February 1771, flush with the success of his stay and bearing a letter from Prince Grigory Orlov, Catherine's favorite, recommending him to General Rumiantsev. From Catherine, Potemkin carried with him a personal request to purchase for her a Turkish horse and possibly the permission to begin corresponding with her.

The intervening years from 1771 to early 1774, when Potemkin assumed the position of favorite, are shrouded in obscurity. While Potemkin clearly spent most of his time in the south with the army, he had undeniably captured the empress's eye and was increasingly looked to as a worthy advisor. Catherine had particular need of such men during these years, a period that constituted the most serious crisis of her reign, both personally and politically, since coming to the throne in 1762.

From the late 1760s, discontent had been growing in the Guards regiments, among the very men who had put Catherine on the throne. Many had come to feel that Catherine had forsaken their interests, and they increasingly resented the overweening power and influence of the Orlov brothers. Tensions climaxed in June 1772 when Grigory Orlov was sent by Catherine to the peace talks with the Turks at Fokshany. A plot was uncovered among members of the Preobrazhensky Guards to overthrow the empress, banish the Orlovs, and place Grand Duke Paul, Catherine's son who came into his majority that year, on the throne. The plotters went so far as to contemplate murdering the deposed tsaritsa and her son should the latter refuse the crown. During these frightful days Catherine left St. Petersburg for the relative safety of Finland to confer with a handful of her most trusted advisors. Potemkin was among them.

Catherine put down the plot, just as she had put down earlier attempts to topple her, though not without paying a price: the events of the summer of 1772 made it clear to her that Orlov, the man who had captured her heart and put her on the throne a decade earlier, would have to go. Her reasoning was both political and personal. The plot exposed to Catherine the depths of the anti-Orlov sentiment, and about this time she also had to face up to her favorite's countless infidelities. In the end, Catherine made the difficult decision to cut her ties to Orlov and his brothers. Not long after returning from Finland, Catherine appointed as chamberlain Aleksandr Vasilchikov, a twenty-eight-year-old lieutenant in the Horse Guards with no affiliation to the Orlovs. On 30 August, Vasilchikov was made adjutant-general to the empress and moved into the palace rooms adjoining Catherine's that had earlier belonged to Orlov. Upon hearing the news, Orlov raced back to the capital from Fokshany, but he was too late. Prohibited from seeing Catherine, the furious Orlov was forced to accept Vasilchikov's appointment as a fait accompli and to graciously receive the gifts the empress showered upon him as a sign of his dismissal.

Although the taking of Vasilchikov as her new favorite helped Catherine through the crisis of 1772, it did not put an end to the court intrigue swirling around Grand Duke Paul, whom elements critical of Catherine continued to regard as Russia's savior, or to the fierce competition between the competing clans centered around Nikita Panin, the de facto foreign minister, and Orlov, who returned to state service in 1773. On top of these troubles, a new threat to Catherine's rule appeared in September 1773 in the guise of Yemelian Pugachev. A scruffy Don Cossack deserter claiming to be the deposed (and actually dead) Tsar Peter III, Pugachev united a motley band of Yaik Cossacks, serfs, Old Believers, and various non-Russian peoples into a huge popular rebellion that quickly engulfed much of eastern Russia before spilling into the Volga River basin and eventually posing a threat to Moscow itself. What started out as but a minor disturbance along Russia's frontier had become a dangerous insurrection that tore at the very foundations of the empire. The situation was all the more precarious given the fact that the troops needed to put down the uprising were encamped far away fighting the Turks.

It was during these dark days that Catherine wrote to Potemkin, then with the army besieging the Turkish fortress at Silistria on the Danube, to express to him her high regard for his person (Letter 3). It has been suggested that this letter was intended as an invitation to Potemkin to return to St. Petersburg, although there is little to support the notion. Yet, to a bold and ambitious young officer such as Potemkin, who had most likely been attracted to Catherine for several years already, it might have been all the prompting needed. After quartering the troops for the winter, Potemkin galloped back to St. Petersburg in January 1774.

Whether Catherine was already in love with her dashing hero and so quietly summoned him to her side, or whether Potemkin saw for himself an opportunity and chose to seize it, the young lieutenant-general was not immediately allowed to take the position he sought. Rather, as she writes in her "Sincere Confession" (Letter 4), Catherine took the time to test Potemkin in order to see if he truly loved her, as she had been told he did and as she so desperately hoped. For the passionate Potemkin, to be so near now to Catherine, to be among her intimate circle at court, yet to be kept at arm's length became increasingly difficult to bear. According to legend, Potemkin, who always displayed a gift for the dramatic, decided to force Catherine's hand. He abruptly abandoned court sometime in late January and retreated to the Alexander Nevsky Monastery, where he grew a beard and took up the life of a monk. Potemkin would force her to decide between him and Vasilchikov.

For Catherine the question presented no difficulty. By now she was not only convinced of his great passion for her, she was even more sure of his intelligence and the keen advice he could give her, which she needed at this time and would come to rely on for nearly two decades.

At six o'clock on the evening of 4 February 1774, Potemkin arrived at the magnificent imperial palace at Tsarskoe Selo outside St. Petersburg. He was presented to the empress, and together they retreated to her private apartments. Though they met several more times in the following days, the way had yet to be cleared for their love to blossom. Ever the more jealous and insecure of the two, Potemkin demanded of Catherine that she give a full account of all her past loves. The presumption on the part of Potemkin is astounding: who was he, after all, to demand such a thing from the empress? Equally remarkable is the fact that Catherine acceded to his demand. It was a sign of how deeply she loved him and how much she needed him.

Throughout the day of 21 February, Catherine never left her private chambers in the Winter Palace. It is possible that she spent this time writing one of the most revealing letters ever penned by a European monarch. In her "Sincere Confession," Catherine shared with Potemkin the intimate details of her personal life beginning with her marriage as a young girl to Grand Duke Peter; she told him of her previous loves, of the painful disappointments she had suffered, and of the passionate nature of her soul. Finally, she let him know of her hopes and fears for their future together and begged him to love her and to always tell her the truth. Catherine called him her *bogatyr'*, or knight. The bogatyri were the mythical heroes of the medieval Russian epic songs. Characterized by their youth, immense physical strength, military valor, and religiously infused patriotism, they had defended ancient Russia against all foes. Besieged by foreign war and domestic revolt, Catherine believed that in Potemkin she had found her bogatyr'.

＊＊＊

1. POTEMKIN TO CATHERINE

24 May 1769   In the camp of Prince Prozorovsky[1]

Your Most Gracious Majesty!

Your Majesty's unprecedented concern for the common good has made our Fatherland dear to us. The subject's duty of responsibility demands that everyone conform to your wishes. For my part, I have carried out my duties in complete accordance with Your Majesty's desires.

It is with gratitude that I have viewed Your Majesty's Royal charities for the Fatherland, and I have endeavored to understand your wise legislation and have tried to be a good citizen. However, the Royal favor, with which I have been especially rewarded, fills me with excellent zeal for Your Majesty's person. I am obliged to serve my Sovereign and benefactress. And so, the only way to express my gratitude in all its splendor is to shed my blood for Your Majesty's glory. The current war has presented such an opportunity, and I have not remained idle.

Permit me now, Your Most Gracious Majesty, to throw myself at Your Majesty's feet and request Royal injunction that I be placed on active duty in the corps of Prince Prozorovsky, in whatever rank it pleases Your Majesty, not entering me forever in the military roll, but only for the duration of the war.[2]

Your Most Gracious Majesty, I have tried to be worthy in whatever way possible for your service. I have a special disposition for the cavalry, the details of which I boldly confirm to know. In addition, concerning the military art, I have learned by rote this rule more than anything else: the best means for achieving success are fervent service to one's Sovereign and disregard for one's life. Your Most Gracious Majesty, this is what military tactics and that general, under whom I request Your Royal permission to serve, have taught me. You will be pleased to see that my zeal for your service will compensate for the deficiencies of my talents, and you will have no cause to regret your decision.

Most Gracious Sovereign
Your Imperial Majesty's most humble servant
Grigory Potemkin

---

1. Major-General Prince Aleksandr Aleksandrovich Prozorovsky (1734–1809) was in command of the vanguard of the Russian First Army.

2. Catherine respected his request and ordered on 23 June 1769 that Chamberlain Potemkin be transferred to the military roll.

2.   POTEMKIN TO CATHERINE

21 August 1770   Camp near Kilia

Your Great, Most Gracious and Supremely Powerful Majesty
Empress and Autocrat of All the Russias
Your Majesty Most Gracious
I had the good fortune to receive Your Imperial Majesty's most gracious deed and the Order of St. George, even though I find myself lacking the necessary strength to merit that imperial charity in actual fact.[1] I feel even less capable of expressing in words my most loyal gratitude. There is nothing more precious to me than life, and mine is sincerely devoted to Your Majesty. Only its end will conclude my service.

Permit me, Your Most Gracious Majesty, to express my most humble congratulations on the subjugation of another Turkish town on the Danube.[2]

Prostrating myself at Your Imperial Majesty's blessed feet, I remain with slavish devotion

Most Gracious Sovereign
Your Imperial Majesty's most humble servant
Grigory Potemkin

---

1. Potemkin received the Order of St. George third class on 27 July 1770 for his deeds in the Battle of Larga.

2. The fortress of Kilia fell to the Russians on 10 August 1770, just weeks after the capture of Ismail, in which Potemkin participated.

3.   CATHERINE TO POTEMKIN

4 December 1773

Sir Lieutenant-General and Chevalier. I suppose you have your eyes so thoroughly trained on Silistria that you haven't time to read letters.[1] And although I do not currently know whether your bombardment has been a success, nonetheless I am certain that everything you undertake can be ascribed to nothing but your ardent zeal toward me personally and toward the dear Fatherland in general, which you love to serve.

But since for my part I very much desire to preserve fervent, brave, clever, and skillful individuals, so I ask you not to endanger yourself for naught. Upon reading this letter, you may well ask: why was it written? To which I can offer you the following reply: so that you had confirmation of my opinion of you, for I am always most benevolent toward you.

Catherine
Say thank you as well to Brigadier Pavel Potemkin for receiving and entertaining the Turks so well when they came to destroy your battery on the island.[2]

1. Potemkin was with the Russian army besieging the Turks at Silistria on the Danube throughout much of 1773.

2. Pavel Sergeevich Potemkin (1743–1796) was Potemkin's second cousin. Thanks in part to his relative's exalted position, Pavel went on to a successful military career. Two battalions under his command repulsed a Turkish landing on an island in the Danube in the fall of 1773, where Grigory Potemkin had set up a battery to bombard the fortress.

4.   CATHERINE TO POTEMKIN

[21 February 1774]

A Sincere Confession

Maria Choglokova[1] saw that after nine years things remained the same as they'd been before the wedding, and often having been scolded by the late Empress for not having tried to change them, she found no other means than to have both parties choose freely from those persons she had in mind. One party chose the widow Groot, who's now married to Lieutenant-General of the Artillery Meller;[2] the other—Sergei Saltykov, and him chiefly because of his obvious inclination and Mama's[3] persuasion, who'd been driven to this by dire necessity.

Two years later Sergei Saltykov[4] was sent away as an envoy, for he had conducted himself indiscreetly and Maria Choglokova no longer had enough power at the Great Court[5] to retain him. After a year spent in great sorrow, the present Polish King arrived.[6] We took no notice of him, but good people, with their empty suspicions, forced me to notice that he existed, that his eyes were of unparalleled beauty and that he directed them (though so near-sighted he doesn't see past his nose) more often in one direction than another. This one was both loving and loved from 1755 till 1761. But a three-year absence, that is from 1758, and the efforts of Prince Grigory Grigorievich,[7] whom again good people forced me to notice, changed my state of mind. This one would've remained for life had he himself not grown bored. I learned of this on the very day of his departure to the congress[8] from Tsarskoe Selo, and as a result I simply decided that I could no longer trust him. This thought cruelly tormented me and forced me, out of desperation, to make some sort of choice, one which grieved me then and still does now more than I can say, and especially at those moments when other people are usually happy.[9] His every caress has aroused tears in me, so much so that I think I've never cried since my birth as I have this past year and a half. At first I thought I'd get used to it, but the further along, the worse it got; and as for the other party, he began to pout, sometimes for three months at a time, and I must admit that I was never as happy as when he would get angry and leave me in peace, for his caresses only made me cry.

Then came a certain knight.[10] Through his merits and customary kindness, this hero was so charming that people, upon hearing of his arrival, were already saying that he should take up residence here. But what they didn't know was that we'd called him here, on the quiet, with a note[11] secretly intending, however, not to act blindly upon his arrival, but to try to discover whether he truly had the inclination which Briussha[12] told me many had long suspected he had, that is, that which I wanted him to have.

Now, Sir Knight, after this confession may I hope to receive absolution for my sins? You'll be pleased to see that it wasn't fifteen, but a third as many: the first, chosen out of necessity, and the fourth, out of desperation, cannot, in my mind, be attributed to any frivolity. As to the other three, if you look closely, God knows they weren't the result of debauchery, for which I haven't the least inclination, and had fate given me in my youth a husband whom I could've loved, I would've remained true to him forever. The trouble is that my heart is loath to be without love even for a single hour. It's said that people try to conceal such vices under the cloak of kindness, and it may be that such disposition of the heart is more of a vice than a virtue. Perhaps it's wrong for me to write this to you, for after reading it you might fall in love with me or might not want to go off to the army fearing that I shall forget you. But I really don't think I'd make such a foolish mistake, and if you want to keep me forever, then show me as much friendship as love, and more than anything else, love me and tell me the truth.

---

1. Maria Semyonovna Choglokova (1724–1756) was the chief stewardess of the young court. She was charged by Empress Elizabeth with finding out why, after nine years of marriage, then Grand Duchess Catherine had yet to produce an heir. With the help of Chancellor Aleksei Bestuzhev-Riumin, she brought Catherine together with Sergei Saltykov.

2. The widow Groot's first husband, Georg Christoph Groot (d. 1749), was a portraitist of some recognition. Her second husband, Ivan Ivanovich Meller (or Miller) (1725–1790), was a decorated veteran of the Seven Years' War and the First Russo-Turkish War. He died in the assault on the fortress of Kilia in the Second Russo-Turkish War. Young and attractive, widow Groot was apparently selected to test the potency of Grand Duke Peter's seed. It is not known for certain whether she became pregnant by him.

3. Empress Elizabeth.

4. Sergei Vasilievich Saltykov (1726–after 1776) was a chamberlain and Catherine's lover from 1752–1754. In her memoirs, Catherine implies that Saltykov, and not her husband, Grand Duke Peter, was the father of her son Paul. Many of Catherine's contemporaries believed this to be true, and historians have generally agreed.

5. The court of Empress Elizabeth, as opposed to the young court centered around the grand duke and duchess.

6. Count Stanislaw Poniatowski (1732–1798) arrived in St. Petersburg in the retinue of the British ambassador, Sir Charles Hanbury Williams, in 1755. Handsome, intelligent, and well-mannered, Poniatowski immediately charmed the young Catherine, who fell deeply in love with him and would later try to keep him in St. Petersburg at great personal risk. He is believed to have been the father of Anna Petrovna, born to Catherine in December 1757. Catherine played a decisive role in the election of Poniatowski as king of Poland in 1764.

He died in St. Petersburg, having abdicated the throne in November 1795.

7. Prince Grigory Grigorievich Orlov (1734–1783).

8. Orlov left to conduct peace talks with the Turks in Fokshany in April 1772. His numerous infidelities were made known to Catherine around this time.

9. A reference to taking Aleksandr Semyonovich Vasilchikov (1740–1804) as her lover. His favor lasted from the end of August 1772 until his dismissal in 1774 to make way for Potemkin.

10. Potemkin.

11. Possibly Letter 3.

12. Countess Praskovia Aleksandrovna Bruce (1729–1786) became Catherine's closest female friend after her accession to the throne. She was the sister of Field Marshal Pyotr Aleksandrovich Rumiantsev, under whom Potemkin had successfully served in the First Russo-Turkish War.

2. Lovers—1774-1775

atherine's confession assuaged the jealous and seemingly hesitant Potemkin and removed whatever obstacles remained from his assuming the position she had prepared for him. On 1 March 1774, Catherine officially marked Potemkin as her new favorite by bestowing upon him the title of adjutant-general, which he had been so bold as to request for himself (Letters 6, 9). The pitiful Vasilchikov remained at court during these undoubtedly trying days and could do little more than watch as Catherine and the man she had chosen to replace him yielded to their passion. Always generous to her past favorites, Catherine awarded Vasilchikov fifty thousand rubles, several estates, and a large annual pension, and sent him off to retirement.

Potemkin's rapid rise and the general perception that Catherine's feelings for him represented something new and unusual created a great stir among the factions at court. Grigory Orlov and his family's supporters sought to counsel her on the danger of her actions and apparently plotted to have Potemkin removed from court (Letter 5). Unsuccessful, they summoned from Moscow Aleksei Orlov-Chesmensky, hero of the First Russo-Turkish War and the most decisive of the five Orlov brothers, to speak with Catherine about the nature of her relationship with Potemkin. The haughty Aleksei laughed in the empress's face when she admitted her love for Potemkin (Letter 11). Nevertheless, Catherine refused to be intimidated by the Orlovs and prudently instructed Potemkin not to cross them (Letters 8, 11). The Orlovs soon realized that whatever hopes they might have had for removing the new favorite and reestablishing their own power were futile.

Shortly thereafter Aleksei returned to the Russian fleet, then in the Mediterranean, and the following year left state service; Grigory abandoned court for his estates, but not before quarreling bitterly with Catherine, and then departed on a lengthy trip abroad. In August, Zakhar Chernyshev, president of the War College and an ally of the Orlovs, resigned his post. The Orlovs' rival, Nikita Panin, was happy to extend a welcoming hand to Potemkin on the principle that one's enemy's enemy is one's friend. Potemkin gladly accepted Panin's support, in part because he hoped to use him to neutralize Grand Duke Paul, who was wary of the new favorite.

The changes then taking place at court were not overlooked by the representatives of the various European powers, most of whom rightly sensed something different in Potemkin. Count V. F. von Solms, the Prussian ambassador, appraised Potemkin's intelligence and talents highly and believed that Potemkin would use the empress's inclination toward him to become one of the most influential men in all of Russia. By early May, the British representative, Sir Robert Gunning, noted that none of Potemkin's predecessors had ever acquired so much power.

Potemkin was indeed quickly amassing considerable power, both formal and informal, as well as numerous titles and honors. On 15 March, he was appointed lieutenant-colonel of the elite Preobrazhensky Regiment, whose colonel was Catherine herself; in early May he began attending the meetings of the State Council, created in 1768 to coordinate Russia's war effort against the Porte; that same month Potemkin was made vice president of the War College with the rank of general-in-chief and was named governor-general of New Russia, the expansive territory to the south bordering the Crimean Khanate and the Ottoman Empire. In July he was put in charge of Russia's irregular troops (the Cossacks) and the cavalry. On 21 April, Catherine's birthday, he received the Order of St. Alexander Nevsky and the Order of the White Eagle from the king of Poland. Other orders soon followed from Prussia, Sweden, and Denmark. In July, Catherine made him a count of the Russian Empire and five months later awarded him the Order of St. Andrew.

Potemkin moved into the imperial Winter Palace in St. Petersburg in April 1774. So as to prove that he had nothing in common with his insignificant predecessor, he refused to occupy Vasilchikov's old chambers and had a new suite of rooms decorated for himself. Beautifully appointed, they were located directly beneath those of the empress and were connected by a private spiral staircase. It was up and down these green-carpeted stairs that Potemkin and Catherine would hurry to their assignations during the coming months. Rooms were also prepared for Potemkin in the other imperial residences. Since they lived according to different clocks—Catherine preferring to retire and rise early, while Potemkin talked and gamed until the wee hours and then rose late in the morning—they generally did not spend the night together, but slept alone in their separate quarters. Along with their private chambers, another favored meeting place was the *bania*, the traditional Russian baths, in the basement of the Winter Palace (Letters 7, 11).

Catherine was utterly swept away by the intensity of her love for Potemkin. Following her difficult break-up with Orlov in 1772 and the icy interlude with Vasilchikov, Catherine, now forty-four, was ready for a strong lover, one who could be more her equal, and she reveled in the emotional rebirth she experienced in Potemkin's arms. Ten years her junior, Potemkin, too, was no longer in his youth, though the years had clearly done little to dampen his sexual appetite or to lessen his attractiveness, a fact which Catherine herself acknowledged (Letter 8).

Although the letters from these years constitute only one side of a conversation, they afford revealing glimpses into the personalities of Catherine and Potemkin and the nature of their relationship. One is immediately struck by the intensity of Catherine's love for Potemkin and the degree to which it consumed her. She repeatedly writes to him of how she has lost her mind and her senses, of how this passion has robbed her of all reason (Letters 8, 18, 21, 23). So exhilarating were the early days of their affair that for several nights in a row she simply could not sleep, and when sleep finally did come to her, Potemkin filled her dreams (Letters 5, 20).

As Catherine admitted in her "Sincere Confession," she was loathe to be without love for even an hour (Letter 4), and part of her feelings can be attributed simply to her love of the idea of being in love. But there was more to it than that. For someone who led a highly regimented and often tedious daily routine that afforded little opportunity for spontaneity, the rush of emotion she experienced with Potemkin must have been liberating. Even if she were not free to be with him whenever she wanted, she could at least lose herself in thoughts of him and in the memories of his caresses as she sat for hours on end reading papers and listening to reports. It is in fact thanks to the highly regulated nature of court life that so many letters exist: because she was not free to see Potemkin whenever she wished, Catherine took to penning these *tsydulki* or little notes while attending to the affairs of state that forever demanded her attention. Before the official day began or between audiences, Catherine would steal a few moments to write to Potemkin, if only to tell him she loved him or to inquire after his health (Letter 51).

The Catherine that emerges from these letters is playful, tender, and loving, though she can at times display signs of vanity and insensitivity. She loved coming up with pet names, turning "Grigory" into "Grishenka," "Grishatka," "Grishootka," and even "Grishifushechka" and "Grishefishechka." He was her "golden pheasant," her "dear sweet lips," her "little pussycat," her "sweet doll" (Letters 28, 88, 96, 145). In him she claimed to have found her "angel," her "marble beauty," her "cher Epoux," and "beloved husband" (Letters 29, 38, 47, 98). She comforted him like a concerned mother when he was ill, urging him to take care and offering her own medical advice (Letters 68, 99, 125).

One of the things that most attracted Catherine to Potemkin was his marvelous sense of humor and gift for mimicry, and she loved losing herself in the laughter he could so easily draw from her (Letters 12, 25). Yet witty as he was, the letters show that he was just as easily prone to sulky depressions, fits of anger, and moodiness. Theirs was never a serene love. Part of this was a result of Potemkin's temperament, for throughout his adult life he suffered from violent mood swings—deep, crippling lows followed by periods of intense activity and seemingly boundless energy—that today would be labeled manic depression. But that is only part of the story. Equally important was the difficult position Potemkin found himself in as favorite. Potemkin was made uneasy by the thought that he owed his lofty station solely to the favor of the empress and that just as he had replaced Vasilchikov, so, too, might he be replaced one day. For Potemkin, who was so supremely confident of his talents and convinced of his own superiority, the vulnerability that came from knowing his position depended solely on the whim of the ruler was especially disturbing.

Catherine was not insensitive to his insecurities. The letters from these years are filled with her soothing words, and she was forever attempting to assure him that he was irreplaceable and their love unique (Letters 17, 29, 30, 32, 34, 124). When gentle reassurances were not enough, she would try to scold him out of his funk in a teasing, playful way. He was no longer her sweet doll, but her worst enemy: a giaour (infidel), a Yaik Cossack, a Pugachev, or a Muscovite (Catherine never did like Russia's former capital, which she viewed as an atavistic remnant of old Muscovy) (Letters 18, 26, 30, 46).

Yet at times her letters must have only made matters worse for Potemkin. Catherine's assertions that no king could ever compare to him and that he would have her protection for all time, while well meaning, may not have had the intended effect (Letter 29). Potemkin was well aware of the great social and political chasm that separated him from Europe's crowned heads, and he could never forget that he was but a subject in Catherine's empire; he surely did not need her to remind him of these facts, whatever her intent. When she jokingly inquired whether she were still in his "favor," or referred to him as her "master," could Catherine not have realized how such jests only fed Potemkin's worry (Letters 86, 119)?

It is quite likely that even if she were not fully aware of how such comments might have been unsettling to Potemkin, these remarks probably did register on some level of her conscience. After having only recently freed herself from the Orlov clan, Catherine was no doubt wary of giving up too much authority to a new favorite. Nevertheless, she found herself vulnerable to Potemkin's charms and subject to her desire. The power of the love she felt for him quite literally frightened Catherine as she found that with each passing hour she was becoming ever more hopelessly entangled in his "webs" (Letters 10, 26). But the power Potemkin held over Catherine was not simply emotional. Rather, by the end of 1775 she had become increasingly aware of the political hold her favorite had on her, admitting that she owed him a debt of gratitude for having given her "the means to reign" (Letter 167).

What lay behind this admission may never be known, or what Potemkin may have done to warrant such a startling confession, but it is known that from the very beginning of Catherine and Potemkin's affair, Potemkin had never been a mere *amant en titre*. From the day he was made adjutant-general, indeed, even well before that, Potemkin had been advising Catherine on a range of issues and was heavily involved in the most important matters of state. As head of the War College, he administered Russia's massive army; as governor-general of New Russia, he worked to secure the empire's southern border. Most of his administrative activity is not reflected here, although several of the letters do demonstrate the degree to which the relationship between Catherine and Potemkin was as much an affair of state as of the heart (Letters 49, 72, 133, 143). Catherine quickly came to seek out Potemkin's opinion on every possible subject, even how to deal with her spendthrift son (Letters 134, 135). So much did Catherine rely on and trust her favorite, that she would sign documents he presented to her that she admitted not to understand (Letter 80).

By the beginning of 1775, the court crisis that had brought Catherine and Potemkin together was over. The Pugachev Rebellion had been crushed, its leader captured, tried, and executed. The war against the Porte had been led to a brilliant and unanticipated conclusion. The Treaty of Kuchuk Kainardji granted Russia freedom of navigation on the Black Sea, a small but solid foothold on the sea's coast between the Bug and Dnieper rivers, the establishment of an independent Khanate of the Crimea, and four and a half million rubles in war indemnity. Russia was once more at peace.

But no sooner had Catherine managed to put out the domestic and foreign fires that had raged around her for several years than her relationship with Potemkin began to show signs of strain. Their quarrels were becoming more frequent and more intense. The tender warmth of their early days had begun to fade. Catherine found to her dismay that Potemkin was no longer just sulky, but was growing increasingly cold and more prone to wrathful outbursts. She claimed to have a "broken heart," and bemoaned that she could no longer expect even a "weary caress" from him (Letters 160, 162, 163, 164). Exasperated by his stony silences, Catherine spewed forth her frustration at this "wolf," "tiger," and "lion in the reeds" (Letters 137, 159). Their affair was nearing its end.

• • •

5.   CATHERINE TO POTEMKIN

[26 February 1774]

Thank you for the visit. I don't understand what kept you. Is it possible that my words were the cause of this? I complained that I wanted to sleep solely so that everything would quiet down sooner so I could see you sooner. And you, scared by this and so as not to find me in bed, didn't even come. But please, don't be afraid. We too are quite shrewd. No sooner had I lain down and the people left, than I rose again, got dressed and went to the doors in the library to wait for you, where I stood in a drafty wind for two hours. And not till midnight was fast approaching did I return out of grief to lie down in bed where, thanks to you, I spent the fifth sleepless night. And now I'm racking my brains trying to figure out what gave you cause to alter your plan, which you seemed to have approached without the slightest aversion. I think I shall go to the Maidens' Monastery today if they don't cancel the comedy there.[1] After that, I want to and must see you no matter what. The one you called the chemist[2] was here, and he frowned at me a great deal, but without success. And I didn't show a single tear. He wanted to prove to me the wantonness of my actions toward you, and finally finished by saying that out of respect for my good name he will try to convince you to leave for the army, to which I agreed. They're all starting to lecture me quite openly, and I listen to all this, but deep down they, and especially the Prince,[3] do not find you disagreeable. I've not admitted to a thing, nor have I justified myself in such a way that they could reproach me for lying. In a word, I've a great deal to tell you, and especially on matters similar to what I said yesterday between eleven and one o'clock, but I don't know whether you are in the same mood as yesterday and whether your words often correspond so little to the facts as in recent days. For you assured me over and over that you'd come, but didn't. You can't be angry that I reproach you. Farewell, God be with you. I think of you every hour. Oh my, such a long letter I've scribbled. Sorry, I forgot you don't like them. I shan't do it again.

---

1. St. Petersburg's Smolny Monastery housed the Imperial Educational Society of Noble Maidens, whose members performed dramatic works.

2. Possibly Ivan Ivanovich Betskoy (1704–1795). One of Catherine's trusted advisors and collaborators for years and a supporter of the Orlovs, Betskoy headed the Corps of Cadets and the Academy of Arts. He had been close, and supposedly quite intimate, with Catherine's mother after their arrival in Russia in the 1740s.

3. Grigory Orlov.

6.   POTEMKIN TO CATHERINE

27 February 1774

Your Most Gracious Majesty!

Having appointed my life to your service, I have not spared it in any way whenever there was an opportunity to glorify Your Royal name. Having set this as my foremost duty, I have never considered my own condition, and if I saw that my zeal corresponded to Your Imperial Majesty's will, I considered myself already rewarded. Finding myself almost from the moment of my joining the army the commanding officer of troops always nearest the enemy, I have not neglected to inflict upon him all possible harm, as proof of which I refer you to the army's commander and the Turks themselves. I remain unmotivated by envy toward those who, while younger than I, have nevertheless received more signs of Royal favor than I, but am solely offended by the possibility that in Your Imperial Majesty's thoughts I am considered less worthy than others. Being tormented by this and having prostrated myself at the blessed feet of Your Imperial Majesty, I have chosen to be so audacious as to beg, that should my service be worthy of your favor and should the munificence and the lofty monarchical mercy toward me not be diminishing, my doubt be resolved by rewarding me with the title of adjutant-general to Your Imperial Majesty.[1] This will offend no one, and I shall take it as the zenith of my happiness, especially since, finding myself under the special patronage of Your Imperial Majesty, I shall be worthy to receive your sage commands and, grasping them thoroughly, to become more capable in the service of Your Imperial Majesty and the Fatherland.

> Most Gracious Sovereign
> Your Imperial Majesty's most loyal servant
> Grigory Potemkin

---

1. Potemkin's request was honored by Catherine on 1 March.

7.   CATHERINE TO POTEMKIN

[27 February 1774]

My dear, if you desire to have some meat, then know that everything is now ready in the baths. But by no means take food to your quarters from there, or then everyone will know that food is being prepared in the baths.

8.   CATHERINE TO POTEMKIN

[28 February 1774]

Grishenka isn't dear to me, he's more than dear. I slept well, but am very ill; my chest and head ache, and truly I don't know whether or not I shall go out today. But if I do, then it'll be because I love you more than you love me, which I can prove as easily as two and two make four. I'll go out just to see you. Few have as much control over themselves as you do. And what's more, few are so clever, so nice, so agreeable. I'm not surprised that the entire city has ascribed to you a countless number of women as your lovers. No one on earth is better at busying himself with them, I suppose, than you. It seems to me there is nothing common about you, but that you distinguish yourself greatly from others. I only ask you not to do one thing: don't damage and don't even try to damage my opinion of Prince Orlov, for I should consider that to be ingratitude on your part. There's no one whom he praised more to me and whom, quite evident to me, he loved more, both in former times and now till your very arrival, than you. And if he has his faults, then it is unfit for either you or me to judge them and to make them known to others. He loves you, and they are my friends, and I shan't part with them. Now there's a lesson for you. If you're wise, you'll heed it. It wouldn't be wise to contradict it since it's the absolute truth.

In order for me to make sense, I must close my eyes when I am with you or else I might truly say what I have always laughed at: "My gaze is captivated by you." This is an expression that I considered silly, improbable and unnatural, but that I now see might be possible. My silly eyes will become fixed watching you; not even an ounce of reason can penetrate my mind and God knows how foolish I'm becoming. If at all possible, I must not see you for three days or so for my mind to calm down and to regain my senses, otherwise you will soon tire of me, and rightly so. I am very, very angry with myself today and gave myself a good scolding and tried my hardest to be smarter. On the off-chance I somehow actually get the strength and firmness, I shall take a page from your book—the best example I have before me. You are clever, you are firm and steadfast in the decisions you have made, proof of which is that even for many years, you say, you strove in our midst, and I did not notice, though others told me.

Farewell, darling, about three days remain for our rendezvous, for it will soon be the first week of Lent—days of repentance and prayers when it will be impossible to see you since this would be bad in many ways. For I must fast. Oh! I can't imagine it and nearly cry from these thoughts alone. Adieu, Monsieur, please write how you are today; pray, did you sleep, well or not, and does your fever persist and is it high? Panin[1] will say to you: "Sir, kindly try some quinine, quinine, quinine!" How merry it would be if we could sit together and talk. If we loved each other less, we'd be smarter, merrier. For even I am a merry soul when my mind, and especially my heart, are free. For you won't believe, my love, how important it is for conversation that it not be excessively influenced by love.

Pray write whether you laughed upon reading this letter, for I fairly roared with laughter while reading what I'd written. What nonsense I've scribbled, the hottest fever mixed with gibberish. Well, off it goes—perchance you too will amuse yourself a little.

---

1. Count Nikita Ivanovich Panin (1718–1783). Panin served as Russia's de facto foreign minister for close to two decades. His dismissal in 1781 came with the shift from his pro-Prussian orientation to the pro-Austrian orientation favored by Potemkin. As the head of the so-called Panin Party and governor to Catherine's son Grand Duke Paul Petrovich (later Paul I, born 1754, reigned 1796–1801) until 1773, Panin stood in opposition to the Orlov faction.

9.   CATHERINE TO POTEMKIN

28 February 1774

Sir Lieutenant-General! Mr. Strekalov[1] handed me your letter this morning. I found your request so moderate with regard to your services rendered me and the Fatherland, that I ordered an edict prepared rewarding you with the title of adjutant-general.

I admit I am also very pleased that your trust in me is such that you addressed your request in writing directly to me, and did not go through any intermediaries. Rest assured I remain toward you benevolent

Catherine

---

1. See Letter 6. Stepan Fyodorovich Strekalov (1728–1805) was one of Catherine's state secretaries.

10.   CATHERINE TO POTEMKIN

[1 March 1774. St. Petersburg]

My dear, my precious Grishenka, though you went out early, still I had the worst night's sleep. And even before that my blood had become so agitated that I intended to send for the physician in the morning to let some blood, but I fell asleep toward morning and am now calmer. Don't ask who is in my thoughts; know for certain that it is you forever. I say forever, but, as time passes, will you wish to remain there forever and will you yourself not erase from my mind my thoughts of you? My great endearment toward you frightens me. Very well, should I find the means, I'll be fiery for you, as you are wont to say, but I'll try to hide it from you. But you can't prohibit me from feeling. This morning I shall sign, according to your desire, the edict promised yesterday, which has now been prepared. Ask Strekalov so that you can thank me without others present, and then I shall let you into the Diamond Hall,[1] for otherwise where can we hide in this instance our mutual feeling from curious onlookers? Farewell, my dear.

---

1. Part of the empress's personal apartments in the Winter Palace, the Diamond Hall contained the imperial jewels.

11.   CATHERINE TO POTEMKIN

[1 March 1774]

I often forget to tell you what I must and what I had planned to say, for when I see you, you occupy my entire mind, and so I write. Aleksei Grigorievich[1] asked me this today while laughing: "Yes or no?" To which I answered: "About what?" To which he said: "On the subject of love?"

My answer: "I can't lie." He inquired again: "Yes or no?" I said: "Yes." Upon hearing this, he burst out laughing and said: "And you meet in the baths?" I asked: "Why do you think so?"

"Because," he said, "for about four days a light in the window has been visible a bit later than normal." Then he added: "It was apparent even yesterday with your design not to show any signs of concord between you while among others, and this is very good."

Tell Panin to have a third party persuade Vasilchikov to go to the waters. I feel suffocated by him, and he often has chest pains. Later he could be appointed envoy somewhere where there isn't much to do. He's boring and suffocating.

---

1. Count Aleksei Grigorievich Orlov-Chesmensky (1737–1807).

12.   CATHERINE TO POTEMKIN

[After 1 March 1774]

Sweetheart, what nonsense you spoke yesterday. Your words still have me laughing even today. What happy hours I spend with you. We spend some four hours together, and I'm not bored in the slightest and must always force myself, reluctantly, to part. My precious dear, <u>I love you extraordinarily;</u> you're nice, and clever, and merry and amusing, and I don't need the rest of the world when I'm sitting with you. Never in my life have I been as happy as when I'm with you. I often wish to hide from you my inner feelings, but my heart usually blurts out its passion. It must be that it's full to the brim and so spills over. I didn't write to you the other day since I got up late and you would have been attending to your day's affairs.

Farewell, brother, behave cleverly around others so that no one can say straight away what is or is not on our minds. I find a little dissembling terribly amusing.

13.   CATHERINE TO POTEMKIN

[After 15 March 1774]

Hello, Sir Lieutenant-Colonel. How are you after the baths? We are well and merry, thanks in part to you. Do you know what we talked about after you left? You can easily guess—you sometimes even guess others' thoughts. It was you, sweetie. We assessed your value, but didn't fix a price: there is none.

Farewell, busy yourself with the regiment, busy yourself with the officers all day today.[1] But I know what I'll do. I shall think, and about what precisely? For the sake of the rhyme, you might say: about him.[2] The truth be told, Grishenka alone is on my mind. It's not that I love him, but I do feel something extraordinary for which no words have yet been found. The alphabet is short and the letters few.

---

1. On 15 March 1774, Catherine made Potemkin a lieutenant-colonel in the Preobrazhensky Guards Regiment.

2. "[. . .] ia budu dumat', dumat' ob chem? Dlia virshi skazhesh' ob nem."

14.   CATHERINE TO POTEMKIN

[After 15 March 1774]

Grishenka, hello. I'm well and slept well, and didn't make a mistake with that first word, for I wrote it based on your written declaration. I am afraid you'll lose my letters. People will steal them from your pocket and your book thinking they are banknotes, and will put them in their pockets as if they were an ivory rook. You forbade quarreling; it's high time, by the way. I haven't the slightest desire and am by no means angry. Rather, I'm analyzing Grishenka as intelligent people do, without becoming impassioned. Be so good as to write me: in what manner did your master of ceremonies lead my ambassador to you today and did he kneel as is his usual custom?[1]

Kindly ask Panin either in writing or verbally about that certain letter. How will it be received? His answer will give me many grounds for investigating that gang's ideas, but I suspect their heads are filled with a good deal of foolishness and that they themselves were often bored.[2]

I'm sending herewith what you deigned to request. But I don't understand, why do you need them?

Kindly accept some friendly advice from me and restrain yourself, for I fear that if you don't, love's most gratifying aspect will be lost, and you have come to a somewhat false conclusion about me. With time you'll see that you were mistaken and that I told you the truth. If your fever doesn't force you to stay home today and you get the notion to visit me, then you'll see a new arrangement. First of all, I'll receive you in the boudoir, shall seat you near the table, and you will be warmer there and won't catch cold, for there's no draft from under the floor there. And we'll read a book, and I'll let you go at half past ten. Farewell, sweetheart, I haven't time to write. I got up late. I love you very much. Write of your health.

---

1. The kneeling master of ceremonies is a reference to Ivan Perfilievich Yelagin (1725–1793), the director of court music and spectacles. A writer and translator, Yelagin was a longtime, devoted servitor of the empress as well as a leading Freemason. Potemkin was then staying with Yelagin in his Petersburg home before moving to the Winter Palace.

2. Apparently a reference to the endless intrigues among the various court factions. Catherine sought to protect her new favorite by keeping him on good terms with powerful figures such as Nikita Panin.

15.   CATHERINE TO POTEMKIN

[Before 17 March 1774]

I very much wish to finish all of today's promotions, those for the Guards and the army as well, but don't know whether I shall manage. And because of this I must then expect many discontented persons and faces, all of which, I suppose, I shall see this very day or tomorrow. Days such as these are as agreeable to me as taking pills. Oh, how nice it is to be in my place! Allons, encouragés-moi avec quelque chose.[1] Pavel Sergeevich is to become a major-general, did you know that? I shall order him to go to Bibikov.[2] About my endearment there's nothing to say: you saw for yourself how I was yesterday, and so I am today as well. Had you granted me three more days, I could have organized and prepared everything with great order, and nothing would have been lost because of this. Farewell, Lordkin.

---

1. "Come now, cheer me up with something or other."

2. Upon the recommendation of his cousin Grigory Potemkin, Pavel Potemkin was promoted to the rank of major-general on 17 March 1774. He was recalled to the capital and then sent to join General Bibikov. Aleksandr Ilich Bibikov (1729–1774) was commissioned late in 1773 to put down the Pugachev Rebellion, a task which he carried out admirably until his death from fever.

16.   CATHERINE TO POTEMKIN

[Before 19 March 1774]

I wanted to send you a letter just now when your note was delivered to me. And now I'm vexed that you beat me to it, and am sad, my dear, that you're not well. If you've been sweating, then it's best you don't go out. Nevertheless, I remember you whether I am idle or busy with affairs, whatever they may be. An odd man passed through my room into the manège, and appeared exactly as yesterday.[1] If you don't go out, send someone to tell me. Adieu, mon tonton.[2]

---

1. Possibly a reference to Vasilchikov, who moved out of the palace and into his brother's home on 19 March.

2. "Farewell, my top." With "tonton," Catherine most likely did not mean "uncle," but "toton," a top, as in a child's toy, one of her nicknames for Potemkin, forever whirling with energy.

17.   CATHERINE TO POTEMKIN

[After 19 March 1774]

No, Grishenka, it's quite impossible that my feelings for you will change.

Be fair with yourself: could I love someone after you? I think there's no one like you, and I don't give a damn about everyone else. In vain the empty-headed wench judges me according to her own self. But be that as it may, my heart is constant. And there's still more I shall say to you: I don't like change of any kind. Quand Vous me connaîtrés plus, Vous m'estimerés, car je Vous jure que je suis estimable. Je suis extrêmement véridique, j'aime la vérité, je hais le changement, j'ai horriblement souffert pendant deux ans, je me suis brulé les doigts, je ne reviendrai plus, je suis parfaitement bien: mon coeur, mon esprit et ma vanité sont également contents avec Vous, que pourrai-je souhaiter de mieux, je suis parfaitement contente; si Vous continués à avoir l'esprit alarmé sur des propos de commère, savés Vous ce que je ferai? Je m'enfermerai dans ma chambre et je ne verrai personne excepté Vous, je suis dans le besoin de prendre des parties extrêmes et je Vous aime au-delà de moi même.[1]

---

1. "When you get to know me better, you will esteem me, for I swear to you I am estimable. I am extremely veracious, I love the truth, I hate change, I have suffered horribly for two years, I have been burned, I shall never go back, I am perfectly well: my heart, my mind, and my pride are equally content with you, what more could I desire, I am perfectly content. If you continue to be alarmed by the talk of gossips, do you know what I shall do? I shall lock myself up in my room and shall see no one but you, I must take extreme measures, and I love you more than my very self."

18.   CATHERINE TO POTEMKIN

[After 19 March 1774]

Darling, really now, I suppose you thought I wouldn't write to you today. You're quite mistaken, sir. I awoke at five o'clock, it's now after six—I should write to him. But only so as to speak the truth, and kindly take heed what sort of truth: I don't love you and don't want to see you anymore. You won't believe it, my love, but I can't abide you at all. Yesterday we chatted till twelve o'clock, and then he was sent away. Don't be angry— indeed, as if one couldn't do without him. The dearest thing of all that came from that conversation is that I learned what they say among themselves: no, they say, this is no Vasilchikov, this one she treats differently. And he is indeed worthy. No one is surprised, and the affair has been accepted as if they have long been expecting it. But no—everything must be otherwise. From my pinky to my heel and from these to the last hair on my head, I have issued a general prohibition today against showing you the least affection. And my love is being kept in my heart under lock and key. It's awful how cramped it is in there. With great difficulty it squeezes itself inside, so mind well—it might just pop out somewhere. Now see here, you are a reasonable man, could so few lines contain more madness? A flood of foolish words has sprung from my head. How you can enjoy spending time with such a deranged mind I do not know. O, Monsieur Potemkine, quel fichu miracle Vous avés opéré de déranger ainsi une tête, qui ci-devant dans le monde passoit pour être une des meilleures de l'Europe?[1]

It's time, high time indeed to start acting sensibly. It's shameful, it's bad, it's a sin for Catherine the Second to allow this mad passion to rule over her. Such foolhardiness will make you loathsome even to him. I'll begin repeating that last verse to myself often, and I hope this alone will be enough to lead me back onto the true path. But this won't be the final proof of your great power over me. It's time to stop or I'll scribble a complete sentimental metaphysics that will finally make you laugh, though this will be its sole benefit. Well, my nonsense, off you go to those places, to those happy shores where my hero dwells. If, perchance, you don't find him still at home and are carried back to me, then I shall toss you directly into the fire and Grishenka won't see this extravagant behavior, in which, however, God knows, there is much love; but it would be much better if he didn't know of this. Farewell, giaour, Muscovite, Cossack. I don't love you.

---

1. "Oh, Mister Potemkin, what strange miracle have you performed in so thoroughly deranging a head that earlier was considered by society to be one of the best in Europe?"

19.   CATHERINE TO POTEMKIN

[After 23 March 1774. Tsarskoe Selo]

I thank you for treating me yesterday. And though I was a little embarrassée,[1] still I recall all your affection, which filled me with joy upon going to bed and awakening. Do me a favor and tell me what our nephew said when you were left alone.[2] I suppose our lunacy seemed very strange to him. I can't help but laugh when I think about how the dogs went over to keep him company. Farewell, Grishenka, for I suppose that if you truly do remain behind my chair I shall become red as a lobster. Lord, let it be cold in the gallery. When I get up from the table, I'll say: Ooh! But you too must dine, don't forget, and I shall send you away, just as you did Aleksandr Nikolaevich yesterday.

---

1. "embarrassed,"

2. Aleksandr Nikolaevich Samoilov (1744–1814) was the son of one of Potemkin's sisters. A trusted adjutant to his uncle, Samoilov served with distinction in the Second Russo-Turkish War and became procurator-general in 1792.

20.   CATHERINE TO POTEMKIN

[After 23 March 1774]

Hello, sweetheart. A most wondrous thing has happened to me: je suis devenu Somnambule.[1] I strolled in a garden in my sleep, and I dreamed that I was walking around in some sort of handsomely decorated chambers. There were walls resembling gold, richly embroidered with flowers and doves. I found there a dais, on which a most handsome man did not stand, but lay. And he was dressed in gray garments trimmed with sable. This man was very kind to me and thanked me for coming, and we talked about insignificant matters for a time. Then I left and awoke. It had obviously been a dream, for it sent shivers up and down my spine. And now I am looking everywhere for that handsome man, yet he is nowhere to be found, though his image will never be erased from my memory. He's so dear! Dearer than the entire world. Oh, if only you could see him you would not take your eyes off him. Darling, when you meet him, give him my regards and kiss him for me. For he truly is worthy of that. And it may well be that you'll meet him, if, upon getting out of bed, you turn to the right and glance at the wall.[2]

1. "I have become a somnambulist."
2. In all likelihood Catherine is referring to a portrait of Potemkin that hung next to this bed.

21.   CATHERINE TO POTEMKIN

[After 26 March 1774]

Sweetie, Grishenka, hello. I know, what will Praskovia Aleksandrovna[1] say about me? She will say that I've lost my mind and my senses. And about you? Well, brother, you know for yourself what she'll say. I shan't guess, I'm not certain, I don't know, I'm afraid, I'm a coward. She will say, she will say, what will she say now? She will say: "And he too loves her." What else? Sweetheart, is it possible that these lines upset you? Have a good look, take note from where they spring. There is no reason to be angry. But no, it's time to stop giving you assurances. You must be most, most, most certain by now that I love you. And there you have the entire story, but some stories are not just stories. And still other stories—oh, but you've simply confused me. How bad it is for one with a mind to lose it! I want you to love me. I want to appear desirable to you. But I only show you madness and extreme weakness. Ugh, how bad it is to love so extraordinarily. It's an illness, you know. I'm ill, only I don't send for the chemist nor do I write long letters. If you want, I shall paraphrase this page for you in three words and cross out all the rest. Here it is: I love you.

1. Countess Praskovia Bruce.

22.   CATHERINE TO POTEMKIN

[March–April 1774]

Sweetie, I got up very merry and more enlightened than when I went to bed. They say the Greeks were such resourceful people in the past: the arts and sciences took root among them, and they were very clever at inventing things. All of that is written in the *Encyclopédie*, but much nicer, smarter and more handsome than they is the one who has been copied to the letter in the article délicieux,[1] that is, Grishenka, my beloved.

1. "delightful,"

23. CATHERINE TO POTEMKIN

[March–April 1774]

Grishenka, hello. It seems to me this morning that not only do you love me and are you affectionate, but that it's all with as much sincerity as I feel for you. And you must know, that those conclusions I draw in the morning become rules till such time as experience provides reasons for their refutation. But should you, contrary to any expectation and probability, use some sort of deception or cunning, then you ought to know, that it's unforgivable for any intelligent person, as you are, to stick to such foolish methods when you yourself are the first and best method for controlling for life the heart and mind of a most sensitive person. Indeed, you know that this might well produce nothing but a certain kind of mistrust and anxiety not at all compatible with candor and sincerity, without which love can never be firmly established.

God be with you, brother, farewell. I am much smarter in the morning than at the setting of the sun. But be that as it may, my mind is upset. And should this continue, then I shall stop attending to my affairs, for I can't keep my mind on them, and I've been acting like a chicken with its head cut off. I truly shall try to use this week to my advantage, and may God grant me the reason and the good sense to seize the true path. For you know I've always been a raisonneur de profession,[1] although with the occasional delirium.

------

1. "philosophizer by profession,"

24. CATHERINE TO POTEMKIN

[March–April 1774]

Precious darling, Grishenka, I love you extraordinarily. Be so good as to take note—here is yet another new [letter], though it came about quite by accident. I just came across this sheet, so kindly look at it closely; it was written out crosswise. You'll probably say that this must be Finnish. Fine, search high and low for any cunning in my love for you. Should you find anything but pure love of the foremost sort, I permit you to put all of this into some cannons in place of a charge and to fire it at Silistria or wherever you want. Hmmm, hmmm, I'm muttering to myself—that was foolishly said, but nothing cleverer came to mind. Surely, not everyone is as clever as I know who, but shall not say. God forbid I become so weak as to tell you who I think is cleverer than I and everyone I know. But no, sir, and kindly don't try to find out—for you won't.

I have cheered up. Oh, my God, how foolish one is when he loves extraordinarily. It's an illness. One should cure people of it in hospitals. Il faudroit des calmants, Monsieur, beaucoup d'eau fraîche, quelques saignées, du suc de citron, pointe de vin, peu manger, beaucoup prendre d'air, et faire tant de mouvement qu'on rapporte le corps à la maison,[1] and the devil only knows whether after all that I might still get you out of my head. I think not. Adieu, you five French volumes in folio.

---

1. "One would need calmatives, sir, a lot of fresh water, some bloodletting, lemon essence, a drop of wine, to eat little, to get lots of fresh air and to move about so much that one comes home exhausted,"

25.   CATHERINE TO POTEMKIN

[March–April 1774]

My darling, my darling, hello. Pray read this with the accent of Maria Aleksandrovna.[1] A propos, I had a dream about her in which she was sitting on one side and Anna Nikitichna[2] was on the other, and they had a great many guests, including you. Aleksandr Aleksandrovich[3] kept running around the table and encouraging everyone to eat and drink, which I truly do not like. And because of this I became quite angry with him and awoke from my irritation, and lay there in a great fever, and tossed about after that till morning unable to sleep.

Now there's a tale for you. I think the fever and the agitation of my blood come from the fact that already for many evenings, so it seems to me, I go to bed very late, though I don't know why. It's always one o'clock. I am accustomed to going to bed at ten o'clock. Be so kind as to leave earlier in the future. Indeed, it's wrong. Sweetheart, write me how you are and whether you slept peacefully. I love you, but haven't time to write, nor anything to say.

---

1. Maria Aleksandrovna Izmailova (*née* Naryshkina) (1730–1780) was the sister of the influential courtiers Lev and Aleksandr Naryshkin.

2. Anna Nikitichna Naryshkina (*née* Rumiantseva) (1730–1820). A close friend of Catherine's for many years, she was made a lady-in-waiting in 1773.

3. Aleksandr Aleksandrovich Naryshkin (1726–1795). As chief cup-bearer of the imperial court, Naryshkin was responsible for the wine served at the empress's table.

26.   CATHERINE TO POTEMKIN

[10 April 1774. St. Petersburg]

I'm writing from the Hermitage where there's no chamber-page. I suffered from colic last night. Grishenka, it's awkward to come to you here in the mornings.[1] [. . .] The ice hasn't gone out on the river yet, just a bit is holding the water back, and people are strolling about on it. Issue an edict in my name prohibiting Mr. Fat Man[2] from crossing the river. He has a wife and children. Besides, he serves me well; by no means do I want him to drown. I very much liked how he replied yesterday that he served in order to serve and to carry out that which had been placed upon him. Ce sont les sentiments d'un honnête homme et d'une âme remplie de candeur, cela ressemble à son père.[3]

But enough talk of others. Order me to talk about us. Thanks to you I awoke cheerful. Vous faites mon bonheur, Dieu donne que je puisse faire le Vôtre.[4] And though I got a little angry and punished you in order to make a point, my heart has recovered and now I am exceedingly gracious and exceedingly courteous toward you. Kindly note my little rhyme—so-and-so is associating with you, Sir Yaik Cossack. My sweet darling, I am exceedingly tender toward you, and were I to give freedom to my indiscreet heart, I would scribble an entire page, but you do not regard long letters with favor, and so I am compelled to say: farewell, giaour, Muscovite, Cossack, angry, sweet, excellent, intelligent, courageous, brave, enterprising, merry one. Do you know you have all those qualities I love, and thus I love you so much it is impossible to express it. Mon coeur, mon esprit et ma vanité sont également et parfaitement contents de Votre Excellence parce que Votre Excellence est excellent, délicieux, très aimable, très amusant et précisément tout ce qui me faut et il faudroit je crois se donner au Diable pour pouvoir Vous quitter.[5]

For you see, one cannot free oneself from your webs, but with each hour becomes more entangled. And should you somehow lessen my passion, you will make me unhappy. But even then I would probably not stop loving you. And I pray to God that I die upon the hour that it seems you are not the same toward me that you have deigned to be these seven weeks. But be that as it may, I must think that you love me, and the slightest doubt about that troubles me cruelly and saddens me unspeakably. My dear, you have a good heart. Love me, even a wee bit, for my being sincerely attached to you. I suppose a fidget won't have the patience to read this letter. So fling it into the fire; that's fine with me. Just be merry.

---

1. The court returned to St. Petersburg on 9 April after a little over two weeks at Tsarskoe Selo. Potemkin now occupied the apartments especially prepared for him in the palace.

2. Possibly Prince Nikolai Mikhailovich Golitsyn (1727–1786), a devoted servant of Catherine's and chief marshal of the court in the 1770s.

3. "These are the feelings of an honest man and a transparent soul. This resembles his father."

4. "You provide my happiness; may God grant that I can provide you yours."

5. "My heart, my mind, and my pride are equally and completely satisfied with Your Excellency, for Your Excellency is excellent, delightful, very kind, very amusing and exactly everything that I need, such that I believe it would be necessary to give myself to the devil in order to be able to forsake you."

27.   CATHERINE TO POTEMKIN

[After 10 April 1774]

Hello sweetie. I couldn't come to you as usual, for our borders are sepa-rated by all sorts of roaming animals. So I greet you in my mind only and wish you health, and us—your love and friendship. And we remain to-ward you today the same as yesterday and tomorrow. By the way, how did we seem to you yesterday?

28.   CATHERINE TO POTEMKIN

[After 10 April 1774]

My dear, I came after seven o'clock, but found your valet standing across from the doors with a drinking glass in his hand. And so I didn't come in to you. I write you this so that you know why I violated our dear, established arrangement. Adieu, mon faisan d'or. Je vous aime beaucoup, beaucoup.[1]

---

1. "Farewell, my golden pheasant. I love you very, very much."

29.   CATHERINE TO POTEMKIN

[15 April 1774]

My sweet beauty to whom no King can compare. I am very gracious and affectionate toward you, and my protection you have and will have for all time. The archpriest's cross has left for Moscow, and so you needn't concern yourself anymore with sending it. I suppose you are even better looking and cleaner after the baths; still, it's a strange thing: I don't love you at all. You won't believe it, my love, but I can't stand you. Is this easy? Tell Mikhail Sergeevich[1] that you are now in complete disfavor. Only don't tell him all of a sudden or he will die of grief. Ivan Ivanovich Betskoy promised me something today. Don't be-come angry, but I shan't say what. And I dare say, even Friedrichs,[2] no matter how shrewd, still won't tell your brother-in-law.[3] I can't imagine how he will enter the former billiards room: two things are possible—either I shall die laughing or shall become red as a lobster. Faudra t'il l'admettre au petit souper pour faire pendant à Elagin?[4]

I'll puff myself up. I'll think I'm sitting in the Senate. I wonder how he'll wish to entertain himself: will he force us to jump rope? Precious dar-ling, please don't introduce many more like him, for it'll be just like sit-ting in a steam bath. Listen you, my marble beauty, I rose terribly merry and not at all friendly toward you; mon coeur, il faut de la variation dans le style et pour cela je dis,[5] that I am unfriendly. You do understand anyway, even though you are a man of reason.[6] Adieu, mon bijou.

---

1. The younger brother of Pavel Potemkin, Mikhail Sergeevich Potemkin (1744–1791) arrived in the capital bearing a rare Turkish standard captured in the war, and he presented it to Catherine. Called the "Saint" by Potemkin because of his earnest nature, Mikhail went on to a distinguished military career.

2. The court banker Ivan Yurievich Friedrichs (1723–1779).

3. Nikolai Borisovich Samoilov (1718–1791) was married to Potemkin's eldest sister, Maria, and was the father of Aleksandr Samoilov.

4. "Must he be admitted to the small evening supper in order to counteract Yelagin?"

5. "my love, it is necessary to vary one's style, and so I say"

6. "[. . .] razumeesh', vit' khotia ty razumovskii." A play on words on the name of Elizabeth's favorite Aleksei Razumovsky, which can be translated as "man of reason."

30.   CATHERINE TO POTEMKIN

[16 April 1774]

Grishenka, I have just received your letter. It's true we both needed rest yesterday, but I can in no way own, my darling, that I allegedly let you go without showing any affection. And I don't understand how you can come to such a conclusion. I love you extraordinarily, and when you cuddle up to me, my caresses always hasten to respond to yours. I slept well and am not sad, and shall be utterly merry as soon as I see you. There's no greater pleasure in the world than that. We waited for Mikhail Sergeevich. Pavel must be sent for—don't forget. And as soon as he arrives, two things must be taken care of: first, his disorganized domestic situation must be set right or else he will be in no condition to do what I expect of him, unless he is rebuked in some fashion. Second—he must be prohibited from squandering money and going into debt. Just based on the promissory notes protested against him, he owes about eleven thousand, which I can show you, even the names of every single person.[1]

Farewell, darling, I'm sad you won't be with me either today or tomorrow. Farewell, Muscovite, giaour, Cossack.

---

1. Before Catherine sent Pavel Potemkin off to join General Bibikov, she wanted to see that he brought his financial matters in order.

31.   CATHERINE TO POTEMKIN

[Before 21 April 1774]

My dear, I am sending you along with this a letter to Count Aleksei Grig-orievich Orlov. If I have made any spelling errors, please make the necessary corrections and then return it to me. To those who do not like the appoint-ment of Messrs. Demidov as counselors in the College of Mines, in which field, however, they have considerable knowledge and may be used to advantage, it may be said that the Senate often arbitrarily confers ranks even on tax-farmers. And so I suppose that even I, given my authority, may reward ruined people from whom (through the orderly administration of manufactories) trade and state revenues have received significant profit for many years.[1] I also suppose that they will be no worse than Sir Bilistein, the General's fool, on whose be-half the entire city labored.[2] But here we all love to see only the negative side of things, and I have grown accustomed to not giving a damn about that and have long known that they are mistaken who think that you can please every-one simply because their intentions are so irreproachable. My dear top, don't be angry that I've expressed in writing what you wouldn't let me finish saying or wouldn't hear out while together. Every person seeks his own justification, except for me, who is subjected hourly to countless reproaches and criticisms from clever and foolish people. And so, once my ears have been stuffed with all this, my mind as well whirls about it just the same, and my thoughts are not as cheerful as they would naturally be could I please everyone.

Should you have time, please write to me about Bibikov, Prince Golit-syn, Freyman, Mansurov and Reinsdorp.[3]

I shall now discuss something that will perhaps be more pleasant for both of us. Namely, that Ivan Chernyshev[4] lied to you when he said that I am unable to love from a distance, for I love you even when I don't see you. And I see you, in my opinion, only seldom, though in fact it's not seldom. Kindly attribute this to passion: you don't hunger to see someone you don't love. Farewell, darling.

---

1. Wealthy industrialists Nikita and Yevdokim Demidov had their manufactories destroyed during the Pugachev Rebellion.

2. Baron Karl Leopold Andreu de Bilistein was made a member of the Commerce Commis-sion in 1765. Beginning in 1769 he served in the army under General Pyotr Panin, who, along with his brother Nikita, was Bilistein's patron.

3. General Aleksandr Bibikov, Major-Generals Prince Pyotr Mikhailovich Golitsyn (1738–1775), Magnus Freyman (1725–1796), Pavel Dmitrievich Mansurov (1726–after 1798), and Lieutenant-General and Governor of Orenburg Ivan Andreevich Reinsdorp (d. 1781) all received awards for their efforts against Pugachev on 21 April 1774. Bibikov was already dead by then, though word had not yet reached the capital.

4. Count Ivan Grigorievich Chernyshev (1726–1797) was vice president of the Naval Col-lege. The conversation with Potemkin probably happened earlier, possibly in 1770, since Ivan Chernyshev was absent from St. Petersburg for all of 1774.

32.   CATHERINE TO POTEMKIN

[21 April 1774]

Hello, sweetheart. The truth must be told—we are both so dear to one another. There's nothing like it in the world. As soon as I got up, I sent a letter to the Vice Chancellor requesting the ribbons and wrote that they were for Lieutenant-General Potemkin; and after Mass I'll put them on him.[1] Do you know him? He's a beauty, so good-looking, so clever. And he loves me in equal measure to his good looks and cleverness, and is loved by me just the same. It would be difficult to prove that one loved the other any more or better. I have attached some notes that I prepared today for declaration this very day. Please return them to me if you don't find anything to correct. But if you find something that needs changing, then write it down, my sweet darling. Adieu, mon bijou. Do be merry today, for thanks to you, I am very, very merry, and you don't leave my thoughts even for a minute.

---

1. On her birthday, 21 April 1774, Catherine presented Potemkin with the Order of St. Alexander Nevsky and with the Polish Order of the White Eagle, given to him by King Stanislaw August Poniatowski. Vice Chancellor Aleksandr Mikhailovich Golitsyn (1723–1807) was a prominent diplomat and member of the State Council.

33.   CATHERINE TO POTEMKIN

[22 April 1774]

Hello, darling, congratulations upon receiving the White Eagle, and the two red ribbons, and the striped scrap of cloth, which, however, is the dearest of all since it's the work of my hands.[1] It can be expected as something appertaining to merit and valor. We ask that henceforth you don't humiliate us, but that you cloak all our vices and mistakes and don't expose them to others, for that cannot be agreeable to us. This is quite inappropriate with a friend, and still less with one's wife.[2] Now there's a reprimand for you, though the gentlest sort. I woke up merry, thanks in large part to yesterday evening and your amusement and merriment. I love it terribly when you're merry. I suppose there'll be a lot of trying on today. Adieu, mon bijou, souvent Vous n'avés pas le sens commun, mais toujours Vous êtes fort aimable.[3]

You forgot either to write or talk to me about Reinsdorp.

---

1. The "striped scrap" refers to the black and orange ribbon of the Order of St. George third class that Catherine had presented to Potemkin in 1770 in recognition of his bravery in fighting the Turks.

2. Catherine refers to herself as Potemkin's wife, although the likely date of their marriage is still a month and a half away.

3. "Farewell, my precious, you often lack common sense, but you are always very kind."

34.   CATHERINE TO POTEMKIN

[After 22 April 1774]

Bonjour, mon coeur! Comment Vous portés Vous?[1]
Oh, my darling, you should be ashamed. What need do you have of saying that he who takes your place hasn't long to live? Does using fear to
compel someone's heart look like the right thing to do? This most loathsome method is utterly contrary to your way of thinking in which no evil
dwells. For this would be the work of ambition alone, not love. So cross
out these lines and banish even the thought of this, for it's nothing but
nonsense. It resembles the fairytale about the peasant whose wife cried
when he hung an axe on the wall since it might fall down and kill their
small child who never was and never could've been for they were both
about one hundred years old. Don't be sad. You'll sooner tire of me than I
of you. But be that as it may, I form strong attachments and am constant,
and habit and friendship only strengthen my love. Vous ne Vous rendés
pas justice, quoique Vous soyés un bonbon de profession. Vous êtes excessivement aimable.[2]

I must admit that even in your apprehension there is tenderness. But
you haven't the slightest reason to fear. You have no equal. I burned
my fingers on a fool.[3] What's more, I gravely feared growing accustomed to him, which would have either made me unhappy for life or
shortened my life. And had he remained another year and you not arrived, or had I not found you upon your arrival, as was desired, I may
have grown accustomed, and this habit would have taken the place
prepared for you by my inclinations. Now read my heart and soul. I
open them sincerely to you in every possible way, and if you don't feel
and see this, then you won't be worthy of this great passion that you
awoke in me by your waiting. For truth, I love you immensely. See for
yourself. And we ask that we humbly be paid in kind, or else there will
be many tears and much sadness, both inward and outward. For we,
when we love with all our soul, are cruelly tender. Pray satisfy our tenderness with like tenderness, and not with something else. Now there's
a lengthy little note for you. Will it be as pleasing for you to read as it
was for me to write, I don't know.

---

1. "Hello, my love! How are you feeling?"
2. "You do not do justice to yourself although you are a bonbon by calling. You are excessively kind."
3. Vasilchikov.

35.   CATHERINE TO POTEMKIN

[April 1774]

The man whose spirit cannot be troubled by any deed is capable of carrying out great deeds. Speak less when drunk. Never get angry when eating. Hurry along the matter that is slow to bear fruit. Accept magnanimously what the fool has done.

36.   CATHERINE TO POTEMKIN

[8 May 1774]

I so terribly want to quarrel with you. I came to wake you, and not only weren't you asleep, you weren't even in your room. So, I see sleep overcame you merely as an excuse to run from me. At least in the city you would sit with me, although after dinner only out of a sense of compulsion, in response to my entreaties, or in the evening. But here you only visit me on forays. Giaour, Cossack, Muscovite. You visit me and then hurry as best you can to be off. You will assuredly frighten me away, and I shan't desire to be with you—just like Prince Orlov. Well fine, should you one day compel me to master my greedy desire to be with you, then I shall indeed be colder. You'll laugh at this, but, really, I don't find it amusing that you're bored with me and that there's always somewhere more important for you to be than with me.

G:M:C: C:M: Y:S:B:M:S:[1] and all the abuse in the world, but not a single caress. I am sending for Bauer.[2]

---

1. "Giaour:Muscovite:Cossack: Cossack:Muscovite: You:Son of a:Bitch:My:Spouse [?]"

2. Catherine jokes that she is going to send for Friedrich Wilhelm Bauer (1731–1783), a Swede in Russian service, who at the time was directing the construction of a water supply system at Tsarskoe Selo.

37.   CATHERINE TO POTEMKIN

[After 8 May 1774]

My sweet dear, pray, what are you sighing about as you lie on your bed? I didn't overhear this standing behind the screen; rather, your "Oh!" reached my ears through all the galleries and rooms, making its way even to the divan. Pray tell, what does this "Oh!" mean? Oh, Jesus Maria, it means I love you extraordinarily.

38.   CATHERINE TO POTEMKIN

[15 May 1774. Tsarskoe Selo]

I am sitting on the leather sofa covered with sponges and my legs stretched out because I wandered about the hills and hollows for two hours. But for three maids-of-the-bedchamber and Avdotia's[1] dog, I didn't run into a soul.

Having just gotten to work, I love you immensely and am gladdened by your love for me, my own sweet and priceless friend, my dear, my angel.

––––––––––

1. Avdotia Petrovna Ivanova was one of Catherine's maids-of-the-bedchamber.

39.   CATHERINE TO POTEMKIN   [In French]

[30 May 1774. Tsarskoe Selo]

General, do you love me? Me love general very much.

40.   CATHERINE TO POTEMKIN

[1 June 1774. Tsarskoe Selo]

The end of your letter clearly demonstrates the contradictions in the words of a madcap. I could not have been bothered by requests for ranks, for you received the only rank that you clearly deserved. And you could not have requested more ranks, for there were only two ranks above the one you already had. One has been given to you, and as for the other—I do not even recall that you requested it,[1] for you, as much as I, knew and shared my principles, mais cette mauvaise tête[2] compose et décompose les phrases à sa fantaisie, il prend d'une un mot et l'attache à une autre; cela m'est arrivé cent fois avec lui et je ne doute pas que Vous et bien d'autres ne l'aient remarqué, il se pourroit aussi que dans ce moment, où il est enragé, il n'y eut de la méchanceté dans son esprit et que ne pouvant se racrocher il ne cherche à bouillonner et qu'il ne soit soufflé à cela peut être par d'autres. J'espère que Vous aurés déja des nouvelles de la personne qui s'étoit perdue hier pendant l'ennuyeux entretien que Vous aves essuyé. Adieu, mon Ami, portés Vous bien. Je suis bien fachée que Vous soyés tracassé par un fou.[3]

––––––––––

1. On 30 May 1774, Potemkin received the rank of general-in-chief, then the second highest military rank just below that of field marshal.

2. Count Zakhar Grigorievich Chernyshev, president of the War College. Chernyshev (1722–1784) had long ago attracted the eye of a young Grand Duchess Catherine, some of whose intimate letters to him from those early years have survived. After her feelings for

Chernyshev were noticed, he was sent away to the army. Though he later married into the Panin family, Chernyshev was a supporter of the Orlovs. He was greatly upset by Potemkin's being made vice president of the War College.

3. "but that trouble maker composes and decomposes phrases according to his fantasies, he takes a word from one phrase and attaches it to another; this has happened a hundred times in my dealings with him, and I don't doubt that you and many others have noticed this; it is also possible that although there is no evil intent in his mind, he is not able to steady himself at that moment when he is enraged and so is only letting off steam and it is possible others incited him to do this. I hope that you already have news from that person who left yesterday during the boring conversation you endured. Farewell, my friend, take care of yourself. I am very sorry that you are being pestered by a fool."

41.   CATHERINE TO POTEMKIN

[4 June 1774. Tsarskoe Selo]

Baten'ka,[1] I shall be there tomorrow and shall bring with me those you write about.[2] Order Field Marshal Golitsyn to have his boat ready across from Sievers's wharf, should he not be able to dock any closer.[3] Farewell, be well, and we shall be so merry toward you that it will be a delight to see. Call Monsieur le Gros,[4] if you so desire. Adieu, mon Ami.

---

1. For the meaning of this and the handful of other terms of address left in Russian, see the Note on the Translation.

2. The court returned to St. Petersburg from Tsarskoe Selo on 5 June. Catherine was possibly bringing with her her chambermaid Maria Perekusikhina and her chamberlain Yevgraf Chertkov, who both reportedly participated in Catherine and Potemkin's secret wedding.

3. Possibly preparations for readying a boat to take the couple and their witnesses directly from the Summer Palace, where Catherine spent that summer, to the Church of St. Samson located down the Neva River at the city's edge. Field Marshal Prince Aleksandr Mikhailovich Golitsyn (1718–1783) was a hero of the Seven Years' War and leader of Russia's forces in the First Russo-Turkish War until his replacement by Rumiantsev. He was in charge of the capital during the empress's absence.

4. "Mister Fat Man"—possibly Chief Marshal Prince Nikolai Golitsyn.

42.   CATHERINE TO POTEMKIN

[After 8 June 1774]

Grishenok, priceless, rarest and sweetest in the world, I love you madly, extraordinarily, my dear friend, I kiss and embrace you with all my body and soul, dear husband.

43.   CATHERINE TO POTEMKIN

[After 8 June 1774]

Baten'ka, my dear, as if there could be anything awkward about your asking me to come and snuggle. This is all quite natural for me, sweet and priceless darling, husband dear.

44.   CATHERINE TO POTEMKIN

[12 June 1774. St. Petersburg]

Let him go, precious darling.[1] My body and soul are tormented by my foolish and inappropriate grumbling over our caresses. I shall die should you change your behavior in any way. My dear friend, gentle husband, forgive with magnanimity the foolishness of a slumbering mind and body.

---

1. Catherine instructed Potemkin to allow Pavel Potemkin to leave having just the day before been put in charge of the Kazan and Orenburg secret commissions investigating the Pugachev Rebellion. She ends by apologizing for being unable to see him one final time.

45.   CATHERINE TO POTEMKIN   [In French]

[Before 28 June 1774]

General, my head is spinning from your project. You won't receive any rest from me after the festivities till you present your ideas to me in writing. You are a charming and rare man. I love you and shall esteem you forever with all my heart.

46.   CATHERINE TO POTEMKIN

[Before 28 June 1774]

Bonjour, mon coeur. I awoke so cheerful it's frightening. Oh, my love, don't be angry, for you love it when I am cheerful. Today you won't hear a thing but rubbish. There is, however, one serious matter about which I can speak, for it occupies my senses completely. But I shall end this note with it, and now à propos de cela,[1] I very humbly request that you not delay the lieutenant-colonel list with your comments, or I fear Kuzmin[2] will flog me and Chernyshev[3] will once more befoul his room with smoke.

My darling, my dear, my beloved, je n'ai pas le sens commun aujourd'huy.[4] Love, love is the reason. I love you with my heart, mind, soul and body. I love you with all my senses and shall love you eternally.

Precious darling, I kindly beg you—do me the favor and love me too. For you are a good and generous person. Do your best to make Grigory Aleksandrovich love me. I tenderly beg you. Also, write me how he is— is he merry and well?

I thought my dog had gone mad today. She came in with Tatiana,[5] jumped up in bed with me, sniffed a bit, and shuffled on the bed, and then began to move about and to snuggle up to me as if she were happy to see someone. She loves you very much, and so is even dearer to me. Everyone on earth, even the dog, confirms your place in my heart and mind. Consider how dear Grishenka is. He doesn't leave my mind for an instant. Truly, my love, it's frightful, frightful how dear you are.

---

1. "with respect to that,"

2. Catherine's secretary Sergei Matveevich Kuzmin (1724–1788).

3. Military promotions were handed out on 28 June, Catherine's accession day. Potemkin, as vice president of the College of War, had been entrusted to go over the list of promotions, having usurped this prerogative from Zakhar Chernyshev.

4. "I have lost all common sense today."

5. One of Catherine's chambermaids.

47.   CATHERINE TO POTEMKIN

[22 July 1774. Peterhof]

Dearest darling, cher Epoux,[1] pray come cuddle with me. Your caresses are so sweet and pleasing. My thanks for them. There's going to be a concert, and regarding Lolli,[2] pray order the Marshal-of-the-Court yourself. Priceless husband.

---

1. "dear spouse,"

2. The Italian violinist and composer Antonio Lolli (1733–1802) resided in St. Petersburg from 1773 to 1778.

48.   CATHERINE TO POTEMKIN

[After 23 July 1774]

My dear, I expect Tatiana woke you with her howling. She was laughing so loudly because my wet-nurse had grabbed me by the head and refused to let go for a long time as she smothered me with kisses. You too will like my wet-nurse's way of thinking when you hear that she has a son, an artillery captain, who was sent to the Archipelago with Spiridov's squadron five years ago, since when she has not seen him.[1] And she hardly even receives any letters. She came to me today and said: "Thank

God that peace has been established and I shall see my son once more. I wrote to him: Though everyone will begin to request to leave there, you, however, stay. I don't want to hear that you didn't serve where needed." Ma foi, il y a de la vigueur à cette façon de penser d'une femme du commun.[2] I gave her a thousand rubles and let her go, and you, precious darling, I embrace you in my mind a thousand times for yesterday's caresses, but I can't come, for the anteroom is full.

---

1. Admiral Grigory Andreevich Spiridov (1713–1790) participated in the historic naval victory over the Turks at Chesme in 1770. "Archipelago" refers to the Aegean Sea, with its many islands between Greece and Turkey.

2. "Honestly, there is strength in this way of thinking, especially for a woman of the common folk."

49. CATHERINE TO POTEMKIN

[29 July 1774]

You will see, my dear, from the items attached herewith, that Sir Count Panin deigns to make his brother a potentate with unlimited power in the best part of the empire—that is, the Moscow, Nizhny-Novgorod, Kazan and Orenburg Provinces. And, sans entendu,[1] there are other issues as well; namely, that if I sign this not only will Prince Volkonsky be both grieved and humiliated, but I myself shall not be protected in the least, and out of my fear of Pugachev I shall be praising and promoting above all other mortals in the Empire before the entire world the foremost liar who has personally insulted me.[2] Here's a book for you: pray read it and admit that the pride of these people is greater than all others. I am also attaching to this Bibikov's instructions for confrontatie.[3] That point which states that all persons, wherever they may be, he may [execute and pardon][4] how, where and when he desires isn't bad.

---

1. "it goes without saying,"

2. The recent sacking of Kazan by Pugachev unleashed panic in Moscow and Nizhny-Novgorod. Desperate, Catherine decided to call out of retirement Count Pyotr Ivanovich Panin (1721–1789), a hero of the First Russo-Turkish War, a harsh critic of Catherine, and supporter of the opposition centered around Grand Duke Paul. Panin demanded extraordinary powers before agreeing to accept the commission. Such a move would have indeed been confusing to Prince Mikhail Nikitich Volkonsky (1713–1789) since Catherine had earlier entrusted him with the task of spying on Panin in Moscow.

3. "comparison."

4. Though these exact words are not in her letter, such were Count Pyotr Panin's demands.

50.   CATHERINE TO POTEMKIN

[Before 1 August 1774]

My dear, I shall tell you something strange. This morning I got it into my head to look at the plans for Moscow's Catherine Palace. I found that the rooms that could be yours are quite far away and offer practically no access to mine, and I remembered that I purposely made them that way myself a year and a half ago, for which I was scolded; but I left them that way, claiming that there were no other rooms.[1] But I have now found six rooms for you: and they couldn't be any better or closer to mine. Avec Vous tout devient aisé; voilà ce que c'est que d'aimer veritablement.[2]

Farewell, my darling.

---

1. Preparations were being made for the court's trip to Moscow in the coming year to celebrate the victory over the Turks. Catherine purposely kept the rooms that had been intended for Vasilchikov at a distance from hers, despite his objection. His replacement with the much preferred Potemkin caused her to change her plan.

2. "With you everything becomes easy; this is what it means to truly love."

51.   CATHERINE TO POTEMKIN

[18 August 1774. Tsarskoe Selo]

Permit me to report, my dear and obliging friend, that I do remember you. And right now, after having listened to reports for three hours, I wanted to send someone to inquire about you. Since it's not past ten o'clock, I feared I'd wake you if I did it any earlier. So there's nothing to be angry about, but there are people in this world who love to find other people guilty when they should say thanks for all their many tender attentions.

Lordkin, I love you like my soul.

52.   CATHERINE TO POTEMKIN

[After 18 August 1774]

My darling, I'm very sad that you aren't well, and especially that with my words, which you found unpleasant yesterday, I perhaps worsened your illness, for it seems to me they upset you. Sweet darling, believe that I love you without end.

53.   CATHERINE TO POTEMKIN

[After 18 August 1774]

Lordikins, my angel, you should be the healthiest person in the world were your health to depend on my love for you.

Dear husband, priceless darling.

54.   CATHERINE TO POTEMKIN

[Before 23 August 1774]

Intelligent people, just as fools like us, are prone to mistakes. You're mistaken, my love, in thinking that I turn my thoughts to Chernyshev in the slightest.[1] All your other conclusions in this instance are of the exact same soundness. Adieu, Amour ou congé.[2]

---

1. In August 1774, Zakhar Chernyshev requested permission to retire from the War College.
2. "Farewell, love or take leave."

55.   CATHERINE TO POTEMKIN

[23 August 1774]

A trial does not begin before it has first heard out the justification of the accused. I got up after seven o'clock, and then went to the baths. Upon leaving, I listened to the Procurator-General. And since I had your lectures about not waking someone who is ill on my mind, I only sent someone once I thought that, perhaps, you'd awakened. Mon Ami, je suis bien fâchée que Vous êtes malade,[1] but I've no doubt that this is not from your being cross or vexed, for I know there's nothing to be cross or vexed about. It's high time I visit the sick ones.

---

1. "My friend, I am quite vexed that you are ill,"

56.   CATHERINE TO POTEMKIN

[Before 30 August 1774]

Mon très cher Epoux,[1] I shan't come to you because I sweated a bit during the night, because my bones ache as yesterday, and because it's quite cold. Precious darling, I slept well and love you with all my heart.

---

1. "My very dear spouse,"

57. CATHERINE TO POTEMKIN

[August–September 1774]

My sweet dear, I thank you for your hospitality. My Grishenok, you fed me and gave me to drink yesterday, but that surely wasn't wine. Please send me Galakhov's[1] notes.

---

1. A captain in the Preobrazhensky Regiment, Aleksandr Pavlovich Galakhov (b. 1739) had been sent on a secret mission to capture Pugachev.

58. CATHERINE TO POTEMKIN

[August–September 1774]

Baten'ka, I slept till nine o'clock. I'm up now and am well, though most terribly weak. Tell me, Lordikins, how are you and am I in your good graces? My darling, you know nothing is as dear to me as when you tell me that you love me. So say it, and for my part I love you extraordinarily. Kindly send me the letters from Panin and Kazan.[1]

---

1. Pyotr Panin wrote Catherine of his successes against the rebels, and from Kazan Pavel Potemkin wrote to complain of Panin's brutal methods.

59. CATHERINE TO POTEMKIN

[13 September 1774]

Sweetie, I wish you a happy birthday, dear friend to my happiness.

60. CATHERINE TO POTEMKIN

[14 September 1774]

Il n'y a rien de plus impertinent que ce "slave".[1] If I intended to quarrel, I would have some kind of an excuse. But I don't intend to, do you hear me, Lordikins? I am well, but not merry, nor sad, and I was glad to see you in the window.

---

1. "There is nothing more impertinent than that 'slave'." Petitions and letters to Russian tsars were traditionally sent not from their "subjects," but "slaves." Catherine found the practice abhorrent and was most likely reacting to Potemkin's use of it.

61. POTEMKIN TO CATHERINE

[14 September 1774]

Why, matushka, are you neither merry nor sad?

[Catherine] What a good answer. It couldn't be any drier. Is it truly necessary to be either merry or sad?

62. CATHERINE TO POTEMKIN

[21 September 1774]

My true friend, I am very sorry you're not well. I was compelled to leave Mass (my head ached so) and having held audience for the Swedish Chamberlain, I've gotten undressed and am eating alone. It's unbearable, such pain.

63. CATHERINE TO POTEMKIN

[Before 23 September 1774]

My darling, I think that if there is no other way to bring the blinded Grand Prince to see reason regarding Razumovsky, then might not Panin convince him to send Razumovsky away to sea, so that the rumors about him here in the city might die down?[1] Make use of the attached letter as you see fit.

---

1. Count Andrei Kirillovich Razumovsky (1752–1836), a close friend of Grand Duke Paul's. The rumors refer to Count Andrei Razumovsky's relations with Grand Duchess Natalia Alekseevna (*née* Princess Wilhelmina of Hesse-Darmstadt) (1755–1776), the first wife of Grand Duke Paul. Despite his close relationship with the grand duke, Razumovsky is reported to have begun an affair with Natalia, which Catherine told her son about, but which he refused to believe. A proud and decisive young woman, Natalia Alekseevna was rumored to have had her sights on the Russian throne soon after her wedding, and her desire might not have been unknown to Catherine.

64. CATHERINE TO POTEMKIN

[Before 24 September 1774]

After twelve. If you're now having your hair cut and curled, I guess you'll be dining at home. I'll find a place for your brother-in-law, and I am not at all against doing this. But do tell your brother-in-law to keep his eyes and ears open, for just as I, of course, do not want ruin, I also do not want the Crown to come out of this affair cheated and suffering any loss.[1]

---

1. Nikolai Samoilov was appointed chief procurator of the First Department of the Senate on 24 September 1774.

65.   CATHERINE TO POTEMKIN

[5 October 1774]

My sweet little dear. Everything in the world is subject to interpretation. I suppose that even these lines will be subjected to such interpretation, however, I shall not take this into consideration, but shall write the truth according to my conscience.

The Yaik Cossacks need rest, which they haven't had for four nights, or else they'll collapse.[1] One of them already feels that he is definitely not well and complains of a headache, sore back and a slight fever. He even has boils on his chest and a wound that usually produces a fever as it heals. Kindly let them rest, at least this sick one. I know you will say that he is a rogue and a scoundrel, but be that as it may, even rogues and scoundrels need rest.

I'll now report to you on the most important matter: I love you extraordinarily and shall for all time, only do not take from me this delicacy of feeling and do not deny me in my humble request that serves to increase this delicacy. Bonjour, mon coeur.

---

1. As head of Russia's irregular forces (the Cossacks), Potemkin presented to the empress on 5 October 1774 leaders of the Yaik Cossack Host who had fought against Pugachev.

66.   POTEMKIN TO CATHERINE

[Before 26 October 1774]

My beloved and priceless matushka. I've arrived, but am frozen to the bone. First and foremost, I wish to know of your health. I thank you, my benefactress, for the three frocks. I kiss your tender little feet.

[Catherine] Batia, I'm glad you've arrived. I'm well. Go to the baths and warm yourself up. They've been heated.

67.   CATHERINE TO POTEMKIN

[8 December 1774. St. Petersburg]

Mon cher Ami et Epoux,[1] upon hearing you were ill, I set off to see you, but I encountered so many people and officers in the corridors that I returned. I am extremely worried about your illness, for I was assured that you'd come home so you could clean up. You're not the only one who's ill. There are even those in town whom the arguses left behind this evening for the comedy. Sweet darling, send someone to tell me whether I am to see you today and when.

---

1. "My dear friend and spouse,"

68.   CATHERINE TO POTEMKIN

[8 December 1774]

Sweetie, your letter made me quite happy, especially since Lev Katansky[1] told me you weren't well and gave me to understand you weren't merry. The thought occurred to me, as it is wont to, that perhaps I annoyed you somehow. I reckoned it must've been my letter. Obviously, he didn't find it endearing. So, for a second time I intended to allow my feelings for you to write, and these feelings are in essence full of endearment for you, my Lordkin. My unparalleled darling, I regret you're not well. From now on, don't run up and down the stairs barefoot, and if you want to quickly get rid of your runny nose, then take a tiny pinch of snuff. You'll be better that very instant. Adieu, m'amour, mon coeur,[2] husband dear, splendid, sweet, and everything nice, pleasant and clever that you can imagine.

---

1. "Lev Katansky" was a nickname for Lev Aleksandrovich Naryshkin (1733–1799). Famous at court for his wit and humor, Chief Equerry Naryshkin had known Catherine since her early years in Russia and had at one point almost become her lover, an honor that he lost to Sergei Saltykov.

2. "Farewell, my passion, my love,"

69.   CATHERINE TO POTEMKIN

[9 December 1774]

My dear, my darling. How are you? Send word how you're doing. I have arrived home, so if you need me, of which I have no doubt, then send word, Lordikins. I'm not quite myself knowing that you're not well. If I may not come see you now, let me know when I may.

70.   CATHERINE TO POTEMKIN

[After 9 December 1774]

My precious darling, I'm truly sorry you're not well, and I ask you not to forget us. For we are firmly devoted to Grishatka for life with our heart and soul.

71.   CATHERINE TO POTEMKIN

[14 December 1774]

I'm returning to you the signed edict. My dear, tell me, what's the regiment to be called: the St. George Regiment or the Regiment of the Order?[1]

The fact that you, my dear darling, are pleased with my letter or resolutions has made me exceedingly happy. God grant that you are as pleased with me as I am with your love. I'm very worried that you're ill. And though I too am not well, still I'm not given a minute's rest. God only knows how much I've already dispatched and how much still awaits. And all my bones ache.

----

1. On 14 December 1774, Catherine signed an edict changing the name of the Third Cuirassier Regiment to the Cuirassier Regiment of the Military Order of the Great Martyr and Vanquisher St. George.

72.   CATHERINE TO POTEMKIN

[Before 17 December 1774]

Baten'ka, my friend. I'm infinitely sad that you're ill. I'll send the main ideas for the manifesto within the hour and I beseech you, if it's not too much trouble, to read them over. Should you be pleased with them, then hand them over to the bishop so he can compose the manifesto.[1] And if he needs it, I'll give him the file to read as well, however, it's very large, and he won't select anything different from what I've written. However, in order to ensure that the precision of the rituals be maintained, it is necessary that the bishop read the manifesto on Mirovich,[2] in which he will see how the trial was set up.

----

1. Following the conclusion of the investigation into the Pugachev Rebellion, Catherine began composing a manifesto that would proclaim Pugachev's crimes and set down the guidelines for the trial and sentencing. The final text was to be written out by Archbishop Gavriil (1730–1801), Metropolitan of St. Petersburg.

2. In 1764, Second Lieutenant Vasily Yakovlevich Mirovich (1740–1764) led an attempt to replace Catherine with former Emperor Ivan Antonovich (Ivan VI), who had been overthrown in 1741 and was still sitting locked up inside the Schlüsselburg fortress. Ivan Antonovich was killed during the failed coup and Mirovich was caught, tried, and executed.

73.   POTEMKIN TO CATHERINE

[March–December 1774]

Beloved matushka, pray allow me to indulge my curiosity: was Yelagin with you yesterday? And please let me have a brief look at the plan of your baths.

[Catherine] Yelagin was here and everything he brought me was signed. I'll send the plan of the baths in half an hour; I sent someone to get it from Pavlov.[1]

----

1. A court servant.

[Letters 74–130 are from Catherine from March–December 1774]

74.
Bonjour mon coeur. Although I do not at all love to go for walks through the mud, still it's merry and nice being with you wherever it may be.

75.
You talk gibberish, precious darling. I love you and shall love you eternally against your will.

76.   [In French]
My dear friend, be so kind as to pick out some present for my spirit,[1] and let me know, if you can, how are you feeling? Having no direct communication, and what with Mr. Fat Man[2] not here, I am forced to disturb you, for which I send my apologies.

---

1. Potemkin.
2. Possibly Prince Nikolai Golitsyn

77.
Baten'ka, my dear friend. Come to me so that I might calm you with my infinite caress.

78.
Sweetie, why don't you say a word to me or write? I just heard you're not well and are not going out. Est-ce que Vous êtes fâché contre moi et pourquoi?[1]

---

1. "Are you angry with me and why?"

79.
Baten'ka, but for weakness, I don't feel a thing now.

80.
Either the decree and the letter are in essence not clear to me, or I am muddle-headed today. But since I trust your honesty, I've signed and am returning them.

81.

You lie, precious darling. I'm not the haughty one, I'm not the unfriendly one, I was simply very engrossed in my project. Nevertheless, I love you very much.

82.

If I haven't made any spelling mistakes, return this and I'll seal it. But if I have, please correct them, and do send word, may I come to you or not? And I beg you not to venture out into the cold anteroom after the baths under any circumstances. Adieu, mon bijou.

83.

Be off, my dear, and be merry.

84.

Precious darling, you're very puffed up. Will you deign to appear today and play billiards? Please send someone to tell me—either yes or no, since letters can't be read in the comedy without glasses. Hmmm, you're puffed up, precious darling.

85.

Grishenok, you aren't angry are you? Even if you are angry, I hope you've ordered your anger to desist more than once. As for me, I have even stopped grumbling at Panin and his King,[1] and I'll never grumble at you.

_____

1. As a sign of her willingness to make peace after a quarrel with Potemkin, Catherine writes that she has even given up arguing with Count Nikita Panin, who pursued a pro-Prussian policy. "His King" refers to King Frederick II (the Great) of Prussia.

86.

Precious darling, although you don't need me in the least, still I need you very much. How's your health, and have I fallen out of favor or not? To you I proclaim God's as well as the Empress's every blessing.

87.

Grishenka, did you know you're priceless? Only do send word—how you are after the baths?

88.
My little pussycat, are you well? I am well and love you very, very much.

89.
Grishenka, hello. Say what you like, nevertheless I love you extraordinarily.

90.
Baten'ka, I don't dare come as it's late, still I love you as my soul.

91.
My dear friend, I don't know why, but it seems to me you're angry with me today. If not and I'm mistaken, tant mieux.[1] And as proof, run to me. I'm waiting for you in the bedroom. My soul hungers for you.

1. "so much the better."

92.
You naughty little thing. Are you going to pout for long?

93.   [In French]
Good evening, my love. I'm going to bed.

94.
As you please, my sweet Grishifushechka, however, I am not jealous and love you very much.

95.
Hello, sweetie. Know that there is no one dearer than you in the world. Precious darling, my Grishenok.

96.
Sweetie, dear sweet lips, my life, my joy, my merriment. Lordikins, my precious dear, mon faisan d'or. Je Vous aime de tout mon coeur.[1]

1. "my golden pheasant. I love you with all my heart."

97.

Oh, you, I shall punish you with a kiss straight on the lips for slandering me with the charge of haughtiness. I'm well and rejoice in your health.

98.

Baten'ka, sweet Lordikins, beloved husband, true friend, my finger hurts and a soothing plaster has just been applied.

99.

My sweet, priceless and unparalleled darling, I can't find the words to explain how much I love you. Don't worry about your diarrhea. It'll clean out your stomach. But you must take care of yourself, dear husband, Lordkin.

100.

I think about Grishenka always, and he never leaves my thoughts. And I love him as my soul.

101.

Hi, sweetie. I'm kissing and caressing you in my mind.

102.

Lordikins, may I come see you and when? I'm dying, I want to see you, my very own Grishatka.

103.

Sweetie, as you so order: should I come to you or do you desire to come to me? How are you this evening?

104.

I thank you for your most affectionate letter filled with both praise and zeal, which, upon having read, I immediately flung into the fire along with my returned letter.

105.

Sweetheart, I'm sorry you had a bad night on my account, I, however, slept tolerably well. Nevertheless, my arms and legs feel a bit tired. Rogerson[1] says my pulse is not normal. I don't know whether or not to go out. Give me your advice.

---

1. The Scotsman Dr. John Rogerson (1741–1823) was the court physician from 1769 until Catherine's death.

106.

Do you intend on leaving your things here with me for long? I humbly beseech you not to throw your kerchiefs all about as the Turks do. Nonetheless, I say a profound thank you, verbally as well as in writing, for your visit, and I love you very much.

107.

Baten'ka, they say that something odd happened last night: it turns out I apparently wandered throughout the palace and entered various rooms. I wasn't in your room, was I? I suppose you had quite a fright.

108.

Sweetheart, I am going to bed, and they will lock the doors. But if you come, even though I don't expect you to, and they are locked, then I truly shall cry tomorrow. And so I most humbly request that you stay at home and be certain that no one can love you more than I love you, precious darling.

109.

Grishenka, my friend, send word when you want to come to me, in the meanwhile I've sat down to read the newspapers.

110.   [In French]

My love, I came to you, but through the door I saw the back of either a scribe or an adjutant, and I ran away as fast as I could. Nevertheless, I love you with all my soul.

111.

No, not even at nine o'clock can you be found asleep. I came to you, Lordikins, but found people walking about, coughing and cleaning. And I had come to tell you that I love you extraordinarily.

112.

Baten'ka, I came to tell you how much I love you but found the door locked.

113.

Bonjour, mon coeur. Je me suis levée tard, je n'ai dormi, que quatre heures.[1] I don't dare go to you, I fear an encounter. My dear, sweet angel, my very own friend, my husband.

---

1. "Good day, my love. I got up late, I only slept four hours."

114.

Sweet Lordikins, priceless friend, Grishootka, hello. God grant you everything to your liking. I am well and love you to excess. I sought a path to you, but found so many footmen and lackeys along the way that I abandoned this undertaking to my deepest regret, for I so very-very much wanted to kiss you. My dear, send me Bariatinsky's report once it's been copied.

115.   [In French]

The doors will be open and everything will depend on the desire and the possibility of the one this concerns. As for me, I am going to bed.

116.

Precious darling, I beg you not to reproach us. I so overslept that I didn't get up till almost ten. And when I came to you, your windows were already open, and so I was afraid to enter. However, believe that I love you in exemplary fashion.

117.

Giaour, Muscovite, Cossack, do you want to make up? Put out your hand if your rage has passed and a glimmer of love remains within you. If not, I shall send for your brother-in-law. Giaour, Cossack, Muscovite.

118.
Hello, sweet darling. Since it'll be difficult to go for a ride today without freezing one's nose, I'm not going. But I love you very much and desire to hear that you, Grishefishechka, are well.

119.
Lordikins, I don't recommend you come to me, for you might easily catch cold. I'm glad you are feeling well after the baths, parce que je Vous aime, ma commande.[1]

_____

1. "because I love you, my master."

120.
Good night, sweetheart. I'm sorry you're not well. God be with you; I, however, am going to bed.

121.   [In French]
My friend, I am writing you this to learn how you are feeling, I am dying of boredom. When shall I see you again?

122.
Mon Ami, je m'ennuye si je ne puis Vous voir, envoyés moi quelqu'un pour jaser.[1] Lordikins, my dear friend.

_____

1. "My friend, I am bored if I cannot see you. Send me someone to chat with."

123.
It's been a hundred years since I last saw you. As you wish, but clean your chamber before I come from the comedy so I might visit you. Otherwise the day will be unbearable, and it's been sad enough already. The Devil led Fonvizin to you. Fine, precious darling, clearly he's much more amusing than I. Nevertheless, I love you, while he loves no one but himself.[1]

_____

1. Russian dramatist Denis Ivanovich Fonvizin (1745–1792). Catherine's assessment of Fonvizin's character was not unjustified.

124.

My dear, I'll write my answer tomorrow, but today my head aches. I am not cross and beseech you too not to be angry and not to pine. In short, I'll remain your true wife to the grave, should you so desire; if not, you're a giaour, Muscovite, Cossack.

125.

Baten'ka, if you absolutely must see me, then send word. I have had the most horrific diarrhea since five o'clock. I fear passing through the cold gallery in such damp weather will worsen my colic, and I sincerely regret you are ill. Tranquillisés-Vous, mon Ami. C'est le meilleur conseil que je puis Vous donner.[1]

---

1. "Calm down, my friend. That's the best advice I can give you."

126.

See here, sweetheart, twice you prevented me from attending to a most important affair with your silly little notes. I had intended to answer later, but ran out of patience—I threw out Kuzmin. Lordikins, I sincerely regret you are ill. I'll come visit you after dinner, as long as you don't have any Hussars, or Arnavuts,[1] or any odd specimens, originali[2] that is, with you.

I sent you a snuffbox. What sort of an object is that on your nose? Of course, it's that object that golden pheasants have instead of a mantilla. It actually grows and it is so necessary, proper and appropriate.

Adieu, mon beau faisan, je Vous aime de toutes mes facultés.[3] I order you to be well and merry.

---

1. Albanians, based on the Turkish. A now rather obscure play on words: the Turks used the term "Arnavut" in reference both to the Albanians and to a special type of military force whose guards were Christians. The term also came to mean a monster or cruel person.

2. "eccentrics"

3. "Farewell, my handsome pheasant. I love you with all my faculties."

127.

Three gloomy and by no means fair rescripts were read to me, and then scribbled all over and corrected in many places. For all my labors I have but one comfort. Amid many ingratitudes from everyone, your affection alone pleases me. If I could be caressed by it again, I should wish that you stood before me, but not at all in the form of an angry Pluto, but an ingratiating little idol. Having told you this, I shall add to my weakness by saying as well that should you find in this the slightest difficulty, then I shall prefer your will to my occasional whims which you find burdensome.

128.

I got up early, and the thought occurred to me to write down my rambling thoughts in the form of a letter. I'm sending them to you. I would by no means insist that this letter be sent were there a word in it at odds with the state of affairs. Please note que cette lettre est écrite d'un seul trait de plume[1] without any design and there's no copie.[2] I'll do one of two things: either fling it into the fire or send it.

---

1. "that this letter was written with a single stroke of the pen"
2. "copy."

129.

Your long letter and stories are quite excellent, but what's quite foolish is that there isn't a single affectionate word in them. What need do I have of someone who lies backwards and forwards? It seems to me that you, while telling tales according to your own liking, were obliged to remember that I too am in this world and that I have a right to desire affection. Fool, Tatar, Cossack, giaour, Muscovite, morbleu.[1]

---

1. "damn it."

130.

Having torn it to pieces, I am hereby returning this unpleasant note. I regret that you have become impassioned for nothing. But since this heart lacks reason, so I hope that this affair doesn't produce any lasting consequences, car coûte que coûte je Vous aime de tout mon coeur et Vous estime de même.[1]

---

1. "for come what may, I love you with all my heart and respect you just the same."

131. POTEMKIN TO CATHERINE

[18 February 1775. Moscow]

Matushka, après demain c'est le jour de naissance de notre esprit.[1] I kiss your tender little hands. My runny nose has been tormenting me. Donnés-moi conseil, que faut-il lui donner?[2]

1. "the day after tomorrow is our spirit's birthday." Perhaps a reference to a conversation held on 20 February 1774 in which Catherine and Potemkin discussed their mutual feelings, which resulted in the "Sincere Confession" of 21 February.

2. "Give me some advice, what should I give it?"

132. CATHERINE TO POTEMKIN

[19 February 1775. Moscow]

Il y a trois jours que je ne Vous ai pas vu à mon grand regret.[1] Your runny nose has been tormenting you, and me a pain in my head. But as I am better, so I can come to you this evening. However, before I do, please write what you wanted to say yesterday par rapport au jour de naissance, qui est demain, de l'esprit.[2]

1. "I have not seen you for three days to my great regret."
2. "in respect to the spirit's birthday, which is tomorrow."

133. CATHERINE TO POTEMKIN

[March 1775]

I received your cross letter after getting up from the table. I admit, it's all my fault that I demand that contradiction be avoided in my decrees, and what was said were only guidelines, whatever they may be, given to you to choose from freely. I do not intend to fool you, and what is more, I do not readily wish to be known as a fool. Your letter's other outbursts I take as hotheadedness, to which I shan't deign to answer, and still less become impassioned in vain, for you know yourself that you wrote nonsense.

Once you have properly written out the decree,[1] please send it to me for signing, and at the same time stop abusing and cursing me when I do not deserve it in the least. Fool, giaour.

1. As a gesture of royal charity, Catherine issued a decree lowering the tax on salt on 21 April 1775, her birthday.

134. CATHERINE TO POTEMKIN

[After 21 April 1775]

The Grand Duke was here and said that he was afraid lest word reach me and I become angry. He came to tell me himself that he and the Grand Duchess are in debt again. I said that this is not pleasant for me to hear and that I wish they wouldn't live so high on the hog and would forgo unnecessary expenses. He told me that her debt was from this, that, and the other thing, to which I answered that she had an allowance (just as he does) like no one else in Europe, and, what's more, that this allowance is simply for clothing and passing fancies, but that the rest—servants, table, and carriage—is provided them, and that on top of all that she had been furnished with clothing and everything else to last her for about three years.[1] And I said it might be better were they to put their house in order and not buy and order all sorts of rubbish and rags. He said that the journey had been expensive for them.[2] To which I answered that I cart them about and have spent twice as much because of them than if I had traveled alone. In response to this he sought to convince me that some of my expenses had been charged to them. In a word, he requests more than twenty thousand, and I fear there will be no end to this. Tell Andrei Razumovsky to stop this squandering, for it's depressing to pay their debts in vain and without any thanks. If you count everything, including what I gave, then more than five hundred thousand has been expended on them during the year, and still they are in dire straits. But not a single thank you nor an ounce of gratitude.

---

1. The grand duchess received a yearly allowance of fifty thousand rubles.

2. The entire court traveled from St. Petersburg to Moscow in January 1775 and remained there most of the year largely to celebrate the victory over the Turks.

135. CATHERINE TO POTEMKIN

[After 21 April 1775. Moscow]

My dear and priceless friend. I suppose we can also threaten the Grand Duke by having Razumovsky or somebody else say to him that this reputation as a spendthrift sets a bad example to young people, for they will point to him when getting money from their parents to pay for their wastefulness. Oh, this is depressing.

136. CATHERINE TO POTEMKIN

[After 21 April 1775]

Sweetie, I'm merry, I'm not angry, and there's nothing to be angry about. Dearest Grishenka, I shan't exclude yesterday from among the happy days, for it ended quite agreeably. If only it could be so in the future. I, precious darling, shall be compliant, and you, my darling, be indulgent as well, clever little Adonis. I'll give you the portrait at the peace celebration.[1] I am telling you in advance so as to avoid any misunderstanding. Adieu, mon bijou, mon coeur, husband dear.

1. The celebrations marking the Peace of Kuchuk Kainardji, ending the First Russo-Turkish War (1768–1774), were held in Moscow from 10–23 July 1775. On the first day of the celebration Potemkin was made a count and received a diamond-encrusted miniature of the empress like the one worn by Grigory Orlov.

137. CATHERINE TO POTEMKIN

[After 3 June 1775]

I'll never ever again go pray to God. You're so cold to me it makes me sick. Giaour, Muscovite, Cossack, wolf, bird.

138. CATHERINE TO POTEMKIN

[8 June 1775. The Village of Kolomenskoe]

My darling, our own true holiday is today,[1] and I would celebrate it most gladly, but it's too bad that you ache all over, and with all my soul I wish to see you well, merry, content, for I love your charities to excess.

1. Possibly the one-year anniversary of their marriage.

139. CATHERINE TO POTEMKIN

[After 15 June 1775]

My dear Sir, Grigory Aleksandrovich.
I wish Your Excellency every possible success, but it's imperative that you lose at cards tonight, for you completely forgot me downstairs and left me all by myself as if I were some lone post marking the city border.

[Potemkin] [A line of fanciful Arabic letters] that is, an answer; if I dare say or report, everything written here is false, for you were impatiently waited for here.

140. POTEMKIN TO CATHERINE

[Before 28 June 1775]

Permit me, Your Majesty, to absent myself today. I have been called away on a visit.

[Catherine] Have fun, but see to it that you promote those men from yesterday's list (whom you presented) to the rank of colonel.

141. CATHERINE TO POTEMKIN

[June 1775]

I noticed that your dear mother[1] was quite dressed up today, but she has no watch. Give her this one from me.

---

1. Catherine gave Daria Vasilievna Potemkina (*née* Kaftyreva) (1704–1780) many expensive gifts and made her a lady-in-waiting in 1776.

142. CATHERINE TO POTEMKIN

[Before 10 July 1775. Moscow]

To help console your mother, name as many of your nieces as you desire maids-of-honor.[1]

---

1. Potemkin received word from his brother-in-law Vasily Engelhardt of his sister Marfa's death shortly before the peace celebration and took steps over the years to help his several nieces. Aleksandra (then 21 years old) became a maid-of-honor on 10 July 1775; Varvara (18 years old) in 1777; Nadezhda (16 years old) in 1779; Yekaterina (14 years old) in 1776; and Tatiana (8 years old) in 1781.

143. CATHERINE TO POTEMKIN   [In French, except for last word]

[After 10 July 1775]

My friend, must the Field Marshal always be given the title Zadunaisky?[1]

---

1. One of Russia's great generals, Field Marshal Count Pyotr Aleksandrovich Rumiantsev (1725–1796) received the honorific title "Zadunaisky" (literally, "beyond the Danube") for his important victories over the Turks south of the Danube River in June 1775.

144. CATHERINE TO POTEMKIN

[2 August 1775]

My doll, either you're pig-headed or you're angry, and so I've not seen a single line from you. Fine, precious darling, I'll punish you, just you wait—I'll smother you with kisses. It seems to me you've gotten used to being without me. I haven't seen you for almost an entire day, but Shcherbachev[1] and other riff-raff, who aren't worth my little finger and who don't love you as much, are always allowed to enter into your sight, while I have been pushed aside. Fine, I shall become a Général des Jamchiks[2] in your service, and then I'll gain admittance to Your Excellency.

1. Aleksei Longinovich Shcherbachev (d. 1802) was a major-general, senator, and head of the Coachmen's Office.

2. "General of the Coachmen"

145. CATHERINE TO POTEMKIN

[4 August 1775]

Precious darling, I have only now gotten up and don't think I'll have time to come to you, and so I write. I have been asleep since one o'clock and slept very well till this very hour. Later, around twelve o'clock, I'm taking my daughter-in-law for a ride, and he's coming along on horseback.[1] The weather is heavenly, and they already talked to me about this yesterday. And though it seems ridiculous to our gentlemen that she is going out for a ride today, I am taking responsibility for this. I'll say that I took her away. My sweet doll, I love you extraordinarily. Farewell.

1. On 4 August 1775, Catherine took Grand Duchess Natalia, who had been ill of late and had recently become pregnant, for a ride in her phaeton to visit the village of Kolomenskoe outside Moscow. The grand duke accompanied them on horseback.

146. CATHERINE TO POTEMKIN

[15 September 1775]

Respecting your request, which is filled with gratitude and recognition toward Sir Zagriazhsky (and coldness toward me, hmm-hmm), I permit him to prostrate himself at my blessed feet, when and where you like.[1] What is more, I allow you to use the word "you" the entire morning when in my absence, as much as you please, as long as I don't hear it, neither in writing, nor verbally.[2] Oh, how cold, how very cold it is! It must be the windows are open somewhere. And such a violent wind is blowing: it must be ringing for Sir Zagriazhsky. [. . .]

1. Catherine and her suite paid a visit to Zakhar Chernyshev's estate in Yaropoletz on 15 September 1775. In response to Potemkin's request, she took time the next day to meet Chernyshev's neighbor, General-in-Chief Aleksandr Artemevich Zagriazhsky (1716–1786), a relation of Potemkin's mother and an old family friend.

2. Catherine and Potemkin freely switched between the informal "thou" (*ty*) and the formal "you" (*vy*) in their correspondence. In this instance, Catherine is teasing Potemkin for his use of the formal "you."

147. CATHERINE TO POTEMKIN

[Before 7 November 1775]

We ask and entreat you to place a small cross like this "+" at each article in order to signify your approval. The exclusion of an article as well we ask you to mark so "#". And the alteration of an article we ask you to write out exactly.[1]

---

1. Throughout the spring and summer of 1775, Catherine worked on a plan to reform the administration of Russia's provinces. Potemkin played a minor role in helping to draft the Statute for the Administration of the Provinces, promulgated in November 1775.

148. CATHERINE TO POTEMKIN

[Before 7 November 1775]

Of the papers sent, I first read with great pleasure the general plan and everything pertaining to it and found that everything was compiled with a sound mind and after considerable reflection, for which many thanks. I see throughout it ardent zeal and your thorough understanding.[1] I also read the second papers, concerning the provinces, and ordered to speak with you about them, for the number of inhabitants in some of the districts exceeded the accompanying proportionality. Better to increase them, the districts, that is.[2]

---

1. Potemkin was also putting together a defense plan for Russia's borders.

2. See Letter 147n1.

149. CATHERINE TO POTEMKIN

[After 13 November 1775]

Baten'ka, three times I tried to come to you, but each time I encountered lackeys and stokers. And so I'm sending Madame Popova[1] to find out how you are.

---

1. Yelizaveta Mikhailovna Popova married one of Catherine's valets on 13 November 1775 in the presence of the empress.

150. CATHERINE TO POTEMKIN

[Before 14 December 1775]

Baten'ka, kindly don't say anything more about it. I'm exceedingly content with your caresses. For they are, of course, my comfort. And so, je

Vous prie d'agir comme si de rien n'étoit,[1] and everything will pass, and my bottomless passion will abate of its own accord, and nothing will remain but pure love.

Kindly consider what a cunning swindle Matonis[2] has carried out. Who among those people can you trust after this?

---

1. "I beseech you to act as if it were nothing,"

2. Secretary of the Heraldmaster's Office, Nikolai Nikolaevich Matonis (b. around 1739) is believed to have fallen victim, along with his friend, Grigory Kozitsky, a creature of Orlov and one of Catherine's state secretaries, to court intrigue. Matonis was dismissed from service on 14 December 1775; Kozitsky committed suicide shortly thereafter.

[Letters 151–167 are from Catherine from 1775, except 154, which is from Potemkin to Catherine]

151.

My doll, I've come from the concert during which you never left my thoughts. I don't know whether or not I may come to you. Do you wish to come to me?

152.   [In French]

May I know what new madness you've dreamed up?

153.   [In French]

If your own company pleases you, I am very glad. But this is no reason to forget your friends. Keep in mind that pride is not a virtue. May I have the honor of seeing you, my Lord?

154. POTEMKIN TO CATHERINE

To Her Imperial Majesty.

A Most humble Petition.

Prostrating myself at your feet, I request your leave to dine with Lazarevich[1] today.

Your Majesty's servant

G.P.

[Catherine] I grant you leave on one most gracious condition: that there be neither gluttony nor drunkenness, lest after that illness ensue.

1. Ivan Lazarevich Lazarev (1735–1801) was a court jeweler who went on to become one of Russia's wealthiest bankers. His son was an aide-de-camp to Potemkin.

155.

Well, baten'ka, I waited till twelve o'clock thinking that given my pain yesterday you'd send someone to ask how I'm feeling. But I see that my waiting was in vain, although I know that this is by no means because I am not in your thoughts. Nevertheless, since you are occupied by affairs, while I have already freed myself from mine, so I write this to you in order to know whether you are alive, for I am.

156.

My God, shall I see you today? How lonely it is, what boredom. I desire your political assembly to meet anywhere it wants, but as for me, I want to be with you.

157.

Control your anger, you little idol. You're spouting drivel. You're not going to move to the Sech[1] or to a monastery.

1. The Sech was the name of the headquarters of the Zaporozhian Cossack Host located on an island in the Dnieper River. As part of her policy of exerting greater state control over the Cossacks, Catherine abolished the Sech in 1775.

158.   [In French]

Ill-humor and impatience are injurious to one's health. Everything one does with ill-humor and impatience is badly done and disagreeable; when one abandons oneself to ill-humor one always makes the worst decisions out of spite and unreasonableness. That is what I just read in a book. If you think my book is right, come to me.

159.

It's not the first of April after all when one might send a piece of paper without writing anything on it. This is obviously the result of your dream not to spoil me with excess kindness. But as I poorly learned how to be sly, so it may be that sometimes even I don't understand what it means to keep silent. Be that as it may, whereas I am obliging, you prefer to repay us with an unequal coin.

Giaour, Muscovite, Yaik Cossack, Pugachev, turkey cock, peacock, exotic tom-cat, golden pheasant, tiger, lion in the reeds.

160.

Something has been written on this sheet. It's probably abuse of some sort, for yesterday Your Excellence in relation to me consisted[1] of your haughty heart, while I, with a broken heart, was obliging, and searched with a light for your love's weary caress; yet though I searched till evening's arrival, still I was unable to find it.

What exactly has happened? Oh, God! My cunning has put right what my sincerity had spoiled. Our quarrel was born three days ago as a result of my seeking in a sincere and friendly manner and without the ruse of cunning and scheming to explain myself to you regarding those thoughts that I couldn't have imagined anyone might find reprehensible. On the contrary—they were actually in your own favor. Nevertheless, yesterday evening I acted with deliberate cunning. I confess that I deliberately didn't send anyone to you till nine o'clock in order to see whether you would come to me; but when I saw you weren't going to come, I sent someone to inquire about your health. You came and came all in a huff. I pretended not to notice. And being more stubborn than you in every way, I calmed down your heart and huffiness and saw with pleasure that you were quite glad to be rid of it. You'll say that you asked me to write you an affectionate letter and that instead I am giving a recapitulation of our quarrel. But wait just a moment, permit my wounded heart to calm down. Affection will return of its own accord everywhere that you afford it room. My affection is of the bustling sort—it bustles to and fro and goes everywhere but from where it's pushed away. And even when you push it away, still it whirls about you, like an evil demon, in order to find a post it might occupy. When my affection sees that it cannot make its way with sincerity, it immediately cloaks itself in the garments of cunning. See how cunning my affection is? It's happy to take on any appearance simply in order to reach you. If you strike it with your fist, it will jump aside and will immediately seek a new place to land so as to get closer—no, not to its enemy, but to its true friend. And who's he? His name is Grishenka. It overcomes his wrath. It forgives him his distorting of her words. It confers a softening meaning upon his harsh words, allows his hot-tempered ones to pass by its ears, doesn't take the insulting ones to heart or tries to forget them. In a word, our affection is the most sincere love and a love most extraordinary. But be angry, if you can, and make us stop, should you find the means, from being true. Great will be the profit you find. Think it over well, blow your top, but please, follow my example, even if only a little, and then we shall both be content.

1. Another one of Catherine's untranslatable wordplays: "[. . .] ibo prevoskhoditel'stvo Vashe peredo mnoiu vcheras' v tom sostoialo [. . .]"

161.

I have received your affectionate letter with its mad proposal, and since I am in my right mind and have all my wits about me, I shall throw it into the fire as a superfluous and useless scrap of paper. I accept this without being cross, for my thoughts are not malicious, and I cannot want a person in this or any other post thinking that he is suitable and capable in others. And of the others, it seems no mention has ever been made. You were in the mood to quarrel. Please inform me once this inclination passes.

162.

Precious darling, I took a cord with a stone and tied it around the necks of all our quarrels, and then I tossed it into a hole in the ice. Don't be angry that I acted so, precious darling. And should this please you, pray do the same. Hello, my dear, I write to you free of any tension, dissension or contention.

163.

You are such a fool, and so I shan't order you to do anything, for I don't warrant such coldness, but attribute it to my villain, this damned depression. Vous affichés il me semble cette froideur, sachés que cette affiche tout comme cette froideur sont deux bêtes ensemble.[1] However, if this affiche[2] is only to get me to say something affectionate, then know that this is a futile effort, for I swore that nothing but affection shall I repay with affection. I want caresses, and what's more, tender caresses of the very best sort. But your foolish coldness together with my foolish depression gives birth to nothing but anger and vexation. Did it really cost you that much to utter either "darling" or "my dear"? Is your heart really silent? My heart certainly is not.

1. "It seems to me you make a show of this coldness; know that this show and this coldness are together two beastlinesses."
2. "show"

164.

It's high time that we live in harmony. Don't vex me with your intolerable behavior and then you won't be treated coldly. I shan't repay rudeness with affection. I love being candid, and my soul has no difficulty in doing this. I'm sorry you're ill, my dear. Calmés Votre esprit, il lui faut du repos. Au reste Vous devés Vous en fier à la bonté de mon coeur, qui n'aime point à voir ou à faire souffrir; j'aimerais bien à trouver la même disposition dans les autres hommes vis à vis de moi.[1]

---

1. "Calm your spirit, it must have rest. Moreover, you must trust the goodness of my heart, which doesn't like to see or cause suffering. I should like to find the same inclination in others toward me."

165.

Even though you said to me that you aren't affectionate toward me, still I am content, since this has given me cause not to be affectionate toward you and to say this to you, were this to reflect my thinking. But since I don't have a single unfriendly fiber in me, so, unlike you, I don't intend to lie, since it is base for me to say something that doesn't reflect my feelings, giaour!

166.

I shall be merry, sweet darling, really and truly! I am so moved by your love and your regret that I wish I could find the means to make you forget the past day and everything that happened and to keep this from ever being mentioned between us again. My Lordikins, my priceless sweetheart.

167.

Your gentle behavior toward me shines everywhere, and the incoherence of your words is always the same when you least expect it. Then everything comes crashing down. So now, when every word is a misfortune, pray bring your words and conduct into agreement when you say that you wish to live in perfect harmony and not to have any secret thoughts. To a madcap like you there's nothing sweeter than your own vexation as well as mine, and for you tranquility is an extraordinary and unbearable condition. The gratitude I owe you has not vanished, for I suppose there has never been a time when you haven't received signs of this. But at the same time it's also true that you gave me the means to reign while taking away the powers of my soul, incessantly harrowing it with new fabrications abhorrent to mankind. A fine position, for which I ask you to tell me—must I thank you or not? I always thought that health and restful days were esteemed for at least something in this world. I should like to know, how could there be either of these with you?

3. Breaking Up—1776

fter spending most of 1775 in Moscow, the court returned to St. Petersburg on 26 December. To all outward appearances, it seemed that relations between Catherine and Potemkin remained strong and that her favorite was solidifying his position. On 1 January 1776, he was entrusted with command of the St. Petersburg troop division and his mother was made a lady-in-waiting to the empress. Several of Potemkin's nieces and nephews had recently joined Catherine's intimate circle. Nikolai Vysotsky, the son of Potemkin's sister Pelageia, was made an aide-de-camp to the empress, and Aleksandr Samoilov was appointed to Catherine's State Council as a secretary. Aleksandra Engelhardt, a maid-of-honor since July 1775, had quickly become a fast friend of Catherine's. And to add to Potemkin's growing collection of titles, Catherine wrote to her ambassador in Vienna on 13 January instructing him to seek the title of prince of the Holy Roman Empire for her favorite.

Despite these signs of Potemkin's ever increasing power, rumors soon appeared in early 1776 that Potemkin's days as favorite were ending and that his fall from grace was imminent. The cause for such gossip was the recent appearance of a new man by Catherine's side, Colonel Pyotr Zavadovsky, whom the empress had designated as her favorite with the seldom used title of "general's adjutant" on 2 January. Although Zavadovsky's status would not be officially proclaimed for another six months, his appointment marked an important change in Catherine's personal life and signaled the beginning of a period of crisis in her relationship with Potemkin, a crisis that was to last until the end of July 1776.

Zavadovsky, a handsome and well-educated thirty-seven-year-old Ukrainian (the same age as Potemkin), first caught Catherine's eye in Moscow in the summer of 1775. He had been recommended to the empress by Field Marshal Pyotr Rumiantsev, under whom he had labored with much success for several years, and was appointed Catherine's cabinet secretary on 10 July. Before the end of the month he was dining at Catherine's table, and soon thereafter he became part of her suite, accompanying her on short trips throughout the Moscow countryside. He assisted Catherine with her drafting of legislation to reform Russia's provinces and was duly awarded for his efforts on this and other projects with estates, serfs, and decorations.

Upon returning to Petersburg, Catherine set up a most unusual *ménage-à-trois* with Potemkin and Zavadovsky. Potemkin kept his rooms in the Winter Palace and continued his duties much as he had before. Yet he and Catherine were henceforth joined by Zavadovsky, who worked closely with them and dined with them alone or with others in small groups. The most private details of this arrangement, namely with whom Catherine was sharing her bed—Zavadovsky or Potemkin or, rather unlikely, both—are not known. Nor are Catherine's motives for establishing this arrangement altogether clear. It is possible she was playing them against each other, perhaps in the hope the competition between them would reinvigorate Potemkin's flagging ardor.

Matters were further complicated when Grigory Orlov appeared in the capital in the middle of January, fresh from his European travels. His warm reception at court set tongues wagging that the Orlovs' influence was yet again ascendant. Individuals desirous of Potemkin's fall found further cause for hope when Potemkin received the title of prince from Joseph II of Austria in February, for it was well known that Orlov's dismissal had coincided with his being granted permission to use this title. There was talk that Zavadovsky had eclipsed Potemkin in Catherine's estimation and that Orlov had enough power to protect him. Potemkin was rumored to be so outraged by Orlov's return and new-found respect that he was even trying to poison him.

The letters that have survived convey the painful uncertainty of these months when Catherine and Potemkin's future was so much in doubt. Whereas the year before Potemkin had turned cold to Catherine, now he appeared to be contemplating abandoning court and leaving her altogether. When he asked Catherine, "Where should I go, where should I hide myself?" (Letters 172, 180), Catherine told him to come to her, that she would greet him with open arms. But her assurances of continued affection did little to ease his doubts. Potemkin was often in a rage. He began insulting her, implying she was a "monster" and a "beast." He was forever making scenes, crying, charging into her room to quarrel and then stomping off, slamming the door behind him (Letters 174, 175, 184, 194, 201). Even though there still were moments of tenderness between them, these were becoming rare. Given the peculiar *troika* Catherine had assembled, it is not surprising that Potemkin had come to doubt her sincerity. Potemkin accused her of being "two-faced," and he put the justifications for her actions down to so much "craftiness" (Letters 174, 193).

The leitmotif that runs throughout Catherine's letters is a desire for peace and harmony. She had by now begun to weary of Potemkin's outbursts, and though Catherine continued trying to pacify his wrath, an unmistakable restraint had crept into her letters. The gushing pronouncements of her undying love were gone, replaced by more reserved assurances of her friendship and attachment (Letters 169, 177, 189, 201). The problem with their relationship, as she saw it, was that while she was guided by dispassionate reason, he, on the other hand, was in the grips of an overly active imagination that kept him from seeing the truth of her actions (Letters 189, 198, 201). She repeatedly told him that it was in his power to change his behavior should he so desire. Catherine's letters suggest that if Potemkin did not change his ways, she would have no other choice but to withdraw her affection as a means of self-preservation (Letters 175, 177, 201). She claimed to have done everything for him and made reference to the "bonds of Holy Matrimony" that bound them together, a reminder that there was no greater sign of devotion she could give him. And he, in return, had plunged a dagger into her heart (Letters 173, 184, 195).

The specific causes and sequence of events that led to the collapse of their affair are murky. It is generally believed that Potemkin was the first to cool, sometime in mid-1775. The position of favorite had never been a comfortable one for him; he had not been able to master the insecurity he felt in this role and possibly grew to resent Catherine's inability to understand the depth of his unease. Given his boundless ambition, the life of favorite was too confining. Potemkin sought greater autonomy of action; it was not enough to be Catherine's pupil and to organize his days according to her schedule. Despite the honors Catherine showered upon her lovers, being a favorite was, as Vasilchikov once ruefully remarked, like being a kept woman. While Potemkin was clearly no Vasilchikov, nevertheless, he, too, was susceptible to such feelings. Indeed, the strain was probably much greater for Potemkin given his ambition. Catherine observed that they quarreled about "power, not love," and even though this assessment was more a reflection of her desire than the true state of affairs, the ever more confident, knowledgeable Potemkin was in fact seeking greater political power (Letter 174).

While Catherine appears to have initially sought to keep Potemkin from estranging himself from her, she came to realize that she was going to have to make some sort of decision. She, too, had grown tired of the never-ending quarrels brought on (in her opinion) by his petty jealousies and uncontrollable anger. She had initially sought in Potemkin a refuge from the loneliness and stresses of her position, but with time their relationship had ceased to be a comfort and become yet one more burden. The placid, diffident Zavadovsky, ever aching to please her, offered Catherine the reassuring warmth she sought but could no longer find in Potemkin. Moreover, Potemkin's anger had started to take on a public face: their fights were no longer their own business, rather Potemkin had started to discuss them with his friends and family and to make open displays of his displeasure, actions that Catherine could not help but interpret as damaging to her authority (Letters 190, 200, 201).

Sometime in the early months of 1776, Potemkin wrote Catherine in an attempt to make up after yet another fight. He told her of the awkwardness their love caused him and of his desire to be first among all others in her heart, "since no one has so loved you as I." He admitted to being the work of her hands, and asked that she secure his peace (Letter 186). In the margin of his letter, Catherine scribbled in a cramped hand a reply and sent it back. She told him to "be calm," that she had placed him "firmly and solidly" in her heart and that he was and would remain there before all others. She admitted that securing his peace was her "foremost pleasure." To that end, Catherine ultimately decided that while she could replace Potemkin's affection with another's, she could not do without his political talents.

On 28 June, Zavadovsky was promoted to major-general and granted twenty thousand rubles and three thousand serfs. His position as Catherine's favorite was now official. Several days earlier, Potemkin departed to inspect the Novgorod province and did not return until late July. His absence from the capital, combined with Catherine's gift to him of the Anichkov Palace, appeared to confirm the rumors of Potemkin's definitive fall from favor. Few realized at the time, however, that the prince's greatest triumphs still lay before him.

◆ ◆ ◆

168. CATHERINE TO POTEMKIN

[1 January 1776]

Baten'ka, Lordikins, I received your affectionate New Year's letter with the same tender feeling with which I accept everything that comes from you. May God grant you too everything you might wish. I sincerely love you, and if you are my friend, then know, of course, that I too am the most loyal one you have. I fulfill your requests and ask you not to consign mine to oblivion as well. Farewell, sweet darling, I shall now call for Morsochnikov and shall order him to bury Countess Vorontsova at my expense.[1]

1. Ivan Mikhailovich Morsochnikov (1717–1785) oversaw the collection and dispensing of court monies. Countess Anna Karlovna Vorontsova (*née* Skavronskaia) (1722–1775) was a cousin of Empress Elizabeth and the wife of Chancellor Count Mikhail Illarionovich Vorontsov (1714–1767), who had played a role in the coup that put Elizabeth on the throne in 1741. Anna Karlovna died greatly in debt, and Zakhar Chernyshev wrote to Potemkin asking that he request three or four thousand rubles from Catherine to pay for her funeral.

[Letters 169–187 are from February–March 1776]

169. CATHERINE TO POTEMKIN

Baten'ka, I was filled with both gratitude and tenderness upon receiving your letter and marvelous present. Please be assured, that my candid friendship and sincere attachment to you will remain a part of me always without fail. Be well and merry, and so give me even greater pleasure. Farewell, my dear charge, I wish you a good night. I'm going to bed now.

170. CATHERINE TO POTEMKIN

My head truly is bad, it's spinning and weak. I'm not angry and am not cross with you. It's your choice as to how to treat me. I don't intend to cause you any pain. You've no reason to worry about that. I desire to see you at peace and to be so myself. My true friend, I speak the truth, turn your ear to the truth. But for my very own self, there's no one else to speak it to you.

171. CATHERINE TO POTEMKIN

The very first sign of loyalty is obedience. I am not accustomed to showing ingratitude. Your life is precious to me, and so I don't wish to alienate you.

172. CATHERINE TO POTEMKIN

Dearest darling, having read your letters it's not difficult to decide: stay with me. And as for your political proposals, they're all quite reasonable.

173. CATHERINE TO POTEMKIN

It's shameful to wake someone who's ill. Batenk'ka, Stackelberg[1] told me you're sleeping. I'm sending this now to find out how you are. I ordered him to write out the instructions on his own, and I expect that this will take care of the matter.[2] Darling, I do everything for you, so I wish you'd encourage me just a wee bit by showing me some affection and composure. Je ne suis jamais mieux que quand les mouvemens de mon bon coeur ne sont pas gênés.[3] Lordkin, dear husband.

---

1. Count Otto Magnus von Stackelberg (1736–1800) was the Russian ambassador to Poland from 1772. He visited St. Petersburg in early 1776.

2. Potemkin was then seeking for himself the throne of the duchy of Courland, which belonged to Duke Peter Bühren, the son of Empress Anna Ioannovna's favorite, Ernst Bühren. Ambassador Stackelberg had been entrusted with interceding on Potemkin's behalf in Poland and Courland. Nothing came of the idea, in part because Catherine wanted to keep Potemkin with her in Russia.

3. "I am never better than when the movements of my good heart are not constrained."

174. CATHERINE TO POTEMKIN

Listening to you talk sometimes one might say that I am a monster who has every possible shortcoming, particularly that of being a beast. I am frightfully two-faced, and if I'm grieved, if I cry, this is not the result of my sensibility, but something entirely different altogether, and consequently this must be ignored and I must be looked down upon. Such an exceedingly tender way of behaving can only have a positive effect on my mind. As mean and as horrible as this mind is, however, it knows no other way of loving than to make happy the one it loves. For this reason it's impossible for it to be on bad terms with the one it loves even for a moment without despairing, and it's even more impossible for it to be continually occupied every moment of the day reproaching the one it loves with this or that; on the contrary, my mind is busy finding the virtues and merits in the one it loves. I love to see in you all marvels. Pray tell, how would you behave if I continuously reproached you for the shortcomings of all your acquaintances, of all those whom you most respect or employ, if I held you responsible for their blunders? Would you be patient or impatient? If, seeing you impatient, I were to be offended, were to get up, were to stomp away, slamming the doors behind me, and after that were to be cold to you, were [not] to look at you, and were to act even colder than I in fact were; if I were to add threats to all this—would you conclude from this that I'd been putting on airs with you? Finally, if after this your head were also inflamed and your blood boiling, would it be most surprising

if both of us had by then lost all common sense, if we couldn't understand each other or if we both spoke at the same time?[1]

For Christ's sake, find the means to keep us from quarreling ever
again. Our quarrels always arise from nothing but irrelevant rubbish.
We quarrel about power, not about love. Now there's the truth for you.
I know what you'll say, so don't bother saying it. For I shall indeed not
answer you since, as concerns me, I, of course, do not intend to become impassioned. Voulés Vous me rendre heureuse, parlés moi de
Vous, je ne me facheré jamais.[2]

---

1. Entire paragraph in French.
2. "If you want to make me happy, speak to me of yourself. I shall never become angry."

175. CATHERINE TO POTEMKIN

Though I've frequently caressed you till now, still I haven't succeeded in a
single thing. No one can be compelled to caress, to compel is indecent,
and to feign is an attribute of base souls. Pray comport yourself in such a
manner that I may be content with you. You know my disposition and
my heart, you know my good and foolish qualities, you are smart, so I
leave it to you alone to choose accordingly the appropriate behavior. You
worry needlessly, you suffer needlessly. Common sense alone will show
you the way out of this uneasy state. This calls for nothing drastic, you
damage your health for no good reason.

176. CATHERINE TO POTEMKIN   [In French]

My friend, you're angry, you're sulky with me, you say you're vexed, and
why? Because I wrote you a letter this morning devoid of all common sense.
You returned this letter to me, I tore it to pieces in front of you and burned
it the very next moment. What more satisfaction could you desire? Even
the Church aspires to no more once a heretic has been burned. My note has
been burned. You should not want to burn me too, yet if you continue being sulky with me, you will ruin all my merriment till this passes. Peace, my
friend. I stretch out my hand to you, do you wish to take it?

177. CATHERINE TO POTEMKIN

I'm ready to live in perfect harmony, but only so long as my sincerity
never causes me harm. And should I see that I shall suffer because of it,
then charité bien ordonnée commence par soi-même.[1]

Stop the remittances, since the Dutch will now often put this money into the Black Sea. Sweet darling, my head aches, it's difficult to write.

---

1. "charity begins at home."

178. CATHERINE TO POTEMKIN

Your Irate and Excellent Sir General-in-Chief and Chevalier of various Orders. I am finding that this week abounds in fools. If your silly depression has passed, then please let me know, for it seems to me quite protracted since I gave you neither the slightest reason nor cause for your rather great and protracted anger. It seems this has been going on for long, but unfortunately I see that it seems this way to me alone, and you are an evil Tatar.

179. CATHERINE TO POTEMKIN

It's time to be fair. I'm not proud, I'm not angry. Stop worrying and give me peace. I shall say to you with all sincerity that I'm sorry you're not well. But I shall not spoil you with words that have been forced upon me.

180. CATHERINE TO POTEMKIN

Mon mari m'a dit tantôt:[1] "Where should I go, where should I hide myself?" Mon cher et bien aimé Epoux, venés chez moi, Vous serés reçu à bras ouverts.[2]

---

1. "My husband said to me earlier:"
2. "My dear and beloved spouse, come to me. You will be received with open arms."

181. CATHERINE TO POTEMKIN

I wrote a letter and then tore it up because it contained nothing but rubbish. Since you are very smart, so you will find an answer to everything, yet I shall not give you a weapon to use against me. So do as you please. There's no use in my giving you orders. Know, however, that I too try to make sense of your thoughts and actions that produce a reaction in me only because I find in them those sentiments I hope to find.

Je Vous avoue outre cela que j'aime mieux voir Votre visage que Votre dos.[1]

1. "Moreover, I confess to you that I like looking at your face more than your back."

182. CATHERINE TO POTEMKIN

Baten'ka, deary, do me this one divine favor for my sake: be calm, be hale and hearty, be certain that we share every feeling equally. I'm a bit merrier after my tears, and only your agitation grieves me. My dear friend, my darling, stop tormenting yourself, we both need tranquillité[1] so our thoughts can settle down and become bearable, or else we'll end up like balls in a jeu de paume.[2]

1. "peace"
2. "game of tennis."

183. CATHERINE TO POTEMKIN

Like a blind man judging colors, so you judge the condition of a person whose thoughts you do not know. It's true, I'm bored. I revealed this to you out of trust, and I don't know anything more about myself than this, and, what's more, can't know, since it's impossible to judge the condition of objects and places that are far removed from one's eyes and view. There is no way to estimate or to measure such distance. So I'm putting this off till the time is ripe, and do not at all want to gallop off to the post, for I'm offended.

184. CATHERINE TO POTEMKIN

My Lord and Cher Epoux![1] I shall begin my answer with that line which touches me most of all: who ordered you to cry? Why do you give greater authority to your lively imagination than to the proofs that speak in your wife's favor? Was she not attached to you two years ago by the bonds of Holy Matrimony? My dear, you deign to suspect the impossible in regard to me. Have I changed my tune, could you be unloved? Believe my words—I love you and am attached to you by all bonds. So now, consider for yourself: were my words and deeds in your favor stronger two years ago than now?

1. "dear husband!"

185. POTEMKIN TO CATHERINE

[Potemkin]

My darling is priceless,
you know I am all yours,
and I have only you alone.
I am loyal to you till death,
and need your sympathies.
For this reason,
and also according to my desire,
your service and the timely
use of my talents is
most agreeable to me.
Having done something for me,
you truly won't regret it,
and will see its benefit.

[Catherine's response in the margin]

I know
I know, I'm certain.
The truth.
Without a doubt.
I believe it.

Proven
long ago.

With pleasure, what?
I'm happy with all my heart,
but obtuse. Say it more clearly.

186. POTEMKIN TO CATHERINE

[Potemkin]

Allow me, my precious dear, to say
these final words that, I think, will
end our row.
Don't be surprised that I
am so uneasy about
our love. Beyond the
innumerable gifts you've bestowed
on me, you've placed me
in your heart.
I want to be there alone,
preferred to all former ones,
since no one has so loved you
as I. And since I am
the work of your hands, so I desire
that you should secure my peace, that
you should find joy in doing me
good, that you should devise
everything for my comfort
and find therein repose from the
great labors that occupy your lofty
station.
Amen

[Catherine's response in the margin]

I permit you.

The sooner the better.

Be calm.
One hand washes the other.

Firmly and solidly.
You are and will be.

I see and believe it.

I'm happy with all my soul.
My foremost pleasure.
It'll come by itself.
Let your thoughts be calm, so
that your feelings can freely
act; they are tender and will find the
best way themselves. End of quarrel.
Amen.

187. CATHERINE TO POTEMKIN

21 March 1776

Prince Grigory Aleksandrovich!
We most graciously permit you to receive the diploma from the Roman Emperor granting you the princely title of the Roman Empire and deign that henceforth you be called Prince of the Roman Empire everywhere in accordance with the authority of this diploma.[1]
Rest assured we remain as always benevolent towards you.

Catherine

---

1. Intent upon improving relations with Russia, Joseph II (1741–1790), the Holy Roman Emperor (from 1765) and sole ruler of Austria (from 1780), fulfilled Catherine's request and awarded Potemkin the title of prince of the Holy Roman Empire on 16 (27) February 1776. Henceforth Potemkin was called "His Serene Highness," or "Serenissimus," or simply "The Prince."

188. CATHERINE TO POTEMKIN

[After 21 March 1776]

Baten'ka, Cher Epoux, your little depression comes from bathing in cold water. I have told you that they come over me as well. I just received news from Riga that Prince Henry intended to arrive in Riga around the evening of the 21st of March, that is last Monday, and will come here, I think, at the beginning of the Passion Week.[1] We'll find a little country house for him. Write to Browne[2] to look for one. Batia, my darling, my dear sweet friend, be merry, cast away your depression.

---

1. The younger brother of Frederick the Great, Prince Henry (1726–1802) visited Russia in the spring of 1776 in an attempt to shore up Russo-Prussian relations, which had suffered during the First Russo-Turkish War.
2. Irishman George Browne (1694–1792) was governor-general of Livonia.

189. CATHERINE TO POTEMKIN

[After 21 March 1776]

When neither words nor deeds can serve as proof, then one's imagination must be filled either with emptiness and capriciousness or an equally empty suspicion. Be that as it may, since neither my heart nor my soul harbors an abusive thought toward you, I remain hopeful that these ravings will end very soon, for it's truly high time.

190. CATHERINE TO POTEMKIN

[After 21 March 1776]

Such rage ought to be expected from Your Highness should you wish to prove to the public, as well as to me, how great is the extent of your unruliness. This will of course be an indisputable sign of your ingratitude toward me, as well as your slight attachment to me, for it's both against my will as well as incongruous with the state of affairs and the status of our persons.

The Viennese court has no equal. Thus, one must realize how much trust I have in those persons whom I recommend to it for its loftiest titles. And so this is how you show your concern for my glory?

191. CATHERINE TO POTEMKIN

[After 21 March 1776]

Batia, Prince! Before I was born the Creator appointed you to be my friend, for He created you to be so disposed to me. I thank you for your gift, and equally for your affection, which I see with or without a telescope wherever I turn.

192. CATHERINE TO POTEMKIN

[10 April 1776. St. Petersburg]

I was there at four o'clock, and she was racked with labor pains.[1] Then the pains abated, and I went to drink some coffee. After I had finished my drink, I went back again and found her in torment, which soon stopped once more and she then fell into such a deep sleep that she snored. Seeing that this business was going to be a lengthy one, I went to get cleaned up. After I'd cleaned up, I went back again. The severe pains have stopped, and the baby is forcing his way out. This could go on for quite a long time. I ordered them to fetch me if they see that the matter is becoming more serious. Oh, my back aches, just as hers does, from anxiety, I suppose.

---

1. The grand duke woke Catherine at four in the morning on 10 April 1776 to tell her that his wife, Grand Duchess Natalia, was going into labor amid incredible pains. Catherine spent much of the next several days at her daughter-in-law's bedside.

193. CATHERINE TO POTEMKIN

[12 April 1776]

Monsieur, my prophecy has come true. This inappropriate air of superficiality that you have adopted is causing me harm and is distancing you from your wishes. And so, for God's sake, please don't abuse my passion for you, rather hear out my timely and appropriate arguments, which truly are not founded upon frivolous excuses.

I can't now answer either for Thursday, Friday, or for Sunday. I know that you will take all this as rubbish, as craftiness, however, it's the absolute truth. So listen to me just this once, even if only so I might say that you listened. Farewell, my darling, I love you extraordinarily and am very merry, and well too, though it was a rough night.[1]

---

1. Natalia's anguished labor continued on into the second day. Catherine maintained her vigil, and the leading doctors and physicians were called in, though to no avail. The baby was unable to descend into the birth canal. With Catherine and Grand Duke Paul looking on, Natalia was read her last rites on 14 April and died at 5 o'clock in the afternoon of the following day.

194. CATHERINE TO POTEMKIN

[After 15 April 1776. Tsarskoe Selo]

Should you not find pleasure in constantly quarreling with me, should there be the slightest spark of love in you, then I beseech you to dampen somewhat your hot-temper and to occasionally heed even my words without giving way so to your passion. But for yesterday, I've been suffering from an ineffable agitation ever since Friday. Should my peace be dear to you, do me a favor and stop grumbling. Make room for those sentiments united by peace and quiet that may consequently be more pleasing than the present state.

I truly am someone who loves not only affectionate words and behavior, but an affectionate face as well. But sullenness often produces the opposite. In expectation of the effect you will allow this letter to have upon you, I remain, however, full of good hope, without which I too, just like all other people, could not live.

195. CATHERINE TO POTEMKIN   [In French]

[May 1776]

Over an act at bottom worthy of respect you have plunged a dagger into my breast by saying that such an act on my part weakened your love for me. Honestly! Is that not a fickle love? There's nothing to warrant this since I didn't do anything to offend you, and I neither have nor shall have such an intention despite everything that, given your usual impetuosity, your animated and moody spirit might permit you to imagine. But whatever you might say, I am not worried about your feelings for me. I know very well that while at any moment your words might show little respect or consideration for me, there is in fact a lot of the one and the other in your heart and in your mind. I don't regret writing that letter. But I'm deeply grieved by the effect it has had on you, and I foresee that you will punish me sufficiently by harping on this matter continually with all conceivable imprecations. As usual, I shall submit with obedience, courage, and patience. So then, have at me! There is but one thing I would not endure—if you truly were to stop loving me.

196. CATHERINE TO POTEMKIN

[May 1776]

Read my answers with patience, for I read your letters without tedium. Here's an answer for you to the first line: may God forgive you, as I desire, not only your baseless despair and rage, but also the injustices you've shown me, which stem from the reasons you give and which ought to be nothing but pleasant for me. But if possible, We ask you to forget this unpleasantness. Catherine was never insensitive. Even now she is attached to you with all her heart and soul. Having borne the offenses and insults, she hasn't told you anything to the contrary (read her letter of yesterday), and you will see that you'll always find her just as you might desire. I don't understand why you call yourself unloved and repugnant, and me gracious to everyone but you. Don't be angry, these are but three lies. Even now you are first in my good graces. Repugnant and unloved you can hardly be. The word "loathing" tears not only at your soul, but mine as well. Je ne suis pas née pour la haine, elle n'habite point dans mon âme, je ne l'ai jamais sentie ni n'ai l'honneur de la connaître.[1]

I believe that you love me, though quite often your words lack any trace of love. I believe because I am scrupulous and just, I don't judge people by their words when I see that they are at odds with common sense. You deign to write from the perspective of the past, you deign to say "was, has been." Yet throughout all these days my actions have been dedicated to establishing harmony at the present moment. Who desires your peace and tranquility more than I? Now I hear that you were content with former times, but at the time nothing seemed to be enough for you. But God will forgive, I do not reproach you, I do justice to you and shall say to you what you've not yet heard: namely, that although you've greatly insulted and vexed me, nevertheless there's no way I can hate you, and I think that since beginning this letter and seeing you with all your senses and in your right mind things seem to be as they once were. If only you would remain this way, and if you do, you'll indeed not regret it, my dear friend, my darling. You know how sensitive my heart is.

---

1. "I was not born to hate, hatred does not dwell in my soul. I have never experienced it nor had the honor of making its acquaintance."

197. CATHERINE TO POTEMKIN

[May 1776]

If there's a drop of blood in you that's still attached to me, then do me a favor—come and speak plainly to me of your rage. For truth, my heart is innocent before you.

198. CATHERINE TO POTEMKIN

[May 1776]

Baten'ka, believe me, I'm not angry and I desire to see you at peace. I have repeated to you a hundred times that your conduct alone can give us a life in keeping with our position. My friend, who desires as much as I to live in peace and harmony and who possesses a gentler character? Let reason, not fantasy, be your guide. It causes you to act in a manner out of keeping with your nature.

199. POTEMKIN TO CATHERINE

[May 1776]

You deigned to order me: "Turn a blind eye to so-and-so." Your Most Gracious Majesty, when I direct my sight in any direction, then it's not with a blind eye. I renounce any position in which matters will be removed from my oversight. However, should my talents and desire at some time cease, then someone better than I can be selected, to which I shall readily and fully consent.

[Catherine] I'm not the cause of mischievous rumors. I've never said "turn a blind eye to so-and-so," rather I said, "It was so-and-so's oversight." And this I said in reference to Tolstoy,[1] for it's inexcusable for him to leave the regiment or, better said, so many soldiers without undergarments. I have enough sense to know that a lieutenant-colonel can't be a quartermaster-sergeant.

1. Fyodor Matveevich Tolstoy (1748–1789). Although Potemkin was the leader of the elite Preobrazhensky Guards Regiment, he did not have the necessary time to devote to this duty and so entrusted the command of the regiment to Tolstoy, his comrade during the First Russo-Turkish War. In an attempt to further weaken his faltering position, Potemkin's ill-wishers had apparently been spreading rumors about the poor order among the Preobrazhentsy. Potemkin's seeming reference to his own disability (he was blind in one eye) is merely a felicitous coincidence of translation, the Russian idiom being "to look through one's fingers."

200. CATHERINE TO POTEMKIN   [In French]

[May–June 1776]

You scolded me all day yesterday for no reason. Thank God you found one today. I wrote a letter that upset you, but if you could consider this for a moment with some dispassion, you would see that this is a letter from an Empress to a subject who has offended her by his thoughtlessness, extravagance, and lack of judgment, and that this Empress has punished him as she was duty bound a subject who has offended her; but at the same time she has not forgotten that this subject has often risked his life, as his service required. Here is a dispassionate and reasoned assessment of this letter, which deserves to be printed.

201. CATHERINE TO POTEMKIN

[May–June 1776]

To oblige you I read your letter, and having read it through, I've found no trace of your words from yesterday—not those said after dinner, not those I heard in the evening. This doesn't surprise me, for I have grown accustomed to seeing frequent changes in them. But consider, which one of us constantly creates discord and which one of us never fails to establish harmony once more? A conclusion may easily be drawn from this: which one of us is truly frank, sincere, and eternally attached to whom? Who is indulgent, who is able to forget insults, oppression, and disrespect? I know, my words don't count. But I at least display and prove this every hour through my very deeds, and there is no possible sentiment in your favor that I wouldn't have and wouldn't be glad to show. For God's sake, come to your senses and compare your actions with mine. Is it not in your power to do away with this discord and is it not in your power to conceal any weakness should it appear? Even the opinion of the stupid public depends on whatever respect you intend to give this matter.

You ask for Zavadovsky's removal. My glory will greatly suffer should I carry out this request. With this our discord will become firmly established, and I'll only be considered the weaker for it, and in more than just one respect. I'll add that this would be to do injustice to and to persecute an innocent person. Don't demand injustices, stop your ears against slanderers, heed my words. Our peace will be restored. Should you be moved by my grief, then dispel even the thought of estranging yourself from me. For God's sake, I find just imagining this intolerable, which proves again that my attachment to you is stronger than yours and, I dare say, is not dependent upon événements.[1]

Your arrangement with Gagarin, Golitsyn, Pavel, Mikhail, and your nephew[2] to present this comedy to society is highly regrettable, for it's a triumph for your enemies and mine. I did not know till now that you have been implementing this group's decisions and that they were so thoroughly informed of what goes on between us. In that I still have a different opinion than you. I have no confidant in matters that concern you, for I honor our secrets and do not disclose them to anyone for discussion. We all arrange our thoughts and actions in accordance with our own sensibility and respect for those individuals toward whom We are obliged or inclined. And as I have never been able to think differently of other people than I do of myself, so I expected the same from others.

I didn't banish you from my room or from anywhere else. You can't be in a state of loathing forever. I repeat and have repeated this to you a hundred times. Stop your raging, be so kind pour que la douceur de mon caractère puisse rentrer dans son état naturel, d'ailleurs Vous me ferés mourir.[3]

---

1. "circumstances."

2. Gagarin is probably Prince Gavrila Petrovich (1745–1808), a relation of the Panin brothers, who served with Rumiantsev during the First Russo-Turkish War. Through Potemkin's patronage, Prince Sergei Fyodorovich Golitsyn (1749–1810) became an aide-de-camp to the empress and later went on to a distinguished military career. The final three names refer to Pavel Potemkin, Mikhail Potemkin, and Aleksandr Samoilov. Potemkin had apparently shared with them, united either by relation or by shared interests, intimate details of his deteriorating relationship with Catherine.

3. "so that my character's tenderness might return to its natural state, otherwise you will be the death of me."

202. POTEMKIN TO CATHERINE

[After 2 June 1776]

Matushka, here is the result of your agreeable treatment of me over the past several days. I clearly see your inclination to get along with me. But you have let things go so far that it is becoming impossible for you to be kind to me. I came here to see you since without you life is tedious and unbearable. I noticed that you were incommoded by my arrival. I do not know whom or what you are trying to please; I only know that it is not necessary and to no purpose. It seems to me you have never before been so ill at ease.

Your Most Gracious Majesty, I shall go through fire for you. But if it has finally been decided that I am to be banished from you, then at least let it not be before the entire public. I do not tarry to withdraw, although this is equal to losing my life.

[Catherine] Mon Ami, Votre imagination Vous trompe.[1] I am glad to see you and am not embarrassed by you. Rather I was vexed by an unrelated matter, which I shall tell you about when an opportunity permits.

---

1. "My friend, your imagination deceives you."

203. CATHERINE TO POTEMKIN

[After 3 June 1776]

Pray tell Yelagin[1] yourself or write to him to find and buy and fix up a house to your liking. I'll confirm all this with him, and what's more I gladly give credence to all your assurances because these thoughts are in agreement with honesty and a good heart.

---

1. Ivan Yelagin.

204. CATHERINE TO POTEMKIN   [In French]

[After 7 June 1776]

Listen here my friend, your letter would call for lengthy discussions were I to answer it in detail; I have selected two essential points from it. First, the Anichkov house. In Moscow they wanted four hundred thousand rubles for it.[1] That is an enormous sum that I wouldn't know where to get, but Yelagin has only to ask the price—perhaps it's cheaper. The house is uninhabitable and threatened by ruin; one of the walls is nothing but cracks; I think upkeep and repairs will not be insignificant. The second point is friendship. I dare to assert that there is no more loyal a friend than I, but what is required of a friend? I always thought it was mutual trust, which has been complete from my side. For a long time now I've told you what I think of this. It remains to be seen in which direction the scales have been tipped, and in what regard . . . etc.; but no more discussions: I don't intend either to argue or to vex; I know how to assess and I know the value of things.

1. Despite the mention of the Anichkov house, Catherine is probably speaking of the Moscow home that previously belonged to Aleksandr Bibikov, which was almost purchased for Potemkin. The complaint about the expense cannot be taken seriously: Catherine clearly did not want Potemkin to leave the capital, and her, for Moscow.

205. CATHERINE TO POTEMKIN

[Before 21 June 1776]

Baten'ka, God knows I don't intend to drive you out of the palace. Please live in it and be calm. It's for that very reason I've given you neither house nor spoon nor saucer.

If you wish to divert yourself by traveling around the provinces for a while, I shan't stand in your way.[1] Upon your return, pray occupy your quarters in the palace as before. As God is my witness, my attachment to you remains firm and unlimited, and I'm not angry. But do me one favor—menagés mes nerfs.[2]

1. Potemkin left the capital on 23 June to inspect the troops belonging to the St. Petersburg division located in the Novgorod province.

2. "spare my nerves."

206. CATHERINE TO POTEMKIN

22 June 1776. Tsarskoe Selo

Prince Grigory Aleksandrovich, We bestow upon you the Anichkov house, which We have purchased from Count Razumovsky, for your eternal and hereditary possession.[1] Pray receive it from Yelagin, who has been ordered to repair and decorate it according to your taste, using for this purpose up to one hundred thousand rubles.

Catherine

1. In July 1776, Catherine purchased for Potemkin the Anichkov Palace, which had been built by Empress Elizabeth for her favorite and probable husband, Count Aleksei Grigorevich Razumovsky (1708–1771) on St. Petersburg's Nevsky Prospect. Potemkin never lived in it, but did like to throw lavish parties there.

207. POTEMKIN TO CATHERINE

5 July [1776]. Novgorod

Your Most Gracious Majesty!
Having learned from Ivan Perfilievich[1] of my being presented with the Anichkov house, I kiss your feet. I express my humblest gratitude. Most

merciful mother, God, having given you all resources and power, did not give you, to my misfortune, the means to know human hearts. God Almighty! Make known to my Sovereign and benefactress how grateful I am to her, how devoted I am and that my life is dedicated to her service.

Your Most Gracious Majesty, keep in your protection and care a person devoted to you body and soul, who remains in the most sincere manner till death

Your Majesty's most loyal and most devoted servant
Prince Potemkin

----

1. Yelagin.

4. Partners—1777-1781

When Potemkin returned to the capital in July 1776, he did not move out of the Winter Palace. Rather, he quit the apartments he had occupied until then and moved into a small building known as the Shepilov house, attached to the palace by a covered walkway that afforded Potemkin and Catherine private access to each others' rooms. The Shepilov house was to remain Potemkin's St. Petersburg residence for the rest of his life.

Potemkin's move from the apartments of the favorite into the Shepilov house reflected the change in the nature of the relationship between Catherine and the prince. Although he was no longer the official favorite, Potemkin remained physically close to Catherine and continued to enjoy a unique relationship with her. He was now her consort, friend, advisor, and de facto chief minister. The letters from 1771–1781 attest to the new partnership Catherine and Potemkin had managed to fashion out of the ruins of their love affair. These are not the *billets-doux* of passionate hearts nor the angry missives of hurt lovers, but the letters of a mature couple united by shared interests and mutual respect. At once intimate and official, they convey something of the complexity of the bond that had developed between Catherine and Potemkin as wife and husband, sovereign and subject.

The output of their correspondence for these five years was much less than it had been previously and less than it would be in the coming years. The reasons for this are largely twofold. First, after the great passion and then the emotional turmoil of their break-up—which had generated so many letters—had passed, their main reason for writing disappeared. The tender pronouncements of love they had once penned to each other were now being addressed to others. Second, unlike the years ahead, which found them separated by great distances, Potemkin and Catherine were never long apart between 1777 and 1782 and so had less cause to write. When not with the court in St. Petersburg, they were typically together at the imperial palaces at Tsarskoe Selo and Peterhof or at Potemkin's nearby estates of Ozerki and Osinovaia roshcha.

Catherine's replacement of Potemkin with Zavadovsky marked the beginning of a quick succession of imperial lovers over the next several years. While the originally compliant and dutiful Zavadovsky had provided the perfect antidote to the irascible Potemkin, Catherine soon cooled toward him. He began to manifest many of the same anxieties born from the stresses of his position that his predecessor had, although with few of the compensating benefits. While her love for Zavadovsky had been real, Catherine grew tired of his tears and fits of bad nerves, and by May 1777, he was already on his way out. Apparently it was Zavadovsky himself, crumbling under the strain of court gossip and intrigue, who requested his retirement. Catherine made the usual grant of serfs, silver, and rubles—though in this instance she was far less generous than she had been with Orlov and Potemkin and would be with her future favorites—and sent him off to his Ukrainian estate of Lialichi in early June (Letter 208).

No sooner had Zavadovsky departed than a new candidate for favorite was put forward. A major in the Hussars, Semyon Zorich was a handsome, dark-haired thirty-two-year-old of Serbian extraction who had displayed uncommon bravery in the First Russo-Turkish War. After several years in a Turkish prison, the ambitious Zorich eventually made his way to St. Petersburg, where he sought the patronage of Potemkin. The prince quickly realized Zorich's potential, and after taking him as an adjutant, he casually introduced Zorich to Catherine in the hope of Zorich taking the place of Zavadovsky. Seemingly overnight, Zorich became the new favorite in June 1777 and was immediately showered with titles, decorations, and money. The dazzling ascent proved to be too much for Zorich to handle, however. He was soon buried under a mountain of gambling debts and was apparently foolhardy enough to attempt to free himself from Potemkin's patronage, supposedly even challenging the prince to a duel. Neither Catherine nor Potemkin would permit such outlandish behavior, and after a mere eleven months in favor, Zorich was dismissed (Letters 209–221).

On 26 May 1778, Catherine and her suite dined at the Kekerekeksinsky Palace outside the capital. They were joined there by Potemkin and his new adjutant, Major Ivan Rimsky-Korsakov. Sensing Zorich's imminent fall, Potemkin sought to make certain that he, and not the Orlovs, would have his hand in the selection of the next favorite and was eager to make certain the young Guards officer caught the empress's eye (Letter 221). The court next journeyed to Potemkin's estate at Osinovaia roshcha for several days, where Catherine's attraction to Korsakov, whom she dubbed "Pyrrhus, King of Epirus" in reference to his classical beauty, grew (Letters 222, 225). In early June, Korsakov was appointed the favorite, and for a little over a year Catherine was entranced by his beauty and enthralled by the sounds of his fine singing voice. It was not long, however, before Korsakov began sharing his charms with others. When, in September 1779, Catherine learned that on top of other illicit amours, Korsakov had secretly been conducting an affair for months with her own lady-in-waiting and close friend Countess Praskovia Bruce, Korsakov's days were through (Letters 223–225, 228, 236, 238).

Wounded by this betrayal, Catherine did not take another favorite for six months. It was perhaps around this time—between the late spring of 1779 and February 1780—that she and Potemkin exchanged several curious letters with references to Cagliostro, the great eighteenth-century adventurer then visiting St. Petersburg. These letters convey a genuine warmth of feeling and might be read as playful expressions of a renewed sexual relationship that perhaps developed after Korsakov's dismissal (Letters 232–235).

By the spring of 1780, the favorite's apartments in the Winter Palace had a new occupant. Another protégé of the prince, Aleksandr Lanskoy was a former Guards officer and an unusually obliging and gentle soul. Over thirty years Catherine's junior, Lanskoy idolized the empress. Content not to meddle in politics (though members of his family made certain to take advantage of his position), Lanskoy was happy being Catherine's companion and her eager pupil. For her part, Catherine believed she had finally found someone to share the rest of her life with, though fate was to intervene only four years later (Letters 244, 247, 248, 250).

As for Potemkin, his intimate affairs during these years were possibly even more dramatic. According to legend, it was at this time that he began a series of affairs with his nieces, the Engelhardt sisters, maids-of-honor at court. While their letters lend nothing to support the legend, they do show that Catherine and Potemkin were very much involved in the young women's lives and sought to guide them as best they could. They looked on with amused curiosity, for example, when Aleksei Bobrinsky, Catherine's son by Grigory Orlov, fell in love with Yekaterina Engelhardt, and they later debated the merits of her plans to marry the eccentric Count Pavel Skavronsky (Letters 241–243, 255). They quite naturally took an interest in such matters given the political implications that would result from the marriages of the prince's nieces. Thus, in November 1781, Catherine and Potemkin helped to arrange Aleksandra Engelhardt's wedding to Grand Hetman of the Polish Crown Ksawery Branicki in order to strengthen Russia's ties to the magnates in Poland.

Along with the considerable influence Potemkin had come to exercise over Catherine's personal life, he was beginning to exhibit comparable authority in matters of state. This was becoming particularly apparent in the realm of foreign relations, in which Catherine encouraged Potemkin to take an ever more active role. Evidence of this can be seen in King Gustav III's visit to Russia in 1777, when Catherine selected Potemkin to accompany the king during his stay, or in British envoy James Harris's courting Potemkin in the hope of gaining an alliance with Russia in 1779–1780 (Letters 209, 211, 237, 250).

But by far the most significant foreign policy development during these years, one in which Potemkin played a decisive role, was the conclusion of the secret Austro-Russian alliance of 1781. The treaty with Austria marked a major reorientation in Russian foreign policy. Since the reign of Peter III (1762), Russia had been allied with Prussia. Count Nikita Panin continued to support the union throughout the 1760s and 1770s and had sought to make it the basis for his "Northern System," an alliance of European powers intended to act as a balance against the Habsburgs and Bourbons. By the late 1770s, Potemkin had come to represent a competing vision of Russia's foreign policy that shifted the focus away from the states of Europe and toward the south. For Potemkin, Russia's future lay in the lands along the northern coast of the Black Sea, and it was Austria, not Prussia, who could best help Russia achieve its expansionist goals in this area. Joseph II of Austria avidly sought to acquire the electorate of Bavaria and, knowing Russian support was critical, worked to entice Russia away from Prussia, Austria's foremost enemy. Catherine, who distrusted Frederick the Great and had tired of the Prussian alliance, was growing increasingly enamored of Potemkin's bold southern strategy and so was inclined to look favorably on such an alliance.

On 9 May 1780, Catherine and her suite departed Tsarskoe Selo for Mogilyov where she was to meet Joseph II—traveling incognito as "Count Falkenstein"—and discuss the possibility of an alliance. Along the way she wrote to Potemkin, who had gone on ahead to make the necessary arrangements for the meeting, that they would "together try to figure out how to handle Falkenstein" (Letters 246, 247). The Russian empress and the Holy Roman Emperor, joined by Potemkin and his niece Aleksandra, spent six days together in Mogilyov getting acquainted and exploring the possibilities of a Russo-Austrian rapprochement. Before returning to Vienna, Joseph journeyed first to Moscow, where Potemkin served as his tour guide, and then on to St. Petersburg for further talks and sightseeing (Letters 248, 249). The death, in November of that year, of Joseph's mother, Maria Theresa, an opponent of the alliance, removed the chief obstacle to the alliance, which was finally concluded in May 1781 after months of negotiations (Letters 251–254).

The Austro-Russian alliance was a major triumph for Potemkin. It signaled the defeat of Nikita Panin, who was dismissed as foreign minister in the fall of 1781, and the rise of the prince's influence in the sphere of foreign relations. As a result of Potemkin's urging, Russia's energies were now being shifted to her recently acquired southern territories over which Potemkin ruled as the governor-general of New Russia, Azov, and Astrakhan. Beginning in the mid–1770s, Potemkin worked to develop these lands and to establish them as a base for Russian expansion into the Crimea and the northern reaches of the Ottoman Empire.

• • •

208. CATHERINE TO POTEMKIN

[Before 14 May 1777]

I sent word to him to ask whether he had something to say to me.[1] He asked me in response, just as he did yesterday, whether it would please me were he to choose someone, and after receiving my permission, he chose Count Kirill Grigorievich Razumovsky.[2] He said all this through his tears, and requested that he not be deprived of being able to come to me, to which I consented. Next, after many bows, he also requested not to be deprived of my favor et de lui faire un sort.[3] I replied that both requests were just and that he should expect to have the former and the latter; having thanked me for this, he left in tears. The entire conversation lasted fewer than five minutes. I'll now await the Field Marshal.[4] When will he come? Not today, of course.

Farewell, darling, have fun with your books. They're equal to your stature.

---

1. Catherine describes her final conversation with Zavadovsky before his departure for his estate. He returned to court in 1778 following Zorich's dismissal and resumed his previous administrative duties.

2. Count Kirill Grigorievich Razumovsky (1728–1803), chosen by Zavadovsky to be his intermediary with the empress, was the younger brother of Aleksei Razumovsky. President of the Academy of Arts and Hetman of Little Russia, Razumovsky played a significant role in the coup of 1762.

3. "and that he be provided for."

4. Kirill Razumovsky.

209. CATHERINE TO POTEMKIN

[22 May 1777]

After ten o'clock
I just received word that the Swedish King[1] wanted to leave Stockholm yesterday. He plans to be here within two or three weeks, that is, the week

after Whitsunday. He wants to deport himself in every respect like everyone else and to be on equal footing with everyone, just like the Emperor now in France;[2] he wants to visit everyone, to run and travel here and there, to take a back seat to everyone. He's dispatching Minister Scheffer[3] and his chamberlains on ahead and doesn't want to receive any honors. He'll be here under the name of the Count of Gotland and requests that he not be called His Majesty. I am ordering Nolken[4] to come here on Friday, and he will ride out to meet him. I have sent an order to Count Chernyshev that yachts or a frigate be sent to meet him as soon as possible.

Give this little letter I've enclosed to Seniusha.[5] Oh, how I miss you. Adieu, mon cher et bien aimé Ami.[6]

1. Gustav III (1746–1792), king of Sweden from 1771 and Catherine's first cousin (whom she called "Brother Gu"), visited Russia from 5 June to 5 July 1777.

2. Joseph II visited France in 1777 under the name of Count Falkenstein. Much was made in the press about how he traveled without his suite and, ignoring rigid court etiquette, tried to act like an unexceptional nobleman.

3. Count Ulrik Scheffer (1716–1790) was Sweden's chancery-president and its de facto foreign minister.

4. Baron Johan Frederik von Nolken (1737–1809) was the Swedish extraordinary envoy to St. Petersburg from 1773–1788.

5. Semyon Gavrilovich Zorich (1745–1799). After his dismissal as favorite in May 1778, Zorich left for Europe and later returned to his magnificent estate in Shklov, where he carried on an opulent lifestyle.

6. "Farewell, my dear and beloved friend."

210. CATHERINE TO POTEMKIN   [In French]

[27 May 1777]

Sima[1] doesn't have a watch. Give him this one from me, my dear friend.

1. Zorich.

211. CATHERINE TO POTEMKIN

[Before 10 May 1777]

Periusha,[1] Lordikins, be so good as to dress us up for Peterhof in such a manner that everyone's eyes will pop out[2] and so that as much talk will be made of our procession as of the Swedish King's arrival. Je crois qu'il y a des chevaux turks à mon écurie, ils sont à Votre choix. Je Vous baise les mains et j'ordonne à la Perruche de les becqueter.[3]

What a funny creature you have acquainted me with.

1. From the French "la perruche"—parrot or parakeet—Catherine's pet name for those who liked to dandy themselves up in fancy dress.

2. Catherine's playful desire to dress up may well be connected with the appearance of the colorful new favorite, Semyon Zorich.

3. "I believe there are some Turkish horses in my stable; they are at your disposal. I kiss your hands and order the parakeet to peck at them."

212. CATHERINE TO POTEMKIN

[24 June 1777]

My little Prince, I've received the plume and given it to Sima, and Sima paraded about, thanks to you.[1] Vous lui avés envoyé une canne superbe. Il ressemble au Roy de Suède avec la sienne, mais il surpasse celui-ci en reconnaissance pour Vous.[2] It saddens me to the bottom of my heart that you're not well. Do be well tomorrow, and merry, or I shall be quite displeased. Adieu, mon Ami.

1. Potemkin had given Zorich a diamond plume with which he adorned his hat. Catherine compared her new favorite to Gustav III, a coxcomb in his own right.

2. "You sent him a splendid walking-stick. He looks like the King of Sweden with his, but he surpasses the latter in his gratitude toward you."

213. CATHERINE TO POTEMKIN

[After 19 August 1777]

Thank you for the note. Do amuse yourself at that Kingston lady's.[1]

I'm dying to see you here in good health. It's warmer here, we've been walking all about the entire morning, and everyone, including myself, is well. Adieu, mon bon Ami, portés-Vous bien.[2] I write in a hurry.

1. The scandalous Elisabeth Chudleigh, duchess of Kingston (1720–1788), arrived on her yacht in August 1777, having been forced to abandon England after being charged with bigamy. She entertained members of Russian society on her richly appointed vessel and at her house on the Neva River. She met the empress on at least two occasions, but her rumored wish to be made a lady-in-waiting went unfulfilled. She made two more trips to Russia in 1779 and 1784 and lived out the rest of her days in France.

2. "Farewell, my good friend, take care of yourself."

214. CATHERINE TO POTEMKIN

30 September 1777[1]

Prince Grigory Aleksandrovich, I send you my best wishes on a double holiday—your birth- and name-day.[2] I ordered one hundred fifty thousand rubles given to Friedrichs which are to be placed at your disposal so you can pay your debt. I remain toward you perfectly benevolent.

Catherine

1. On that day Catherine took her carriage to the Anichkov Palace. After a tour of the palace, a festive dinner was given in honor of its owner, Potemkin. The guests included Countess Praskovia Bruce, Prince Grigory Orlov, Field Marshal Zakhar Chernyshev, Pavel Potemkin, Aleksandra, Varvara, and Yekaterina Engelhardt (Potemkin's nieces), and Semyon Zorich.

2. Potemkin's birthday was 13 September; his name-day, the day celebrated for the saint after whom he was named, was 30 September.

[Letters 215–220 are from Catherine during 1777]

215.

My dear, Prince, you've gotten upset for nothing. Just a short while ago I told you to be assured that nothing you said disturbed me in the least. So, be well and merry, and I shall be pleased.

Parania,[1] Leonus,[2] Magnus,[3] Lodi, Mimi,[4] and I beg our compliments to you.

1. Countess Praskovia Bruce.
2. Chief Equerry Lev Naryshkin.
3. Possibly Major-General Magnus Ferdinand von Freyman.
4. Lodi and Mimi were two of Catherine's dogs.

216.

Listen, my dear, Varenka[1] is very ill. Si c'est Votre départ qui en est cause, Vous avés tort.[2] You'll be the death of her, and she is becoming very dear to me. They want to bleed her.

1. Potemkin's niece Varvara Engelhardt. Potemkin had planned on leaving St. Petersburg for a few days, but delayed his trip upon learning of her illness. It has been suggested that Varvara was then her uncle's lover, and Potemkin's planned departure was the cause of her illness.

2. "If your departure is the cause of this, you are in the wrong."

217.　[In French]
In a short while I shall have the honor of telling you, my parakeet, that I love you with all my heart.

218.
Voila qui paye les dettes de la Perruche.[1]
Oh, Periusha, Periusha, Periusha.

---

1. "Behold who pays the parakeet's debts."

219.
I gratefully accept the lavish gifts you sent me and everything you write me on this occasion. Such manner of thinking is characteristic of a noble soul, and I leave it to the world to judge whether or not I am grateful.

220.
Baten'ka, I regret not having seen you for a long time and am indignant about your fire. I thank you for the enameled picture and am sending you a homegrown melon. Eat to your heart's content.

221. CATHERINE TO POTEMKIN

[25 May 1778]

Batia, I'll be pleased to receive the plan of operations from your hands.[1] We'll talk about Golitsyn[2] in town. I reproach you, sir, for speaking to me in parables. My mind can't guess who you're taking aim at. God only knows whom you are indebted to and who among your kin feels he has this powerful claim over you.

Parlés net ou bien je me fâche, mais j'aimerais mieux que Vous me disiés à la fois toutes ces belles choses et ce que Vous souhaités, [not] in snatches tous les jours quelques choses.[3]

The little kiddy[4] left et puis c'est tout: du reste nous parlerons ensemble.[5] My most humble thanks for the snuffbox of Osinovaia roshcha.[6] Have you forgotten that you are to dine tomorrow dans le château de Tunderthentrunk, en grec Kekerekeksina?

Adieu, mon bijou, que le ciel Vous bénisse et surtout que je Vous voye gai comme un pinson demain, ou bien je ne ferai que bouder à Espenbaum.[7]

1. In October 1777, an uprising broke out in the Khanate of the Crimea against Shagin Girey (1746–1787), who had been elected khan with Russian backing earlier that year. The revolt was put down with the aid of Russian troops in February 1778. Potemkin apparently drafted a plan of operations in case of a falling out with the Porte over Russia's actions in the Crimea.

2. Probably a reference to Field Marshal Prince Aleksandr Golitsyn who sought to be relieved of his duties due to illness.

3. "Speak plainly or well, I shall be offended. I would prefer that you tell me all at once all those beautiful things and what you wish, and [not] in snatches a few things everyday."

4. The new favorite, Ivan Nikolaevich Rimsky-Korsakov (1754–1831), was an officer in the Preobrazhensky Guards Regiment and became an adjutant to Potemkin on 8 May 1778, approximately three weeks before his appointment as the favorite.

5. "and that is it. We shall discuss the rest together."

6. Potemkin was given the country estate of Osinovaia roshcha (Aspen Grove) several versts outside the capital near the village of Pargolovo in August 1777.

7. "in the castle of Thunderthentrunk, Kekerekeksina in Greek?

Farewell, my precious, may heaven bless you, and above all may I see you tomorrow merry as a lark, or else I shall do nothing but sulk at Osinovaia roshcha."

Catherine and her suite dined on 26 May 1778 at the Kekerekeksinsky Palace (from the Finnish "Froggy Bog"). Catherine's words about Voltaire's Baron Thunder-ten-tronckh (*Candide*) may be a reference to the pseudo-Gothic style in which her palace had been built. Among those who dined with the empress were Potemkin and Korsakov. The final reference to Semyon Zorich in the court journal was on 13 May.

222. CATHERINE TO POTEMKIN

[Before 1 June 1778]

I fear burning my fingers and so it's better not to lead into temptation, and especially not to reveal it to Paraclete.[1] Even so, I fear yesterday gave everyone the impression of an attraction, which, however, I hope is only one-sided and which your clever guidance could easily put an end to. And so, We want without wanting and without wanting We want.[2] Morbleu, voila qui est clair comme le jour.[3]

1. An advocate or counselor. In Christian theology, the Holy Spirit, in the sense of a comforter, intercessor, or advocate. It is not clear to whom Catherine is referring.

2. While visiting Osinovaia roshcha, Catherine wrote of her budding attraction for Korsakov and told Potemkin that he could easily put an end to this should he so desire. Catherine initially expressed uncertainty about her feelings for and intentions toward Korsakov.

3. "Oh, hell, now there is something clear as day."

223. CATHERINE TO POTEMKIN

[Before 1 June 1778]

There wasn't a hint of shyness; you conducted yourself in the most agreeable manner. C'est un Ange, grand, grand, grand merci.[1]

---

1. "He is an angel. A big, big, big thanks." Her mind made up, Catherine thanked Potemkin for introducing her to Korsakov—the "angel" in question. He was made an aide-de-camp to the empress on 1 June 1778.

224. CATHERINE TO POTEMKIN

[After 1 June 1778]

Baten'ka, my dear, I'm very glad you're better. Rogerson[1] was here and said that he had given you some medicine. Blackhead[2] has orders to convey all my tender words to you. I forget you as much as I forget myself.

I have already given the order concerning Aleksandr-shants, and shall now hurry this matter along.[3] Adieu, mon cher et bien aimé Ami, je Vous embrasse.[4] I am very bored, I anticipate a boring parting.[5]

---

1. The court physician.

2. Korsakov.

3. On 31 May 1778, Catherine approved Potemkin's plan for building a new town on the Dnieper River to serve as a port and shipbuilding center. While Ivan Chernyshev, vice president of the Naval College, preferred the location of Glubokaia pristan as the site for the future city of Kherson, Potemkin selected Aleksandr-shants, an old fortress further up river that was less vulnerable to attack.

4. "Farewell, my dear and beloved friend, I kiss you."

5. Possibly a reference to a meeting with Zorich, who was about to go abroad.

225. CATHERINE TO POTEMKIN

[Before 28 June 1778]

Batia, concerning Kherson, it doesn't matter to me where it's to be located, only that I have ships built there and that we don't have to build another fortress again or do other similar work.

I've received the decrees, but they must be rewritten. Would you believe Pyrrhus, King of Epirus is protesting the rank of gentleman-of-the-bedchamber? You forgot that Putiatin too was to have been entered into the list. Concerning Davydov, I'll have the honor of speaking with you.[1] Adieu, mon bijou, grâce à Vous et au Roy d'Epire je suis gaie comme un pinson et je veux que Vous soyés aussi gai et bien portant. Grand merci pour les fruits. Les dessins je les regarderai aujourd'huy où je n'ai rien d'autre chose à faire.[2]

1. Potemkin was preparing the annual list of promotions given on Catherine's accession day (28 June). Korsakov—Pyrrhus, king of Epirus—sought the rank of chamberlain, which was higher than that of gentleman-of-the-bedchamber recommended by Potemkin. Korsakov got his way. Prince Nikolai Avramovich Putiatin (1744–1818) was made a gentleman-of-the-bedchamber. Davydov has not been identified.

2. "Farewell, my precious, thanks to you and the king of Epirus I am as merry as a lark, and I want you to be as merry and in good health. Thank you so much for the fruit. I shall look at the drawings today since I have nothing else to do."

226. CATHERINE TO POTEMKIN

[After 29 June 1778]

Prince Grigory Aleksandrovich, who's smart, so very smart and such a little smarty and is devoted to her very self without reservation. Je Vous embrasse mille fois, mon Ami, pour Votre lettre d'aujourd'huy,[1] and you're right: without you Kherson won't be built.[2] And if you say your decree doesn't contradict Hannibal's,[3] then I trust your saying so. J'étais très malade hier de la tête, mais aujourd'huy je me porte bien. Adieu, mon Ami, Vous êtes charmant et Vous avés de l'esprit comme un ange.[4] Thank you, a thousands thanks in fact, for not boasting. Be well and merry.

1. "I kiss you a thousand times, my friend, for your letter of today,"

2. Catherine signed a decree on 25 July 1778 ordering the construction of Kherson at Aleksandr-shants.

3. Ivan Abramovich Hannibal (1735–1801) was the eldest son of Abram Petrovich, son of an Ethiopian prince and a ward and favorite of Peter the Great. Ivan's brother, Osip, was the grandfather of the poet Alexander Pushkin (1799–1837). As a member of the Naval College, Hannibal was put in charge of the building of Kherson per Potemkin's request.

4. "I had a very bad headache yesterday, but today I feel fine. Farewell, my friend, you are charming and you have the spirit of an angel."

227. CATHERINE TO POTEMKIN

[Before 5 August 1778]

We're living, and have been living, from minute to minute in anticipation of your arrival.[1] I'm most sorry you're not well. The child[2] asked me to kiss you on the lips should you arrive during his absence.

I thank you for the Italian and Swiss scenes. Be sure to get well soon and to come to us. In ten days we'll already be together in town. Adieu, mon cher Ami, je Vous embrasse et je désire beaucoup Vous voir, parce que je Vous aime de tout mon coeur.[3]

1. Potemkin was absent from court from 24 July to 4 August 1778. He and Korsakov accompanied Catherine back to the capital from Tsarskoe Selo on 5 August.

2. Korsakov.

3. "Farewell, dear friend, I kiss you and long to see you very much, for I love you with all my heart."

228. CATHERINE TO POTEMKIN

[21 September 1778]

My little Prince, baten'ka, I thank God you're better. As long as you're weak, do take care of yourself, don't go anywhere and for my sake show some concern for your health. I'm well. Yesterday passed in quite a peaceful and proper manner. I suppose Volkov told you what I have ordered concerning Gorich. If he's found, order that he be treated as the laws dictate.[1]

Be assured that I love the little kiddy. He wrote to you himself what he got out of me with his begging:[2] je n'ai [pas] pu lui refuser une chose aussi aisée à faire pour le rendre content, d'autant plus qu'il agit par reconnaissance. Adieu, mon Ami. Quand je Vous reverrai en bonne santé, je Vous embrasserai de tout mon coeur.[3]

[. . .]

1. Dmitry Vasilievich Volkov (1718–1785), police-master general of St. Petersburg, had been ordered to locate and then try Lieutenant-Colonel Ivan Petrovich Gorich-Benesevsky, who was wanted for his participation in a duel. Gorich had earlier served under Potemkin, and the prince helped him to escape to Poland. Gorich was later cleared of any charges and returned to fight in the Second Russo-Turkish War.

2. Korsakov received the Polish Order of the White Eagle on 20 September 1778.

3. "I could not refuse him something so easy to do that would make him happy, so much the more since he acts out of gratitude. Farewell, my friend. When I see you again in good health, I shall kiss you with all my heart."

229. CATHERINE TO POTEMKIN

[1778–1779]

Many thanks for coming. Could you not come to me for an hour, even if only on the small staircase? Je voudrais Vous parler.[1]

1. "I would like to speak to you."

230. POTEMKIN TO CATHERINE   [In French, except first word]

[1778–1779]

Matia, we have returned, and now want to sup.

[Catherine] My God, who would've believed that you would return? Have you been invited to Gatchina?[1]

---

1. The Gatchina estate then belonged to Grigory Orlov. Although Catherine worked to maintain smooth relations among her current and past favorites, tensions simmered just below the surface. It was around this time in the fall of 1778 that the Orlov brothers, led by Aleksei, who nurtured a profound hatred for Potemkin, sought to topple him one final time.

231. POTEMKIN TO CATHERINE   [In French]

No, I wasn't invited. Madame Orlova[1] is difficult to please, and I didn't return in order to go there, but because I had promised you. My dear, I can't imagine this annoys you.[2]

[Catherine] My dear friend, I'm delighted to know you're here, but am very sorry that you are ill. Don't ask me to come see you.

---

1. Princess Yekaterina Nikolaevna Orlova (*née* Zinovieva) (1757–1781) married Prince Grigory Orlov, her cousin, on 5 June 1777. The match was vehemently opposed by his brothers and the Russian church, which sought to annul the marriage and was only persuaded to drop the matter by the empress three years later. His wife's death in Lausanne destroyed Grigory Orlov. He returned to Russia a broken man and died a year and a half later.

2. This sentence in Russian.

232. CATHERINE TO POTEMKIN   [In French]

[Spring 1779–February 1780]

My dear friend, I ask you to send or to give this enclosed note to Mr. Fat Man.[1] It's for the spirit of Cagliostro.[2]

---

1. Possibly Prince Nikolai Golitsyn.

2. Freemason, alchemist, and necromancer, Giuseppe Balsamo (a.k.a. Count Alessandro di Cagliostro) (1743–1795) was one of the century's most famous adventurers. In the spring of 1779, he arrived in St. Petersburg supposedly seeking the patronage of the empress. Catherine appears never to have met Cagliostro during his stay and later satirized him and his followers in several plays. He most likely departed Russia for Warsaw in late February or March 1780, although some sources suggest he left as early as October 1779. Legend has it that Potemkin had an affair with Cagliostro's wife, Lorenza, during their stay. Although Lopatin dates these letters (232–235) to 1774 and 1776, this period is likely more accurate.

233. POTEMKIN TO CATHERINE

[Spring 1779–February 1780]

Matushka, l'esprit de Cagliostro[1] will go for a walk along the river bank across from the Hermitage. Will you not go to the Hermitage?

[Catherine] Cela s'appelle se moquer des gens.[2]

---

1. "the spirit of Cagliostro"
2. "That is called ridiculing people."

234. CATHERINE TO POTEMKIN   [In French]

[Spring 1779–February 1780]

My dear friend, despite the feeling of well-being that the spirits of Cagliostro produced, I very much fear that I exceeded your patience and inconvenienced you with the length of my visit. My watch had stopped and the time passed so quickly that at one o'clock it still seemed as if it were not yet midnight. I have still another regret, namely, that instead of that "cold soup" you didn't have at hand for the past year and a half the chemical medicine of Cagliostro that is so gentle, so agreeable, so handy that it perfumes and lends an elasticity to the mind and the senses.[1] Basta, Basta, caro amico,[2] one mustn't bore you for too long. We are full of gratitude and every possible sentiment of gratitude and respect for you.

---

1. A self-styled healer, Cagliostro concocted for his clients various potions intended to cure maladies of all kinds.
2. "That's enough, enough, dear friend,"

235. CATHERINE TO POTEMKIN   [In French]

[Spring 1779–February 1780]

I am writing this note to tell you that the spirits of Cagliostro appeared to me in my dreams last night, and they said to me, "Every dream is a lie," but then they wrote: "Prince Potemkin is concocting a chemical mixture for you in which he uses all sorts of superb and very healthy herbs." They told me all the herbs by their names and nicknames. I could compile a separate catalogue (but since it won't ruin the matter and doesn't enter into it, I shall put that aside for another time). "But," the little one-and-a-half-inch-tall spirits added, "there are two herbs that grow on one and the same stalk that he scorns or neglects to include. Nevertheless, it is essential for you and your happiness that they be included. These herbs are gentleness and delicacy. They have no other names, but the stalk from which they emanate has a sacred name for souls of noble origin." I was astounded by what the spirits told me. I hurried to carry a twig of these herbs to your alembic without which, the spirits had told me, everything else would be reduced to nothing. But although I walked on my tiptoes, barely was I able to approach your alembic when I saw you in my way. You pushed me aside with such force that I suddenly awoke, and my eyes filled with tears since the sole herbs that could make a good, healthy, and agreeable mixture for me were precisely those you neglected and about which you didn't even want to hear spoken. Having awakened, I gathered myself and said: He must know my dream. There it is. If it doesn't amuse you, it is worth your telling Cagliostro to keep his spirits under control so that they stop appearing to me. I'll get by just fine without them.

236. CATHERINE TO POTEMKIN

[22 June 1779]

Greetings to ya, Prince, your place is here with us. Even without you everything on the steppe will be in good order thanks to your instructions. I love ya, Prince, I shan't forget ya. So the little kiddy[1] ordered me, in jest, to write you. He sends ya his regards and kisses, Prince. I shall arrive tomorrow after five in the afternoon and shall be merry. I'm sending a newspaper, please don't lose it.

Adieu, mon bijou. Parasha[2] ordered that I beg her compliments.

---

1. Korsakov.
2. Countess Praskovia Bruce, whose affair with Korsakov brought a quick end to his favor.

237. CATHERINE TO POTEMKIN

[After 23 July 1779]

You thank me very much, although I truly don't know what for. The French say: Voila comme les gens de qualité se ruinent.[1]

In your first letter you deign to write you'll be receiving some more income. I was curious to learn how from Prince Viazemsky.[2] In speaking with him, however, I learned that instead of an increase in income, you're simply collecting your current one ten years in advance. Ma fois je m'étonne comment Vous trouvés cela si réjouissant. Si cela peut payer Vos dettes ou si cela les paye, encore à la bonne heure, cette idée peut rejouir, mais si cet argent, tiré du sanctuaire auquel il ne faudroit, en bonne économie, jamais toucher, est employé en choses dont on peut se passer et que Vous resties chargé de dettes; je Vous avoue que je regretterai in-finiment ce que je fais par complaisance pour Vous cette fois,[3] and for the reason that this won't do anyone any good. Although I had desig-nated yesterday for a meeting with the English Minister,[4] I only saw him standing by the gates as I drove by since you had left. Farewell, baten'ka, till we meet. With all my heart I'm sorry that the heat gave you a headache. Mais malgré cela il faut gronder les jeunes gens comme Vous, quand leurs amis voyent qu'ils font mauvaise économie, et qu'ils man-quent de parole.[5]

---

1. "That's how the well-born go to ruin." Despite his immense income, Potemkin was for-ever in debt. Catherine issued a decree on 23 July 1779 increasing his yearly salary to the staggering sum of 750,000 rubles.

2. A trusted advisor of Catherine's, Prince Aleksandr Alekseevich Viazemsky (1727–1793) was Russia's procurator-general, and so the state treasurer, for almost thirty years.

3. "Really, I am astonished how you find this so amusing. If this could pay your debts or if it pays them, then fine, this gladdens me; but if this money, taken from the sanctuary that, under good management, should never be touched, is used for things one could do without and if you remain saddled with debts, I confess to you that I shall infinitely regret what I am doing this time out of my goodwill toward you,"

4. At war with France and the American colonies, Britain desperately sought an alliance with Russia. To that end, British ambassador James Harris (1746–1820) had been sent to St. Petersburg in 1777. Harris cultivated a relationship with Potemkin as a means to influence Catherine, though without success.

5. "For all that, one must reprimand young people like you when their friends see that they are wasting money and are not keeping their word."

238. CATHERINE TO POTEMKIN   [In French]

[After 5 August 1779]

My dear friend, I am infinitely sorry that I may have contributed to your headache. I suppose my letter hastened your return. Excuse the ardor that it contained. My situation yesterday was so cruel that everything put me out of patience; it was an unbearable day;[1] this morning's stroll was a balm to my soul. I don't dare ask you the fate of my short letter of yester-day. I clearly see that he didn't become a courtier of King Pyrrhus since if he were here, I think he would have deigned to honor it with a word in response; perhaps my expectations are too great as well, but that is be-cause for several days my judgment has been cloudy.

---

1. Zorich reappeared at court quite unexpectedly on 5 August. It is possible that the return of the fiery, unpredictable Zorich led to some sort of friction with Korsakov.

239. CATHERINE TO POTEMKIN

[Before 20 September 1779]

Sir, it seems it's been an entire year since I last saw you.[1] It's time you abandoned the Finnish woods and swamps and returned to us. Baten'ka, the bears and elks of Osinovaia roshcha truly do not know your worth. We, on the other hand, love and respect you. Is it proper to flee your friends and to abandon them for the desert? The storm-clouds heartened me the day before yesterday when I saw that they were heading toward that bank of the river, and I hoped they would perhaps chase you back to us. Adieu mon cher Ami, portés-Vous bien et revenés au plus tôt trouver Vos Amis qui Vous aiment.[2]

---

1. Potemkin spent three weeks in September at Osinovaia roshcha.

2. "Farewell, my dear friend, take care of yourself and return soon to find your friends who love you."

240. CATHERINE TO POTEMKIN

[Before 20 September 1779]

Mon Ami, il fait si froid ici, que j'ai pris la résolution de m'en aller demain ou ce soir à Czarsko Selo.[1]

Baten'ka, I hear you are living in a camp. I'm quite worried you'll catch cold. Do come stay in one of our rooms: whichever one you choose, it'll be warmer and drier than any tent. It seems to me it's been a year since I last saw you. Halloo, halloo, my dear falcon. Let yourself be lured here. For a very long time now you've been off in flight.[2]

---

1. "My friend, it is so cold here that I have decided to go to Tsarskoe Selo tomorrow or this evening."

2. Potemkin returned to St. Petersburg sometime before 20 September. Ten days later the forty-year-old prince celebrated his name-day at his Shepilov house in the company of Catherine, Nikita Panin, Semyon Zorich, Korsakov, and many of the prince's relatives.

241. CATHERINE TO POTEMKIN   [In French]

[4 December 1779]

I have the pleasure of informing you that Monsieur[1] says that Katenka[2] is more pleasant and more attentive and prettier than all the other current young ladies. He speaks most eagerly of her, he finds being with her most agreeable. That's what I know at present. Madame Ribas[3] will come soon, and I shall inform you of everything she tells me.

1. The son of Catherine and Grigory Orlov, Aleksei Grigorievich Bobrinsky (1762–1813) was raised without a clear idea of who his parents were. He traveled for a time in Europe and then studied in Leipzig before returning to Russia and enrolling in the Noble Corps of Cadets. In the 1780s, he racked up enormous debts while abroad and was placed under the guardianship of the former favorite Zavadovsky.

2. Potemkin's niece Yekaterina Vasilievna Engelhardt (1761–1829), a maid-of-honor at court.

3. Anastasia Ivanovna Ribas (1745–1822) served as a maid-of-the-bedchamber to Catherine for fourteen years until her marriage in 1776. Her husband, José de Ribas, was responsible for overseeing Bobrinsky's education at the Noble Corps of Cadets.

242. CATHERINE TO POTEMKIN   [In French]

[After 5 December 1779]

Young Bobrinsky says that Katenka has a better mind than all the other women and girls of the city. We wanted to know what he based this opinion on. He said that, in his opinion, this is proven simply by the fact that she wore fewer feathers, less makeup, and fewer jewels than the others. While at the opera he took it into his head to break the railing on his box because it kept him from seeing Katenka and being seen by her. I don't know how, but he finally succeeded in enlarging a gap in the railing and then—goodbye opera. He paid no more attention to it. He defended himself like a lion yesterday against Prince Orlov who wanted to tease him about his passion. Finally, he answered him with such wit that he reduced him to silence: he told him that Katenka wasn't his first cousin.[1]

1. Prince Grigory Orlov was obviously uncomfortable with the idea of a match between his son by the empress and one of Potemkin's nieces. On Orlov's own controversial marriage, see Letter 231n1.

243. CATHERINE TO POTEMKIN

[After 5 December 1779]

Selon ce que Ribas[1] m'a dit hier son élève n'aime pas beaucoup qu'on le moralise ainsi; je crois que ces prêcheurs ne feront pas grand effet sur lui, d'ailleurs je sais que le ton de papa ne lui plaît pas toujours.[2] He[3] has greater sensibility than is characteristic for his age, he doesn't like lying, and he who expects to get something from him or to ingratiate himself through flattery would not always succeed. Il a beaucoup de candeur et de franchise.[4]

1. José de Ribas (1743–1800) was a Spanish adventurer in Russian service from 1772. Patronized by the Orlovs, he made a successful career in Russia, first as a tutor to Bobrinsky, later as an officer in the Second Russo-Turkish War, and finally as the builder of Odessa.

2. "According to what Ribas told me yesterday, his pupil doesn't like it very much when he is preached to in that manner. I don't believe these sermons will have a great effect on him; moreover, I know that this fatherly tone doesn't always please him."

3. Bobrinsky.

4. "He has a good deal of candor and sincerity."

244. CATHERINE TO POTEMKIN

[After 19 April 1780]

Aleksandr Dmitrievich[1] has just returned and told me that your head is filled with worries. These are all nothing but meaningless fantasies, and what's more I know that my soul and his are quite innocent in regard to you; I shall retain my peace of mind till such time you deem it worthwhile to speak to me. I do not doubt in the least that all slander and falsehood will yield to that true friendship that you will always find without fail in my soul and in the soul of one who is devoted to me and who loves and respects you as much as I do. Our only regret is that you are so worried.[2]

---

1. Aleksandr Dmitrievich Lanskoy (1758–1784), the new favorite, sprang from a poor Smolensk noble family and served in the Izmailovsky Guards and later Chevalier-Gardes before becoming an adjutant to Potemkin on 6 October 1779. Within a month he had been made an aide-de-camp to Catherine and was officially installed in the palace as the favorite in the spring of 1780.

2. A possible cause of Potemkin's worry might have been the resistance he was encountering at the time from Nikita Panin and other pro-Prussian elements, including the Orlovs and Grand Duke Paul, who were opposed to Potemkin's pro-Austrian orientation, and to his growing influence in general. The prince's enemies at court were trying to block Lanskoy's appointment as favorite and to put forward their own candidate around this time.

245. CATHERINE TO POTEMKIN   [In French]

[After 19 April 1780]

My dear friend, I have finished my dinner and the door onto the small staircase is open. Should you desire to speak to me, you may come.

246. CATHERINE TO POTEMKIN

[22 May 1780]

Baten'ka, I just received your letter from Mogilyov upon my arrival in Sennoe, that is at ten o'clock in the evening. I attribute Count Falkenstein's[1] very endearing words more to his desire to please than anything else. Russia is great all on Her own; whatever I might do is no different than adding a drop of water to the sea. I have no doubt that his words about me make you merry, for I know how much my obliging and grateful charge loves me. I leave it to Count Falkenstein to decide what day and at what time we should meet so that we can make each other's acquaintance without others present.

Si je n'avais suivi que les mouvements de mon impatience et ma vivacité naturelle, dès que Votre lettre m'est parvenue, c'est-à-dire à dix heures du soir, je me serais remise en carrosse et aurais couru sans m'arrêter nulle part tout droit à Mohilef, où j'ai beaucoup de regret de savoir que Mr. le comte de Falkenstein m'ait devancé. Mais comme cela aurait fait une brêche à son incognito, la réflexion a retenu mon premier mouvement, et je m'en vais suivre ma route, comme Vous saves qu'elle a été réglée. Je coucherai demain à Shklov[2] et dimanche je viendrai pour la messe à Mohilef.[3] It's just that I don't know how best to arrange our meeting so that others won't be present, for upon my return from Mass, I'll be surrounded by a throng of people. It wouldn't be courteous to postpone it yet again till after dinner. Perhaps he could come when everyone is at Mass, so that upon entering my inner chambers, those before my bedroom, that is, I would find him already there. Let me know if you find a better way, though it seems this way might be handy as well. Considering that Count Rumiantsev[4] writes me that our guest doesn't want to dine anywhere, so I assume that he doesn't want to dine even with me at the main table; I shall await word on this. I'm enclosing his letter, so that you know what and how he writes. Rien de plus flatteur ni de plus agréable que cette lettre que Vous m'avés envoyée. Je Vous prie de réitérer à Mr. le comte de Falkenstein les assurances que mon premier désir est de me conformer en toute façon à tout ce qui pourra lui rendre le séjour de Mohilef supportable.[5]

Farewell, my friend, we long for you terribly. I so very much wish to see you as soon as possible.

---

1. Joseph II of Austria.

2. Semyon Zorich hosted Catherine and her retinue at his estate in Shklov on 23 May.

3. "Had I only followed the impulses of my impatience and my natural vivacity, as soon as your letter reached me, that is at ten o'clock in the evening, I would have gotten back in the carriage and would have hastened without stopping straight on to Mogilyov, where, I am very sorry to learn, Mr. Count Falkenstein has preceded me. But as this would have damaged his incognito, consideration held back my first impulse, and I am going to follow my route as you know it was laid out. Tomorrow I shall sleep at Shklov, and Sunday I shall arrive for Mass at Mogilyov."

4. Field Marshal Pyotr Rumiantsev arrived in Mogilyov before Joseph II and was the first to speak with him.

5. "Nothing could be more flattering and more pleasant than that letter you sent me. Please reiterate to Mr. Count Falkenstein the assurances that my first desire is to accommodate myself in every way to that which will render his stay in Mogilyov tolerable."

247. CATHERINE TO POTEMKIN

[23 May 1780] from Shklov, at 11 o'clock in the evening

I just received your letter, my true friend. I hope to reach you early tomorrow;[1] we all find it so dull without you. I see your friendship for me in everything you write. Together we'll try to figure out how to handle Falkenstein. Good night. Sasha Dmitrievich[2] begs his compliments and longs for you terribly.

-----

1. Catherine arrived the following day. Talks in Mogilyov lasted until 29 May when the parties departed for Shklov, where they were treated to lavish entertainments by Zorich.

2. Lanskoy.

248. CATHERINE TO POTEMKIN

From Mshaga, 9 June, 1780

Baten'ka, Prince, upon arriving here after nine o'clock this evening, I received your letter from Viazma, from which I learned that Count Falkenstein, and you right behind him, has taken off for Moscow.[1] We, including your children,[2] are all well. I'm carrying them along speedily, and I think we'll arrive home on Friday. I'm hurrying so you don't overtake me. If I find you in Novgorod, I'll take you with me. You think I'm delirious; no, I'm not delirious, but I know that I'm dealing with clever folks. Should our guest still care to know my opinion of him, then you may say that je pense qu'aucun Souverain présentement vivant ne l'approche en fait de mérite et de connaissances et de politesse; je suis enchantée d'avoir fait sa connaissance; comme particulier même ce serait une excellente connaissance à faire. Adieu, mon bon Ami.[3]

Be assured that my friendship for you is equal to your attachment to me, which I consider priceless. Thanks for the cakes. Aleksandr Dmitrievich asked me to send you his compliments; it's so dull without you, goodness knows how long it's been since we last saw you.

-----

1. Legend has it that on her return trip, Catherine, together with Potemkin, visited the prince's native village of Chizhevo. From there, Catherine returned directly to St. Petersburg, and Potemkin galloped off to meet Joseph II in Moscow.

2. Potemkin's nieces Aleksandra and Yekaterina Engelhardt.

3. "I think no other sovereign now alive can approach him in terms of merit, knowledge, and civility. I am enchanted to have made his acquaintance; even as a private person he would make an excellent acquaintance. Farewell, my good friend."

249. CATHERINE TO POTEMKIN

From Novgorod, 11 June 1780, that is, on Thursday

We arrived here safely at four o'clock this morning, and after dinner I'm leaving straight away for Tsarskoe Selo.[1] I'm well, as is everyone with me, first and foremost the children[2] you entrusted to my care. Baten'ka, I do so wish to know how you're doing. I'm hurrying so you don't overtake me along the way. I suppose I've been winning so far with my greater speed. Mon bon Ami, it's lonely without you. Farewell, baten'ka. The Hierarch received me without any oration, which must be attributed to his modesty as he didn't want to disturb me in the middle of the night.

How are you getting along there? For no one writes to me about that.

---

1. Catherine arrived in Tsarskoe Selo on 12 June, with Joseph II six days behind her. They continued talks about their defensive alliance until his departure on 8 July.

2. See Letter 248n2.

250. CATHERINE TO POTEMKIN

25 September [1780], Friday, after eight o'clock in the evening

Baten'ka, I just now received your letter of the 24th and we, Sasha[1] and I, that is, were very gladdened by it. He was given the enclosed note, and I send his reply herewith. I'm so pleased you'll soon be returning, although that doesn't mean I'm forgetting you. We were talking about you the very minute your sweet letter was delivered, and we doubted that you would return by Tuesday, but now I regret to learn that you won't even be here on Wednesday, your name-day.[2] But be that as it may, at least be well and of us be assured that we are quite fond of you.

I sent someone to Aleksandra Vasilievna to get her letter to you, but I suppose she had already left to visit Harris,[3] and so don't be angry but you won't have a letter from them today.

---

1. Lanskoy.

2. Potemkin did arrive in time and celebrated his name-day, having turned forty-one earlier that month, with the empress and a small party of guests.

3. As part of his strategy for winning over Catherine and Potemkin to the idea of an alliance with Britain, Harris courted Aleksandra Engelhardt, Potemkin's niece, and supposedly sought to buy her cooperation with money. His endeavors having failed, he left Russia in 1783.

251. CATHERINE TO POTEMKIN

[After 14 January 1781]

Since I feared that Panin would return Cobenzl's proposals to him without sending them to me, I ordered yesterday that he and the Vice Chancellor report to me what Cobenzl has proposed to them and what the Emperor has written to me.[1] As a result, I am also sending along the following papers. I'll now demand from them their opinions about this, but shall then decide the matter as I please.

---

1. Count Ludwig Cobenzl (1753–1809) was the Austrian ambassador to Russia since 1779. He took part in the discussions at Mogilyov, and in January 1781 he presented to Catherine the emperor's proposal for a defensive alliance between Austria and Russia. He represented Joseph II in the ensuing discussions that led up to the secret alliance between the two powers. Catherine was worried that given his pro-Prussian sympathies, Nikita Panin might try to undermine the negotiations.

252. CATHERINE TO POTEMKIN

[Before 25 January 1781]

It is proper to compare, not out of cowardice but for the sake of honesty, since we have obligations and it would be dishonest to violate them. A treaty of equal friendship is not a dishonest matter based on the principle that when not at war a power will try to live in peace with any other power. War is not declared without reason and without need. I do not wish to be dependent on any of the powers. The Viennese court may well boast that I am comparing them with a twenty-year-old ally even though ten years ago that court refused any union with us at an important moment for us and undertook every possible dirty trick at the time.[1]

I regret with all my heart that you are weak, and I do not know what to attribute this to. So I shall examine you myself. Farewell, my good friend. The draft treaty, which you read, was presented by Cobenzl. Our counter-treaty is being prepared.[2]

---

1. Potemkin had apparently accused Panin of cowardice for wanting to compare the terms of the alliance with Austria with those between Russia and Prussia, who had been allied since 1762. Catherine makes reference to Prussian subsidies paid to Russia during the First Russo-Turkish War and points out that during the war Austria had aided the Porte against Russia.

2. Russia objected to Austria's attempt to lessen its obligations in the event of a Turkish attack.

253. CATHERINE TO POTEMKIN

[February–March 1781]

If Cobenzl says to you, as he often has said, that there can be no alternative between the Emperor and the Russian Empress, then please tell him to abandon such nonsense, which will bring the matter to an unavoidable halt, and that my principles have in fact been not to take anyone's place and not to concede my place to anyone.[1]

---

1. Diplomatic protocol required that when agreements were signed by crowned heads two copies be drafted: the sovereign who signed first would then sign the second copy after the other sovereign, thus ensuring that each would have his signature first on one of the texts. Joseph II wrote Catherine on 23 February (6 March) 1781 that as Holy Roman Emperor he could not abide by this "alternative." Disagreement over this formality delayed the conclusion of the alliance for months.

254. CATHERINE TO POTEMKIN   [In French]

[April 1781]

I am curious to know what Cobenzl will have in his bag, and once he has emptied it, I have an idea that will help solve everything: that is, that in dropping all discussions and idle talk of the alternative, each Sovereign set down in writing a copy of the treaty that begins so: I or We, by the grace of God, promise to give to Our Dear Brother (Sister) this and that pursuant to the articles' terms, which will be agreed upon, and that each will sign and these signatures will be exchanged, and then . . . [1]

---

1. Catherine recommended a way out of the problem created by the alternative: both sovereigns would draft letters containing the treaty articles, sign and then exchange them. These letters would have the same force as a regularly drafted treaty. On 18 May 1781, the alliance was concluded. In the event of a Turkish attack on Russia, Austria would offer military support; Catherine, in turn, vowed to defend the integrity of her ally's lands in the event of a Prussian attack.

255. CATHERINE TO POTEMKIN[1]

[Before November 1781]

My dear friend, permit me to explain myself to you on a matter that acutely concerns us and is so near to us and that you spoke to me about three days ago, and that I see makes you anxious, and given my friendship for you disturbs me as well.

You are of the opinion that I am opposed to these young peoples' attachment to each other,[2] whereas I can truthfully say that neither have I ever been opposed nor am I now opposed. I think we desire the same thing; you and I both want them to be happy. But in order for them to be so, it's necessary that, on both sides, this affair be decided by themselves and their attachment to each other. I promise you that I shall not oppose it, either directly or indirectly. But I can't hide from you that this young man is anything but mature, that he is foolish and awkward, and that it could well be that at present no woman will find her happiness with him, a fact which will not fail to disturb their well-being and cause a great deal of grief.

My honest opinion is to give them the freedom to come to an agreement among themselves, as they see fit, or else, God forbid, both of them will harshly reproach us should they not find happiness in marriage. Till such time that they both come to an agreement, keep an eye on him where he is now, and continue to watch over him so that his youth, lacking supervision, doesn't commit something wanton.

I have spoken my mind with sincerity and friendship; if my view is too narrow, and if you can supply me with sounder ideas, I shall listen to them with friendship and pleasure.

---

1. First, second, and final paragraphs in French.

2. Potemkin's niece Yekaterina Engelhardt was being courted by the wealthy Count Pavel Martynovich Skavronsky (1757–1794), a gentleman-of-the-bedchamber. She married him in the chapel of the Winter Palace in the presence of the empress on 10 November 1781. Two days later her sister Aleksandra (1754–1838) married the Polish Hetman Ksawery Branicki (1731–1819).

5. Annexing the Crimea—1782-1783

*T*n 1781, a rebellion broke out in the Khanate of the Crimea against the rule of Khan Shagin Girey. By April 1782, the revolt had spread throughout the Crimean elite and the khan's own army, forcing him and the Russian consul to flee Kaffa by boat for the Russian fortress at Kerch on 14 May. The rebels immediately elected Bahadir Girey, Shagin's brother, their leader and sent a delegation to Constantinople to request the Porte's recognition of the new khan and its support. The overthrow of Shagin Girey left Catherine facing a difficult decision: should she accept the rebellion against her own puppet as a *fait accompli* or use military force to put Shagin Girey back on the throne, for a second time, at the risk of provoking a war with the Ottoman Empire?

The origins of the Crimean Khanate stretch back as far as the mid-fifteenth century when its leaders managed to establish their independence from the Golden Horde, a remnant of the Mongol Empire that had dominated Russia and most of Asia for centuries. The khanate soon came under the authority of the Ottoman Empire, which sought to use it as a buffer state against Muscovy and the Polish-Lithuanian Commonwealth that were beginning to move into the steppe region north of the Black Sea. The existence of the hostile khanate hurt Russia in several ways. First, numerous Tatar raids made the establishment of permanent settlements on the steppe difficult. Russian peasants who sought land as well as freedom from serfdom settled on the southern steppe and were often captured on such raids and sold into slavery. Second, by controlling the northern shore of the Black Sea, the Crimean

Tatars denied Russia access to the sea and so cut her off from vital trade routes to the outside world. In addition, Russians had been forced to accept being subjects of the more powerful Tatars for centuries. Even as late as the beginning of the eighteenth century, in fact, Russia was still paying a burdensome tribute to the Crimean khans. Not surprisingly, the Russians had come to resent the Tatars and their threatening presence along Russia's frontier.

Beginning in the final decades of the seventeenth century, Russia staged repeated military campaigns against the Crimean Khanate, none of which produced a lasting solution to the problem. Catherine herself ordered three separate invasions of the Crimea: the first, in 1771, led to the creation of an independent Crimea under the rule of Khan Sahib Girey; he was chased from the throne by Devlet Girey in 1774, which prompted Catherine to mount a second invasion in November 1776 that put Shagin Girey, then in exile in Poltava, in power. Catherine first met Shagin in St. Petersburg in 1771 when he impressed her with his good looks and European polish, the product of several years spent in Venice as a boy. He became Catherine's protégé, and she saw to it that he was elected khan in 1777. Shagin Girey's inept rule led to a revolt later that year but was put down in February 1778, though only after Russian forces were sent back into the Crimea for a third time. During his second reign (1778–1783), Shagin continued to implement the same unpopular westernizing reforms that had led to the rebellion of 1777. Thanks to the overwhelming Russian military presence, however, he had been able to maintain his grip on power until the new unrest of 1782.

On 3 June 1782, just weeks after the khan had fled to Kerch, Catherine wrote to Potemkin, then away in Moscow, of the revolt in the Crimea and asked him to hurry back so they could discuss the situation (Letter 256). Potemkin raced back to Tsarskoe Selo where he and Catherine conferred on the best course of action. Not without some urging from Potemkin (Letter 257), Catherine soon decided to put down the revolt with Russian troops and to reinstate Shagin Girey, despite her fear that this action could lead to war with the Turks. On 1 September 1782, Potemkin departed for the south to oversee the invasion himself. Traveling at great speed, he first visited Kinburn, located across the Liman from the Turkish fortress of Ochakov, to see whether the Turks were indeed preparing for war. He next galloped off to the Petrovsky fortress on the northern shore of the Sea of Azov to meet with the khan and to assure him of Russia's support (Letter 258). Just days after Potemkin's meeting with Shagin, Russian forces led by Generals Anton de Balmen and Aleksandr Samoilov marched into the Crimea in late September and quickly made their way for Bakhchisarai, the khan's capital. Potemkin and Shagin Girey departed the Petrovsky fortress by boat for Kaffa where they met up with Russian troops from

Kerch. By the end of October, the rebellion had been crushed, and Potemkin had raced back to St. Petersburg to discuss with Catherine the fate of the khan and the Crimea.

Having put Shagin Girey on the Crimean throne for a third time, Catherine began to waver in her support. She was unhappy about the huge sums being spent on propping up the khanate (over seven million rubles since 1774), and it was now clear that without Russian arms the present khan had no chance of maintaining power. To make matters worse, Shagin had begun a brutal campaign of retribution against his enemies that had threatened to ignite a third rebellion. Potemkin had long been a vocal proponent of annexation, and when he returned to St. Petersburg he sought to convince Catherine that the time to act was at hand. In a bold, forceful letter, which artfully played to the empress's vanity and insecurity, Potemkin tried to push the hesitant Catherine toward annexation (Letter 259). The international situation seemed to favor immediate action. Britain and France were still at war and so would not come to the Porte's aid; Joseph II had expressed Austrian support for Russia's actions; and Constantinople was reeling at the time from riots and an outbreak of the plague. Potemkin's arguments began to wear down Catherine's hesitancy. On 14 December, she issued a secret rescript to Potemkin permitting him to annex the Crimea, but only under certain conditions—should Shagin Girey die, for example, or should he refuse to grant Russia Akhtiar, or should another rebellion break out. Despite the restrictions, the underlying message was not lost on Potemkin: Catherine was slowly warming to the idea of annexation.

The prince remained in St. Petersburg throughout the first few months of 1783. During that time he worked out defensive plans for Russia's borders in the event of war with the Porte and proposed to Catherine a major reform of the Russian army intended to strip it of all pointless and harmful European accouterments and replace them with more practical items, many of which had long been used by the Cossacks. Although the recommendations Potemkin made in his memorandum did not all originate with him, in their clear disdain for mindless imitation of the West, their pride in native traditions, and their progressive concern for the well-being of the common soldier, they bear Potemkin's unmistakable imprint (Letters 260, 261).

By the spring of 1783, Catherine had been made to see the necessity of immediate annexation. Potemkin's incessant urging had overcome her earlier hesitancy. He was able to point out that Russian troops had faced almost no resistance in 1782 and that since then he had been working hard to win over the local elite to the idea of joining the Russian Empire. In addition, Britain and France had signed peace preliminaries on 9 (20) January and so would soon be free to impede Russia's plans. Time was running out.

Finally, on 8 April, Catherine signed a manifesto on the annexation of the Crimea, which was not to be made public until Potemkin had completed the annexation. That same day she issued instructions to Potemkin on what to do in the event the Porte declared war.

Potemkin arrived in Kherson in early May. During the trip south, he and Catherine exchanged letters on the European powers' reaction to what was happening in the Crimea. Potemkin instructed Catherine not to heed the threatening sounds emanating from various capitals, for, he correctly averred, none of them would do a thing to prevent Russian seizure of the Crimea. Nonetheless, Catherine still worried that annexation might provoke a war, especially if it dragged on too long, and she urged Potemkin to hurry matters along (Letter 262–268).

Yet, things were not going as smoothly as might be hoped. Before the Tatars would agree to take an oath of allegiance to the empress, the khan had to renounce his throne and leave the Crimea for Russia. It had originally been proposed, and Shagin Girey had agreed, that he was to be given a handsome pension and to be made ruler of a new state in the eastern Caucasus on the border with Persia. But Shagin was delaying his departure as he waited to see how the Porte would react to Russia's actions, and he began to demand from Catherine a higher price for relinquishing power. Nevertheless, Potemkin was finally able to inform Catherine on 1 June that Shagin had begun to send his wagons to the Petrovsky fortress and would soon be joining him in Kherson (Letter 269). The wily Shagin Girey had different plans, however.

Along with coordinating the annexation, Potemkin was also engaged in numerous other activities that demanded considerable attention. The construction of Kherson needed his supervision, ships had to be built, Kinburn required fortifying, and troops and artillery needed to be brought into position in case of war. Potemkin was simultaneously negotiating with Heraclius II, the king of Kartli-Kakheti in the Caucasus, seeking to place his land under Russian suzerainty. To add to all this, a plague epidemic broke out in the Crimea and soon began to spread, despite Potemkin's efforts to establish a quarantine. In the latter part of June, Potemkin left Kherson for the Crimea to direct the fight against the plague himself and to make the final preparations for administering the oath (Letter 272).

Potemkin had initially hoped to administer the oath on 28 June, Catherine's accession day, but events had conspired to prevent his plan, and it was not until 10 July—almost an entire month since he had last written Catherine—that the prince was able to congratulate the empress on the acquisition of the Crimea, which had been largely completed (Letter 275). Meanwhile, Catherine was becoming increasingly anxious. On 15 July she wrote to ask why she had had no word from him for so long.

Catherine intimated that dark rumors about troubles in the Crimea had begun circulating at court and complained that she had no solid information with which to dispel them. She had expected the annexation to be completed by the middle of May, and here it was the middle of July, yet she still knew no more about the situation than "the Pope himself" (Letter 276).

The tension that developed between Catherine and the prince as a result of the delay soured what should have been an unmitigated triumph for them both. From his camp at Karasubazaar, Potemkin defended himself against Catherine's angry letter of 15 July by asserting that due to numerous unforeseeable obstacles the annexation could not possibly have been carried out before the middle of June (Letter 281). Days later he was able to congratulate Catherine on yet another victory, namely the signing of the Treaty of Georgievsk that made Heraclius's Caucasian kingdom (part of today's Georgia) a Russian protectorate. Like a true courtier, Potemkin heaped praise upon Catherine: "What Sovereign," he asked, "has ever compiled such a brilliant epoch as you?" More than mere politics, the annexation of the Crimea was for Potemkin an achievement tinged with mysticism (Letters 282, 283). Catherine's frustration had largely subsided by now, and while praising Potemkin's feat, she clucked with barely contained glee at their coup (Letters 284, 285).

But they were not yet out of the woods. Instead of heading for Kherson, Shagin Girey had taken off in a different direction, making his way to Taman, from where he began inciting the Nogais, Tatar nomads, to rebel against their new Russian masters. The Nogais, then being forcibly resettled from the Kuban, responded by rising up. Upon learning of the unrest in the Kuban, Potemkin sent General Aleksandr Suvorov to restore order, which he did, crushing the rebels on 1 October. Meanwhile, Shagin Girey managed to flee Taman and escape capture.

Surrounded by the plague and weary from his labors, Potemkin fell seriously ill in late August. A severe fever lay him low for more than a month and left him so weak that he had to be carried out of the Crimea, first to Kremenchug and then to Nezhin. From there he wrote Catherine on 23 September of his torment and intimated that he was near death (Letter 286). Catherine responded with worried letters, and implored him to take greater care of his health. A feeling of foreboding that she might lose Potemkin came over her. She begged God to preserve him, and asked Potemkin to hurry back. "Oh, for truth," she cried, "I'm very often lost without you" (Letters 287, 288).

Potemkin returned to the capital in late November 1783. Amazingly, instead of being hailed as a hero, as Russia's conqueror of the Crimea, he was shunned and ignored. Count Bezborodko, an ally at court, told Potemkin that his successes had sparked jealousy in the souls of his enemies, who

were spreading rumors about his mishandling of the plague and other supposed blunders. Even the favorite, Aleksandr Lanskoy, was reportedly involved in the effort to discredit Potemkin. Rather surprisingly, Catherine
believed the rumors and turned cold toward Potemkin. He stopped visiting her for a time, stayed away from court, and even talked of going
abroad. The street before his Shepilov house, usually choked with carriages while he was at home, was empty.

Potemkin's icy reception is shocking in light of what had been accomplished. With the annexation of the Crimea, Russia had added over eighteen thousand square miles to its territory and had rid itself of an age-old
problem. With the disappearance of the Crimean Khanate, Russia's southern territories could now be safely settled and developed. Control over the
Crimean peninsula finally gave Russian ships access to the Black Sea and
permitted the construction of a significant naval presence there. And all of
this had been done without provoking war. The European powers, though
they threatened war at times, in the end never raised a finger to stop Russia. What is more, they pressured the Porte, which officially recognized
the annexation in late December 1783, not to risk a war over the Crimea.
The balance of power in the Black Sea region was shifting ever further
away from the Ottoman Turks, and the states of Europe did not fail to take
note of an expanding and increasingly confident Russia.

• • •

256. CATHERINE TO POTEMKIN

3 June 1782. Friday morning

Baten'ka, Prince Grigory Aleksandrovich. Not only my desire to know of
your good health compels me to send this messenger to you, but matters of state as well. In the Crimea the Tatars have once again begun to
make not insignificant disturbances, which forced the Khan and Veselitsky[1] to leave Kaffa by water for Kerch. They were received coldly by Filisov.[2] It's now necessary to give the Khan the promised defense, to protect our borders and his, our friend's. You and I could've taken care of
all this in half an hour, but now I don't know where to find you. I beg
you in every possible way to hurry your arrival, for I fear nothing more
than to say the wrong thing or to make a wrong move. Adieu, mon cher
Ami, revenés au plus vite, portés-Vous bien,[3] and of me be assured that I
love you like my soul. I'll send money and fit out the vessels, but as
concerns the troops, I'm relying on you, or whomever you choose to
send. For you're the best at choosing the right person. Cette affaire me
paraît délicate parce qu'elle peut avoir des suites, qu'il serait bon
d'éviter encore quelque tems.[4]

The English have inflicted great losses at sea; a French Admiral together with four ships were captured off the islands of Domingo near Jamaica.[5] I'm enclosing a little note from someone who is extremely attached to you and who cruelly yearns for you.[6]

---

1. Pyotr Petrovich Veselitsky was Russia's resident to the Crimean Khanate.

2. Major-General Fyodor Petrovich Filisov (1731–1784) met the khan at Kerch on 17 May 1782 after his flight from Kaffa (Theodosia).

3. "Farewell, my dear friend, return as fast as possible, take care of yourself."

4. "This business seems ticklish to me since it could have consequences that would be good to avoid for some time still."

5. At the Battle of the Saintes on 1 (12) April 1782 near Martinique in the West Indies, British Admiral George Bridges Rodney (1718–1792) defeated the French fleet and captured the French Admiral Count de Grasse (1722–1788). The victory offered some solace after British defeats at the hands of the colonists.

6. Aleksandr Lanskoy.

257. POTEMKIN TO CATHERINE

[Before 3 August 1782]

It's clear from Envoy Bulgakov's[1] latest dispatches how subtly the Turks dissemble. In addition to the inevitable and constant incitement of the Tatars against Russia, the present act of sending the Pasha of the Three-Tailed Mace to the environs of Taman clearly signals their intentions.[2] The Reis-Efendi[3] recounted to Bulgakov the Tatars' complaints against the Khan; he gave a great many reasons, all of them laughable. But he kept to himself the main thing that worries them—namely, the Khan's attachment to your person; and he also did not mention that which especially marked him as a Russian: the fact that the Khan has accepted a military rank in the Guards.[4] They intended to kill him, which they've not yet succeeded in doing, but their intention will remain forever, so even if the Tatars were to submit, how could the Khan live among them without protection? The opportunity to send troops into the Crimea is now at hand, and there is no reason to delay. Your loyal ally and the absolute Sovereign of his land requests your aid in suppressing the rebels. If you do not give him assistance, some will interpret this to mean that the rebels have a right to rise up against the Khan. So order the Khan to leave Kerch for the Petrovsky fortress, from where, together with regiments located nearby, he will enter Perekop. These same troops will remain in the Crimea as long as they are needed.

I can assure you that the greater number of Tatars, upon seeing the troops, will recoil from the request raised by the Porte and will lay all the blame on the leaders of the revolt.

1. Potemkin's former Moscow schoolmate, Yakov Ivanovich Bulgakov (1743–1809) served as Russia's extraordinary envoy and minister plenipotentiary to the Sublime Porte. His diplomatic tact helped bring about a peaceful resolution to the crisis over the Crimea in 1782–1784.

2. By sending the pasha (equivalent in rank to a full Russian general) to Sudzhuk Kale near Taman, which was part of the Crimean Khanate, the Turks signaled their support for the rebellion against Shagin Girey.

3. The Turkish foreign minister.

4. Shagin Girey visited St. Petersburg in 1771 and accepted an honorary rank in one of the Guards regiments.

258. CATHERINE TO POTEMKIN

30 September 1782

With all my heart I wish you many happy returns on your name-day. I regret that I'm not celebrating it together with you. Nonetheless, I wish you well and, most of all, good health. Of my customary friendship toward you please do not doubt in the least, just as I in equal measure rely on your attachment to me even more than stone walls. Your letter of 19 September from Kherson has been delivered to my hands.[1] The description of Ochakov's poor condition, which you observed from Kinburn, fully reflects that empire's concern for the common and private good to which it has belonged till now.[2] How dare that puny town put on airs before the young Colossus of Kherson! I shall gladly receive the plans for Kinburn's new fortification, and I am ready to support its completion by any means. Forced to fight against nature, Peter the First faced more obstacles with his establishments and buildings in the Baltic than we do in Kherson. But had he not carried them out, then we would be lacking in many of the means that we have made use of for Kherson itself. For the building of the fleet there, I have ordered that carpenters from the Okhtensky suburb, and from Olonchan, be found and sent there in groups. I'll let you know how many they're able to find. I gather from Veselitsky's letters from the Petrovsky fortress that soon after you sent your letter you had a meeting with the Khan. As a result of your good instructions Bahadir Girey and Arslan Girey[3] will melt away like wax before a fire, together with their partisans and protectors. That the Tatars are herding their cattle in the shadows of our fortresses, I dare say that I was the first to look upon this with favor and, what is more, even before the war I always encouraged gentle treatment of them through my instructions and have not placed restrictions on them, as was done in former times. People are saying here that the Turks will not permit a war, but I say: cela se peut.[4]

According to the latest reports, it seems they are in a pinch. The courier says that along his entire route there was not a single town nor a single fortress that was not locked up as a result of the convulsions taking place inside every one of these towns and fortresses.[5]

The Prince of Württemberg[6] arrived today and will visit me tomorrow. Farewell, my true friend. Katia,[7] your niece, is better, but she still has some boils.

---

1. This letter has not been found.

2. Potemkin left St. Petersburg for the south on 1 September 1782. He reached Kherson on 16 September. After visiting the fortress of Kinburn on the Liman, he rode to meet Shagin Girey at the Petrovsky fortress (now Berdiansk).

3. The khan's brothers, who had led the revolt against him. They were abandoned by the rebels and later captured by Russian troops.

4. "it is possible."

5. The courier sent by Bulgakov testified to the unrest in many Turkish towns.

6. Prince Frederick William of Württemberg (1754–1816) was a brother of Grand Duke Paul's second wife, Grand Duchess Maria Fyodorovna (*née* Sophia Dorothea) (1759–1828), whom Paul had married on 26 September 1776. He entered Russian service and was awarded numerous honors before being banished for his brutal treatment of his wife.

7. Yekaterina Skavronskaia was pregnant at the time, and so her illness was of significant concern.

259. POTEMKIN TO CATHERINE

[Before 14 December 1782][1]

If only the Emperor[2] had ordered his Minister at the Porte as we had ours simply to insist that the Porte honor the Khan in no other way than as an absolute Sovereign and as fully independent of their court,[3] especially since the objections were incorrectly raised and were nothing but mere fabrications. Moreover, as they are by no means in the vicinity of the Porte, they cannot be any disturbance.

Given the recognition of the Khan as independent, any joint decree with him will be forceful. It would be inopportune to compel the Austrians to discuss, through the aid of the Porte, conceding to us the harbor of Akhtiar,[4] for this will create more suspicion than benefit. In this way we shall surely only create suspicion before we need to. Moreover, it is better not to involve the Turks in the Khan's affairs so that they don't even entertain the thought of becoming lords in the Tatar domain.

Your Most Gracious Majesty, I always remind you of matters as they are and of where you need all your perspicacity so as to place all possible conditions in your control.

If you do not seize [the Crimea] right now there will come a time when everything that we might now receive for free, we shall obtain for a high price. Pray consider the following.

With its geographic position, the Crimea cuts across our borders. Whether caution must be exercised with the Turks along the Bug or in the area of the Kuban lands—in both instances we must take the Crimea into account. So it is quite obvious why the Turks find the present Khan troublesome: he does not allow them to come into our lands, into our very heart, so to speak, by way of the Crimea.

So now imagine that the Crimea is yours and that wart on our nose is no more. The state of our borders suddenly becomes excellent: along the Bug the Turks share a border with us, and so must conduct business directly with us themselves, and not through others. Their every step there will be visible. In the Kuban lands, in addition to the local fortresses supplied with troops, the Don Host, with its large numbers, is always at the ready there.

The allegiance of the inhabitants of the New Russia province will then be beyond doubt. Navigation upon the Black Sea will be unrestricted. Pray take note that otherwise your ships will find it difficult to leave port, and even more difficult to return. And what is more, we shall rid ourselves of the difficulty of maintaining fortresses now located at distant points in the Crimea.

Your Most Gracious Majesty! My infinite zeal for you compels me to say: scorn the envy that is incapable of impeding you. You are bound to raise the glory of Russia. Consider, who was ever rebuked for having acquired something? France took Corsica, and the Austrians took more from the Turks in Moldavia without a war than we. There is no power in Europe that would not be willing to seize parts of Asia, Africa, and America for itself. Acquiring the Crimea can neither strengthen nor enrich you. It can only secure peace. This would be a powerful blow—against whom? The Turks. And this obliges you even more to do it. Believe me, with this acquisition you will achieve immortal glory such that no other Sovereign in Russia has ever had. This glory will pave the way to still another even greater glory: with the Crimea will also come supremacy over the Black Sea. Upon you depends whether the path of the Turks is to be blocked and whether they are to survive or to perish.

Reward the Khan with whatever you see fit in Persia; he'll be happy.[5] He'll deliver the Crimea to you this winter, and the inhabitants will freely present their request for this. As glorious as the acquisition, so much will be the shame and reproach heaped upon you by posterity should you not act. With each difficulty they will say: yes, she could have, but didn't want to or let the opportunity slip through her fingers. Should meekness be your strength, then there need be a paradise in Russia. Kherson in the Tauride! From you piety flowed to us. Now watch how Catherine the Second introduces to you anew the meekness of Christian rule.

---

1. Written after Potemkin's return to St. Petersburg from Kherson in October 1782 and before Catherine's secret order to Potemkin on annexing the Crimea composed 14 December 1782.

2. Joseph II.

3. Despite recognizing the Crimean Khanate as independent in the Treaty of Kuchuk Kainardji (1774), the Turks had continued to meddle in the khanate's affairs.

4. During the revolt of 1782, the khan had proposed ceding Akhtiar (the future site of Sevastopol) to Russia. Potemkin, then pushing Catherine to annex all of the Crimea, did not want to consider the question of taking just Akhtiar.

5. Shagin Girey expressed interest in being made ruler over some land along the Caspian Sea which then belonged to Persia.

260. POTEMKIN TO CATHERINE

[February–March 1783]

Enclosed is a roster of troops for the territories bordering Sweden from which Your Majesty may see the degree to which its numbers make it sufficient against a state whose entire military forces total forty thousand.

Till there be future need, send nothing more than one corps volant to the Swedish border, which should be stationed together with regiments of the Finnish division along that border. I see no need to arm ourselves against the King of Prussia. His feints will not be directed against us, however, there is a chance he will in fact set his sites on Danzig. This will certainly wake up the Emperor, and we shall buy some time.

But were the King of Prussia to try to seize Poland instead of Danzig, then rouse the Poles, directing against him part of Saltykov's corps and the remaining regiments in Russia; a force will be put together that, together with the Austrian troops, will be charged with preventing him from taking any land from Poland.

Our dealings with the Turks will not come to a halt: Prince Repnin's corps is holding them back along the border at Khotin and Bender. I shall establish a detachment on the Bug, and both of these units will be used for defensive purposes. We'll put off the siege of Ochakov for the time being, but we'll occupy the Crimea, hold on to, and secure its borders. And we shall make the biggest possible demonstration of force with the Kuban and Caucasus Corps and in this way force the Porte to concern itself with that side. Arrange the fleet for the summer so that it is facing Stockholm, and make the naval preparations as deceptively as possible. You don't need to keep an eye on the Swedish King, but tell His Majesty that although at another time you would consider military camps near your borders amusing, in current circumstances this smacks of a provocation. Declare to him in all seriousness that you will henceforth not fail to use everything necessary to rid yourself of such troubles.

Putting the Little Russian forces into the best possible order for combat will in no small way serve to deter our ill-wishers. According to your wish, I shall soon complete this matter, as well as matters concerning the uniforms, consoling myself in advance that I shall, of course, receive Your Majesty's approbation.

261. POTEMKIN TO CATHERINE

[March–April 1783]

On the Clothing and Arming of the Forces

Executing Your Imperial Majesty's Royal will concerning the fitting out of the chevaliers in the most advantageous manner for soldiers, I did everything possible to avoid excess and, in attiring his person, still gave him, however, everything that might serve to maintain his health and to protect him against foul weather. Presenting this for Your Royal approval, I can assure Your Imperial Majesty, and time itself will show, that such care on your behalf will serve as eternal proof of your motherly charity. Freed from torment, the Russian Army will not cease to offer up prayers. The soldier will be healthier and, having lost his foppish fetters, of course, more agile and more courageous.

In former times in Europe, when every man who could went off to war and fought with cold steel as was then the custom of battle, each burdened himself with metal armor according to his wealth. Such protection extended even to horses. Upon undertaking distant campaigns and forming themselves into squadrons, they then began to lighten themselves. Full armor was replaced by partial and finally even that was reduced to the point where in the cavalry all that remained of that gothic gear was the breastplate and a casque on the hat and, in the infantry, insignia—and then only on the officers. Since in those days they fought more hand-to-hand, so such protection offered significant defense, most especially against spears, and thus this protection was respected for good reason. Over time this respect developed into a type of military pedantry that in turn lent value even to those accouterments that were in no way protective. But since everything seemed light in comparison with that metal gear, along with the change in equipment a multitude of superfluous and absurd things were introduced.

When the military discipline was introduced to Russia, foreign officers arrived with the pedantry of that time. And our officers, who did not know the true worth of military equipment, considered everything sacred and mysterious. It seemed to them that such discipline consisted of pigtails, hats, flaps, cuffs, manuals of the rifle and the like. Occupying themselves with such nonsense, even now at the present day they still do not know well the most important things, such as how to march, to put together different formations and to execute facings. Regarding the proper working order of the rifle, they prefer a good buffing and polishing to readiness. And they are barely able to shoot. In a word, the clothing and munitions of our troops are such that it would be almost impossible to imagine anything that could oppress the soldier more, especially since he, after having been taken from the peasantry, must almost at the age of 30 become familiar with narrow boots, a multitude of garters, a tight under-garment and a mass of things that shorten his life.

The beauty of the military uniform follows from its consistency and from the correspondence between things and their usage: clothes should serve the soldier as cover, not as a burden. All foppishness must be rooted out, for it is the fruit of luxury, requires much time, means, and servants, which a soldier cannot have. For this reason I submit in order the following proposals on those elements that comprise his munitions.

The tricorn is a good-for-nothing piece of attire. It does not cover the head and, with its ends sticking out in all directions, always puts the soldier in danger as he tries not to crumple it; it makes it particularly difficult to lay one's head down and, being three-cornered, impedes turning it around, and, what is more, it does not protect the ears against extreme cold.

The caftan and camisole with sleeves. As these are not worn at the same time, one of them must be superfluous. The cut of the caftan affords great opportunity to make it in various styles, consequently there can be no uniformity.

In the cavalry the breeches are buckskin and they must be worn for a long time. Thus, in order to preserve them the soldier must make another pair of breeches from cloth at his own expense, which constitutes an unbearable and unjust expense. Moreover, cleaning them and the difficulty of putting them on cause the men great trouble. In the winter they are cold, and in the summer, hot. One cannot wear linen clothing beneath them. Buckskin clothing is no longer necessary. In olden times the men wore it since they used metal armor, and since buckskin could stand up better than cloth, so it was preferred.

The boots are made so narrow that they are quite difficult just to put on, and getting out of them is even more difficult, especially when they get wet. What is more, there are so many garters to keep them taut and so much buffing to make them shine!

A sword is an unnecessary burden for a foot soldier. It is a difficult weapon to use, and everyone's primary concern with it is how to put it on in the most comfortable manner so that one can march and move about more freely. Many armies do not use swords in the infantry, but carry bayonets.

The Hungarian saddle is the best of all saddles. Proof of this is that all nations that ride use it: the Hungarians, Tatars, Circassians, Cossacks and Poles. They are light and do not injure the horses at all. They can be made in the regiments and are less expensive than the old ones.

On the dressing of the hair. Curling one's hair, powdering it, weaving braids—is this really the business of a soldier? They have no valets. What need do they have of curls? Everyone must agree that it is healthier to wash one's head and comb one's hair than to burden it with powder, grease, flour, hairpins and braids. The soldier's toilet must be so—once he's up, he's ready to go. If one could only count how many canings have been given out in the regiments because of this foppishness and how many courageous souls have departed for the other world from this! Can one forgive the fact that the keeper of the Fatherland's safety has been dispirited by the fancies that originated with feather-heads and oft reckless persons too?

The soldiers' usage of curls and braids is attended by the following disadvantages: 1. It uselessly deprives them of time and exhausts them, for when a detachment is on watch the men usually need 6 hours to help each other do their hair, and 12 are necessary when a squadron or an entire regiment is called to formation. They are bothered with this the entire night and do not get any sleep, as a result of which an inescapable neglect of other necessary repairs inevitably follows. As they have thus passed the night in exhaustion, they have neither time nor strength to tend to their other affairs, for example, cleaning and feeding their horses. If they do not neglect this duty, then, not being fortified with sleep, they are weak, sluggish and largely unable to perform those actions that require vitality, liveliness and strength.

2. It demands a ruinous expenditure from poor soldiers who, already in a position of great want as a result of their small salary, must still spend at least 1 ruble 5 kopecks of it yearly on powder, pomade and hair ribbons.

Cloth breeches are preferable to buckskin in that cloth ones are intended to be worn for only one year, whereas buckskin are for 4 years, and so those in the lower ranks are compelled to replace them with cloth ones, buying them with their own pay, which costs each soldier no less than 60 kopecks a year. In autumn and in rainy weather buckskin breeches are a great nuisance, especially newly fitted ones. Moreover, in winter they provide no warmth at all. Buckskin breeches are more costly for the soldiers since not only must they often be treated with ocher, which costs at least 20 kopecks a year, but what is more, it is necessary to keep about three pairs of boot-stockings along with them, which costs at least 30 kopecks a year, and the new-style cloth breeches require nothing of the sort.

Wide boots and socks or puttees have the following advantages over narrow boots and stockings: 1. In case one's feet get wet or damp with sweat, at the first convenient moment one can quickly kick them off, wipe the feet dry with the puttee and, after wrapping them up again with the dry end, soon put one's boots back on and thus protect them from dampness and chills. But in narrow boots and stockings there is no way this can be done as they are inconvenient to take off and are impossible to put back on freely. Besides, it is not always possible to change or dry out the stockings, and so the poor soldiers, whose feet are continually wet, frequently suffer from colds and other illnesses.

2. Since they do not find it necessary to bind their feet tightly, as with narrow boots, the soldiers can both walk more freely and withstand greater labor while on their feet, and what is more, blood circulation is not cut off.

If all of these very obvious inconveniences in the uniform and in other elements are corrected, then the soldier, beyond the many other advantages, will be left with up to 2 rubles more of his pay than now.

The helmet, in addition to its overall advantage and greater utility in relation to the hat, is also to be preferred since it gives the soldier a comely appearance and is an item of apparel that is characteristic of the military.[1]

---

1. Potemkin's suggestions were approved by the empress in a decree on 4 April.

262. CATHERINE TO POTEMKIN

14 April 1783. Good Friday

Mon Ami. J'ai reçu hier une lettre de l'Empereur dont je Vous envoye copie, c'est la réponse à ma dernière, j'ai ordonné de Vous envoyer un résumé de tout le bavardage de Cobenzl. Je ne fais aucune réflexion sur tout cela parce que je suis très fermement résolué de ne compter sur personne que sur nous-même.

Quand le gâteau sera cuit chacun prendra l'appétit.[1]

I rely on my ally as little as I fear and respect the French thunder or, better said, summer lightning. I regret that I've not seen a single line from you since Narva. Please don't leave me without news of yourself and of affairs so that I may be informed of everything and shan't worry unnecessarily. Be well and do write more often.

Aleksandr Dmitrievich[2] begs his compliments and goes to the post every day to ask whether there are any letters. Is Tatiana Vasilievna[3] well? Adieu, mon cher Ami, je Vous souhaite santé et bonheur.[4] My best wishes to you on the approaching holiday.

---

1. "My friend. I received yesterday a letter from the Emperor which I am sending you a copy of; it is the response to my last letter. I have ordered that you be sent a summary of all of Cobenzl's twaddle. I am not making any mention of all this since I am very firmly resolved not to rely on anyone but myself.

Once the cake is baked everyone's appetite will be whetted." In a letter from 27 March (8 April) 1783, Joseph II expressed Austria's support against the Porte, although after Russia made known to the European courts its intention of annexing the Crimea (19 April 1783), Austrian minister Cobenzl, acting on his government's instructions, wavered on the question of Austrian support. Catherine notes that once they have taken the Crimea, then the other powers will want in on the spoils.

2. Lanskoy.

3. The youngest of Potemkin's nieces, Tatiana Vasilievna Engelhardt (1767–1841), became a maid-of-honor in 1781. She departed St. Petersburg along with her uncle in April 1783 in order to visit her sister Aleksandra Branicka, who had recently given birth to a son, at her estate of Belaia tserkov.

4. "Farewell, my dear friend, I wish you health and happiness."

263. POTEMKIN TO CATHERINE

22 April [1783]. Dubrovna

Your Majesty! The enclosed copy of the Emperor's letter[1] doesn't show much firmness, but believe me, he will speak differently, just as you correctly guess, once your proposals are put into action. That sneaky Kaunitz[2] is acting just like a snake in the grass trying to create a new political system, but they are all tied up by France now, as if caught in its pincers, and so don't dare break with it, even though this may be to their benefit. They are also attempting to instigate a quarrel between you and the Prussian King, and this is their main goal. I think that their ignorance of our movements is tormenting all of them. Matushka, take up the mantle of strength in your struggle against all these endeavors, and especially against the Bourbons both here and abroad.[3] Whatever happens will be nothing more than an empty gesture, for in fact they too will all want to seize something. Do not rely on the Emperor for too much, however, it is necessary to continue acting friendly toward him. Still, there really is no great need of his help anyway, we just don't want him to impede matters.

Be assured, my beloved matushka, that I shall not miss any opportunity to further your advantage and shall always act with the ardor that fills my heart. I shall soon be in a position from where I'll inform you without interruption of everything that is happening. I received reports from the Crimea while on the road, but there was nothing important in them, nor anything worth reporting, except that there is no pasturage and so it is difficult to move the cavalry regiments. But I do hope there will be some soon. We had a long winter this year.

Time will prove to you how wisely you acted in not sending the fleet.[4]

Farewell, matushka, I kiss your tender hands.

I remain till death your most loyal servant

Prince Potemkin

Say thanks to Aleksandr Dmitrievich.[5]

---

1. See Letter 262n1.

2. Statesman Prince Wenzel Anton von Kaunitz-Rietberg (1711–1794) directed Austrian foreign policy for most of the second half of the century. He played a major role in the Diplomatic Revolution (1756) that led to the Austro-French alliance and later supported an alliance with Russia as an obstacle to Prussian expansion.

3. France opposed the annexation. Potemkin paints domestic opponents of annexation as supporters of France.

4. In a letter from March 1783, Potemkin had recommended to Catherine that the Baltic fleet be sent to the Archipelago to engage the Turkish fleet, as had been successfully done in the First Russo-Turkish War, and so distract them from the Crimea. The fleet, however, was never sent.

5. Lanskoy.

264. CATHERINE TO POTEMKIN

From Tsarskoe Selo. 4 May 1783

Upon receiving your last [letter] of 22 April from Dubrovna, I became so terribly ill with a pain in my cheek and a fever that I was forced to take to my bed and have some blood let. But I recovered just as suddenly as I had been taken ill, and the worst of the illness ended with colic on the third day. So the Tsaritsa was healed without any medicine, much as it is written in the "Tale of Fevei."[1]

I already wrote you that I received two letters from the Emperor that are again in a different tone. I don't rely upon him in the least, and he won't cause any trouble. I am not paying the least heed to the Bourbons here and abroad, but I think war is unavoidable. We are having wonderful, warm weather, and judging by this I suppose even where you are the pasturage is ripening. The order has been given in Little Russia that the tax be paid according to souls.[2] It would not be bad to issue such orders also in the territories of the Poltava and Mirgorod Regiments that are attached to the province of New Russia, while excluding the new settlements, which have been given years of preferential treatment.

I have ordered that Tutolmin[3] be released to you. Farewell, my true friend. Please be as certain of my absolute friendship for you as I am of your loyalty to me. Farewell, be well and merry, and may you enjoy success in all things.

---

1. Catherine was the anonymous author of "Tale of the Tsarevich Fevei" (1783), which was written for her two grandsons, Alexander and Constantine. In the story, one Reshemysl (Mr. Resolute), supposedly representing Potemkin, sends someone to heal the sick tsaritsa.

2. Throughout the 1770s and 1780s, Catherine instituted a number of major administrative reforms. As part of her program to replace local practices with a uniform, nationwide system of laws, Catherine recommended taking away from Little Russia (left-bank Ukraine) the special advantages it had enjoyed due to its status as a border territory.

3. The former governor of the Tver province, Timofei Ivanovich Tutolmin (1740–1809) was appointed governor of the newly created (upon Potemkin's recommendation) province of Yekaterinoslav ("Catherine's Glory") out of the former provinces of New Russia and Azov.

265. POTEMKIN TO CATHERINE

11 May [1783]. Kherson

Your Majesty. Since arriving in Kherson I've not been able to make any sense of matters at the Admiralty[1] and am now dog-tired. Everything has been neglected, there are no orderly records for anything. All the other work has been done just as carelessly. The high cost of the contracts and the carelessness of the contractors has resulted in a great loss of money and time. I have ordered Vice Admiral Klokachev[2] to establish a commission to put matters in order. Not one person charged with overseeing things was at his post, not even the captain in charge of the port. They had all been removed, and everything was in the hands of Hannibal's secretary, Prince Shakhmatov,[3] whom he had taken away with him leaving behind here not a soul with any experience to keep on eye out. When you issued your edict to the College of the Admiralty to build seven ships this year, he reported to the college that they would be ready. It now turns out they didn't even prepare enough wood for the ships, and much of what was prepared has rotted. I have ordered matters to be repaired and to find out who the contractors are, and shall later send a detailed report on everything I uncover.

My zeal and strength will, of course, suffice to repair everything as much as is possible. I only request that you be so gracious as to note how matters were up till now and how they are being managed under my care.

I sent instructions to our superior officer in the Crimea warning him about his indecision.[4] Since then, nothing significant has happened. I shall ride there myself in the coming days and, whatever happens, shall report without fail.

I greatly lament having heard nothing of you for a long time, my beloved matushka. I pray God that you are well. I kiss your tender hands and faithfully remain

till death
your most loyal servant
Prince Potemkin

[. . .]

---

1. The Admiralty in Kherson had been established to build ships and to oversee the requirements of all Russian naval forces on the Black Sea.

2. Rear Admiral Fedot Alekseevich Klokachev (d. 1783) was the ranking naval officer on the Black Sea. Under his command a detachment of Russian warships occupied the harbor of Akhtiar in May 1783.

3. Possibly Prince Nikolai Shakhmatov, in state service from 1756.

4. Potemkin secretly ordered Lieutenant-General Count Anton de Balmen (1741–1790) to prevent any situation from arising that would delay annexation and to try to convince the khan to leave for Russia. A veteran of the First Russo-Turkish War, Balmen had led troops in the 1777–1778 invasion of the Crimea and again in the autumn of 1782.

266. POTEMKIN TO CATHERINE

16 May [1783]. Kherson

Your Majesty. Without my having to ask, you have bestowed all your favors upon me. Do not now refuse me that one which I consider most necessary, namely that you preserve your health.

Once the Khan departs the Crimean affairs will soon end.[1] I am trying to get them to request subjecthood themselves since I think, matushka, this will be more to your liking. I am now stationing regiments, which had wintered far away, near the Crimea so that the peninsula can be more reliably seized.

Oh, matushka, how confused are matters here with the Admiralty and how terribly have its resources been pilfered. I had been very satisfied with Klokachev till now. Believe me, they began working only once I arrived. I attribute all the disorder to nothing but laziness, nevertheless it is an unpardonable laziness and carelessness exceeding all limits. You will be astonished to learn that for five years he did not once visit a single work site, and his secretary, Prince Shakhmatov, a downright swindler, has plundered everything and left no accounts. I am fighting like mad with this administrative region. The fortress and buildings are no less neglected, but this can be quickly corrected.

The heat here is unbearable, especially since there is no cover. They hadn't the sense to plant any trees. I have ordered some planted. I wrote to Bezborodko[2] of the great need of affairs so that he can inform you. I have established commissions for both the city and Admiralty administrative regions to reckon and count the sums.

Farewell, my beloved matushka, milady. God grant you health, which I wish for with the purest heart.

Your most loyal servant
Prince Potemkin

[. . .]

Just like a profiteer, the Prussian King[3] is serenading the French and wooing them with all the possibilities before them. I wish he would succeed in convincing the King to send French troops here. We would give them a good hiding in true Russian fashion.

---

1. Shagin Girey refused to leave the Crimea as he waited to see how the Porte and the European powers would react to the news of the annexation. The former khan complained to Potemkin of his poverty and requested a pension and other privileges.

2. Aleksandr Andreevich Bezborodko (1747–1799) began his service in the chancellery of Pyotr Rumiantsev, then governor-general of Little Russia. Recommended by him, along with Pyotr Zavadovsky, to the empress in 1775, Bezborodko became one of Catherine's secretaries and was soon one of her most trusted advisors. In the 1780s, Bezborodko formed part of a triumvirate together with Catherine and Potemkin that consulted on and decided the most pressing matters of state. Joseph II awarded him the title of prince in 1785.

3. Frederick II (the Great) of Prussia (1712–1786, reigned from 1740). Prussia was then try-ing to convince France to block Russia's moves in the Crimea. France was unable to enlist support for intervention from Britain, and gave up all hope of action upon learning of the secret Austro-Russian alliance.

267. POTEMKIN TO CATHERINE

Kherson. 28 May [1783]

Your Majesty. My not having any news of you for so long troubles me con-siderably. God forbid that you are forgetting me. At present the Khan has still not departed, which prevents me from publishing the manifestoes. The Tatars will not be free to act till he leaves the Crimea. Proclaiming them with him still there would be interpreted by the people as a ruse and as efforts undertaken at his request. So I'll wait another week, and then act. Thanks to the strictest measures, the plague has not broken out again.

You cannot imagine, matushka, how many troubles I have in this land from the Admiralty alone. I've still not been able to set matters right. There's no rhyme or reason to anything. Much money has been spent, but I'll never learn where it's gone. The building of ships has been going suc-cessfully since my arrival. I've sent for more wood, which there is not enough of. Do me the favor of sending me the required number of offi-cers, a list of which I've enclosed. There is a shortage of blacksmiths here. I sent to Tula for some. In addition, mistakes have been made throughout the province. The governor[1] here has greatly eased my troubles, and I have now sent him where he is most needed. One thing lightens my bur-den—that is the purchasing of grain, which is inexpensive and has been successful. [. . .]

Farewell, beloved matushka, I am fully prepared to leave for the Crimea. I await the Khan's departure at any moment.

I kiss your tender hands.

Your most loyal servant
Prince Potemkin

---

1. Apparently Tutolmin, then visiting Kherson.

268. CATHERINE TO POTEMKIN

From Tsarskoe Selo. 30 May 1783

I received yesterday your letter of 16 May from Kherson, and, in response to your request, I inform you that I am well, however, I was so ill in early May that on the first of the month instead of going for a walk, I had to lie down and have some blood let.

Along with your letter I received from Vienna a courier with a letter from Joseph the Second, a copy of which I have enclosed.[1] From it you'll see, my true and intelligent friend, that your prophecy has come true: l'appétit leur vient en mangeant.[2]

May God grant that the Tatar or, better said, Crimean affair ends soon. I think the less you tarry now the better, so that the Turks aren't able to hinder this enterprise in whatever way possible should they learn of it before it has been completed. Don't pay any attention now to the Tatars' request, and according to Pavel Sergeevich's letters the Nogais are beginning to discuss becoming subjects anyway.[3]

I regret that work on the military and civilian buildings in Kherson is not as would be desired. I hope that through diligence everything will be corrected. The entire month of May here has been so nice that we could wish for nothing better.

[. . .]

Adieu, mon Ami, portés Vous bien. Sasha[4] begs his compliments and will write to you himself.

You'll receive the instructions that have been prepared in response to your various representations. On the eighth of June I'm leaving for Finland for ten days where I'll meet with the Swedish King in Fredrikshamn.[5]

---

1. Joseph wrote on 8 (19) May congratulating Catherine on taking the Crimea, of which she had recently informed him, without firing a single shot. He lamented the greater means at her disposal and expressed his support against the Porte.

2. "their appetite grows with eating."

3. Potemkin had sent Pavel Potemkin, in command of the Caucasus Corps, to the Kuban to subjugate the Nogai hordes. At the same time, the prince ordered Aleksandr Vasilievich Suvorov (1730–1800) and his troops to act in concert with Potemkin's in Taman and the southern Kuban. One of Russia's greatest military commanders, Suvorov later served under Potemkin in the Second Russo-Turkish War. Their names have long been linked together, usually to the detriment of Potemkin, who has unfairly been portrayed as having been jealous of Suvorov's military success and having sought to harm his career.

4. Lanskoy.

5. Gustav III hoped the annexation of the Crimea would lead to war between Russia and Turkey. A distracted Russia would allow him to attack Denmark and so regain some of Sweden's lost Baltic territories. In the spring, he proposed a meeting with Catherine to discuss the possibility of an alliance that would free his hand to act. For her part, Catherine agreed to the meeting as a way to communicate to the Porte that they could not count on Sweden's support against Russia.

269. POTEMKIN TO CATHERINE

1 June [1783]. Kherson

Your Majesty! The Khan has already begun sending the carts with his belongings to the Petrovsky fortress. And then he'll soon be in Kherson himself. The reason I am not promulgating the manifestoes while he is still there is that the Tatars themselves say that they cannot announce their desire to become Russian subjects until the Khan has departed and they are certain he has given up the Khanate. The fact that they subjugated themselves voluntarily will be all the more beneficial to your affairs since then no one at all will make threatening noises about how they were forced to become subjects. I am not failing to take every last thing into account in order to prepare the peoples' minds for this.[1]

Repairs to the fortress are beginning in Ochakov; little by little troops are arriving. I have now begun to bring Kinburn into defensive readiness, which due to its location had not been entrusted with any corps for protection, and so it must be prepared for a lengthy defense.[2]

The Admiralty here doesn't have a single kopeck, and so even the workers can't be paid, though there is some money to pay the carpenters. I have established a commission to investigate the expenditures. This cannot be done quickly, however, and, what's more, there will be little profit from it as well. They'll find only high prices, but no money. In order to keep the work going, which has now begun with great zeal, be so good as to support it. Regarding the town's buildings, these can be adequately mended with their own funds.

[. . .]

Repeating my request to supply the Kherson Admiralty with money and men, I report that the first ship to be launched will be "Catherine's Glory." Permit me to give it this name, which I take upon myself to warrant by making it a reality.[3]

I kiss your tender hands.

Your most loyal servant
Prince Potemkin

I beg my compliments to Aleksandr Dmitrievich.[4]

---

1. Potemkin worked hard to make it appear the annexation had been a response to the expressed desire of the local populace.

2. In response to the Crimean affairs, the Turks were fortifying their fortress of Ochakov, located directly across the Liman from Kinburn, which belonged to Russia.

3. The sixty-six-gun ship of "Catherine's Glory" line was launched from the Kherson shipyards in September 1783.

4. Lanskoy.

270. CATHERINE TO POTEMKIN

From Tsarskoe Selo. 5 June 1783

Two days ago a special messenger from the Swedish King arrived with a note for me that he had safely arrived in Åbo after 22 hours at sea. And

then yesterday he sent another messenger with word that while inspecting his troops on horseback near Tavastehus, he fell off his horse, which
had jumped unexpectedly after being spooked by a cannon shot, and His
Majesty broke his left arm in two between his shoulder and elbow. The
messenger says that the King was carried from the spot on a chair to
Tavastehus. He wrote to me himself with his right hand, asking that I
agree to postpone the meeting till June twentieth; his physician is hopeful that by then he can come meet me with his arm bandaged. I sent
him my regrets and a gentleman-of-the-bedchamber to inquire after his
health, and agreed to the postponement. Pardi, mon Ami, voilà un
héros bien maladroit, que de tomber comme cela dans une manoeuvre
devant ses troupes.[1]

I've received, my dear friend, your letter of 18 May. To satisfy the
Khan's wish regarding the light-blue ribbon and at the same time to
preserve everything that he and I must preserve, I've ordered a light-
blue ribbon prepared which is to be worn over the shoulder with an
oval medallion, upon which, amid diamonds, is the word "Loyalty"
taken from the inscription of the Order of St. Andrew.[2] I have also ordered a diamond star with the very same inscription. Yet for all that, he
must be told that neither can he wear a cross nor can I give him one
because he is not a Christian. Nevertheless, I am giving him the light-
blue ribbon together with the inscription of the Order of St. Andrew
and the privileges of that order and the rank of lieutenant-general. I
impatiently await from you news of the conclusion of the Crimean affair. Do occupy it before the Turks manage to stir up resistance against
you. I've ordered that Pavel Sergeevich and you be sent the presents—
furs and things—that you requested.[3]

[. . .]

Field Marshal Rumiantsev has written to me requesting the General
Staff, engineers and additional monies. I ordered that his letters be communicated to you. He fears the Turks will forestall him. Since war has not
been declared, so it seems everything can be gotten ready in time.[4]

Adieu, mon Ami, portés Vous bien. [. . .]

Zorich was to come here, but I sent word to him that till a decision on
the Zanovich affair has been made he's not to appear before my eyes.[5] He
then asked if he could go to Sesvegen, which I permitted him.

---

1. "Good Lord, my friend, this is a rather clumsy hero to fall down in this manner while
maneuvering before his troops."

2. Shagin Girey had asked Potemkin to communicate to Catherine his desire to receive Russia's highest order—St. Andrew. A special star and medallion devoid of all Christian symbols
were prepared for him.

3. Potemkin had requested the gifts to give to members of the Crimean nobility.

4. The aging Rumiantsev was then rusticating on his Ukrainian estate. Despite Catherine's reassurances, he was quite certain war would soon break out. To calm him she sent 100,000 rubles and saw that all his demands were met.

5. Years of extravagant living on his Shklov estate had led Semyon Zorich deep into debt. A pair of Dalmatian adventurers posing as noblemen, Mark and Hannibal Zanovichi, offered a way out: they set up a press to make counterfeit bills on his property. By the time they were all caught, some one million rubles had been printed. Zorich was prohibited from visiting St. Petersburg, and the Zanovichi brothers were imprisoned for five years.

271. CATHERINE TO POTEMKIN

From Tsarskoe Selo. 9 June 1783

I received today from the hands of Aleksandr Dmitrievich your letter from the 28th of last month. I hope, my little Prince, that my letters have now reached your hands, and when you deign to write : "God forbid that you are forgetting me," that is what we call "to write rubbish." Not only do I often remember you, but often regret and grieve as well that you're there and not here with me, for I'm lost without you. I beg you in every possible way: don't tarry over the occupation of the Crimea. I am now frightened by the threat the plague poses to you and everyone else. For God's sake, do be careful and order all possible measures be taken against it. I very much regret that you and Field Marshal Rumiantsev were not able to meet somewhere. All the world's troubles he bears now on his shoulders: he requests the general staff, engineers, more money, and news from Bulgakov. He also fears being forestalled by the Turks and something being overlooked. Seeing this, I've ordered everything possible sent to him. Let's hope this helps, or it'll all prove a waste. I believe that you have many troubles, but know that you and I are not vexed by them. Word that the shipbuilding is proceeding swiftly is very pleasing to my ear. I'll try to send the required number of men. [. . .]

The Swedish King broke his arm at his camp at Tavastehus, and so our meeting in Fredrikshamn has been postponed till the 20th of this month. Adieu, mon Ami.

[. . .]

272. POTEMKIN TO CATHERINE

13 June [1783]. Kherson

Your Majesty! God alone knows how exhausted I am. Every day I hasten to the Admiralty to force the men there to keep working, and I am beset by a multitude of other concerns as well: the fortification of Kinburn, supplying provisions everywhere, keeping the troops in order and stamping out the plague, which didn't fail to appear in Kizikermen, Yelizavetgrad and even in Kherson. Precautions have been taken everywhere, however, and, thanks to God, it has been stopped. The most alarming aspects of this plague are the reports coming out of the Crimea, where it has appeared in different districts and in our hospitals. I rushed there as soon as I learned of this and took measures to separate the sick from the uninfected, and saw to it that all their clothing was fumigated and washed. I divided the sick according to their illnesses; thank God there are only five as of now. I shan't describe the beauty of the Crimea, which would take much time, leaving this for another occasion. I shall only say that Akhtiar is the best harbor in the world. Petersburg, situated upon the Baltic, is Russia's northern capital; Moscow is its central, and may Kherson of Akhtiar be my Sovereign's southern capital. Let them see which Sovereign made the best selection.

Matushka, do not be surprised that I have not yet promulgated the manifestoes. It truly hasn't been possible without first increasing the number of troops, for otherwise there would be no way to use force were it to be necessary. [. . .]

Back to the subject of shipbuilding. You will see from the list, which I'll submit following this letter, in what state of disorder everything was. In a word, the only honest man in the entire lot was one master shipwright;[1] all the rest were thieves. Admiral Klokachev truly is a solicitous man, but what can he accomplish without helpers? I earlier requested that the following men be sent here to work on the ships. Then we'll have everything we need. [. . .]

Regarding the Emperor, do not impede him. Let him take what he wants from the Turks. This will help us a good deal. And it would be a great service were he to create a diversion. I received intelligence from the consul in Bucharest that the Austrian pickets have already driven off the Moldavian frontier guards while also declaring that they intend to occupy the land. This has been communicated to the Porte.

The postal boat sent by the Kapudan Pasha[2] to Ochakov, which Bulgakov mentions, really was in Ochakov and has departed for Tsar Grad.[3] My compliments to Aleksandr Dmitrich. Farewell, beloved matushka, I kiss your tender hands.

Your loyal servant
Prince Potemkin

[. . .]
I'm leaving for the Crimea in three days.

---

1. Probably Aleksandr Semyonovich Katasanov (d. 1804), one of the main builders of the ships in the Black Sea fleet.

2. Kapudan Pasha was the title given to the grand admiral of the Ottoman navy.

3. As the Russians called Constantinople, "the city of the Caesars."

273. CATHERINE TO POTEMKIN

From Tsarskoe Selo. 13 June 1783

My true friend, I received your letters of 1 June from Kherson the day before yesterday. It is quite desirable that you occupy the Crimea as soon as possible so that our adversaries don't find a way to create any additional obstacles, though it seems vague rumors about the occupation have already reached Tsar Grad. There's no reason to consider whether the Tatars are going along with it or whether or not they are voluntarily giving in. News from everywhere confirms that the Turks are taking up arms. I have ordered that at the earliest convenience you be sent one hundred thousand rubles for your needs in Kherson. Since you did not specify a sum in your request, so I did not know how much to send for your needs there, but simply chose to send this amount. I ordered a number of men sent to the Admiralty, and hope that with this detail service will be put in good order. [. . .] Kindly do not give the ships very grand names, afin que des noms trop tot fameux ne deviennent à charge et qu'il ne soit trop difficile de remplir une pareille carriere,[1] however, as you wish with the names, ma bride en main, parce qu'il vaut mieux être que paraître et ne pas être. Adieu, mon Ami.[2]

Regarding your other requests, I refer you to the supplied instructions.

Be so good as to let me know whether the plague continues, whether it is abating or has been stopped. This frightens me. I fear its stealing into Russia again as a result of some blunder along the frontier. Farewell, be well. I've set the day after tomorrow for my departure to Fredrikshamn. I don't know how the King with his fractured arm will withstand the journey. I've sent someone to inquire. Alexander the Great was never so clumsy as to fall off his horse in front of his troops.

Sasha begs his compliments.

---

1. "so that names too soon famous do not become a burden and so that it does not become too difficult to measure up to this designation,"

2. "I give you free rein, because it is better to be than to seem and not be. Farewell, my friend."

274. CATHERINE TO POTEMKIN

29 June 1783. From Tsarskoe Selo

My true friend, best wishes on the recent holidays.[1] I returned from Fredrikshamn last Saturday where I met with the Swedish King, who suffers greatly from his broken arm. You know him, and so there's nothing to write about.[2] J'ai seulement trouvé qu'il étoit excessivement occupé de sa parure se tenant fort volontiers devant le miroir, et ne permettant à aucun officier de se présenter autrement à la Cour qu'en habit noir et ponceau et point en uniforme; ceci m'a choqué parce que selon moi il n'y a point d'habillement plus honorable et plus cher qu'un uniforme.[3]

[. . .] I shall now answer your letter of 12 June from Kherson.[4] I am quite sorry that you are exhausted; you know that I need you very, very much. So I ask that you do everything to preserve your health. Men have been and are being dispatched to the naval armory; I hope it is not a bad selection of men. The Admiral-General[5] was entrusted with this himself. Regarding all the measures you have taken to fortify Kinburn, to supply provisions everywhere and to strengthen the troops, I firmly hope that everything goes as you desire. The only thing that scares me is the plague spreading. For God's sake, don't neglect a single known precaution against it, for yourself as well as for everyone else. I sometimes also fear it may steal its way into Russia again. [. . .] Your plan for Sinop and the other places should war be declared is not bad. Word has reached me from all over that the Turks are heavily arming themselves, but their friends are holding them back from declaring war for now. Our thoughts on the Emperor are quite in agreement, as long as he isn't in the same position as in the last war. Whatever else he can give us will be of use. I'll order Mikhail Sergeevich Potemkin[6] to go to you, as you requested. I hope that the fate of the Crimea has been decided by now, for you write that you are going there.

Adieu, mon cher Ami, portés Vous bien, je Vous embrasse de tout mon coeur.[7]

Sasha begs his compliments.

---

1. Catherine's accession day (28 June).

2. Catherine and Gustav met for three days in June. The Swedish king left disappointed after Catherine rejected his proposal for an alliance.

3. "I simply found that he was excessively occupied with his dress, so very pleased to stand before the mirror, and did not permit any officer to present himself at court except in a black and crimson dress-coat and not in uniform. This shocked me, for in my opinion there is no attire more honorable and dearer than a uniform."

4. Actually from 13 June. Letter 272.

5. Grand Duke Paul was the admiral-general and president of the Naval College. Catherine entrusted him with selecting officers for the Black Sea fleet then being built.

6. The prince had recommended his nephew for the position of chief of the commissary. Mikhail Potemkin was given the office in June and was then sent to join his uncle.

7. "Farewell, my dear friend, take care of yourself. I kiss you with all my heart."

275. POTEMKIN TO CATHERINE

10 July [1783]. Camp near Karasubazaar

Your Majesty. In three days I shall congratulate you upon your acquisition of the Crimea. The entire elite has already taken the oath, and now all the others will follow. You will find even more pleasant and splendid the fact that they all gladly placed themselves under your authority. True, there were many difficulties due to the timidity of the Tatars, who feared violating the law; however, as a result of my assurances, extended to their envoys, they are now as peaceful and as cheerful as if they had lived under us forever. So far nothing has been discerned on the Turks' side. It seems to me they are afraid we might attack, and all their troops have been placed on the defensive.

In three days a courier dispatched from here will deliver detailed reports, and so I shall cut my letter short by throwing myself and all those who have labored, on whose behalf I shall intercede, at your feet. As for me, I am all worn out. For truth, I alone must put everything in motion and run to and fro. Before this I was terribly ill with spasms in Kherson and left for the Crimea while still weak. Thank God, I've now recovered. The plague surrounds the camp, but so far God protects us. Goodbye, matushka, I kiss your tender hands. Do not forget

your most loyal servant
Prince Potemkin

The Prince of Württemberg has taken up his command and serves with great enthusiasm.[1]

I beg my compliments to Aleksandr Dmitrich.

---

1. Potemkin had placed the grand duke's brother-in-law in command of a unit in Kherson.

276. CATHERINE TO POTEMKIN

From Tsarskoe Selo. 15 July 1783

You can imagine how worried I must be not having received a word from you in more than five weeks.[1] What is more, false rumors are being spread here, and I've nothing with which to refute them. I expected the Crimea would be occupied by the middle of May at the latest, and here it is the middle of July and I still don't know anything more about the situation than the Pope himself. This inevitably produces all sorts of talk that I do not find at all agreeable. I beg you in every possible way: inform me more often, afin que je reste au fil des choses: l'activité naturelle de mon esprit et de ma tête forge mille idées qui me tourmentent souvent.[2]

All sorts of tales about the plague are also making their way here. Frequent reports from you will calm my mind. I've nothing else to write. Neither I nor anyone else knows where you are. My best guess is to send this to Kherson. As always, Field Marshal Rumiantsev seeks all sorts of ways to make himself difficult.

Adieu, mon Ami, portés-Vous bien. Quand est-ce que Votre histoire de la Crimée sera une fois terminée?[3]

---

1. A slight exaggeration: the last reports Catherine had received from Potemkin were dated 14 June.

2. "so that I can remain in the course of events. The natural activity of my mind and my head fabricate a thousand ideas that often torment me."

3. "Farewell, my friend. Take care of yourself. When will your Crimean tale finally end?"

277. POTEMKIN TO CATHERINE

Camp near Karasubazaar. 16 July [1783]

Your Majesty. I request charity for the generals serving under me: for Suvorov, the Vladimir cross, and for Pavel Sergeevich as well. For Count Balmen, the Alexander cross.[1] And do not overlook Lashkarev, God knows he is a zealous man, and I tormented him a good deal.[2]

I'm now engaged in composing a topographical description of the Crimea. The villages have all been inventoried, and this only needs to be translated into Russian. I am hurrying to present everything, including the crops grown here as well as information on the harvests. I can now only report that such a fertile land can rarely be found: this year there simply won't be enough people to gather the entire harvest.

This pleasure notwithstanding, the Tatars are alarmed by a rumor begun by the Turks at Ochakov that we intend to recruit them into the army. In response I assured them that such a rumor was started by their villains and is groundless. Were you, matushka, to issue an edict freeing them from this, they would be completely put at rest. They also persistently request that they be allowed to pay tax based not on souls, but on land and on everything they produce, one tenth, that will generate much more revenue and is fairer to them. And if this is done, then believe me that the manifestoes could be sent to Anatolia, and even the people there would freely become subjects.[3]

Having compiled a table of revenues, I shall present my comments on how they must be allocated in order to please the Mohamadans, such as on the maintenance of some mosques, schools, and public fountains. This last point they consider a great blessing, and it will make them very happy should you order a large and fine one to be built in your name. And from such a bagatelle will come resounding glory that will not reflect well on the Turkish Sultan.

The Turks are presently quiet everywhere. According to reports, they are making repairs, although not intensively, and are not augmenting their garrisons. They are afraid we shall attack them. They are fortifying the passage through the Bosphorus in all manner of ways, and even in Tsar Grad the order has been given to repair the fortifications. If there is to be war, then it won't be this year. Ramadan is now approaching and ends on the twentieth of August, so not much time remains till autumn. I am not surprised by the Swedish King's affectation; what else can he do? He does well by not wearing a full-dress uniform given that theirs look more comical than serious. Matushka, I am writing some of my political observations to Bezborodko, which he will report to you.[4]

Farewell, my dear matushka.

Your most loyal servant
Prince Potemkin

My compliments to Aleksandr Dmitrievich

---

1. Commanders of the Caucasus, Kuban, and Crimean Corps that played a decisive role in the annexation, all three were decorated as Potemkin requested.

2. Sergei Lazarevich Lashkarev (1739–1814), a prominent diplomat and Russia's resident at the court of Shagin Girey, helped to convince the khan to give up the throne and leave the Crimea. He was rewarded with a village in White Russia and the rank of Councillor of the Chancellery.

3. Potemkin's recommendation for the inhabitants of the Crimea were followed.

4. Among other matters, in his note to Bezborodko, Potemkin railed against France's futile attempts to stop the annexation and instructed Catherine to remain firm in the face of any French threats.

278. CATHERINE TO POTEMKIN

From Tsarskoe Selo. 20 July 1783

After a long wait I finally received yesterday your letter, dear friend, of the 10th instant from Karasubazaar with the pleasing news that the Crimea and the two Nogai Hordes have taken the oath of allegiance. For all this, I thank you. Perhaps this time everything will pass without further trouble. I now await the courier with the detailed reports. Please assure those who have toiled that they will not be abandoned, and I'll expect representations of this from you. I only regret that you were ill and that while weak were forced to toil so. The plague scares me. God grant that you have been able to protect your men from it and to stop it in the Crimea. I'll tell the Prince of Württemberg's sister[1] that he serves with enthusiasm. We expect her to give birth at any moment now.

Sasha was so severely hurt by an English horse that he lies in bed practically motionless. He's not in any danger, however. This happened yesterday morning, exactly twenty-four hours ago now.

Adieu, mon cher et précieus Amie, portés Vous bien.

[. . .]

---

1. Grand Duchess Maria Fyodorovna.

279. CATHERINE TO POTEMKIN

From Tsarskoe Selo. 26 July 1783

As you wish I am sending Major Glazov[1] back to you and have ordered
him to present you with this short letter with which I inform you, my true
friend, that I answered your letter about the occupation of the Crimea
with the last courier. This event has altogether gladdened the public here:
seizing objects is never disagreeable to us; it's losing them we don't like.

Write me whether you have sent the light-blue ribbon to Shagin
Girey, and send me the names of the men who are worthy of being made
majors in the Izmailovsky Regiment, for Olsufiev[2] has died. [. . .] Aleksandr Dmitrievich is recovering from his unfortunate fall from his horse.
We've been waiting for the Grand Duchess to deliver any minute now
for the past month, but so far in vain.[3] Adieu, mon Ami, portés Vous
bien, I am well.

---

1. Pavel Mikhailovich Glazov, a major in the Hussars, entered Potemkin's service in May
1783. Potemkin had chosen him to deliver the news of the completion of the Crimean affairs to Catherine.

2. Major-General Fyodor Yakolevich Olsufiev had been serving in the Izmailovsky Regiment. In his letter of 29 July (this section has been excised here), Potemkin recommended
either Prince Aleksandr Ivanovich Lobanov-Rostovsky (1752–1830) or Colonel Fyodor Fyodorovich Buksgevden (1750–1811), hero of the First Russo-Turkish War, former adjutant of
Grigory Orlov, and an aide-de-camp to the empress.

3. Grand Duchess Maria Fyodorovna gave birth to a daughter, Aleksandra Pavlovna
(1783–1801), three days later.

280. POTEMKIN TO CATHERINE

Camp near Karasubazaar. 29 July [1783]

Your Majesty. I am writing my justification in a special letter and shall
here make my report on the Crimea. I am sparing no effort to put together
a detailed description, but the plague, which has sprouted in almost every
village, hampers making an accurate count of the inhabitants. This is an

unspeakably abundant and a most suitable land, both for the fleet and for trade, and for the many establishments befitting a warm climate.[1] This peninsula will be better still in every way were we to rid ourselves of the Tatars and send them away. Many means for this can be found. For truth, they are not worthy of this land, while the Kuban would make a decent home for them.[2]

Till now our neighbors here have been quiet. They are gathering their main forces near Ismail and have stationed a post near Kochibei. We shall find a way to separate them in the field from our corps stationed in Poland, which, together with a supplement from part of the regiments earlier appointed to Saltykov,[3] will constitute a good army. It will be even stronger since there will be no need to divide it, for I do not intend to advance any farther, but to maintain my grip on the places we now occupy. We need to buy time in order to strengthen the fleet. Then we shall become their masters.

Leave me and the Caucasus Corps—please spare us—under your direct command, otherwise everything will be turned upside down.[4]

After dispatching the courier I'll leave for Akhtiar to determine how best to fortify it, and shall present my opinion about that place as well as about the entire border system.

Matushka, we've never had such an engineer like Korsakov.[5] The way he finished off Kinburn it looks truly grand. We need to hold on to this man.

[. . .]

I kiss your tender hands. Farewell, beloved matushka, I was very ill upon Prince Dashkov's[6] departure, but, thank God, have recovered.

Your most loyal servant
Prince Potemkin

I beg my compliments to Aleksandr Dmitrievich.

P.S. The plague continues unabated in the Crimea, but since I have been here only one person in the Third Greek Regiment has died, and only three are ill from the disease. In Kherson every precaution has been taken. Matushka, for truth I stand guard and have a big helper in Sergei Nikolaevich Saltykov,[7] who is my orderly general. I call your attention to him as someone quite suitable for use in state affairs. He's no mollycoddle. Would you be so charitable as to make him equal to his comrades by bestowing upon him the Order of St. Anne, just as you did Vice Admiral Klokachev?

[. . .]

---

1. Despite the ever-present plague, Potemkin traveled throughout the peninsula selecting sites for the construction of fortresses and towns. He had also ordered a topographical description of the area prepared.

2. Potemkin later changed his mind and did not attempt to remove the Tatars.

3. General-in-Chief Count Ivan Petrovich Saltykov (1730–1805) was a veteran of the Seven Years' and First Russo-Turkish wars.

4. Potemkin requested that the Crimean, Caucasus, and Kuban Corps not be placed under the command of Rumiantsev, who would lead them (and so Potemkin too) in the event of war.

5. One of the best engineers in the Russian army, Nikolai Ivanovich Korsakov (1749–1788) was the chief builder of Kinburn and Kherson. He died tragically during the siege of Ochakov when, while inspecting the batteries, he slipped, plunged into a deep ditch and impaled himself on his own sword.

6. Prince Pavel Mikhailovich Dashkov (1763–1807) was an aide-de-camp to Potemkin. His mother, Princess Yekaterina Romanovna Dashkova (*née* Vorontsova) (1743–1810), was one of the most accomplished European women of the day: director of the Russian Academy of Sciences, founder and president of the Russian Academy, member of the American Philosophical Society (having been nominated by Benjamin Franklin), and author of numerous plays and articles.

7. After serving admirably in the Crimea, Major-General Sergei Saltykov, in service since 1757, retired.

281. POTEMKIN TO CATHERINE

Camp near Karasubazaar. 29 July [1783]

Your Majesty! It is true, I am to blame for not having written you, my benefactress, for a long time, and I have grieved for having kept you ignorant of my affairs for so long. However, the reason for this was that beginning on the 14th of June Count Balmen kept reassuring me with every courier that the manifestoes would be published. He dragged out matters till the last day of the month and then finally let me know that the Tatar officials had still not all assembled. I realized that their gathering depended upon their will and that he had failed to do what I had ordered him to earlier from the road with these words: "Adopt the tone of a military leader." And so, I decided to gallop there myself, and three days later I proclaimed the manifestoes despite the fact that not all had assembled. Everyone told me that the clergy would protest, and then the rabble after them, however, it turned out that the clergymen were the first to support it, and then everyone else after them.

You deigned to mention in your letter, matushka, that you had expected the Crimea to be subjugated in the middle of May, however, the orders that were given me explicitly stated that I was to undertake this at my own discretion once I deemed it appropriate. Bezborodko wrote me that should this take place in the middle of May he would consider it timely to announce this to the ministers of the foreign courts. Your Majesty, I had only then just arrived in Kherson, and the regiments could not have entered the Crimea before the middle of June, indeed only today did the last of the regiments arrive that had to come from afar. Most of the regiments had a march of seven hundred versts. And what is more, they had to cross the Dnieper and the Ingulets two, and others three, times, and the shorter crossing held up each regiment for four days. If only you knew how much I had to work to find ferries, which there were none at all of.

Your Majesty, I conduct your affairs with heartfelt desire and unlimited care. A thousand difficulties confronted me, and I surmounted all of them while struggling with the climate, with the water and with various natural shortages. Not sparing myself in the slightest and having but a small number of helpers, I had to do everything myself, and, in the midst of a large plague outbreak, I was able to procure all the necessary supplies at the least possible expense. Thanks to God's help the plague is no longer spreading—neither among the troops nor in your province, and what you write about rumors of the contagion, these are being spread by cowards who wouldn't bother to come this way even if there were no plague: they prefer to gather in Spa and Paris.

[. . .]

I shall say once more, matushka, that I am unintentionally guilty of having failed to inform you of affairs for a long time. But as conerns the occupation of the Crimea, the closer this is to autumn, the better, since then the Turks will decide in favor of war that much later and so will have less time to prepare.

I wrote to Bezborodko just what came to mind. It's not particularly clever, but it's filled throughout with zeal.[1] Farewell, Your Majesty, and be assured that as concerns my zeal for service, no one is my equal, and as concerns the disposition of my heart, I can say no one is more loyal than

your faithful servant
Prince Potemkin

---

1. A reference to the letters Potemkin wrote to Bezborodko that duplicated the ones he sent Catherine.

282. POTEMKIN TO CATHERINE

5 August [1783]. Camp near Karasubazaar

Your Majesty. There you are, my benefactress, the Georgian affairs have also been brought to an end.[1] What Sovereign has ever compiled such a brilliant epoch as you? And this is not merely splendor's luster. There is also great benefit in all this. The lands upon which Alexander and Pompey merely glanced, so to speak, you have bound to the Russian scepter, and Tauric Chersonese—the source of our Christianity, and thus our humanity as well—is now within its daughter's embrace. There is something mystical in this.

The Tatar nation was once Russia's tyrant and in more recent times its hundredfold ravager, whose might Tsar Ivan Vasilievich did fell.[2] But it was you who destroyed its root. The new border promises Russia peace,

Europe envy and the Ottoman Porte fear. Take up this trophy unstained by blood and order your historians to prepare more paper and ink.

I shall soon send another courier following this one with many representations, and for this reason I now ride to the Crimea to inspect the necessary places. I'm writing to Bezborodko some necessary remarks before the investiture of Tsar Heraclius.[3] [. . .]

I kiss your tender hands, beloved matushka, and am leaving this hour for Yenikale, though I arrived from Akhtiar but two days ago.

Your most loyal servant

Prince Potemkin

Is Aleksandr Dmitrich not ashamed to be riding on a mad horse that's already kicked him once before? I sincerely wish him relief.

---

1. On 24 July 1783, Heraclius II (1720–1798), king of Kartli-Kakheti, signed the Treaty of Georgievsk, making his lands a Russian protectorate.

2. In 1480, Tsar Ivan III (the Great) defeated Khan Ahmed, leader of the Great Horde (a remnant of the Golden Horde), on the Ugra River southwest of Moscow in a battle that marked the end of the centuries-old "Tatar yoke."

3. Following the Treaty of Georgievsk, Heraclius was invested with the marks of imperial Russian authority and received the Order of St. Andrew. Russian troops were dispatched to his lands.

283. POTEMKIN TO CATHERINE

Camp between Ak-mechet and Karasubazaar on the Buruncha. 9 August [1783]

Your Majesty. While preparing to dispatch this courier with my answer regarding Admiral Elphinstone,[1] I received the messenger with Your Most Gracious rescript and the decorations for the generals I had recommended.

My beloved matushka, enter into my heart, you will see how faithfully I lead my life, especially regarding my service, and if you have the kindness to look with favor on my affairs, then I shall gladly go through fire and water. [. . .]

What a pleasing concurrence of events God has ordered in giving you your granddaughter Aleksandra Pavlovna at this time. The laurels planted on the shores of the Euxine will grow along with Alexander and Constantine, and for her a grove of olive trees will rise on the promontory that was called the Parthenon in ancient times, that is—the temple of the maiden. In this isolated grove near Balaclava there stood a temple of Diana in ancient times. Iphigeneia was its priestess.[2]

Preparing to dispatch Lieutenant-Colonel Popov[3] with the description of the Crimea along with this letter, I shall write no more at present, but kiss your tender hands. I remain till death

your most loyal servant

Prince Potemkin

1. The brave though vainglorious Scot Rear Admiral John Elphinstone (1722–1785) had served in the Russian navy during the First Russo-Turkish War until being forced to resign his commission for negligence in 1771. Given Elphinstone's history, Potemkin chose instead Vice Admiral Klokachev to head the Black Sea fleet.

2. According to Greek myth, Iphigeneia, the daughter of Agamemnon and Clytemnestra, was saved from sacrifice at the hands of her father by Artemis who carried her off to Tauride (the Crimea) where she became a priestess. The story is the basis of Euripides's tragedy *Iphigeneia in Tauris*.

3. Vasily Stepanovich Popov (1743/1745–1822). This is the first reference in the correspondence to Potemkin's closest assistant and the head of his private office. Popov remained by Potemkin's side until his death and became one of Catherine's most trusted helpmates.

284. CATHERINE TO POTEMKIN

From Tsarskoe Selo. 13 August 1783

My true friend, I have received your letters of 29 July from your camp near Karasubazaar, and since you have sent me your explanation, I shall make no more mention of what has transpired. Thank God that amid the intense Crimean plague you and the troops with you in the camp are well. It would be good if every Tatar village could be made to follow those procedures against the plague that every village here has followed in similar circumstances. The plague would be stopped sooner. I cannot adequately express to you my gratitude for all your dedicated and unlimited care for my affairs. You know yourself how sensitive I am to services rendered, and yours are excellent, just like my friendship and love for you. May God grant you health and may He keep your body and spirit strong. I know you'll come through with honor.

Be assured that I shall not place you under anyone's command but my own. A mighty thanks as well for carrying out the work so inexpensively. But please do take care of yourself for my sake. I had a good laugh over what you wrote about those who spread rumors of the growing plague gather in Spa and Paris. C'est un mot delicieux.[1]

I think that after Bayram[2] the Turks' pending decision will be evident, and so as not to be mistaken, I'm betting they'll declare war.

[…]

Farewell, my true friend, God be with you.

Sasha begs his compliments.

1. "That is a capital remark."

2. Turkish for the Feast of Fast-Breaking that ends the month-long celebration of Ramadan. In 1783, the feast began in the middle of August.

285. CATHERINE TO POTEMKIN

18 August 1783. From Tsarskoe Selo

I received yesterday your letter of the 5th instant from Lieutenant-Colonel Tamara,[1] who also delivered the Georgian file, for which my thanks to you once again. Voilà bien des choses de faites en peu de tems.[2]

That's just like you—my true friend! I gaze most calmly upon Europe's envy: let 'em clown around; we're conducting business.

Judging by your representations, affairs won't remain idle for long. [. . .] God grant you health and every possible happiness and satisfaction. And as for me, know that I remain the same toward you forever.

Sasha has recovered and thanks you for your compliments.

----

1. Lieutenant-Colonel Vasily Stepanovich Tamara (1740–1813) played an active role in the negotiations with Heraclius II and delivered the Treaty of Georgievsk to Catherine.

2. "Here are a great many things accomplished in a little time."

286. POTEMKIN TO CATHERINE

23 September 1783. Nezhin

Your Most Gracious Majesty!

Extremely exhausted from my severe and protracted illness and so not being in any condition to write to Your Imperial Majesty myself, I must rely on the help of another. Your Most Gracious Majesty, I dared to seek refuge from my sufferings, though I did not find any in Kremenchug, which has been overrun by fever. I hastened to withdraw from there, but my illness stopped me hourly. It took nearly a week to convey me to Nezhin, and I have been forced to stay here several days in order to gather the remains of my weakened strength and to fortify myself for the remaining journey, which I was no longer able to continue. Your Most Gracious Majesty, I don't know how my sufferings will end. In the meantime I have ordered all the affairs and troops that Your Majesty has entrusted to me in such a way that they have not and will not suffer the slightest neglect, and as soon as I find some relief, I shall once more be fully back in Your Imperial Majesty's service.[1]

Using his influence among the hordes, Khan Shagin Girey continues to bend the Nogais to his plans and shows no intention of leaving for Russia, maintaining, incidentally, that he already is within the borders of the Russian Empire.[2] He requests that his courier be dispatched to Petersburg, but since he is doing this in the hope of buying time, so I have ordered him told that he can dispatch this courier once he arrives in the Russian Empire. He recently summoned Lieutenant-Colonel Rakhmanov,[3] who serves as his deputy, and said to him that he wanted to write of his condition to the foreign ministers in Constantinople. I have therefore sent an order to Sir Lieutenant-General and Chevalier Suvorov that he be sent from Taman to the interior of Your Imperial Majesty's Empire. I hope to end soon all his conceits.[4]

Your Imperial Majesty's most faithful servant

Prince Potemkin

---

1. Potemkin fell severely ill in August and began to regain his strength only in October. Too weak to write, his correspondence was conducted by Vasily Popov.

2. Instead of traveling to Kherson, where he was to meet Potemkin, Shagin Girey had tricked the Russians and gone to Taman, which he asserted was part of the Russian Empire.

3. Possibly Colonel Nikifor Mikhailovich Rakhmanov. In service since 1761, he was made a captain in the Preobrazhensky Guards Regiment, then under Potemkin's command, in 1775.

4. A reference to Shagin Girey's stay in Taman and his efforts to incite the Nogai hordes. Shagin, who had fled beyond the Kuban during the uprising, was lured back to Russia 1784. He stayed there until 1787, and then left for Turkey. The grand vizier had him executed later that year.

287. CATHERINE TO POTEMKIN

From Petersburg. 28 September 1783.

I have just now received, my dear friend, your letters of the 23rd instant from Nezhin, which cause me extreme worry, for despite my thinking you were better, I see that you are weaker than before. I beg God to preserve your days and to strengthen your body and spirit. I'm extremely grieved by your condition. Je serais dans des inquiétudes mortelles si Vous me laissiés longtems sans nouvelles. Adieu, mon cher Ami, portés-Vous bien, quand Vous Vous porterés bien, tout le reste ira.[1]

Nothing so amazes me as how you gallop about while extremely ill. This will only make your illness worse. A sick person needs rest.

---

1. "I shall be mortally worried if you leave me without news for a long time. Farewell, my dear friend, take care of yourself. Once you take care of yourself, everything else will go fine."

288. CATHERINE TO POTEMKIN

16 October 1783

I have received your letters of the 6th and 7th instant,[1] my dear friend, and although you assure me that you are better, still I worry and will continue to till I know that you have fully recovered, for I know how you are when you're ill. As for me, it's been a black year: Field Marshal Prince

Aleksandr Mikhailovich Golitsyn died this week, and it seems to me that whoever falls into Rogerson's hands is already a dead man.

I hear that Summers isn't with you and this worries me too. God grant you get well soon and return here to us. Oh, for truth, I'm very often lost without you. Most importantly, show me this one kindness—take care of yourself. I do not write of affairs; you'll learn of them from the reports and my other letters. It seems whether there's to be war or peace over the Crimean affairs will be decided this winter. Adieu, mon Ami, I fear disturbing you with a lot of reading.

[. . .]

---

1. These letters have not been found. In a report dated 7 October, Potemkin informed Catherine of Shagin Girey's secret communications with the Nogais and his flight from Taman and of Suvorov's actions in the Kuban, among other things.

289. POTEMKIN TO CATHERINE

22 October 1783. Chernigov.

Your Majesty! Thanks to God I am now better with each passing hour. I'm leaving Chernigov for Krichev, and once I've fully recovered shall leave there to visit my beloved matushka for a short while. There's no sign of the Turks moving along the borders. Farewell, my benefactress.

Your most loyal servant
Prince Potemkin

I beg my compliments to Aleksandr Dmitrich.

6. Southern Visions—1784-1787

he tension that had developed between Catherine and Potemkin at the end of 1783 did not last long, and by the beginning of the next year, their customary trust had reestablished itself and Potemkin was once more in Catherine's good graces. On 2 February 1784, she appointed him governor-general of the new district of Tauride, formed out of the defunct Crimean Khanate, and also made him president of the War College with the rank of field marshal, the highest military rank. The new offices added greatly to Potemkin's already immense power. He had now become Catherine's viceroy for all of southern Russia, ruling over a massive territory that stretched from the Bug River in the west to the Caspian Sea in the east.

The years between the annexation of the Crimea and the Second Russo-Turkish War saw Potemkin largely devoted to developing his southern provinces, where, beginning in 1784, he spent approximately half of every year. As he looked out over these broad, sparsely populated expanses, Potemkin envisioned new farms and manufactories, towns and cities, bustling with trade and exhibiting the best of the arts and culture, and he worked with a dogged persistence to make this a reality. The range of his activities was remarkable. One of his first goals, dating from 1775, was to promote migration to the new territories. Potemkin granted incentives to encourage settlers from throughout the empire and abroad to come to southern Russia, and his efforts brought hundreds of thousands of colonists to these territories (Letter 307). The settlers provided the necessary labor to begin the construction of towns. Following the establishment of Kherson in 1778,

Potemkin laid the foundations for Mariupol, Sevastopol, Simferopol, and Yekaterinoslav—"Catherine's Glory"—the grand vision for which Potemkin presented to Catherine in October 1786 (Letter 297). He saw to his territories' economic development, too, and gave special encouragement to the production of wool, the establishment of silk manufactories, and the planting of vineyards (Letter 298). As early as 1783, Potemkin began developing Sevastopol as the main port for the Black Sea fleet. Yet another product of Potemkin's bold imagination, Potemkin created this fleet from nothing and became its grand admiral in 1785. In just a few years, Potemkin built a significant number of vessels that when added to the Baltic fleet placed Russia among the major European naval powers. Potemkin's purview also included the Caucasus, where he oversaw the growing Russian presence, based on settlement and the building of new fortresses at Yekaterinograd, Stavropol, and Vladikavkaz.

Although separated from Catherine now by great distance, Potemkin continued to play a guiding role in the empress's personal life. Her reliance on Potemkin was never more apparent than at times of crisis, as, for example, when Aleksandr Lanskoy died unexpectedly on 25 June 1784 following a brief illness. Lanskoy's death devastated Catherine. When the usual medical procedures (bloodletting, purges, etc.) failed to lift her spirit, her doctor and close advisors agreed that only the prince could revive her, and so Count Bezborodko wrote Potemkin begging him to hasten to Tsarskoe Selo for the sake of Catherine's health. Potemkin received Bezborodko's urgent letter in Kremenchug, and he raced back in a mere seven days, arriving at Tsarskoe Selo on 10 July.

Despite Potemkin's arrival, Catherine fell ever deeper into despair over the loss of Lanskoy, with whom she had hoped to spend the rest of her life. She remained in bed for weeks at a time and did not appear in public for months. Unwilling to accept Lanskoy's death, Catherine refused to allow him to be buried for over a month; when his rotting corpse was finally committed to the ground, she could not bear to attend. Catherine returned to the capital in early September and to the great relief of the entire court finally reappeared in public on the eighth, after two and a half months of seclusion. By the end of 1784, Catherine was slowly returning to her usual self. Potemkin was now confident he could leave her side, and in January 1785 he returned to the south, where he remained throughout the winter and spring.

Catherine did not take another favorite for almost an entire year after Lanskoy's death. As the months passed, talk at court intensified over who would be chosen to occupy his apartments in the Winter Palace, and the various factions sought to draw Catherine's attention to their respective candidates. Potemkin, too, looked about for a replacement, and he eventually found one in Aleksandr Yermolov, a thirty-one-year-old officer in the prince's service, whom he presented to Catherine in the spring of 1785. Not terribly bright, good looking, or decent, Yermolov ranks toward the bottom of the list of Catherine's lovers. His insignificance is reflected by his complete absence from Catherine and Potemkin's correspondence.

Like Zorich before him, Yermolov made the mistake of thinking that he, together with Potemkin's enemies, could break the prince's hold over Catherine. This error of judgement cost Yermolov his position, and in July 1786, he was dismissed and sent abroad. Yermolov barely had time to fetch his belongings from the Winter Palace before the new favorite moved into his chambers. Aleksandr Dmitriev-Mamonov, aged twenty-six (to Catherine's fifty-seven), was a distant cousin of Potemkin and one of his adjutants. In addition to being handsome, Mamonov was refined, cultured, fluent in both French and Italian, and charming. Catherine dubbed him "Red Coat" in reference to his beloved attire and fell madly in love with him. Titles, wealth, and influence followed shortly thereafter. Though not base by nature, Mamonov later returned Catherine's favors with betrayal.

On the morning of 7 January 1787, Catherine and Aleksandr Mamonov, accompanied by the empress's suite and the envoys of France, Britain, and Austria, set out from Tsarskoe Selo on a grand voyage to inspect the progress made by Potemkin in developing his southern provinces and to marvel at his achievements. They would be away for over six months and would travel over six thousand kilometers. The entourage included hundreds of servants, dozens of footmen and washerwomen, several physicians, apothecaries, and even a few silver polishers. This itinerant court was transported by fourteen carriages and over a hundred sledges that glided across the snowy landscape. Nearly six hundred fresh horses were kept ready at each post station to relieve the exhausted beasts upon their arrival.

The idea for the trip first arose in 1784, although Catherine had been forced to postpone it until 1787. There were several reasons for the journey. First, the empress was curious to see these new territories of her empire where her prince had spent so much time and labored so hard. Second, Potemkin's enemies at court had long been denigrating his achievements in these lands, asserting that the millions of rubles Potemkin had received for his numerous projects had in fact been wasted. Catherine, therefore, wanted to see for herself what Potemkin had managed to accomplish, and so shut the mouths of his detractors. In addition, by bringing along the foreign ambassadors, she sought to demonstrate to all of Europe the growth of Russian power along the northern Black Sea littoral.

Their itinerary took them through Smolensk en route to Kiev, where they arrived on 29 January. Catherine and Potemkin, then making the final preparations for her arrival in the south, exchanged letters as they made their separate ways to Kiev (Letters 299–302). They remained there until the ice went out on the Dnieper River and then embarked in late April on seven opulent, gold and scarlet galleys—each with its own orchestra—that Potemkin had especially built for the voyage. A flotilla of eighty boats carrying three thousand troops followed behind. Three days later the floating party dropped anchor at Kaniev, where King Stanislaw Poniatowski impatiently awaited their arrival. It had been more than a quarter of a century since the former lovers had last seen each other, and the Polish king was nervous with excitement, not only at the thought of seeing the empress after so many years, but also because this would be his best chance to gain the Russo-Polish alliance he sought (and which Potemkin also favored) and the promise of support for his reforms in Poland. Their meeting proved a disappointment, however. Catherine felt none of her former passion and made little attempt to hide this. She refused to endorse his proposed alliance and even rejected his polite request that she delay her departure a day or two. Embarrassed and dejected, Poniatowski was rowed back to shore from Catherine's galley that evening. It was to be their final meeting (Letters 303, 304).

Catherine was in a hurry to weigh anchor since Joseph II, once more traveling incognito as Count Falkenstein, was expected soon in Kherson and would be waiting for them. The two sovereigns met several days later outside Yekaterinoslav and traveled on together from there to Kherson and then into the Crimea, arriving at Bakhchisarai on 20 May. So moved was the empress by the former capital of the Crimean Khanate, that she wrote to Potemkin of her feelings in verse, a skill it is generally recognized she lacked (Letter 305). The party next visited Sevastopol in order to inspect Potemkin's new Black Sea fleet, and then, after a brief tour of the peninsula, Joseph II took his leave of Catherine on 2 June and set off for Vienna. Catherine and the rest of her entourage headed north to Poltava, the site of Peter the Great's triumph over the Swedes in 1709, where Potemkin staged a reenactment with fifty thousand troops. The following day Catherine bid farewell to Potemkin and turned toward home (Letter 306).

The voyage of 1787 quickly passed into legend and became the basis for the myth of the "Potemkin villages," the sham settlements Potemkin supposedly fabricated along the Dnieper River in order to deceive Catherine as to the true state of Russia's southern territories. The claim—actually concocted by Potemkin's enemies *before* the voyage—that Potemkin had built nothing in his provinces and that the towns, armies, and fleet of which he spoke existed only on paper never was true, and historians have long agreed that what Potemkin had managed to achieve in the south in such a short time and in the face of so many obstacles was indeed remarkable. Catherine herself acknowledged the significance of Potemkin's achievements, as her letters attest (Letters 308–310, 312, 314). In recognition of his labors, on 8 June 1787 she awarded him the honorific title of

"Tavrichesky"—literally "of Tauride," the classical name for the Crimea. For his part, Potemkin basked in Catherine's approbation and showered her with gratitude (Letters 311, 313).

Both Catherine and Potemkin viewed the grand southern journey as a resounding success and it left them with their spirits buoyed. The success was all the sweeter given the fact that while Catherine had been enjoying a relaxing stroll "about my garden, which has grown up nicely and is beautiful," much of Europe was embroiled in a fight over the Netherlands (Letter 346). The warm afterglow of the voyage did not last long, however.

As early as July 1786, Potemkin began writing to Catherine of trouble brewing in Constantinople. Although they had been forced to recognize the Russian annexation of the Crimea, the Ottomans had never been able to accept the growing presence of their infidel neighbor in the Black Sea region and were waiting for the right moment to attempt to reassert their influence. The French and especially the Prussian and British ambassadors to the Porte encouraged the advocates of war by playing to their resentment of Russian expansion and making vague promises of support (Letters 295, 296, 302). Catherine's southern voyage only served to heighten tensions with the Ottomans, who quite rightly viewed the trip as a pointed display of Russian power directed largely at them. Indeed, the larger geopolitical significance Potemkin attached to the newly acquired southern territories was succinctly communicated in an inscription across the archway before his town of Kherson: "This is the road to Byzantium." Yet even if Russia truly harbored intentions of one day marching into Constantinople, neither Potemkin nor the empress felt they would be ready for such an enterprise for at least another two years. And so, when the Porte began demanding concessions from Russia in early August 1787, Potemkin urged the Russian envoy, Yakov Bulgakov, to be conciliatory. On 19 August, Catherine wrote Potemkin from St. Petersburg recommending he take steps to avert war, which she felt was quite possible, though not likely. Little did she know at the time, it had already started (Letter 316).

• • •

290. POTEMKIN TO CATHERINE

[Early 1784]

Matushka, the instructions are sufficient and quite good.[1] I would only like to remind you of one thing, that Greek be made the primary language of study, for it is the basis of all others. It is unbelievable how much learning and delicate style it lends a great multitude of writers who are distorted in translation, not so much by the translators as by the frailty of other languages. This language possesses a most pleasing harmony and, in the way its words are put together, much play of thought. The technical words of the arts and sciences signify the essence of the very thing and have been adopted by all languages.

Concerning your decision to read the Gospels in Latin, in this instance the Greek language is more appropriate, for they were originally written in it.

[Catherine] Make the recommended changes.

---

1. Potemkin's reply to Catherine's program of instruction for her grandsons, Alexander and Constantine.

291. CATHERINE TO POTEMKIN

17 May 1784

I have received, my true friend, your letter from Kremenchug. I'm glad that the plague has stopped in places, and I hope that as a result of your excellent orders it will also be stopped in Kherson. We are receiving so much and such detailed information from England and Denmark about the Swedish King's ventures against Norway and even against the city of Copenhagen, which practically resemble lunacy, that without being mistaken in the slightest one can have practically no doubt about it. He can't attack Denmark without dealing with us.[1] And in order to check his mischief as quickly as possible, I have ordered the General Staff to prepare ten thousand infantry and three thousand cavalry, as well as forty artillery guns, for the military camp located beyond the Neva, and also a store—in Finland—with provisions and forage for an entire year. You are to send here two regiments or up to two thousand Don Cossacks.

The Danes are preparing themselves just in case. Our naval force will be such that we shall be able to crush all of Sweden, and namely: five ships from Livorno, three from the town of Arkhangelsk and 7 from Kronstadt, and the Danes will have six in the Sound. I ordered the Swedish minister told that such rumors are in the air and that although it seems there is little truth to them, nonetheless they should know that it would be inconvenient for them to attack the Danes, for they are, in fact, allies of Russia.

You saw that even the words the Swedish King exchanged with Markov were similar.[2] We'll see whether his foolish tricks will diminish now that he has left France. I think he can expect little help from the Turks and their illustrious treaty of alliance of which he boasts.

We have been having uninterrupted hard frost here, and the leaves on the birches are no bigger than silver kopecks; as for the lime-trees and oaks, they've not begun to even think about putting out their leaves. The Grand Duchess is pregnant again and expects to deliver in November.

Let vessels be built in Smolensk, and as to how they are to be moved—

this can always be arranged. Farewell, be well. It was pleasant to hear that you are also engaged with matters concerning the provinces. Success is beyond doubt, for when you undertake something yourself, it comes off without a hitch. Adieu, mon Ami, je Vous aime beaucoup et avec raison.[3]

---

1. Despite being rebuffed by Catherine the previous year, Gustav III, who was arming with French subsidies, still sought to seize Norway from Denmark, Russia's ally.

2. Arkady Ivanovich Markov (1747–1827) was Russia's envoy to Sweden from 1783–1786. He reported to Russia of Sweden's hostile intentions.

3. "Farewell, my friend, I love you much and for good reason."

292. CATHERINE TO POTEMKIN

[After 28 June 1786][1]

I am extremely worried, are you well? So many days now with neither sight nor sound of you, and the weather has been so grand yesterday and today that I have by now begun to fear you have crossed the Voksha. And so I'm sending a special messenger—I must know where and how you are. Adieu, mon Ami, je prie Dieu que Vous Vous portiez bien.[2]

Friday after eight o'clock in the evening.

---

1. Tensions mounted in the spring of 1786 between Potemkin and the current favorite, Aleksandr Petrovich Yermolov (1754–1834), that strained Catherine's relations with the prince. Potemkin abandoned court unexpectedly toward the end of June, perhaps in an attempt to force Catherine to dismiss Yermolov.

2. "Farewell, my friend. I pray God to keep you well."

293. CATHERINE TO POTEMKIN

[Before 20 July 1786][1]

I received a watermelon as big as Turchaninov[2] if not bigger. You couldn't see him behind the watermelon as he carried it into my rooms. Thank you, Sir Thoroughbred.[3] First of all, I considered you to be on the way to the Voksha, but you deigned to turn up on the way to Schlüsselburg. I'll discuss the Field Marshal's reports with you when we see each other.[4] This is my letter's second point. The third consists of my desire to see you, for it seems it's been a year since I saw you last. Farewell, God be with you. Je Vous embrasse, mon Ami.[5] Arrive merry and well or you'll be beaten.

---

1. Apparently written around the time of Potemkin's return to court on 20 July, five days after Yermolov's dismissal.

2. Pyotr Ivanovich Turchaninov (1746–after 1823) had been the director of Potemkin's chancellery before being made a state secretary to the empress in 1783.

3. "Spasibo Vam ili tebe, Barin-skakun." Catherine plays here with the informal and formal forms of "you": first she uses the formal "you" (*vam*), and then switches to the informal "thou" (*tebe*).

4. Field Marshal Pyotr Rumiantsev had reported to Catherine of the Turks' preparations for war.

5. "I kiss you, my friend."

294. POTEMKIN TO CATHERINE

[20 July 1786]

Matushka, after touring Petersburg, Peterhof and Oranienbaum, I've returned and kiss your tender feet. Paraclete[1] has been brought back safe, healthy, merry and obliging.

[Catherine] Baten'ka, a grand effort. Sir, not having slept, how's your health? I'm very glad you've arrived.

---

1. The new favorite, Aleksandr Matveevich Dmitriev-Mamonov (1758–1803).

295. POTEMKIN TO CATHERINE

[26 July 1786]

Count Bezborodko always receives from Bulgakov the reports' more secretive items. He always gives them to me to read, and as there is now more than ever a need to know, so I have read them and present them here.

Pray take note, matushka, of the cabal at work there: I know for certain that the French are seeking to win the Porte's aid by not allowing our fleet into the Archipelago and by lending them officers. I almost suspect that they even intend to use Custine[1] against us in some way, and there can be no doubt that the Prussians are making assurances, though only verbally, to the Turks.[2]

There are many tales about Sheikh Mansur,[3] but I wonder—was it not a different one or was it in fact that one that the Turks secretively dispatched to him?

Once you have read them, please return these papers to me so I might make a copy of the figure of Mansur and question those who have seen him.

It seems to me France is cooking up this fine mess in order to cause us worry. They fear the Prussian King's approaching death, at which time they, of course, imagine the Emperor will begin his enterprise against Bavaria.[4] What makes this all the more likely is that the entire cavalry in France has been ordered to be outfitted with horses, which they never do unless they intend war.

Even though the French have assured the Turks that they will not let us into the Archipelago, nevertheless we must keep the fleet at the ready.

Order that you be given a report on the ships and frigates with a description of each one's readiness. The mood in Sweden, it seems, is in our favor, but is our minister there competent to handle the present situation in which everything possible must be done against the French?[5]

These latest reports from Bulgakov seem probable to me for many reasons. But nonetheless, I am certain that the French ambassador, having gotten in touch with Bulgakov, will turn these matters around in an attempt to merit your praise.[6]

A large packet from Constantinople has been delivered to Count Ségur.[7] He is to dine with me tomorrow; I shall not begin the conversation, but should he, then from this a conclusion can be drawn. The main thing is to buy a little time.

---

1. General Count Adam Phillipe Custine (1740–1793), who had distinguished himself in the American War of Independence, was the governor of Toulon, France's main naval base in the Mediterranean Sea. At the same time France sought to improve relations with Russia, French officers were assisting the Turkish military, and French engineers were helping to fortify the fortresses of Ochakov and Ismail

2. Prussia, uneasy about the Austro-Russian alliance, sought to incite the Turks against Russia.

3. The Russian protectorate over Kartli-Kakheti and the growing Russian influence in the Caucasus in general were met with resistance by local peoples. One such resister went by the name Sheikh Mansur (d. 1794) and claimed to be an heir to the Prophet. He declared a holy war on Russia and, after initial success, was captured in 1791 and later died in captivity.

4. Frederick the Great died on 7 (18) August 1786. France feared his death would upset the balance of power in Europe: Joseph II of Austria would make a play for Bavaria and so possibly start another European war. The French hoped to use Turkey to keep Russia occupied.

5. Potemkin's worry was not without foundation: Count Andrei Razumovsky, Russia's ambassador to Sweden, proved unable to prevent a rupture with Sweden and its consequent declaration of war in 1788.

6. France's ambassador to the Sublime Porte, Count Choiseul-Gouffier, was reportedly willing to aid Russo-Turkish rapprochement.

7. Count Louis-Phillipe Ségur (1753–1830) served as the French envoy to Russia for five years. He established close relations with Catherine and Potemkin and is remembered for his memoirs of his stay there.

296. CATHERINE TO POTEMKIN

[26 July 1786][1]

There's no doubt that the French are cooking up a fine mess. We must prepare for war. I consider all that about Imam Mansur a mere tale. [. . .]

---

1. Catherine's response to Letter 295.

297. POTEMKIN TO CATHERINE

6 October 1786

Your Most Gracious Majesty!

Laying the plans for the building of the city of Yekaterinoslav at Your Imperial Majesty's blessed feet, I dare to request for their completion all revenues remaining after the provinces have paid their expenses. Though this part of Your Empire is, so to speak, still in its very infancy, nevertheless it possesses all the provincial ranks and expenditures, pays out the assigned three million rubles for the construction of fortresses and other buildings in Tauride, and still the balance will be enough for the creation of a celebrated city.

Your Most Gracious Majesty, where else but in a land dedicated to your glory should there be a city of magnificent buildings? And for that reason I have undertaken to compile plans worthy of this city's lofty name. First of all, I envision there a magnificent temple, an imitation of St. Paul's outside Rome, dedicated to the Lord's Transfiguration as a sign that your labors have transfigured this land from a barren steppe into an abundant garden, and the dwelling-place of beasts into a favorable refuge for people arriving from all countries.

I envision a court of law resembling the ancient basilicas in memory of your beneficial legislation. There will be stores arranged in a semi-circle resembling the propylaea or the Athenian portico, with a bourse and a theater in the middle.

I envision state chambers with a magnificent and vast canopy in the middle in the style of Greek and Roman buildings where the governor-general will also live. There will also be an archbishopric at the Cathedral Church of the Transfiguration with a consistory and a school of religion.

Since this province is a military one, there will be an invalid home with all possible benefits and with the appropriate magnificence to care for meritorious, aged warriors.

I envision a governor's house, a vice governor's, a noblemen's house and an apothecary. There will be cloth and silk mills. There will be a university complete with an academy of music and a conservatory.

For all these buildings enough of the necessary supplies has been stockpiled. Two hundred thousand rubles, left over from the extraordinary sum, will be required for their construction.

Your Imperial Majesty's most loyal
Prince Potemkin

298. POTEMKIN TO CATHERINE

[Before 13 October 1786]

Since the legislation has now reduced the bank interest, so the capital in the Yekaterinoslav bank, accumulated by me through various economies and amounting to three hundred forty thousand rubles, cannot maintain the university with its academies of the arts and music and its surgical college and public school. Your Most Gracious Majesty, have the kindness to allot for all this sixty thousand rubles from the revenues of the Yekaterinoslav Province. Yekaterinoslav is near Poland, Greece, the Walachian and Moldavian lands and the Illyrian peoples, and so a multitude of youths will pour in to study, who will later return home with permanent gratitude toward your munificence and with attachment to Russia. And the capital now in the bank can then be turned into capital for manufactories that are so suited for that area, given the low price of grain, and are so necessary for Russia.

The southern climes of Your Empire abound in fleece-bearing livestock, almost more than all of Europe combined possesses. Having converted this into the best wool through reliable and simple means, Your Empire will surpass all other states in the quantity of cloth produced. From all those places where the best sheep are found, I have requested males of the species, which I expect next summer. The master craftsmen, however, have already arrived, and their headman is so skillful that even in Holland he stood out among all others. France sacrificed a lot of money to establish such a manufactory there. But it will cost Your Majesty almost nothing. In addition to producing cloth at this manufactory, apprentices from the nobility will be accepted, as a result of which this craft will be spread throughout the entire State.

Mulberry trees, which already grow naturally in the Crimea in great number, have been ordered planted throughout all of Tauride and the Perekop steppe. Within ten years we shall of course be swimming in silk. For this reason, silk manufactories in Yekaterinoslav are advantageous. Even now they will have enough work processing the silk brought in from Bursa and the Morea, which I arranged to exchange for salt, which is worthless, as if we had traded pure sand for it.

Without exception all the silk mills in Russia are inadequate. Neither do their goods have any beauty nor do they have the requisite strength, especially those types of materials that demand a smooth surface. Those of Lazarev are better than the rest, but even his material does not maintain its beauty for long. Excluding that mill, all the others are of unreliable condition, buying silk on credit, on bad terms with unbearable interest and using primarily Persian silk so badly spun that nearly a third of it is always wasted. Owing to such difficulty, people take to various forms of trickery, such as making the base thinner than necessary or adding combings to the woof where good silk is needed, and in this manner they produce material that looks like old rags.

Catherine the Great, Empress of All the Russias. (Fyodor Rokotov)

166

Field Marshal Prince Grigory Aleksandrovich Potemkin-Tavrichesky from the late 1780s. (James Walker, after Johann Baptist von Lampi, the Elder) © Copyright The British Museum

Catherine the Great dressed for her coronation. (S. Torelli)

168

Catherine II. va trouver Potemkin dans
son hermitage.

A late eighteenth-century French engraving depicting Catherine
visiting Potemkin at his hermitage after he fled court in the early 1760s.
(unknown artist)

O NIMIVM FORTVNATI SVBDITI !—VT HOS INFANTES , ITA VOS AMAT ,

Catherine surrounded by her family and closest courtiers in St. Petersburg in 1782: (l. to r.) Potemkin, Count Aleksandr Bezborodko, Grand Duke Alexander, Grand Duke Constantine, Grand Duchess Maria Fyodorovna, Catherine, Ivan Betskoy, Grand Duke Paul, Prince Nikolai Repnin, Count Nikita Panin, Aleksandr Lanskoy, Lev Naryshkin, and Count Ivan Osterman. The caption reads: "Oh, you all-too-fortunate subjects! As she loves these children, so does she love you." (unknown artist)

Potemkin as he might have looked about the time of his break-up with Catherine. (unknown artist) © Copyright British Museum

170

Catherine in Kiev in 1787 in the travel costume she wore while on her journey to the Crimea. (M. Shibanov) Hillwood Museum, Washington, D.C.

Potemkin, flush with his victories over the Turks, depicted as a mighty knight
ca. 1790. (Johann Baptist von Lampi, the Elder)

The storming of Ochakov, 6 December 1788. The original painting was commissioned by Catherine. Potemkin is shown to the right of center leading the charge, although he entered Ochakov only after it had been taken. (Barch, after Kazanov)

A plump, somewhat disheveled Potemkin in his later years. (unknown artist)

An aging Catherine walking with one of her Italian greyhounds in the gardens at Tsarskoe Selo in the early 1790s. The model for this painting was Maria Perekusikhina, Catherine's trusted maid and possibly one of the witnesses to her wedding to Potemkin. Perekusikhina posed for the artist wearing the empress's clothes. (V. Borovikovsky)

The death of Potemkin, 5 October 1791. Potemkin's secretary, Vasily Popov, who was not present at Potemkin's death, commissioned this historically inaccurate depiction of the prince's end, and he is shown here clasping his hands and gazing heavenward. Aleksandra Branicka, who was present, is wailing over her uncle's dead body. (Skorodumov)

To aid and benefit these mills, I intend to set up in Yekaterinoslav a store of dyed and well-spun silks from the silk left over after it has been used by the local manufactories, which will be distributed on credit at 6 percent. This will bring the price back down, and the mills will not need doublers, spinning mills and dye-works, which is even better since given Yekaterinoslav's climate it will not be necessary to dye in the winter months, for silk not dried out in the sun has a very different quality.

I spare nothing in executing Your Imperial Majesty's will, which has been made known to me, to increase the revenues and to further the arts. Colonies of craftsmen have been sent for; I have assembled a large number of factory workers in White Russian villages who will be conveyed down the Dnieper on ships with their tools to their destination in anticipation of the construction of housing in Yekaterinoslav, which will be ready by next autumn.

Concerning the Tauride region, cultivation there intensifies from year to year. The Hungarian vines have already borne their first fruit; better wine than before is being made. Cognac is being distilled that is better than the real thing, and in a year there will of course be a large quantity of it.[1]

---

1. Catherine approved his request on 13 October 1786.

299. CATHERINE TO POTEMKIN

18 December 1786

My friend, Prince Grigory Aleksandrovich, your two letters reached me to-day.[1] One by way of Count Bezborodko, and the other by way of Aleksandr Matveevich.[2] Prince Repnin's delightful proposal compelled me on the day of St. George to put on the Guards uniform and take great pride in it, just like a peahen.[3]

I fear the Dnieper might play a trick on us, just as on you. You are not the only one having balls, so are we, and, what's more, endless troubles as well. Les étrilleries du Prince de Württemberg ont enfin obligé sa femme de se retirer chez moi, parce que réellement elle étoit en danger de sa vie; j'ai saisi cette très favorable occasion pour les renvoyer tous les deux d'ici, et sous peu de jours nous en serons quittes. J'ai fait ce que j'ai dû faire et j'ai fait bien, la femme ira chez les parens et le mari où il voudra.[4]

It's odd that you liked Prince Nassau[5] considering his universal reputation is that d'un cerveau brûlé,[6] still it's well known that he is brave. Your conversations with him improve my opinion of him.

I regret very much that I shall not see you before Kiev. Two weeks from to-day, that is on 2 January, I shall depart here without fail.[7] I read with pleasure the Emperor's letter to you.[8] It's most affectionate, and he does write the truth. Concerning his voyage, I don't doubt that you'll take all necessary measures. I thank you for the rings with the ancient cameos. We all desire nothing more than that God would soon carry us from here. I read your letter to Aleksandr Matveevich[9] with extreme pleasure, and you were not mistaken: he loves you with his heart and soul and he becomes kinder with each passing hour. Farewell, my friend, be well. If it's to be that we can't see each other sooner, then we'll see each other in Kiev. Your nieces departed here yesterday. All of society is galloping off, such that one can't help but be envious.

---

1. The letters have not been found.

2. Mamonov.

3. Catherine donned the uniform of the Order of St. George for the celebration on 26 November 1786. Prince Nikolai Vasilievich Repnin (1734–1801) fought bravely in the First Russo-Turkish War and was Russia's envoy to the Sublime Porte from 1775–1776. He later fought in the Second Russo-Turkish War.

4. "The Prince of Württemberg's beatings have finally forced his wife to seek refuge with me, for she truly was in danger for her life. I seized this very favorable opportunity to send them both away, and in a few days we shall be rid of them. I did what I had to do and I did well: the wife is going to her parents and the husband wherever he wants." Princess Augusta was the victim of extreme violence at the hands of her husband, Prince Frederick of Württemberg, the brother of Grand Duchess Maria Fyodorovna. To protect her, Catherine eventually sent Augusta with a small retinue to live near Reval. She then forced Prince Frederick to resign his post over the objections of the grand duke and duchess.

5. The German adventurer Prince Charles Nassau-Siegen (1745–1808) arrived in Russia in 1786 seeking to sell Polish goods along the Dnieper. He became a favorite of Potemkin's, who placed him in command of the oared flotilla on the Liman during the Second Russo-Turkish War.

6. "of a hot-head,"

7. Catherine did not depart until 7 January.

8. Joseph II wrote to Potemkin that he was looking forward to seeing him again on the upcoming trip with the empress to the south.

9. Mamonov.

300. POTEMKIN TO CATHERINE

Simferopol. 7 January [1787]

Your Majesty! I kiss your tender hands and thank you for the gracious missive. The verdure here is starting to appear in the fields. I think the flowers too will soon come up. The roads here are all dusty, while in Perekop there is still snow. May God grant this land the good fortune of pleasing you, my benefactress. This is my chief pleasure. Farewell, my beloved matushka, I am consoled by the thought of appearing before you soon.

Your most loyal and most grateful subject

Prince Potemkin

301. CATHERINE TO POTEMKIN

Smolensk. 17 January 1787

I received today your letter, my true friend, here in Smolensk where I have stopped for four days longer than I expected because Aleksandr Matveevich was ill. And everyone was tired, and many complained of trouble with their eyes. Where you are the verdure has begun to appear, while here it's very cold. There are great mounds of snow here. I do not doubt that Tauride will please me and everyone else. I'm departing tomorrow morning. God grant that we'll see each other soon and that you're well. I put on a very large ball here today. I am well. Farewell, my friend, till we meet.

302. POTEMKIN TO CATHERINE

1 February [1787]. Kremenchug

Your Majesty. Owing to how extremely busy I am, and being particularly occupied with the arriving troops, who I fear might freeze, I must remain here for yet a while longer.[1] Moreover, the Moldavian Hospodar has appeared inside Your Majesty's borders seeking refuge. He is now in Olviopol. I have dispatched a special courier to him to learn of conditions there, and after that I shall not tarry to Kiev.[2] I shall be here two more days, and in three shall have the pleasure of seeing you, my beloved matushka.

Bulgakov's dispatches demand that we deal with the Turks ourselves and in this way show them how ridiculous is the gossip of the extraneous powers. Upon arriving he will himself receive from Your Imperial commands the authority for this affair.[3] As for the rest, I've sent everything to Count Bezborodko. I remain till death

your most loyal subject
Prince Potemkin

---

1. Potemkin was busying himself with his newly formed light cavalry regiments, which he was especially intent on showing Catherine.

2. The Turks overthrew the Moldavian hospodar Alexander Mavrocordato (1745–1819) in late 1786, which constituted a violation of the Treaty of Kuchuk Kainardji. Fearing execution should he return to Constantinople, which was a common fate of deposed hospodars, Mavrocordato fled to Russia.

3. Yakov Bulgakov, Russia's ambassador to the Porte, met with Catherine in Kherson and received from her instructions for dealing with the Turks, who were being pushed toward war by Britain and Prussia.

303. CATHERINE TO POTEMKIN

[25 April 1787]

Aleksandr Matveevich told me of our guest's desire that I remain here for another day or two, but you yourself know that this is impossible given my meeting with the Emperor.[1] And so kindly let him know, in a polite manner, that there is no possibility of making changes in my journey. And moreover, as you yourself know, I find any change in plan disagreeable.

---

1. Catherine and Stanislaw Poniatowski, king of Poland, met on the Dnieper River near Kaniev on 25 April 1787. The king asked Mamonov to convey to Catherine his request that she stay on a while longer. She turned him down, citing her need to meet Joseph II.

304. CATHERINE TO POTEMKIN

[25 April 1787]

The dinner proposed for tomorrow was suggested without any regard for what is possible. His Majesty must return today by water to Kaniev— 7 versts. We'll send for him for dinner tomorrow—7 versts. He'll come— 7 versts. Having dined, he'll be brought back—7 versts. The launches will return here—7 versts, and then we'll set out on our way. And what time will that be exactly? After having traveled three versts we'll have to anchor again because the launches, which will have already done twenty-eight versts, will be tired. When I make a decision there's a reason for it, unlike as is often the case in Poland. And so, I'm leaving tomorrow as planned, and I wish him all possible happiness and benefit.

Baten'ka, I truly am tired of this.[1]

---

1. Despite Poniatowski's insistence, Catherine refused to change her plans.

305. CATHERINE TO POTEMKIN

[20–21 May 1787][1]

> I lay at eve in the summer-house of the Khan,
> Amidst the infidel and the faith Mohammedan.
> 'Cross from the house there stood a mosque most tall,
> Whither five times a day an imam the people did call.
> I thought to sleep, my eyes barely shut for the night,
> When, with ears stopped, he did roar with all his might . . .
> Oh, miracles of God! Who amongst my kin of yore
> Slept calmly, free from the Khans and their hordes?

And disturbed from my sleep amidst Bakhchisarai
By tobacco smoke and cries. . . . Is this place not paradise?
Praise to you, my friend! This land you did seize,
Secure it now with your vigilance, as you please.

---

1. Catherine and her party arrived in Bakhchisarai, the former capital of the Crimean Khanate, on 20 May. The empress showed her poem in praise of Potemkin to Khrapovitsky, her secretary, who corrected (and possibly rewrote) it.

306. CATHERINE TO POTEMKIN

[9 June 1787]

Papa, I do so hope you will let me go tomorrow without a lot of ceremony.[1]

---

1. Catherine parted with Potemkin and set off for Tsarskoe Selo on 10 June.

307. POTEMKIN TO CATHERINE

22 June 1787

The Yekaterinoslav Province and the Tauride region possess excellent lands, yet they lack the inhabitants to cultivate them, and these beautiful places remain uninhabited.

Since it is my duty to care for the welfare of Your Majesty's lands entrusted to me, I dare to solicit from the senate a Royal Edict whereby subjects desirous of moving to this province and to Tauride from throughout the provinces be sought. The number of volunteers will, of course, be very large, particularly from among the single-homesteaders, who are in extreme need of land.

Russia will feel the benefit of such resettlement, the fertility of these lands will spread abundance throughout her, and her fields, which are so exhausted from their constant burden, will bear fewer inhabitants and so will rest and mend themselves. This will put an end to the flight of your subjects, which is undertaken out of need. And as there has been no way to stop them, the alternative would be to deny the state any benefit from the fugitives' stay here. And then Poland would make use of them.

Your Imperial Majesty has deigned to revive all this land, and by populating it, you will become the foundress of Your Empire's new strengths.

Prince Potemkin-Tavrichesky[1]

---

1. On 8 June, Catherine ordered the Senate to reward Potemkin with the honorific title of "Tavrichesky" ("of Tauride"). The request was approved on 3 July 1787.

308. CATHERINE TO POTEMKIN

The village of Kolomenskoe. 25 June 1787

My friend, Prince Grigory Aleksandrovich. I arrived here in good health, having dined in the village of Dubrovitsy, which is exactly as you described it. And if you intend to sell it, then I am a certain buyer, but in the deed of purchase We'll enter the name of Aleksandr Matveevich, your major.[1] We'll spend the holidays[2] here, and then continue on. I've no letters from you. Be well. We here are boasting about our journey and Tauride and the orders of the governor-general there whose good deeds are without end and are felt everywhere.

Farewell, God be with you.

---

1. Potemkin had purchased the Golitsyn family estate of Dubrovitsy in 1782 for eighty thousand rubles. Catherine purchased it from him to give to Mamonov.

2. Catherine celebrated the twenty-fifth anniversary of her accession on 28 June in Moscow.

309. CATHERINE TO POTEMKIN

Tver. 6 July 1787

My friend, Prince Grigory Aleksandrovich. When I started to write to you from Moscow, your letters of 22 June from Kremenchug were so packed away that in my haste I simply couldn't find them. I finally discovered them here in Tver, where I arrived yesterday. Forgive me, my friend, for such carelessness. Now I can respond to them. First of all, the disposition of minds and spirits in Kremenchug upon my departure was very pleasing to me, and your own feelings and thoughts are all the more so dear to me since I love you and your service, which springs from pure zeal, so very, very much, and you are yourself priceless. I say and think this every day.

We reached Moscow and this place in good health, and thanks to the rains that followed us we have not been disturbed in the least by either dust or heat. It seemed empty to you in Kremenchug without us, but along the entire route, and especially in Moscow, we were simply lost without you.

We proclaimed Platon[1] Metropolitan in Moscow's Uspensky Cathedral on the day of St. Peter, and We sewed onto his white klobuk[2] a diamond cross over twelve inches long, and the entire time he acted like a Kremenchug peacock.

Amid the intense heat that you have there in the south, I beg you most humbly, do me a favor, take care of your health for God's sake and for Ours, and be as content with me as I am with you. Farewell, my friend. God be with you. After dinner I'm leaving to spend the night in Torzhok.

I thank you for the four squadrons of Cossack regulars. For truth, you're a rare and fine fellow, which I preach to everyone.

---

1. Catherine appointed Archbishop Platon (born Pyotr Yegorovich Levshin [1737–1812]), a remarkable preacher whose sermons Catherine praised to Voltaire, Metropolitan of Moscow on 29 June.

2. The headdress worn by Orthodox monks.

310. CATHERINE TO POTEMKIN

Tsarskoe Selo. 13 July 1787

My true friend, Prince Grigory Aleksandrovich. Two days ago we finished our six-thousand-verst journey having arrived at this station in perfect health, and since that very hour we've been exercising our brains discussing the delightful condition of the places—the provinces and regions—entrusted to you, your labors, successes, effort, zeal and care, and the order that you have established everywhere. And so, my friend, our almost incessant conversations are solely devoted, either directly or indirectly, to your name or your work.

Please, please, please be well and come to us free of harm, and I, as always, remain both amicable and benevolent toward you.

The Emperor has arrived in Vienna. Flanders and the Brabant continue to rebel. He is sending 30,000 troops there.[1] For two days the Dutch held the Princess of Orange, the Prussian King's sister, under arrest.[2] We'll see how her dear old brother takes that. Louis XIV would've made them beg for mercy for such a thing. The English are outfitting 12 ships and are already helping the Orange faction with money. That's the news as we have it from here.

Only here in the north did we come upon warm weather and fruits, and you have neither hot weather nor fruits; now we're going to tantalize you with them. Sasha[3] is very sweet. We ask you to love him and be nice to him, for he loves you so with all his soul.

---

1. The Austrian Netherlands were then revolting against the Habsburgs and demanding the return of the former privileges of the local nobility, church, and towns that Joseph II had taken away.

2. Fredericka Sofia Wilhelmina (1750–1820), wife of Stadtholder William V of Orange (1751–1802), was forcibly held by members of the pro-French Patriot Party, in opposition to the stadtholder. Backed by the British, Prussian troops marched into the United Provinces in September 1787, crushed the Patriot Party, and restored William V. This marked the warming of Anglo-Prussian relations, and in August 1788 the two countries signed a defensive alliance, directed against France, Austria, and Russia.

3. Mamonov.

311. POTEMKIN TO CATHERINE

17 July [1787]. Kremenchug

Your Majesty! I received your gracious missive from Tver. God knows how sensitive I am to its expressions. You are dearer to me than my own mother since your concern for my well-being is freely rendered. This is not blind luck. How much I owe you. How many signs of distinction you have given me. How widely you have showered your blessings on those attached to me. But most of all, malice and envy have never been able to incite anger in you toward me, and all the stratagems against me have been completely unsuccessful. That is what is rare in this world. Steadfastness of this degree was granted you alone.

This land will never forget its good fortune. You are an eternal part of it, for it considers itself to be your estate and has complete confidence in your charity.

I thank you for Katenka,[1] who speaks with great affection of the blessings rendered her. In general, all is well with us. To escape this unbearable heat I am leaving for Yelizavetgrad: it sits on higher ground. Nevertheless, there is, thank God, no disease present, and when someone does fall ill, he soon recovers. Farewell, my benefactress and matushka, God grant me the opportunity to show the entire world how much I owe you, being till death

your most loyal servant
Prince Potemkin-Tavrichesky

---

1. Potemkin's niece Yekaterina Skavronskaia accompanied the empress on her return.

312. CATHERINE TO POTEMKIN

From Tsarskoe Selo. 27 July 1787

My friend, Prince Grigory Aleksandrovich. I received your letter of 17 July the other day, and from it saw how happy my letter from Tver made you. Just between you and me, my friend, I'll tell you the state of affairs in a few words: you serve me, and I am grateful. And that's all there is to it. With your zeal toward me and your fervor for the affairs of the Empire you rapped your enemies across the knuckles. I'm glad you're well. Please abstain from all fruit. Thank God there's no disease and no one is ill.

Affairs in Europe are getting complicated. The Emperor[1] is sending troops to the Netherlands. The King of Prussia is arming himself against the Dutch. France, which has no money, is setting up camps. England is sending out its fleet and is giving money to the Prince of Orange. The other powers keep watch, yet I stroll about my garden, which has grown up nicely and is beautiful. Farewell, God be with you.

1. Joseph II, the Holy Roman Emperor.

313. POTEMKIN TO CATHERINE

1 August [1787]

Your Majesty. Glory be to God who kept you well throughout the entire difficult journey, which will remain for all time the most pleasant of memories for us. Be well, my beloved matushka, and fully content. I would give my soul to you were it possible. So many favors you have showered upon me. In the autumn we shall sow forests and plant gardens, and our descendants will say: Here is the grove that Catherine the Great ordered sown; here are the chestnut trees she ordered planted in sandy places; and having drunk the clear water, they will recall your care. Twenty springs have now been found all around Yekaterinoslav. In Kremenchug the heat is sultry and unbearable. I am departing to go live in the country some seventy versts from here. Everyone else is leaving too.

What you write to me, matushka, about Aleksandr Matveevich I too shall say the same of him. And what's more, believe that I love him very much.

How wonderful it would be, matushka, if Holland drove the French into a fight with the English.

Farewell, my precious benefactress. I remain till death your most loyal and most grateful subject

Prince Potemkin-Tavrichesky

314. CATHERINE TO POTEMKIN

12 August 1787 from the City of St. Peter, which is on the Neva banks and which is terribly handsome, but is built in a very bad climate.

My friend, Prince Grigory Aleksandrovich. I received your letter of 1 August two days ago. I arrived here in town almost a week ago, and while you in Kremenchug celebrated my safe return, I celebrated here the Day of the Transfiguration, attended Mass in the regiment's church, dined with the officers and drank to the health of the lieutenants-colonel together with the subalterns. And I didn't forget as well to talk about what I had seen on my trip and how the man in charge there distinguishes himself like a true governor-general. I am well, as are all those who arrived with me. Since my arrival, for an entire month that is, it's done nothing but rain here, and but for one day we have not had any warm weather. Nothing but the thickest layer of clouds and gloomy weather. Such are the St. Petersburg holidays. I practically live in the Hermitage and leave the weather to do what it will.

I wish you much success in the sowing of trees and the planting of gardens. Having done this, you'll mitigate the sun's intense heat, attract the rains and so give those places exactly what they lack. I was also pleased to note that springs had been located. Cela s'appelle faire du bien à la contrée. Vous lui donnés ce qu'elle n'a pas.[1]

Please, please be well, avoid all fruits et ne Vous exposés pas trop à la chaleur.[2]

The letters from Tsar Grad clearly show that the Turks are playing games.[3] It appears as if the English want to profit from the French shortage of money and for this reason have gotten themselves entangled in Dutch affairs.

Thank you for fondly loving Sasha. He's an honest and noble man. Farewell, my friend, be well. Katia[4] has arrived.

---

1. "This is called doing good to the region. You give it what it lacks."

2. "and do not expose yourself too much to the heat."

3. Encouraged by the British and the Prussians, the Porte demanded from Russia changes in the Treaty of Kuchuk Kainardji, the recall of the Russian consul in Moldavia, the renunciation of the protectorate of Georgia, the opening of a Turkish consulate in the Crimea, and the handing over of the Moldavian hospodar.

4. Yekaterina Skavronskaia.

315. POTEMKIN TO CATHERINE

14 August [1787]. The village of Mikhailovka

Your Majesty. I have fully recovered,[1] but the drought in Kremenchug and Kherson has led to an increase in illnesses. I am taking all measures against them and place my hope in God. I've stopped all the work being done in Kherson till the middle of September. This will serve to relieve the forces. I'm not going there lest rumor of my arrival cause our neighbors to draw greater attention to Ochakov. Nonetheless, I have ordered the troops to prepare for Olviopol.

I should skip a page; ink is seeping through onto the back side. There is no water in the streams here, and the windmills are all motionless. I have already started buying grain. Profiteers, who have arrived from various places, have driven up the price threefold.

My beloved matushka, remain gracious toward me always. I remain till death

your most loyal and most grateful subject
Prince Potemkin-Tavrichesky

---

1. Potemkin fell ill in Kremenchug in July.

316. CATHERINE TO POTEMKIN

19 August 1787

My friend, Prince Grigory Aleksandrovich, your letters of 7 August have reached my hands.[1] I am very sorry that in addition to the current troubles you were ill for a spell. Please do take care of yourself and remember this request of mine. In light of the first courier from Tsar Grad, I am anticipating one of two probable adventures: either the mad Vizier[2] and Reis-Efendi will be removed or war will be declared. It seems that the French interest requires that court's ambassador to work for a change of ministry; and since the Sultan himself wants peace, and not war, so this seems all the more likely.[3] I'm composing a long answer in response to a long letter.[4] If you think that the removal of Consul Selunsky[5] is necessary, then he can be recalled from there for a time under the pretense of a temporary holiday.

Farewell, my friend, be well. We are all well, and Sasha is quite a dear.

---

1. Potemkin wrote to Catherine on 7 August of his recent illness and of Turkish demands presented to Bulgakov in Constantinople. Potemkin had written to Bulgakov to accept them and so avoid war.

2. Grand Vizier Koja Yusuf Pasha (d. 1800) led the partisans for war with Russia.

3. France could not see any gain for itself from a Turkish declaration of war. Yet since it no longer enjoyed the same influence it once did with the Porte, it was unable to dissuade the Imperial Council from attacking Russia, despite the fact that the aged Sultan Abdul Hamid I (reigned 1774–1789) was inclined toward peace.

4. A reference to Letter 318 that Catherine wrote in response to a report from Potemkin of 1 August.

5. Russian Vice Consul Selunsky resided in Jassy in Moldavia. Potemkin did in fact consider it necessary to recall him to help prevent war.

7. War—1787

O n 13 August 1787, the Sublime Porte declared war on Russia. For months Grand Vizier Koja Yusuf Pasha had led the call for immediate war as the only way to make amends for Turkey's past defeats. While no one at the Porte was against the idea of war, there was disagreement over the exact timing. Sultan Abdul Hamid and Gazi Hasan Pasha, grand admiral of the Turkish navy, believed that the country was not yet ready. They maintained more time was needed to prepare for the inevitably long and costly fight and that concrete promises of support first had to be gained from Britain and Prussia. Throughout the spring and summer of 1787, Yusuf Pasha, with the support of the Janissaries and the imams, incited the masses of the capital to demand war against the infidel. By June, there were reports of rioting in Constantinople and rumors that if Abdul Hamid did not declare war, he would be overthrown. Confronted with unrest in the streets and intense pressure from his top officials, the sultan succumbed. On 5 August, the Russian envoy was summoned and told that the Porte had renounced its existing treaties with Russia and demanded that Russia evacuate the Crimea and Georgia. The demands were intended to provoke war, and Yakov Bulgakov rejected them out of hand. He was arrested and thrown into the Seven Towers fortress. The Ottomans would have war.

As soon as Potemkin learned of Bulgakov's arrest and the rupture of relations with the Turks, he dashed off a short letter on 21 August to tell Catherine the news and to instruct her to order a large levy of recruits (Letter 317). While Potemkin's courier rode northward, he was passed by one heading southward bearing a letter from Catherine written three days later (on 24 August) about the reports of war coming out of Moldavia, which the empress was inclined to believe (Letter 318). Catherine compared her situation with that which prevailed upon the outbreak of the First Russo-Turkish War in 1768 and found reason for confidence given the gains made over the intervening years in advancing Russia's borders and developing her military potential in the south.

Yet while back in the capital Catherine faced the threat of war with cautious optimism, in the south a profound despair descended on the prince and deepened as the days and weeks progressed. Not unlike their Turkish counterparts, Catherine and Potemkin had expected war, but not so soon. They had hoped for another two years of peace in which to make the necessary preparations, but as Catherine observed, "the bubble has burst ahead of time" (Letter 318). Part of Potemkin's despair may be explained as an expression of regret over his own actions toward the Porte during the past year. In October 1786, Catherine had put Potemkin in charge of Russia's relations with the Porte, and although he had taken concrete steps to avoid war in the summer of 1787, his actions up until then had only served to increase tensions and to make the outbreak of hostilities more likely. The saber-rattling exhibited on the 1787 voyage served as the final straw that pushed the Porte to declare war, and the cocksure bravado Potemkin had displayed during those weeks evaporated as soon as he realized the Turks had called his bluff.

The primary objective of the Turkish forces was to seize the Crimea using the approximately 24,000 men of the Ochakov garrison. Supported by the Turkish fleet, which greatly outnumbered the Russian navy in the Black Sea, these troops planned to take the fortress of Kinburn and then Kherson before advancing into the Crimea. Next, Turkish troops would secure the coast as far west as the Bug River. Forces were also to be dispatched to Anapa in order to incite the inhabitants of the Kuban against the Russians.

Russian military aims centered on the network of Turkish fortresses located along the northern Black Sea littoral at key positions on the Liman, Dniester, Pruth, and Danube rivers. These fortresses allowed the Turks to maintain their grasp on the Black Sea's northern shore. The Russian army dared not advance beyond them to the west since this would expose its supply lines to disruption, or worse. This situation dictated the use of siege warfare and required the taking of each fortress, one by one, before advancing westward. The conduct of Russia's war effort was placed in the hands of Potemkin, commander in chief for both the army and the navy. His responsibilities included overseeing operations against the Turks in the south and ensuring the defense of Russia's western border with Poland and its northern border with Sweden. Russia's ground forces were divided into two armies: the Yekaterinoslav Army, comprising over 80,000 men, was placed under Potemkin's direct command, and a smaller, reserve Ukrainian Army, with approximately 40,000 men, was entrusted to Field Marshal Pyotr Rumiantsev. Russian forces were also deployed to the Caucasus and the Kuban. Russia's original plan had been to seize the fortress of Ochakov with Potemkin's army, and so secure the Liman and ensure the safety of the Crimea. Given the early beginning of hostilities, however, Potemkin was forced to conduct a defensive campaign and to put off the siege until the following year.

On 18 August, Potemkin, fearing a Turkish attack, sent an order to General Suvorov in Kherson to heighten his vigilance and keep an eye on the Turks' movements at Ochakov and on the Bug. Fighting broke out the following day when Turkish ships off Ochakov opened fire on two Russian vessels attempting to escort recently constructed warships out of the Liman. In early September, the Turks began bombarding Kinburn in preparation for an assault. Suvorov rushed there himself, and on the night of 14 September, an attempted landing was repelled, although the bombardment continued (Letters 321, 322).

Throughout the first three weeks of September, Potemkin's spirit continued to flag. As the commander in chief, he shouldered immense responsibility, and the strain was taking its toll. On top of this, since August he had been sick with fever and wracked with spasms. He could barely eat or sleep. Potemkin's letters from this period betray a shaky, quivering hand, testimony to the extreme physical and emotional strain under which he labored. For years he had toiled to prepare Russia for this day, and now he was unable to manage it and sought a way to abandon all his cares. He begged Catherine for rest and to allow him to come join her in St. Petersburg, even if only for a while, entrusting command to Rumiantsev in his absence (Letters 321, 322). And then, just when it seemed things could not get any worse, Potemkin received word on 24 September that the Sevastopol fleet, the prince's great accomplishment and the source of so much personal pride, had been caught in a violent storm two weeks earlier and lost at sea. The news dealt Potemkin a crushing blow. He wrote Catherine that day to tell her of the catastrophe and to inform her that he was writing to Rumiantsev to ask him to accept command. His spirit was broken, he told her, and he was now laying down all the titles and decorations she had so graciously bestowed upon him. He sensed the approach of death, and he wanted to meet it alone in some quiet retreat far away from the great stage he had long occupied (Letter 323). That same day he wrote a second letter to Catherine arguing that given the loss of the fleet, the Crimea was now vulnerable to Turkish naval attack and so ought to be evacuated. It was a difficult decision, one that would provoke censure if not more, but one that he felt had to be taken to save the lives of the soldiers stationed there.

From the capital, Catherine sought to calm her worried prince and to reassure him of her unquestioned support. In her letters, she tried her best to project an image of strength and confidence even though these were tense days for her too. Catherine's initial optimism had begun to show signs of fading; she was anxious and prone to uncharacteristic outbursts of anger and fits of tears. It was becoming ever more difficult for her to bear the periods between the arrival of Potemkin's couriers. Impatient for news, she increased the number of horses along the post route to speed the delivery of his letters, which meant the couriers could reach the capital from Kremenchug in about seven days. Word of Potemkin's poor health especially grieved her, and Catherine, writing like a worried wife and mother, repeatedly urged him to take better care of himself (Letters 319, 320, 324).

Catherine was particularly troubled by Potemkin's wish to renounce command and to return to St. Petersburg, which she considered a sign of weakness. In response to his letter of 19 September (Letter 322), she wrote Potemkin on the 25th that she was sending him an order giving command to Rumiantsev, though she asked that he delay doing so as long as possible (Letter 325). A week later she received two letters from Potemkin: first, one dated 26 September arrived, and several hours another dated the 24th (Letter 323). The letter of the 24th, written after Potemkin learned of the loss of the Sevastopol fleet, contained Potemkin's comments on the need to abandon the Crimea. The second letter Potemkin had written soon after receiving the miraculous news that the initial reports about the fleet had been greatly exaggerated; the ships had actually survived the storm and were on their way back to Sevastopol. In her reply dated 2 October, Catherine did her best to be encouraging, but she was finding this increasingly difficult. She strongly disagreed with his idea of giving up the Crimea, which she correctly assumed he had only entertained when he thought the fleet had been destroyed, and in a rare moment of candor, let him know he was acting just like a small child (Letter 327).

Meanwhile, on the night of 1 October, the Turks landed 5,000 Janissaries on the Kinburn spit in an all-out assault on the Russian fortress. In a daring move, Suvorov kept his men inside the fortress and did not fire a shot as the Turks came ashore and approached the fortress. Then, suddenly, the Russians poured out of the fortress and attacked the Turks in three successive waves. The fighting was bloody and lasted throughout the entire day and on into the night. For a time it looked as if the Russians would be defeated. Yet when it was over, almost the entire Turkish force had been destroyed, and although the Russian forces had suffered significant casualties as well, Kinburn had been saved. Potemkin first reported the good news to Catherine on 6 October and then again in greater detail on 1 November, when he praised Suvorov's exceptional bravery and urged her to reward him with the Order of St. Andrew, Russia's oldest and highest order, despite the possible objections of some generals with greater seniority. Past historians have often written of Potemkin's petty jealousy toward Suvorov's successes. His letters to the empress explode this myth and show Potemkin's true appreciation for Suvorov and his exploits (Letters 328, 330).

The victory at Kinburn helped to arouse Potemkin, and by early October the depression and illness that had laid him low for over a month had passed. There were, however, new troubles brewing. On 31 August, recognizing that she needed more advisors to assist her in the war effort, Catherine added several new officials to the State Council, some of whom were sworn enemies of the prince. Concerned at how Potemkin might react, she tried to convince him that he remained in her trust and that she would protect him (Letters 320, 324). Over time, however, Potemkin's enemies in the Council, especially Pyotr Zavadovsky and Count Aleksandr Vorontsov, managed to fill Catherine's head with doubts concerning Potemkin's conduct of the war. Most importantly, they gave her the false impression that Ochakov would crumble before the slightest display of Russian military strength. Even though she knew Russian forces would have to remain on the defensive for the rest of the year, in early October Catherine began pushing Potemkin to explain why he had not yet taken Ochakov, which Potemkin, with palpable frustration, attempted to do (Letters 327, 329, 330).

The international situation was another source of friction between Catherine and Potemkin. Instead of declaring war, as obligated by their alliance of 1781, the Austrians were coyly waiting to see how matters would develop. Frustrated by their ally's stalling and how this aided Russia's foes, Potemkin suggested in mid-November making certain overtures to Prussia to ease the situation. He recommended employing the Prussian minister in Constantinople on some small mission so as to communicate to the Porte that the Prussian king could not be relied on for support. Potemkin also urged appeasing the king with the city of Danzig, long sought by the Prussians. Catherine greeted Potemkin's ideas harshly, interpreting them as signs of indecision on his part. She refused to accept the notion that the Prussian court should be shown any special consideration, and pointedly reminded him that the alliance with Austria had been his idea. Rightly disturbed by the Anglo-Prussian alliance of August 1787, with its unmistakable anti-Russian character, and advised by Count Bezborodko to adopt a hard line toward Prussia, Catherine could not countenance Potemkin's proposals and let him know in no uncertain terms (Letter 332).

Their disagreement led to a breakdown in communication. In the final two months of 1787, Potemkin wrote the empress only five times. From mid-November until mid-December she did not receive a single letter. She was growing desperate for word from him, whatever it might be, and began to reproach him for not realizing the strain his silence placed her under. She trusted Potemkin and wanted to see him succeed, but surrounded as she was by his detractors, it was extremely important that he keep her informed of matters in the south. Finally, on 25 December, Potemkin responded. Deeply offended by her letter of the previous month, Potemkin tried to explain to her his reasoning for reaching out to Prussia and reaffirmed his commitment to the Austrian alliance. Moreover, he pointed out that had she not frowned upon his proposed alliance with the Poles of the year before, they would now be fighting alongside Russia against the Turks, and there would be less need to worry about neutralizing Prussia. He went on to reiterate all the troubles associated with the conduct of the war that he faced as commander in chief, troubles that the courtiers intent on destroying the empress's trust in Potemkin did not have to confront (Letter 333).

On 30 December, Catherine was finally able to write Potemkin with some good news. On the night of 2 December, Austria, without officially declaring war, had launched a surprise attack on the Turks at Belgrade. Although the attack failed, nevertheless it made Joseph's intentions clear to all and would soon lead to war between Austria and the Ottomans, exactly what Catherine and Potemkin had been so urgently awaiting. Still, the empress was vexed. Recent discussions with Versailles over a Franco-Russian alliance had collapsed, and this seemed to be a reflection of the European courts' growing antagonism toward Russia. What troubled her most, however, was Potemkin's neglect in writing, and she begged him yet again to write more often. His silence, Catherine moaned, was causing her to die not once, but a thousand times (Letter 334).

• • •

317. POTEMKIN TO CATHERINE

21 August [1787]

Your Most Gracious Majesty!
War's been declared. Bulgakov's been imprisoned in the Yedikule.[1] I've been pushed to the brink. The regiments can't get here quickly from their quarters. In Kherson there is a dreadful number of sick. In the Crimea there are many as well. It will be difficult to defend the ships in the Liman. God alone has the power to help us. All grain transports will stop. If my life could solve all these difficulties, I would give it. Order a large levy of recruits and add double the number to the reserve regiments in Russia. It will be difficult for us to hold out till some help arrives.

Your loyal subject
Prince Potemkin-Tavrichesky

1. Bulgakov was imprisoned in the Seven Towers fortress (the Yedikule) on 5 August.

318. CATHERINE TO POTEMKIN

24 August 1787

My true friend, Prince Grigory Aleksandrovich, I'm glad you have recovered, but at the same time I quite regret that in Kherson the number of sick has increased. People are talking here as if there isn't a single healthy person there and everyone is ill with diarrhea. You should stock up on rice in Kherson and in those places where diarrhea is a problem. Nothing but rice will cure this diarrhea. Recall that the Tatars, the Turks, the Persians, the Italians and all inhabitants of warm places use rice. Once it becomes inexpensive, then everyone will buy it, however, it can be fed to the sick for nothing. In addition, along with this dish you should order the sick be given a small glass of strong wine. These thoughts simply occurred to me and so I considered it my duty to communicate them to you. I hope they will be of some use. If it were possible, I would send you our rains by post. From July tenth, when I arrived here, till today it's rained every day, and we have seen almost no clear and warm days since the day of St. Peter.

I wrote all that immediately upon receiving your letter of 14 August.[1] But yesterday evening, while coming from the opera "Fevei," I received reports from Consul Selunsky of 11 and 14 August, according to which it appears that the Moldavian Hospodar himself ordered that he be told that war has been declared and that he, together with all Russians, must depart for Russia; et comme pour ne me tromper je mettrai les choses ainsi,[2] that is, I shall consider war to have been declared till I receive news to the contrary, though Selunsky's expulsion may perhaps be a separate matter. For they have been seeking his recall and have said that they will expel him. As for the rest, they look like Moldavian and Walachian reports, which have sometimes been erroneous, mais ceux-ci cependent paroissent avoir le cachet de la vérité.[3] My thoughts therefore are solely directed toward preparing the troops, and since yesterday evening I have begun to compare my situation now in 1787 with that in which I found myself upon the declaration of war in November 1768.[4] Then we expected the war to begin a year later; the regiments were scattered across the entire Empire in their billets; it was late autumn; no preparations had begun; revenues were much less than now; the Tatars were upon us and nomad encampments on the steppe reached to Tor and Bakhmut, and in January they rode into the Yelizavetgrad district. Our war plan amounted to nothing more than turning our defense into an attack. Two armies were sent. One served to defend the Empire, while the other marched toward Khotin. After Moldavia and the lands beyond the Danube had been occupied in the first and second campaigns, then the second army took Bender and occupied the Crimea. The fleet was detailed to the Mediterranean Sea and a small corps to Georgia.

Now our border runs along the Bug and the Kuban. Kherson has been built. The Crimea constitutes part of the Empire and in Sevastopol we have a fine fleet. There are troops in Tauride, fine armies are already stationed on the very border, and they are stronger in fact than were the defensive and offensive armies of the year 1768. God grant we have no difficulty with money, which I'll now do everything possible to secure and hope to be successful. I know that it would have been quite preferable if peace could have been preserved for two more years so that we could have completed the fortresses of Kherson and Sevastopol, and also so that the army and fleet could have been brought to the desired state of readiness. But what is to be done if the bubble has burst ahead of time? I recall that at the very conclusion of the Peace of Kainardji, wise men doubted whether the Vizier and Sultan would ratify it, and then they incorrectly predicted that peace would last no longer than two years, but instead fourteen summers began peacefully. If the Turks have declared war, then I suppose they have left the fleet in Ochakov in order to prevent the ships built in Kherson from reaching Sevastopol. But if they haven't done this, then I suppose it won't be so easy for them to anchor in the Dnieper estuary next year as it would be now.

I rely upon your fervent care that you will keep the Sevastopol harbor and fleet free from harm; in winter a fleet in the harbor is always in danger. Of course, Sevastopol is not Chesme. I admit that only one thing frightens me, namely, the plague. For the sake of God Himself, I beg you— in your three provinces, in the army and in the fleet take all possible measures in a timely manner so that this evil doesn't steal into us again as a result of carelessness. I know that in Tsar Grad itself there is now no word of the plague, but as it is forever present there, so their troops spread it wherever they go. Send me (and for me alone) your plan for how you intend to fight the war in order that I might know it and then might judge you according to your very own ideas. In the past year of 1786 you were given a rescript, and so inform me of everything in detail in order that I might always squelch the slightest ravings here in a timely manner and put a stop to every possible act. It seems the French now have a good reason to deny the Turks any assistance since war was been declared in defiance of their demand that peace be maintained. We'll see what the Emperor does. He is obligated by treaty to declare war on the Turks in three months.

The Prussians and Swedes are the firebrands behind this, but I don't think that the former will create a diversion, and the latter scarcely can, unless the Spaniards give them money, which is most unlikely.[5] And can you achieve much while fighting with someone else's money? [. . .] Farewell, my friend, be well. Everything here is fine, but thoughts of war are brewing in my head just like young beer in a barrel, and Sasha[6] is extremely concerned and tries to calm my agitated noodle.

The Emperor's ambassador still hasn't received a courier.[7] Fitzherbert[8] has departed, Ségur and Ligne wanted to leave on Tuesday, but as soon as he hears of the war, Ligne will most certainly gallop off to you upon receiving the Emperor's permission.[9] I suppose you have no more nails left on your fingers—you've gnawed them all off.

Adieu, mon Ami.

The real reason for the war is and will be that the Turks want to alter the treaties: first—that of Kainardji, second—the convention on the Crimea, third—the commercial one.[10] It is possible that as soon as war is declared they will try to begin negotiations. They acted the same way in 1768. But if my minister has been imprisoned in the Seven Towers as he was then, so will they have to answer for the very same example, for the dignity of the Russian court does not permit paying heed to any peace proposals till this power's minister is returned to her.

[. . .]

1. Letter 315.

2. "and so as not to be mistaken, I shall consider it so,"

3. "but these, however, would appear to have the mark of truth."

4. The First Russo-Turkish War began in 1768.

5. Though generally accurate, Catherine did not give adequate due to the role of the British in provoking the Turks. Sweden was given money by the Porte to attack Russia in the north.

6. Mamonov.

7. Cobenzl had yet to receive word from Joseph II that he had begun military operations in support of Russia.

8. Britain's ambassador to Russia, Alleyne Fitzherbert (1753–1839), was recalled soon after the outbreak of the war.

9. Count Ségur returned to France following the southern voyage of 1787. Prince Charles Joseph de Ligne (1735–1814), a Belgian-born subject of Austria, was a hero of the Seven Years' War, a writer, a wit, and a friend of Joseph II. He took part in the 1787 voyage and joined Potemkin at Yelizavetgrad after the outbreak of the war, where he began to spy on the Russians for the Emperor.

10. Russia and the Ottoman Empire signed a commercial treaty in 1783.

319. CATHERINE TO POTEMKIN

29 August 1787

My friend, Prince Grigory Aleksandrovich. I received this morning the letter you wrote of 21 August, which confirmed for me the Moldavian news concerning the declaration of war. I thank you very much for not hiding from me the dangerous situation in which you find yourself. God Himself demands no greater from man than what he is capable of withstanding.

The Russian God has always been, is and will be great. I place my unshakable faith in God Almighty and rely upon your proven zeal, that, as much as you can, you will make full use of your intelligence to extirpate evil and to overcome all possible obstacles. And for my part, I shall not miss a single opportunity to lend help wherever it may be required of me. I have already ordered a recruitment levy of two men from every five hundred persons, and shall order double the number added to the reserve regiments in Russia, and I beg you in every possible way that in the future you continue to notify me of the true state of affairs with the same exact trust. I know that in difficult and dangerous circumstances one must not be dejected, and so I remain toward you ever friendly and benevolent

Catherine

320. CATHERINE TO POTEMKIN

2 September 1787

My true friend, Prince Grigory Aleksandrovich. My greatest and chief concern and worry now are for your health, for which I zealously pray God. Be so good as to notify me more often how you are. If only God would return you to health, then I would be sure that my friend and favorite would be the same as my opinion of him and the same as my trust in him. I received yesterday your letter of 22 August and see from it that you have taken all possible measures,[1] even though all of the enemy's efforts are now being directed against you. Since you reckoned that our troops will arrive fifteen days after 22 August, so from this day I reckon in four days they will be where they are needed.

I quite regret that there are many sick in Kherson. The Russian God is great in a special way; the border along the Bug will remain free from harm. I ordered a rescript prepared for Field Marshal Rumiantsev, and a copy of it will be sent to you. A levy of recruits has already been ordered, as I wrote you. The ambassador received a courier yesterday and announced to the Vice Chancellor that the Emperor recognizes *casus foederis*[2] and is ready to fulfill his obligations and to command his troops to go to the Turkish borders. I enclose herewith a copy of the Emperor's letter to me. I am now being as vigilant as possible to ensure that no one creates any obstacles for you in whatever way, be it even with a single word. Rest assured that I intend to defend and to protect you just as much as you do me from the enemy, and I have become so sensitive about all that concerns you that I even take the measure of every expression and word, and weigh them on a scale, such as I have never done in all my born days.[3] And as you give me in every instance unquestionable proof of your zeal and loyalty, rest assured that you yourself can expect from me in every instance unquestionable signs of friendship and genuinely friendly support. May God fortify your physical strength, and you, my friend, will use your spiritual and intellectual gifts for the good of the Empire and of my affairs.

May the evil tongues see how splendid is my ward and favorite, and may he in his glory be solicitous and in his good fortune not proud, but exactly as I desire to see him. Perhaps you will laugh at my words and will say they are unnecessary, but to this I shall say to you: let them be unnecessary, with whom can one speak of unnecessary things if not with one's friend. Farewell, true friend, you will be well, and I shall be calm.

Were I in Sevastopol now, I would take a seat with Voinovich[4] on that ship I was on during my stay in that port. Its role may perhaps be brilliant should God bless them, as I heartily desire, with fortune and reason and valor. Adieu, mon Ami.

----

1. Potemkin ordered Suvorov, who had been put in charge of the defense of Kinburn, to be ready for a Turkish assault.

2. By recognizing *casus foederis* (literally, a reason leading to a dispute under treaty), Joseph II signaled his intention to abide by his treaty obligations with Russia toward the Porte.

3. Having added several new members to the State Council, including enemies of Potemkin's such as Pyotr Zavadovsky and Count Aleksandr Romanovich Vorontsov (1741–1805), Catherine attempted to reassure Potemkin of her continued support and trust.

4. Rear Admiral Count Mark Ivanovich Voinovich (1750–1807) was in charge of the Black Sea fleet. Haughty and indecisive, Voinovich was relieved of command by Potemkin in 1790.

321. POTEMKIN TO CATHERINE

16 September [1787]. Kremenchug

Your Most Gracious Majesty! Couriers arriving practically one right after the other have delivered to me your most precious letters. My patroness, you truly write to me like my own mother, but it is beyond my power to be worthy of your ineffable favors.

First of all, I'll begin by noting that the enemy is mercilessly bearing down on Kinburn, directing all his bombardments upon it, and for 4 days and for 4 nights now he cannons and bombards without ceasing. So far he has inflicted only minor damage. We have had 4 killed and 10 injured. God instills our soldiers with courage. They are not dejected. I have ordered everyone there to distribute wine and meat to the men. That detachment is under the command of Major-General Rek,[1] a Courlander, brave and smart, who understands Russian like a native, which means a good deal to the men. The commandant there, Tunzelman,[2] is a well-tried man. Above them all both here and in Kherson is Aleksandr Vasilievich

Suvorov. The truth must be told: now there is a man who serves not only with every ounce of sweat, but every drop of blood as well. I shall rejoice when God gives me an opportunity to recommend him. Kakhovsky[3] in the Crimea would climb atop a cannon with the same nonchalance as onto a couch, but he lacks the energy of the former. Matushka, do not think of Kinburn as a fortress. It is a cramped and foul castle with very weak retrenchments, so you should consider how hard it will be to hold on to it. The more so since it is a bit over a hundred versts from Kherson. The Sevastopol fleet left for Varna. May God protect it.

Count Pyotr Aleksandrovich[4] has sent me two infantry regiments, two of carabineers, and has ordered General Kamensky[5] to follow with his unit from Orel. But he still hasn't set out, except for the Rostov infantry regiment which has already arrived in Kremenchug from Belagorod. Things will be easier for me once he arrives here. I shall then lead him into Poland, however, I shall act with the detachments stationed along the Bug, for the border will then be safe.

Matushka, raise no fewer than 60 thousand recruits. If you don't do this now, the army will never be brought up to full strength and as a result of this shortage it will immediately exhaust itself. Given the high cost of grain, the populace will not grieve over this.

Thank God the Emperor has decided to take part; the sooner he declares war the better.

In the meantime, order the English and the Prussians be stroked. The fleet intended for the Archipelago must be made ready. No fewer than twenty ships of the line are needed, however, prepare 40. Tell the French of the ships' departure so as to convey to them that you do not doubt that they will extend to our fleet the necessary advantages while on their shores. The same thing to the English. Then you will see how each responds.

Your Majesty, as for me, unless God gives me strength I shall remain extremely weak, beset by millions of troubles, and the most severe hypochondria. I haven't a minute's rest. For truth, I'm not certain I can go on like this much longer. I can't sleep or eat. All these games I must play to ensure that nothing be lost. If only I could withdraw or steal away so that the world would hear nothing more of me! Such an accursed defensive position. The Crimea and Kherson alone have 20 infantry regiments. What an army that would make! But the sick, oh, they so greatly reduce our forces.

Farewell, matushka, I can't write any more. If only Ivan Petrovich[6] would arrive sooner. Permit me to come to Petersburg for a short while during the winter months. There's no way to write, to explain everything.

Your most loyal and most grateful subject
Prince Potemkin-Tavrichesky

1. Major-General Ivan Grigorievich von Rek (1737–1795) commanded a detachment defending Kinburn.

2. Colonel Yegor Andreevich Tunzelman (b. 1736) was the commandant from 1784.

3. General-in-Chief Mikhail Vasilievich Kakhovsky (1734–1800), one of Russia's most talented generals, was in charge of the Crimean forces.

4. Rumiantsev.

5. Mikhail Fedotovich Kamensky (1738–1809).

6. General-in-Chief Ivan Saltykov served in Rumiantsev's Ukrainian Army. His forces were to march to the right bank of the Dnieper to provide cover for Potemkin's troops operating in the lower reaches of the Dnieper and the Southern Bug.

322. POTEMKIN TO CATHERINE

19 September [1787]

Your Most Gracious Majesty. There's no news from the fleet. The Turks do not stop cannonading Kinburn, and several times they tried to land at night, but have found our men ready for them. I have ordered that an attempt be made on the Turkish gunboats with all possible vessels. We need five days to prepare for this. Lord knows when Kamensky will finally arrive. Part of the infantry, the battalions of grenadiers, that is, are ready; the other part won't be ready before the middle of next month. Yet I, matushka, am extremely ill. Spasms torment me, and I'm truly useless. Dispassion is needed now and not the great sensitivity that I possess. And God forbid we suffer some loss, for then, if I don't die from grief, I'll probably lay down all my titles at your feet and shall hide myself in obscurity. Be kind, allow me to rest, even if only a little. For truth, I cannot go on. I have done everything possible till now: I'm confidant about our grain supply, and that the troops, which are being formed, will be ready. But I don't know what to do this year. Count Pyotr Aleksandrovich's troops must now act in concert with those here, so he should have full command. And the Emperor's cordon abuts his flank. It will be easier for him to discuss matters with them having already dealt with them. Were you to give him command and to allow me to come to Petersburg, I would recover on the journey. Matushka, God sees I've no more strength.

Your most loyal and most grateful servant
Prince Potemkin-Tavrichesky

323. POTEMKIN TO CATHERINE

24 September [1787]. Kremenchug

Your Majesty, I've become despondent. Though I've taken every possible measure, still everything is topsy-turvy. The Sevastopol fleet has been smashed to pieces by a storm; its remains are in Sevastopol—all the small and unreliable vessels, or, to put it better, the useless ones. The ships and large frigates have been lost. God strikes us, not the Turks.[1] On top of my illness, this has struck me an extreme blow; my spirit's broken, I'm at my wit's end. I have requested that command be entrusted to another. Believe me, I truly feel this way; do not allow matters to suffer because of this. Oh, I'm almost dead. I lay before your feet all the favors and possessions I've received from your munificence; I want to end my life, which I think will not last much longer, in seclusion and obscurity. I'm writing now to Count Pyotr Aleksandrovich requesting that he take up command, how-ever, not having an order from you, I don't think he will accept it.[2] And so, God knows what is to be. I relieve myself of everything and remain a common man. But that I was devoted to you, God is my witness.

Your most loyal and most grateful servant
Prince Potemkin-Tavrichesky

1. The Black Sea fleet was battered by a powerful storm beginning 9 September while out at sea. According to initial reports, the entire fleet had been lost.

2. Rumiantsev did agree to accept command from Potemkin, but only temporarily while the prince was away in the capital.

324. CATHERINE TO POTEMKIN

24 September 1787

My dear friend, Prince Grigory Aleksandrovich. After a seventeen-day wait for a letter from you, I received yesterday all at once your letters of 13, 15 and 16 September, in response to which you will receive my decisions forthwith.[1] I shall enclose a list of them as soon as I end my reply to your personal letter, and I shall begin my reply by saying that I am quite pleased to see that you give my letters their true worth: they are and will be nothing but sincerely friendly. Your health worries me a great deal. I know how solicitous you are, how zealous you are, exerting yourself with all your might. For God Himself, for me, take better care of yourself than you have been. Nothing frightens me, except your illness. Dans ce mo-ment-ci, mon cher Ami, Vous n'êtes pas un petit particulier qui vit et qui fait ce que lui plait; Vous êtes à l'état, Vous êtes à moi; Vous devés, et je Vous ordonne de prendre garde à Votre santé; je le dois, parce que le bien, la défense et la gloire de l'Empire sont confiés à Vos soins, et qu'il faut se porter bien de corps et d'âme pour faire la besogne que Vous avés sur les bras; après cette exortation maternelle, que je Vous prie de recevoir avec docilité et obéissance je m'en vais continuer.[2]

I saw from the letter you wrote that Kinburn is under siege and had by then already withstood four days and nights of cannonade and bombardment. God grant that it not be lost, for any loss is unpleasant. But suppose it is—there's no reason to be dejected over this; rather we must try in whatever way possible to avenge ourselves and to take revenge. The Empire will remain an Empire even without Kinburn. Haven't we won and lost more important things? The best of all is that God is instilling our soldiers there with courage, and here too the people have not become dejected. But the public flatters itself with its own lies: it captures cities, it conducts battles at sea, it dreams up battles in its head and has Voinovich bombarding Tsar Grad. I listen to all this in silence and think to myself: even if something unpleasant were to happen somewhere, were my Prince well, everything would still be all right and would be mended.

It is very good that you ordered wine and meat given to the besieged men. May God help Major-General Rek and Commandant Tunzelman too. Aleksandr Vasilievich Suvorov's zeal, which you so animatedly describe, quite gladdened me. You know nothing can have a more pleasing effect on me than doing justice to the labors, fervor and talents of others. It would be good for the Crimea and Kherson if Kinburn could be saved. We must now await news from the fleet.

[. . .]

Recruits are already being levied, however, I shall now levy still more and think that not 60 but 80 thousand will be levied in total. I hope this will be enough.

As you will learn from the papers sent to you earlier, the Emperor is preparing 120 thousand men, with which he intends to act, and has granted us a great many generals, Ligne among them.

Stroke the English and Prussians you write. The minute Pitt[3] learned that war had been declared, he wrote to Semyon Vorontsov[4] asking him to come. Upon Vorontsov's arrival he said to him that war had been declared and that in Tsar Grad and in Vienna it is being said that their ambassador talked the Turks into this, and he swore that their ambassador has no such instructions from Great Britain's Ministry. I believe this, however, the foreign affairs of Great Britain are not under the direction of the English ministry now, but of the malicious King[5] who operates according to the rules of the Hanoverian ministers. His Majesty has already lost fifteen provinces through his good governance. So is it so odd for him to give orders to his ambassador in Tsar Grad that are contrary to the interests of England? He is governed by petty personal passions, not the interests of the state and the nation.

Regarding the Prussians, they have been shown nothing but gentle strokes till now, but they do not pay us back with gentle strokes, though this may be because of Hertzberg[6] and not the King.[7] Their troops have indeed entered Holland. We shall now see what the French say. [. . .]

I'll order a large fleet outfitted for next year, for the Archipelago as well as for the Baltic, and the French can say whatever they want. I am not accustomed to ordering my affairs and actions in any other way except in mutual agreement with my interests and those of my Empire, just as the other powers—friend and foe—do what they please.

I pray God to give you strength and health and to calm your hypochondria. Since you do everything yourself, so you have no rest. Why not take on a general who could tend to all the small matters? Tell me whom you need, and I shall send him. A field marshal is given full generals for such things so that one of them can occupy himself with trivialities and the commander in chief need not be bothered by them. I'm certain you won't fail, but in any case don't become dejected and guard your strength. God will help you and won't abandon you, and the Tsar is your friend and supporter. And yes, as you write in your own words, it is "an accursed defensive position," and I don't like it either. Try to turn it into an offensive one soon. Then things will be easier for you and for everyone else. And then there will be fewer sick, for they won't all be in one place. Having written me seven pages, and much else besides, you're surprised that you are weak! When you see that you can leave, then come to us, I shall always be very glad to see you.

[. . .]

Farewell, my friend, a recruitment levy has been ordered. [. . .] You write that Greig[8] should be sent with the fleet—I shall send him, but wouldn't the name of Aleksei Grigorievich Orlov-Chesmensky speak more loudly? This is just between us, however, and neither he nor I are calling for this. Rather, given my profusion of ideas, I simply wrote what came to mind. The money will be sent. And artillery as well has been added to both armies. The discharge of non-commissioned officers and cadets has been ordered, and everything else mentioned in your letters and reports that requires my action has been fully taken care of. I pray God to return you to health.

Sasha[9] could not possibly be kinder or more reasonable.

---

1. This letter is largely a response to Letter 321.

2. "At this moment, my dear friend, you are not an insignificant private person who lives and does as he pleases; you belong to the state, you belong to me. You must and I order you to take care of your health. I must do this because the good, the defense and the glory of the Empire are confided to your care, and because one must have a healthy body and soul in order to do the work that is in your hands. After this maternal exhortation, which I ask you to accept with docility and obedience, I shall now continue."

3. William Pitt (the Younger) (1759–1806) became the British prime minister in 1783 at the age of twenty-three and headed the government until 1801. He followed an anti-French and anti-Russian foreign policy that almost led Britain to war in 1791.

4. Count Semyon Romanovich Vorontsov (1744–1832) was Russia's ambassador to Great Britain.

5. King George III (1738–1820).

6. Count Ewald Frederick von Hertzberg (1725–1795) served as chancellor under Frederick William II.

7. Nephew of Frederick the Great, Frederick William II (1744–1797) came to the throne in August 1786.

8. Admiral Samuel Greig (1736–1788), a Scot, joined Russian service in 1764 and distinguished himself in the victory at Chesme in 1770. Greig was to have taken his squadron from the Baltic to the Archipelago, but the presence of the Swedish fleet forced him to remain in the Baltic.

9. Mamonov.

325.   CATHERINE TO POTEMKIN

25 September 1787

My friend, Prince Grigory Aleksandrovich. About an hour ago I received your letter of the 19th instant and your communiqué of the very same date, from which I see that the Turks continue to cannonade Kinburn and that twice they attempted landings, which, however, were repulsed. God grant that your endeavors against the Turkish gunboats are successful and that you are able to save Kinburn. [. . .] Your own condition and your spasms weigh upon my breast. Your sensitivity and fervor, produced by diligence, which I quite understand, arouse impatience in you. I myself am quite often in the very same condition, especially when facing matters of such importance as now. But you could do nothing worse than to lay down your titles and so deprive me and the Empire of the most needed, capable and loyal man, who is my best friend as well. Abandon such a doleful thought, take heart, raidissés Votre esprit et Votre âme contre tous les évènements, et soyés assuré que Vous les vaincrés tous avec un peu de patience, mais c'est une vraie faiblesse[1] to, as you write me, lay down your titles and hide. From what? I don't know. I don't forbid you from coming here if you see that your arrival will not upset what you have begun or are about to achieve or if you judge that your stay here is rather more necessary than it is there where you are now. I am sending you the order for Field Marshal Rumiantsev to take up command upon your giving it to him. Should you follow my desire and counsel, you will deliver it to him as late as possible. As for me, I remain, albeit with a mournful spirit, nevertheless with my customary friendly benevolence.

When you leave your current post, to whom will you entrust the Caucasus Corps? Field Marshal Rumiantsev has no knowledge of this nor of affairs there and will scarcely be able to manage them, and I don't know what is to come of all this. You yourself know how difficult it is for me to accept any idea for which I am in no way prepared, however, I have decided to take this step, which I find difficult, since you say that your health requires it. I need your health. I desire it for you, and equally the continuation of those deeds that bring glory to you and the Empire. God grant that you change your mind about giving command to Field Marshal Rumiantsev. I don't understand how one man can command such a terribly large mass. Except at such a time when we truly shall be safe from any attack or enterprise by the enemy.

---

1. "strengthen your spirit and your soul against all occurrences and be assured that you will vanquish them all with a little patience, but it is a true weakness"

326. POTEMKIN TO CATHERINE

2 October [1787]. Kremenchug

Your Most Gracious Majesty. If you could see my unending troubles and that it is a rare night I sleep, you would not be surprised that I have been reduced to a state of extreme weakness. The destruction of the Sevastopol fleet delivered me such a blow that I do not even know how I withstood it. [. . .] I am weak, every day spasms torment me and occasion such a powerful hypochondria that I regret being alive. It was at that hour that I requested my dismissal. Now I have it, and so shall be more secure, for if I reach the point of complete exhaustion, then I shall be able to rest, and, of course, only in the extreme shall I send for Count Pyotr Aleksandrovich.

It would not be at all bad if Prince Repnin were here.[1] He is older than my generals and we could divide the duties between us. The armed vessels will reach Kherson any day now. I have ordered the Ochakov fleet attacked by both our force and our cunning. May God send his help, which I beg for from the bottom of my heart. It is true, as you deign to write, that even without Kinburn the Empire will remain an Empire. However, given the present circumstances it is extremely important. I have two fortresses, neither of which defends either the men or the location, but which must be defended, and now the fleet in Sevastopol too.

Whether I shall be sick or well, nevertheless, once everything here has been put in order, I should and must out of necessity come to Petersburg before the coming month, for it is impossible to discuss everything in writing.

Don't be surprised, matushka, that I disturb you: I am not to blame for being sensitive. As for the last two reports, God knows, I wrote them in a fever. And two days ago I had a most severe paroxysm.

With the next courier I shall describe everything in detail and what I had to do, to order, to build, and then you will see how great is my burden. If you grant me Prince Repnin, I shall be greatly relieved. Till death I remain your most loyal and most grateful subject

Prince Potemkin-Tavrichesky

P.S. It would be most fitting to send Count Aleksei Grigorievich to command the Archipelago fleet. But Admiral Greig must also be sent there, because we don't understand navigation or how to make use of the winds. I now see that had we missed the Equinox the Sevastopol fleet would have remained intact.

---

1. In Letter 324 (this section has been excised), Catherine suggested to Potemkin that he receive Prince Repnin, who had written to the empress that he was willing to serve wherever needed. Repnin arrived at Potemkin's army on 23 October.

327. CATHERINE TO POTEMKIN

2 October 1787

My friend, Prince Grigory Aleksandrovich. This morning first the courier you sent on the 26th arrived with news that the fleet, having endured the storm, is preparing to leave for Sevastopol, and then a few hours later I received your letters of the 24th of September.[1] Of course, none of this is good news; however, nothing's been lost. Perhaps the storm was as harmful to the enemy as it was to us. Is it possible that the wind blew only against us? As neither you nor I were the cause of this, I shan't say another word about it, but shall trust in your good orders to repair the ships and to cheer up the men if they are downcast, which, however, I haven't noticed.

I most terribly regret that you are in such an extreme state, as you write, that you want to give up command. To me this is the saddest of all.

In your letters of the 24th you mention withdrawing the troops from the peninsula.[2] If you carry this out, the question arises: What will happen and where shall we put the Sevastopol fleet? I think even in former times the wharf at Glubokaia was deemed to be inconvenient. I hope you wrote this as a sudden impulse when you thought that the entire fleet had been lost, and that you won't act on such an idea except as a final resort. I think the best thing would be if it were possible to launch an attack on Ochakov, or on Bender, in order to turn our defensive position, which you yourself have deemed undesirable, into an offensive one. But to begin the war by evacuating such a province, which to this very day is not in danger, seems to be rushing for no good reason. And likewise, I hope you will refrain from giving up command, renouncing your titles, ranks and God knows what else, for I see neither reason nor need for it, and attribute all this to your excessive sensitivity and ardent zeal and to your not having attained the expected degree of success. In such circumstances I always ask others to take heart and to keep in mind that a hale and hearty soul can set right even a failure. I write all this to you as to my best friend, my ward and pupil, who sometimes has a stronger spirit than even I myself. But in this instance I am merrier than you since you are sick while I am well.

According to reports from Tsar Grad there were still no ships in the Black Sea in the final days of August.

In accordance with your wish and so as to please you, I have sent you the rescript you desired on giving up command, but admit that I find this order by no means dear or agreeable. No one on earth wishes you more good than I, and for this reason I tell you what I think. If in fact you've already given up command, then I ask that you quickly come here so that I might have you near me and so that you can learn for yourself my thoughts and my opinion of this. You'll find here that as always I am full of friendly and sincere benevolence for you. Farewell, God be with you.

And here is my opinion of this: Que Vous êtes impatient comme un enfant de cinq ans, tandis que les affaires dont Vous êtes chargé en ce moment demandent une patience imperturbable. Adieu, mon Ami.[3] Neither time nor distance nor anyone on earth can change my attitude toward you and my way of thinking about you.

P.S. The thought occurred to me, concerning what you write about withdrawing the troops from the peninsula, that as a result of this the road, so to speak, into the heart of the Empire[4] would once again be open to the Turks and Tatars, for it would scarcely be expedient to concentrate our defenses on the steppe. We occupied the Crimea in former times in order to strengthen our defenses, and now the Crimea is in our hands. Once the fleet is repaired, I hope this notion will completely vanish, and I hope it appeared only when you thought that the fleet had been lost. But if you want, I shall order you to construct a nice little dozen frigates on the Don. Why, the Sevastopol fleet uses them even now.

---

1. Potemkin wrote on 26 September that though the ships had been heavily damaged and lost their masts in the storm, still the men had survived and the ships were limping back to Sevastopol.

2. In a second letter written on 24 September (written after Letter 323), Potemkin, who at that time still thought the entire fleet had been lost, urged that Russian troops be pulled out of the Crimea, now vulnerable to Turkish attack.

3. "That you are as impatient as a five-year-old child, whereas the affairs with which you have been entrusted at this moment demand an unshakable patience. Farewell, my friend."

4. Catherine used Potemkin's own words of 1782 against him. See Letter 259.

328. POTEMKIN TO CATHERINE

Yelizavetgrad, 6 October [1787]

Having received here on the 4th Aleksandr Vasilievich's report on the fierce battle near Kinburn, I could not immediately send a courier to you, Your Most Gracious Majesty, since his dispatch was so brief that I was unable to glean any details from it.[1] Yesterday, however, I received a complete communiqué, which weakness following his labors and wounds prevented him from writing earlier. The Turks fought with unprecedented ardor and desperation. Had God not helped, Kinburn would have fallen, and bad consequences would have followed. Justice must be done to Aleksandr Vasilievich's zeal and valor. Although wounded, he remained till the end and thus saved everyone.[2] Everything had been thrown into confusion and the befuddled men ran from the place, with the Turks right on their heels. And who stopped them? A grenadier from the Schlüsselburg Regiment by his example and encouraging words.[3] The men who were running away stuck by him, and the momentum shifted. They smashed the enemy and the cavalry struck; they took back the cannons and slaughtered the Turks mercilessly, so much so that even the General-in-Chief himself couldn't persuade them to spare him just three men. [. . .]

I had a severe paroxysm today and have become so weak I can't write much. Forgive me, matushka.

I departed Kremenchug and hurried here in order to head for Kherson, but have become so weak that I truly am no longer strong enough. In a couple of days I shall set out and shall visit Kinburn. [. . .]

Grain in Poland is in short supply and expensive. Try as I might, I've been able to purchase only a very small amount. Farewell, Your Most Gracious Majesty.

Your most loyal and most grateful subject
Prince Potemkin-Tavrichesky

[. . .]

---

1. On 4 October, Suvorov sent Potemkin a brief report of the Turks' landing near Kinburn and the intense battle of 1 October.

2. Suvorov was wounded both in the side and the hand.

3. Stepan Novikov's heroics—he single-handedly dispatched three Turks near Suvorov—helped turn the tide of the battle.

329. CATHERINE TO POTEMKIN

9 October 1787

My friend, Prince Grigory Aleksandrovich. I have received your letters of 2 October. I understand your innumerable troubles, and quite regret that you are not sleeping nights and are extremely weak. The loss of the Sevastopol fleet delivered a blow not only to you alone, I share this misfortune with you. Neither I nor anyone else has any doubt that you did not neglect a thing, and all your instructions are in full accord with the complete trust I have placed in you. Thank God that you were able to fill the magazines.

Concerning your spasms, I am of the belief that they are nothing else but winds et qu'en chassant les vents Vos spasmes seront soulagés, essayés je Vous prie, et faites Vous donner des choses qui chassent les vents. J'ose croire que les spasmes s'en iront avec les vents; je suis d'opinion que tout spasme est causé par les vents.[1]

I know how agonizing they are, especially to sensitive and impatient persons like you and me. I am heartened that you are now more at ease, and hope you will take care of your health, as you do my affairs, every time you recall that I need and require you. I have written to Prince Repnin to join you.

Write me of what is happening with Kinburn; you've already sent two couriers without mentioning Kinburn. God grant that you have been able to defend it successfully, however, were Ochakov in our hands, then Kinburn itself would be made safe. I do not demand the impossible, but only write what I think. Please be patient and read what I have to say; after all, nothing will be ruined or harmed by my words—the worst that can happen is my quill will go dull, but that's no matter. Be well, and not ill, that's what I wish. If you're well and come here, we shall discuss what's necessary. I think little of my worry and pay it no heed: God will perhaps give me the strength to withstand it. There is one way to lessen my worry: write to me more often and inform me of the state of affairs. I impatiently await the promised details. And don't forget to write to me about Kinburn as well. I'll inquire with Count Aleksei Grigorievich about his trip, Greig, however, must go, either with or without him. Of course, it would've been better had we missed the Equinoxe, but what is to be done? What's done is done. Could the storm have hit only us, did it not inflict damage on the Turks? Did nothing happen to the Ochakov squadron as a result of the storm? Adieu, mon Ami, I've written enough, I suppose you don't have time for reading. God be with you.

---

1. "and that by discharging the winds your spasms will be relieved. I ask you to try it and have yourself be given something to discharge the winds. I dare think that the spasms will leave with the winds. I am of the opinion that every spasm is caused by winds."

330. POTEMKIN TO CATHERINE

1 November [1787]. Yelizavetgrad

Your Most Gracious Majesty! Who could be more heavy-hearted about Ochakov than I? All the unspeakable cares associated with that matter accost me. I would not be lacking in goodwill if I saw some opportunity. There's no way it can be seized, and given the lateness of the season there can be no formal siege, and such great preparations must be made for it. They are still teaching the miners in Kherson how to make mines, and other things as well. Up to one hundred thousand fascines are required and many gabions are needed. You are aware that there is no wood in the area; I have already cut some in my Polish forests, and from there it will be delivered where needed. I've given still more orders to meet all the other demands.

I return to Ochakov. Of course, we must take this place, and so we must use all reliable methods to attain this objective. This town wasn't destroyed in the last war, and the Turks have been fortifying it in peacetime without interruption. Deign to recall from my plan of attack, that given their preparedness there I did not intend to take it before those other places where they are weaker. If it only meant sacrificing myself, then be certain, Your Majesty, that I would not hesitate for a minute. However, I am obliged to move with certain steps in order to preserve such precious men and must not make a doubtful attempt should it mean that after losing several thousand men we shall depart without having taken it and shall fall into such confusion that, having lost our experienced soldiers, we shall be weak for the next campaign. Moreover, not having defeated the enemy in the field, how are we to set about storming the towns? Doing battle with the Turks in the field might be called a plaything, however, in towns and tight places doing business with them is bloody. And they abandon the towns anyway once they have lost the battle.

You deign to write, matushka, about my thoughts of how to properly reward Aleksandr Vasilievich.[1] I have an idea, but let me first describe in detail his heroic deed. Having appointed him commander of the Kherson unit, I could not demand of his rank that he take the forward-most post in place of the main corps in Kherson. But after the attack on our two vessels by the Turkish fleet,[2] he anticipated an assault on Kinburn and moved there altogether. Even before 22 squadrons of cavalry and 5 regiments from the Don had arrived, he withstood their not infrequent gunfire and bombardment, and he repulsed their attempted landing on our shore. They intended to allow the enemy to land his troops as soon as our regiments arrived; it was then agreed that once the aforementioned regiments had arrived, he would move them closer to Kinburn and then hide the men inside the fortification over the next two days and nights and prohibit them from showing themselves around it. The enemy, arrogantly assuming that either no one was in Kinburn or that there were only very few men, approached to within a short distance with all their vessels and opened up a heavy cannonade and bombardment. For a day and a half he withstood all this, not answering with a single cannon, and he allowed the enemy to land their troops and to make retrenchments. And after they had all landed on our shore and had led their first attack against the fortress, the first shot was then fired from the fortress, and even this was grapeshot. He ordered General Rek to attack, who expelled them from several fortifications and was wounded in the leg. And so he was the only one left. Seven times they drove us back. Three times they received reinforcements. Night descended. Given how small and constricted that place is, a great many cavalry and infantry became crowded together and got mixed up with the enemy, forming a mass that was by then difficult to bring into formation. He kept the men in place by remaining in the very front rows the entire time. The soldiers themselves repeated to the men who were running away: "Where are you going? The General is in front of us!" With these words they were turned back. Wounded by a bullet and having received a contusion from the grapeshot, still he did not leave his place. Finally, having denied the enemy, our soldiers became fully enraged, and the tales of the Turks, Greeks and others from Ochakov all unanimously testify that no more than eight hundred men out of more than 5 thousand who were there survived, almost all of whom were wounded and more than half of them died while returning. Such a large number of Turks has never before been killed.[3] As a result of the slaughter of their very best fighters, their large fleet sailed away as soon as ours appeared in the Liman. Who, matushka, could possess such leonine valor? Though he has received all the decorations one could possibly earn, the General-in-Chief serves in his sixtieth year with the zeal of a twenty-five-year-old still needing to make his reputation. This important victory has stayed us from those bad consequences that might have followed had we been unsuccessful in holding on to Kinburn.

Having described everything, I expect your justice to reward this worthy and venerable old man. Who more than he has earned decoration?! I don't want to make any comparisons, for by citing other names I might lessen the dignity of Saint Andrew: how many there are in whom there is neither faith nor loyalty. And how many there are in whom there is neither service nor valor. To award a deserving man with an order is to do honor to that order. I shall begin with myself—give him mine.[4] But if you put off rewarding him till a future occasion, which, of course, he will not be long in providing, then reward him now with what you will. He has already said that he desires neither villages nor money and will be offended by such an award. Appoint him

Lieutenant-Colonel of the Guards (according to regulations there are to be three in the Preobrazhensky) or Adjutant-General—either this or the other with the addition of a sword richly decorated with diamonds, for he has an ordinary one. The significance of his service is intimately clear to me. You know for certain, matushka, that I am dispassionate when showing my approval, whether it concern my friend or villain. My heart bears no stain of envy or vengeance.

Before directing the troops to their winter billets, I shall erect a bridge over the Bug and send some detachments beyond Ochakov and toward Bender to clear the steppe. And once the rivers freeze over there will be a good deal of trouble here to protect our quarters, especially since the new Khan[5] will, of course, try to attack. With God's help, I shall try to make certain it is they who receive a good fright. It would be inappropriate for me to leave such troubles to another, thus, important as it is for the state and for my own personal affairs that I visit Petersburg, even if only as a courier, I shall, nonetheless, stay here; and so, the happiness of seeing you will be delayed. I am, however, thank God, on my way to the fortress. I intend to ride out along the border and into Tauride to tend to a good many matters. For life I remain

your most loyal and most grateful subject
Prince Potemkin-Tavrichesky

1. Suvorov. In a letter dated 16 October, Catherine asked Potemkin how best to reward Suvorov for his actions at Kinburn in light of the fact that too grand a reward would offend those generals with greater seniority.

2. A reference to the outbreak of hostilities on 19 August when the Turks attacked two Russian vessels escorting the ships "St. Vladimir" and "St. Alexander" out of the Liman to Sevastopol.

3. Almost all of the five thousand men the Turks landed on the Kinburn spit on 1 October were killed.

4. Catherine hesitated giving Suvorov the Order of St. Andrew, Russia's highest order whose motto was "Faith and Loyalty." Potemkin offered to give Suvorov his. Catherine did later decide to give Suvorov the order. See Letter 331.

5. Even though the Crimean Khanate had ceased to exist, the Ottomans appointed a new khan, gave him money, and sent him to Kaushany to gather Tatars and Turks to fight the Russians.

331. CATHERINE TO POTEMKIN

9 November 1787

My friend, Prince Grigory Aleksandrovich. I received today your letters of 1 November[1] at the very moment I was preparing to speak to Nassau, and now, having spoken with him, I have so much to write you that I truly don't know where to begin. Ségur has also made an offer here of his court's willingness to enter into an alliance with us, as you might have seen already from the reports sent to you and from the answer given to him.[2]

Nassau told me in our conversations of the French court's present disposition and of the changes in their way of thinking. I received all this with a pleasant countenance and said that I was pleased to see that they think differently than previously, and I thanked him for the zeal he had displayed and for his good efforts and I expressed concern that this court may once more change its good disposition. To which he himself responded that should he notice upon receiving the first courier the slightest wavering in the thinking of the French ministry, he will gallop back to France and will use all his power to reinforce that court's good disposition toward us. As he spoke of our rapprochement through an alliance, I said that I would not hide from him that we are in quite delicate circumstances regarding our trade with England and the great naval arms which we receive from there, and that for this reason we have grown accustomed to finding refuge in English ports. In response he offered France's, and I said that the former's geographic location was more convenient, that all this is said, however, primarily so as to find, together with him, the advantages and disadvantages of this or another location, and that I recognize and have already seen the various advantages of a friendship with Louis XVI. So we parted quite agreeably, and everything that might have been was discussed. They are arming and will have war, for they themselves recognize that if they leave the Dutch affair as it is, their reputation will be entirely ruined.[3]

Nassau told me that the French think they have the Swedish King in their pocket, but I told him that they should not rely on this person too much, which his trip to Copenhagen and, they say, even to Berlin proves, and that the Swedish King will be in the pocket of whoever gives him money, which the enemies of France could also make use of at times. My dear friend, there you have an honest confession of what took place between me and Nassau.

I now return to your letters. First of all, thank you for them and for writing me in such a candid and truly friendly manner and for not failing to inform me in detail despite all the troubles associated with that location and with your office. I look upon this with an excellent and sincere feeling and am extremely content with you. You have presently displayed to the world such broad and skillful knowledge and behavior that does honor to my selection and to you, and I love you twice as much as before. I see that Ochakov is causing you concern: giving you complete freedom in this matter, I simply pray God to bless your good enterprises.

Your letters have made Aleksandr Vasilievich Suvorov's service known to me in detail, and so I have decided to send him Saint Andrew in recognition of his faith and loyalty, which this courier is bringing to you.

May God help you to purge the steppe from beyond Ochakov and around Bender and to defeat and to drive away the new Khan from our dwelling places.

Ségur has letters from Choiseul[4] stating that the Vizier is allegedly already wavering and that they are allegedly grumbling at him for having declared war and still not having taken any action.

I most regret that your troubles won't permit you to come here, even if only for a short while. I would gallop off to you, would this not add to your troubles.

Word that your health is improving comforts me greatly, for I love you so and am very, very content with you.

I'll order the frigates built with large artillery and according to your draughts. I'll speak no more of the loss of the ship "Mary Magdalene": what's done is done, and this goes for the other lost vessels too.[5] [. . .]

Farewell, my friend, God be with you, and may it never enter your thoughts that you could be forgotten by me.

Aleksandr Matveevich[6] loves you like his soul.

Kindly write how the injured and sick are, and did you send my first letter to Suvorov?

---

1. Along with Letter 330, Potemkin wrote two more letters on 1 November in which he described the suffering the damage to the Black Sea fleet cost him and requested Catherine to order several frigates built on the Don River.

2. France was then trying, unsuccessfully, to conclude an alliance with Russia, using for this purpose both Prince Nassau-Siegen and Count Louis-Phillipe Ségur, the French ambassador.

3. In fact, France chose not to intervene in the struggle taking place in the United Provinces.

4. Count Marie Gabriel August Florian de Choiseul-Gouffier (1752–1817) was the French ambassador to the Porte.

5. One of three ships of the line in the Black Sea fleet, "Mary Magdalene" lost its way in the storm of 9 September and ended up in Constantinople, where it surrendered to the Turks.

6. Mamonov.

332. CATHERINE TO POTEMKIN

23 November 1787

My friend, Prince Grigory Aleksandrovich. After a twelve-day wait for a letter from you, a courier finally arrived with your letters of the 12th instant.[1] As a result of your good command it can now be expected that the Tatars will have no more success in their winter operations than the Turks had in their autumn ones, and in the past war the Tatars would soon turn back during their attacks even when they encountered but little resistance.

I attribute the Emperor's still not having declared war on the Turks to the intrigues of the Prussians and the English. These courts are spreading tales that they have found a means to lure us to their side, despite the fact that they incited the Turks to declare war on us and we are obliged to dance to their tune. We cannot try to influence Prussian politics by giving them Danzig, for even in the friendliest of times it was proposed and acknowledged that anything concerning Danzig would constitute casus foederis. My ancestors and I gave that city signed guarantees of their freedom and that they will remain as they are now, and this has been reaffirmed once more in the convention on the partition of Poland.

Concerning the Emperor, I'll also say that he anticipated war no more than we did and so is also unprepared, and now nothing can be expected from him till March, for it is written in the treaty that during December, January and February the troops are not to be moved. But that they are busy making great preparations, this is known to everyone.[2] I shall order the ambassador here reminded more often, and you speak to Ligne. It is also true that in the last war we fought alone against the Turks and fought successfully. Yet since we have a treaty and hope to receive assistance, it is proper to rely on it at the present time and is, at least, more reliable than the favors and good intentions or dispositions of those courts from whom we have experienced the villainous act of declaring war upon us. The system with the Viennese court is your work, and from the earliest times it has been preferred for our southern affairs and border, for it is in keeping with the local conditions of those lands and with our general interest. Panin himself, before he had yet been blinded by the Prussian flattery, looked upon other ties as pis-aller[3] that in regard to the common enemy, the Turks that is, did not compensate us for the loss of the Austrian alliance. From your many letters I might think you are wavering in carrying out your plan, which you yourself designed and have already begun in regard to the Turks, and that which is related to it, but in no way do I permit myself these thoughts and I drive them from my head, since I cannot imagine that your thoughts waver so, for there is no glory, no honor, no profit in undertaking a venture and ardently moving it forward, and then, not having completed it, willfully ruining it, only to start something else.[4] You defended our borders with complete success. God grant you health, my friend, and then you'll successfully conduct the offensive operations as well.

Preparations are being made here to arm the navy. I wrote to the Counts Orlov and received their answer, according to which it seems they refuse the journey.[5] I would have considered this to be a refusal to accept command had they not also written at the same time that they are coming here. This trip has now been postponed for a time by the death of Count Vladimir Grigorievich's elder son.[6] I think this is why they've stayed on for a while in Moscow. Admiral Greig is now considering up to five thousand regular troops for this naval armament here. In the past war a total of 2,370 men of all ranks were sent—from the Guards as well as from the Schlüsselburg Regiment, the artillery and the cuirassiers. I need your advice now: what should we send? It seems to me Greig requests a lot, and the cuirassiers are indeed unnecessary. From which regiments should they be sent? Should they be sent as regiments or as battalions drawn from various regiments? A general to command the troops on land must also accompany this troop detail with the fleet. He could go directly to Italy, and it would be desirable if he were a man from whom some use might be expected. Give me some advice, whom should I send?

[. . .]

[. . .] Write me—is it true what the Turks and other ill-wishers are shouting from the roof-tops, namely that the ship "Catherine's Glory" is in their hands, and that they seized it at the mouth of the Danube, and that Voinovich slipped away on a launch? Be so good as to rename that ship if we still have it. Should this happen, God forbid, I don't want scoundrels to boast that they have "Catherine's Glory" in their hands.[7]

Farewell, my friend. God be with you. Be well and safe, my thoughts are constantly with you.

---

1. On 12 November, Potemkin wrote to Catherine to tell her of Prince de Ligne's arrival and of the prince's ideas for trying to neutralize Prussia.

2. Joseph II did not officially declare war on the Porte until 29 January (9 February) 1788.

3. "the lesser of evils"

4. According to Potemkin's earlier plan, after the Ukrainian Army under Rumiantsev had successfully stymied any attempt by the Turks to enter Russian territory, his Yekaterinoslav Army was to seize Ochakov. The lack of action by the Russian forces, and particularly the indecision over the Crimea, was fueling Potemkin's detractors back at court.

5. Catherine offered command of the planned Archipelago expedition to Aleksei Orlov-Chesmensky and his brother Fyodor (1741–1796), who had also taken part in the battle of Chesme. They declined her invitation.

6. The youngest of the five Orlov brothers, Vladimir (1743–1831) lived quietly with his family in Moscow. His son Aleksandr died of consumption in France on 12 October.

7. The rumor, then prevalent at court, was false.

333. POTEMKIN TO CATHERINE

25 December [1787]. Yelizavetgrad

Your Most Gracious Majesty. After having received your most gracious missives in Kherson, I received your very insulting letter upon my return in which you suppose that my thoughts are wavering.[1] I don't know when I could have given you cause to come to this conclusion about me. Was it my service, in which my lone goal consists of demonstrating to you my zeal and that is so steadfast that death alone can rend me from it? If my idea about stroking the Prussian King is not to your liking, I can say that this does not involve a change in our alliance with the Emperor; rather, by stroking him we can avoid any obstacles he might erect.[2]

I proposed using their ministers to our advantage at the Porte so as to show the Turks that their hopes for these courts were futile. There was no intention of using them for anything other than some unimportant matter, rescuing Lombard, for example, which even the Emperor could not find suspicious. I spoke of the article on Danzig not knowing that it was so important. [. . .] In a word, I thought and still do think that it would not be bad for us were he too to enter into our plans, even if only for the sake of Poland, lest he create some sort of interference. And this can be achieved by stroking him.

You deign to mention that the alliance with the Emperor is my doing. This proceeded from my zeal. It was from this as well that the Polish alliance in Kiev also sprang. The Lubomirski estate was purchased with this in mind, since by becoming its proprietor this conferred upon me the right to participate in their affairs and in the military command. You may see what sort of alliance this would have been from the plan enclosed herewith.[3] They would already have been fighting for us by now, and that would have been helpful, for the harder we come down on the enemy, the easier we'll achieve our goal. My counsel always proceeded from fervor. If I am out of place, then, of course, in the future I'll speak only on those matters that have been entrusted to me.

After returning to Kherson I was tormented for a long time by such a headache that I couldn't do a thing. I'm better now; the pain left me slightly deaf, though this has now passed. Between the fourth and the tenth of November winter turned cruel. It lasted for eight days, all the rivers froze, and then everything melted. But now everything is freezing over again. Imagine how great must be my concern for quartering the troops on the steppe. When it comes time to do battle in the summer, trust me that it won't be any easier.

Your Most Gracious Majesty, it is difficult to calculate all my cares. In the midst of wartime I must build lodging, teach men how to shoot, prepare for a siege, repair ships, transport provisions, form troops anew—and that amid extreme changes in temperature—and combat disease as well. From afar these problems are not obvious, but close up they are much more trying than those successful matters which are more respected and much discussed. God help us hold out till summer and manage to set things right. Then I shall not give you cause to goad me on. Your Majesty, it is tearing me apart inside that I am unable to show you now those good turns that I would wish.

The enemy is constantly adding a few men to his forces in Orsova. The Khan is in Kaushany, and the Sultans and the Tatars are near Ochakov, at Delagel and further up toward Olviopol. They ride out along the Bug and inspect the fords, acting as if they are getting ready to cross. Some of them are even on the Dniester.

I am trying to lure away from them the Zaporozhians who serve as their guides and without whom they wouldn't dare poke their noses into the area. I have gathered about 500 unmounted Cossacks who were formerly with me on the Danube. They are so effective in the Dnieper estuary that the Turkish patrols won't dare show themselves in their small boats. Their Ataman is Sidor Bely. They are called the Loyal Cossack Host in contrast to those with the Turks. They asked me to petition land for them, namely at the tip of the Kerch Peninsula or at Taman, where large numbers of them will go to live. This will be quite useful. They will form a barrier against the Circassians, and through this we shall rid ourselves of bad tillers of the soil. The majority of them are already married now, and so will establish orderly settlements there, and they will be joined by many from Poland.[4]

I don't know what to do with the sick whose numbers are already increasing in some villages and amongst the peasants. There is an epidemic of diarrhea.

[. . .]

I remain with steadfast fervor and zeal till death

your most loyal subject
Prince Potemkin-Tavrichesky

---

1. Letter 332.

2. A reference to his suggestion to appease the Prussians with Danzig. The question of Danzig figured in the so-called Hertzberg plan (named for the Prussian chancellor), a complex territorial swap that involved Poland ceding Danzig and Thorn to Prussia in exchange for Galicia from Austria.

3. The plan has not been located. Attempts at a Russo-Polish alliance, which Potemkin had backed in 1787, were revived in 1788, though they proved fruitless.

4. With the outbreak of war, Potemkin ordered Suvorov to organize the Zaporozhian Cossacks into a fighting force. Their Ataman, or chieftain, was Sidor Bely (1730?–1788), a veteran of the First Russo-Turkish War and an acquaintance of Potemkin. Later renamed the Black Sea and Yekaterinoslav Host, they served with great distinction throughout the entire war.

334. CATHERINE TO POTEMKIN

30 December 1787

My friend, Prince Grigory Aleksandrovich. It is known to you with what Nassau arrived here, and after he arrived I heard him out. Shortly thereafter Ségur sent a courier to France, whose return he and Nassau impatiently awaited. This courier did indeed return during those days, and after that Ségur held a conference with the Vice Chancellor in which he tried to make it appear as if I am looking to establish an alliance with France and for this reason the authority was sent hence to France in order that this matter be discussed there and not here. For his part Nassau requested that I admit him to me, and after arriving he said that in complete openness and with profound grief he must tell me that the French court completely disavows everything he says here and that that court is in negotiations with London, which he does not hide from me. How much truth or perfidy there was in all these or the previous conversations I leave to you to ascertain. But of one matter I've little doubt—that this and the other is more the doing of the court than Nassau and Ségur. The former is now on his way to you, for he does not want to remain here any longer. And should he act in accordance with his court's wishes, he'll try to deter you from any undertaking against the Turks, toward whom, it seems, the inclination of the French as well as the English ministry and court is equally strong at the present time. Lord Carmarthen's proud and arrogant letter to Fraser, the political pup here, has been sent to you.[1] No court has the authority to demand from another such an account. And they offer us nothing in exchange; what's more, they're not recalling their rabid ambassador[2] in order to give us satisfaction. In a word, both courts are acting equally perfidiously and distressingly while they have never seen us inflict any grief on them or employ any chicanery, and we have at least treated them with respect.

I suppose you are already aware of the Austrians' unsuccessful attempt on Belgrade. The best part of this incident is that this action has made the Emperor's intention manifest to the world and that after this war will unavoidably follow between him and the Turks.[3]

I would be extremely content with you, my friend, if you could force yourself to write to me more often and to dispatch a courier every week without fail. Not only would this calm my spirit, it would preserve my health against needless worries and would avert more than a thousand inconveniences. At this very hour it's been exactly a month since I had my last line from you.[4] From every province, except from the one bearing my name, I receive news twice a month, but from you and the army not a line, even though that's the place toward which my every thought and wish is directed. C'est me faire mourir de mille morts, mais pas d'une.[5] You can show your attachment and gratitude to me in no better way than by writing to me more often, but to write from month to month, as now, is the harshest act, which causes me constant suffering and which could have the wickedest and most unexpected and most undesired consequences for you.

Farewell, God be with you.
I wish you a happy New Year.

---

1. Britain expressed its position on the war to Russia in a letter to its temporary representative in St. Petersburg, Charles Fraser, stating that it felt equal friendship for both Russia and Turkey. Catherine clearly put little stock in such expressions.

2. Russia unsuccessfully sought the recall of the British ambassador to the Porte, Sir Robert Ainslie (1730?-1812). He served on in Constantinople until 1792.

3. On 2 December, Austria attacked the Turks at Belgrade and were badly defeated.

4. Catherine is mistaken. Two weeks earlier on 16 December, she wrote Potemkin to say she had received his letter of 30 November.

5. "This is to make me die not one but a thousand deaths."

8. The Siege of Ochakov—1788

The beginning of 1788 found Potemkin at the small garrison-town of Yelizavetgrad where he had established his headquarters for the winter. In the eighteenth century, warfare was largely a seasonal occupation, and armies typically sat out the winter waiting for the warm, fighting weather of the summer months. In his wooden palace, Potemkin put together his own court complete with orchestra, officers and adjutants, a host of foreign adventurers, and lovely young women. He whiled away the hours gambling, playing billiards, feasting, and making love to several beauties, including Yekaterina Samoilova, the wife of his nephew Aleksandr, and Praskovia Potemkina, married to his cousin Pavel. At the same time, the prince did not lose sight of his chief objective, and also busied himself with the preparations for the siege of Ochakov. There was much to be done: the army had to be strengthened, recruits had to be gathered, bombs and shells needed to be produced, and a large flotilla for the Liman had to be built.

The new year brought with it many problems. The especially harsh winter inflicted hardship on Potemkin's men, a great many of whom suffered from illness and disease. Their plight was exacerbated by a severe shortage of grain as a result of drought the previous year. The shortage had profound economic and social consequences. Not only did it lead to soaring grain prices, but to overall inflation and devaluation of Russia's paper currency, which ate away at the soldiers' pay. Grain was the pillar of the Russian economy, and so shortages and inflation meant higher taxes might have to be imposed to finance the war effort. Additional financial burden on the

Russian populace combined with the fear of famine threatened to ignite a new jacquerie à la Pugachev. The threat of unrest proved particularly frightening to the authorities given the fact that Russia's troops had been removed from the provinces to protect the borders and thus would not be readily available to put down any disturbance. Sensitive to the seriousness of the situation, Catherine spent millions to buy grain from abroad (Letters 337, 339).

Russia's ally had still done little to help shoulder the burden against the Turks. When Potemkin sent an adjutant to the Austrian forces in Bukovina to inquire how things were proceeding, the fellow returned to tell Potemkin in early January that the Austrians and Turks were acting as if they were old friends. Following a second failed attempt on Belgrade, Joseph II and his army went on the defensive, and their long line, stretched out across central Europe, did little more than keep the Turks in place and prevent them from all turning toward Potemkin. The one bright spot came when Joseph officially declared war against the Turks on 29 January (9 February) (Letters 337, 339, 340).

Frustrated by Austria's inaction and fearful of losing the Poles to the Turks or someone else, Potemkin continued to urge Catherine to seek an alliance with Poland. Catherine, though skeptical, was open to Potemkin's ideas for an alliance, and in January the two countries began exchanging proposals. In June, a final version was forwarded to Warsaw (Letters 339, 340, 345). Word of the proposed alliance enraged Count von Hertzberg, the Prussian chancellor. For months Prussia had been trying to insinuate itself in Russia's affairs as a mediator in the conflict with Turkey. Prussia's primary goal, known as the Hertzberg plan, was to negotiate a peace to its own advantage: Russia would receive Bessarabia and Ochakov, Austria would be given the Danubian principalities by Turkey and would return Galicia to Poland (taken in 1772), Turkey's lands south of the Danube would be guaranteed, and Prussia—without losing so much as a single man—would be given Danzig and Thorn from Poland. Prussia had been angered by Catherine's rejection of the Hertzberg plan in March and now sought to kill the proposed Russo-Polish alliance, which had been poorly received in Warsaw, by portraying Prussia as the Poles' true friend and protector.

By the middle of May, Potemkin's forces had almost all reached the Bug River and were preparing to cross it on their way to Ochakov. Potemkin himself finally left Yelizavetgrad on the twenty-seventh. The month had been a difficult one for him. Not only did he have to fight the Turks, but Potemkin also felt he now had to do battle with his enemies at court and with the Austrians too. Prince de Ligne, Joseph II's spy at Yelizavetgrad, had been reporting on the prince's dragging pace and unwillingness to cooperate, and in early May, Potemkin wrote Catherine to complain that Ligne was leading an effort to remove him from command. Angry and frustrated, Potemkin defended himself and his army and once again offered his resignation (Letters 344, 346). The day Potemkin departed Yelizavetgrad, Catherine wrote to commend all his efforts so far and to refute his claim that the Austrians were bent on subverting him. She did, however, strongly react to his plan for pulling Russian forces out of the Crimea and abandoning it to the Turks, which Potemkin, anxious that the Turkish fleet might trap Russian troops in the peninsula, had proposed earlier that month (Letters 345, 347).

Potemkin's fears, though not unwarranted, were dispelled the following month when the Russian Liman fleet scored an important victory over the Turks. On 20 May, Gazi Hasan Pasha, the feared grand admiral of the Turkish navy known as the "Crocodile of Sea Battles," had arrived off Ochakov with nearly one hundred ships, several more than the Russians had. The massive Turkish fleet riding at anchor beneath the walls of Ochakov not only protected the Turkish fortress from attack by sea, but also threatened Kinburn and Russia's hold over the Crimea. Potemkin rightly believed that only once the Turkish fleet had been beaten and Russia had seized control over the Liman would Ochakov fall. He set against Gazi Hasan his newly constructed Liman fleet, comprising a flotilla of oared gunboats, under the command of Prince Charles of Nassau-Siegen, and a sailing flotilla under John Paul Jones, hero of the American War of Independence who had arrived in Russia earlier that year. On 7 June, the Turks' oared flotilla sailed up the Liman and attacked the Russian gunboats, but were driven back (Letter 350).

Angered at the defeat and intent on crushing Potemkin's Liman fleet, Gazi Hasan returned on the sixteenth to do battle again, yet this time with his entire fleet of ships. At 4 a.m. the following day, the Russian fleet launched a surprise attack on the Turks, whose large craft, helpless in the shallow waters of the Liman, ran aground on the shoals. The fighting lasted for two days, and when it was all over Russia had become master of the Liman. The Turks lost over a dozen vessels, most of them large warships, and several thousand dead. Gazi Hasan was forced to flee the Liman with the remains of his fleet, which was pounded by Russian guns near Kinburn as it retreated to the open waters. On 19 June, Potemkin wrote Catherine to tell her the wonderful news. He was, he wrote, "beside myself with joy" (Letter 352).

Potemkin's letter reached Catherine on the morning of 26 June. Unfortunately, the empress did not have long to savor the news of the splendid victory, for only hours later word arrived that the Swedes had attacked the Russian fort at Nyslott just days before. Russia now faced war on two distant fronts. Although anxious, Catherine tried not to reveal it to Potemkin. "He who laughs last laughs loudest," she wrote upon hearing of the attack, "justice, right and truth are on our side"

(Letter 353). In private, however, she cried, and preparations were quietly made to abandon St. Petersburg if necessary.

As early as March, Catherine had heard rumors that Gustav III was preparing for war, though Potemkin had played down the likelihood of a Swedish attack (Letters 341, 342, 350). Inspired by his desire to avenge past defeats at the hands of the Russians and seeking to quell opposition at home with military successes, Gustav sought to take advantage of Russia's war with the Ottomans by launching a preemptive strike. Preoccupied by the southern war and thus unable to mount an effective campaign against the Swedes, Russia would be forced, or so the king hoped, to return the Baltic territories lost to Russia following the Great Northern War (1700–1721) and Finnish territory lost at Åbo in 1743.

The Swedish plan was to ferry the main force to Oranienbaum and from there to march on St. Petersburg. A smaller, diversionary force was to attack Fredrikshamn and Vyborg in an attempt to divide the limited Russian forces. At the same time, the Swedish fleet would attack Kronstadt, the main base for Russia's Baltic fleet. But the Swedish king had miscalculated. The Russian fleet intended for the Mediterranean had not yet departed, and on 6 July it met up with the Swedish fleet off the island of Hogland. Although the Battle of Hogland produced no clear victor, the Swedish fleet was forced to retreat to its base at Sveaborg, thus ruining Swedish plans for a landing at Oranienbaum. As a result, the Swedes, led by Gustav himself, had to focus their assault in Finland, which very quickly bogged down in the face of Russian resistance. Following the outbreak of hostilities, Catherine left Tsarskoe Selo for the capital to encourage the city's inhabitants. She wrote Potemkin in mid-July that St. Petersburg had taken on the appearance of an armed camp and noted that on the day of the Battle of Hogland the smell of gunpowder filled the air. Catherine, too, was now at the front (Letters 347, 353–355, 357).

News of the Swedish attack greatly worried Potemkin, and he begged the empress to keep him well informed of matters from the capital lest he "die of sorrow." Still her bogatyr', Potemkin bragged that were he there, entire provinces would follow him into battle against the Swedes (Letter 356). Potemkin had by now crossed the Bug and with his 50,000 men encircled Ochakov. Given Ochakov's size—its garrison held some 24,000—its excellent defenses, and Potemkin's justifiable unwillingness to risk heavy casualties, the prince never intended to seize the fortress with a *coup de main*, rather to attempt to force the Turks into surrender. Batteries were put in place and trenches dug. By early summer, the long-awaited siege of Ochakov had finally begun.

Meanwhile, despite another Russian victory over the Turkish fleet on 3 July off the island of Fidonisi, Gazi Hasan managed to return to Ochakov at the end of the month, break through the Russian blockade and deliver fresh troops and supplies to the fortress. Only days before, Aleksandr Suvorov, responding to one of the many Turkish sorties at Ochakov, foolishly (he was reportedly drunk) let himself be drawn into a pointless fight that resulted in the death of more than 150 Russian soldiers. Potemkin was furious at Suvorov's lack of discipline. To add insult to injury, in August one of Russia's ships accidentally blew up while bombarding Ochakov, and shortly thereafter a major explosion rocked Kinburn while shells were being loaded. All of these setbacks began to wear on Potemkin. He was chewing his nails now so furiously that he developed whitlows—painful, pussy infections—on the fingers of his right hand, making it difficult to write (Letters 356, 358, 360).

From St. Petersburg, Catherine informed Potemkin of their successes against the Swedes in Finland. Though outnumbered, Russian troops had managed to repulse an attack on Fredrikshamn, and in August the momentum shifted to the Russians. Catherine confidently predicted peace, perhaps even as early as the coming autumn. Aware of the strain under which Potemkin was conducting the siege, she wrote him to be patient, not to hurry matters along and so needlessly place the men at risk. Upon reading of his whitlows, she worriedly inquired whether he were hiding an injury from her (Letters 357, 359, 361).

Potemkin's siege of Ochakov dragged on throughout the summer and fall of 1788. The foreigners around him, especially Nassau and Ligne, expressed growing frustration at his unwillingness to storm the fortress. The prince's fondness for spending the days playing billiards, arranging fêtes, and conducting love affairs with the officers' wives as he waited for the stubborn Turks to surrender did little to help his critics see the necessity of waiting. In early November, the wet autumn suddenly gave way to an uncommonly snowy and cold winter that made life miserable at camp. Food was running scarce and dysentery descended upon the troops in their trenches. Still, Potemkin waited. He was determined to win Ochakov for the least possible price and remained confident that the blockade and the constant cannonading would eventually bring the Turks to their knees. With each passing day, the number of Potemkin's supporters dwindled. He was becoming increasingly isolated.

Although Catherine had supported Potemkin's patient approach at Ochakov and had herself urged caution lest the army suffer heavy casualties, by the autumn of 1788 she, too, was growing impatient. The international situation had taken a drastic turn for the worse. Prussian meddling among the Poles had helped to ignite an outburst of anti-Russian sentiment that threatened to destroy the Russian protectorate over Poland and to win it over to the Prussians. In addition, Prussia threatened to invade Denmark, Russia's ally who had joined the war against Sweden in August, if the Danes did not call off their advance in southern Sweden.

While intimidating Russia's ally, Prussia, together with Britain (its partner with the United Provinces in the Triple Alliance established that same year), brazenly offered to mediate the wars between the Swedes, Turks, and Russians. Prussia's actions infuriated Catherine. Potemkin's enemies at court, well aware of his policy of placating the Prussian king, urged her to be firm and not to tolerate Prussia's affronts to her honor and that of the empire. In a meeting of the State Council on 25 September, it was decided to turn down the Prussian offer and to send Russian troops to the Polish-Prussian border as a sign that St. Petersburg could not be intimidated.

Potemkin threw up his hands in disgust upon hearing of the decision. What with the poor showing of the Austrians in the war, the tenacity of the Turks, and the unforeseen hostilities with Sweden, Potemkin feared Russia quite simply lacked the manpower to wage a new war against Prussia. Russia needed fewer not more enemies, he reasoned, and the only way out of the present crisis was through clever diplomacy. Had he not foreseen all this trouble, Potemkin asked, and had he not urged her to prevent it from happening? Utterly dismayed at what Catherine was proposing, Potemkin again offered his resignation (Letters 363–365).

Potemkin's angry letters hurt Catherine. She sought to defend herself and her actions, noting that she was only human and so susceptible to mistakes. Particularly unsettling was Potemkin's threat of resigning, which the empress considered a "mortal blow," and she repeated that she was doing everything possible to placate the "all-powerful dictator." To Catherine, the way out of the present crisis lay in Potemkin's hands: "Seize Ochakov and make peace with the Turks," she instructed him on 27 November, then Russia's enemies "will melt away like snow on the steppe after a thaw" (Letters 366, 368).

Potemkin did not wait for Catherine's order, however. On 1 December, the prince signed the order to storm the fortress with six columns attacking from different directions. Early on the morning of 6 December, three shells were launched into the dark sky over Ochakov to signal the attack. After an hour and a quarter of fighting, Ochakov fell to the Russians. Potemkin wrote to Catherine the following day from inside the fortress to give her the long-awaited news. The fighting had been especially brutal: approximately 10,000 Turkish men, women, and children were killed; Russian casualties numbered more than 2,500. The bodies lay so thick on the ground it was difficult just to walk. Potemkin's courier arrived in St. Petersburg at 7 p.m. on 15 December. Overjoyed, Catherine wrote to congratulate her prince and to convey to him her profound gratitude. It appeared to Catherine that peace with the Ottomans might now be achieved (Letters 369, 370).

Sadly, although the fall of Ochakov should have been for Potemkin one of his proudest moments, the hard-won victory was tainted by what he perceived to be Catherine's criticisms of him, as expressed in her letters of November, and by the persistent conniving of his enemies at court. At the end of December he wrote to justify his counsel on dealing with Prussia, stating that he was motivated by zeal and loyalty for his empress and not by any love for the Prussian king. For the conqueror of Ochakov, this was not easy to write. It had become quite clear by now to Potemkin that in his absence his enemies had managed to insert themselves between him and the empress. It was time he returned to St. Petersburg (Letter 371).

• • •

335. POTEMKIN TO CATHERINE

Yelizavetgrad. 3 January [1788]

Your Most Gracious Majesty. A courier for Ligne arrived today and brought with him from the Emperor a description of the Belgrade affair, rumors of which reached here two days earlier. After having attired themselves in different uniforms, 130 Imperial soldiers together with an officer were led into Belgrade. The guards at the gates had been bribed, the gates had been left open, and all that the 12 battalions had left to do was enter. However, they were apparently impeded by fog, and so those in the town could not wait for them any longer and had to leave. And in this way this business came to an end. I have, however, a true account from the other side, which is now being translated from the German for me, and I shall attach it hereto.

If the Emperor would recall my proposals, which I communicate to him through Ligne, about taking Khotin, which is so poorly defended at present, and would establish a post in the Banat, position part of his forces in Megadia, which is near Orsova, and part by the Rymnik; and would station those forces on the Olt near the castle of Braniovan, as well as in a line from Kronstadt toward Cimpolung and Cimpino—he would then be placing his entire weight on the Turks' shoulders. Two hundred thousand would suffice for this.[1] Then everything would begin to shudder. What with his forces in the enemy's side throughout almost all of Walachia, the enemy will find collecting grain and dues and, what is more, moving their troops to be dangerous. Should this create an awful mess for them, so much the better for us, and may God grant us success.

Your Most Gracious Majesty! Convince Poland to make war with us. And although I swore to forsake speaking, still my zeal compels me: at the same time stroke the Berlin court. Then, with God's help and encountering no obstacles, we shall step lively and go far.

I request once more for your benefit that you order me to act regarding the Cossacks and the purchase of private estates as outlined in my proposals. Through these actions we shall increase our number of light forces which will be directed against the enemy everywhere, and should God give us success, will pursue and destroy him. Be assured that this is necessary and beneficial.[2]

I wrote about Kingsbergen. Order that he be sent here to the fleet.[3]

By completing the fortifications, as much as was possible, we have finished with Kinburn. Kherson is being brought into a state of defensive readiness. Preparations are being made for the siege of Ochakov. Ships are being built for the Zaporozhians.[4] My heart is now heavy with the Tatars. The Khan is preparing to attack either from the Bug or Poland. The troops are arranged in such a way that, with God's help, great success cannot be expected, but it is not possible to defend all the settlements which are little more than small groupings of peasant homesteads, from one to four in number. Till now God has been merciful: the Bug has not yet frozen over.

[. . .] I am well and shall remain till the end of my life
your most loyal and most grateful subject
Prince Potemkin-Tavrichesky

---

1. Instead of stretching their forces out along the entire Turkish line, Potemkin suggested to the Austrians that they concentrate their forces at key strategic locations.

2. Potemkin increased the size of the army by creating new Cossack forces from the single-homesteaders (*odnodvortsy*) and Old Believers of New Russia. He also sought to strengthen the borders by having the state purchase private estates and charging the inhabitants with the defense of these areas.

3. Dutch Admiral Jan-Henrik Kingsbergen (1735–1819) had fought for Russia in the First Russo-Turkish War. Despite Russian pleading, he was unable to fight for Russia again.

4. This flotilla of small oared craft secretly built near Kremenchug played a decisive role in the victories over the Turks off Ochakov in June and July 1788.

336. CATHERINE TO POTEMKIN

11 January 1788

My friend Prince Grigory Aleksandrovich. Your letters of 25 December and 3 January have reached my hands. From the first I see with pleasure that you were offended by the notion that vacillation could have a place in your thoughts, which I too did not suppose. We are treating the Prussian court with respect, but considering its hostile conduct during the break in Tsar Grad, we can expect little good from it. I'm sending you herewith my comments on the Polish plan.[1] I'm quite sorry that you were ill upon your return from Kherson; I too was indisposed, but am now better. In one day here it's gone from well above freezing down to between twenty and twenty-five degrees below zero.

That your cares are great, I've little doubt, but you, my light, will withstand them all, both great and small. I know the spirit and mental strength of my pupil and have no doubt that he can endure everything. Nevertheless, be certain that I thank you very much for your numerous labors and efforts. I know that they flow from your ardent love and zeal for me and our common cause.

Please notify me in writing how many vessels you lost last autumn so that I might distinguish the universal lies from the truth, and in what condition is the Sevastopol and Dnieper squadron now? God grant you health amid such great troubles. Be certain that although we are apart, still I am always with you in my thoughts and I take to heart all your worries given my sincere friendship for you. And I quite understand that future successes very much depend on the current preparations and efforts. May the Almighty help you in everything and everywhere.

If you are successful in enticing the Zaporozhians, then the other good thing to do is to settle them in Taman, je crois que c'est vraiment leur place.[2] The sick and the illnesses frighten me. I shall not send Mikhelson[3] to the fleet, but am thinking of talking Zaborovsky[4] into going. He is coming here. Mikhelson has gout, and besides, he's needed here, should the Swedes start playing tricks.

Although the Emperor's unsuccessful undertaking against Belgrade is not very good for them, it is, nevertheless, good for us since it moves this matter further along, and an end has been put to this doubt. Perhaps matters will be resolved as you presupposed. Orders will be prepared regarding Poland and the Cossacks. And as regards the purchase of villages along the Bug, there is no question about it, since you found the money yourself.

I think Kingsbergen has already been engaged. A courier departed long ago on this mission for Holland, and I'll write to you when I hear how things went. What you write about the finishing of Kinburn's fortifications, about the defensive readiness of Kherson and about the preparations for the siege of Ochakov—all this serves to comfort and please me. The Turkish ventures will perhaps be weaker now than previously, but if they do cause some trouble somewhere it will most likely not amount to much and will cost them dearly. [. . .]

Zorich left the Empire under another name, was in Vienna and left there saying that he would soon return from Hungary, but he never came back. So order someone to ask Neranchich:[5] where did his brother go?

Farewell, my true friend, be well. I pray God to strengthen your body and soul.

The Grand Duke is now preparing to leave for the army, but since there is a chance she is pregnant, this may stop him. But so far nothing can be said for certain.[6]

Adieu, mon Ami voilà un embarras de plus pour Vous que je serais enchantée de Vous épargner.[7]

1. These have not been found.

2. "I believe that is their true place."

3. Lieutenant-General Ivan Ivanovich Mikhelson (1740–1807) had fought in the First Russo-Turkish War and led troops in the decisive victories over Pugachev. Despite being ill, he later took part in the fighting against the Swedes.

4. Lieutenant-General Ivan Aleksandrovich Zaborovsky (1735–1817) was to be sent to the Archipelago with a fleet carrying a landing force but was prevented from leaving due to Swedish aggression that summer.

5. Major-General David Gavrilovich Neranchich (1751–?) was the brother of Catherine's former favorite Semyon Zorich. He was serving at the time in Potemkin's army.

6. The grand duchess was indeed pregnant, and so Grand Duke Paul was not able to join Potemkin's army, to the latter's great relief.

7. "Farewell, my friend, here is one more kiss for you since I should be delighted with your thrift."

337. POTEMKIN TO CATHERINE

15 January [1788]. Yelizavetgrad

Your Most Gracious Majesty. A courier will depart from here every twelve days. Believe me that my head ached so that I couldn't apply myself to a thing upon arriving from Kherson. It has been three days now since my senses have returned. I think Nassau expressed to me straight from the heart what you deign to write about him, and the French want to discuss matters at Versailles since it is customary for every court to want to put on airs. But be that as it may, my earnest advice is not to embitter anyone, but to acquaint everyone with your plans, while showing them how they serve their own advantage.

The Belgrade affair will forever be a mystery. They[1] are again on friendly terms with the Turks everywhere, and they are trading and paying each other visits. I received news this hour that the Turkish force is beginning to march out of Bender for Balta, and the fleet is hurrying to depart from Tsar Grad.

You deign to write that I should watch out for Nassau, that he will, perhaps, distract me from my undertakings.[2] For God's sake, Your Majesty, could anyone distract me from my duty to serve? No one will rouse me to an undertaking if it lacks purpose, and no one can distract me when a beneficial opportunity presents itself.

There are now very many sick in the force this winter, when illnesses usually come to a halt, but God grants us victories, and our hope should be placed in Him, and not in thick battalions.

It will cost ten rubles a quarter to purchase and deliver grain from Smolensk and White Russia to Kremenchug. Last year this would have cost two hundred thousand, but now two million. Yet what is to be done?

Things are inordinately expensive everywhere. Lord have mercy upon us in the coming summer. Till now they have been promising good crops, still nothing will drop to its former price. The exchange of paper money for coins is being made at a rate of 12 and 15 kopecks to the ruble. As a result the soldiers are losing one sixth of their salaries. I am expecting copper coins and for this reason gave the order to wait a bit before paying out the salaries.[3] Farewell, Your Most Gracious Majesty. While alive I remain

your most grateful and most loyal subject
Prince Potemkin-Tavrichesky

---

1. The Austrians.

2. Prince Charles of Nassau-Siegen arrived in Yelizavetgrad early in 1788 to serve under Potemkin.

3. The outbreak of war had resulted in a drop in value of Russia's paper money. At the same time, the country was experiencing a shortage of coinage.

338. CATHERINE TO POTEMKIN

26 January 1788

My friend, Prince Grigory Aleksandrovich, your letters of 15 January have reached me. God grant that this missive found you in complete health. Here everyone is sick with a runny nose and cough. I think a third of the city, at least, is bothered by this and catarrhal fevers.

The Grand Duchess is big with child and will give birth in May, and so now he won't leave before the child's birth.

[. . .]

It is quite sad for me to hear that there are many sick with you. God grant that the illnesses soon cease.

You have been sent copper coins. Everything is terribly expensive, may God grant you the strength to endure all troubles, both discernible and indiscernible. I've been well of late.

It occurred to me that you love my nice little fur coats, and I suppose those you have are already old, so I took it into my head to provide you with a new one. Wear it in good health. Farewell, my friend, be assured that I am your true friend and that I love you as always. Adieu, mon Ami.

Sasha[1] is mad about your letters, and he loves you like his soul and is extremely grateful. Is it true you moved your Kremenchug home to Yelizavetgrad?[2]

---

1. Mamonov.

2. It was rumored at court that Potemkin had moved the wooden governor-general's palace, built for Catherine during her voyage, for Grand Duke Paul's use.

339. POTEMKIN TO CATHERINE

[5 February 1788]

Your Most Gracious Majesty. I became very [weak] after my last illness which, however, thanks to God, has completely passed. There are many sick here with me, which is sad to recall. God is my witness as to how much I look after them, however, my strength is not sufficient. Till now things have been quiet here. Some Tatars have come once again to Ochakov, and the Khan himself has moved toward Dubossary. I have already reported on our arrival in Nania, which caused great alarm in Jassy.[1] Parties are heading out daily in every direction from my border cordon to reconnoiter on the other side of the Bug, often traveling up to forty versts across the steppe near Ochakov. Our loyal Zaporozhians ravaged the village of Adzhigiol in recent days, but the inhabitants had already left. I frequently harass them to keep them from moving. If the winter weren't so severe I would send the parties farther, but there has been no opportunity. The Emperor's agent hasn't left Jassy in recent days, though he practically ran to his cordon. The troops that were in Sniatin have advanced toward Bukovina, and they say that the war manifestoes are to be published any day now.[2] I also know that a second attempt is being made on Belgrade and with large forces. It is already high time for the enterprise to end. May God grant success. All the grain that was gathered in Jassy and then densely stored in a monastery rotted since it had not been barn dried, and more has now been ordered harvested, but that'll be difficult.

How good it would be, matushka, if we could quickly come to a decision about the Poles. And so, to entice the entire nation, they must be promised parts of the Turkish lands, for without this it cannot be done. When you deign to approve new brigades for their nation's army, order that the one given to Count Branicki be attached to my army. What marvelous people and, one might say, horsemen. It is a pity that you are not favorably disposed to giving me command, if not over the cavalry of the entire nation, then at least over one brigade. I'm as much a Pole as they are.[3] I would do much good. [. . .] Count Damas[4] has arrived here, a true child, but modest and excellently civil. Addressing himself to me, he said that if he is not permitted to serve as a volunteer, he would enlist as a common soldier in some regiment. We ought not reject those Frenchmen who are devoted to us. Better to have them here with us, than with the Turks. You do deign to recognize the ardor of this nation: should they hear that they are tolerated here, and, still more, should someone from among them succeed in distinguishing himself here, then it will immediately become fashionable to raise the battle cry for Russia.

Your Majesty, loving your profit, glory and my land, I speak freely of what I have been able to devise as for the best. It is your will which of my ideas are to be approved.

Illnesses, the dearness of materials and a great many obstacles trouble us, along with the complete scarcity of grain and, as you deigned to write, that also in Petersburg there are many who are not well. In this situation, what are you to do? Have patience and do not doubt that you can rely on God. Christ will help you. He will send an end to our misfortunes. Go over your life, you will see how many unexpected blessings, born of misfortune, came to you from Him. You found yourself in situations when it appeared that every path was blocked. Yet suddenly, success was yours. Place all your hope in Him and believe that He cannot be denied. Let others think as they wish, but I believe that upon your accession the Apostle passed on his blessing: "I commend to you our sister Phoebe, a deaconess of the Church at Cen'chre-ae, that you may receive her in the Lord as befits the saints, etc."[5]

Man cannot perceive why God permits grief. But one must know this, that in such situations one must turn to Him. You know me, and that this does not make me superstitious.

[. . .]

Whoever said that I moved my house from Kremenchug to Yelizavetgrad has, of course, gone soft in the head. I bought a house in Mirgorod from retired Major Stankevich and moved it to Yelizavetgrad, and even that I didn't do for myself, but since I had heard that Their Highnesses were on their way here. As for me, I would live wherever I happen to land, for I don't think too highly of myself and haven't even taken for myself a guardhouse befitting my rank. What has been brought here from Kremenchug is some furniture. Forgive me, Your Majesty, I am so weak my head is spinning.

[. . .]

I kiss your tender hands, I thank you for the fur coat. It is so cold that I've had to warm myself. If I could be furnished with two Chinese dressing-gowns I would be extremely grateful. One I would simply wear, and the other would serve as a lining for my full-dress frock-coat. Farewell, Your Majesty. May God grant that the time will come when I might present my loyalty to you and my boundless zeal for service. I remain till the grave

by my loyalty and gratitude
your subject Prince Potemkin-Tavrichesky

---

1. On 15 January, Potemkin reported on the successful attack of a Don Cossack force on the village of Nania, near Olviopol on the road to Jassy. When news reached the Moldavian hospodar in Jassy, he prepared to flee the town.

2. Potemkin did not yet know that Joseph II had issued the manifesto declaring war against the Porte on 29 January (9 February) 1788.

3. According to the union treaty being negotiated by Potemkin and others, Russian subsidies were to be used to create three brigades of Polish cavalry. One was to be entrusted to Count Ksawery Branicki, married to Potemkin's niece, Aleksandra. By calling himself a "Pole," Potemkin is making reference to his family's descent from Smolensk's Polish gentry, his large land holdings in Poland, and his official recognition of Polish noble status as conveyed by the certificate of *indigenat*.

4. French Count Roger de Damas (1765–1823) arrived in Yelizavetgrad seeking to volunteer in the Russian army. He enjoyed the patronage of Nassau, and Potemkin appointed him to serve in his patron's flotilla. He distinguished himself in the battles in the Liman in June 1788 and in the siege of Ochakov.

5. Potemkin cites Romans 12, verses 1–2.

340. CATHERINE TO POTEMKIN

22 February 1788

My friend, Prince Grigory Aleksandrovich. Prince Vasily Dolgorukov[1] is bringing you my letter, with which I inform you that the distinguished Paul Jones[2] wants to enter our service. And as I see that the arrival of Kingsbergen is ever more distant, and that if he does come he will come late, and will, perhaps, not come at all, so I have ordered that Paul Jones be admitted into our service and he is leaving straightaway for you. Even among the English he is regarded as the second man in the navy: Admiral Howe[3] is the first, but he is the second. He defeated the English four times while with the Americans. [. . .]

My friend, I quite regret you were weak and had many sick there with you when you sent your last letter. Send me at least one report monthly about them, and also about our losses. I am quite certain that you are looking after the sick. May God fortify your strength.

The Tatars' enterprise has, to all appearances, lessened somewhat over that of past years and centuries. Based on news from abroad, all the Christians are awaiting their fellow believers as the Israelites did the Messiah. It is praiseworthy that the loyal Zaporozhians are serving loyally, however, with time try to replace the Zaporozhians' name with something else, for the Sech, which was destroyed by the manifesto, hasn't left a pleasant ring to the ears. For we don't want ignorant people to begin dreaming about the need to reestablish either the Sech or the name.

Your praiseworthy command has forced the enemy to hold you in high regard throughout the entire winter. Winter here has been very harsh, and I see it's a source of complaints there too. It seems to me that the Austrians put on a bear garden outside Khotin not much different from their previous one at Belgrade.[4] Their manifesto on the declaration of war has been published everywhere.

An order will now be issued to decide the matter of the Poles. Count Branicki's brigade will be attached to the troops under your leadership and command, and then it won't be difficult to place other Poles under your command as well. Regarding volunteers, I shall say to you that till now I have granted permission neither to our own subjects nor to foreigners to join the army for the reason that it had already been decided in the final campaign of the previous war not to accept any volunteers. Those from society's highest ranks were a burden to the commanders. And now, when grain is lacking and is very expensive everywhere (and volunteers have been showing up by the hundreds), so I thought that many superfluous mugs in the army would worsen the shortage and drive up the already high prices. You yourself have been complaining about writers of erroneous news. I even ordered the consuls expelled from Kherson, or there would've been even more. You can't even imagine how many of them were showing up: indeed, by the hundreds. It's not possible to sort them out and to say—you good one, we'll take you, but you bad one, stay there. Thirty Danes came, 50 Prussians, our subjects enlisted in entire regiments. Frenchmen, Italians, Spaniards, Germans, Swedes, Dutchmen—it was raining volunteers. In this way I got away with not accepting anyone. Once God gives us sufficient and ample provisions, then this general prohibition can be repealed, mais à toute armée les bouches inutiles l'on tâche de les éloigner ou diminuer.[5] It's fine to let Count Damas remain with you. [. . .]

Regarding the Kremenchug house, there was a rumor going around the city. I find it nice that you're not proud: he who's not proud is never dejected. Only for God's sake, be well. More than anything I am frightened by your frequent complaints about your head and by the fact that as of now you have still not fully recovered. I attribute this to your frightful labors and cares.

[. . .]

All the newspapers have been written about the massive size of our fleet.[6]

Farewell, my friend, I'm glad you liked my nice little fur coat. I'm sending two Chinese dressing-gowns. I do not doubt that I shall see everywhere your love, loyalty and zeal for me. And as for me, Your Lordship, I love you very, very, very much.

Farewell, God be with you.

I'll send the Preobrazhensky bombardiers to you by the post-chaise. Sasha loves you and regards you like his own father, and he's extremely attached to me and you, which all his words and deeds clearly show.

[. . .]

---

1. Lieutenant-General Prince Vasily Vasilievich Dolgorukov (1752–1812), a veteran of the First Russo-Turkish War, took part in the storming of Ochakov, for which he received the Order of St. George second class. Dolgorukov's beautiful wife, Yekaterina, joined her husband in the south and became one of Potemkin's mistresses.

2. A hero of the American War of Independence, John Paul Jones (1747–1792) was living in Paris when Catherine invited him to join Russian service. His service in the Black Sea fleet proved a disappointment.

3. Admiral Lord Howe (1726–1799) was the first lord of the Admiralty. In making the comparison between Howe and Jones, Catherine exaggerated the latter's stature.

4. Austrian troops under the command of General Prince Frederick of Saxe-Coburg-Saalfeld (1737–1817) made a failed attempt on the Turkish fortress of Khotin early in the year.

5. "however, throughout the entire army our task now is to get rid of or diminish the useless mouths."

6. As Potemkin had earlier suggested, Catherine ordered that a rumor of the departure of a large Russian naval fleet for the Archipelago be floated. The hope was that upon hearing it, the Turks would not be able to send their entire fleet to Ochakov.

341. CATHERINE TO POTEMKIN

24 March 1788

My friend, Prince Grigory Aleksandrovich. A rumor is going around Sweden that the Swedish King intends to pick a fight with us. Count Razumovsky discussed this rumor with old Count Fersen,[1] who told him that one would have to be mad to believe this, mais que d'un cerveau un peu dérangé on peut tout attendre.[2] The truth about this business is that an order has been sent to Karlskrona to arm twelve warships and several frigates. Money is being negotiated in Holland, and camps are being prepared in Swedish Finland. In addition, three colonels were called from Finland to present themselves to the King in Stockholm and were then sent back to Finland. General Posse[3] is touring the entire border and is preparing a magazine—14,000 barrels of all types of grain, and the King himself has left for Uppsala for a time. Having seen and heard all this, prudence demands that without becoming alarmed precautions appropriate to the situation be taken in order to prevent any dirty tricks. And so, in addition to arming the fleet heading for the Archipelago, arm five ships here, and just as many ships and frigates from the town of Arkhangelsk, keep the galleys and the oared vessels at the ready and instruct them to patrol our borders in order to defend against an unexpected landing and the like. The local regiments and the Baltic garrisons are to be brought up to full strength, as well as the artillery and everything pertaining to it. As for men, all this will require up to eighteen thousand recruits. Even before all this, the Church hierarchs reported that there are as many as twenty-four thousand extra church peasants;[4] there might be some among them suitable for military service, others are themselves demanding to be enlisted.

[. . .]

Farewell, my friend, be well. God be with you. I received from König[5] your portrait in marble. It's extremely good, and an empreinte en pâte[6] has been made from it and placed in my collection. C'est charmant.[7]

---

1. Count Fredrik Axel von Fersen (1719–1794) was then the leader of the anti-royalist "Patriots" opposed to Gustav III.

2. "but from a slightly deranged mind anything can be expected."

3. Lieutenant-General Count Fredrik Arvidsson Posse (1727–1794) commanded Swedish forces in Finland.

4. Peasants living on church lands were traditionally exempt from recruit levies. Catherine

suggested, and Potemkin agreed, to use them in regiments directed against the Swedes.

5. Georg Heinrich König (d. early 1800s) was a German sculptor and die-sinker who lived for a time in Russia.

6. "paste impression"

7. "It's charming."

342. POTEMKIN TO CATHERINE

6 April [1788]. Yelizavetgrad

Your Most Gracious Majesty. Here's my reply to the courier who arrived late the day before yesterday. Razumovsky's reports consist of only superficialities; either he is not well informed or isn't solicitous enough. It's not enough simply to say that twelve ships have been ordered outfitted; do they even have them? I think the King was able to divert several of the army's regiments in the last war, and so thinks he can do a service to the Turks again in the same way.[1] In all the dispatches to us, their spying and everything else is done in so obvious a manner that this seems more to resemble a demonstration. Preparations must be made, but not with too much seriousness, for this will send him into a rage. Since we have 10 ships, several frigates and other vessels and the help of the Danes as well—there is no danger of a landing. His magazine is not very large. We could use a diligent minister there.

[. . .] It wouldn't be difficult in the present situation to explain to the Swedes why they should seek to show us their good intentions instead of unkind acts. They could attach Russia to themselves through a favorable disposition and have in her a most useful friend. I think if we explain all these matters well to their minister everything will end quietly.

[. . .]

I am expecting any hour the arrival of the Turkish fleet. For my entire life I remain devotedly

your most loyal and most grateful subject
Prince Potemkin-Tavrichesky

P.S. I enclose herewith a copy secretly made of a letter of Prince Ligne's son in which the Emperor's actions are described.[2]

---

1. Razumovsky's reports warned of the seriousness of the situation. Sweden had aided its ally Turkey in the First Russo-Turkish War by forcing Russia to divert troops to the north, and was threatening to do so again.

2. Prince de Ligne's son, Charles (1759–1792), a colonel in the Austrian army, wrote to his father then living with Potemkin. His letter, in which he describes the shortcomings of the Austrian forces preparing to do battle with the Turks, was secretly copied by Potemkin's staff.

343. CATHERINE TO POTEMKIN

20 April 1788

My friend Prince Grigory Aleksandrovich. Your letters and reports of 6 April I received on the very day of the celebration, on the occasion of which I send you best wishes, and I desire for you the very greatest happiness, health and mental and physical strength. Thank you for answering without delay my letters about the Swedes' armaments. They do indeed exist, but whether will they be put to use against us—time will tell. In the meanwhile, common sense demands that we take every possible step concerning that side, especially all those means that depend on us: and so, as you are already aware of, on the sea 10 ships and the rest are being prepared. And yesterday I signed a levy of churchmen. And so our posture now is quite respectable. The Danes have also been told not to neglect their duty, which they won't refuse to carry out, I am certain. We shan't show, of course, any unnecessary alarm. According to the rumors going around the city about war with the Swedes, Nolken explained himself to the Vice Chancellor and said, among other things, that his King could not undertake such a step unless he were mad, but that from the youth surrounding him every kind of absurdity ought to be expected, and if this comes to pass, then he, Nolken, will go live in Livonia. They say that the Swedish nation will not look upon this with favor, and it very well may be that the King, wheedling money from various powers under the guise of buying arms, will then abandon them.

Razumovsky has been written to from here, and I hope everything will end with mere words. The copied letter of Ligne's son does not add much respect to our ally's discipline; still it's better to have him with us, rather than against us, as in the last war.

[. . .]

Farewell, my friend, be well and merry. According to intelligence received from Tsar Grad, the Kapudan Pasha[1] is simply biding his time till the Turks' first failure in order to avidly seek peace, and word is being spread everywhere that it will be concluded by autumn. Let's hope to God it's the truth. I wish for this with all my heart and that you return here, for then I wouldn't be lost, as now.

Once you take Ochakov with God's help, this will end the matter, and I suppose Bulgakov is already in Livorno now, for they wanted to let him go in the middle of March, by sea.

---

1. Gazi Hasan Pasha (1713–1790) served as the grand admiral (kapudan pasha) of the Ottoman fleet (1774–1789) and later as grand vizier (1789–1790). He was considered to be a proponent of peace.

344. POTEMKIN TO CATHERINE

[Before 5 May 1788]

Your Most Gracious Majesty. Practically from the beginning of my existence on this earth, I have not missed a single opportunity to offer proof of my loyalty, especially to Your Person, and all the truly outstanding favors of distinction that I possess I have received directly from you, having made no use of anyone's patronage, nor any intrigue on my behalf. I have not followed others' example—I did not assemble a party and thus arm myself against the growing strength of my haters. I have tried to serve equally both those whom I love as well as those who envy me. I am flattered by the distinction of the ranks you have given me since it has always provided me the means to render you my services, to which I have applied myself with true zeal.

Permit me to reveal directly to you, as my mother, as my benefactress, the circumstances that oppress me. The Austrians, who seek my ruin in every possible way, are laying a trap for me. They have learned that I discern their stratagems better than others and that I shall not trade my state's interests for theirs; hence they reckon that they cannot always succeed in their intentions with me, and so have been seeking of late to find an opportunity to damage me in your eyes. Prince Ligne, an empty-headed man whose character is devoid of anything sacred, is the instrument for this loathsome undertaking. He has written to Count Cobenzl[1] by special courier that I am not one who would want to conduct matters here to his Sovereign's advantage, and that by no means do I want to make any movements that would distract the Turkish forces from their borders, and that I doubt their sincerity. In a word, that it's high time to shove me aside. He added to this, in response to Cobenzl's inquiry about what my thoughts were concerning precautions against the Prussian King that had been sent to him, that I had not answered according to their wishes, although my answer was that till we had finished with the Turks, he was to be treated with care. Even this they did not like. He proposed to Cobenzl a way to find an occasion when you are dissatisfied with me to use Zavadovsky to damage your opinion of me. They have never exerted such a strong effort against me till now [. . .]

Your Majesty, I am certain of your firmness, however, the anxiety of having to defend myself against envious persons cannot but trouble me. And should it be necessary that they be left in peace, then I shall myself depart and leave everything behind with pleasure, though not as a victim; but as they are so indomitable in their malice, let them be free of me. I am tired of looking at their loathsome ingratitude. With true devotion till death I remain
your most loyal and most grateful subject
Prince Potemkin-Tavrichesky

P.S. I am certain that Cobenzl will not easily confess since he is not so empty-headed. But nevertheless, in his letter he mentioned that upon their declaration of war on the Porte, I should be certain of the Emperor's true participation.

---

1. Austria's ambassador to Russia.

345. POTEMKIN TO CATHERINE

Yelizavetgrad. 10 May [1788]

Your Most Gracious Majesty, some of the regiments are approaching the Bug, and the others are also on the move. I'll soon go there, and when the advance troops arrive, I shall then have them cross from the Crimean Steppes toward Ochakov and Bender. From Witt's[1] enclosed letters and the testimonies of the captured Turks, kindly note the extreme situation in which Khotin finds itself. Austrian Colonel Fabré[2] even captured a transport with money heading for Khotin. It is time that our men showed up in more equal numbers in that region and along the border as well where there is lodging and provisions; and then we must start crossing over to that side. We shouldn't abandon the Austrians, who in all seriousness have already begun operations in Moldavia. Your Majesty, we have yet to fire even a pistol in that region.[3]

[...]

I've ordered the Caucasus and Kuban Corps to move; I directed those in the Crimea to defend themselves by allowing the enemy to land and then cutting him off from his vessels. May God help us. But for all that, I remind you of my previous idea, that since we don't have any reliable fortresses there nor a strong fleet yet, it would be much better to abandon it and then, after having allowed the enemy to enter, to drive him out. The troops there, which are located beyond Perekop, could have operated in response to the given circumstances and increased our numbers that are once again small; but now, besides providing defense, for which reason they are attached to Sevastopol, they must remain in Tauride as if trapped inside a sack.

Your Most Gracious Majesty, I shall go there and shall act with the utmost fervor, despite the inexperience of my infantry, which is almost entirely made up of recruits. I shall set an example everywhere, I shall gladly sacrifice my life for you, my mother, for the state, and, one might say, for Christianity, expecting without any doubt that God will help me. I have taken all possible precautions everywhere against enemy attacks, but since military successes are subject to change, so even if despite all my efforts the enemy has made some gains, do not consider this, Your Most Gracious Majesty, to be my fault. God sees how I burn with desire to bring you glory.

There's a great ferment now in Poland, especially among the young, and Count Branicki is no less agitated than all the others. Matushka, order matters hurried along, for another might win them over to their side. Make use of their good disposition toward us. [. . .]

[. . .] While alive I remain with constant devotion

your most loyal and most grateful subject
Prince Potemkin-Tavrichesky

---

1. Polish General Joseph de Witt was the commandant of the fortress of Kamenets-Podolsk.

2. An officer fighting under Coburg, Fabré captured a load of supplies being sent to the Turks at Khotin in the spring, and then later helped to seize Jassy. He was promoted to the rank of general.

3. Potemkin instructed Rumiantsev in May to march with his Ukrainian Army into Moldavia to work in consort with the Austrian forces there.

346. POTEMKIN TO CATHERINE

Yelizavetgrad. 19 May [1788]

Your Most Gracious Majesty! I received word of Her Imperial Highness's delivery and celebrated it the next day.[1] On the very same day the standards belonging to the excellent Cossack force that you permitted formed out of the Yekaterinoslav single-homesteaders were consecrated.

The Greeks are out cruising and have displayed considerable bravery and preparedness. It would be good if our naval men resembled them, but they have been ruined by science, which they use more for making excuses than for taking action. I promoted those men who battled near the enemy's fleet to the rank of midshipmen. Apparently the Turks are watching where we are directing our forces in order to head in that direction themselves. Almost all the troops have arrived at the Bug, including the Cossacks who were held up by the Dnieper. Everything needed for the siege is being readied; I would already be on the Bug, however, my presence is needed here in order to incite those in the rear to get moving more quickly. The Bug will be crossed in two places: the 1st pontoon bridge will be placed two versts below Olviopol, where, together with part of the infantry, almost all the light troops and advance cavalry will cross, which I formed out of the Olviopol and Voronezh Light Cavalry Regiments. [. . .]

As soon as the first party crossing the Bug reaches that point on the other side across from Aleksandrovka, then another bridge will be laid there, and everyone else will cross. After uniting the forces there, I'll make my way to Adzhigiol, where 6 infantry battalions will join me after crossing over in craft from Kherson, and the siege artillery will cross over at the Russian spit to the mouth of the Bug. At the same time, all the vessels will approach Ochakov, and Aleksandr Vasilievich[2] will attack with his troops from sea, and I on land, God willing.

Your Majesty! I hear that the Emperor supposedly complained through his ambassador to you and the Vice Chancellor[3] of the armies' lack of cooperation. On what basis do they drag me into this matter? The forces entrusted to me must primarily defend the borders; my offensive force, on the other hand, is directed against one spot, that is, against Ochakov. Hence it cannot serve them as a diversion, and for this reason I must make the proper preparations and take every measure so that we don't drag along as they did with Dubica, which is nearly defenseless. Because of this unexpected war I had to do in 4 months what should have been done in two years. Very well, another might have summoned the spirit to repair a fleet completely ravaged by the weather, to build such a great number of oared craft fit for use at sea, to form completely anew sixteen infantry battalions, ten thousand entirely new cavalry as well, to put together a large mobile magazine, to supply the artillery with a frightful number of oxen, to use all his wits to supply sustenance—and all this in 4 months while protecting your borders, along which, thank God, everything has been kept safe—on the steppes, without sufficient billets, and especially in the area around Kinburn, where in three weeks housing for more than ten thousand men had to be built.

In light of their position, they ought to look only to the Ukrainian Army for assistance, which could move anywhere given that it is surrounded by fine settlements. [. . .]

Your Most Gracious Majesty, you will see with what desire I shall go forth, being till death

your most loyal and most grateful subject
Prince Potemkin-Tavrichesky

P.S. Aleksandra Vasilievna[4] would have left us here for the other world had God not suddenly and unexpectedly provided His help.

---

1. Grand Duchess Maria Fyodorovna gave birth to a daughter, Yekaterina (1788–1819), on 10 May.

2. Suvorov.

3. The son of one of Peter the Great's ministers, Count Ivan Andreevich Osterman (1725–1811) had been made vice chancellor in 1774 thanks to Potemkin's support.

4. Potemkin's niece Countess Aleksandra Branicka.

347. CATHERINE TO POTEMKIN

27 May 1788

My dear friend, Prince Grigory Aleksandrovich. Yesterday, while I was preparing a thorough reply to your letter of the 10th instant, Ribeaupierre[1] arrived with his dispatch of 19 May. Your meticulous and detailed description of the condition of affairs and operations, as well as the more frequent dispatch of couriers than before, pleases me and calms my soul. I see from your letters your altogether judicious command, also that everything is already in motion and that in every situation and setting you completely confirm my trust and my choice. Carry on, my friend, as you've begun. I hope that God will bless your zeal and fervor for me and for our common affair and will crown your undertakings with successes. And rest assured—you've a loyal friend in me.

It's been ages since I received any letters from Field Marshal Rumiantsev. I don't know what he's doing, and I only know about this from his letters that you have sent to me. I suppose he'll say that his mother's death has caused him such grief he couldn't write.[2]

[. . .] Ribeaupierre told me that you received Paul Jones quite affectionately, which gladdens me all the more since he was a bit worried that you wouldn't like him.[3] But I assured him that you are quite easily pleased by demonstrations of zeal and fervor and that you were impatiently awaiting his arrival, and with this he departed. After he left I sent him Simolin's original letter, which I had by then received, in order to reinforce his good disposition, since in it was written how you sought to obtain Paul Jones, and this could serve as proof to him of how well disposed you are to him and what you think of him.

Say what you will, but I cannot agree on abandoning the Crimea. Over it the war is being fought, and if we abandon this nest, then both Sevastopol and all our labors and good establishments will be lost, and the Tatars will make raids into our interior provinces once again, and the Caucasus Corps will be cut off from you, and we shall once again be occupied with trying to take Tauride and shall not know where to put our warships, which will find refuge neither in the Dnieper nor in the Sea of Azov. For God's sake, don't entertain these thoughts, which are difficult for me to understand and seem inappropriate to me, for they deprive us of much advantage and benefit acquired through peace and war. When one is sitting on a horse, one doesn't get off so as to hold on by the tail. Nevertheless, rest assured that your thoughts and actions, based upon zeal, fervor and love for me and for the state, will of course, whatever their success, never be held against you.

A courier was sent to Poland long ago with a plan of the treaty, and I think this business is already well underway. We have already received here official word on the convening of the Sejm.[4] [. . .]

I see from your letter of 19 May that you received my notice on the birth of my granddaughter Yekaterina. This time her parents acted more affectionately toward me than previously since they think that I somehow saved the mother's life, because for two and a half hours her life was in considerable danger solely from the affectionate gestures and cowardice of the doctors surrounding her, and seeing this I was able to offer some good counsel in a timely and opportune manner, which served to end the matter successfully. She is now well, and he[5] is getting ready to join you with the army, to which I assented, and he is thinking of leaving here on the twentieth of June, that is six weeks from the day after tomorrow, assuming Swedish affairs do not detain him. Should the half-witted Swedish King start a war with us, then the Grand Duke will stay here, and I shall appoint Count Pushkin[6] commander of the army against the Swedes, and as for Bruce[7]—well, he can be as furious as he wants to: how can I, at the present time, entrust such an important post to an idiot who has failed everywhere he has served?

Swedish Affairs are now in a state of extreme crisis. You'll learn from the papers conveyed to you by this courier what's being and has been done about them. Every court, the Swedish court included, has been informed of our arming for the Mediterranean Sea, and the Swedish King feigns that he views all this as directed against him, and he truly is arming himself heavily in Karlskrona. He entrusted command of this fleet to his brother, and has now left for Karlskrona to bring the ships out on a raid, and before that he assembled the Senate and announced to them that since Russia is arming against him and is trying to provoke a war with him in every possible way (to this he added lies and slander against us and his minister Nolken), so he must prepare for war as well. All the Senators praised his vigilance. After departing the Senate, he ordered galleys be outfitted and his Guards and six regiments as well be prepared for the crossing to Finland, for where, upon returning from Karlskrona, he himself intends to set out. It is suspected that the Porte gave him the money for these arms. [. . .] [P]erhaps the matter will end with the King exchanging compliments with me, as usual, upon arriving in Finland and being content with his demonstration. But if he takes it into his head to fight, then we shall try to defend ourselves, but that he received money from someone, of this there is no doubt. [. . .]

I'm glad the Greeks with you are displaying great courage, and it may well be that our men have been ruined by science. The Turks appear to be in considerable confusion. [. . .]

My friend, whoever told you that the Emperor complained to me and through his ambassador to the Vice Chancellor about your army's lack of good offices completely lied. Neither I nor the Vice Chancellor have heard even a single word about this at any time—neither directly nor indirectly.

Besides, who knows as much as I do myself how many labors you have had since the beginning of the war: you repaired and built the fleet, formed anew the infantry and cavalry, put together magazines during a lean time, supplied the artillery with oxen and horses, protected the borders so that throughout the entire winter not even a tomcat got across (NB. This is without precedent and has amazed me numerous times) and you have preserved Kinburn.

[. . .] I'm very sorry about Aleksandra Vasilievna's Illness. The trees she sent me have taken root, but will they withstand the winter—I don't know; the gardeners speak as if not.

I'm quite pleased with the zeal for Russia that the Poles with you have shown. My friend, I would be happy to permit you to put together a force, but I don't know whether I'll have enough money for more troops.

[. . .]

Farewell, my friend, God be with you. I wish you health, happiness and success.

Aleksandr Matveevich[8] has received the title of Count from the Emperor, and since he behaves like an angel, so I have made him an adjutant-general. You have loved him like a son, and so I've no doubt that you will gladly share in this.

Do hurry and send me your plan on the formation of the Cossack troops from the coachmen and petty townsmen, as well as the Cossack lieutenant-colonels.

God knows, I do not doubt that you will act as honor and good faith dictate, and now even more I rely on your good and irreproachable disposition.

---

1. Born in Alsace, François de (a.k.a. Ivan Stepanovich) Ribaupierre (1750–1790) joined Russian service in 1778. He became an adjutant to the prince and later a confidant of the favorite Mamonov.

2. Rumiantsev wrote Potemkin of the bitter tears he shed following the recent death of his mother, Maria Andreevna (1698–1788), chief stewardess of the court and a lady-in-waiting.

3. Potemkin put Jones in command of the Liman flotilla of sailing craft on 20 May.

4. Russia's plans for a treaty floundered in part due to Stanislaw Poniatowski's wish to make the Polish throne hereditary, which Catherine was unable to support. The so-called Four-Year Sejm, which lasted from 1788–1792, was virulently anti-Russian, opposed the king, and instituted a series of constitutional reforms.

5. Grand Duke Paul.

6. Count Valentin Platonovich Musin-Pushkin (1735–1804), a veteran of the Seven Years' War and the First Russo-Turkish War and vice president of the College of War, was made commander in chief of the Finnish Army in 1788.

7. Though he had distinguished himself in the Seven Years' War and First Russo-Turkish War, General-in-Chief Count Yakov Aleksandrovich Bruce (1732–1791) did not shine as a military leader. He served as the governor-general of St. Petersburg and Moscow and was married to Field Marshal Rumiantsev's sister, Countess Praskovia, one of Catherine's close friends mentioned in her "Sincere Confession" (Letter 4).

8. Mamonov.

348. POTEMKIN TO CATHERINE

Yelizavetgrad. 27 May [1788]

The Kapudan Pasha has arrived at Ochakov with a huge fleet.[1] I despatched Paul Jones to the Liman and Kinburn to have a look, however, I'm still awaiting his answer: due to a large storm on the Liman, they were unable to make the crossing. Your Most Gracious Majesty, I would already be on the other side of the Bug myself, where the troops are now located, but I must await word from Paul Jones in Kherson. The enemy's fleet is large and is well manned. As they arrived, our double-launch, which was standing guard, had just sailed off when more than thirty different vessels rushed after it. Its commander, Lieutenant-Captain Saken, was unable to outrun them and went up in the air together with his vessel.[2] Such courageous resolution merits recompense for those he has left behind. Matushka, affairs here are serious. It is imperative that others take action as well, or else everything will be directed against a single place. My offensive forces comprise 22 infantry battalions; the cavalry are sufficient. All the rest are out on watch. I must preserve the fleet as well, and the so-called Kinburn fortress. Farewell, Your Most Gracious Majesty, I remain for my entire life

> your most loyal and most grateful subject
> Prince Potemkin-Tavrichesky

---

1. Suvorov reported to Potemkin on 21 May that ninety-two Turkish vessels had arrived at Ochakov.

2. On 20 May, Second Captain Reinhold Osten-Saken's guardship was outrun by enemy vessels on its way from Kinburn to Glubaia pristan' where it was to meet up with the main fleet. At the mouth of the Bug, he unloaded his crew and then blew up his ship, killing himself and inflicting damage on the nearby Turkish vessels.

349. CATHERINE TO POTEMKIN

4 June 1788

My dear friend Prince Grigory Aleksandrovich. Your letter of 27 May with the news of the arrival of the Turkish fleet at Ochakov was delivered to my hands yesterday. Lieutenant-Captain Saken's courageous act fills me with great sorrow. I intend to give his father a house in the country, which he can have for nothing, and I have ordered that his brothers be found in order to ask them how I might show them my charity.

Field Marshal Rumiantsev writes me that he is going to visit you on the other side of the Bug so that the two of you can agree on joint operations. While the Turkish forces are directed against you, the Swedish King, having received money from the Turks, has armed at least twelve warships and is moving troops to Finland. All these demonstrations are aimed, I think, at stopping our fleet which has been fitted out for the Mediterranean Sea. Nevertheless, this fleet will depart on its journey, and if obstacles are placed before it along the way, then it will seek to destroy these obstacles.[1] Yet opinions here are divided: the Vice Chancellor says—"Before leaving, let us strike the Swedish fleet, even if they don't attack us first," and others say—"Once our fleet departs, then the Swedes will attack." But it seems to me they will not attack, and will merely continue with their demonstrations.[2] Only one question remains to be answered: should the demonstrations be tolerated? Were you here, I would discuss matters with you for five minutes and would then decide what to do. Were I to follow my inclination, I would order Greig's fleet and Chichagov's[3] squadron to smash the demonstration to pieces: the Swedes wouldn't build any more ships for the next forty years. But in so doing, we'll have two wars, not one, and this might well produce unforeseeable consequences as well. And so as to avoid this, as the Swedish Minister in Stockholm told the Danish envoy to report here, which he has done in writing, clarification ought to be brought to the matter; but in the meanwhile, hurry and write me your opinion, I need it in order to stop my rambling thoughts. Twelve days or so do not make the least bit of difference—only hurry and tell me what you think, and even if Greig were to head out to sea we shall still have twelve ships, excluding the Danish ships, and with Greig we shall have a total of twenty-seven war ships, excluding the frigates. While not wishing to be careless, all this makes me just itch for a fight. The truth be told, the defeat of the Swedish naval force would send a warning to the Turks as well, however, I don't wish to lend credence to the Swedish King who is loudly proclaiming that he is arming supposedly since he fears that we are preparing to attack him and that supposedly for this reason we have moved Kalmyks and Tatars up to his borders, which is a downright lie, as you know yourself.

We are having the nastiest cold weather and for five days now it's been storming so hard that the trees are being snapped to pieces.

Farewell, my friend, we both have plenty of cares. God, however, is merciful. He knows, God grant, how to get us out of this safely. Be well and happy.

We must also not start matters since if he attacks us, then according to their constitution he will not receive any help from the Swedish nation; but if we attack, then they must offer help. And so, I think I'll give him this free time to play his childish tricks, spend all his money, and eat up his bread.

1. The fleet intended for the Mediterranean Sea did remain in the Baltic to battle the Swedes.

2. There was considerable disagreement in St. Petersburg over whether or not to send the fleet. Vice Chancellor Osterman was the lone voice calling for a preemptive strike against the Swedes.

3. An experienced seaman, veteran of the First Russo-Turkish War, Admiral Vasily Yakovlevich Chichagov (1726–1809) commanded a squadron on the Baltic and headed the entire Baltic fleet after Greig's death in 1788.

350. POTEMKIN TO CATHERINE

15 June [1788.] Camp on the Bug

Your Most Gracious Majesty! Your idea of not picking a fight with the Swedes and of sending the fleet to the Mediterranean Sea is sacred, for if we do pick a fight, then the nation will give the King both the necessary power and the means. It would be good if we could destroy their fleet for certain; however, as soon as they see we are on the move, they will withdraw to their fortified ports, and so we shall begin matters for naught and shall detain our fleet, which is all we have to divert the Turkish naval forces, for you know how terribly unequal our forces are here on the Black Sea. Better to remain on the defensive and to reassure the Swedish court as publicly as possible, so that their people learn of this as well, how much you desire to preserve the peace with them for all eternity, that this is the immutable law of our state. If it somehow came to be that you and the King began to correspond directly with each other, that would put an end to everything; then it would be possible to say to him in all candor that he should take as much as he wants from the Porte, that this is even to your advantage, just as long as he sits there quietly. What if under these circumstances we suddenly needed to win over the Prussian King, for even without this there will still truly be many difficulties. [...]

Oh, if only we could find a way to make peace quickly here, then in a sensible and swift manner we could give a good lesson to the Swedish King, but we must keep this most secret.

I would already be outside Ochakov by now, however, unusually strong rains denied me the means of crossing the river at the most convenient spot. The Bug, having spilled over its banks, has become unapproachable. With difficulty we found a spot by going 35 versts back up the river. The trouble we had moving the bridges upstream cannot be described. But nevertheless, everything has been rectified, and tomorrow everything will be on the other side of the Bug. Half has already been between Solonikha and Chichakleia for a long time now.

Among the fleet remaining in the Baltic, order for the sake of reinforcement 18 pounders added to the frigates, this will make them frigates of
the line. Also add more howitzers and unicorns to the ships and frigates:
their charges inflict incomparably greater damage. On 7 June three Turkish vessels vanished all at once, some into the air, others into the water,
and if the Kapudan Pasha had remained for another hour, many would
have gone up in flames.

Your Most Gracious Majesty, Prince Nassau's flotilla conducted the entire battle. He is tireless and zealous, do not leave him unrewarded, and
with this you will turn the heads of all the Frenchmen—what is more, justice demands it.

Paul Jones will be quite useful to us, with him a considerable addition to our service has been made; he also has a thorough knowledge of
shipbuilding, is fully satisfied with me, and I, of course, shall give him
every advantage; nevertheless, I cannot hide from you how many people have been grieved by his joining our service. Practically no one
wanted to remain; all the Englishmen wanted to quit our service, as
well as many of our own naval officers.[1] Brigadeer Alexiano, who had
been the commander of the squadron that I entrusted to Paul Jones, almost went mad from grief; he and all the other Greeks with him wanted
to quit our service. How many troubles this has caused me to put everything back into good order. I sent the orderly officer, a brigadeer, wrote
to many of them, and through kind words and threats was able to retain them, although with difficulty.

Alexiano, a good man though stubborn and direct, was so angry that
he was barely persuaded. He said he was angry with me and, what's more,
with you too. This was in the morning, but that evening he came and announced that he was staying because the enemy is the foe of our Faith,
and all the Greeks, following his example, stayed.[2] And what happened
next? On 7 June each outdid the other with the fervor that was bursting
inside him to enter the fray, and since the sailing ships could not move
due to a headwind, and only Prince Nassau's flotilla engaged the enemy,
so everyone, including even the sick, arrived on launches. Paul Jones on
Nassau's launch served as his adjutant, and Alexiano led the Zaparozhians,
who were used to pull the boats along on ropes, while shouting the whole
time to aim at the Kapudan Pasha; he displayed a coolness that amazed
everyone—the trust in him is extraordinary. Have mercy, matushka, do
him the favor and promote him. He is truly worthy. It would be a pity to
lose him. Even Paul Jones himself speaks on his behalf.

[. . .]

Farewell, Your Most Gracious Majesty!
Till death I remain your most loyal and most grateful subject
Prince Potemkin-Tavrichesky

1. Jones's appointment as rear admiral in command of the Liman squadron enraged the British officers in Russian service who considered him a traitor and a pirate.

2. Panaioti Alexiano (d. 1788), a Greek volunteer, decorated veteran of the Battle of Chesme, was replaced as commander of the Liman sailing squadron in favor of Jones by Potemkin in May. Suvorov attributed to him Russia's victories on the Liman. He died shortly after being made a rear admiral.

351. CATHERINE TO POTEMKIN

16 June 1788

My dear friend, Prince Grigory Aleksandrovich. I received yesterday your letters of 8 June from your camp on the Bug between Chichakleia and Chortitsa.[1] I'm quite sorry that, having departed Yelizavetgrad, you fell ill and became weak from the intense heat on the way and that this and other obstacles kept you from sending us your letters. We, however, lived for two weeks in expectation amid intense heat, which, one must admit, didn't lessen the mugginess. I'm glad you're much better.

The enemy is strengthening his fleet day by day near Ochakov, particularly with oared vessels (even though theirs are more maneuverable and carry more men than ours), and although this has caused you to worry very much about what may be, in truth they have provided us an opportunity for overcoming all difficulties, which I see from your letter, written at the very moment of the courier's departure, which I'll reply to below. I hope that you will surmount in equal fashion the difficulties in crossing the Bug. That the Turks have become more careful and are not moving out from under their canons—this should be attributed, perhaps, less to tactics than to danger. Pyotr Aleksandrovich writes me that he wanted to meet up with you on the Bug. Do you have any news—where is the Vizier or that part of the Turkish army directed against us?

[. . .]

Here rumors of the Swedes' arming and of the Swedish King's intention of declaring war on us are increasing daily and hourly. He has moved and continues to move regiments to Finland. His fleet has already left Karlskrona, and he himself is expected any day in Finland. He sent for Count Hord[2] in Berlin to command the Finnish army against us. We saved this man's life, for the late Empress Elizabeth Petrovna, who had held him as her prisoner, did not hand him over to the Swedes, who wanted to execute him, as they executed Horn and Brahe in 1756.[3] [. . .]

18 June

The Danes have begun speaking to the Swedes in a firm tone. I shall be quite glad to make peace, but nothing can bring this peace about with greater haste than your successes, and especially the taking of Ochakov, which, God willing, I hope to hear of soon.

19 June

We received news yesterday about the Swedish fleet: it encountered three of our one-hundred-gun ships, which had set out for the Sund, and the Swedes demanded that Rear Admiral von Dessen[4] salute them, to which he sent an answer stating that according to article 17 of the treaty between Russia and the Swedish Crown of 1743, it is agreed not to salute each other anywhere, however, since the Duke of Sudermania[5] is the brother of the King and a cousin of the Empress, so he will send best wishes—and so he fired 13 guns, and the Swedes responded with 8 guns, and then ours departed for the Sund, and theirs—from Gotland to the east.

I'll now answer your letters written as the courier was departing. Our public here is unspeakably gladdened by the victory achieved on the Liman, with which I congratulate you from the bottom of my heart. For three days we forgot to talk about Sweden's arming. I quickly sent your news of this to everyone. I now await from you details and shall gladly distribute decorations in honor of this occasion and of any other like it, where utility and encouragement for service demand it.

Farewell, my dear friend, be well and safe, and may Our Lord God help and bless you.

20 June

A courier arrived from Stockholm this morning with news that the Swedish King sent word to Razumovsky that he is to leave Stockholm, using as a pretense his having written "King and nation" in a note delivered in order to clarify their arming—an expression that, however, is used in all treaties with all powers, but that seemed insulting to the Swedish King. It's obvious from this that he was simply looking for an easy pretext.[6]

[. . .]

---

1. Potemkin wrote Catherine twice on 8 June. His second letter was written upon learning of the Russian victory over the Turks on the Liman the day before.

2. Swedish aristocrat Count Johan Ludvig Hord (1719–1798) was captured fighting for the Prussians in the Seven Years' War. He was freed by Tsar Peter III and later returned to Swedish service.

3. Counts G. J. Horn and Erik Brahe were publicly executed in 1756 in Stockholm as the leaders of a failed revolution to restore the power of the monarchy.

4. Rear Admiral V. P. von Dessen (1740–1826).

5. Prince Karl, duke of Sudermania (1748–1818), was the brother of Gustav III and head of the Swedish navy. Later reigned as Karl XIII.

6. Sensitive to noble opposition and mindful of the fact that by declaring war he was violating the constitution, Gustav III was greatly angered by a reference in a note presented by Russia's ambassador Count Andrei Razumovsky to those members of the "nation" who, together with the king, helped govern the country. The king forced Razumovsky to leave Sweden and prepared for war.

352. POTEMKIN TO CATHERINE

Camp on the march toward Solonikha. [19 June 1788]

Beloved matushka, Your Most Gracious Majesty! I congratulate you on an outstanding victory.[1] The Kapudan Pasha,[2] who wanted to devour us and arrived with frightful forces, has departed with difficulty. It appears God is helping us. With our boats we smashed their fleet to pieces and destroyed the best craft, and nothing survived but rubbish with which he is leaving for Varna. Matushka, be generous toward Nassau, how great have been his labors and zeal, and toward Alexiano, who fights beside him. Our pirate, however, is not their equal.[3] Reward all who labored. After the Kinburn affair I enjoyed such great confidence that you entrusted me with several Chasseurs crosses, which I did not put to ill use. If I am to be equally as fortunate now as well, then send me, matushka, 16 crosses, including 4 of the third class. This will drag on if you wait for a detailed report. And there's greater benefit in rewarding the men promptly.

For the first battle[4] I requested the second class for Prince Nassau, but for this he must be generously rewarded with an estate and in so doing attach him to us forever. How much he has accomplished and how often he has put his life in mortal danger. The same with Alexiano too. How happy I am that this took place on the holiday from which flowed all my well-being. I am beside myself with joy, yet it is unbearable—so many cares: everything must be forced along. I'm now on my way to the forward-most corps. Oh, were God to grant me the chance to lay Ochakov at your feet. Beloved matushka, I remain till death

your most loyal and most grateful

subject

Prince Potemkin-Tavrichesky

P.S. Now you see, matushka, how many troubles there were to build in two months what we are now using to beat the enemy. Do not tell anyone, but the Archipelago fleet can now stay completely put, and send in its place as quickly as possible two thousand good sailors, in addition to navigators and others with the necessary ranks, as well as officers. God will assist us—we shall manage from here [. . .]

---

1. Russia's victory over the Turkish fleet in the Liman on 17–18 June.

2. Gazi Hasan lost his own ship in the battle and was forced to flee on a small boat.

3. John Paul Jones had proved indecisive in battle, and Potemkin, among others, had begun to question his ability.

4. The battle in the Liman of 7 June.

353. CATHERINE TO POTEMKIN

26 June 1788

My dear friend. I received this morning from Count Apraksin[1] your letters with which you inform me that the Almighty has conferred a victory upon us; that the Kapudan Pasha's fleet was destroyed by the oared flotilla; that six ships of the line have been destroyed by fire, two have run aground, and thirty damaged vessels have escaped to their fortress; that the Kapudan Pasha's and the Vice Admiral's ships have been destroyed and we have captured more than three thousand men; and that General Suvorov's batteries have inflicted much damage on the enemy. This has made me most glad. It was God's great mercy that miraculously allowed our oared vessels to defeat warships. You will receive a rescript listing the decorations. I'm giving Nassau three thousand souls, Alexiano—six hundred, and the crosses have been sent. And you, my friend, I thank for your labors and cares, and may God Himself help you. We await the details of all this most impatiently, and I ask you to pass along a mighty thanks to everyone from me.

From here you'll receive some not entertaining news: the Swedes have attacked Nyslott, where two companies of Chasseurs were stationed, but war has not been declared. Cela s'appelle agir en forban.[2] We are gathering troops from all over. I shall leave for town the day after the holiday and shall reside there in order to cheer up the people, although spirits have not fallen; all the troops, however, are on the move. Rira bien qui rira le dernier; la justice, la raison et la vérité sont de notre côté.[3]

I just now signed an order to Greig that, God willing, he seek out the Swedish fleet and try to attack and destroy it. My friend, I hope I might soon give you good news from here, I know it would gladden you, just as it would me. And with all my heart I congratulate you on your victory. May God grant you to take Ochakov without any losses, and be well. We here dare not now contemplate losing a single sailor. Couldn't you make use of the Greek prisoners? We'll send what we can once we know what is what here. However, everything on this side has been put to use. Farewell, my friend, may God help us.

I have promoted Count Apraksin to Lieutenant-Colonel of the Preobrazhensky Guards Regiment and have given him a snuffbox and five hundred chervontsi.

---

1. Count Fyodor Matveevich Apraksin (1765–1796).

2. "That is called acting like a pirate."

3. "He who laughs last laughs loudest. Justice, right and truth are on our side."

354. CATHERINE TO POTEMKIN

Saint-Petersburg. 3 July 1788

My true and dear friend, Prince Grigory Aleksandrovich. In expectation of your courier with detailed information on the victory on the Ochakov Liman of 17 June, I am sending this courier to you in order to inform you of unpleasant events here. After firing on Nyslott for two days, the Swedes set to pillaging the Nyslott district. I ask you—what's there to pillage? Then the Swedish secretary demanded an audience with the Vice Chancellor and handed him a note upon arriving that had been signed by him upon the King's order, in which, through the use of many words insulting to my very self and the state, His Majesty proposes to me conditions for peace.[1] A copy of this mad note will be sent to you with this same courier. I responded by ordering the deliverer of this note be deported. It is said that the Swedes and Finns are equally dissatisfied with the King's behavior toward us. He oft said and reassured everyone that he was going to act defensively, but has instead gone and attacked. News arrived today that he has left Abborrfors and gone 15 versts into Finland, and is on his way to Fredrikshamn.

As many of our regiments as possible have left, Pushkin has left, and Mikhelson has been there for a long time and has taken up positions from Villmanstrand to Vyborg. They say Fredrikshamn can hold out for several weeks. Greig will join up with the fleet, I think, today or tomorrow; may God grant success. For this I pray to Almighty God, who has never abandoned me or the state at any time.

The Swedish King has forged for himself armor, a cuirass, brassards and cuisses and a spiked helmet with the most ghastly plumes. Upon departing Stockholm he told the ladies that he expected to offer them breakfast at Peterhof, but upon taking his seat in the galleys he said qu'il s'embarque dans un pas scabreux.[2] He ordered that the Swedes and his troops in Finland be told that he intends to surpass and to overshadow the deeds of Gustav Adolph[3] and to finish the undertakings of Charles XII.[4] The latter may come true, for he began Sweden's ruin. He also assured the Swedes that he would force me to lay down my crown. The conduct of that treacherous Sovereign resembles madness.

With this courier you will receive my manifesto on the declaration of war.[5] The insults against us are many, we have never heard any complaints from him in all our born days, and so now I don't know why he's gotten so angry. Now God will be our judge; should God help us, then his plan will be to leave for Rome, to adopt the Roman faith and to live as Queen Christina did.[6]

It's most ghastly hot and muggy here, I have moved to town to live. A great anger against the Swedish King has arisen among the people here, and there is no manner of abuse that the great and the small have not heaped upon him. The soldiers march with a hungry desire and say they'll lead the traitor here by his whiskers. Others say they'll finish the war in three weeks; they request permission to march without rest in order to reach the Swedes sooner; in a word, the disposition of spirits here and in his force is in my favor. This is a difficult time for me, that's true, but what is to be done? I hope to receive in a short time a great supplement of men and materials, which are being brought from all over.

Farewell, my beloved. What's happening with the Ochakov siege? Be safe and well.

Enclosed with this is the manifesto and a copy of the mad note.

---

1. Sweden demanded, among other things, that Russia return Finland, part of Karelia, and everything gained by the Peace of Nystad (1721) and Åbo (1743) to Sweden, and that Russia return the Crimea to the Porte.

2. "that he was embarking on something a bit dubious."

3. Sweden became a major European power under King Gustav II Adolph (1594–1632), who, by conquering lands in the Baltic, effectively cut off Russia's access to the sea.

4. King Charles XII of Sweden (1682–1718). Peter the Great's defeat of Charles at the Battle of Poltava (1709) marked the beginning of Sweden's decline as a great power.

5. The manifesto was issued on 30 June 1788.

6. After the death of her father, Gustav II Adolph, in 1632, Christina (1628–1689) was crowned queen of Sweden, though the country was governed by a regent until 1644. She secretly converted to Catholicism and, after abdicating the throne in 1654, lived out the rest of her life in Rome.

355. CATHERINE TO POTEMKIN

17 July 1788

Yesterday evening, my true friend Prince Grigory Aleksandrovich, Kishensky arrived with the flags and standards and delivered your letters.[1] I'm sending the trophies to the Peter and Paul Cathedral with ceremonious display today, and though spirits here are not downcast, this will nevertheless serve to encourage the people. The iron you requested for Kherson will be sent to you. [. . .]

God Grant you take Ochakov without any loss of men. This frightens me, but our northern affairs have now taken a somewhat reassuring turn, for the Swedish King, but for his follies, is doing very little. Everyone, including even the English Prime Minister,[2] admits that the King's conduct is le comble de extravagance.[3] His captured vice admiral is the biggest featherbrain, and he's one of his best men.[4] The King lost his best opportunity while landing his troops in Finland, and till now they've done nothing, and wherever they encounter our men, the Swedes always run away. They have been attacking Nyslott from time to time. They placed two cannons before Fredrikshamn, one 18 pounder and another 24, and they fired them from a great distance several times and stopped. We now have 20 infantry battalions, 800 Cossacks and two regiments of cuirassiers in Finland: I think there have never been so many in Finland in all its days. This new enemy has aroused great popular zeal and our men can't wait to begin fighting. [. . .] In a word, it seems that our prospects have changed much for the better, especially after the naval battle, and I hope you'll say that I've turned matters about quite nimbly. There is also a small trick that I am preparing for the Swedish King in the north, about which I don't yet dare speak, but will perhaps have greater impact than anything else.[5]

It was so hot here that the thermometer read 39 1/2 + in the sun. In Portugal no one can recall higher than 44. While sitting here in town in this oppressive heat, I was oppressed by the Swedish affairs as well. Pétersbourg a l'air dans ce moment d'une place d'armes et moi même je suis comme au Quartier Général.[6] On the day of the naval battle, 6 July, gunpowder could be smelled here in town; ainsi, mon Ami, j'ai aussi senti la poudre.[7]

[. . .]

I'm glad Voinovich and the Sevastopol fleet are well.[8] I think that the Kapudan Pasha feared that you might undertake some operation behind him and for this reason he turned and went back. Adieu, mon cher Ami, portés Vous bien. Be well, happy and safe. As for me, I've now taken a little rest, since it seems that affairs here are taking a turn for the better, and we are quite unconcerned about matters on your side. I hurry to dispatch this letter to you, for I see from your letters that you worry, while we have calmed down a bit.

---

1. Potemkin had sent Colonel Fyodor Ivanovich Kishensky to Catherine with the trophies taken during the victory of 17–18 June, which included the flag of the kapudan pasha.

2. William Pitt the Younger.

3. "the height of folly."

4. Swedish Vice Admiral Count Klas Adam Wachtmeister (1755–1828) was captured at the Battle of Hogland on 6 July.

5. Namely, the pact of Anjala (1 [12] August) in which 113 officers in the Swedish army united to denounce Gustav's war as unconstitutional. The Anjala League collapsed several months later and its leaders were arrested.

6. "Petersburg at this moment has the appearance of an armed camp, and it is as if I myself am in the headquarters."

7. "and so, my friend, I too have smelled the powder."

8. Rear Admiral Voinovich's fleet had defeated the Turks off the island of Fidonisi (Zmeiny) on 3 July.

356. POTEMKIN TO CATHERINE

18 July [1788]. Camp near Ochakov

Beloved matushka, Your Most Gracious Majesty. From the enclosed communiqué kindly observe the actions of the Sevastopol fleet. My sole desire was that we not lose anything. Even with such superior numbers the Kapudan Pasha acted quite timidly.[1] This is proof of God's mercy upon us. Voinovich did not know of our successes here, though even if he had known, he could not have taken advantage, since he was down wind. This affair is quite important given our small numbers in relation to the enemy. I am now unloading the fascines and the last of the artillery. It's unusually cold and windy here. Once everything has been received, I'll begin the attack, taking extreme precaution to keep the men out of harm's way. Your troubles torment me. Oh, were I with you I would find the means to recruit as many as three thousand Hussars in Petersburg alone. The Novgorod Province, and particularly Livonia and Estonia—they'd all follow me. Our fleet must act courageously since it has a superiority in incendiary weapons. Should it fulfill its duty, how can we not win!

I never liked fortresses, and particularly our Finnish ones which present no obstacles, but require many men. I always said, though this may have appeared to be a joke, that all the Finlanders ought to be settled throughout the state, and the land be made impassable by cutting down a great number of trees. Then the capital would be safe. [. . .]

Order Nesselrode dispatched forthwith.[2] As soon as the Prussian King calms down, then all will be well. There you have it, Your Majesty, I have spoken out of zeal and with the foresight of continuing to abide by our treaty with him, which cannot disturb the Emperor. This ally of ours has halted all his operations, and the Turks are saying that they have an agreement not to act. I assure you he is a bad helpmate.

I've heard nothing about our Field Marshal.[3]

Farewell, Your Majesty. Put your Faith in God. Christ will help us. Believe without any doubt, that He will not abandon us.

I would have undertaken a raid against the fortress of Berezan, but the weather kept us pinned down here. Having called upon God's help, I'll now begin the siege.

Matushka, have mercy, do not leave me long without news of what is happening there with you. Or else I shall die of sorrow.

Your most loyal and most grateful subject
Prince Potemkin-Tavrichesky

---

1. Though outnumbered, the Sevastopol fleet, under the command of Voinovich, forced the Ottoman fleet to retreat at the island of Fidonisi.

2. Count Wilhelm Karl Nesselrode (1724–1810), a native of Westphalia, served in several European countries before finally joining Russian service as envoy extraordinary to Lisbon. In 1788, he was sent as Russian envoy to Berlin.

3. There is a gap in Potemkin's correspondence with Rumiantsev from 30 June to 22 July.

357. CATHERINE TO POTEMKIN

28 July 1788

My friend, Prince Grigory Aleksandrovich, I received your letter of 18 July from Flag-Captain Seniavin,[1] upon whom, if you deem that he should be promoted and this will not offend others, you may convey a rank in my name. But since you do not mention him, so I didn't promote him, leaving this to your discretion.

The actions of the Sevastopol fleet gladdened me very much: it is almost unbelievable with what small force God helps us to defeat the powerful Turkish arms! Tell me, how can I make Voinovich happy? You have been sent crosses of the third class; would you give him one, or a sword perhaps?[2] May the Creator Himself help you take Ochakov; most of all, try to keep the men safe, it's better to be more patient.

Regarding our troubles with the Swedes, I shall tell you that on the 22nd they arrived at Fredrikshamn with a large force and surrounded it from the sea and on land and busied themselves with the construction of batteries till the 24th, but that night they hastily jumped back into their craft again and sailed out to sea into the wind, and those on land ran off to Abborrfors and were never to be seen again. Our men didn't know what such a flight should be attributed to, but the superintendent of Fredrikshamn, having been released from Swedish captivity, together with one of their compatriots, solved the matter, as you'll see from the enclosed copy of the Vyborg Governor's report.[3] The hand of God is visible here, punishing perfidy. The Hussar Regiment is being recruited, however, the Cossack lieutenant-colonels, which you promised, are still not here yet. Please send Cossacks from the coachmen for the unit. Greig has departed once more in search of the Swedes, and it seems our affairs are beginning to go well enough. The Prussian King has announced that he won't take part in this Swede's foolish behavior. The Danes are preparing for war. The three-decker ships will return with the Arkhangelsk squadron. Nesselrode will leave immediately.

I have ordered that Field Marshal Rumiantsev be written that he is doing nothing. I, of course, hope that God will help us, and am now already much calmer. My friend, now you are asking me to inform you more often; judge now for yourself how it was for me not having word from you for three weeks at a time. Yet I write and have written to you almost weekly. God be with you, be well and safe, and happy and merry, and content and calm. Adieu, mon Ami.

---

1. One of Potemkin's favorites, Dmitry Nikolaevich Seniavin (1763–1831) went on to a distinguished career in the Black Sea fleet.

2. Voinovich received the Order of St. George third class.

3. Poor coordination among the three attacking Swedish corps and the inability to land more troops doomed the Swedish assault on Fredrikshamn.

358. POTEMKIN TO CATHERINE

6 August [1788]. Near Ochakov

Whitlows on two fingers of my right hand, on my thumb and index finger, prohibited me from writing. They're getting better now. Your Most Gracious Majesty, the Kapudan Pasha has again arrived with his fleet and has positioned his small boats near Berezan and the large ones on the far side of Berezan.[1] And one group has left for Khadjibey. The Ochakovites are defending themselves most stubbornly. Before the arrival of the Kapudan Pasha, Aleksandr Vasilievich Suvorov committed a considerable folly, which cost us four hundred men killed and wounded from Fisher's battalion alone. On my left flank 6 versts from here, he engaged the enemy in a skirmish after dinner, and after uniting two battalions with some Cossacks, he ran off with them all without informing anyone, and without any cannons, and the Turks cut them off using the ravines, of which there are many along the shore. They wounded him, he galloped back to camp, and all the rest were left without a superior. And fortunately he was wounded or he would have led all the rest there. Upon first hearing of this affair I didn't believe it. Finally some cannons were sent, under which they withdrew, having lost 160 killed and the rest wounded.[2]

Having had no news for a long time, I'm extremely tormented by anguish wondering what is happening. Your Majesty, I cannot write, my fingers ache so.

Your most loyal and most grateful subject
Prince Potemkin-Tavrichesky

[. . .]

---

1. On 29 July, Gazi Hasan's large fleet appeared once again off Ochakov. Russian attempts to stop the fleet proved unsuccessful, and the Turks were able to supply the fortress with provisions and reinforcements. The grand admiral finally departed for the winter on 4 November.

2. Potemkin's report on Suvorov's costly folly of 27 July. The exact number of Russian casualties is not clear, but Potemkin's estimate appears about right. Wounded in the fighting, Suvorov left Ochakov for Kinburn to recover.

359. CATHERINE TO POTEMKIN

14 August 1788

Listen here, my true friend, Prince Grigory Aleksandrovich, the Swedish war doesn't worry me now, for the Finnish troops are mutinying and don't want to attack us. It also seems that the Swedes too aren't displaying much eagerness to carry out the arbitrary desires of a Nobody-Knight that are contrary to their laws.[1] But your whitlow worries me, of which you inform me in your letter of 6 August after a three-week silence. It seems to me you are wounded, but are hiding this from me. Sinelnikov was of course close to you when he was wounded. Could it be that that same shot struck your fingers?[2] I do see that your current situation near Ochakov demands a good deal of care and is more difficult than I had imagined. And so I'm now more sensitive to all your worries than to the foolish Swedish war, the recent events of which are laughable and which will apparently end with a gathering of the Sejm in Finland and Sweden, followed by peace negotiated between us and the estates. And should this happen soon, which there can be practically no doubt of, then we'll detail the fleet for the Mediterranean Sea, perhaps even by this autumn. May God simply grant that now, just as before, you are able to manage the Kapudan Pasha's fleet that has again arrived. But I beg you for the sake of God Himself: order our ships back to port during the Equinox. Let the storm pound the Turks, as long as ours are safe. It's quite a pity that Aleksandr Vasilievich Suvorov lost so many men and was himself wounded.

Be so good as to make it a habit of writing me more often, or else I shan't live to see peace. I laid in bed for two days just now d'une colique bileuse[3] and quite a fever. Today is my first day out of bed. Write me how I might best reward Sinelnikov's wife and children.

Farewell, my dear friend, be well and happy, as best you can.

---

1. A reference to the Anjala League and general displeasure with the war in Sweden.

2. Major-General Ivan Maksimovich Sinelnikov was mortally wounded by a Turkish cannonball while reconnoitering the fortress of Ochakov. Potemkin was standing close by when it happened, and Catherine feared Potemkin might be hiding from her a serious injury.

3. "with a bilious colic"

360. POTEMKIN TO CATHERINE

Camp near Ochakov. 22 August [1788]

Your Most Gracious Majesty, it's not with the desired joy that I write to you. I still cannot inform you of success here at Ochakov. The enemy stubbornly or, better said, desperately defends himself. We are already working close to their fortifications. You cannot imagine how hard the ground is here and with what difficulty we work. Till now we have been driving back their sorties and inflicting damage on them, although we don't get off scot-free.[1] Were success to depend on my self-sacrifice, then, of course, I would not hesitate for a moment. But the men must be and need be spared.

In recent days I have had two unpleasant incidents. First—my bombardier blew up from its own fire during operations.[2] Second—the magazine with shells belonging to the flotilla mysteriously caught fire in Kinburn. A great number of bombs fell in all directions, and as this happened on a Sunday, hence many people in the nearby church were injured. And twenty people were killed. Aleksandr Vasilievich was injured as well, but he's now better and is out of danger.[3] During this misfortune God's mercy became evident in an incident surpassing all possible likelihood. A great number of the bombs which exploded had been lying on barrels of gunpowder, more than a thousand poods of it. And the gunpowder remained intact during this powerful explosion, and not one barrel exploded. Otherwise Kinburn, the camp and flotilla, and the squadron, which is stationed along the shore, would have been blown sky-high. These events confirm to me that we are blessed in the eyes of God.

Matushka, given my sensitivity, you can judge the condition of my heart. There's no end to our troubles, and we're facing a mass of deficiencies that demand such zeal. If we had cannons and shells, then I would have a frightful fleet at sea, for I believe that at sea it is not the size of the vessels, but the caliber of the guns that is decisive. And so for now I gnaw on my fingers and watch the Kapudan Pasha, to whom I can do nothing.

If the Swedes, and particularly the Finns, don't follow the King, we can achieve much here through our politics. When they request your help in deposing the present Autocrat, you should state that you have suffered the change in government till now, which is in conflict with the last treaty's stipulation, because the nation did not protest. But now, as the nation calls for your assistance, you cannot refuse given your obligations to it. Your King will end up alone, just like a fico.

[. . .] Farewell, Your Most Gracious Majesty. I remain till death
your most loyal and most grateful subject
Prince Potemkin-Tavrichesky

I have sent the Cossack lieutenant-colonels for the levy.

The Turks have smashed the Imperial forces to pieces on the borders of the Banat of Kraiovsky, and have taken away their cannons and transport.

---

1. The Turks continued their sorties in August. On the eighteenth, Count Roger de Damas and other officers were injured repulsing a sally.
2. The vessel blew up on 13 August while bombarding Ochakov. The entire crew was killed.

3. A massive explosion occurred on 20 August while shells were being loaded onto ships in Kinburn. Adding insult to injury, Suvorov, who was there recovering from his wounds, suffered burns and contusions from the blast.

361. CATHERINE TO POTEMKIN

31 August 1788

My friend, Prince Grigory Aleksandrovich. I received today your letter of 22 August. I'm quite sorry that you are so troubled by the siege of Ochakov. Patience overcomes everything. Better to go slowly, but safely, than quickly and so expose yourself to danger, or to risk losing men. One can clearly see how hard the ground is there from the need to plow with oxen. I do not doubt in the least that you will do everything possible and won't overlook a thing. I pity every last man lost, even in the successful repulsing of a sortie, but what is to be done if there's no other way? I was horrified to learn of the two unpleasant incidents—first, the bombardier, which blew up from its own fire during operations, and second—the burning down of the magazine with the flotilla's shells in Kinburn. And what greater harm might still have occurred had the hand of God not preserved the barrels of gunpowder containing as much as a thousand poods, which remained safe!

[. . .]

Till now the Swedish fleet has been blockaded at Sveaborg. Our squadron alone, also positioned near Hangö, is holding their army fleet in the skerries. And the Swedes, but for the post at Högfors, have now left all of Finland. The King himself is sitting either in Helsingfors or God knows where in some corner in Finland and is carousing with his men, who don't listen to what he says about the need to go on the offensive against us; nevertheless he is filling them with various fanciful ideas and nonsense. I ordered them told that I can't listen to a thing till they leave of their own accord or are driven out of Högfors. I'll make use of your timely thoughts on the matter.

The Cossack lieutenant-colonels for the Cossack recruitment levy have still not arrived; it seems those here were unwilling to begin the recruiting of Cossacks: they said that they, the Cossacks, are ready to serve everywhere and that there's no need of this since there's enough of them to serve everywhere. I think that they think that once there are Cossacks here, we shall then have less respect for those men from the Don. Taking note of this, I have put a halt to this business till you send the lieutenant-colonels, and now I have ordered a Hussar Regiment and an Estonian Corps of Chasseurs formed. [. . .] Look at what a bold warrior I've become. Laugh at me if you want, however, kindly give your approval to that which is good, parce qu'il faut encourager le mérite naissant.[1]

Farewell, my dear friend, be well, safe and happy.

Write to me how Kutuzov[2] is doing, and how was he injured? Order someone to inquire after him on my behalf.

---

1. "because one must encourage budding merit."

2. Hero of Russia's war against Napoleon, Mikhail Illarionovich Kutuzov (1745/1747–1813) was one of the officers wounded during a Turkish sortie on 18 August. At the time it was thought he would die from his wounds.

362. POTEMKIN TO CATHERINE

11 September [1788]

Your Most Gracious Majesty. The enemy cannot be pushed any harder, and I never could have imagined such tenacity and patience from the Turks. I shall intensify the pressure still more and shall carry on. What it is God wishes, we shall see in the future. [. . .]

Khotin should already be in our hands by now, for they have nothing there to eat.[1] In Ochakov, there are unfortunately large stores of everything.

In recent days I reconnoitered the fortress from the water and found it more fortified than I had expected. As powerful as the storm was here, it must have been twice as powerful out at sea. Still nothing happened to the enemy's vessels. The entire Sevastopol fleet has entered the harbor, and the frigate "The Virgin's Protecting Veil" has joined them. Only the Greeks are out cruising, having not suffered any losses. Should my idea about Count Wachtmeister please you, would it not be better to send him to Krechetnikov[2] in Kaluga or to Tula, and show him the way from there, should there be time to let him out him. Or else he will hear a lot of rubbish in Moscow, and besides, there will be many more people flocking about him than necessary. He'll also find there many brothers de la stricte observance.[3]

[. . .]

I spare neither my labor nor my life. Everyone is a witness to this. The other day I reconnoitered on a launch at such proximity that Turkish grape-shot flew directly over our launch. But God protects me everywhere. Here was an occasion to have been killed, sunk and taken into captivity. Matushka, you will deign to say once again that it was not necessary to do this. But duty tells me what is necessary. And so it is that every general must scurry about amid the cannons.[4] Farewell, matushka, for my entire life I remain

your most loyal and most grateful subject
Prince Potemkin-Tavrichesky

---

1. The Austrians had by now finally taken Khotin (on 4 September), although the news had not yet reached Potemkin.

2. Lieutenant-General Mikhail Nikitich Krechetnikov (1729–1793) was the acting governor-general of Tula and Kaluga.

3. "of the Strict Observance." Captured Vice Admiral Wachtmeister was a prominent Freemason. Suspicious of the fraternal order, Potemkin warned against sending him to Moscow, which had become the major center of Masonic activity in Russia.

4. Together with Damas, Nassau, and Prince de Ligne, Potemkin reconnoitered the citadel from the Liman on 5 September. Wearing his orders and medals, Potemkin was clearly visible to the Turks who took direct aim at him. Potemkin and the others were saved by Prince Repnin, who opened fire on the Turks from his battery.

363. POTEMKIN TO CATHERINE

17 October [1788]

Your Most Gracious Majesty. My reports now being sent had already been prepared several days ago, however, the various movements of the Turkish fleet and rumors that the enemy was planning to come to the aid of Ochakov from Akkerman and Bender, which had also been confirmed by Count Pyotr Aleksandrovich's report, kept me from sending them. I have sent two parties of Don and Loyal Cossacks to Khadjibey and Palanka and shall learn the truth from them. Though they have yet to return, since I have positive reports from them sent from posts along that road, I am sending them along now. It seems the parties reached Khadjibey, for throughout the entire night and on into the day as well cannon fire could be heard from that direction. The fleet is continuing to move about, however, no definite purpose can be discerned, and so it is impossible to know whether it intends to depart or is preparing to land troops.

Their gunboats anchored off Ochakov, which were damaged in the last battle, have been repaired. I ordered Prince Nassau either to seize or burn them. Though he made two attempts, he did not succeed or, better said, good fortune did not offer its services. Having been confronted with this challenge, he has departed for Warsaw under the pretext of illness. Two days later these vessels departed Ochakov for their fleet and passed by the flotilla and the slumbering Admiral Paul Jones, who before this had let slip by under his nose three Turkish vessels on their way to Ochakov in one day, the largest of which ran aground. I ordered him to burn it, and twice he tried but turned back both times fearing the Turkish cannons. I ordered him to abandon this enterprise and ordered the Zaporozhians instead. Colonel Golovaty,[1] together with 50 Cossacks, set it ablaze at once, despite the cannonade, and blew up the vessel with the gunpowder on board.

Your Most Gracious Majesty, the benefit of your affairs is as dear to me as my own life. This man[2] is unfit to lead: he's slow, lacks zeal and is perhaps even afraid of the Turks. And besides, he has a black soul. I can't trust him with any enterprise. He will do no honor to your flag. Perhaps he ventured to undertake this out of cupidity, however, he has never commanded many ships. He's new at this business, has neglected his entire crew and is good for nothing: not knowing the language, he can neither give nor comprehend orders. Hence everything ends up all muddled. He's held in contempt by all the officers. Given the extreme situation, I ventured to inform him that you deigned to request his presence in Petersburg in order to commission him with an expedition in the north. This I dared do for the benefit of your affairs. I could have placed him under the command of Mordvinov, however, he will not serve under anyone's command. Believe me, matushka, he understands nothing. Perhaps as a pirate with a single vessel he is suitable, but he's incapable of commanding, and as a pirate can he compare to Lombard? Deign to note what he achieved. And should God not abandon him, he will work miracles.[3]

[. . .]

I thank you, Your Majesty, for the stone and the fur coat. The former is a mark of charity and springs from Monarchical munificence. The latter—from maternal concern. And this is dearer to me than beads and gold. You deign to write whether or not I received the platter and sword.[4] Did you truly think I had forgotten to thank you? Why did you not realize, matushka, that I was comforted by the thought of repaying you in a worthy manner and was waiting for the opportunity. But what am I to do, the second plot has now been uncovered in Ochakov, and its leaders executed.[5] I am more worried about this than everything else. I am attaching a plan in light of the current situation. Should I learn from the returning parties that no one is approaching me, I shall intensify the cannonades and shall, God willing, direct all my forces against the retrenchment. The French, however, displaying their customary kindness, constructed a defense out of guns in this retrenchment that surpasses all their other fortresses. We have recently drawn close and begun to strike them with our guns, which has quieted them down. [. . .]

With gratitude Aleksandr Nikolaevich[6] prostrates himself before your feet. He was even bespattered with earth from a bomb that landed in front of him. His battery is the nearest of all to the enemy. I can safely say that he serves as one should. The ground here is so hard that everyone is using axes to do their digging, and you can walk about on it as if it were rock. Twice I walked through the trenches, and it was so hard on my souls they developed blisters, and now I am sitting here dead on my feet.

[. . .]

In order to defend the borders I have detailed 5 infantry regiments, all of them formed out of recruits near Kremenchug whom I had desired to keep safe. You deign to write that the Swedish Amadis has addressed himself to everyone. Matushka, things aren't so simple. A league has been formed against you. On your reason depends whether Russia can be delivered from calamity and, perhaps, even whether Europe can be delivered from Prussian dictatorship.[7] My zeal compels me to say: while feigning as if you do not suspect this plot, inform him that you are not against peace with everyone as long as your ally is also included. Matushka, permit me to say what our politics have wrought. In our war with the Turks, to which everything should have been reconciled, we have, so to speak, made a mess of everything. The Bourbons laid a trap for us, and so far things are going according to their plan, even as regards the Swedish episode. They whipped up the Turks, and then were unable to restrain them. Others made use of this by presenting themselves as useful to us. The former announced themselves to be bankrupt and absolutely powerless, while the others speak the kindest words as they impede us everywhere. And impede us they will. How shall we stop them if the war doesn't quiet down? The Prussian King, who sought to keep the treaty in force, is keeping a tight rein on himself. As a result we might be able to establish accord between him and the Emperor, and so lead the Polish affairs in the desired direction. By ruining the commercial treaty with England that was so beneficial and so fitting, we've behaved as if we were quarreling. Our lone ally is the Danish court, and they'll make mincemeat out of them. I predicted all this and issued my warning out of my boundless zeal for you. You deigned not to heed this. Unfortunately, things have come to pass as I predicted, and so will it be henceforth. What might my personal advantage or designs be in this? Good God, may this all end here and now. I shall take my rest. May everything remain just as desired—they can all intrigue to their hearts' content. Whenever our ally is present things go badly. He set out after the Turks. And they, with only four cannons, were able to force him to build parapets in his camp. All this scared him, so he left. The draymen thought the enemy was pursuing them. They cut the traces and scattered. Two infantry regiments, also thinking that they were being pursued by the enemy, began shooting at their own men and killed many of them. He ended up in this crush of bodies and almost got himself shot. They marched for three days straight, and believe me there weren't all that many Turks. He left them Transylvania and Megadia to ravage. To put it in a word, they're now busy burning and slaughtering.[8] The French Queen[9] said when Lacy[10] took it into his head to defend the borders by using a defensive cordon: "que Lassy étranglerait avec son cordon et le Banat et la Transilvanie,"[11] which is true.

I've exhausted all means here to contain the enemy and force him to surrender. I must make up my mind to move with force, and then it'll be in God's hands. Let His will be done. But I shan't spare my life. My main obstacle is the Kapudan Pasha and his fleet, which has stuck to me like a Spanish fly,[12] and constantly strives to land behind me, particularly should help come from the land forces.

Farewell, Your Most Gracious Majesty, I remain till death
your most loyal and most grateful subject
Prince Potemkin-Tavrichesky

[. . .]

1. Anton Andreevich Golovaty (1744–1797) formed the Loyal Cossack Host together with Sidor Bely and Zakhar Chepega who also played a significant role in the war. Golovaty himself took part in the storming of Ochakov and Ismail and received numerous military honors.

2. John Paul Jones.

3. Disappointed with Jones's indecisiveness, Potemkin sent him back to St. Petersburg. He was replaced by Rear Admiral Nikolai Semyonovich Mordvinov (1754–1845). Giuliano de Lombard (d. 1791), a native of Malta and a hero of past battles in the Liman, was then in Turkish captivity.

4. Catherine had sent Potemkin a platter of gold and a richly decorated sword as gifts in honor of the recent victories in the Liman. He thanked her in a letter from 29 September, which she had apparently not yet received.

5. Potemkin had spies among the Ottoman military at Ochakov through whom he hoped to convince Husein Pasha to surrender. The spies were found out and executed.

6. Potemkin's nephew, Aleksandr Samoilov.

7. Russia now faced a strong coalition aligned against her: Prussia, Britian, the United Provinces, Turkey, Sweden, and Poland.

8. Joseph II had joined his troops that year and proven that he was no great field commander. When the Turks attacked his camp at Lugosch on the night of 9 (20) September, Joseph barely escaped.

9. Marie Antoinette (1755–1793), Joseph II's sister and the wife of King Louis XVI.

10. Field Marshal Franz Lacy (1725–1801) was the president of Austria's Hofkriegsrat.

11. "'that with his cordon Lacy would strangle the Banat and Transylvania,'"

12. Lytta vesicatoria, common name Spanish fly or blister beetle. In addition to its purported aphrodisiac properties, the dried, crushed Spanish fly was widely used at the time in tinctures to treat various maladies.

364. CATHERINE TO POTEMKIN

19 October 1788

My true friend, Prince Grigory Aleksandrovich. While you've been busy with affairs at Ochakov, this is what's been happening here: the Prussian King has made two declarations—one to Poland against our alliance with the Poles[1] (which even before this I realized could cause a fire to break out, and so I have ordered that it be suspended till an opportune time); the other to the Danish court, threatening to send thirty thousand troops into Holstein should the Danish court, aiding us, enter Sweden. The Danes, however, have actually already entered and have captured a Swedish lieutenant-general with 800 men and ten cannons, but it is still unknown what sort of answer the Danes gave the Prussian King.

The Prussian envoy here sent the Vice Chancellor the Prussian King's declaration to the Danish court together with an excerpt from the Royal letters, which is not of the best tone: that is to say, that with every passing day their intention and adopted plan not only to cause us all manner of harm, but also to provoke us at the present time, which is already difficult enough for us, is coming to light. They succeeded with the Dutch affair. Now they are adopting the exact same dictatorial tone with the Danes, and in this manner they are trying to get us as well. I am doing everything to avoid giving them an excuse to seize on the least thing, nevertheless it will not pass without comment that without having received from us an answer to their offer of mediation, which the Swedish King delivered to six courts, they had already made such a declaration to the Danes that was favorable only to him and was injurious to us, despite the fact that the first quality of an intermediary must be disinterestedness. But in this instance the opposite is clearly obvious: my ally is threatened with attack for offering me aid, and I am obligated to defend him or, at least, to help him in equal measure as he helps me. I have prepared a letter to Count Nesselrode on this matter, and am attaching a copy of it herewith. I shall intentionally send it with the post: let them open it and read it, perhaps this will shame them or give them cause to think a bit, but I don't expect it to have any greater effect than this. But in case the Prussian King acts on his intentions, which are harmful to Russia and her ally, then: 1. The army of Field Marshal Count Rumiantsev is to be directed against the Prussian King, as was intended in your general plan, and is to be brought up to full strength with regiments of musketeers according to the new eight-company military statute. 2. In order to close the borders and to increase the number of active troops, maintain a corps of up to thirty thousand troops stationed in Livonia and White Russia; for its formation I hereby appoint the newly formed Estonian Corps of Chasseurs and the infantry regiment located in Riga, as well as the four cavalry regiments here and in White Russia. In addition, six army regiments and one regiment of Dragoons are also needed, along with a thousand Don or Ural Cossacks. I leave it to your discretion from which regions it would be most appropriate to select these regiments. More than anything else, every effort must be made so that by spring they can arrive here, that is to White Russia and Livonia.

The army in Finland is to remain as it is; I am bringing the Guards up to strength.

Kindly write to me about this in greater detail and soon so that nothing of importance to me be overlooked, and, most importantly, once Ochakov has been taken make every attempt to begin peace negotiations. But don't forget that Bulgakov is still being held in the Seven Towers.

I also received yesterday the bad news that after a three-week illness and to universal regret, Admiral Greig died from fever combined with jaundice in the Reval harbor on the one-hundred-gun ship "Rostislav."[2] I sent Rogerson to him two weeks ago when I heard that he was so dangerously ill, but nothing could save him from God's will. Spiridov[3] has already returned to Kronstadt with six ships, and all the rest are already heading in for the winter. I cannot begin to say how deeply moved I am by the Admiral's death, and in this instance this loss is a misfortune for the Empire, for we have no one in the fleet with his degree of skill and reputation with which to replace him.

Farewell, my dear friend, may God grant you health, happiness and good fortune. We await news from you—may God grant, good news.

[. . .]

---

1. On 13 October, Catherine received word from the Russian ambassador in Poland that Prussia would not allow Poland to conclude an alliance with Russia.

2. Admiral Greig died on 15 October.

3. Son of the famous naval commander Grigory Spiridov, a hero of Chesme, Aleksei Grigorievich Spiridov (1753–1828) had served under Greig. He was later promoted to admiral.

365. POTEMKIN TO CATHERINE

3 November [1788]. Near Ochakov

Your Most Gracious Majesty, what I predicted has now come to pass. Recall what I wrote at the very outbreak of the war. We cannot end these troubles through successes against the Turks, but by sorting out what kind of political system is most important to us; that is, should we find the means to achieve peace with the Turks and, possessing all possible powers in our hands, to devise a profitable bond, then in this manner we might construct a beneficial political arrangement. You deign to say that Count Rumiantsev's army is to be directed against the Prussian King, as I stated in my plan. But that plan was to have been put into operation two years hence once everything had fully developed and was ready. Had that been the case, we would have then seized for nothing everything along the Danube in a single campaign at the beginning of our war against the Turks. But now, thanks to the perfidy of all of Europe, the Turks have foiled our plans by declaring war. The Emperor has conducted an odd war, he has exhausted his army with its defensive position, and everywhere he has taken part himself he's been beaten up along with his best troops. Many of his corps have fled without even having seen the enemy. But as for our side, and particularly here in my territory, where they exhibited the strongest intentions of crossing the borders, of ravaging our lands, of seizing the Crimea, of occupying Kherson and so on, God has protected us, and it's they who've grown weak, not us. And what's to be when our large forces, which, however, are very poorly organized due to the fact that they consist of a large number of recruits, are diverted? The Emperor was incapable of overcoming the Turks even when he directed everything against them. But if he sends some troops against the Prussian King, then you can be assured that the Turks will march into Vienna, and the Prussian King will grow even stronger. Now the Turks march against us reluctantly, but upon learning of our reduced forces, they'll hurl themselves at us in droves. How shall we then protect our vast borders which are divided by bodies of water and require special barriers at every location? Our fleet here has only begun to recover, and together with the help of the land forces it could have struck a blow against the enemy in the heart of his domain, but now even this will not be possible. Your Most Gracious Majesty, how dispirited my heart has become having seen everything that inevitably was to come. The means to avert this was simple. I did not forget to mention it on numerous occasions. God Himself knows what my heart feels. Just think in what state of complete lethargy the Bourbons are—they'll betray us too, just as they did the Dutch. It is a powerful league: England, Prussia, Holland, Sweden, Saxony. And many Imperial Princes will join them. Poland will burden us more than the other states. Instead of starting a new war for which we lack the strength, do everything possible to make peace with the Turks and direct your cabinet to lessen the number of Russia's enemies. Believe me, no good will come from this. How can we overcome all those armed against us? The Prussian King will become even more of a dictator than now. He who would tell you otherwise you should consider to be both your villain and the Fatherland's. Regarding the infantry regiments, I don't know where to find six of them at this point. This will create nothing but confusion regardless where they're taken from. And so, issue whatever orders you please. As for me, deliver me from command, for I do not find the means nor the possibility to command and to protect that which remains.

[. . .]

Your most loyal and most grateful subject
Prince Potemkin-Tavrichesky

366. CATHERINE TO POTEMKIN

7 November 1788

My dear friend, Prince Grigory Aleksandrovich. Your letters of 17 October have been delivered to my hands, from which I'm glad to see that everything is fine there. The plan for the siege revealed to me all the obstacles facing you. May God lessen the obstinacy of the Ochakov garrison. I am astonished at how the Kapudan Pasha is able to hold out at sea this late in such a stormy autumn. I suppose he fears returning to Stambul and the Vizier's depriving him of either his position or his life.[1]

It's regrettable that Prince Nassau was unable to burn the vessels that had been repaired in Ochakov. Paul Jones had, as you yourself know, an enterprising reputation till now. If you send him back here, we'll find a place for him.

[. . .]

You will see what an odd armistice agreement the Prussian King forced the Danes to make or, to say it more accurately: the Danes unwisely quailed before the Prussian threats.[2] I do not doubt in the least what you write me about a league having been formed against me. They have been told, as you write, that I am not against peace as long as my allies are included, but they, the league, that is, are not even content with that: they demanded that I not conclude an alliance with Poland, saying that was not in their interests. And I even agreed to this and ordered that this plan for an alliance with Poland be dropped. Now they're demanding that I withdraw my troops from Poland. The truth be told, it would be difficult to agree to this. They want to deprive me of my allies, are acting in the interests of the Swedes and the Turks, prescribe laws to me, threaten me should I not carry them out, and, what is more, complain about me and seek to revile me and harm me through all manner of dirty tricks. As a result of all that they are doing to aid the Swedish King, the French will be the winners, and Elliot,[3] the English minister, is the one doing this.

You will recall, my friend, that the Prussian King made the proposal about the treaty at the very moment he learned that the Emperor had recognized *casus foederis*; this proposal was made precisely so as to prevent the help anticipated from that party.[4] In no way did I break the treaty with England: they did not want to renew it after it had expired, and they entered into one with the French instead, and together with them acknowledged the principles of neutrality, which they refused to do with us.[5] Please don't blame me for this set of circumstances. For truth, I'm wracking my brains trying to find the best solution, but when things go wrong I never complain since successes and failures happen every day. If I overlook something, then this is excusable, for I am human, and only God Himself is free of sin.

I'll be very sorry if you decide to withdraw and shall take this as a mortal blow, all the more so since in so doing you'll be abandoning me in the midst of intrigues, for which, I suppose, you don't expect any thanks from me. But I hope that once everything ends successfully, then, out of your love for me, this notion will pass and you will be as you were, my most loyal one.

No one could've known last year that the Austrians' affairs would not go as desired. Farewell, may God grant you happiness, health and every possible good.

You can't imagine how foolishly Princess Dashkova is behaving in her quarrel with Chief Cup-Bearer Naryshkin! Every single day they put on some new farce, and everyone is laughing at them.[6]

There's nothing I want more in the world than for you, after having taken Ochakov and having issued your commands for the winter, to come here this winter if only for an hour so I might, first, have the pleasure of seeing you after such a long separation, and second, discuss a great many things with you face to face. Farewell, God be with you.

---

1. There existed a long, irreparable hatred between Gazi Hasan and Grand Vizier Koja Yusuf Pasha. "Stambul" refers to Istanbul (Constantinople).

2. Under pressure from Britain and Prussia, Denmark signed an armistice with Sweden on 28 September (9 October).

3. Britain's envoy to Denmark, Hugh Elliot (1752–1830) worked to pull the Danes out of the war.

4. In early March, Catherine turned down an offer for a Russo-Prussian alliance given her antipathy to the Hertzberg plan and her treaty with Austria.

5. Britain chose not to renew the Anglo-Russian commercial treaty in April 1787.

6. Princess Dashkova and Aleksandr Naryshkin were neighbors in the countryside outside St. Petersburg. They quarreled terribly over Naryshkin's pigs, who liked to cross over into the princess's property and trample her flower beds.

367. POTEMKIN TO CATHERINE

17 November [1788]. Near Ochakov

Your Most Gracious Majesty. A heavy snow prevented carrying out the assault. So large was the snowfall it left behind impassable drifts. For truth, we are suffering, but the enemy suffers even more. I am using all means to provide the men with winter boots and clothing; I brought here in advance some felt, cloaks and fur coats. Everything possible has been put to use. I let the fleet go for the winter. Berezan is an unassailable place, however, it's of no use to us. I have ordered everything removed from there and that it be abandoned.[1] The Loyal Black Sea Cossacks should receive what is due them according to the regulations for what they have captured, and Lieutenant-Colonel Golovaty should receive a military decoration as well. And the other one—Captain Mokei—should receive the Order of Vladimir. I shall present him with one of those that were sent to me in the name of Your Imperial Majesty.[2] [. . .]

The Pasha here was an Aga of the Janissaries and was persecuted by the Vizier for his favorable disposition toward Russia. Thus, I have decided to accord him all advantages and respect.[3] I treated the other Turks most kindly as well and explained to them how the Porte was unjust in starting the war. Although this group of Turks is not large, nevertheless they represent a select group and are equal in number to the garrison at Dubica.[4] The breach-battery will end in three days, and despite winter and the cold I'll commence the assault after first having called on God's help.

[. . .] According to Count Stackelberg's letters—things are bad in Poland, which, of course, they wouldn't be had my plan been followed. But so be it. We must now do everything possible to stop the league's undertaking and not to allow this act. If you are successful in this, then everything can be repaired later. As your most loyal and devoted subject, I repeat: Hasten to turn matters around—make peace with Sweden by using the Prussian King to persuade the Swedish King to address himself to you. For the time being, put on a peaceful and friendly countenance in your dealings with Prussia. In this way you will put everything right. Do the same with England. Later you will see how best to get your revenge. I give you my honor on this. Farewell, matushka, while alive I remain

> your most loyal and most grateful subject
> Prince Potemkin-Tavrichesky

P.S. General Maksimovich was a courageous and zealous servant. He perished by neglecting to be cautious. Being courageous, he put too much faith in this. He leaves behind a wife.[5]

I present herewith the reports and letters received from Count Pyotr Aleksandrovich. The Pasha confirmed that the Emperor has concluded an armistice with them.[6]

---

1. After the departure of the Turkish fleet on 4 November, Potemkin's Cossack force captured the island of Berezan, where provisions and supplies for Ochakov had been stored. With Berezan taken and the Turkish fleet gone, Potemkin had hoped to be able to time the attack on Ochakov with Catherine's name-day (24 November), although a heavy snowfall ruined his plan.

2. Potemkin noted that the Cossacks should receive their share of the booty from Berezan. In addition, Golovaty was given the Order of St. George fourth class, and Captain Mokei the Order of St. Vladimir fourth class.

3. Osman Pasha of the Two-Tailed Mace, commander of the garrison at Berezan, had been captured by the Cossacks. Potemkin insisted, and Catherine agreed, that he and his assistants be released as a goodwill gesture to the Turks at Ochakov.

4. The Austrians seized the Turkish fortress of Dubica on 15 August 1788, and hailed it as a major victory.

5. Major-General Stepan Petrovich Maksimovich was killed on 11 November during one of the frequent Turkish sorties. In keeping with custom, the Turks lopped off his head and mounted it on the walls of Ochakov for all to see.

6. Rumiantsev wrote Potemkin that the Austrians, in response to the sudden, heavy snowfall in Moldavia, had brought their troops to their winter quarters.

368. CATHERINE TO POTEMKIN

27 November 1788

My friend, Prince Grigory Aleksandrovich. I received yesterday your letters of 17 November and see from them that you have snow and extremely cold weather just as we do here. I highly praise your efforts to provide the men with winter clothing and boots. I was pleased to learn of the capture of Berezan. I pray God that Ochakov too will soon surrender. It seems that now, with the Turkish fleet having departed, they must be without a single hope.

I grant freedom to Osman Pasha of the Two-Tailed Mace captured in Berezan and to all those you promised it to. Order that he be released with honor. Friends of the Kapudan Pasha in Tsar Grad are soliciting the freeing from our captivity of a certain Turkish ship's captain, as you'll see from the rescript, about which you were written. We should demand Lombard in exchange, who is going mad and nearly cut his own throat. [. . .]

A great hatred toward us has arisen in Poland, and, in contrast, a fervent love for His Royal Prussian Majesty. I suppose this will last till he deigns to introduce his invincible troops into Poland and occupies the better part of it. I, of course, can't prevent this and I don't even dare to think that any reasoning, words or action could in the slightest stand in the way of His Royal Prussian Majesty. The entire universe must submit to His Supreme Royal will.

You repeat to me your counsel that I should hurry and make peace with the Swedish King by using His Royal Prussian Majesty to win him over to peace. Yet if it pleased His Royal Prussian Majesty to do this, he would not have allowed the Swedish King to go to war. You can be certain that no matter how I might try to make overtures to this all-powerful dictator, my wishes will surely be crushed for this no matter what I might say, and the most agreeable conditions will be prescribed to me, such as, for example: giving away Finland, and perhaps giving away Livonia to Sweden, White Russia to Poland and the land along the Samara River to the Turks. And should I not agree to this, then I can have war. In addition to all this, their manner is so rude, and foolish as well, that there's never before been anything like it; the Turks exhibit the gentlest manner by comparison.

I swear to Almighty God that I am doing everything possible to withstand everything that these courts, and most especially the Almighty Prussian one, are doing. But he has become so puffed up, that unless he stumbles upon some obstacle, I see no way to agree to all his desires without disgracing myself; and even now he himself doesn't know what he does or doesn't want.

The English King is dying now, and if he drops dead then perhaps we'll have success establishing concord with his son (who till now has been obeying Fox and the patriotic English party, and not the Hanoverians).[1] I know that the German league was very unhappy with the Prussians' actions in Denmark.

Permit me to say that I am beginning to think it would be best for us not to have any allies rather than for us to be changing them willy-nilly, as if we were reeds being helplessly blown about by a storm. What's more, wartime is not the moment for establishing alliances. I am not inclined toward revenge, however, that which is contrary to my honor and that of the Empire and to its essential interests is injurious to it as well: I shall not give up province after province. Those who permit others to dictate laws to them will end up in disgrace, for no one has ever been able to get away with such a thing; they have forgotten themselves and who they're dealing with. This is precisely what the fools are counting on, that we shall be compliant!

Seize Ochakov and make peace with the Turks. Then you'll see them melt away like snow on the steppe after a thaw and they'll crawl off like water running down a slope. Farewell, God be with you. Be well and safe. I'm very sorry about Maksimovich.

---

1. King George III actually outlived Catherine by twenty-four years, dying in 1820. His eldest son, later King George IV (from 1820–1830), was drawn to the opposition centered around Charles James Fox (1749–1806), who opposed Pitt's plans for war with Russia.

369. POTEMKIN TO CATHERINE

From Ochakov. 7 December [1788]

Your Most Gracious Majesty. I had intended to deliver Ochakov to you as a gift on the day of St. Catherine,[1] but circumstances impeded my plan. The fortress's fortifications had still not been adequately broken down to make it possible to scale the walls, and the line of communications had still not had time to cover the left flank's column making its assault, without which they all would have been shot down.

I congratulate you with the fortress that the Turks guarded more than anything else. The operation went as splendidly and smoothly as our exercises generally do. Of the practically twelve thousand crack troops who made up the garrison, no fewer than seven thousand lost their lives here, which is quite plain to see. And many were killed in the magazines and dugouts as well. Our casualties were moderate, though many officers who acted with fiery zeal and courage were injured and wounded. Major-General Prince Volkonsky was killed on the retrenchment and Brigadier Gorich on the wall.[2] Oh, how sorry I am for them. The Cossack Host of single-homesteaders, just recently formed by Your Majesty's edict, served as the infantry during the assault and worked miracles. They were led by colonels from the Don—young men—who displayed uncommon valor.

Your Majesty, what hardships my army suffered and how many casualties it inflicted on the enemy cannot be described all at once: You will hear about it from the Turks.

The prisoners, and especially the women, are a burden to me. Winter here is cruel, like in Russia. Sending them away will require much effort. Our cannons inflicted damage on the town's buildings. Many need repairing. There are other concerns as well—the regiments have to be settled in their billets, and on top of this the Poles do not want to allow them to enter.[3]

Aleksandr Nikolaevich entered the fortress first, and then Anhalt from the other side.[4] My army is practically to a man made up of recruits, but when we have God's help, it can defeat everyone.

I'll soon send the Pasha and his officials to Petersburg.[5] And the standards too. I'll be able to report on everything in detail only in five days.

Your most loyal and most grateful subject

Prince Potemkin-Tavrichesky

P.S. Lieutenant-Colonel Bauer[6] of my regiment was with me the entire time as my orderly and he often put himself in danger. You were kind to his father. Confer upon him the rank of colonel.

---

1. 24 November.

2. Major-General Prince Sergei Avraamovich Volkonsky. Brigadier Ivan Petrovich Gorich-Benesevsky (the Elder), not to be confused with his younger brother of the same name (see Letter 266), was a Circassian in Russian service. He and his brother were patronized by Potemkin.

3. In November, the Sejm demanded that Russia remove its troops from Polish Ukraine.

4. Aleksandr Samoilov received the Order of St. George second class for his heroism at Ochakov, as did Prince Viktor Amadeus Anhalt-Bernburg-Schaumburg (1744–1790).

5. Husein Pasha and the captured Turkish officers were presented to Catherine in St. Petersburg on 11 March 1789.

6. Karl Fyodorovich Bauer was dispatched with the news of Ochakov's fall. He was promoted to the rank of colonel and presented with a snuffbox of gold and diamonds. He returned to the south bearing Potemkin's rewards: the Order of St. George first class (set in diamonds) and a diamond-encrusted sword worth sixty thousand rubles.

370. CATHERINE TO POTEMKIN

16 December 1788

Having grasped you by the ears with both hands, my true friend, Prince Grigory Aleksandrovich, I'm kissing you in my mind out of gratitude over the news delivered by Bauer on the taking of Ochakov. This happy event has gladdened everyone most extremely. And I think it will greatly serve to bring about the ultimate resolution of this business. Glory be to God,

THE SIEGE OF OCHAKOV 275

and to you I render praise and thank you so very much for this acquisition that is so important for the Empire in the present circumstances. With the utmost gratitude I accept the fervor and zeal of the troops, from the highest to the lowest ranks, under your command. I greatly regret the loss of valiant men; the illnesses and injuries of the wounded touch me, I hope and pray God for their recovery. I ask you to thank them all for me and to convey my gratitude. I impatiently await your reports on the details so that my generous hand might reward the deserving. I can imagine the army's difficulties during the harsh winter, and so it's fitting that it be given half-a-year's pay from the extraordinary sum in advance. Quarter the army for the winter in Poland without the slightest worry; as a result, the Poles' attitude will return more quickly once more to normal; à une armée de conquérant l'on n'a encore jamais refusé de quartier.[1] It'll now be easier to make peace, and I shan't overlook any means to achieve it soon.

My true friend, you've silenced everyone, and this happy occasion provides you another opportunity to show magnanimity to your blind and empty-headed critics. Farewell, my friend, till we meet. Be well and safe.

You know, I suppose, that the English King has gone so completely mad that four men can hardly control him when he's overcome by rage.[2]

I take it as a certainty, that once you have attended to your army's needs, I shall have the pleasure of seeing you here, as I have already written to you in my previous letters and am now repeating.

---

1. "a conquering army has as yet never been refused quarters."
2. "rage" in the original.

371. POTEMKIN TO CATHERINE

Ochakov. 26 December [1788]

Your Most Gracious Majesty, I've not been able to send my reports till now due to powerful snowstorms that have made it impossible to travel a single verst. Things have calmed down now. There's nothing I can say about the attack, about how it all happened, for it was unlike anything ever before. One can confidently say that simple maneuvers cannot be carried off with such precision. Believe me, matushka, that it was like the most powerful whirlwind that in a short time sent people to their graves and turned the town upside down. It was dear to see how everyone set off with such joy and confidence. Once I have settled matters here, I'll come to Petersburg with your permission, which you deigned to grant in your next to last letter. Your affairs as well as my own require it most emphatically.

Matushka, you expressed your anger in your last letters in vain.[1] My zeal does not merit this. I do not base my ideas on the arguments of Count Panin, but on the state of affairs. I'm not in love with the Prussian King, I don't fear his troops, but I shall always say that they, more than anyone else, must be shown the least disdain. My ideas are based upon loyalty to you. I am not one who would want to see your honor tarnished. But to begin anything without first making peace with the Turks cannot bring you glory. And this must be avoided in every possible way, for we surely shall lose if we poke our noses in everywhere.

The great distances separating our borders do not allow us to move our troops where they are needed as can be done in smaller countries. It's awkward having two enemies, and this would mean having five. God has helped us here. And so shall we manage to make the next campaign a glorious and easy one. But were we to run off to the other side, everything here would come to naught, and although we were on the path toward completing matters, this would set them back. You deign to say that I should pay no heed to the Europeans' schemes. Your Majesty, I am not a cosmopolitan, I have little need of Europe, but when its madness affects those affairs entrusted to me, then I cannot remain indifferent. You often deigned to remind me—"Take Ochakov." When did I report to you that I would retreat without having taken it? And I boldly say that there's no way it could have been taken earlier. You have deigned to know what interest it held for the Sultan and the Porte. This you can judge by the way it was supplied with weapons and men. The army stationed there was a select one, and as of this spring it truly was 20 thousand men strong, not counting the fleet. Now there are over twelve thousand, not a soul of whom will go back. Your Majesty, I do not lie, as others do, and my so-called army, in which three quarters of the infantrymen are recruits, does not comprise 14 thousand. But God is merciful toward me, He did not grant the enemy any success. You deign to write that it's not time to think of rest. Matushka, I was not writing of bodily rest, still it is time to calm the spirit. So much have I been forced to attend to: hourly troubles, vigilance along several thousand versts of border entrusted to me, an enemy on land and on sea whom I neither fear nor disdain. There are villains whom I do disdain and whose designs I do fear: namely, this band of ungrateful men who think of nothing but their own gain and peace.[2] Armed with perfidy, they play all manner of dirty tricks on me. There is no slander they would not direct against me, and unable to make you waver, they unleash their devoted scoundrels everywhere to defame me. There you have their business, while mine is to forgive them. They cheat, and I serve. Your Most Gracious Majesty, I have sacrificed my life to you everywhere, and I may truly say that no one has taken greater risk than I. I do not take advantage of those benefits that others find in the magnificence of my title. It would be difficult to be simpler than I. From this one can conclude that I serve for your sake and for the sake of utility. My orderly general, who was sent along with the reports, can report in detail on everything that happened, and I beg for him Your Royal charity.[3] I'll bring with me further details on the men who distinguished themselves. While alive I remain

your most loyal and most grateful subject
Prince Potemkin-Tavrichesky

P.S. You deign to write that there is no more money. Having no knowledge of the state's resources, I have never said this, but I do say that the current high prices are unbearable. The entire fleet will have to be put into action in the next campaign. Finishing the vessels together with building some new ones will require a horrific sum. The fleet alone can decide matters with the Turks once we have pushed them back to the capital itself. I have requested sailors. Since I have not received them, it is best to leave everything at the dockyards. I didn't receive the cannons in time as well. Meanwhile, that article, about which I shall report, may be of some aid. You deign to say that I am burrowing like a mole. Given how cold the winter is here, it wouldn't be a bad idea to live in a dugout, but as the truth about me is rarely reported, so once again people have lied. I had been living at my headquarters, which I've handed over to the wounded, but am now living in one small kibitka, and even that belongs to someone else.

---

1. Letters 366, 368.

2. A reference to Potemkin's enemies at court.

3. Major-General Nikolai Mikhailovich Rakhmanov (1744–1793) was sent by Potemkin to St. Petersburg with the detailed reports of the storming and the keys to the town. Catherine rewarded him with the Order of St. Vladimir second class and a jewel-encrusted sword.

9. A Gallant Campaign, the Count's Betrayal, and Blackie—1789

*A*fter garrisoning Ochakov and quartering his troops for the winter, Potemkin set off for St. Petersburg where he arrived early on the evening of 4 February. It had been more than two years since His Serene Highness had last visited the capital, and the entire city was filled with nervous anticipation at the thought of his return. Mikhail Garnovsky, the prince's steward at court, noted in early January that a sense of the approaching Second Coming—when the good would be rewarded and the wicked punished—had descended upon the city. Catherine herself was anxious about Potemkin's return. They had last seen each other in June 1787 at the end of the triumphant southern tour and would now be meeting for the first time since the outbreak of the war. Frequently ill in the past days, the empress felt a growing need to be with Potemkin and spoke of never letting him leave her side again. At the same time, however, well aware of his strong opinions on Russia's foreign relations, she fretted over what his return would mean to the present political system.

Potemkin remained in St. Petersburg for three months, during which time he devoted himself to a range of pressing matters including building up the army, procuring provisions, and planning the coming year's campaigns along the southern and northern fronts. Potemkin laid out his plans in several undated letters to Catherine. In the south, the prince intended to place Russia's ground forces on the offensive and direct them against the Turks in Bessarabia and after strengthening the fleet to send it out to destroy the Turkish navy. In the north, Potemkin argued for trying to cut Finland off from Sweden and then occupy it. Once in Russian hands, Finland would be given its own political administration whose advantages would surpass anything the Finns had seen before, and thus Russia would win them away from Sweden. But the most urgent, thorniest issues had to do with Russia's relations with Prussia and Poland. Here Potemkin continued to stand by his earlier argument, namely, that Prussia be calmed by promising to restore its former confidence with the court of St. Petersburg, by permitting it to satisfy its hunger for Polish territory, and by making peace with the Turks. As for the Poles, whose anger toward Russia was growing daily, they were to be placated by the offer of former Turkish territories. At the same time, Potemkin pressed for a new commercial treaty with Britain that would help dissuade it from worsening its relations with Russia any further. The alternative to his recommendations was a new war against Prussia and Poland, backed by Britain, for which neither Russia nor Austria was prepared (Letters 373, 379).

While Catherine was pleased with Potemkin's plans for the coming campaign, she refused to accept his arguments concerning her neighbors to the west. And although some minor conciliatory gestures were made to Prussia and Catherine agreed to remove Russian troops from Poland, marking the temporary end of Russian sway over Poland, she rejected Potemkin's proposals (Letter 374).

Russia's hopes to attain peace with the Ottomans and to forestall the Prussians were dealt a severe blow when Sultan Abdul Hamid I died in March and was replaced by the young Selim III, who did not share his predecessor's interest in peace and was receptive to the bellicose encouragement of Russia's European enemies. Immediately after being officially installed, Selim ordered the grand vizier to resume the campaign against the enemy as soon as possible. Despite the Porte's defeats during the past year and a half, there would be no peace. To her great regret, Catherine knew Potemkin could no longer remain with her, and on 6 May he bade Catherine farewell and departed Tsarskoe Selo for the south.

A few weeks after Potemkin's return to the army, a crisis erupted in Catherine's personal life that was to have profound implications for the prince. The past year had brought an obvious cooling in relations between Catherine and her favorite, Count Aleksandr Dmitriev-Mamonov, and after various distressing conversations Catherine finally decided to release Mamonov from a position that he had clearly come to find odious and offered to find him a wealthy bride. Mamonov's response to Catherine's generous offer struck her a cruel blow. He informed Catherine that for a year he had been in love with Princess Daria Shcherbatova, one of Catherine's maids-of-honor, and had plans to marry her. Overcome by emotion after having finally revealed his secret to Catherine, Mamonov broke down, prostrating himself before her and confessing all the details of his betrayal. After several meetings and a great many tears shed all around, Catherine, betrayed yet again by a young favorite, rose above whatever personal desire for revenge she may have felt and agreed to the couple's request that they be allowed to marry. On 1 July, Mamonov and the young princess wed in a small ceremony at the palace church at Tsarskoe Selo and then quietly abandoned court two days later. Garnovsky observed tears in Catherine's eyes on the day of the wedding.

Catherine first wrote Potemkin of the Mamonov affair on 20 June in a secret letter that she sent with a special courier. Catherine's letter subsequently disappeared, and it is quite possible that she destroyed it after the prince's death when her letters were returned to her. Several days later, she composed a second letter describing the entire scene with Mamonov and Shcherbatova, and this letter did survive. In it she questioned Potemkin's role in Mamonov's illicit love affair and asked why he had not told her about it. Potemkin admitted to having some knowledge of the amour, but claimed that because he had no concrete proof, he had decided not to press the matter when Catherine did not respond to his subtle hints.

Of course, the prince had good reasons not to force the issue with Catherine. First, Potemkin knew of Catherine's attachment to the count and did not want to cause her undue sorrow by forcing her to see the truth. Second, Mamonov was his man, and he had proved useful to Potemkin as a source of information and as a beneficial influence on Catherine's thinking. Potemkin's standing would in no way be served by seeking the ouster of Mamonov, whose place might well be filled by someone much less sympathetic to him. And this is indeed what happened. Within days of her falling out with Mamonov, Catherine took notice of a dark-haired officer at court named Platon Zubov. He was twenty-two, she was sixty. She dubbed him "le Noiraud," Blackie. He was to be her final favorite. The coming together of the two was not accidental, but had been carefully orchestrated by Nikolai Saltykov, then vice president of the War College and Zubov's patron, and Anna Naryshkina, a lady-in-waiting and an old friend of the empress, both of whom were opponents of Potemkin. On 3 July, Zubov was promoted to colonel and made an adjutant to the empress, who bestowed ten thousand rubles upon him. He in turn thanked Anna Naryshkina for her efforts on his behalf with two thousand rubles.

Potemkin was not pleased with the change in favorites. True, Mamonov had lost Potemkin's favor by being unfaithful to Catherine, but Potemkin's not having been permitted any role in selecting his successor and the new favorite's links to Potemkin's critics must have been troubling. Potemkin truly sought Catherine's happiness, yet he feared his enemies might take advantage of the current situation to harm him, and he told Catherine this in no uncertain terms. For her part, Catherine sought to reassure him that no one could damage her trust in him and that his place with her was secure against any threat. Perhaps fearing an angry response, Catherine asked him to understand her actions. She pleaded with him not to insult her, but to see how marvelous this "most innocent soul" was and to know how her fragile health depended on him. Potemkin could clearly see how Zubov had revived Catherine's spirit in the wake of the Mamonov affair, and this was important to him for political and personal reasons. In the end, there was little he could do but accept the change (Letters 380–387).

With Catherine again happy and content, Potemkin was able to devote greater attention to the war against the Turks. The primary goal for that year's campaign focused on the lands of the Danubian principalities (Moldavia and Walachia): Potemkin's army aimed to win control over the Dniester and then continue toward the Danube, where it would meet up with Austrian troops under Prince Coburg. Meanwhile, the main Austrian army, led by Field Marshal Loudon, would attack Belgrade. The allies faced a Turkish army of 100,000 under the command of the new grand vizier, Jenâze Hasan Pasha. The vizier's strategy consisted of trying to prevent the Austrian and Russian forces from ever joining: first he would destroy Coburg's forces and then slip in behind Potemkin and attack from the rear. As a diversion, the Turkish navy would attack the Crimea.

The Turks' initial attempt against Coburg resulted in a resounding defeat near Fokshany on 12 July. As some 30,000 Turks advanced, Coburg sent a desperate message for aid to General Suvorov, who arrived with his small but disciplined "flying corps" of 5,000 men. Though greatly outnumbered, the joint forces beat back the Turks. In the meantime, Potemkin raced back and forth between Olviopol, Kherson, Kaushany, and Ochakov seeing to the fleet, directing his troops toward the Dniester, and preparing the attack on Khadjibey (Letters 385, 387). On 12 August, Potemkin's army crossed the Dniester, and the prince set up headquarters at Dubossary, where he waited to see what the Turks would do next (Letter 388). In early September, the Turkish forces made a second attempt to break through the gap between the Austrian and Russian armies as the grand vizier himself marched toward Fokshany at the head of 80,000 soldiers. Again, Prince Coburg sent a frantic request for help to Suvorov, who led his men on an arduous forced march to save the Austrians. They arrived to find that the grand vizier's army outnumbered their combined forces by more than three to one. Still, Suvorov pushed the indecisive Coburg to attack. The Battle of the Rymnik (11 September) proved to be the decisive engagement of the war: the Turkish forces were routed, and the grand vizier and the remnants of his army (15,000 men had been killed) retreated south across the Danube. News of the victory thrilled

Potemkin. He praised Suvorov's heroism to Catherine, urged her to reward him properly, and complained of the Austrians' cowardice and baseless pride (Letters 391–393, 395, 397).

The autumn of 1789 saw many victories over the disorganized and disheartened Turks. On 13 September, Potemkin captured Kaushany; the next day Russian forces seized Khadjibey (Odessa). On the final day of the month, the fortress of Akkerman (Belgrade-on-Dniester) surrendered to the Russians, and in early November so, too, did the massive fortress of Bender. Not a single Russian soldier was lost taking Bender, which made Potemkin's success all the sweeter. Russia now controlled all the land between the Bug and Dniester. Potemkin was bursting with pride at his achievements. "Were I a braggart," he wrote with false modesty on 4 November, "I would say that I'd executed to the letter all the plans for the coming campaign that I presented to you in Petersburg." And when, after heartily congratulating him on his "gallant campaign," Catherine gently counseled him not "to be haughty, not to become proud," Potemkin's thin skin got the better of him: he replied that although he was motivated solely by zeal, although he gave himself up in selfless devotion to his empress, and although he had been hailed in Vienna as a great victor, what he truly sought was not a crown of laurels, but a bishop's miter and a quiet retreat. Catherine, realizing her mistake, sought to smooth his ruffled feathers: "The bishop's miter you will assuredly never receive from me. And a monastery will never be the home of a man whose name resounds throughout Asia and Europe. It is too small for him" (Letters 392, 399–407).

Catherine could not afford to lose Potemkin to a monastery (though there was little likelihood of his acting on the threat) since there was still much that required his attention. The recent campaign created the possibility for peace with the Porte, and Catherine instructed Potemkin to open negotiations with the Turks. Initially, peace seemed to be within reach. In November, the grand vizier sent Potemkin a letter with the Porte's peace proposal, and Bulgakov, the Russian envoy, was released from the Seven Towers fortress. The sultan, however, did not share the peaceful sentiments of his grand vizier and would only agree to a temporary armistice, which Potemkin rejected. Selim's desire to continue the war—despite the disastrous defeats of the past year and rioting in the streets of Constantinople—received support in November in the form of an offer for a formal alliance from the Prussian ambassador. By December it was not only clear that Russia would need to prepare for another season of war, but it was also beginning to appear as if it might have to carry on without the support of the Austrians, who were trying to make their own separate peace with the Porte, given the approaching death of Joseph II, unrest in the Netherlands and Galicia, and the threat of war with Prussia.

The prospect for peace looked equally poor in the north where the fighting between Russia and Sweden during the year had been indecisive. Gustav III had managed to strengthen his position, however, by defeating the Anjala League, by executing a successful coup d'état in February that increased the authority of the monarch vis-à-vis the nobles, and by signing an alliance with the Porte that promised Sweden a large subsidy for continuing the war with Russia. In the west, Russia had effectively lost control of Poland to the Prussians who, backed by Britain, were inciting the Poles to war with the promise of regaining the land lost to Russia in the first partition of 1772.

Far from bringing peace, the victories of 1789 over the Turks had only served to incite Russia's enemies all the more. The situation in which Russia found itself at the end of 1789 was decidedly more dangerous than that of a year before. "We are now in a crisis," Catherine observed in late December, "we shall either have peace or a third war, that is, with Prussia."

* * *

372. CATHERINE TO POTEMKIN

2 February 1789

My true friend, Prince Grigory Aleksandrovich. I have just received your letter of 31 January from Dubrovna. I'm very glad you're hastening toward us and was pleased to learn that the ship "Vladimir" has safely arrived in Sevastopol, though I'm sorry that Count Voinovich has hurt himself.[1] The ice is thick everywhere, even in the harbors in the Mediterranean Sea, so they say; I don't know whether this is true or not, for I haven't done any measuring myself. Your journey from Kremenchug to Mogilyov resembled the flight of a bird, and yet you're surprised that you're tired. You simply do not take care of yourself, and there's no one to soothe you: should you arrive here ill, then no matter how happy I shall be at your arrival, nevertheless, be certain that the moment I lay eyes on you I shall tug your ears. Go ahead and make a face, but don't fool around with your health. That's the kind of greeting we're preparing for the victor!

Farewell, till we meet, God be with you.

---

1. Potemkin had written Catherine on 31 January from Dubrovna, where he was resting for a few days after arriving from Mogilyov quite exhausted. In his letter, he told her that "Vladimir" had become trapped by ice in the Liman in January while on its way to Sevastopol and that Rear Admiral Voinovich had fallen and injured himself the same month while inspecting the shipyards in Kherson.

373. POTEMKIN TO CATHERINE

[After 4 February 1789]

The taking of Ochakov with God's help frees our hands to extend our victories to the Danube and to dispirit the enemy to the extreme at which point we shall deliver the final blow. The fleet must be strengthened, and with the prepared ships it should be strong enough if we can find sufficient sailors and artillery. The Kuban troops together with forces from the Caucasus could nevertheless carry out a diversion, just as they are doing now, and so be able to keep the Turkish forces from leaving Anatolia.

The Ukrainian Army should have every opportunity to force the enemy out of both Principalities.[1] One might say that after Ochakov everything seems possible. Nevertheless, conditions in Poland, the danger presented by the Prussian King and England's assistance to him not only present us with an obstacle, they also constitute a great danger. Our neighbors the Poles are located behind the backs of our troops, and since they are stretched out along our borders, they will cause much harm unless they can be won over to our side. This will be especially so should the sale of grain be prohibited.

Your Most Gracious Majesty, I am loyal to you, I am grateful to you, I honor you like a mother, I love the Fatherland. For me personally, wherever I might lay down my life for you I consider good and splendid, and not only have I not retreated from this, but have sought it out. Yet your reign's honor demands a change in the present critical state of affairs. All of your subjects expect this and place their hopes in your talents. Nothing appears impossible to me, provided that you act with greater haste in the realm of politics and entrust matters to those men faithful to you. First of all, placate the Prussian King by luring him with the hope of gaining your former trust, which can be done by conveying to him in a tender manner word of our reconciliation with the Turks, concurring with the Emperor at the same time so as to avoid any suspicion on his part. If you inform the Poles that you intend to give them some land beyond the Dniester upon concluding peace with the Turks, they will all come over to you, and they will place at your service the arms they are now preparing. Hasten to supply England with a commercial treaty. With this you will gain for yourself a nation that has cooled toward you. Marshall all forces to achieve these two goals. We shall later not only curse, but shall strike the Prussian King. Otherwise I do not know what is to be. The Emperor cannot divert strong troops against Prussia, for even with all his forces he was unable to fight a handful of Turks. The French will not send a single brigade, and so the Prussian King can easily divert 80 thousand of his own troops and 25 [thousand] Saxons against the Emperor. He would send 80 thousand against us, as well as about 50 [thousand] Poles. Pray consider, what would we use to fight against this without first having finished with the Turks? I am the first to think that the Prussian King must pay, however, let us first make peace with the Turks.

I turn now to the military plans against the Turks. It is simply impossible to make a report on the troops on that front without knowing whether the Ukrainian Army, either all or a part of it, is to remain in place or will move to the other side.² If it is to stay here, then we shall have an entirely different type of war. In accord with your command, I have dispatched from here four infantry regiments for Lubny for the sake of sending them to Livonia, along with ten squadrons of Dragoons.³

I read the plans of Baron Sprengtporten and Jägerhorn and found them almost identical, except for their methods, which differed somewhat. It would be good to support the oppressed nobility by distracting the Finns, however, since the two other orders have risen up against them, were we to commence actions in Finland this would represent another threat to the noble estate from the aforementioned orders since it would provide yet another reason for attacking them, the nobles, that is, as evildoers against the Fatherland.⁴ What is more, the winter season prohibits us from using military subterfuge, which the local geography would have made possible in combating their superior troop strength. Would such action not force the Prussian King, before being truly ready, to venture to introduce his army into Poland at a time when the Prussians' influence there is beginning to weaken a bit and would certainly vanish were matters conducted according to my ideas and in a manner commensurate with my zeal for you? In this case the entire Polish cavalry, with the reinforcement of our corps, would be directed against Prussia and would, of course, destroy its entire cavalry in a single campaign.⁵ But this fervor of mine is known in all its purity to God alone.

I conclude with matters concerning the Finns. Should God give our fleet superiority, then toward the end of the next campaign we, disrupting Sweden's communications with Finland, shall gather all our forces and occupy the latter principality. Having firmly established ourselves there, we shall create, with their help, and give them a new form of government with all possible advantages beyond what they currently possess, giving every estate the opportunity to take note of these fruits, and in so doing tempt the Swedes too. Otherwise the current enterprise will be nothing more than an experiment and will quite easily end up to be fruitless, and as a result our plan will become known and precautions will be taken against it. I am repeating myself somewhat, however, the fleet must be directed with all possible strength to inflict the decisive blow. But if it acts in a disunified manner, then instead of all these fruits it will know nothing but loss.

There is much I could say about Poland, but I'm unable to read and write much now. In the event that we enter Finland, should God bless these future actions, all provisions must be prepared in advance and kept secret. This should be preceded by a manifesto. I shall say at another time what I think it should contain.

A decision about the Ukrainian Army must be made soon so that steps can be taken, for what's been disordered requires mending. It is possible that by the time I arrive they won't have a slice of bread. And we've but little time. I spare no labors and gladly suffocate under their weight, yet speed is required.

---

1. The Danubian principalities of Moldavia and Walachia.

2. In the event of war with Prussia, the Ukrainian Army, under the command of Rumiantsev until 3 March when it, too, was placed under Potemkin's control, was to move to defend the western border against attack, leaving the Yekaterinoslav Army to fight the Turks.

3. In accordance with Catherine's order, a new army was being formed near Riga, with some of the forces stationed in White Russia, to defend against a possible Prussian attack.

4. The Anjala League, led by Baron Göran Magnus Sprengtporten (1741–1819), a Finn in Russian service, and Major Jan Anders Jägerhorn, collapsed in January 1789, in part due to its members' call for Finnish independence from Sweden and to Gustav III's ability to turn the lower orders against the noble opposition. See also Letter 355n5.

5. A reference to an earlier plan of Potemkin to create three Polish cavalry brigades to use against the Turks, which Catherine had rejected. See Letter 339.

374. CATHERINE TO POTEMKIN

[After 4 February 1789]

There's no question but that you write out of zeal, yet as I've done everything possible, so it seems to me it is not possible that even more be expected of me without offending my honor. And without this I have no need of either my life or my crown. To give Poland any of the Turkish lands now would result in His Royal Prussian Majesty immediately and assuredly protesting this with threats against us in that rude tone that he's adopted with us, which we would either have to swallow or avenge. And so I think it best to avoid this, not to promise the Poles anything and to allow them to indulge their whims till they stop. In other words, let them ruin things and do what they want among themselves, however, I shall not send for them, and so let the regiments directed to Lubny go on to White Russia.

I am of the opinion to recall Field Marshal Rumiantsev from the army and to entrust you with both armies so that things will go more harmoniously.[1]

My friend, I don't think I used angry words with you, and for my receiving the Prussian King's insults with impatience and the appropriate sentiment—I beg you not to condemn me, for I would be unworthy of my position and title were I not to possess this sentiment in my soul.

Everything you write about the army's operations is quite good, and my opinion was always that Bender and Bessarabia should be the objects of this campaign, and there's no reason for trying to go as far as the Olt.

---

1. On 3 March, Catherine placed both Russian armies under Potemkin's command. Upset at having been relieved of command of the Ukrainian Army, Rumiantsev resigned from service and requested permission to leave to take the waters. Although his request was granted, Rumiantsev, refusing to leave, remained in Jassy, from where he criticized the Russian war effort.

2. Austrian ambassador Cobenzl had tried to talk Potemkin into directing his forces far to the west, nearer to the Austrian border and the Olt River. Potemkin refused, and Catherine supported his decision.

375. POTEMKIN TO CATHERINE

[10 May 1789]

Your Most Gracious Majesty. I have received Voinovich's report along with some oranges.[1] I am sending all of them on to you. For truth, I didn't eat a one. I galloped into Smolensk yesterday two and a half days after departing Tsarskoe Selo. I'm leaving this hour and shall stop in Dubrovna to repair the carriages and mend myself. I'm extremely exhausted, but shall remain there no more than two days.

Kamensky reports that the men are without shoes and shirts because the Poles will not let them through. But I think that they wanted to bring their weapons with them. A special shipment of the yearly accouterments might be made, but I won't be able to sort things out till my arrival. But in the meanwhile, I'll write to Prince Repnin to do everything possible to put things right. I'll send a report from Dubrovna. Whatever it is that's lacking, I'll write.

I fear that a strong current not seen for a long time will prevent us from erecting bridges on the Bug. Kremenchug is completely flooded, and they have taken to riding about there on boats.

Your Majesty, you have not written to me the French letter that I might show to General of the Artillery Count Potocki. I shall need it so that I may show it to him, for you do note his true patriotism. It wouldn't be bad if you included in it your compliments to his wife.[2]

Note from Count Voinovich's reports the shortage of officers for the ships being prepared on the Sea of Azov. I shall do everything possible, however, it would be a pity if we are not that strong because of our fleet which, if it had enough men, would terrify the enemy. Farewell, beloved matushka, honest to God I could hardly write this, I've become very weak.

Your most loyal and most grateful subject
Prince Potemkin-Tavrichesky

1. Voinovich reported on the successful operation against the Turks on the shores of Rumelia by eighteen Greek vessels. The oranges were part of the booty seized from the Turks.

2. Count Felix Potocki, commander of forces in Polish Ukraine, and his wife, Josephine Amelia, were members of Poland's pro-Russian party. Upon Potemkin's request, Catherine wrote the couple on 13 May expressing her support for them.

376. POTEMKIN TO CATHERINE

22 May [1789]. Kremenchug

Your Most Gracious Majesty. I was both tired and a bit feverish and so was unable to travel any farther without rest. Upon arriving in Kremenchug, I found it completely flooded, and after the water recedes there will certainly be serious illnesses, for the water is settling in the low places. The stoves in every house have been ruined by the water, and I have ordered that the administration be moved to the new Yekaterinoslav.[1] All the inhabitants are leaving as well.

Matushka, if some retired naval officers are to be assembled, then they should be sent straight away, we've extreme need of them.

I can't describe how weak I am. My finger hurts once again, I've irritated it with all this writing: down to the last trifle I've been writing all the official correspondence myself.

Farewell, Your Majesty, be kind and do not forget me. I am leaving here tomorrow. Only the building housing the provincial administration has not sunk, and I am living in it. It can't be said that I am not where I belong.

Your most loyal and most grateful subject
Prince Potemkin-Tavrichesky

1. The administration of the Yekaterinoslav province was temporarily located in Kremenchug.

377. POTEMKIN TO CATHERINE

23 May [1789]. Kremenchug

Now that it has quieted down, my carriages have been able to cross over, and I, Your Majesty, shall leave here tomorrow, though I'm weak from fatigue. Since sending my reports I've had no news from Jassy. Our manufacturers in Poland have committed quite a few follies. They took it in their heads to send knives to sell to the army. They hid them in some oil. The Poles found them and got suspicious. I am awaiting reports from Lieutenant-General Krechetnikov in Kiev about all the transports whose routes I laid out.[1]

Farewell, Your Majesty, do not forget that I remain till death
your most loyal and most grateful subject
Prince Potemkin-Tavrichesky

---

1. To improve the supplying of the Ukrainian Army, Potemkin ordered Krechetnikov to send transports to Olviopol via Kiev.

378. Catherine to Potemkin

31 May 1789

My true friend, Prince Grigory Aleksandrovich. I received yesterday and the day before your letters of 22 and 23 May from Kremenchug, for which I thank you. I'm most sorry that you're tired. I see from them that you are sending the inhabitants to Gorodishche and the administration to Yekaterinoslav. The naval officers are being sent to you as they become available. Our oared flotilla departed for Kronstadt and will leave there in about two days. There is news that the Swedish fleet might be out cruising near Karlskrona. The Reval and Kronstadt fleets have joined up.

May God grant the Swedish and Prussian Kings whitlows on every finger, and that your fingers stop hurting. Don't worry, I shan't forget you. Your writing often calms my spirit.

The Poles will calm down and will be sorry when they see that we are conveying everything past them and have our own road. Punish them by not purchasing anything from them.

Farewell, my friend, God be with you. I love you like my soul.

379. POTEMKIN TO CATHERINE

Olviopol. 25 June [1789]

I've not yet received an accurate map of the necessary places and so, Your Most Gracious Majesty, am even now unable to present a system for the borders. I have ordered, however, a stone castle constructed, by Turkish prisoners brought from Moldavia, on the Bug at Sokal, from where ship travel begins downstream. Another will be constructed on the Vitovka, where a monastery is also planned.

My civil behavior toward the Poles so frightened the Prussians that they have turned to playing dirty tricks on me personally. Lucchesini[1] has secretly composed a libel, which I'm enclosing herewith, and it only makes me laugh. Nevertheless, order, Your Majesty, that their new envoy[2] be treated most kindly. Bring about a change in the Prussian King, find ways to make them hope to gain our friendship, and in so doing free your hands. Then you will do what you want with them, and will punish them as you please. We must prepare ourselves against Poland. I am increasing the Black Sea Cossacks as much as possible. Indeed, we must prepare arms for any possible situation. So as to hide my intentions, I shall order them from Tula as if they were intended for the Cossacks formed out of the petty townsmen and coachmen. We need a great deal of such weapons since all the weapons were confiscated from everyone in Poland belonging to our faith.[3] I hope to complete transporting the magazines soon, which will be followed by the withdrawal of our troops from Poland.

Some of the regiments have arrived here at the Bug, some are nearby. Grain is being brought. Once everything has arrived, I'll go to take up position. The Cossacks acted gallantly near Bender.[4]

I, thank God, am well. Prince Württemberg[5] has arrived and is most civil and compliant. I don't know whether Count Saltykov[6] has departed, but he must set out.

[. . .] Farewell, Your Most Gracious Majesty, I remain till death your most loyal and most grateful subject

Prince Potemkin-Tavrichesky

[. . .]

---

1. Marquis Giralamo Lucchesini (1751–1825) was the Prussian ambassador to Poland from 1789. His efforts to undermine Potemkin and the pro-Russia party in Poland were successful and resulted in the Prusso-Polish alliance signed on 18 (29) March 1790.

2. Count Bernhard von der Goltz was made ambassador to Russia in 1789.

3. Following an uprising in 1768, Polish authorities relieved the Orthodox inhabitants of Polish Ukraine of all their weapons. Potemkin began stockpiling weapons for them in the event of an attack by the Poles and Prussians.

4. A small party of Cossacks managed to defeat nearly 3,000 Turks who had attacked a convoy bearing Turkish prisoners.

5. The brother of Grand Duchess Maria Fyodorovna, Major-General Prince Karl Friedrich Alexander of Württemberg fought in that year's campaign under Potemkin.

6. Although he had been given orders to depart for the Caucasus, General-in-Chief Ivan Saltykov lingered in St. Petersburg, causing considerable confusion.

380. CATHERINE TO POTEMKIN   [In French]

[29 June 1789]

Apothegm

One must tell one's intimate friend things as they are. On 18 June, upon leaving the table (N.B. it was a Monday) Count Mamonov came to tell me that I no longer treated him as well as before, that I didn't respond to the questions he had posed to me at table, that he wasn't pleased that a lot of people, who had noticed this, were making faces, and that he was tired of the role he was playing. It wasn't difficult to respond. I said to him that had my conduct toward him changed, this wouldn't be at all surprising considering that since the month of September he had behaved in such a manner as to bring about such a change; that he had said and repeated to me that other than attachment he had no other sentiments for me; that he had impeded all of mine and that if they no longer were the same he might lay the blame for this on himself, having suffocated them, so to speak, with his own hands; that I didn't hear his questions, and that I could not be responsible for the facial expressions of others, assuming they were not simply figments of his imagination. To this he said to me: you acknowledge, then, that you no longer have the same feelings for me. The same answer to this question on my part. In response he said to me: then it's necessary that I now act accordingly. My reply: you'll do what you deem necessary. Upon which he entreated me to give him advice on what he ought to do. I replied that I would think it over, and then he left. A quarter of an hour later he wrote to inform me that he could foresee all the troubles and humiliations and contempt to which he would be exposed, and once more he asked for my advice. I answered that as he had hardly followed my advice till now, so I was not about to risk giving him any at present; but seeing that he begged me for it, I would tell him that a splendid way out of this affair might present itself, that Count Bruce would be on duty next Sunday, that I would order him to bring his daughter,[1] that Anna Nikitichna[2] was here, and that I would do my best to put in a good word for him and to obtain for him the richest heiress in the entire Empire, and that the father, as I believed, would willingly consent to this. I believed to be doing something agreeable to all interested parties.

I received in reply to this note a written confession from Count Mamonov in which he confesses to me that he has been in love with Princess Shcherbatova[3] for a year and requests my formal permission to marry.[4] I nearly collapsed from shock, and I had still not recovered when he entered my room, fell at my feet and confessed to me his entire intrigue, his assignations, his correspondence and his secret dealings with her. I said to him that he had only to do what he desired, that I did not stand in the way of anything, that I was only offended that for one whole year instead of deceiving me he hadn't told me the truth, and that if he had he would have spared me, and him too, much grief and worry. He had nothing to say to this, but desired that Anna Nikitichna be called. She came and scolded him in a way that I've never seen anyone scolded in my entire life. The following day he requested that I make some promises, which I carried out on Wednesday.[5] Then he requested a wedding, which will take place on Sunday, 1 July; Lent does not permit them to wed any sooner. But what is so odd is that the fiancé and the fiancée do nothing but cry, and neither one nor the other leaves their chambers. The newlyweds are leaving for Moscow the day after the wedding. I was the one who demanded this, for I could foresee the moment when he would desire to stay here despite his marriage. And if I may speak the truth, there are some peculiar contradictions in his behavior, of which I have almost certain proof. As for me, I seek ways to amuse myself; I had believed that I could win him back, but I always foresaw that this expedient could be dangerous.

Next week I shall tell you more with regard to a certain Blackie.[6] Whether we shall make each other's acquaintance may well depend entirely upon me, but I shall undertake this only as a final resort. Farewell, take care of yourself.

The other day I called for Ribaupierre,[7] who was his confidant for a year. I found him silent and trembling. I said to him that they had been wrong to trick and deceive me with all this for an entire year and, what is more, not to have confided even in you. After this I recalled all your words, my friend. You said many things that have remained in my mind. For example, "There isn't any little amour, is there?" And after that you asked me: "Are you not jealous of Princess Shcherbatova?" And a hundred times you repeated to me: "Oh, matushka, to hell with him."[8] And you never gave me the least hope when I complained. But, if you knew of this love, why were you not frank with me? This would have caused me much grief at the time, but would have cured me for certain, for I have never been a tyrant to anyone. It's true that at that time there was no prospect of Blackie. Tell me, did you or did you not know of the intrigue? If you knew of it, I shall think you concealed it from me to protect my feelings, but you did wrong; you should have told me. Farewell, I kiss you with all my heart.

---

1. Count Yakov Bruce's daughter, Yekaterina, was only thirteen years old at the time.

2. Naryshkina.

3. "Shcherbatova" in Russian.

4. The empress's adjutant-generals and maids-of-honor had to receive her permission to marry. Princess Daria Fyodorovna Shcherbatova (1762–1801) had been raised at court by her aunt. As a young girl, she had written to Potemkin requesting that she be made a maid-of-honor, which he helped her to become in 1787.

5. Catherine betrothed the couple herself on 20 June. Around this time she gave Mamonov 2,250 serfs and 100,000 rubles.

6. Platon Aleksandrovich Zubov (1767–1822).

7. Mamonov's confidant, François de Ribaupierre. After Mamonov's marriage, Ribaupierre left court to join Potemkin's army. He died heroically at the siege of Ismail.

8. Quoted words of Potemkin in Russian.

381. POTEMKIN TO CATHERINE

[5 July 1789][1]

Your Most Gracious Majesty, nothing is more necessary than your peace; and as it is more precious to me than anything, so I always told you not to try to get to the bottom of everything. I also gave you hints about his attraction to Shcherbatova, however, you told me something quite different about her. In time the details of this intrigue will come to light.

I am in your favor, and so under no circumstances do I expect any harm to come to me, however, the wretches aligned against me are indefatigable in their villainy. They will, of course, try anything. Beloved matushka, free me from such vexations: but for peace, I must also have a free head.

I am just, by no means do I consider Count Bezborodko my ill-wisher, just the opposite;[2] there are, however, many others.

Count Pyotr Aleksandrovich is not leaving Moldavia, I don't understand this mystery. Farewell, beloved matushka, I impatiently await news from the north. For my entire life I remain

your most loyal and most grateful subject

Prince Potemkin-Tavrichesky

---

1. A response to Catherine's missing letter of 20 June.

2. Although Bezborodko and Potemkin remained essentially allies and shared similar views (most importantly on foreign affairs), the former had long resented the power of Potemkin's latest protégé, Mamonov.

382. CATHERINE TO POTEMKIN

6 July 1789

My true friend, Prince Grigory Aleksandrovich. I have received your letters of 25 June from Olviopol, and this courier is bringing you my answers and resolutions concerning affairs. I haven't the slightest doubt that you disdain the Polish or, better said, Prussian libel. I received Goltz warmly, and he is more modest than his predecessor. Count Saltykov has almost reached Moscow, and I shall urge him on from there. Just as Nassau moves forward with the galley fleet, so do the Swedes retreat in equal measure. In about six days, I think, the fleets will meet up. Having quarreled with Denisov, Mikhelson has reported sick, and my Grenadiers are so angry at Mikhelson they are calling him a traitor.[1]

After marrying Princess Shcherbatova on Sunday, Count Aleksandr Matveevich Dmitriev-Mamonov departed on Monday with his spouse for his parents, and were I to tell you everything that happened during these two weeks, you would say he has gone completely mad; even his friend and confidant Ribaupierre[2] himself says he's acting just like a madman: imaginés Vous qu'il y avait des traces, qu'il avait envie de rester avec sa femme à la cour comme ci-devant, enfin mille contradictions et idées contradictives,[3] and bizarre behavior such that even those closest to him do not excuse him. I'm enclosing herewith a letter of recommendation to you from a most innocent soul, who possesses the best possible disposition along with a good heart and an agreeable turn of mind.[4] I know that you love me and won't insult me in any way. Imagine for yourself in what fatal state for my health I might find myself without this person. Adieu, mon Ami, caress us, so that we might be utterly merry. Anna Nikitichna acted like a very good friend toward me and did not leave my side till yesterday.

---

1. Highly decorated hero of Russia's wars against the Turks and protegé of Potemkin, Don Cossack Fyodor Petrovich Denisov (1738–1803) was transferred from the south to Finland in 1789. Lieutenant-General Mikhelson quarreled with Denisov after the latter had to rescue Mikhelson and his men following a botched attack the previous month. Mikhelson was forced to resign his command and then Potemkin transferred him to his army.

2. Ribaupierre had been called back to court from the army by Catherine, who wished to learn from him of his role in the affair.

3. "imagine, there were signs that he desired to remain at court with his wife just as before; in short, a thousand contradictions and contradictory ideas,"

4. The letter was probably from Platon Zubov.

383. CATHERINE TO POTEMKIN

14 July 1789

My true friend, Prince Grigory Aleksandrovich. I received yesterday your letters of 5 July from Olviopol. I'm curious to know what news you'll receive from a certain personage by way of the messenger you sent to him in Poland.[1] Concerning the Prussian King, it seems everything possible is being done to restrain him and to soothe his anger. After you remove the magazines from Poland, he will have to dream up new lies and slander in order to incite the Poles.[2]

The Swedes have now been driven back to Anjala, and all that remains is to hound them out of the post at Kymmenegard.[3]

In response to your second letter,[4] which I received from Nikolai Ivanovich Saltykov, I shall say to you that I recalled all of your words and what you told me during the winter and spring, however, I acknowledge that there is a good deal of inconsistency here. Ribaupierre knew about everything, he and his wife's brother arranged the match.[5] I don't know whether or not he spoke candidly to you about this, however, I remember that once you told me that Ribaupierre said to you that his friend deserved to be banished from me, which surprised me. If you learned of this in winter, why did you not tell me then? This would have put an end to much affliction and he would have long since been married.

I have never been anyone's tyrant and I hate coercion, est il possible que Vous m'ayés méconnue jusqu'à ce point et que dans Votre esprit la générosité de mon caractère Vous ait échappée et que Vous m'ayés cru un vilain égoiste, Vous m'auriés guérie tout d'un coup en me disant la vérité.[6]

You speak the truth when you write that you are in my favor to such an extent that there are no circumstances that could inflict harm upon you. Please keep this trust in me; it's precious to me and I have earned it. Of course, your evildoers cannot have any success with me, mais, mon Ami, ne soyés pas aussi ombrageux sans aucune raison et mettés-Vous au dessus des ombrages minutieux.[7] I'll, of course, do everything possible to spare you from any disappointment. And as for you, comfort me, caress us.

N.B. We have a good heart and a most agreeable disposition, which is free of malice and perfidy, et un désir très déterminé de bien faire.[8] We have four rules and try hard to preserve them, namely: to be loyal, modest, devoted and grateful to the extreme, avec cela ce Noiraud a de fort beaux yeux et ne manque pas de lecture, en un mot il me plaît et aucune sorte d'ennui jusqu'ici ne s'est glissé entre nous; au contraire voilà la quatrième semaine qui se passe très agréablement.[9]

I ordered Count Bezborodko to drive Field Marshal Rumiantsev out of Jassy: they know better how than I. This is the second installment of his Danzig stay.[10]

Farewell, my friend. Sorry if my letter and your having to read it bored you.

---

1. A reference to the letter Catherine sent to the Potockis.

2. As a gesture to the Poles, Potemkin offered to move all Russian magazines from Poland and not to send any more transports through their territory.

3. Russian troops, under the command of Denisov and General Bogdan Fyodorovich Knorring (1746–1825), had made significant, though temporary, gains fighting the Swedes in Finland.

4. Letter 381. Potemkin had written another letter that same day concerning purely official matters.

5. Mamonov and Shcherbatova had met in the St. Petersburg home of Ribaupierre and his wife, Agrafena Aleksandrovna, a maid-of-honor at court and the daughter of General Aleksandr Bibikov. Her younger brother referred to here was Aleksandr.

6. "is it possible that you did not know me to such an extent and that the generosity of my character escaped you and that you believed me to be a vile egoist. You would have cured me all at once by telling me the truth."

7. "but, my friend, do not be so suspicious for no reason and place yourself above petty suspicions."

8. "and a very determined desire to do good." The compliments in this paragraph refer to Platon Zubov.

9. "along with this Blackie has rather beautiful eyes and is well read; in a word, I like him and not the slightest tension has crept in between us. On the contrary, it has been four weeks now and things are still very pleasant."

10. In command of troops fighting Prussia during the Seven Years' War when Catherine seized the throne, Rumiantsev had refused to swear the oath of loyalty to her. After being relieved of command, he stayed on for a time in Danzig, refusing to return to Russia.

384. POTEMKIN TO CATHERINE

Olviopol. 18 July [1789]

Beloved matushka![1]

Vous me nommés Votre ami intime, c'est vrai dans toute l'éntendue du terme:[2] be certain that I'm faithfully devoted to you. None of these strange happenings surprise me, for though I've spent little time with him, still I know him better than others. Mais par ma coutume d'apprécier les choses je ne me suis jamais trompé en lui: c'est un mélange d'indolence et d'égoisme. Par ce dernier il étoit Narcisse à l'outrance. Ne pensant qu'à lui, il exigeait tous sans paier d'aucun retour; étant paresseux il oublioit même les bienséances; n'importe que la chose n'ait aucun prix, mais sitôt qu'elle lui ploit, selon lui, elle doit avoir tout le prix du monde. Voilà les droits de la Princesse Sczerbatof.[3] Is it possible to appear so foolishly and so strangely before all of society? As things come to light, so the signs are becoming more visible: this little amour had been going on for a long time. Upon hearing last year that he was sending her fruit from the table, I immediately made a note of this, however, since I didn't have concrete evidence, matushka, I couldn't confidently present you with this. But I did hint at it. My benefactress, it grieved me to see you, but more intolerable for me were his rudeness and feigned illnesses. Be certain, he will tire of his Dulcinea. Even before this he had difficulty paying for things, and she's thirty thousand in debt, and he spends money very begrudgingly. They're a pack of deceivers; so many various shams they cooked up in order to conceal this intrigue. Matushka, you're not vengeful, and so I recommend that without any malice you send his friend and mentor[4] to Switzerland, for example, to serve as our minister there, pourquoi le retenir ici avec sa femme qui est une exécrable intrigante? Vous avés très bien fait de l'expédier à Moscou, mais ne croyés pas, matushka, aux conjectures que Vous faites: il n'y a rien du tout, pourquoi Vous lui faites tant d'honneur?[5] I have written him a short but rather strong letter. God grant you health and much needed calm and, what's more, a clear head so you can solve these many problems. For the most part, matters here are not going poorly, so long as the Turks do not head for the Straits of Yenikale. For till the troops arrive at Taman, that would not be good for our defenseless ships near Taganrog. I have used everything possible for their defense. Their landing forces are not dangerous, but I simply fear losing our ships.[6]

Having covered seven hundred versts in an unbearable heat, I'm extremely exhausted. All the troops are now on the other side of the Bug. Farewell, beloved matushka, God grant you all the best, and in expectation of the promised letter I remain till death

your loyal and most grateful subject
Prince Potemkin-Tavrichesky

[. . .]

---

1. Potemkin's reply to Letter 380.

2. "You call me your intimate friend, this is true in every sense of the word:"

3. "But given my way of judging things, I never misjudged him: he is a combination of sloth and selfishness. Because of the latter he became an extreme Narcissus. Thinking of no one but himself, he demanded everything without giving anything in return; being lazy he even forgot decency. It is not important that the object is worthless, for as soon as he takes a liking to it, it must be, according to him, the most valuable thing in the world. Such are the rights of Princess Shcherbatova."

4. Ribaupierre.

5. "why keep him here with his wife who is an execrable schemer? You did very well in sending him [Mamonov] to Moscow, but do not put, matushka, any stock in your conjectures: there is nothing to them, so why do him this honor?"

6. Potemkin feared the Turkish fleet would intercept two Russian ships built at Taganrog that were bound for Sevastopol. He sent troops to help defend them, and they passed safely through the Straits of Yenikale and met up with the rest of the fleet at Sevastopol in September.

385. POTEMKIN TO CATHERINE

30 July [1789]. Olviopol

Mon Dieu, que je Vous dois pour Vos attentions vraiments Maternelles.[1]

My beloved matushka, could I not sincerely love the man who pleases you? You can be certain that I shall feel a sincere friendship for him because of his attachment to you.[2] Matushka, do not think that I knew of this vile intrigue and concealed it. I did not have convincing proofs, although I was firmly certain of it myself: their various machinations were suspicious to me, and I was extremely surprised by his true friend's[3] desire—completely contrary to his own advantage—that he be sent away. The entire family[4] was in on the secret, including General Apraksin.[5] Tell me, my benefactress, how did you not deign to notice? He sent her fruit from your table, and when he went upstairs he always exhibited the greatest lethargy, yet in the morning he would eagerly run to and fro. Now I hear that she would meet him in the morning, and that they kept a house on Vasilievsky Island pour rendez-vous.

Thank God, the united forces soundly defeated the enemy near Fokshany.[6] Our losses were small. Brigadiers Levashov and Westfalen[7] were lightly wounded. The Austrian Colonel Auersperg was killed. General Suvorov lauds their Barko Hussar Regiment.[8] Pavel Sergeevich[9] will arrive at Dubossary on the first of August together with two corps of Chasseurs, 10 squadrons of cavalry and a thousand Cossacks, and the remaining troops are approaching Balta.

Once I'm with the fleet, I'll decide how to bring it out and how to approach Khadjibey by land so as to seize it and to provide support for our vessels there. This matter requires, however, great skill and bravery. Placing my hope in God, I have called upon His help and shall try to entirely surround the enemy. I've received word from Taganrog that two battalions of Chasseurs have reached the ships and other vessels, and I am now less worried about matters on that side. The ships' cannons have begun to arrive. I'm here all by myself. Tomorrow I'm leaving for the fleet to take care of a good many matters and shall gallop off straightaway from there to the army, which I intend to catch up with within two-days' march of Balta. My piles, however, are giving me a bad headache.

Matushka, God grant you health. My sincere compliments to Anna Nikitichna for her having stayed by you.

Farewell, my benefactress, I remain till death

your most loyal and most grateful subject
Prince Potemkin-Tavrichesky

[. . .]

---

1. "My God, how much I owe you for your truly maternal care."

2. Over a month had passed since Catherine had written Potemkin her "Apothegm," and yet she still had no response from him about the new favorite. Potemkin finally forced himself to make polite reference to Platon Zubov.

3. Ribaupierre.

4. The Ribaupierres and Bibikovs.

5. Major-General Stepan Stepanovich Apraksin (1747–1827) was a friend of Mamonov.

6. On 21 July, 17,000 Russian and Austrian troops under the command of Suvorov and Prince Coburg defeated 30,000 Turks near Fokshany in Moldavia.

7. Fyodor Ivanovich Levashov (1752–after 1817); Friedrich von Westfalen (1749–1798).

8. Count Auersperg hailed from a prominent aristocratic family. Major-General Baron Felix Barko (1756–1829) commanded a Hussar regiment bearing his name.

9. Potemkin.

386. CATHERINE TO POTEMKIN

From Tsarskoe Selo. 5 August 1789

My true friend, Prince Grigory Aleksandrovich. You'll learn of the state of affairs of the Finnish war from the rescript signed by me today.

I am quite pleased with your letter of 18 July from Olviopol. Your arguments are just. I now impatiently await your answers to the letter I sent you avec certaine incluse qui me tient fortement au coeur à cause du fort aimable caractère du personnage.[1] Your making his big brother one of your orderlies has made this one unspeakably happy. He writes and boasts of your nephews' kindnesses.[2] He has a younger brother, who is here now on guard duty in his place: an absolute child, an extremely handsome young lad.[3] He's a lieutenant in the Horse Guards. With time, help us bring him up in the world. Il n'y a rien encore qui presse et nous sommes très modestes et point du tout impatients, car nous sommes très occupés, mais nous aimons cet enfant qui réelement est très intéressant, il n'a que 19 ans.[4]

I'm well and merry and have revived like a fly in summer. We are now awaiting news from everywhere, and I hope that affairs will soon take a turn to your pleasing. May God grant you health and every happiness and pleasure to your heart's content. Farewell, my friend. I love you like my soul, and I know you love me too.

[...]

---

1. "with a certain enclosure that is exceedingly close to my heart due to this person's very pleasant character." Catherine eagerly awaited Potemkin's response to Platon Zubov's first letter to him included in the empress's letter of 6 July. The prince replied in a letter dated 12 August.

2. Potemkin chose the eldest of the Zubov brothers, Nikolai Aleksandrovich (1763–1805), to be one of his orderly officers, together with the prince's nephews Aleksandr Samoilov, Vasily Engelhardt, and N. P. Vysotsky.

3. The youngest and most gifted of the Zubov brothers, Valerian Aleksandrovich (1771–1804) served valiantly in the Second Russo-Turkish War.

4. "As of yet there is nothing urgent, and we are very modest and not at all impatient, because we are very busy. But we love this child who truly is very interesting; he's only nineteen years old."

387. CATHERINE TO POTEMKIN

12 August 1789. From Petersburg

My true friend Prince Grigory Aleksandrovich. I was most gladdened to receive your courier of 30 July from Olviopol and immediately arranged to have a service performed on Thursday, that is, two days after the courier's arrival, and I myself went straight to the Kazan Church upon arriving in the city, where we gave our thanks to God with genuflection for the gift of victory at Fokshany, and everyone is ineffably gladdened by this victory. May God grant you successes and victories everywhere, which you warrant through your examples of zeal for me and our common cause, through your fervor and your labors. Be well and safe, that's what I sincerely wish for you with all my heart.

Your enclosed letter of reply I immediately handed to its intended recipient,[1] and it was received with fiery eyes filled with happiness, and since his heart and mind are comprised solely of feelings, so does he consider it his duty to be both grateful and sincere. He will not fail to express this himself.

Of the intrigue that lasted for an entire year and ended with a wedding, there's nothing more to say. I purposely saved his last letters concerning this matter, in which he places God's judgement on those people who led him to this, and in which he writes as if his head is all a muddle. Ah, forget about him; I'm only sorry he didn't reveal all this to me sooner.

I thank you for the beautiful stamp that Platon Aleksandrovich handed to me from you. I am sending this letter to you through him. [. . .] I am most satisfied with the actions you have taken. I am well and much merrier than when you left me, although matters here are not going as one might desire.[2] Still, nothing bad's happened.

Farewell, God be with you. I love you with all my heart, as my truest friend.

I conveyed your compliments to Anna Nikitchna, and she begs her compliments to you.

---

1. To please Catherine, Potemkin wrote to Platon Zubov.

2. Catherine chose not to inform Potemkin of the Swedish victory on 8–9 July over Major-General Baron Wilhelm von Schultz, which cost Russia 600 men, or of Admiral Chichagov's indecisive engagement with the Swedish fleet on 15 July.

388. POTEMKIN TO CATHERINE

New Dubossary. 21 August [1789]

Your Most Gracious Majesty, upon arriving at the Dniester I didn't find a crossing ready for me, but for two small ferries. I had to build a bridge. My fate is to prepare things for everyone, though no one does for me. Had this been done earlier, I think we'd have a strong fleet on the Dniester by now that would be of great benefit to our service, and many volunteers for it would have been found. The same thing goes for the Pruth. I shall order them built in both places. I have already ordered wood prepared.

The enemy is gathering at Ismail and Brailov. I'll watch in which direction he intends to move, and then, after estimating the time it will take and seeking God's help, shall finish with the one and then turn against the other.[1] Pray see from Prince Coburg's reports that after Fokshany he is making a show of bravery against Walachia, and in a different location against Brailov. Yet his actions are deceiving, for if he's not successful, then he'll slip away into Transylvania near Buzau and abandon us. It nearly happened already, and yet even with all his derring-do he fears losing Khotin.[2] He also speaks here of his borders, even those with Galicia.

The Turkish fleet is positioned in such a manner that were our flotilla to move it would have to pass between their entire line and a shoal at the slightest distance.[3] But I shan't take such a big risk, and shall look for other means.

The Poles do not stop persecuting us in every possible manner. Yes, it's truly awkward to be stuck between two enemies. Moreover, the desertions are creating much disturbance: they are enticing our men to join them. They are constantly playing dirty tricks on me in my villages, and I am certain they would like to find a pretext to clash with us. I would sell them for a song so as to be rid of the nuisance, but I don't wish to since these lands are a great resource for us and, depending on circumstances, people, about whom I shall make a special report, might leave there for other places.

My benefactress, I admit that I'm tired as a dog from all this running around. Count Pyotr Aleksandrovich is still here. He should be ashamed of himself. This cannot help but cause rumors and talk that, although empty, nevertheless are harmful.

You deign to mention Platon Aleksandrovich's brothers. I shall not fail to give the one here opportunities to earn merit and shall not impede his advancement. My nephews share my disposition, and they will, of course, always get along well with him. Write to me about the other one: what about him could differ and so prevent his being promoted?

My beloved matushka, my love for you is unparalleled, and I truly feel utter gratitude toward you. I'm preparing for you my thoughts on the current state of affairs. I am sending them to you in complete candor. Accept them should they meet with your approval, but I beg you, for God's sake, don't be angry. For you know it is your choice whether to accept or simply to disregard them. However, I am sending you what is in my heart.[4] As God is my witness, I'm so weak I wasn't able to finish, and am enraged because there's no transport across the water.

[. . .]

Farewell, my beloved matushka, I kiss your tender feet.

Your most loyal and most grateful subject
Prince Potemkin-Tavrichesky

1. Grand Vizier Jehâze Hasan Pasha (served June–December 1789) intended to send a smaller corps against Ismail and his main force of 80,000 against Prince Coburg near Fokshany.

2. Prince Coburg commanded Austrian troops operating in conjunction with Russian forces, chiefly Suvorov's, against the Turks. Potemkin considered him, like most of the other Austrian commanders, simultaneously incompetent yet arrogant.

3. The Turkish fleet inhibited the oared flotilla under José de Ribas from providing support for Russian ground forces preparing to attack Khadjibey.

4. Potemkin thought at the time that Prussia could be neutralized by promising an alliance with Russia and by assuring the Prussian king that Russia was willing to make peace with Sweden based on the *status quo ante bellum.*

389. CATHERINE TO POTEMKIN

6 September 1789

My true friend, Prince Grigory Aleksandrovich. I have received your letters of 21 and 24 August[1] from Dubossary. They found me still a bit weak from a spasmodic colic which lasted two whole weeks. I am now fully recovered, much of which I attribute to the camomile pillows that the Saint-Petersburg Metropolitan recommended I place around my entire body.

Having spoken of myself, I'll now answer your letters. What's there to marvel at in God's having appointed you to make arrangements or to prepare things for everyone while for you no one got even a crossing ready? In you alone there's more zeal for the common cause and for my service than in all others, and you're cleverer as well. May God help you in all your undertakings. I am quite at ease with your affairs, for last year's campaign completely justified my thoughts in regard to you and my trust. And you write to me often and in detail et par conséquant je suis sans inquiétude de Votre côte.[2] I'm not surprised that Coburg is making a show of bravery after the victory: he's not accustomed to success. Ils ressemblent en cela aux parvenus, qui sont étonnés de se voir des beaux meubles et qui ne cessent d'en parler et de les admirer.[3]

They say that the Turkish fleet is short of men, and that Bulgakov has been freed, though it's possible that neither is true.[4] I desire with all my heart that you will vanquish the enemy and surmount all obstacles. We must tolerate the Poles' dirty tricks till the moment is right.

I am thinking of writing Rumiantsev that his presence in Moldavia is giving rise to rumors harmful to my and our common affairs, and that I desire and demand that he leave Moldavia. I now await your thoughts on affairs; you know my principles: never disavow that which is beneficial, as long as it is in keeping with the honor and dignity of the Empire. [. . .] The French unrest is spreading to Brabant and Holland and is already worrying the court in Berlin. You'll soon hear that it has even shown up in the Prussian provinces, for the people are hungry and the troops are foreign.[5]

I can imagine that you were gladdened by our galleys' victory. You will see from the details sent to you that our loss was less than we thought in the heat of the moment. The Swedes left Högfors and Kymmenegard, but no way has yet been found to compel Pushkin to take advantage of the opportunity and to inflict upon the Swedes the greatest possible harm. I'm very tired of this indecisive oaf; he is indeed incapable of exercising command.[6]

[. . .]

Thanks for your kindness toward Platon Aleksandrovich and his brother. I don't know the brother who is there with you, but the one here behaves as well as could possibly be desired. Il est d'une humeur égale et très aimable and an exceptionally good and noble heart, en un mot, il gagne à être connu.

Adieu, mon Ami, portés Vous bien et soyés assuré de toute mon amitié.[7]

---

1. Potemkin wrote Catherine on 24 August upon hearing the good news about the First Battle of Svensksund.

2. "and consequently I am not anxious about you."

3. "In this they resemble those upstarts who marvel at their fine furniture and do not stop talking about and admiring it."

4. Bulgakov was not released until November.

5. Revolt broke out in the Austrian Netherlands that autumn, and opposition to the stadtholder in Holland grew as well, which Frederick William II and revolutionary parties in France took advantage of.

6. Prince Nassau defeated the Swedish oared flotilla on 13 August at the First Battle of Svensksund. The victory was not as great as it might have been because the indecisive Musin-Pushkin, in command of the ground forces, allowed Gustav III to escape encirclement.

7. "He has an even and very pleasant temperament [. . .] in a word, he grows on you. Farewell, my friend, take care of yourself and be assured of all my affection."

390. CATHERINE TO POTEMKIN

6 September 1789

My dear friend, Prince Grigory Aleksandrovich. Platon Aleksandrovich is very humble, a quality which I, however, find worthy of reward; but you decide—you're the head of the Corps of the Chevaliers-Gardes—do you not need a cornet? I remember you wrote a brief report about this. So first, do send me something of the sort.[1] Shouldn't we give our child a Hussar escort? Write me what you think, however, we've got a worthy man here, and I don't want to insult him in any way. Our child is 19 years old, take note of this. Mais j'aime beaucoup cet enfant et il m'est fort attaché, pleurant comme un enfant[2] if he's not permitted to come see me. Make whatever arrangements you see fit. But for you, I put my trust in no one.

A rumor about Count Mamonov is being spread that he's supposedly going to live separately with his father, and that the old folks aren't pleased with their daughter-in-law. Maria Vasilievna Shkurina has recently asked to leave court, and I have let her go: they say they've invited her to live with them.[3] Adieu, mon Ami, portés Vous bien et aimés moi comme je Vous aime.[4]

---

1. Potemkin acceded to her request on 22 September.

2. "But I love the child very much; he is very attached to me and cries like a child"

3. The daughter of one of Catherine's long-trusted servants, Maria Vasilievna Shkurina (1755–1824) was a maid-of-honor. She was forced to leave court for her part in aiding the affair between Mamonov and Shcherbatova, but not before Catherine gave her 12,000 rubles toward her dowry. She was unhappy living with the couple and left them for a convent.

4. "Farewell, my friend, take care of yourself and love me as I love you."

391. POTEMKIN TO CATHERINE

22 September [1789]. Kaushany

Your Most Gracious Majesty! My best wishes to you, my benefactress, on the anniversary of your coronation, on the day that pleased me so.

A strong storm prevented our fleet from departing, and it just barely spared the small vessels from damage, although some repairs were necessary. Otherwise, the entire Turkish flotilla would be in our hands. Perhaps God will still give us something better. I'm now leaving for Khadjibey by way of Palanka, which I've ordered occupied.[1] I'm gathering all the troops, except those beyond the Pruth, near Bender, and then we'll see what God gives us. I'm preparing warm boots for 12 thousand men and shall act throughout the entire winter. But matushka, please don't let anyone know about this.

I'll say to you in the words of Lomonosov, as he advised Peter the Great: "With the hand and mind were the impertinent and smooth-tongued overthrown!"[2] Matushka, not solely with the hand, but also with the mind must the Prussian King be pacified, for should he notice our bad disposition toward him in advance, he won't now stop causing us harm, and then we shall never be finished with the Turks. Give him some hope—he won't hinder us from reconciling, and then you will do whatever you want with him. Our ally too can be made to agree to this; and then the Poles will have to be pacified, but now is not the time to think about that. Be certain that I shall do everything possible here.

Till death your most loyal and most grateful subject
Prince Potemkin-Tavrichesky

P.S. I'll soon send a detailed communiqué on the Suvorov affair;[3] Matushka, he indeed merits your favor and it was an important battle. I have been thinking about what to give him, but haven't thought of anything. Peter the Great conferred the title of Count for nothing. What if the word "Rymniksky" were added to his name? The battle was on that river.

[. . .]

1. The Russians took Khadjibey on 14 September. Heavy seas kept the Russian fleet from attacking the Turks.

2. Potemkin quotes from Mikhail Lomonosov's epic poem "Peter the Great" (1756–1761).

3. Potemkin had received a brief report on Suvorov's dramatic victory over the grand vizier at the River Rymnik on 11 September.

392. POTEMKIN TO CATHERINE

Belgrade-on-Dniester. 2 October [1789]

Your Most Gracious Majesty. The Belgrade fortress is constructed entirely of stone, its walls are high, and its moat is deeper, I think, than any other in the world. It has large supplies of everything. I can assure you that it is both the best of all Turkish fortresses and in the best condition.[1]

Had it not been for Suvorov, the Austrians would have been routed.[2] The Turks were smashed by this Russian's name. The Austrians had already run away, having lost their cannons, but Suvorov arrived in time and saved the day. This is yet one more time that he has rescued them, but little thanks. They demand, rather, that I give them Suvorov and his corps permanently so that together with him they can pour into Walachia. They are not very gladdened by our successes, and they want to acquire lands with our blood, and expect us to be content with nothing but air. Matushka, be assured, they are a burden. All the Hungarians are inclined to rebel, and they love us, but not the Austrians.

Our sole concern now is Bender. I am sending as many as thirty men, inhabitants of Bender who were captured here, to describe everything they have seen. It would be extremely good if we could take it without suffering any losses. Given its proximity to Poland, this town is harmful to us, and once it's ours, then we can devote everything to the offensive.

Beloved matushka, be kind to Aleksandr Vasilievich. His bravery surpasses all probability. Defeating the Vizier was an important business. Show him favor and in so doing disgrace the parasitic generals, many of whom aren't worth their salaries. I'm dispatching a courier tomorrow with a detailed description of this battle with the Vizier. Farewell, beloved matushka. God grant you health, I, however, am truly exhausted.

Your most loyal and most grateful subject

Prince Potemkin-Tavrichesky

---

1. Akkerman (Belgrade-on-Dniester) surrendered to Potemkin's army on 30 September.
2. A reference to the battle at the Rymnik.

393. CATHERINE TO POTEMKIN

4 October 1789

My friend, Prince Grigory Aleksandrovich. I thank you for your best wishes on the day of my coronation. It's a pity that a storm impeded our fleet. Everyone is most gladdened by the successes of the army under your command, and we impatiently await the details. I beg God to bless your undertakings against Bender and everywhere else. We're doing everything possible to pacify the Prussian Hercules, or his cudgel rather, and the same goes for England. Not only am I never against peace, but I sincerely desire it.

You'll see from the rescript that I have rewarded Suvorov with the title of Count Suvorov-Rymniksky.[1]

[...]

He's been made a Cornet in the Corps of the Chevaliers-Gardes.[2] And as for Valerian, he had already been released earlier and, I think, has already arrived there. [...]

Farewell, my friend, be well and may God help you.

Your new Cornet of the Chevaliers-Gardes is a reliable man, who so far hasn't been misbehaving. I am very pleased with him, I owe him this testimonial. Be kind to the child and show him the true way. He has a good heart and is of good will.

Adieu, mon Ami, je Vous aime de tout mon coeur.[3]

---

1. In addition, Suvorov was permitted to accept the title of count from Joseph II.
2. Platon Zubov.
3. "Farewell, my friend, I love you with all my heart."

394. POTEMKIN TO CATHERINE

Belgrade-on-Dniester. 5 October [1789]

Your Most Gracious Majesty. I have remained here to put everything in order in anticipation of the regiments coming from Khadjibey which must occupy Yanyk, Palanka, and Belgrade. Then I'll turn to Bender, to that place which is most necessary to us. And also for the sake of calm in our billets, and for the sake of placing our troops on the offensive since we no longer have an enemy in our rear. That town's proximity to Poland also does us no good. Requesting God's help, I shall make use of all my strength to supply them. If there's something that worries me and keeps me from sending them off, it is supplying them with provisions. I am, however, doing everything within my power. My benefactress, you deign to write about Platon Aleksandrovich's brother. Be assured that I'll take the best possible care of him.[1]

I've no news of the fleet. I don't even know where it is. I've sent someone to inquire. The flotilla is suffering greatly in the mouths of the Dniester from the extraordinarily choppy waters. For two straight weeks a head wind has been blowing it back toward Ochakov. Attempts to rescue it are causing me considerable trouble. I cannot bring it into the Dniester since the mouth is too shallow. Farewell, beloved matushka. Till death I remain

your most loyal and most grateful subject
Prince Potemkin-Tavrichesky

---

1. Catherine wrote Potemkin on 22 September recommending to him Valerian Zubov. Zubov took the letter with him and personally delivered it to Potemkin upon his arrival at Belgrade-on-Dniester.

395. POTEMKIN TO CATHERINE

[5 October 1789]

Beloved matushka, Your Most Gracious Majesty! I've just received word that Coburg has been promoted to the rank of Field Marshal, even though the victory was entirely the work of Aleksandr Vasilievich. Your glory, the honor of our arms, and justice demands for him superlative recompense, both for what rightly belongs to him and so that such a distinguished and important deed not be attributed to others. Even if he was not the main commander, still it was a general battle: the Vizier was defeated along with the main army. The Austrians would've been beaten had it not been for Aleksandr Vasilievich. And the military order's statute speaks entirely in his favor.[1] He moved swiftly to rescue our allies, arrived in time, helped them and defeated the enemy. The victory belongs entirely to him, just as I reported earlier. Here is Coburg's letter and his report.[2] Matushka, see to it he doesn't become dejected, encourage him and in so doing strike a blow to those apathetic generals in your service. Suvorov stands alone. Of all my infinite obligations to you, I consider one of my foremost to be doing justice to every person. This duty is one of the most pleasant for me.

How many generals, upon hearing of the enemy's great size, would've moved cautiously and slowly, like a tortoise, whereas he flew like an eagle with a handful of men. He achieved swift victory over the Vizier and his great army. He's here with me now waiting for the chance to march on the Sultan himself wherever he makes a move.

Your most loyal and most grateful subject
Prince Potemkin-Tavrichesky

---

1. According to its statute, the Order of St. George first class was to be awarded for victory in a general battle, that is a field battle or the taking by assault of a fortress of the first rank.

2. Writing to Potemkin, Coburg praised Suvorov's role in the victory at the Rymnik.

396. CATHERINE TO POTEMKIN

5 October 1789

There's a rumor going around town here that Count Mamonov has gone mad in Moscow, but I think it's a lie: people have asked his uncle and he doesn't know a thing about it. If it's true, we ought to thank God that it didn't happen last year. I noticed a good deal of confusion in his speech on the very day of his wedding, but I attributed this to the awkward position he was in at the time. Forgive me, my friend, for burdening you now with having to read these lines what with all your other cares, but consider for yourself, were you here now, then we'd simply talk about it, wouldn't we? I have ordered your chambers tidied up.[1] I was walking around in them and found them so dirty and so nasty, that it just wouldn't be fitting to lead a celebrated warlord into them. I don't know, however, whether or not you'll like the way I ordered them done up. I think they're not bad. Knowing your taste, however, I fear you won't like them. But be that as it may, nevertheless they are finer than any dugout or tent. Adieu, mon Ami, je Vous aime beaucoup, beaucoup.[2]

---

1. In August, Catherine wanted to show Platon Zubov and his brother Valerian the prince's collection of paintings in the Shepilov house. Upon seeing the condition of the rooms, she put off the planned visit and ordered the remodel.

2. "Farewell, my friend, I love you very, very much."

397. CATHERINE TO POTEMKIN

18 October 1789

My true friend, Prince Grigory Aleksandrovich. The description you give of Belgrade-on-Dniester in your letter of 2 October shows how important our recent acquisition was to the Turks. The details of Suvorov's and

Coburg's victory over the Vizier have still not arrived. I think the courier, the one you promised to dispatch on 4 October, has fallen ill along the way. Whatever the Austrians may be and whatever burden we may suffer because of them, nevertheless it will always be incomparably less than that presented by the Prussians, which is fully attended by everything abusive and intolerable in the world imaginable. Mon cher Ami, je parle d'expérience, j'ai vu ce joug malheureusement de fort près et j'ai sauté de joie, Vous en êtes témoin, lorsque j'ai aperçu seulment une petite lueur pour en pouvoir sortir.[1]

My friend, do try to make a beneficial peace with the Turks, a good many troubles will then disappear, and we shall be deferential: we can expect this after your present campaign.

May the Lord God Himself help you take Bender. I'm sending you an engraved portrait of the victor of Ochakov copied from a stone carving. Both the stone and the portrait were made in my Hermitage. I'm sending Aleksandr Vasilievich Suvorov the order, a star, epaulettes and a sword decorated with diamonds, it's quite valuable.[2] Having showered him with diamonds, I think he'll look splendid. It's true there are many parasites. I've been of this opinion for a long time. I'm sorry you're worn out: take care of your health, you know that the state and I need it. Adieu, mon Ami. Christ be with you. Be well and happy.

We are stroking the Prussians, but God alone knows what we must suffer in tolerating their words and deeds which are filled with rudeness and abuse. I am waiting for your reply to my letter on changing command of the Finnish Army, and even though you wrote about appointing Count Ivan Petrovich Saltykov, is it not possible that this cup be passed from the Finnish Army?[3] It seems to me that once again nothing will come of this but obstinacy and stupidity. For in truth, two companies have already been lost, and God forbid there be a third filled with stubborn stupidity. Adieu, mon Ami, je Vous aime de tout mon coeur.[4]

---

1. "My dear friend, I speak from experience. Unfortunately I have seen that yoke from quite close, and I jumped for joy, you were a witness thereof, when I saw the tiniest glimmer of how to escape it."

2. For his victories at Fokshany and Rymnik, Suvorov received, in addition to the titles of count and "Rymniksky," the Order of St. George first class, diamond epaulettes, a ring, and a jeweled sword emblazoned with the words "Conqueror of the Vizier."

3. Catherine's displeasure with Valentin Musin-Pushkin as commander of the Finnish Army led to his being replaced by Count Ivan Saltykov in January 1790, despite the empress's doubts about the latter's ability.

4. "Farewell, my friend, I love you with all my heart."

398. CATHERINE TO POTEMKIN

18 October 1789

My true friend, I am writing my third letter to you today: while writing the first two, Zolotukhin arrived and brought me your letters of 5 October from which I see that you are still in Belgrade, where you're putting everything in order in anticipation of the regiments coming from Khadjibey.[1] I beg God to help you take Bender, and especially without the loss of men, and if, contrary to expectation, there are shortages of sustenance or provisions in places, then may God preserve you by making bread and rusk fall from the sky like rain.

Even though an entire cart has been loaded with diamonds for Count Suvorov, I'm also sending the large cross for the Order of St. George as you requested: he's worthy of it, and I am even more pleased with where you intend to send him. May God grant you health. Coburg's letter does them both honor.

Platon Aleksandrovich thanks you very much for his brother. I do not doubt in the slightest that you will keep your word. And they too are very good men, with kind hearts, and they're attached to me and are by no means dishonest.

I am curious to know, who are the generals with Suvorov who stayed behind because of illness? It seems to me that even your Voinovich at sea is rather reluctant to go forward, however, this isn't meant as a criticism of him: I know his strength and that of the Turks. I wish with all my heart that the flotilla and the fleet will remain whole and healthy. And so, farewell for now, my friend. I am well, so you too be well and safe.

---

1. After finishing Letter 397, Catherine received the detailed reports sent by Potemkin along with Letters 394 and 395 on Suvorov's victory at the Rymnik. The courier, Colonel Vasily Ivanovich Zolotukhin (1758–1792), had distinguished himself at Fokshany and the Rymnik and was highly esteemed by Suvorov.

399. POTEMKIN TO CATHERINE

4 November [1789]. Bender

Your Most Gracious Majesty, Bender too is now at your feet.[1] Were I a braggart, I would say that I'd executed to the letter all the plans for the coming campaign that I presented to you in Petersburg. Yet I must not think too highly of myself. All of our successes were gifts from God. Our brave forces obtained our victories. I only contributed my zeal and labor. Of this I can boast. Another would also boast of the fact that the Austrians carried out a good campaign while acting according to my plan.

Though I am well, I've not yet regained my strength and am extremely weak.[2] I hurry to inform you, beloved matushka, and in three days I'll send a detailed report with Popov. Be kind to my generals and to the troops for their labors and fervor.

[. . .]

I have received letters from the Walachian Hospodar with proposals for an armistice, and a letter from the former Kapudan Pasha.[3] I'll send these as well as my answers along with Popov. Here is my plan regarding Poland as well. Should it be welcomed, then we shall need to make the changes soon.[4]

Matushka, you deign to write about a leader for the Finnish forces. Wait three days, and you will receive everything from Popov. Oh, but I've truly become muddle-headed. I'll respond later to all your gracious missives.

See here now, the young man returns in good health and with good news.[5]

Forgive me, beloved matushka, but one cannot get on with the Pashas of equal rank without a good deal of trouble. I remain till death

your most loyal and most grateful subject
Prince Potemkin-Tavrichesky

P.S. I have sent the diamond star and order to Suvorov. The ring and epaulettes I have kept for a later occasion. I have sent the large ribbon and have informed him of the sword.

[. . .]

---

1. Bender surrendered on 4 November.

2. Potemkin fell ill with fever for several days late in October during a visit to Kishinyov.

3. The Walachian hospodar, Nicholas Mavrogeni, had been fighting for the Ottomans. Gazi Hasan Pasha, the longtime grand admiral, had been relieved of command of the navy and put in charge of the land forces in Moldavia in the spring of 1789. His objective was to retake Ochakov and the Crimea.

4. Hopes for an alliance with Poland fading, Potemkin now suggested using Poland's Orthodox inhabitants in the east and those incorporated into Russia via the First Partition of Poland in 1772 to further Russian interests. Specifically, Potemkin asked Catherine to appoint him grand hetman of a revived hetmanate in order to unite the Cossacks of the region and the Orthodox populace against Catholic Poland. Potemkin drew the inspiration for his plan in part from the seventeenth-century uprising of Hetman Bogdan Khmelnitsky against Poland.

5. Valerian Zubov. He brought Potemkin's letter and report to Catherine.

400. POTEMKIN TO CATHERINE

Bender. 9 November [1789]

Your Most Gracious Majesty. God has given us Bender too for nothing. Overall, the troops displayed fervor. In two months the enemy has been defeated everywhere. Four fortresses large and small have been taken. The acquisition of Bender is very important given the fortress's position in the interior: with every move we made, the greater part of our troops had to remain behind. Its proximity to Poland also tied our hands since it cut off communications with our borders. C'est une forteresse royale,[1] with a strong artillery and garrison. It had been finished off exceedingly well. It's much superior to the previous construction. Everything is new.

Well, matushka, did matters not go according to my plan? The enemy, together with the Vizier, has been made to withdraw almost completely to the requisite side of the Danube. What remains of the enemy facing the Austrians is but a trifle. Pray note from the enclosed list that, together with the Austrians, our losses for the entire campaign were just over five thousand.[2]

I must have someone here for the armistice talks. I would be glad to have Bulgakov, for it's awkward for me to be personally involved in the discussions. A subordinate can often claim a lack of authority, and in this way many things can be settled (without requiring my decision). The Austrians' bombast will present a great obstacle. They have just entered Bucharest and are seizing everything. The Turks, however, will be glad to yield to us, though not to them.[3]

Matushka, I agree with what you deign to write about Voinovich being not very bold.[4] But the fleet is still now out at sea. I have already sent an order that it is to turn away from the Turkish shores. Nonetheless, we have already accomplished much. The squadrons had been divided into three groups, and we united them directly under the enemy's nose. This required winds blowing from various directions. Though there were a great number of them, the Turks fled headlong. Three of their gunboats sank and six were captured. I shall tell it to you in verse:

Nous avons pris neuf lançons
Sans perdre un garçon
Et Benders avec trois pachas
Sans perdre un chat.[5]

Though the verses are irregular, nevertheless it's the truth.

I thank you, matushka, for the ring you sent me on my name-day. It was on that day I occupied Akkerman.

Concerning a general to command in Finland, I mentioned Saltykov because he has the most seniority. But do as you please, and it would now seem awkward for him to be obstinate about this. Shuvalov,[6] who spoiled him and gave him advice, is no longer. But if not him, then order Meller. And along with him Lieutenant-Generals Igelstrom and Anhalt; get rid of Knorring and the former clerk.[7] What good can come when a secretary is in command of an army? As soon as I arrive in Jassy, I'll send some good major-generals.

I must tell the truth: by way of his bravery, skill and good conduct, Aleksandr Nikolaevich[8] is turning out to be a worthy general. What is more, his fervor for you is infinite. Vasily Vasilievich[9] is brave, an excellent master. Your Life-Guards Cuirassier Regiment is perfectly smart and orderly, the horses are first-rate, the men are quite well kept: in a word— it's a worthy regiment [. . .]

---

1. "It is a royal fortress,"

2. Though the number is most likely understated, the allies had indeed paid a relatively small price for the considerable territory acquired.

3. Seeking to assert the Emperor's authority over the Russian empress, the Austrians initially tried to assume control of the peace talks with the Porte. Potemkin and the Turks resisted, and Austria and Russia ended up negotiating separately with the Porte.

4. Catherine had expressed some doubts about Rear Admiral Voinovich in a letter dated 18 October.

5. "We have taken nine lansons / Without losing a boy / And Bender with three pashas / Without losing a cat." During the Second Russo-Turkish War, "lansons" was the name given to small vessels with sails and oars common in the Liman and on the Danube. Armed with a few cannons or mortars, they were used as attack craft or for ferrying and landing troops.

6. Count Andrei Petrovich Shuvalov (1744–1789), the son of one of the most powerful men during the reign of Elizabeth and the head of the Assignat Bank, was married to Saltykov's sister.

7. Baron Ivan Meller was a noted artillerist (see Letter 4). The generals Baron Joseph Andreevich Igelstrom (1737–1817)—veteran of the First Russo-Turkish War and former governor-general of Simbirsk and Ufa—and Prince Viktor Anhalt-Schaumburg were sent to the Finnish Army upon Potemkin's recommendation. Part of the trouble with Musin-Pushkin stemmed from the intrigues of General Knorring, the quartermaster general, and Court Counselor Ivan Rusanov, Musin-Pushkin's secretary.

8. Samoilov.

9. Potemkin's nephew Vasily Vasilievich Engelhardt (1758–after 1800) was one of his orderly generals.

401. POTEMKIN TO CATHERINE

[9 November 1789]

A Miraculous Occurrence[1]
The town has eight Bimbashi in charge of their cavalry, and one day six of them had the same dream, though they still didn't know about Belgrade-on-Dniester. On the night it was taken, they dreamed that men came to them and said: "Hand over Bender when they demand it or else you'll be lost. Know that even in Tsar Grad peace is being considered." And then that whole night they saw Russians throughout the town.

They went to the Pasha and informed him of this. And this took root to such an extent that every time they met with our men they would ask: Is there news of peace? It was one of these Bimbashi who took Lombard.

---

1. Potemkin informed Catherine of a remarkable dream that six of Bender's commanding officers ("bimbashi"—Turkish for "one who is head of a thousand") supposedly had before surrendering. The Turks handed Bender over to the Russians without firing a shot. Upon his return to Constantinople, the seraskier of Bender was beheaded.

402. CATHERINE TO POTEMKIN

15 November 1789

My true friend, Prince Grigory Aleksandrovich. It's not for nothing that I love you and have regarded you with favor, you completely justify my choice and my opinion of you. You are by no means a braggart, have carried out all your proposals and have taught the Austrians how to defeat the Turks. God helps and blesses you, you are bathed in glory. I shall be sending you a crown of laurels, which you have earned (though it's still not ready). Now, my friend, I ask you not to be haughty, not to become proud, rather to show the world the magnificence of your soul, which is just as free of arrogance in good fortune as it's free of dejection in failure. Il n'y a pas de douceur, mon Ami, que je ne voudrais Vous dire: Vous êtes charmant d'avoir pris Benders sans qu'il on ait coûté un seul homme.[1]

Your zeal and labor would increase my gratitude were it not that even without them it simply cannot grow any greater. I beg God to fortify your strength. Your illness worried me greatly, however, not having had any letters from you for over two weeks, I imagined you were busying yourself with matters around Bender, or had begun peace talks. I now see that my conjecture wasn't groundless. I shall impatiently await Popov's arrival. Rest assured that I shall do everything possible for the army generals entrusted to you, and equally for the troops: their labors and fervor have warranted this. [. . .] I am curious to see the letters of the Walachian Hospodar and the former Kapudan Pasha about the armistice and your answers. All this already has the smell of peace, and so is not offensive. I'll take a look at your plan for Poland when I receive it and shall not fail to give you a definitive answer as soon as possible. It's extremely necessary that the head of the forces in Finland be replaced. The current one[2] can't be relied on for a thing: I myself was forced to send salt from here to Nyslott, for the men in the fortress were without salt; I ordered meat given to the men, but he sent it to Vyborg, where all the meat spoiled and was lost. He can't make up his mind about anything; in a word, he's incapable of leading, and the generals under him play silly little games and intrigue, but they don't take care of business as they should. You can judge from this how necessary it is to make a change there. I have promoted the fine young fellow[3] you sent to the rank of colonel and made him an aide-de-camp for the good news. L'enfant trouve que Vous avés plus d'esprit et que Vous êtes plus amusant et plus aimable, que tous ceux qui Vous entourent; mais sur ceci gardés nous le secret, car il ignore que je sais cela.[4]

They're extremely grateful for your having received them most affectionately. Their brother Dmitry is to marry Viazemsky's third daughter.[5] Adieu, mon cher Ami, portés Vous bien.

1. "There is no kindness, my friend, that I would not say to you: you are a delight for having taken Bender without losing a single man."

2. Musin-Pushkin.

3. Valerian Zubov.

4. "The child finds that you have more charm and that you are more entertaining and
kinder than everyone around you; but let us keep this a secret, because he does not know I
know this."

5. Dmitry Aleksandrovich Zubov (1764–1836), made a gentleman-of-the-bedchamber in October, married Princess Praskovia Aleksandrovna Viazemskaia (d. 1835), the daughter of
Procurator-General Prince Aleksandr Alekseevich.

403. POTEMKIN TO CATHERINE

Jassy. 22 November [1789]

Your Most Gracious Majesty. The unexpected arrival of winter has caused
me a great deal of confusion and added to my troubles, which I'm already
buried under. I have made use of all possible means to save the men, however, it was impossible to save the livestock. The poor Turks, the first
group of which has left, suffered greatly. I can assure you that I shall never
spare either my life or my efforts for your affairs, however, peace negotiations are more than I can bear. All the more so if I am to be tied to the
Austrians, who are filled with egoism, cupidity, and duplicity. In addition
to this, they are making use of French channels, who certainly do not
wish us well. And what's more, they are held in disdain by the Turks and
want to ingratiate themselves with them at our expense. This is the incon-
testable truth, and in time you will see the results. Kaunitz is already gathering a band of advisors—Thuguts, Herberts and above them Coburg,[1]
who can be led down the garden path by any scribe. Must I really be
thrown together with that wretched lot? All their former ministers in Tsar
Grad fear the Turks like fire, and they act most basely before them. The
Austrian system is to hold on to everything for themselves, and for us to
be satisfied with what we've already possessed for a long time, namely the
Crimea. Together with the French they proposed to the Porte long ago
that we should get nothing, which they would help work out, provided
that they receive Belgrade, Khotin, etc. They're happy to take things with
our help, but want to keep them for themselves. Practically nothing's left
in Moldavia, they've taken all the best places, and I don't know whether
or not this was done by some agreement. My troops and I, however, must
scrounge for every kopeck just like a pauper. Are Russians really mere
swine who must suffer every necessity? We can't touch what's in their
hands, though we must defend it. And besides, they have a dual strategy
concerning peace: if they see an opportunity, they'll make a separate

peace, but if some difficulty arises, then a joint one. We could easily make peace with the Turks ourselves, they, however, will be an insurmountable obstacle, of which you may be certain.

I cannot now present either the naval journal or any other reports. My office hasn't arrived, and I'm here with none of my things. Pray consider that on my last journey I rode ninety versts in four days, through forest and mountains, most of it on oxen and even then only with others' help.

With all my heart and soul I send you my best wishes on the day of your angel. May God give you everything that your most devoted and most grateful charge wishes. There's nothing here worthy of presenting you. Kindly accept these little Turkish cups in memory of my stay in the Turkish towns. I wish that I might mark the occasion in a more memorable way. It's unimaginable how tired I am, yet there's no time to rest. Farewell, matushka, be kind and believe that there is no one more zealously devoted to you than I.

Your most loyal and most grateful subject
Prince Potemkin-Tavrichesky

---

1. In preparation for peace negotiations, Prince Kaunitz sent several experienced diplomats to Coburg, including Franz Maria Freiherr von Thugut (1736–1818), brilliant ambassador to the Ottoman Porte, Poland, Naples, and France and later Minister of Foreign Affairs, and Baron Peter-Philippe Herbert (1735–1802), former envoy in Contanstantinople.

404. CATHERINE TO POTEMKIN

25 November 1789

My true friend, Prince Grigory Aleksandrovich. Popov has arrived with the keys to Bender and with your letters of 9 November. We have conveyed our gratitude to God for Bender, and now I'll say thanks to you once more. Popov has been given the ribbon of Saint Anne as well as some money. I enjoyed seeing him and speaking with him about your gallant campaign, during which your excellent care for the men kept them safe and the enemy's towns were subjugated. I have received the maps of these towns. They prove that God is our helper and that the Turks fear Russian guns and our commanders more than those of the Austrians. With all my heart I now desire for Christ to help you conclude an honorable and advantageous peace, which is what we need most of all, and it seems there is now some hope of achieving it. Your correspondence with Hasan Pasha and Mavrogeni along with your most intelligent answers give cause for hope. It's impossible that your outstanding successes have not made a deep impression on the minds of our enemies and that, sensing the poor state of their own affairs, they won't turn to saving what they have left as soon as possible, rather than relying on the empty promises and counsel of our European enemies. Having subdued Bender, Vous avés couronné l'oeuvre de cette campagne[1] and have executed your plan. I think they'll release Bulgakov to you; it's, of course, awkward for you to be personally involved in the talks. As affairs in Brabant continue to go quite poorly, so one might imagine that the Austrians have as much need of peace as we do, and they're seizing Walachia so as to hold on to what's absolutely necessary.

Volontiers je chanterai avec Vous la chanson que Vous avés faite, que

Nous avons pris neuf lançons

Sans perdre un garçon,

Et Benders avec trois pachas,

Sans perdre un chat.

J'aime à Vous voir en aussi bonne humeur et Vous avés lieu de l'être après une aussi brillante campagne. Soyés assuré que je me rejouis bien sincèrement de Vos succès.[2]

I decided to bring Saltykov here from the Kuban, as well as Igelstrom and Prince Anhalt, and have ordered a courier sent to him. Count Pushkin's clerk is already departing, but please send good major-generals and not only Germans.

I'm sending the Order of Alexander Nevsky to Aleksandr Nikolaevich Samoilov and the Order of Vladimir second class to Engelhardt.

Monsieur le moine, point de moinerie: voilà ce que j'ai à répondre au mot cell, à propos de Vos appartements que je me suis fait un plaisir particulier d'enjoliver.[3]

You will rest once we have peace, and God will fortify your body and soul.

Let the Kuban Corps be under your command as it was. We are stroking the Prussians. Regarding Poland—this must be considered along with other matters and our true situation, so that we do not stir up more trouble than we already have.[4] Once we have peace we can settle things with the White Russians as well. I think the dream of the Bender Bimbashi was made up to give the Divan an excuse for the town's surrender. Adieu, mon Ami, portés Vous bien. We often repeat this wish in our conversations with Platon Aleksandrovich,[5] with whom I'm most pleased and who's extremely attached to me. Here's his testimonial as a Cornet in the Corps of the Chevaliers-Gardes, which I present to its head. Ce garçon est fort aimable, d'un excellent caractère.[6]

---

1. "you have consummated this campaign's work"

2. "I shall willingly sing your song with you, that / We have taken nine lansons / Without losing a boy, / And Bender with three pashas, / Without losing a cat.

I love to see you in such good humor and you have reason to be so following such a brilliant campaign. Be assured that I sincerely rejoice in your success."

3. "Sir monk, stop this talk of monasteries: now there's my reply to the word 'cell' in reference to your apartments, which I had the singular pleasure of beautifying."

4. Although impressed with Potemkin's plan (see Letter 399n4), Catherine hesitated for a while, fearful of the anger the new hetmanate would produce in Poland.

5. Zubov.

6. "This boy is very kind and has an excellent character."

405. POTEMKIN TO CATHERINE

[5 December 1789]

Beloved matushka, Your Most Gracious Majesty! Amid all your favors, your counsel that I not become haughty astonishes me. When in this instance did I give cause for such doubt? What reason is there to expect from me something that is characteristic of scoundrels? And why should I become proud? Fervor and zeal combined with my unlimited duty to you are what move me to serve. But it's God who confers success. If I am proud of anything, then it's the fortunate disposition of my soul to expect all blessings from God. I am a Christian, and so my glory consists in serving. How many of my comrades there are who love to boast and to fill their reports with their person, flattering themselves by claiming they foresee everything, and presenting unexpected events as the result of their plans, which never even existed. Is there any such preening in my communiqués? I solemnly and joyfully confess that every good is given me by God, and I shall say still more, that I alone feel inside that He instills in me the means to undertake matters: how many times have I seen myself miraculously extricated from the midst of calamities by superhuman means? And as for what depends on me, I act unsparingly, I look after your advantage with both my heart and soul. I do not resemble those commanders who are content simply with clearing their names—they merely give orders, but do not give any thought as to whether or not anything gets done. Everyone is a witness to my cares and to my not sleeping nights because of them. Preserving your men weighs heavily on my heart, and God is my witness that I have not lost a one trying to win glory for myself. Gazetteers have never gotten a single ruble from me.

I would gladly place everyone's burdens upon my shoulders were it possible, and then you would see a new Atlas. How many of our comrades sacrifice entire armies for their own sake? But I, of course, would sooner lay myself down for everyone else. Even now, when not a single shot has been fired from your guns against the enemy, when practically no one has been lost, death has still been very close to me. Personal arrogance I leave to those scoundrels who are filled with envy toward me and who repay goodness with dirty tricks, and I shall always remain true to my principles, that is: to surpass everyone with my zeal for you; to serve with all my sweat and blood; to do greater justice to everyone than they would themselves acknowledge; to protect the men entrusted to me better than myself; to dedicate my successes to God; and to await the enemy's esteem.

As much as I may labor and whatever I may do, I shall never merit your favors. These thoughts are firmly planted in my soul, on this I want to pride myself.

The messenger I sent to Vienna with a report for the Emperor was anticipated two hours before his arrival: upon entering the city he encountered as many as thirty thousand people who had turned out to meet him. They were all shouting my name. When an actor made a casual remark about my having sent news about Bender, the entire theater erupted in applause. My courier was given the best seat, and they pestered him during his six-day stay, dragging him from loge to loge. Ladies have taken to wearing sashes and rings with my name on them. I am presenting herewith a ring which Princesse Esterhazy[1] removed from her hand and gave to my courier. Painters have produced an allegorical painting. To whom am I obliged for this if not you, and why are these marks of distinction agreeable to me if not because your charity gave me the means to prove my zeal for you as my true mother? Since I am yours, so do my successes belong wholly to you.

Matushka, you protect me from conceit, and at the same time you crown me with laurels—un ornement pareil appartient aux Héros et je ne suis qu'un Zélé serviteur, ce luxe militaire n'est pas du tout pour ma tête, agissés en véritable mère, prépares moi une bonne mitre Episcopale et un couvent bien situé.[2]

I was ready to send my reports the day before yesterday, but I decided to wait when I was notified that a Turk sent to me from Mavrogeni was on his way. He has now delivered seven letters, one right after the other, all of them about the armistice, however, I shall tell him point-blank that I should not be negotiating with him: he's a big ne'er-do-well.[3] There's still no news from Hasan Pasha concerning his having been made Vizier.[4] The post still hasn't arrived, and I think it will be stopped once they receive the news about Akkerman and especially about Bender. I think there is some confusion in Constantinople.

We must give thought to and forestall Poland, as I wrote earlier. I am using all my powers to placate them, matushka, however, I don't believe Count Stackelberg.[5] He paints a pretty picture with his false reports, and then all of a sudden something unexpected happens. Do as you please, but the Polish King is a mischievous imp and a thoroughgoing Prussian.

I'm presenting herewith a copy of the Emperor's letter.[6] We must assume in advance that there will be another campaign, and we must make a proper show of the troops. But since I don't have any orders concerning the Kuban and Caucasus forces, as I requested, I can't even dispose my own.

The fleet will be positioned near the ground forces' operations, and it will be under my flag since the flotilla will have completely entered the Danube by then. Once I'm close and catch sight of them, then, God willing, we'll have at them.

Farewell, matushka. Once your courier arrives, I'll gallop off for Kherson to prepare the fleet and flotilla for their early departure and shall be gone 12 days, which means I shall not lose anything in my correspondence with the Vizier, for if he truly is the Vizier, then he's no longer in Ismail, but will already be in Shumla.

Till death I remain your most loyal charge

and most loyal and most grateful subject

Prince Potemkin-Tavrichesky

P.S. The Polish Minister in Stockholm has been informing the King and the Republic that there will soon be a revolution here in Russia.

---

1. In French.

2. "such an ornament belongs to heroes and I am nothing but a zealous servant; this military extravagance is not at all for my head. Be a true mother, prepare for me a seemly bishop's miter and a well-placed monastery."

3. Potemkin refused to discuss the idea of an armistice, and answered each letter by flatly asking whether the Turks wanted peace or war.

4. Gazi Hasan Pasha was named grand vizier in November due largely to the fact that he had shown the most success of all the Turkish commanders that year.

5. Potemkin was displeased with Stackelberg, Russia's ambassador in Warsaw, and sought to replace him with one of his own men.

6. Joseph II had written Potemkin to congratulate him on the splendid campaign.

406. CATHERINE TO POTEMKIN

7 December 1789

My dear friend, Prince Grigory Aleksandrovich. From your letter of 22 November I see that you have already arrived in Jassy and that the early arrival of winter has caused you new troubles, that the people have been saved, but that it was impossible to save the livestock. I am certain you will spare no efforts, but what's to be done? It's impossible to fight against the weather. It's still not apparent from Hasan Pasha's letters that the Turks are much interested in making peace. But should negotiations with them begin, then you are by no means obligated to negotiate along with the Austrians. We have had an agreement about this for a long time now—each is to take care of himself and to make the best possible peace he can. I would also desire that this matter not be handled with the help of the French or anyone else but directly. Let Kaunitz's band of advisors remain with Coburg. They've no business either with us or you. Regarding the posts in Moldavia still held by the Austrians, write Coburg that he is to remove his troops to Walachia and to leave them.

I thank you for your best wishes on the day of my angel, and for the beautiful little Turkish cups as well. I'm sorry you're tired and hope God will strengthen your body and soul. Farewell, my friend, I am well and merry.

We recalled the storming of Ochakov yesterday, and I attended services. I give Platon Aleksandrovich the very best testimonial.

407. CATHERINE TO POTEMKIN

20 December 1789

My true friend, Prince Grigory Aleksandrovich. I received today your letters of 5 December[1] and hasten to reply to them with the courier departing for you. You are astonished by my advice not to become haughty—this is how one writes when separated by thousands of versts. Had I spoken with you at that moment face to face, then you, having kissed my hand, would have left me with tears of joy. How could I not tell you not to be haughty upon seeing you adorned with the successes with which God has blessed you? Mon âme, remplie de joye, n'a fait rien autre chose que de Vous avertir un instant, qu'elle souhaitait que Vous évitiés la seule chose qui pouvoit nuire à toute la grandeur de la Vôtre, lisés y mon amitié vraiment maternelle pour Vous, et puis c'est tout; qui a mieux mérité cette couronne de Lauriers que je Vous envoye aujourd'hui que Vous? La voilà; puissiés-Vous la porter cent ans. De mitre Episcopale assurément Vous n'en aurés jamais de moi; et un couvent ne sauroit être habite par celui dont de nom retentit dans l'Asie et dans l'Europe, il est trop petit pour lui.[2]

Based on your news from Tsar Grad it's obvious that they are most despondent there. They really did release Bulgakov, and, as I think you already know, he arrived in Trieste from Vienna on 3 December. As soon as I learned of this I wrote him to go to you, and to Vienna asking that his quarantine be shortened. It's strange we still don't know, who's been made Vizier? I wrote to you by way of Popov concerning Poland, and I await your letters in response on this matter.[3] You will also receive from Popov written information about the Kuban and Caucasus forces.[4] God grant that our enemies are pliable when it comes to the question of peace, but if there is to be no peace, then we must, of course, make every effort to prepare for the next campaign. This piece of news that the Polish minister writes about from Sweden, namely that there is soon to be a revolution here, reached us as well from Finland. The Swedish King began this rumor based on the assumption that I ordered six Guards battalions to come here for the winter since I fear it. For this reason he concluded that this was done out of a fear of revolution, and he said that this is why six regiments have already been ordered to go to Petersburg. Nevertheless, we here are, thank God, in good health.

The Viennese mes dames are cleverer at thinking up sashes and rings than our ladies. I thank you for Princess Esterhazy's ring you sent, je fais de bon coeur chorus avec elle. Adieu, mon cher Ami, portés Vous bien.⁵

[. . .]

1. Despite the reference to "letters," this is a response to Letter 405.

2. "Filled with joy, my soul seeks nothing but to warn you of one thing: it desires only that you shun the lone thing that could harm the great munificence of your soul; detect in this my truly motherly affection for you, and nothing more. Who better merits this laurel crown I am sending you today than you? So here it is; may you wear it a hundred years. The bishop's miter you will assuredly never receive from me. And a monastery will never be the home of a man whose name resounds throughout Asia and Europe. It is too small for him."

3. Catherine sent Potemkin various scenarios drawn up by Bezborodko for preventing a Polish-Prussian alliance, including even promising Moldavia, Walachia, and Bessarabia to Poland. Potemkin stood by his plan.

4. "I gladly add my voice to hers. Farewell, my dear friend, take care of yourself."

5. These two corps returned to Potemkin's authority after Saltykov's departure for the Finnish Army.

408. CATHERINE TO POTEMKIN

21 December 1789

My true friend, Prince Grigory Aleksandrovich. Upon reading your letter of 5 December once more, I was moved to the point of tears by the expression of your heart and soul and by your feelings. May the Lord God Himself bless all your actions. Whatever I may have done for you, you are worthy of everything. Farewell, you clever fellow, be safe and well.

409. POTEMKIN TO CATHERINE

26 December [1789]. Jassy

Beloved matushka, Your Most Gracious Majesty. Popov has arrived. I now humble myself by expressing my gratitude for the countless favors you have shown me. Upon such occasions my confession issues from the great fullness of my heart. You are my only mother, you raised me as an officer from the lowest rank to the highest, you gave me as well the means to prove myself worthy. Whereas the service of all others in my rank consists of organizing the main divisions, I, however, must sacrifice myself everywhere and in every situation so as to set an example, for my obligation is not comparable to that of others. So I am and so I shall be till my final breath.

You are the source of all blessings, from you olives and laurels flow to me, though this has never caused me to be pricked by any thorns. These confessions and feelings of gratitude emanate from the fullness of my heart and are not mere words. Permit me, matushka, to say: I give that worth to those favors that you give so freely.

I am well now, but upon arriving in Jassy I suffered from severe rheumatism in my right hand that made it impossible for me to write. I need the soap liniment you sent me in the beautiful medicine chest very much. And the fur coat is quite timely—I didn't have a single one left.[1]

According to the latest news from Vienna, the Emperor is very ill. I know indirectly that up to twenty thousand men of Laudon's army have left for Galicia: unrest has begun there.[2] In Hungary there is loud grumbling.[3]

Matushka, I truly can't write much, my hand is still bad. Till death I faithfully and steadfastly remain

your most loyal and most grateful subject

Prince Potemkin-Tavrichesky

Your testimonials on my Cornet of the Chevaliers-Gardes are so impressive that they oblige me to ask you to reward him with a decoration.[4]

---

1. On 3 December, Catherine gave Vasily Popov a small chest full of her own medicaments to bring to Potemkin. She also sent the prince a sable hat and fox coat.

2. Field Marshal Gideon Loudon (1716–1790), the aged hero of the Seven Years' War and commander of Austrian forces, had to send troops from his main army in Serbia to fight a rebellion in Galicia.

3. Hungary's nobles, infused with a nascent Magyar national identity, had grown to resent Joseph II's centralizing reforms and also his refusal to be formally crowned king of Hungary.

4. Catherine gladly listened to Potemkin's advice (he was head of the Chevalier-Gardes and so Platon Zubov's superior) and awarded her new favorite with the Order of St. Anne on 3 January 1790.

10. One Paw Out of the Mud—1790

*T*he new year brought with it bad news for Russia. On 20 (31) January, Prussia and the Porte signed an alliance that obligated the Prussians to attack Russia in the coming spring and to help the Turks regain the Crimea. The following month, Joseph II of Austria died. Facing revolts and unrest throughout much of the imperial and Habsburg domains and the threat of a Prussian invasion, Joseph's successor, Leopold II, sought to put his house in order and communicated to Prussia his openness to peace with the Porte. In March, Prussia and Poland signed a defensive alliance whereby Frederick William promised to defend his neighbor from any foreign meddling in its domestic affairs. And that spring, Prussia advanced 40,000 troops toward the border with Livonia, another 40,000 were amassed in Silesia, and 100,000 soldiers were held in reserve. The third war Catherine had feared was becoming ever more likely, and it now appeared Russia would have to stand and fight her enemies—Turkey, Sweden, Prussia, Poland, and possibly Britain—all on her own.

Following the campaign of 1789, Potemkin established his peripatetic court with its usual opulent splendor in Jassy, the capital of Moldavia. From here he contemplated his next move. Despite Russia's military success over the Turks in the past year, Potemkin hesitated to send his forces against the enemy, now located south of the Danube, since this would most certainly bring the Prussians into the war against Russia. Moreover, were he to march south into the heart of the Ottoman Empire, he would inadvertently be playing into the hands of the Prussians: with the Russian army south of the Danube, the road to

Moscow would be wide open. And so Potemkin kept his men in place and continued negotiating with the Turks for peace. But when the treaty between Prussia and the Porte was publicly announced in mid-February, peace talks in Shumla broke down. Any last hope for a quick end to the war was dashed when Grand Vizier Gazi Hasan, a strong advocate for peace, died in March and was replaced by Sherif Hasan Pasha, who obediently followed Selim's order to prepare for war that spring (Letters 411–416).

While unable to direct the Yekaterinoslav Army against the Turks and so deliver the mortal blow, Potemkin did have other options at his disposal. First, he set about preparing the fleet to destroy what remained of the Turkish naval presence in the Black Sea. Second, he devised a secret plan to forestall a joint Polish-Prussian attack. Drawing inspiration from the seventeenth-century Cossack uprising against the Poles led by Hetman Bogdan Khmelnitsky, Potemkin proposed creating a large Cossack army, with himself at its head, that would seize the three Orthodox Palatinates of Kiev, Bratslav, and Podolia—where he owned massive estates—in eastern Poland. Catherine had wavered for a time, but finally gave the plan her approval on 10 January when she appointed Potemkin "Grand Hetman of the Yekaterinoslav and Black Sea Cossack Hosts." Throughout the winter and spring, Grand Hetman Potemkin shifted regiments from his army to White Russia and established new Cossack units. To his enemies, Potemkin's appointment suggested a grand design—on his part—to create for himself an independent kingdom. He scoffed at the notion, calling his new position "more ridiculous than distinguished" (Letters 411, 412). Third, Potemkin advised Catherine to give in to Prussia's demand for Danzig. By throwing Frederick William this "bone to gnaw on," Potemkin believed Prussia's true, rapacious intent would become manifest to Poland and the Porte and so would weaken, and possibly even destroy, their alliances (Letter 413, 415).

Back in St. Petersburg, Catherine approved Potemkin's various plans (save the concession to Prussia) and anxiously waited to see how matters would unfold. These months were especially trying for the empress. Her secretary Khrapovitsky noted that Catherine compared waiting for news of whether there was to be peace or a third war to childbirth. "Our enemies are staring us straight in the face," she wrote on 30 March. She was certain the Prussians together with the Poles intended to march on Moscow, yet she asserted they would not get away without a fight: " . . . it is not enough that we act solely with the pen," she wrote, "our enemies must be shown that . . . we are ready to defend the Fatherland with our teeth" (Letters 414, 416). She was equally worried for her prince. During Potemkin's stay in the capital the previous year, Catherine had openly spoken of Prussian plots against her life, and now she feared the Prussians might have put the idea of poisoning Potemkin into the Turks' heads (Letter 417).

In May, Leopold decided that a show of strength was needed to force the Turks back to the negotiating table. Prince Coburg's army marched toward Rushchuk and acted as if it were preparing to cross the Danube. Yet when the Austrians reached Giurgevo, they encountered such fierce Turkish resistance that they panicked, abandoned all their munitions and supplies, and fled to Bucharest. The Austrian blunder emboldened the Turks to fight on. Leopold was saved, however, by Frederick William, who agreed to call off his planned attack on Austria if Leopold would negotiate a peace acceptable to Prussia. In June, talks between Austria, the Triple Alliance, and Poland began in the Silesian town of Reichenbach, culminating in the Convention of Reichenbach (16 [27] July) that proclaimed an immediate armistice between Austria and the Porte and called for a congress to produce a final peace agreement. Russia's fears had been confirmed: their ally had abandoned them to face its enemies alone. A disgusted Catherine characterized the deal struck at Reichenbach as "shameful" (Letter 429).

Russia narrowly averted catastrophe when on 3 August—fewer than three weeks after the signing of the Convention of Reichenbach—a peace agreement with Sweden was signed in the small town of Verela. News of the agreement thrilled Catherine: "We've pulled one paw out of the mud. Once we pull out the other one, we'll sing Hallelujah," she wrote Potemkin on 9 August (Letter 429). Peace with Sweden followed an indecisive season of fighting in the Baltic. At the beginning of 1790, Gustav still held out hope of capturing St. Petersburg, while Russian war aims centered on driving the Swedish fleet out of the Gulf of Finland and advancing by land into Swedish Finland. The initial naval engagements did not bode well for the Swedes. An inferior Russian fleet under the command of Admiral Chichagov sank two ships of the line in a Swedish attack in Reval harbor in early May; two days later, the Russian fortress at Fredrikshamn turned back an attack by the Swedish oared fleet commanded by Gustav himself. The Swedish battle fleet and the Russian Kronstadt squadron fought an inconclusive battle in the final week of May, which ended with the Swedes retreating to Vyborg Bay to protect Gustav's oared flotilla. The fighting had taken place so close to the Russian coast that Catherine herself heard the ships' guns (Letter 421).

Gustav had embarked on a dangerous gamble. He had pulled Swedish naval forces and some 30,000 men into the Bay of Vyborg in the hope of landing his troops and marching on St. Petersburg. But the Swedes' attempts at landing proved unsuccessful, and their way out of the bay was quickly blocked by the Russians. Running desperately short of food and fresh water, the Swedes tried to break out of the bay on 21 June. What began as a successful operation ended in disaster when a Swedish fireship accidentally collided with two of its own vessels, setting them ablaze. The smoke hung so thick in the air that several ships behind them lost their way and ran aground. Although they managed to break through the Russian line, the Swedes lost twelve ships and Gustav barely escaped capture by the Russians (Letters 423, 426). Despite the rout of the Swedes at Vyborg Bay, Russia managed to snatch defeat from the jaws of victory just days later on 28 June (Catherine's accession day) when Prince Nassau-Siegen unwisely urged his oared fleet to attack the Swedes at Svensksund during a spell of poor weather. The Second Battle of Svensksund proved a resounding loss for the Russians: sixty-four ships were destroyed or taken and over 7,000 men were killed, wounded, or captured. Nassau-Siegen was crushed. He resigned his commission, rank, and honors and requested to be court-martialed (Letter 425, 431).

Russia's defeat contained a silver lining, however. Gustav by now had become thoroughly tired of his war with Catherine, which had dramatically weakened Sweden's battle fleet and seen the rise of Russian naval superiority in the Baltic, and the victory allowed him to negotiate an end to the fighting without losing face. English offers of support came too late to keep Sweden from making peace with Russia on the basis of the *status quo ante bellum* (Letters 428–430).

The end of the Russo-Swedish War greatly improved Russia's international position. Troops from the Finnish Army could now be placed along the empire's western border to defend against a possible Prusso-Polish attack. At the same time, Potemkin's hands were now free to renew operations against the Turks. The radical transformation of affairs had a sudden, positive effect on Catherine and Potemkin: he was finally able to sleep calmly again, and after three years of unremitting stress, she had begun putting weight back on, so much so, in fact, that she had to have all her dresses let out a full size (Letters 430, 431).

Russia's Black Sea fleet had enjoyed considerable success throughout the summer. Under the excellent command of Rear Admiral Fyodor Ushakov, the Russians defeated the Turkish fleet at the Straits of Kerch on 8 July and then also near the island of Tendra south of Kinburn on 28–29 August. Ushakov's victories resulted in Russian control over the Black Sea. The Crimea was now completely safe from Turkish assault, and the way had been cleared for Potemkin to renew the ground campaign (Letters 426, 432).

After visiting Nikolaev and the Crimea to inspect the fleet, Potemkin returned to Bender, where he had moved his headquarters in August, and ordered the commencement of operations in the lower reaches of the Danube in early September. The primary goal was the mighty fortress of Ismail located at a bend in the Danube miles upstream from the river delta. Before besieging Ismail, several lesser forts had to be taken. Potemkin's plan of operations included the use of ground forces to encircle the Turkish strongholds and the positioning of two oared flotillas—one Russian, the other comprising Black Sea Cossacks—commanded by José de Ribas and Anton Golovaty that would fight their way up the mouths of the Danube. After one failed attempt, Russians forces took Kilia on 18 October; two days later, the flotillas broke through into the Danube and quickly seized the forts of Tulcha and Isackcha. By the middle of November, the Russians controlled the river from its mouths as far up as Galatz. Ismail now stood alone to face Potemkin's advancing army.

One of the mightiest of the Turkish fortresses, Ismail, with its elaborate system of ditches, towers, and redoubts, was nearly impregnable. It held almost an entire army of 35,000 men inside and was defended by some 250 guns with enough shells to last for several months. A Russian army of approximately 30,000 invested the fortress on 23 November, but the generals in charge soon came to doubt whether Ismail could be stormed and considered withdrawing. Informed of their indecision, Potemkin ordered General Suvorov to Ismail to take command of the siege, confident that he alone of all the Russian commanders could get the job done. Suvorov arrived on 2 December in time to turn back the troops, who had packed up and begun to move off. After surveying Ismail, Suvorov wrote Potemkin that he would take it within the week. As Potemkin waited in Bender for news of Ismail, he received word from Girolamo Lucchesini, the crafty Prussian ambassador to Poland, of his plan to visit the prince. Lucchesini intended to deliver an ultimatum to Potemkin: either accept the mediation of the Triple Alliance to conclude an immediate peace with the Porte or risk the threat of war with Prussia and Britain. Potemkin, however, stood firm (Letter 436).

On 11 December, Ismail fell to Suvorov and his men after an eight-hour battle. The fighting had been exceptionally bloody—26,000 Turks lost their lives and as many as 10,000 Russians were killed and wounded (Letter 437). The storming of Ismail had great military significance. Russia now controlled all of the lower Danube and had severely damaged the Turks' defenses in the region. News of the defeat unleashed rioting in Constantinople that forced Selim to sacrifice his top officials, even Grand Vizier Sherif Hasan, who was executed in Shumla. In Sistova, where the Triple Alliance powers, the Porte, and Austria had been negotiating a peace settlement, talks were suspended. The Hungarians offered Leopold 80,000 more men to continue the fight against the Porte and force a more just peace. Prussia and Britain were unsure of how best to respond to Potemkin's latest achievement. It seemed, though only for a while, that peace with the Porte was within reach.

• • •

410. CATHERINE TO POTEMKIN

10 January 1790

My true friend, Prince Grigory Aleksandrovich. I received today your letter of 26 December. The sentiment with which you thanked me brought me to tears. God grant you health and every possible blessing, and may He add to your victories the name of peacemaker. We now have the greatest need of this, for there is no doubt but that the Prussian King intends to attack our lands together with the Poles in spring, as you will see from the long rescript sent with this courier.[1] I made certain to order that the entire story be written down and kept in the archive comme une pièce authentique.[2]

Igelstrom is already here, and Ivan Petrovich Saltykov just arrived today. He says that about ten thousand troops could be taken from the Kuban without ruining matters. But you can judge this better than he, and so I place all my trust in you. A courier arrived today from Vienna with a letter from the Emperor himself in which he writes me that he is very ill and grieves the loss of the Netherlands. If there is something that cannot be justified in this business, it's all the changes he made: first he'd take everything away from them, then he'd give it back, then he'd take it away again and then give it back again. Dieu sait ce qu'il faissait, mais l'événement a montré qu'il ne faisait rien qui vaille.[3]

I'm quite sorry, my friend, that your hand is in such great pain. I think there is some camphor ointment or oil or some sort of concoction in your medicine chest. Order your physician to find something that is even more effective against rheumatism than soap liniment. But please don't take it without a physician. I recall telling Popov about it.

Your Cornet of the Chevaliers-Gardes, on whose behalf you request a decoration and who truly is worthy of it, has been bedridden for six days now. The doctors thought it was some sort of a fever. And now he's so weak and thin he doesn't even resemble himself. He's the very picture of a cold, and the veins behind his ears are all swollen. Well, my friend, all we can do is but wait for good deeds from you and your side. I impatiently await the quick arrival of your promised courier. As soon as God allows you to conclude peace, then you will be blessed among men.

Adieu, mon cher et précieux Ami.

---

1. Catherine had recently learned of talks underway in Constantinople between Prussia and the Porte that resulted in their alliance concluded later that month.

2. "as an authentic document."

3. "God knows what he was doing, but events have shown that he was not doing anything worthwhile."

411. POTEMKIN TO CATHERINE

Jassy. 23 January [1790]

Your Most Gracious Majesty. It will seem improbable, but for two weeks now we have had the most severe cold weather. And as the houses here are all built for the summer, there truly has been no way to write given the freezing cold.

There is no doubt that the Turks are trying to buy some time, or that the new Vizier[1] has been given full authority to make peace. Their lands are in complete chaos, and it has pleased God to place me in very good standing with their people. Thus, there is hope that with the very next defeat peace can be achieved, which can always only be done by crushing the enemy under one's foot. Polish affairs need to be resolved quickly. To tolerate their arming without our doing anything about it would be to act like the Trojans who permitted that horse to enter. We must act with a cold heart in what I proposed. This will increase both the Poles' troubles and fear. An unexpected weapon always startles the enemy. The plan will be secret. It will be made known at the right time, and its name should not give anything away. I am not seeking anything for myself with this; if your benefit did not demand it, would I adopt this position, which is more ridiculous than distinguished? It's a means to achieve our goal, however, and there is one thing I can say: however we resolve matters, we cannot give up Poland. Thus, it must, of course, be weakened or, better said, destroyed.[2] From Ambassador Stackelberg's letters enclosed herewith, pray note his disquiet which is all the worse since he is sounding the alarm everywhere. Had he not signed his name, I might have taken his letter for one of Lucchesini's. My Most Gracious mother, I am zealously devoted to you, and so I say openly: do as you please, however, Stackelberg is a dubious man. I'm amazed at how the confederation came about.

Following my appointment measures will be taken to increase my Cossack forces, while not yet involving Poland, and to build this force on a beneficial foundation. They're no longer the same as before. While traveling overland I matter of factly acquainted them with the required order and have inclined the majority of them to marry. On the water they do everything according to signals and are rather keen shooters, which truly is pleasant to see. Their cavalry rides on spirited horses.

I'll now tell you of our ally,[3] of how he, to his misfortune, brought doubt upon himself in his own lands thanks to some bagatelles. Upon his detailing new troops in Hungary, the estates replied to him by saying that they did not have a King as he still hadn't been crowned. It's terrifying to hear how annoyed they are, and they talk so boldly it turns one's stomach.

My beloved matushka, God knows how sensitive I am to your favors, que puis je Vous offrir—mes services, mon Zèle et le peu de succès recevés comme une obole de ma reconnaissance. Je porterai ma couronne de lauriers au jour de St. André sur le chapeau et sur le casque à la tête de mon beau Régiment de cuirassier, Vous verrés, ma très chère mère, comme ce Régiment combattra pour Vous.[4]

My chief concern is to outfit the fleet. Now that we have the entire coast in our hands, from the mouth of the Danube to our own shores, they no longer have any base of support. It's time to give them a scare with our fleet. I shall reconcile the situation on land in such manner that I myself shall have every opportunity to do battle at sea with complete faith in God's mercy, with whose help we have already become a bit stronger at sea than our enemy. And in August we'll become considerably stronger.

Matushka, please let it be known through your conversations, as well as through those of others, that you do not intend to put the Black Sea fleet on the offensive, but intend to keep it along your coast for defensive purposes. This will reach the Turks, and they will come out, fully expecting to be able to leave the channel. Otherwise there'll be no way to lure them out.

[. . .]

I'm sending you, my benefactress, some sheets that they use here to decorate their baths and other rooms. I'll be glad if you can make use of them at Tsarskoe Selo. I remain till death

your most loyal and most grateful subject
Prince Potemkin-Tavrichesky

---

1. Grand Vizier Gazi Hasan Pasha died in 30 March and was replaced by Sherif Hasan Pasha, the governor of Rushchuk, on 16 April (n.s.).

2. The discussion here concerns Potemkin's plan to organize the Ukrainian Cossacks under a revived hetmanate. The prince's enemies had suggested to Catherine that he sought the title of grand hetman in order to create in the south his own, semi-independent territories, of which he would be the ruler. Potemkin sought to reassure her of the absurdity of such notions.

3. Joseph II.

4. "that I can offer you—my services, my zeal, and the few successes, accept them as a farthing of my gratitude. I shall wear my laurel crown on the day of St. Andrew on my hat and on my helmet at the head of my handsome regiment of cuirassiers. You will see, my very dear mother, how this regiment will fight for you."

412. CATHERINE TO POTEMKIN

6 February 1790

My true friend, Prince Grigory Aleksandrovich. I can understand it must've been difficult to write with frozen ink. Not having had any letters from you for three weeks, I finally received your letter of 23 January and am quite sorry that the freezing cold made you ill. Please preserve your health, I need it. From now on when it's cold, use this little flask and goblet, which this courier is bringing to you. Je souhaite que ce petit meuble Vous fasse autant de plaisir, que j'en ai a Vous l'envoyer de bon coeur.[1]

It's possible that the Turks are trying this in order to buy some time, however, it seems to me the Vizier, who possesses absolute power, wants to save his head in advance, and for this reason he and his Pashas wrote to Tsar Grad of the bad position in which he and his troops find themselves, namely that they refuse to leave the provinces to join him and that they have neither money, nor provisions, nor men. With this representation he hopes to wheedle out of the Divan specific instructions or some words that would force him to begin peace negotiations.

I don't doubt in the slightest that peace will quickly come once, God willing, you crush them under foot, as you write. How could you not gain among the Turkish people the trust of their greatest leaders?! First of all, you're smarter than they; second, you treat them magnanimously and humanely, which they've never before seen with their own eyes, nor heard with their own ears, from their countrymen.

Concerning Polish affairs, you have had my permission for a long time now, however, the courier dispatched from here had not yet arrived by the time you sent your letter. Stackelberg has been written that he's to sit quietly and not to make a fuss. And the confederation, as you yourself will recall, was put together in order to conclude an alliance with Poland. The Prussian King rudely prevented this, as you know yourself. I now impatiently await your reply to my rescript and the reapportioning of the troops. The main thing is that they encounter resistance where they want to attack. But I've no doubt that you'll put the troops together in a useful way.[2] Pray toil away, Sir Grand Hetman.[3] You are a most intelligent, good and loyal man, and as for us, we love and caress you. I'm very sorry for my ally. It is strange that though he's rather smart and knowledgeable, still he didn't have a single loyal man who could have said to him: "Do not irritate your subjects with nonsense." Now he is dying hated by everyone.[4] What exactly was so odd about being crowned the King of Hungary, especially considering that its subjects are devoted to the crown? They saved his mother from losing everything in 1740.[5] Were I in his place, I would've waited on them hand and foot. Votre couronne de laurier Vous ira à merveille et je serai charmée de voir un Chevalier de St. André aussi digne de cet ornement, et auquel je l'ai donné parce qu'il l'avait mérité par ses services et sa fidélité.[6]

I couldn't read of your gratitude and what you wrote on this occasion without crying. Your intentions for using the fleet will be brought up in conversation. According to your advice, we'll say that the current bad condition of the roads is the reason why nothing is being delivered and the like. But for God's sake, take care of yourself, don't put yourself in danger unnecessarily, je ne veux pas Vous perdre, mon cher Monsieur.[7]

[. . .] I thank you for the sheets; I'll make use of them at Tsarskoe Selo. Farewell, my friend, God be with you, be safe and well. We are fasting, and your Cornet[8] is wearing the ribbon of St. Anne. His conduct is irreproachable.

---

1. "I hope this little kit gives you as much pleasure as I have in sending it to you."

2. In response to an edict dated 10 January describing the danger of a Prussian attack, Potemkin was developing a plan to move certain regiments of his army to the anticipated areas of attack near Mogilyov.

3. On 10 January, Potemkin was officially given the title of Grand Hetman of the Imperial Yekaterinoslav and Black Sea Cossack Hosts.

4. Joseph II died on 9 (20) February. He was succeeded by his brother Leopold II (1747–1792).

5. The Hungarian nobility had come to the defense of the young queen Maria Theresa (1717–1780) (Joseph II's mother) in 1740 against Frederick the Great in the War of the Austrian Succession. Joseph's opposition to being crowned king of Hungary was based upon his desire to centralize and standardize the Habsburg Empire which was a messy patchwork of kingdoms and provinces.

6. "Your crown of laurels will suit you marvelously, and I shall be charmed to see a chevalier of St. Andrew so worthy of this ornament to whom I gave it since through his services and fidelity he has earned it." Potemkin received the long-promised laurel crown made of gold and diamonds in January, for which he thanked Catherine in a previous letter.

7. "I do not want to lose you, my dear sir."

8. Platon Zubov.

413. POTEMKIN TO CATHERINE

8 February [1790]. Jassy

Your Most Gracious Majesty. I am at a loss as to how I can move anything from here. All the regiments are isolated on the steppe: the men haven't any chance to find shelter from the winter, and the horses haven't any feed. You deign to write, beloved matushka, that Count Saltykov said that ten thousand could be spared from the Caucasus. With this His Highness proved that he can't count. Indeed, when he was there himself he spoke of there being so few men, and for this reason didn't undertake anything. Ce n'est pas son affaire de combiner les choses.[1] I have made my remarks about the rescript.[2] And so shall I now say: can we not do everything possible to divert the Prussian King from his intentions? Let him take Pomerania and whatever he wants. I beseech you as someone who is obliged to you for everything, order that efforts be made to improve matters or else everything will be turned upside down. Where are we to find the troops and the requisite number of commanders and will this not exceed all our energies?! By dividing ourselves into small groups all spread out we'll become weak everywhere and shall achieve no succcess anywhere. The distance separating our borders makes it impossible for one unit to offer help to the other. If you say make peace no matter what, then consider that upon seeing such a large diversion, the Turks will never agree to one. The worst thing is to try to impose on them. I am doing everything to get the Vizier to approach us. Despite considerable effort, the Austrians were unable to gain anything by bargaining, and are now demanding that we negotiate together.

I do not have a good idea of the arrangement of the regiments in the Causcasus. I'll direct some of them from there to White Russia, but only after they arrive. Pray consider for yourself—it's impossible to set out from the Crimea till there is pasturage under foot. As I reported earlier, the regiments of the Ukrainian Army are so thin that a regiment does not comprise even one battalion. Recruits are being gathered, although few have yet to arrive in Kharkov. I had reckoned on putting everything in order and on bringing the troops up to full strength, but that will now be quite difficult to do. If it were possible to gain only six months, then I could repair matters.[3]

We must treat the inhabitants of the Caucasus, and especially the Kabardinians, with kindness and in so doing secure this side, and then we also won't need to keep so many troops there. We've taken much land from the Kabarda, but it's useless to us. For the time being I'll move the provincial administration to Astrakhan. I have taken it upon myself to organize that land and this will allow us to greatly reduce the number of troops there.

Forgive me, beloved matushka, for writing disjointedly: I've been fighting an illness and lay in bed for four days. I'm better now, thank God, following an attack of severe diarrhea, though I'm as weak as a fly.

Things were bad in Hungary and Transylvania. They demanded all the rights that had been taken from them and said they didn't have a King since he hadn't been crowned. The Emperor has returned everything, and has promised to accept both the crown and the conditions. And in so doing he's won over all of Hungary to go to war.

I'm transferring troops to every place possible, and shall report immediately once I am done, however, it would be very good if this could be avoided.

For my entire life I remain your most loyal and most grateful subject

Prince Potemkin-Tavrichesky

---

1. "It is not his place to be putting things together."

2. In a separate report Potemkin wrote his reply to the rescript Catherine sent him with her letter of 10 January. He reiterated that the forces in the south must not be transferred to the Polish border since that would give an opening to the Turks. To defend the Crimea, Potemkin urged sending the fleet to the Kuban region, which would also reduce the number of troops required there. His plans concerning Poland laid out the previous year were approved by Catherine and entrusted to his authority.

3. The goal of gaining six months to prepare for Russia's defense became the primary focus of Russian diplomacy. Special emphasis was given to weakening ties between Berlin and London and to securing an alliance with the latter.

414. CATHERINE TO POTEMKIN

1 March 1790

My friend, Prince Grigory Aleksandrovich. From my signed rescript you'll see the condition of affairs at the present hour and how necessary it is to prepare ourselves to thwart our enemies' evil intentions.[1] All possible measures are being taken—to subdue their malice, to stave off and to extirpate the principles they once adopted so as to humiliate Russia and to involve her in their designs and intentions in accordance with their sham German interests. We must now keep our eyes open—what state of affairs will the Emperor's death bring about? Yet if the future is to be judged according to the past, then matters will remain practically unchanged. For the Berlin court made perfidious, evil and arrogant use of the reports made to it preliminary to the conditions for peace that included a request for their good offices. This proves the mentality of that court and the mad designs of Hertzberg, who rules over the King. Now they demand Thorn and Danzig from Poland. I say let him have them, but I recall that in 1763 Bestuzhev wrote in the Conference minutes that this constitutes *casus foederis* since the treaties and guarantees for Danzig are unique.[2] I know, am aware of and well recall what was said and done against this following that day, and I am trying to change everything for the better and to settle matters so that everything is not turned upside down, as you write.

But it is not enough that we act solely with the pen, rather our enemies must be shown that we can't be taken by surprise and that we are ready to defend the Fatherland with our teeth. They have now gotten the idea that having begun to draw everything to the warring regions, they, together with the Poles, will make their way to Moscow without finding so much as a tomcat at home. Our borders are quite expansive, that's true, but if our enemies don't encounter any resistance, then they'll commence to making them smaller shortly thereafter. We need peace, however, I am quite of the same opinion as you, namely that once the Turks see a powerful diversion, they won't be as quick to make peace as they would themselves desire had they no such hope. But to impose peace or to solicit it from the Turks will produce nothing. The Austrians have ruined many of their affairs by being hasty. We'll see what the new King of Hungary and Bohemia does.

Send me the reapportionment of the troops you are detailing to the White Russian borders. I cannot promise that the six months you request will be gained, but it does seem that we have already gained some time. It will not be at all difficult for me to treat the inhabitants of the Crimea kindly, as you write, however, I do not receive any word of these matters here, and consequently I can't say a thing. I am truly sorry, my dear friend, that you were ill, and I ask you to take the greatest possible care of your health.

We shall see what happens in Hungary and Transylvania under the new Sovereign, but as for the inhabitants of Brabant, they're now just as bewildered as the French. However, the discord among them has stopped England and Holland from recognizing their independence. Pitt is still trying to avoid war, but will perhaps be led into one against his will by the Berlin court and the Princess of Orange. It's now also possible that the election of the Roman King will divert their attention somewhat.[3] Nevertheless, our being prepared won't ruin a thing. Sir Grand Hetman of the Yekaterinoslav and Black Sea Cossacks, live well, do good deeds and be certain that I shall beg God to bless your undertakings in the service of my affairs and the Empire. Farewell, my dear friend, I am well. I give your Cornet an irreproachable testimonial.

---

1. Prussia and the Sublime Porte signed an alliance on 20 (31) January 1790. Catherine's rescript informed Potemkin of this, and that Britain had refused a treaty with Russia. London also objected to Russia's conditions for peace with Sweden and the Porte.

2. Chancellor Aleksei Petrovich Bestuzhev-Riumin (1693–1768) served as one of Catherine's chief advisors in the early 1760s. During the Polish interregnum of 1763–1764, Bestuzhev, well aware of Frederick the Great's territorial desires, had been a staunch opponent of joint Russo-Prussian policy toward Poland.

3. Britain refused all overtures from Russia and was becoming ever more involved with the affairs of the Berlin court. Catherine hoped the election of the new Holy Roman Emperor would temporarily distract the Prussians from their eastern designs.

415. POTEMKIN TO CATHERINE

[10 March 1790]

Your Most Gracious Majesty. The occupation of the three Polish provinces, marked by lines on the map, should be carried out in agreement with our allies, or else we shall be left to face the fire all by ourselves should they come to the defense of these territories. I fear they may do this.[1] And for this reason we need an effective minister there. Prince Golitsyn,[2] however, is an Austrian, and he draws a salary without doing a thing. Out of my unlimited zeal for you, my beloved matushka, I say that Stackelberg is detrimental in Poland. Time will prove to you this truth. Matushka, what you deign to write about Bestuzhev's minutes regarding Danzig is known even without them. One can see that it's better not to give away anything to anyone. But if, given the circumstances, he must be thrown a bone to gnaw on, then let him have it. This will be beneficial—he'll lose credit in Poland, will expose his true self to Europe and, what's more, the Turks and the English will not remain indifferent.[3] We shall gain a means to end the war and shall then immediately direct all our forces against the Prussian King. With God's blessing, after a single campaign we'll leave him with nothing but the Electorate of Brandenburg. Otherwise we'll have many troubles, and he'll be beyond harm's reach. Believe me as your ward who will not spare his life for your honor. Believe me as one devoted to the Fatherland, believe that Russia's glory is dear to me, and that I am greatly honored to have been chosen by you to uphold it. He who does not adapt to circumstances is always lost. We must of course conclude a commercial treaty with England and in this way excite their interest; without this nothing will bind them to us and so the King will win. Order our ministers in Berlin and England not to consider a thing at present so that we might buy some time, even if only a little, for our regiments to get into position. In this way we shall turn things around, otherwise we'll be in a bad state. We've no other means to buy time or to shorten the distances. Order greater use be made of politics. Just imagine, we're experiencing something unprecedented for the season: it's storming and the snow is piling up. How are we to move across the steppe? Both the men and the horses will freeze. We've neither hay nor firewood. That fool Bibikov has marched off beyond the Kuban with nearly all his troops. I have sent a subaltern officer to take command and to bring them back. He will bring ruin to the troops at the present time.[4]

The infantry regiments, which were taken from White Russia, can be taken from the Finnish Army and returned without harm. Honest to God there are enough there, if only there were someone capable of leading them.

We were wrong to demand that reconciliation was only possible if the Swedish King be rendered powerless to declare war. We'll never reconcile in this way. His brother? He could then easily be left a lonely old recluse.[5]

Pray note from the reapportionments that by removing troops from the army engaged against the Turks it will be weakened. All the more so given the terrible shortage of men in the regiments of the former Ukrainian Army. It would be very useful to have troops formed in Russia from among the poor town dwellers, for they would be able to protect the border.[6]

Your most loyal and most grateful subject
Prince Potemkin-Tavrichesky

[. . .]

---

1. According to Potemkin's plan, in the event of a crisis with Poland and Prussia, the grand hetman's Cossack forces were to occupy the territories of Bratslav, Kiev, and Podolia in Polish Ukraine. The plan required that Austria move its troops into Galicia to aid Russia.

2. Prince Dmitry Mikhailovich Golitsyn (1721–1793) had been Russia's ambassador to Austria for twenty-nine years by 1790.

3. Potemkin hoped that by allowing the Prussians to take Danzig from Poland the Poles would see that Prussia, not Russia, represented the real threat to their territory.

4. Attacked by a party of Cossacks from beyond the Kuban in January 1790, Commander of the Caucasus Corps Lieutenant-General Yury Bogdanovich Bibikov (1743–1812) set off in pursuit on his own in the direction of Anapa.

5. Secret peace talks with Gustav III began during the winter break in fighting. Russia put as a condition for peace a return to the former Swedish constitution, according to which only the Riksdag could declare war. Gustav rejected this outright. The reference to his brother, Prince Karl, duke of Sudermania, who was single, apparently refers to the possibility of his becoming king should Gustav renounce the throne.

6. In order to increase the size of Russia's armed forces, Potemkin was permitted to form Cossack regiments from the so-called single-homesteaders of the southern provinces, from the former Zaporozhian Cossacks, from the coachmen, and from the poor town dwellers (*meshchane*).

416. CATHERINE TO POTEMKIN

30 March 1790

My dear friend, Prince Grigory Aleksandrovich. I have received your letters of 10 March from Jassy and am quite sorry about your illness, and it worries me extremely.[1] God grant that I may hear of your recovery as soon as possible. The reapportioning of troops, particularly in the Observation Army,[2] that you promised to send is greatly needed as soon as possible, since upon it depends, so to speak, the integrity and safety of the Empire. For our enemies are staring us straight in the face. Stackelberg's letter to you was mad; I have ordered him recalled, and have appointed Bulgakov envoy to Poland.[3] You will see from the rescript and the papers enclosed with it how they try through their shameful deeds to draw us into humiliation and disgrace and to pull the chestnuts from the fire using our hands. Yet they have signed a fifty-year offensive treaty with the Turks, with the enemies of Christ's name. May God grant that the regiments marching into the Ukraine are able to make their way across the steppe as quickly as possible. Sir, when you have the chance, do order that sheds or clay huts or shelters made of reeds or rushes be built every twenty versts across the steppe. I built some of wood in this province and in Finland every thirty sazhens[4] in which the passing troops fit quite comfortably. A retired soldier lives in each one. So nice are my sheds that while underway the Guards haven't wanted to sleep anywhere else. As I know you love utility more than anything, may even this advice of mine not be disagreeable to you. Have no fear, my friend: only in extreme extremity shall I order the Observation Army to move, for now is not the time to go on the offensive against a new enemy, but rather to remain on the defensive—till they truly lay into us.

There is news that the Prussians are on the move from the direction of Silesia.

Adieu, mon cher Ami, portés Vous bien.

God be with you and may He grant you every success.

1. In a second letter dated 10 March, Potemkin complained of being so sick and weak that he was unable even to lift his head.

2. A reference to the army being put together in White Russia to defend against a Prussian attack.

3. Stackelberg was replaced in August by Bulgakov, who had been freed by the Turks in November 1789 as a sign of goodwill following Russia's numerous victories.

4. A *sazhen'* was equivalent to 2.13 meters.

417. CATHERINE TO POTEMKIN

19 April 1790

My true friend, Prince Grigory Aleksandrovich. Your illness worries me more than anything else. For God's sake, take care of yourself. Though you're not one of those weak souls, nevertheless with age some care is necessary to preserve one's health, more, that is, than in one's first youth. God grant you a full recovery as soon as possible.

It appears the news from Vienna is pleasant: the King of Hungary and Bohemia[1] assures me in his letters that he intends to keep all of his brother's obligations to us. Regarding peace, it seems you've reached a final outcome, however, it's a pity that Hasan Pasha has died.[2] Barozzi's[3] journal shows quite convincingly the state of affairs. Everything now depends on whom they select Vizier: the mad Yusuf or someone inclined toward peace. For Christ's sake, watch out for your Turk. God grant that I am deceived, and do forgive me, but I am most apprehensive that he might try to serve you poisoned food.[4] They do this sort of thing, and you yourself write that Hasan Pasha was almost poisoned. The Prussians gave them the reason and perhaps the idea for doing this, and from these enemies everything ought to be expected, for their malice is mostly personal, against me and, consequently, against you too, whom they fear most of all. I hope that I am deceiving myself, but it wasn't possible to keep silent after this thought came to mind. Of course, on the other hand it is good to show kindness to this man if he is sincere, and in so doing give other Turks cause for overcoming their aversion to us.

A letter was sent this very day from me to Field Marshal Rumiantsev in which I order him unequivocally to leave Moldavia, either for the waters or for Russia, for his stay there is detrimental to my affairs. We'll see what happens.[5]

I thank you for your best wishes on the holiday[6] and hope as well that God will help you in all your acts in the service of the Empire. Farewell, my friend, Christ be with you.

1. Leopold II.

2. Grand Vizier Gazi Hasan Pasha died mysteriously on 18 March. Sultan Selim III had decided against peace, and it is possible that he had Hasan Pasha poisoned in order to replace him with Sherif Hasan Pasha.

3. Ivan Stepanovich Barozzi, a member of the College of Foreign Affairs, had been sent by Potemkin to the grand vizier to undertake preliminary peace negotiations.

4. Early in 1790, Potemkin received a Turkish messenger from the Walachian hospodar named Salig-Aga, the former seraskier of Walachian forces. Potemkin and the highly educated Salig-Aga, who spoke five languages and had traveled throughout Europe, grew quite fond of each other. Salig-Aga stayed on with the prince at Jassy.

5. Despite Catherine's continuing commands for him to leave Moldavia, Rumiantsev, suffering from edema in his legs, remained there and did not depart until 1792.

6. Potemkin had sent Easter greetings to her in a letter dated 1 April.

418. POTEMKIN TO CATHERINE

Jassy. 2 May [1790]

Your Most Gracious Majesty. What dirty tricks that shameless Bibikov has played, that fool, drunkard, and coward. He's brave only when there's no danger before his eyes. He departed after hurriedly gathering some troops, similar to Mazepa.[1] Pray note from Rosen's[2] report that in addition to a shortage of provisions, he refers to odd and unbelievable conditions. I can't even imagine it beyond what we presently know. Was any treachery noted, or did he capitulate in some shameful way, or did the army, as is to be expected in necessary situations, rebel? I think he had with him someone from the enemy who lured him to Anapa, for according to information gathered from men having arrived from Tsar Grad, it is apparent that the Turks sent reinforcements to Anapa long ago. What efforts and troubles will it cost me to repair what has been ruined? And concerning the matter of peace, how many interruptions this will cause: it's impossible that they won't become arrogant.[3]

You deigned to write, and, it seems, to write angrily in your last letter concerning the condition of affairs with the Prussian King.[4] Whatever I say it is for your benefit, and I say it out of true zeal. Many events have justified my thoughts. I shall repeat again that there is little we can do now. Once we've freed our hands here, then you can act boldly. I assure you, that without even engaging in battle I shall destroy his army in a single campaign. I firmly rely on God's help and do boast that I, better than all others, shall find powerful and new methods for dealing with him. We'll simply unleash a swarm of light cavalry and His Majesty won't even be able to dine in peace. This is how one must fight him, always pestering and disturbing him; an occasion will arise for such a desertion that his entire army will vanish. Matushka, if you deign to say on my account, that should God grant us peace, everyone will tell you to leave the Prussian King be, then be just: I am not one who would consent to forget the insults against you and Russia. Pray give me a secret instruction that I may hold in the ready in the event that once God helps us to finish with the Turks I can wage war against Prussia, and you will see whether I hesitate. I owe you too much not to consider it my duty to sacrifice myself for your honor and glory. For this reason I have repeated and repeat again that we must now establish good relations with them, so that once we are free we can act with force. There can be no other way.

It seems the new Vizier was intentionally chosen so as not to disturb the chances for peace, for the courts that have influence with the Porte made an effort on the behalf of Yusuf Pasha and in that case it would've been impossible to pacify the open partisans of war.[5]

The Poles have doubled their civility toward us and have begun visiting my headquarters, which they never dared do before. I hope Bulgakov will be able to turn matters around once it is opportune. Necessity required that I keep him here since I don't have anyone else to conduct the French correspondence.[6] Bühler still hasn't come back from Vienna, but I'll send him[7] tomorrow. I know that Ambassador Golitsyn is beloved in Vienna, but whether he loves Russia, that I don't know, and I see that he sends home little information about the state of the Austrian lands, and he didn't write of the eccentric acts committed by the late Emperor while with the army. Yet such intelligence about our allies is necessary so that we can estimate their true strength and not merely rely on our hopes. The King has now obliged all the departments in many ways, however, the military, which has not received any salutation from him, is grumbling. The army expected to be given a good word.

The Prince of Württemberg[8] injured himself while mounting his horse, and an operation is his only hope, although this too presents more danger than hope. For this reason he requests permission to go to Petersburg so that he might see his dear sister before dying. I have let him go.

While alive I remain,
your most loyal and most grateful subject
Prince Potemkin-Tavrichesky

---

1. Not only had Bibikov marched off in pursuit of the Cossacks without first consulting with Potemkin, as required, he did not take with him the necessary supplies for his men, who suffered terribly from his lack of planning. Ivan Mazepa (1645–1709) was the legendary Cossack leader who fought on the side of Charles XII of Sweden in the Great Northern War.

2. Potemkin sent Lieutenant-General Baron Vladimir Ivanovich von Rosen (1742–1790) to take command after learning of Bibikov's adventure.

3. Potemkin feared that any setback by Russian forces would embolden the Turks then negotiating with the Russians.

4. In a letter dated 8 April, Catherine made reference to the insults she has suffered at the hands of the Prussian king.

5. Koja Yusuf Pasha, who had earlier held the office of grand vizier from 1786–1789, was reappointed on 27 February 1791 (n.s.) following the execution of Sherif Hasan.

6. Bulgakov stayed with Potemkin at Jassy until leaving for Warsaw in August. Meanwhile, the Poles were beginning to chafe under the burdens that came with their new Prussian alliance (increased duties, recruitment levies, etc.).

7. Bulgakov.

8. He returned to St. Petersburg on 28 June and did survive. The prince died in August 1791 of fever while back in the south with Potemkin.

419. CATHERINE TO POTEMKIN

14 May 1790

My true friend, Prince Grigory Aleksandrovich. After I completed yesterday's letters, the courier arrived with your missives of 2 May.[1] I thank you for your best wishes for the holidays and I truly know that they are candid and sincere.

Lieutenant-General Bibikov's expedition is quite odd and unparalleled. I think he has lost his mind: for forty days he kept his men practically in the water and without food. It's amazing even a single man survived. I suppose few returned with him. Let me know how many were lost; I grieve very much for them. If the army did rebel against him, one can't be surprised; rather, one should be more surprised by their forty-day patience. This affair resembles somewhat that of Totleben and Sukhotin during the last war.[2] It's true that it'll cost you much effort and trouble to repair what's been ruined. May God grant you strength and health. Oh, but you did please me so with your letter that I'm now answering. We'll see what needs to be done once God allows you to make peace. I wrote without anger; my sole apprehension is that the insults against the Russian Empire have not always been received with that feeling which the fervor for her dignity has impressed upon my heart, toute ma vie a été employée à maintenir la splendeur de la Russie, il n'est donc pas étonnant que les offenses et les injures qu'on lui fait me soyent insupportables à supporter en silence et à les dissimuler comme nous avons fait jusqu'ici par cette prudence momentanée qui l'exige; mais souvent en les étouffant, de pareils ressentimens intérieurs jusqu'ici, n'en deviennent que plus vifs.[3]

I talk to you as I do to myself, but I'll do what the most dispassionate reasoning indicates to be appropriate and timely. If the Vizier has been selected so as not to hinder peace, then it seems you will soon furnish us with this blessing. As for the other side, matters there have become critical, as you'll see from the official papers.[4] If we had a corps of some twenty-thousand in Livonia, then everything would be safe. Moreover, the change in Poland would speed up.

I wrote you that the smartest thing would be to send Andrei Razumovsky there; his wife is Viennese, and he has connections there; he isn't
stupid, and he's sown his wild oats, et il paroit être devenu beaucoup plus
prudent.[5] He's burned his fingers, so much so in fact that he's lost a good
deal of hair.[6] The Prince of Württemberg has arrived and is in a pitiful
condition. I saw him this morning for the first and I fear last time, on veut
lui faire deux opérations, il est fort résigné; sa soeur croit qu'au bout de six
semaines il pourra s'en retourner à l'armée, mais les chirurgiens regardent
l'opération comme très dangereuse. Adieu, mon cher Ami, je Vous aime de
tout mon coeur[7] and I pray God for your health and for good successes in
peace and war. You're a clever fellow. Thanks too for being kind to Platon
Aleksandrovich. He merits it through his sincere attachment to me and
his good disposition and the qualities of his heart and soul.

I have written to Field Marshal Rumiantsev that he leave Moldavia
immediately.

There's nothing new from Finland at this hour.

---

1. Potemkin had written Catherine a second letter on 2 May in which he sent his belated
birthday greetings.

2. Major-General Count Gotlieb-Heinrich von Totleben (1710–1773), a native of Saxony in
Russian service, had been charged with spying and put on trial in the early years of Catherine's reign. He was later returned to service and sent at the head of Russian troops to Georgia in 1768. His actions there aroused the displeasure of the local authorities and the open
disobedience of forces under the command of Brigadier Aleksandr Nikolaevich Sukhotin
(1726–1805).

3. "my entire life has been spent maintaining Russia's splendor. It cannot be surprising that
I cannot bear to endure in silence and to conceal the offenses and injuries directed against
her as we have done until now as a result of the demands of momentary caution; indeed,
by frequently stifling them, such resentments, which had remained inside up to that point,
only become stronger."

4. Catherine informed Potemkin of the growing crisis with Prussia. Frederick William II,
backed by Britain, demanded that Russia and Austria conclude peace with Turkey and Sweden forthwith on the basis of the *status quo ante bellum*. In addition, Prussia demanded the
role of intermediary in the peace talks.

5. "and he seems to have become much more cautious."

6. In response to Potemkin's criticism of Prince Golitsyn, Catherine recommended Andrei
Razumovsky as ambassador to Austria. In addition to his suspected liaison with Grand
Duchess Natalia, for which Catherine had earlier banished him from court in 1776, Razu-
movsky, a true Don Juan, also got into trouble while envoy to Naples where he fell in love
with Queen Caroline-Marie, the daughter of Maria Theresa. Despite these indiscretions,
Catherine respected his diplomatic abilities, and he was made envoy to Austria.

7. "they want to perform two operations on him. He is fully resigned to this. His sister
thinks he will be able to return to the army after six weeks, but the surgeons consider the
operation to be very dangerous. Farewell, my dear friend, I love you with all my heart". Two
separate operations were performed on Prince Karl. One of the attending physicians, the
Frenchman Massot, would conduct the autopsy on Potemkin's body a little over a year later.

420. POTEMKIN TO CATHERINE

[29 May 1790]

I was ecstatic to learn that the Swedes had been so gloriously repulsed from Reval.[1] Your Most Gracious Majesty, you were kind to the late Prince Anhalt[2] with your promise of villages. His widow finds herself in poverty. Perhaps a pension could be found for her; I am only interested since he bore the name Anhalt. Count Anhalt[3] lives in Petersburg, and through his nasty inclinations is corrupting the morals of the young cadets and doesn't have the time or the ability to look after the Finnish Corps of Chasseurs. Would you please order Major-General Baron Pahlen[4] be made its head. The corps requires mending.

As soon as General-in-Chief Prince Dolgorukov[5] arrives, I'll send him to the regiments gathering in White Russia. It wouldn't be bad to send Razumovsky to Vienna. We have extreme need of an effective minister in Venice. Only there can he can receive accurate intelligence and instructions and by showing kindness to the Republic he can cause the Turks a good deal of worry. I have intelligence that the French treaty with the Austrians runs out in the month of July, and they will approach the Prussians, and that they are secretly courting the Swedes.

The high cost of goods is exceeding all limits: officers' cloth is selling for 8 rubles. It is already difficult, and for many of the officers impossible, to maintain themselves. The honor of the uniform has nothing to do with the quality of its cloth, and the closer it is to the soldiers' the more it resembles a military uniform. While sitting with you, matushka, I recommended that officers up to the rank of Field Marshal, when on active duty and in time of war, should wear uniforms made of the same plain cloth worn by the soldiers! You praised this, and I, having dressed myself in this manner, have ordered all the officers today to do just the same. This is an important matter; it bears a resemblance to Sparta. Praise me for this in a letter, and I shall show it around, and then even all the generals will dress in this manner.

It would be good if Alopeus[6] were removed from Berlin and someone a bit more consequential were sent there to curry favor with the King, and at the same time to court his minister in every possible way. I assure you that if we can buy time till the middle of July, they'll stay put after that. Your expressions of approval about my Cornet of the Chevaliers-Gardes attach me to him all the more and give him the right to expect your favors.

The Preobrazhensky Regiment is yours and it's up to you to reward whomever you so please; however, since you chose me to be its head, so my honor is bound to this regiment. The Guards officers have grown weak from luxury; having joined, so to speak, clubs and theaters they've forgotten about service, and the manly valor that goes with it. They need leaders who are examples of valor and who know of service. Is that soft Vasilchikov[7] such a man? Never having seen war nor having served in the infantry, he's not the one for the present time. Since the St. George Regiment has been attached to the Life-Guards Cuirassier Regiment, so Colonel and Chevalier Morkov, who has served with distinction in two wars, remains. He's as brave as a sword. I am ready to lay him before your feet. He would lead your Guards of this first regiment through fire and water.[8] But what's to be done if he's too late? I must tell you the truth, and you, matushka, pray know how impartial are my endorsements. You ordered me to present worthy men, and I shall soon present many now in service.

Your most loyal and most grateful subject
Prince Potemkin-Tavrichesky

I sent your order to Count Pyotr Aleksandrovich. Here's his answer: he's getting ready to depart any day now, but we'll see what really happens. Nonetheless, no matter where he is, he'll do us no good, so forget about him. Time will make known his schemes, and so I'll hold my tongue.

---

1. In a letter dated 13 May, Catherine wrote of how Admiral Chichagov's squadron at Reval had repulsed a Swedish attack on 2 May.

2. Lieutenant-General Prince Viktor Amadeus Anhalt died from wounds received attacking the Swedes on 19 April. Catherine wept upon hearing of his death.

3. Count Frederick Anhalt (1732–1794) joined Russian service in 1783 and was placed in charge of the Corps of Noble Cadets in St. Petersburg in 1786. Potemkin's harsh judgment does not square with Anhalt's generally positive reputation as an educator.

4. One of the heroes of Ochakov, Major-General Peter von der Pahlen (1745–1826) was dispatched to Finland by Potemkin. After the war, Pahlen played an important role in the diplomatic negotiations with Gustav III.

5. Prince Yury Vladimirovich Dolgorukov (1740–1830).

6. Though he lacked an official position and title, Maksim Maksimovich Alopeus (1748–1822) was Russia's de facto minister to the Prussian court, which he officially became in 1795.

7. Grigory Alekseevich Vasilchikov (d. 1838) was in charge of the Preobrazhensky Regiment in the 1790 campaign against the Swedes.

8. Catherine took Potemkin's advice and entrusted the Preobrazhensky Regiment to Irakly Ivanovich Morkov (around 1750–1829), a veteran of the storming of Ochakov. He later returned to fight against the Turks, participating in the siege of Ismail.

421. CATHERINE TO POTEMKIN

Tsarskoe Selo. 8 June 1790

My dear friend, Prince Grigory Aleksandrovich. I have received your letters from the Day of the Holy Trinity and 29 May. If you were very gladdened by God's miracles at Reval, then their consequences will be no less pleasing to you. When the Swedes learned that Kruse[1] had left Kronstadt together with the fleet, they decided to try to hinder the two squadrons from uniting, and after passing Hogland they attacked the Kronstadt squadron near Seskär on 23 May without any success.² The cannon fire lasted throughout the 24th and 25th, and by then Kruse had already set off in pursuit of them. They kept trying to shoot from afar, and our ships tried to get closer to them. On the final day it was noticed that the Swedes had not fired more than three shots from their broadsides. Throughout these three days the cannon fire could be heard quite clearly, both in town as well as here, and we could also tell that the firing was getting farther away. On 26 May the Swedes learned that Admiral Chichagov was on his way from Reval with eleven ships to join up with the Kronstadt squadron. The Swedes then joined up with their oared flotilla, which pulled them past the shoals, past the rocks and between the islands into the Gulf of Vyborg. And there they continue to thrive till the present moment, having been cut off from the sea by our entire fleet of ships; every possible effort is being made daily on both sides to deny their oared fleet any opportunity from getting out of Björkö Sund. Vice Admiral Kozlianinov³ together with thirty galleys is positioned near Trangsund behind the Swedish fleet, and Nassau⁴ is supposed to head toward Björkö with his oared vessels from the right side of Kronstadt. As for Slizov,⁵ he is to sail from Fredrikshamn toward our own ships and frigates with a good number of gunboats. Bomb ketches and prams are on their way from Reval, and it appears that with God's help they won't get out of this mousetrap in one piece.

Meanwhile, they're madly scurrying about in Vyborg Bay like chickens with their heads cut off. They've begun making landings here and there and are trying to find or to create any possible opening. During the night from the 6th to the 7th of June they attacked Buksgevden⁶ on the Island of Uransaari. They were given a hostile reception, however, and were driven back to the water, and then, amid the confusion, to their boats, whence they departed after having suffered heavy casualties. Forty men, two officers, and four banners were captured. They say their men are being given half rations, and they run away when they're sent for water, which has already happened with some hundred men. Fersen and Rek⁷ are stationed on that side near the coast to the right of Vyborg and are maintaining communications with Sisterbek, where Melissino⁸ is located with the battery. I visited Peterhof and Kronstadt on 29 May; the first three days there the cannon fire was so loud the windows rattled. Such are my activities out here in the country, my friend. There's plenty to keep me busy, and it seems that so far God has offered His help. We pray He'll continue to show mercy.

[. . .]

I wrote to the Prince now in possession of Anhalt-Bernburg⁹ in order to learn the condition of the wife and mother of that house's late Lieutenant-General. I highly praise what you write about your having put on a caftan made of soldiers' cloth, and I desire all my generals and officers to do the same.

I hope we can draw out matters with the Prussians till the middle of July. And I wholeheartedly endorse your plan that you sent on this matter. It's also good that you intend to commission Prince Yury Dolgorukov; I suppose he's already with you. Should you make peace, everything will become easier, however, it's difficult to imagine that the Turks would take up negotiations now save as a last resort. Have a safe trip to Kherson; I wish you health and may your body and soul be strong. Farewell, God be with you.

I hereby attest to the sincere, zealous attachment of your Cornet of the Chevaliers-Gardes[10] and his good character, and once more I entrust to you his brother,[11] that frolicsome lad, and beseech you to take care of him. For his brother is a bit worried about him, though I hope he has no reason to. He doesn't write him.

---

1. Noted for his bravery in the Battle of Chesme (1770), Vice Admiral Aleksandr Ivanovich Kruse (1727–1799) was charged with defending the capital from naval attack and disrupting the activities of the Swedish flotilla.

2. The actions off Styrsudden in the Gulf of Finland, described here by Catherine, did not produce a clear victory for either side. Nevertheless, even though no ships were lost, Russia's naval forces were able to trap the Swedish fleet in Vyborg Bay.

3. Vice Admiral Timofei Gavrilovich Kozlianinov (d. 1798) was one of the commanders of the Baltic fleet.

4. Rear Admiral Prince Charles of Nassau-Siegen, who had earlier fought in the Black Sea.

5. Captain Pyotr Borisovich Slizov commanded the small skerries fleet from the beginning of the war. He was later replaced by Prince Nassau-Siegen.

6. Colonel Fyodor Buksgevden.

7. Major-General Baron Ivan Yevstafievich von Fersen (1747–1799) was one of the experienced commanders recently sent by Potemkin from the south to fight in Finland. Major-General Ivan von Rek had also been transferred from the south to fight against the Swedes.

8. Probably Aleksei Petrovich Melissino (1761–1813), the son of General Pyotr Ivanovich Melissino.

9. Karl Ludwig, the elder brother of Viktor Amadeus.

10. Platon Zubov.

11. Valerian Zubov.

422. POTEMKIN TO CATHERINE

[19 June 1790]

Your Most Gracious Majesty! Having written my dispatch long ago, I had been expecting any day now the return of my messengers sent to the Vizier. I've received the first one, and so am now presenting a copy of the Vizier's letter.[1]

Beloved matushka, amid these circumstances that are a burden to you, do not fail to keep me informed.[2] Do you really not know the extent of my attachment, which is unlike that of all others? How can it be for me to hear ridiculous news from all corners and not to know whether or not it's true? As I am so in the dark, my concerns have rendered me unspeakably weak: deprived of sleep and food, I've become worse than an infant. Everyone can see my exhaustion. Though I must go to Kherson, nevertheless, I'm unable to move.

Should my life be worth anything, then amidst such circumstances at least tell me you are well.

God's mercy has rendered the position of the Swedish fleet most advantageous. We must act as quickly as possible and do what remains to be done. Should it move away, and, even more importantly, should the weather change, various scenarios are possible. There are long cannons in the arsenal that can mow down the enemy at a great distance; by putting them on some craft of whatever kind (galiots and other craft will work), you can strike the enemy with them without exposing yourself to cannon fire.

Five-pood naval mortars mounted on copper bases have a range of up to four versts; yet the best thing to do is to place one's faith in Christ our Savior and to forge straight ahead.

Once my weakness passes I'll send a courier with a detailed description of the enemy's position. While alive I remain

your most loyal and most grateful subject

Prince Potemkin-Tavrichesky

I love my Cornet more and more for his being pleasing to you. Concerning his brother, I shall take every care to make him fit for that military rank in which I shall lead him through all our ordeals. I'll overlook nothing to his benefit, but I shall not spoil him.

---

1. Potemkin was corresponding with the new grand vizier about peace negotiations.

2. Despite the critical situation in which the country found itself, Catherine did not write Potemkin for three weeks (from mid-May until 8 June).

423. CATHERINE TO POTEMKIN

28 June 1790

Well, my true friend, Prince Grigory Aleksandrovich, I've got something to write about. The Swedish King was bottled up together with his fleet of ships and galleys from 27 May till 21 June, as I wrote you. The entire time a westerly wind blew directly against our oared fleet; meanwhile, we managed to build new gunboats to replace those lost by Slizov. Finally, on the 20th a wind favorable to the oared vessels came up, and after entering the

Björkö Sund on this wind, Prince Nassau conducted a five-hour engagement with the Swedish King himself and his rowing vessels. The Swedish King then withdrew and set off further along Vyborg Bay, and after meeting up with his fleet of ships, together they attempted to force their way through our fleet. And what, in accordance with God's power and wisdom, do you suppose happened? After setting three fireships ablaze, the Swedes released them amidst a strong northerly wind in the direction of five ships from Rear Admiral Povalishin's[1] detachment. However, the fireships became entangled with two Swedish ships, and all five of the Swedish ships—but not one of ours—were blown sky high. Then, over the next four hours, the Swedes sailed past Povalishin. You'll see from the list, for my memory fails me, what he captured and what he sank, with Khanykov[2] right behind him. Chichagov, Kruse and Pushkin,[3] who meanwhile weighed anchor, set off in pursuit; please consult the list once more to see what they captured and destroyed.[4] Nassau started after the Swedish galley fleet as well. One 60-[gun] ship surrendered to him. Crown[5] had been waiting at Pitköpas. He's even now still sending captured galleys one right after the other to Kronstadt. One 74- and another 64-gun ship have been brought to Reval, and more are still being captured. In a word, all the fruits of this total victory have yet to be gathered: so far as many as five thousand prisoners, eight hundred cannons and small craft for which we still have no count. Different accounts are being given about the King. Some have it that he left on a long boat between two supply vessels; others that he was on his yacht "Amphion," which sank, and which he supposedly abandoned for some galley. This galley was captured, and from it he jumped onto a launch; this launch was also captured; from the launch he got into a boat, and this boat got away. We captured his breakfast: it comprised six pieces of rusk and smoked goose and two bottles of vodka. The King's brother[6] sailed off on his heavily damaged ship to Sveaborg, before which Chichagov is now cruising.

I send you best wishes on today's holiday and my congratulations on this victory. God has delivered us from this burden, and Chichagov has gladdened you once more, as you see.[7] I held a service here yesterday on the day of the Battle of Poltava, and on Sunday I'm leaving for town where there's to be a service at the Sailor's Church of Nicholas the Miracle Worker.

Farewell, God be with you. They say the Prussians are to get on the march on the first of July, of which I hereby inform you as well. They want to march toward Riga by way of Courland, but the King has been in Breslau for a long time now, and talks are still continuing in Reichenbach.[8]

Your Cornet[9] was gladdened by what you sent and his praiseworthy conduct continues without interruption.

1. Rear Admiral Illarion Afanasievich Povalishin (around 1739–1799) was in command of the Copenhagen squadron. He received the Order of St. George second class for his actions in the fighting in Vyborg Bay.

2. Rear Admiral Pyotr Ivanovich Khanykov (1744–1813) received the Order of St. George third class and a gold sword for his actions.

3. Vice Admiral Aleksei Vasilievich Musin-Pushkin was the flag-officer of the Baltic fleet as of 1789.

4. In the daring breakout from Vyborg Bay, the Swedes lost eight ships of the line, six frigates, two fireships, and several galleys. As many as 3,000 men were killed, and almost 5,000 men, including 200 officers, were captured.

5. Captain Robin Crown (1754–1841), a Scot, had joined Russian service in 1788. He was later made admiral.

6. Karl, duke of Sudermania and brother of Gustav III, served as the admiral of the Swedish navy.

7. Following the Battle of Vyborg Bay, Admiral Chichagov became the first and only naval commander to be awarded the Order of St. George first class.

8. Peace talks among the Triple Alliance powers, Poland, and Austria began at Reichenbach in Silesia on 16 (27) June 1790.

9. Platon Zubov.

424. POTEMKIN TO CATHERINE

Kokoteni. 9 July [1790]

Your Most Gracious Majesty. With all my heart's tenderness, I send you my best wishes on your accession day, an occasion for all to celebrate, and especially me. My health was poor that day and for a few more thereafter, but it's now improving.

The dispatch had been prepared, however, upon receiving news from Belgrade that cannon fire had been heard out at sea from the mouths of the Danube, I postponed sending it in anticipation of reliable information, which I received yesterday, that the enemy's fleet has appeared along the shores of Tauride opposite the tip of the cape of Tarkhanov, from where it descended toward Sevastopol and then headed south; it sailed about 20 versts off the coast on a northerly wind, which made it impossible for our fleet to sail out. As soon as it's possible, Admiral Ushakov will go search for it. I believe it's heading toward Sinop, and from there toward the Straits of Yenikale in the hope of landing its troops. I have written to my men to fight bravely on land and on sea. I pray God to help us.

All the regiments are on the march to their designated locations, but there are many sick. It was very hot, and now it's pouring rain and cold.

The Hungarian King is negotiating with the Prussian King. If only they wouldn't leave us completely out of this game, for they haven't been reporting anything to us here. In Poland the anti-Prussian sentiment is becoming ever more bitter by the day. Matushka, we need Bulgakov there.

I'm sending some camelhair cloth. You may enjoy wearing it in the summer. Farewell, beloved matushka, I kiss your tender hands and stead-fastly remain till death

your most loyal and most grateful subject

Prince Potemkin-Tavrichesky

425. CATHERINE TO POTEMKIN

17 July 1790

My dear friend, Prince Grigory Aleksandrovich, I thank you for your best wishes on the recent anniversary of my accession and for the feelings you expressed thereupon. I know that they are sincere. I regret that your health isn't as I should wish. God grant that the our fleet will deter the Turks' attempt on Tauride just as the Swedes were deterred upon trying to exit Vyborg Bay, which I think you received word of from here soon after sending your letters of 5 July.[1] However, after that truly glorious victory, six days [later] there followed an unfortunate affair with our oared flotilla that caused me terrible grief and distressed my heart more than anything since the smashing of the Black Sea fleet by the storm at the beginning of the current war. You'll see a description of all this in the papers sent to you; worst of all was the great loss of men.[2] Not growing despondent over this misfortune and shutting up my bitter sorrow inside my heart, I am working to see that we regain the advantage in our common cause, as much as is possible. I see from your letters that the regiments are on the move, but that (even with the best care) there are many sick. You complain that it's been very hot there, while here we've still not had a single warm day since the very beginning of spring, and it's so cold you can't even open a window. I think the Hungarian King is trying to drag out the negotiations. Bulgakov has departed for Poland and hasn't been in Moscow or White Russia for two weeks.

I thank you for the material you sent me. I've ordered a dress sewn from it in anticipation of warmer days; according to the calendar we're in the midst of the holidays, however, judging by the weather—it's September itself: almost uninterrupted rains and winds blowing in from the sea.

[. . .] Baron Igelstrom will meet with Chief Gentleman-of-the-Bed-chamber Armfelt on 20 July.[3] I don't know what they'll come up with, however, should the rumors of popular unrest in Sweden be true, then we probably shan't have to wait long for peace. There you have our good and bad news. Christ be with you.

Your Cornet handed me the things you sent and he remains without interruption just the same.

1. On that day Potemkin issued several reports on reorganizing a number of naval battalions.

2. The Second Battle of Svensksund of 28 June.

3. Sweden's victory over Nassau-Siegen's fleet in the Second Battle of Svensksund allowed Gustav to seek peace without a loss of face. Igelstrom met Baron Gustav Mauritz Armfelt (1757–1814), Gustav III's gentleman-of-the-bedchamber and the king's close friend, and reported to Catherine that there was a good chance of making peace with the Swedes.

426. POTEMKIN TO CATHERINE

[20 July 1790]

Beloved matushka, Your Most Gracious Majesty! Having hastened the dispatch of the last courier, I was unable to express all the joy I felt over the victory that God has wrought. This victory[1] is so great, and the help of the Almighty is obvious. All that remains is to end this business, and should everyone possess unanimous fervor, so shall we be blessed. Then I shall sing an Epinikeion[2] to her who is the architect of everything, for without her Petersburg would be empty. Her firm legs, which did not grow weak amid the misfortunes, have provided the foundation for everything.[3]

We haven't taken any vessels here as booty, however, the battle was brutal and all the more glorious for us in that Rear Admiral Ushakov attacked with both ardor and force an enemy who was twice as strong and who included his mentors. As I reported earlier, he defeated them soundly and didn't stop chasing them till nightfall. Three of their ships are so damaged that I don't think they will be able to return to sea during the present campaign, and damaged most of all was the Admiral's ship, whose flag was even captured by a launch from the ship "Georgi."[4]

Rear Admiral and Chevalier Ushakov is a man of excellent merits. He's knowledgeable like Howe, and brave like Rodney.[5] I am certain he will become a great naval commander. Do not abandon him, matushka.

In recent days another Turkish squadron has appeared coming out of the Danube: about six ships of the line, together with frigates and other vessels, about twenty in total, and it looks like their numbers are growing. Admiral Ushakov is on his way back to Sevastopol with the fleet, and if the wind is favorable he'll arrive soon. I fear it may not be. He needs to reach the harbor quickly in order to repair all the damage and to depart immediately for Tendra to join up with two ships as well as the three frigates of the line leaving the Liman, and then sail on to the Straits of Yenikale to meet up with two ships on their way from Taganrog.

The water in the Dnieper is unprecedentedly low. For this reason 20 of the best and largest naval brigantines and lansons did not arrive for

ONE PAW OUT OF THE MUD 353

this campaign. This is all the more to be pitied since the majority of them are meant to carry large naval mortars, and they all ought to have large artillery.

Two frigates of the line built in Khopra ran aground as well. I've now ordered that all vessels are to be loaded to their full capacity so that they can be quickly united with the fleet once it is convenient. The Turks, meanwhile, are cautiously sailing about the sea, and I shall go after them with the approach of autumn.

Matushka, pray learn my thoughts from the memorandum enclosed herewith. I remain till death

your most loyal and most grateful subject
Prince Potemkin-Tavrichesky

---

1. The Battle of Vyborg Bay.

2. A song of victory (Greek).

3. Potemkin joyfully responded to Catherine's letter describing the great damage inflicted on the Swedish fleet. A courier from St. Petersburg, however, was already on his way to Potemkin with news of Prince Nassau-Siegen's bitter defeat several days later in the Second Battle of Svensksund.

4. On 8 July, ships from the Black Sea fleet, under the command of Rear Admiral Fyodor Fyodorovich Ushakov (1745–1817), defeated a larger Turkish naval force in the Kerch Sound.

5. British admirals Richard Howe and George Bridges Rodney. Potemkin's assessment of Ushakov proved prescient, and he went on to become one of Russia's great naval commanders.

427. POTEMKIN TO CATHERINE

3 August [1790]. Bender

Beloved matushka, Your Most Gracious Majesty. How grieved I am by the loss of the flotilla and the great number of men you may judge by my devotion to you and my zeal for you and the Fatherland. You deign to write that after the loss endured by the Sevastopol fleet from the storm nothing has so grieved you. I believe that your feeling for all those involved is the same, but there is a great difference, my beloved matushka. The responsibilities associated with my command are so great they truly exceed my intelligence and abilities. Besides, much has been corrupted by the influence of the corrupt advisors, men such as Langeron, Rodriguez, de Courcy, Zuccotti, and, finally, de Stadt—how much must we Russians grieve as a result of them, how much despair there must be thanks to them.[1] They command lacking any understanding and don't give any thought to their responsibility, they're subordinate to no one, and won't even listen to anyone. That's enough, I don't care to discuss them any more.

Affairs here are taking on an entirely new look since the conclusion of Austrian negotiations: Suvorov and his corps cannot remain in Bucharest, for everything will be thrown upon him.[2] I already ordered him to depart once Coburg communicates with the Turks. I've no more strength to write. I'm leaving tomorrow and don't know how I'll drag myself from here, I've grown very weak. Farewell, beloved matushka, till death I remain

your most loyal and most grateful subject
Prince Potemkin-Tavrichesky

---

1. Potemkin refers to several foreign volunteers in Russian service. Best remembered is the Frenchman Count Alexandre de Langeron (1763–1831). Having fled the revolution in France, he fought for Russia against the Swedes and the Turks and later had a brilliant career under Tsar Alexander I.

2. Suvorov had marched with his men toward Bucharest upon the request of Coburg in late July to defend against a possible Turkish attack. After learning of Austria's departure from the war, on 4 August he moved off to the north and out of harm's way.

428. CATHERINE TO POTEMKIN

From Tsarskoe Selo. 5 August 1790

My dear friend, Prince Grigory Aleksandrovich. God has ordered one paw freed from a tight spot. I received this morning a courier from Baron Igelstrom, who brought me a peace agreement signed without any mediation by him and Baron Armfelt on 3 August.[1] If I dare say, it was thanks to my personal firmness alone that they dropped their demand that we accept their entreaty and the assistance of the Turks in reaching peace. But, hah! They didn't get it. I suppose this peace won't be very pleasant for the Prussian King either. I now pray God to help you do the exact same with the Turks. We celebrated the victory of the Black Sea fleet over the Turks yesterday in town with a service at the Kazan Church, and I was merrier than I remember being for a long time. Please say a mighty thank you from me to Rear Admiral Ushakov and to all his subordinates. You see that with this letter I hastily answer yours of 20 July, and hurry as much as one might to inform you quickly of our not so unimportant news.

For Christ's sake, send me as soon as possible the Ochakov Pasha's receipt for the money he received from the Turks so that the French will stop tormenting the Vice Chancellor about his having received this money. They think we steal such money and keep it as they do in their country.[2]

Farewell, my friend, God be with you.

Given his sincere attachment, your Cornet[3] is unspeakably happy about the peace, which he'll express to you himself.

1. A treaty was hurriedly negotiated and signed based on the basis of the *status quo ante bellum* in Verela on 3 (14) August.

2. The Turks being held by the Russians at Ochakov had indeed received the money, the receipt for which Potemkin sent to Catherine on 10 September.

3. Platon Zubov.

429. CATHERINE TO POTEMKIN

9 August 1790

My true friend, Prince Grigory Aleksandrovich. The peace agreement ratified with the Swedes is being exchanged today in Verela, and this courier is departing in order to inform you of the, in my opinion, shameful ratifications exchanged in Reichenbach that have been sent here.[1] As for us, I instruct you not to send anyone at all under any circumstances to their foolish congress in Bucharest, rather use these instructions which have been signed by me and have been given to you to try to conclude our own separate peace with the Turks.[2]

The Prussian is again trying to finagle the Poles into giving him Danzig and Thorn, this time tempting them at our expense by promising to give them White Russia and Kiev in exchange. He's the world's manager of other people's property. A polite and utterly meaningless reply will be given to Goltz[3] in response to his report on negotiations in Reichenbach. Farewell, my friend, God be with you.

We've pulled one paw out of the mud. Once we've pulled out the other one, we'll sing Hallelujah. A propos de cela,[4] Platon Aleksandrovich gave me Sarti's choruses. Two are very good, and the "Te Deum" is the most masterful of all. It's a pity that it can't be sung in church because of the instruments.[5]

Thank you for sending the music. "Oleg" is now being prepared for the celebrations of the northern peace-making, from which we have achieved a cessation of military operations and, consequently, have saved men and money. As for the Swedes, they will be feeling this for a long time, and His Majesty is becoming most unpopular there. They say that the Prussian King all of a sudden dismissed 120 of his officers in Silesia. No one yet knows why. If you find out, tell me. Hertzberg dit à qui veut bien l'entendre qu'il est, lui, accablé de chagrin,[6] on n'en devine pas la cause, ce ne sauroit être les affaires de son maître qui lui donnent ce chagrin, car elles vont à merveille, ils ont dépensé 25 millions en armement, et en intrigues aussi quelques millions, mais qu'est ce que trente millions pour des gens qui prétendent faire la loy à tout le monde, et qui ont un trésor immense d'argent monnayé.[7]

1. On 16 (27) July, Leopold II gave in to the demands of the Triple Alliance and signed the Convention of Reichenbach, according to which Austria agreed to an armistice with the Porte.

2. The participants of the Reichenbach talks moved to Bucharest, where they invited Russia (who declined) and Turkey to join them in a new round of peace negotiations, resulting in the Peace of Sistova (August 1791) by which Austria concluded peace with the Porte on the basis of the *status quo ante bellum*.

3. Prussian ambassador to Russia.

4. "Speaking of this,"

5. In December 1789, Catherine sent Potemkin a copy of her play "The Beginning of Oleg's Rule," written in late 1786, and asked him to have Giuseppe Sarti (1729–1802), the noted Italian composer and court conductor then directing Potemkin's own personal orchestra in Jassy, compose music for it. Potemkin returned Sarti's compositions to Platon Zubov, who gave them to Catherine. Russian Orthodox churches do not allow the playing of musical instruments, thus making this particular chorus unfit for church services.

6. Hertzberg was incensed by the collapse of Prussian plans to gain Thorn and Danzig.

7. "Hertzberg tells anyone who will listen that he is overcome with grief. No one can guess why, however, he is not greived by the affairs of his master, which are going wonderfully. He has wasted 25 million on arms, and a few million more on intrigues, but what is thirty million for those who aspire to make the laws for the entire world and who possess an immense treasure of coins."

430. POTEMKIN TO CATHERINE

16 August [1790]. Bender

It's not possible to describe the state of my joyful rapture, for not everyone can feel so deeply. The knowledge of your being so near to military operations deprived me of peace, but now, even amid unbearable heat, I sleep calmly.

Matushka, may you prosper with the fruit of your undaunted firmness. As you have already done so much, finish matters by attaching this neighbor to you, secure their lands forever, and so will they be ours.

As for me, be certain that I shall not neglect to do whatever possible here, however, their bond with our enemies is so strong that without them the Sultan will do nothing, no matter what the Turks might lose. If the water doesn't rise, it will be impossible to pass through the mouths of the Danube. I shall consider time to have run out with the return of Lashkarev, who is expecting the Sultan's answer for the Vizier.[1]

I was in Nikolaev, Kherson and Ochakov, saw that everything that need be was taken care of, and returned tired as a dog, having traveled nearly a thousand versts, and having galloped two hundred 40 versts from Ochakov to Bender in fifteen hours.

Amid these happy occasions do not forget to amuse my Cornet. Were I before you, I would not forget to ask you to look favorably upon Count Bezborodko.[2] First of all, in executing all your affairs, I have never encoun-

tered any delays on account of him; second, it is my duty since you selected him, and I must look after such men; third—my good nature moves
me to do so, and most importantly I am encouraged by your benevolence.

Farewell, my benefactress, I kiss your tender hands. We have great need
of Bulgakov at present, or else it'll be too late.[3]

For life I remain

your most loyal and most grateful subject
Prince Potemkin-Tavrichesky

1. Russian diplomat Sergei Lashkarev had been sent by Potemkin to the grand vizier earlier
in the year to clarify the Turkish position on peace. Frustrated by the Turks' stalling,
Potemkin ordered his return. Lashkarev stayed on, however, seeking to convince the Turks
to agree to peace.

2. In anticipation of the awards to be given out in connection with the peace with Sweden,
Potemkin wanted to make certain Bezborodko was not overlooked. Catherine raised the
count to the rank of real privy counselor.

3. Bulgakov, the new ambassador to Poland, had yet to arrive in Warsaw, and Potemkin feared
that a good opportunity to win over the former pro-Prussian nobles there was being lost.

431. CATHERINE TO POTEMKIN

29 August 1790

My dear friend, Prince Grigory Aleksandrovich. With these lines I answer
your letters of 3, 16, and 18 August. Concerning the unfortunate loss of
part of the flotilla to which you refer, here's how I acted in this matter.[1]
The very hour that Turchaninov[2] arrived here with the news, I chiefly
sought to mitigate the misfortune and to repair matters as best as could be
so as not to give the enemy time to inflict greater harm on us. For this reason I made every possible effort to lift the spirits of those who might have
been dejected. We acted largely with the available men, though there
weren't many to select from here, and so I wrote to Nassau. He requested
that I order him to be judged by a military court, but I wrote him that he
had already been judged in my mind, since I recall how many times he
has defeated the enemies of the Empire in battle. I noted that there is no
general who could avoid misfortune in war, that there was nothing more
harmful than dejection and that only in misfortune is the strength of the
soul revealed. I then told him to gather all that could be gathered, to describe the true extent of our loss and to send this along, and to do and account for everything that must be done. Finally, as a result of these actions, within a month this business had once more been advanced to the
point where the Swedish oared fleet was again bottled up and in such a
position that it could have been entirely lost, which in no small way
helped bring about peace.

Knowing your zeal and love for me and our common cause, I don't doubt in the least that you received the news of this peace with great joy. It's endearing for me to hear from your lips that you attribute it to my undaunted firmness. How else could the Empress of All the Russias be, what with sixteen thousand versts at her back and the visible goodwill and the peoples' fervor for this war? Now that God has blessed us with this peace, I assure you that for my part I shall neglect nothing to secure it for us henceforth, and a good foundation for this has already been laid. General Stedingk is traveling here from the Swedish King, and I am sending von der Pahlen for now.[3]

I am certain that for your part you won't neglect a good opportunity to make peace. Do the Sultan and the Turks truly not see that the Swedes have abandoned them, that the Prussians, who promised them in their treaty to attack us and the Austrian court last spring, have quite simply lied to them? It's from them that they'll demand money to pay for their arms. What can the fools be waiting for? They won't get a better peace from us than the one we're offering them, but to listen to the Prussian King—this means they'll never achieve peace since there'll be no end to his greed. I think that were you to write all this to them in your usual style, you would open their eyes.

You have hot weather and drought and waterless rivers, while we haven't had a day without rain since it started in the month of May. The entire summer has been most intolerable, and we've been unable to warm up our chilly hands. You galloped from Ochakov to Bender with unheard-of speed. Is it any wonder that you're weak after such a gallop? Be assured that I shall not fail to bestow charity and distinction upon those whom you have recommended, namely your worthy Cornet and Count Bezborodko. I thank you for the beautiful snuff box and the very nice rug you sent me.[4] I like them both very much, and so do keep your word: you promised to be merry if I liked them, and I love it when you're merry.

I have designated the eighth day of September for the celebration of the Swedish peace here, and I'll do my best to manage. But I often feel, my friend, that there are so many times I would like to talk to you, if only for a quarter of an hour. I'll send Igelstrom to Livonia with the regiments that have served their time in the Finnish War. I'm most sorry that your men are succumbing to illness. There's been an unspeakable number of sick here since spring.

Regarding Field Marshal Rumiantsev and his stay in Moldavia by way of various fabrications, I think it best to send someone to tell him that it's quite possible the Turks will soon take him back home with them should he not leave before they arrive. And if this doesn't help, then send an escort to him who, while protecting him, will send him packing. But in truth, I am protecting him, as much as possible, given his past service, and gratitude alone makes me remember the achievements of his person, but my forebears would've acted differently.

Bulgakov should already be in Warsaw.[5] Our peace with the Swedes has upset the malicious minds there just as everywhere else. We'll see how they react, and should God help you to persuade the Turks, then our most inveterate enemies will calm down. Farewell, my friend, Christ be with you.

Tomorrow on the day of Saint Alexander Nevsky the Chevaliers will carry his relics to that monastery's cathedral and consecrate it in my presence. There will be a banquet for the Chevaliers in the monastery and another for the Grand Duchess, the clergy and the five other classes, as was done under the late Empress Elizabeth Petrovna. I remain with constant benevolence.

Tomorrow, should God grant me health, the "Te Deum" you sent me will be performed together with all the instruments at the banquet in the Nevsky Monastery. As a sign of my recognition for him during the construction of the church, I presented the Novgorod and Petersburg Metropolitan with an emerald panagia today, an extremely good one.

In response to what you write about how calmly you've been sleeping since learning of peace with the Swedes, let me tell you what's happened to me: ever since 1787 my dresses have continually had to be taken in, but during these past three weeks they've started to get tight and will once again have to be let out a full size. I'm becoming much merrier. The pleasing disposition and manners of your recommended Cornet does much toward this end.

---

1. Potemkin wrote Catherine on 3 August of how saddened he was to have received news of Prince Nassau-Siegen's defeat. In what follows here, Catherine describes how she handled the situation.

2. Pyotr Turchaninov, Catherine's state secretary for military affairs.

3. Baron Curt von Stedingk (1746–1836) had distinguished himself in the recent war and was sent as ambassador to St. Petersburg. Catherine dispatched Peter von der Pahlen to Stockholm in the same capacity.

4. Potemkin had sent Catherine a rug made locally in Bender and a snuffbox of lapis lazuli as a belated birthday gift (the snuffbox was so poorly made the prince had to send it first to Viennese craftsmen before forwarding it on to Platon Zubov, who presented it to Catherine).

5. Bulgakov arrived in Warsaw at the end of August.

432. POTEMKIN TO CATHERINE

4 September [1790]. Bender

See here, beloved matushka, God has presented us with yet another victory over the Turkish fleet in which it has been utterly defeated. We captured an admiral, their very best naval commander. It's thought he has already been bestowed with the title of Kapudan Pasha.[1] The captain of the captured ship was also extremely brave; he was killed by cannon fire. What European admiral would not have surrendered after having lost his mast and having half his hold full of water and fire? But not he—and it was only with difficulty that he was persuaded to surrender as his ship was engulfed in flames.

It has been just seven years since the ship "Catherine's Glory" sailed down the Dnieper toward the Pontus.² The already expanded fleet is now victorious and enjoys, thanks to God's blessing, complete and uncontested control of the sea. The enemy didn't even take a boat in the battle, but for Lombard's ship and battery that were carried away by the storm. But that was the will of God. I am happy that I did not dishonor your flag.

Be gracious to Rear Admiral Ushakov. Where could we find someone who so loves to fight? Three battles in one summer, of which that in the Straits of Yenikale was the most intense. The officers strive to outdo each other with their fervor. I do not know another admiral with whom I could introduce the practice of doing battle at close range. Yet with him, the line commences battle at a distance of 120 sazhens, and he himself, together with his ship, was directly across from the "Captain" at a distance of twenty sazhens. He merits the Military Order 2nd class; he only has, however, thirty serfs, and they are in Poshekhone at that. Reward him with 500 serfs, a nice little village in White Russia, and then he'll be a chevalier with a little something to live on.³

I visited the fleet and admired it with tears of joy in my eyes, looking out on more than a hundred vessels together with a flotilla where till you so deigned there had not been a single boat. In the north you expanded the fleet, but here you created one out of nothing. You, unquestionable foundress, love your child that zealously serves you, matushka, and brings no shame. The flotilla is in complete order. I cannot praise Major-General Ribas enough. Along with his excellent bravery, he is filled with unspeakable fervor. The foulest weather prevented the flotilla from reaching the fleet during the battle. And I am in fact glad, or else it would have suffered much damage because of the storm, which came up immediately after the battle. The strong rocking of the ship made me dizzy; I had wanted to dispatch my communiqué from the ship, but was unable to write, and was taken ill during my return. I'm now bringing in a captured ship for repairs, and am preparing the rest in an attempt to seek to inflict harm on the enemy once more with God's help. If only I had greater strength. I'm galloping off to Nikolaev again to hurry matters along and to give the necessary orders. Two corps will be on the move over land toward Tatarbunar during those days, and it's there that I shall find them.⁴

Matushka, how weak in the head I've become; my blood's quite agitated, and this torments me.

[...]

Farewell, my benefactress, I remain till death

your most loyal and most grateful subject

Prince Potemkin-Tavrichesky

1. Ushakov's fleet defeated the Turks near the island of Tendra on 28–29 August. Several Turkish ships were sunk and destroyed, and the naval commander Said-bey, who in fact was not the kapudan pasha, was captured.

2. The Black Sea.

3. Catherine rewarded Ushakov with the Order of St. George second class and 500 serfs.

4. Potemkin had by now given up on waiting for the Turks to decide on peace, and he began making preparations for the coming campaign in the lower stretches of the Danube River.

433. POTEMKIN TO CATHERINE

Bender. 10 September [1790]

Your Most Gracious Majesty. Moving troops toward the Dvina soon will produce great effect. Only order that they be brought up to full strength as quickly as possible and that they be trained according to the instructions I presented to you. Less concern need be shown about Riga, for it's on the other side of the river. I shall send detailed instructions on how the operation ought to be conducted in relation to the general plan. Order the field artillery increased toward that side. See that a dozen armed boats be made on the Dvina from the light ones used there. They can be used to impede any attempt at crossing. Spread rumors to the effect that the troops are being increased. Only the Army of the Dvina should be joined with the one in White Russia. And so, in order to combine them, appoint one of the senior generals-in-chief and instruct him to communicate with me frequently. If not Saltykov, then order Repnin, although there will be a good many troubles with him, for there is no one else.[1]

Given that winter is not far off, I do not expect any action now, but Igelstrom will arrive in time toward spring, and he, of course, will lead them.

The Polish nation is beginning to see they are being deceived, and the majority is inclined toward us. The Sejm, however, is the law, and it is entirely Prussian. I wrote Bulgakov to win the Lithuanian Marshal Potocki, Sapieha and his mother over to our side.[2] It will be necessary to break up and destroy the Sejm by way of a new confederation, or else nothing will change as long as the Sejm continues.

It is amazing that our ambassador seated Malachowski as Grand Crown Marshal,[3] for he is most devoted to the Prussian King. This compels me to think that His Highness is also no small Prussian.

Beloved matushka, the Prussians have been coming after me personally, and there's no dirty trick they wouldn't play on me. I purchased a beautiful, large estate in Poland, and you know that I did so with the intention of bringing much benefit to Russia, primarily for the fleet, the resources for which are to be found solely in the forests there. I am not talking about how they burden me with excessive requisitions and oppress me through the presence of their troops, however, they intend to confiscate my land at the first opportunity, seizing upon some meaningless pretext, or to simply lay waste to it. They've now found some scoundrel to report to the Civil Military Commission that I am ravaging the forests by sending wood to the admiralty and am supposedly exporting subjects to Russia. This denunciation has been sent to Warsaw. These oppressive acts committed by foreign powers do me honor, for they demonstrate my loyalty to you. I am not at all sorry to lose my property, considering that my life is always offered up in sacrifice to you. However, I have sold both Krichev and Dubrovna, having purchased the latter with the money earned from the sale of all my other villages, and for Smila I even sold my villages in White Russia. I now have Koltushy, and in addition a thousand serfs in Yaroslavl and another four hundred in White Russia. I've possessed enough, however, I now have no place where I might lay my head. I beseech you, matushka, grant me that dacha about which I enclosed a note to Count Bezborodko and which I shall consider a great charity.[4] I'm growing weak; this will at least afford me a place where I might rest. I shall truly earn it, being devoted with all my body and soul to you till death.

Your most loyal and most grateful subject
Prince Potemkin-Tavrichesky

---

1. Potemkin considered that the forces being marshaled on the western border to defend against Prussia (the Army of the Dvina, in Livonia near Riga, and the White Russian Army, near Mogilyov) should be united and placed under a single general.

2. Diplomat and Lithuanian marshal, Ignacy Potocki (1750–1809) was a fierce supporter of Prussia during the period of the Four-Year Sejm (1788–1792). Prince Kazimierz Nestor Sapieha (1750–1797), another Prussian supporter, served as marshal of the Sejm.

3. Stanislaw Malachowski (1736–1809) was elected grand crown marshal (one of the senior of the ten ministerial positions) in 1788 and supported the pro-Prussian political orientation.

4. Potemkin had written to Bezborodko requesting the empress give him a house that had formerly belonged to a monastery in a region of the Yekaterinoslav province that he referred to as "heaven." Catherine honored his request.

434. CATHERINE TO POTEMKIN

10 September 1790[1]

My true friend, Prince Grigory Aleksandrovich. I grew extremely tired on the first day of the peace celebrations and lay in bed all day yesterday.[2] I was so weak I could barely lift my head, and only now am I able to take up my pen in order to write you. Your last letter of 29 August informs me that you have left for the fleet.[3] I admit that given how late in the year it is this frightens me somewhat, all the more so since now during the Equinox there are always large storms there, as well as here too. Let the storm disrupt the Turks' naval undertakings, our vessels, however, should wait out the Equinox in their ports. I desire with all my heart that God will help you surmount all difficulties whatsoever, and particularly those associated, as you write, with the transport of provisions.

We too know that the Poles have either a camp or troops in Breslau. Vous verrés, mon Ami, par les registres comment je me suis tirée d'affaire des fêtes de la Paix. J'ai taché d'être juste, et j'ai récompensé avec splendeur et générosité partout là où j'ai pu découvrir l'ombre de service rendus; j'espère que ce nouvel exemple, imité des exemples précedens, servira d'aiguillon pour encourager les gens à bien servir; c'est dommage qu'on ne puisse inculquer à un chacun l'habileté et les talents; cependant je suis bien aise de voir que parmi les jeunes généraux il y en a qui sont et deviennent meilleurs que ceux que j'ai vus dans la guerre de Sept ans finie en 1762.[4]

Bulgakov has arrived in Warsaw. Stedingk has been sent here by the Swedish King; he's a fair man and I received him as well as possible. I'm ordering von der Pahlen sent to Stockholm now. I hereby thank you altogether for the selection of generals sent here. Every one of them did their duty with zealous fervor, and they are all fine men.

[. . .]

Farewell, my friend, I've no more strength to write. My head's spinning from the celebration. I need nothing more now than a few days' rest, and then I'll get back to business. A strange incident occupied our public on the day of the service and the public audience. After leaving church the people gathered in the gallery where the throne had been placed and awaited my arrival, when all of a sudden the Prussian chargé d'affaires Güttel (N.B. Un des principaux employés de Mre. Hertzberg[5]) became dizzy and fell to the ground with such force that his forehead and nose began to bleed, and his blood had to be wiped up off the floor before my arrival. Throughout the entire gallery people began talking about how the Prussian had broken his nose upon the Russian throne. They are most unhappy about the Swedish peace. Adieu, mon Ami, God be with you.

11 September 1790

You will find your Cornet of the Chevaliers-Gardes in the list. I gave him an Alexander's ribbon, and what is written about him is the absolute truth, to which I can attest.[6]

---

1. Catherine apparently started the letter on 10 September and only finished it the following day, probably due to her illness.

2. The celebration marking the peace with Sweden began on 8 September.

3. Potemkin dashed off a short letter to Catherine on 29 August from Bender telling her of the many difficulties confronting him and that he was hurrying off to inspect the fleet.

4. "You will see, my friend, from the accounts how well I managed the peace celebrations. I tried to be just, and I rewarded with splendor and generosity everywhere I could discern a shadow of services rendered. I hope that this recent example, with its resemblance to previous ones, will serve as an incentive to encourage the men to serve well; it is a pity that one cannot instill everyone with ability and talent. Nevertheless, I am very glad to see that among the young generals there are those who are and are becoming better than those I saw during the Seven Years' War which ended in 1762."

5. "One of Mr. Hertzberg's chief assistants"

6. Platon Zubov received the Order of St. Alexander Nevsky on 8 September.

435. CATHERINE TO POTEMKIN

30 September 1790

My true friend, Prince Grigory Aleksandrovich. I have received your letters of 10 and 11 September.[1] I hope it won't be difficult to entrap the Swedish King; we shall live as friends, for he is penniless. All the regiments will be brought up to full strength, and I have ordered boats built on the Dvina, however, His Majesty the King of Prussia has already deigned to convey that he won't attack us, which isn't difficult to believe, all the more so should God help you to defeat the Turks, and then make peace. But till they are defeated, the Turks' allies will do everything to keep the Turks from making peace. I have entrusted Count Ivan Saltykov with command of the Army of the Dvina, and Igelstrom and Prince Yury Dolgorukov to serve under him.[2] It's good that the Poles are beginning to open their eyes. You'll make peace once God permits, and then we'll put together a new confederation, but till that time it is not necessary, and it might even be a burden since it would have to be supported with money and men.

To hell with the Prussians, we shall somehow find a way to take vengeance on them for their dirty tricks.[3]

Forgive me, my friend, that I write little and poorly: I'm not very well, I have a cough, and my chest and back hurt a good deal. I lay in bed for two days thinking I could rid myself of all this if I just lay there in my sweat, but now I'm weak and it's uncomfortable to write. Your Cornet is looking after me and exhibits such care that I can't thank him enough. Farewell, my friend, I send you my best wishes on your name-day, along with this ring. They assure me the stone is rare.

---

1. Potemkin wrote two brief letters on 11 December instructing Catherine to try to win over Gustav and to try to take advantage of the mounting tension between the Poles and Prussians over the question of Danzig.

2. In response to Potemkin's letter of 10 September, General-in-Chief Ivan Saltykov was put

in charge of the unified army along Russia's western border. Saltykov's appointment marked the rising power of Zubov and his supporters: Saltykov's relative Count Nikolai Ivanovich Saltykov (1736–1816) was the vice president of the War College and Zubov's patron.

3. In a short letter dated 11 September, Potemkin had reiterated to Catherine his desire to avenge the insults of King Frederick William once the time was right.

436. POTEMKIN TO CATHERINE

Bender. 3 December [1790]

Your Most Gracious Majesty! The thaw has made the roads so bad that I was unable to receive the flags on time.[1] What is more, General Ribas was severely ill and despaired for his life; his illness has passed, however, and he is already back in service. Having mentioned him, I cannot be silent about his unprecedented fervor. In addition to the obstacles put before him by the enemy, he was obliged to fight against the sea with vessels burdened by large artillery. This alone would deter many, or had it been someone with less fervor everything might have been lost. He found the batteries and a small channel in the estuaries through which to enter. It was a good place for them to unload, to make a landing and to hasten to seek shelter from the approaching bad weather. The fortifications have been taken, the enemy's been driven off, Tulcha's been subjugated, the Turkish flotilla's been defeated, and the fortress of Isackcha, along with the entire Turkish army and flotilla's magazine or depot, has been taken together with a great multitude of various supplies. Up to one hundred fifty vessels have been captured, sunk or damaged.[2] We, however, have lost but one lanson to a bomb, and two have sunk, but their men were saved. We have obtained 120 cannons, as well as 72 in Kilia. It remains to attempt to destroy the vessels near Ismail. I have ordered that the best measures be taken and that an assault be launched; for this reason have detailed there General Count Suvorov-Rymniksky. I cannot absent myself, for our neighbors are watching me closely. I have only to head off in any direction, and they then assume that the entire army has been sent there, and after that the maneuvering begins. What is more, in the case of failure it is less significant if a corps must retreat rather than the army and I. I'll await whatever God grants.[3]

From the enclosed memorandum, pray note, matushka, that Lucchesini intends to visit me. I'll see what he brings, but I can assure you in advance that he won't succeed in deceiving me. I'm enclosing herewith details on the unauthorized disclosures he made during his stay in Bucharest. He's galloped off to Sistova and, after inciting the people there, will gallop back.[4] I do not neglect to suggest to the Turks everything that might open their eyes, but who will listen? The Sultan doesn't give any thought to the stability of the state, and all the rest have been bribed.

You can judge by events on the Danube and by those on land what sort of damage is being inflicted on them: in three naval battles they have lost nearly ten thousand men killed, injured and captured, along with six ships of the line, and yet this means nothing to them. All they do is contemplate how best to lie to the people. I'll now speak of Poland. As long as the current Sejm remains active nothing can be done, and it is difficult for anyone to dare side with us openly, for he who does will lose his head. The King indeed threatens everyone with vengeance. We delivered an ultimatum to the Turks, but they did not accept it, which gives us an opportunity to continue the war, and to expend more money as well. And so, a different ultimatum ought be presented, otherwise how frightened will they be if, while continuing to fight, we stand by the same demands? Why won't you promise some of the territory that has been won to Poland upon the establishment of their union while the Prussian King brazenly whittles away your ancient domains? As for Moldavia, it was not a Turkish conquest, rather it joined voluntarily and thus it has a right to protest when the conditions are violated. Order me to make this promise to the Poles, and with this we shall divert them from any alliances, and the Turks and their confederates will quickly make peace so as to keep this from happening.[5] It is in the interest of the Viennese court to agree to this. Order that England be stroked, or, better said, be treated in a serious manner, however, entrust this to someone who is truly devoted to you, otherwise, believe me, nothing will come of it. Order Count Razumovsky to visit me on his way to Vienna so we can make arrangements and he can receive some instructions from me.[6]

The Prussian King will not make a move toward Riga, for it's impossible to cross so many rivers. And how many troops could he manage to bring with him? Should he incite and support the Poles, then they ought to be diverted. Promise them a guarantee of their possessions, and that we shall not meddle with their form of domestic government. They spurned this guarantee, and it was of no use to us, for this was the Prussian court's perfidy, as well as the affair of the dissidents,[7] intended to incite hatred against us. And now we see the fruits: the good for nothing dissidents are devoted to it. I am most certain that we were used by the Berlin court in every way to embitter the Poles. Much of this is the doing of His Excellency Count Stackelberg.[8] In order to force the Prussian King to speak in a different tone, we should leave some troops—up to about twenty thousand—in Moldavia along the Dniester for the next campaign against the Porte. All the rest are to be directed against the Prussian, and you are to state resolutely and firmly to him that you will defend the dignity of your Empire till the last drop of blood.

Prepare the fleet against the English threats as much as possible,[9] and let me know for my consideration how many vessels there will be, que ca et qu'ils feront ses Messieurs dans la Baltieque; ils n'ont point grand chose pour la descente et tout ce qu'ils mettront par terre doit absolument périr[10] [. . .]

Order the boats for the Dvina be hastened, and should you deem my zealous ideas worthy, let me know: I shall send at once a detailed plan based upon them for the main operation.

Your flotilla will stay in the Danube to prohibit the enemy from crossing over and to destroy their vessels wherever they may be. The fleet will leave early for the Rumelian coast, and then for Anapa. As soon as possible, the Kuban and Tauride forces will launch an attack on Anapa. After that, God willing, it will be on to Sudzhuk Kale, and from there to Sinop as well. I shall not desist from attacking throughout the entire winter wherever possible.

Having said this, I can also not fail to say: do everything possible to attach Sweden to you. For this purpose why not promise to marry one of the Grand Duchesses to their Prince? For truth, my benefactress, this would be good, very good indeed.[11]

How sad I am that you are often not well. With an ardent heart I pray God for you. And I beg you—take care of yourself. My beloved matushka, we are all yours, and I more than everyone else, so how is it that I could forget your men, as you deign to put it? Of course I shall not abandon them: this is my desire and my duty. I kiss your tender hands and remain till death

your most loyal and most grateful subject
Prince Potemkin-Tavrichesky

P.S. Major-General Ribas serves with great merit, and he will achieve even greater successes.

---

1. The Turkish fortress of Kilia on the Danube fell to the Russians on 18 October, on the second attempt. Potemkin wrote to Catherine the good news on 26 October.

2. José de Ribas's flotilla, together with that of the Black Sea Cossacks, had fought its way up the mouths of the Danube as far as Galatz, destroyed the Turkish Danube flotilla, and taken the forts of Tulcha and Isackcha.

3. Instead of joining the forces marshaled outside Ismail preparing for the assault, Potemkin stayed in Bender, fearful that should the assault fail, this would greatly tarnish his and his entire army's reputation.

4. Girolamo Lucchesini, head of the Prussian delegation at the peace talks underway at Sistova, sought to force Potemkin to the negotiating table by threatening to wage war against Russia along her western border. Potemkin was unmoved.

5. As a way to win Poland over to Russia and break the hold of the pro-Prussian magnates, Potemkin wanted to promise it Moldavia and to offer the Poles a guarantee over all their existing lands and complete freedom from Russian intervention.

6. Count Andrei Razumovsky had been appointed Russian minister to Austria earlier that year.

7. A reference to the non-Catholic (i.e., Protestant and Orthodox) population in Poland, which did not enjoy the full political rights granted the Catholic majority. Both Russia and Prussia had used the cause of the dissidents as a pretext for meddling in Polish affairs

8. Russia's former ambassador to Poland.

9. British Prime Minister William Pitt was threatening to send the Royal Navy into the Gulf of Finland to attack the Russian fleet.

10. "and what these gentlemen will be doing in the Baltic. They do not have large forces for a landing, and everything they put on land is bound to completely perish"

11. Potemkin's proposal did almost become reality in 1796 when the future Gustav IV came close to marrying Grand Duchess Aleksandra Pavlovna.

437. POTEMKIN TO CATHERINE

Bender. 18 December [1790]

Beloved matushka, Your Most Gracious Majesty. I present to you my campaign, which has been practically invisible to the eyes of my ill-wishers. They thought that with their deceptions they could put an end to all my actions. But God helped me to wage three splendid naval battles. In the Kuban the army has been defeated.[1] The fortifications at Sulina have been captured, as have Tulcha, Isackcha, Kilia and Ismail—their best and strongest fortress, built in the European manner, and together with it an army of more than thirty thousand confined within. I already wrote about the captives, however, it turns out there are even more: I received a report this hour stating that there are already nine thousand of them. The troops displayed unprecedented bravery in surmounting an untouched fortress and superior numbers. I can boast to you that I was successful in instilling the spirit of order and fearlessness into the army entrusted to me. Our losses are much greater than what we suffered at Ochakov, however, in comparison with the force we have destroyed, they are small.

Valerian Aleksandrovich proved himself worthy of your favor, and I always sought to give him an occasion to win merit. Be gracious toward him and do not tear him away from service.[2] He has great potential, which you may see from the letter his general wrote to Popov. I have yet to receive a detailed report and suppose I shall find it myself in Ismail.[3]

I kiss your tender hands and congratulate you on this unprecedented victory.

Your most loyal and most gracious subject
Prince Potemkin-Tavrichesky

---

1. Russian forces under the command of Major-General von Herman defeated a Turkish army of 25,000 in the Kuban on 30 September.

2. Valerian Zubov was among the troops who approached the fortress on Ribas's flotilla and attacked Ismail from the river. Potemkin sent Valerian back to St. Petersburg with a brief report on the victory. He was awarded the Order of St. George fourth class.

3. Potemkin never made it to Ismail. He sent his secretary Vasily Popov in his place.

11. Death on the Steppe—1791

After the fall of Ismail, Potemkin moved to Jassy, from where he wrote Catherine of his desire to return to St. Petersburg. It had been nearly two years since they had parted, and in light of all that had happened during that time, Potemkin deemed it necessary to see her again. He wrote Catherine that it would be too difficult to attempt to explain everything he wanted to tell her in writing and in a cryptic aside mentioned that he had "news that I cannot entrust to paper," but had to discuss with her *unter vier Augen* (Letters 439, 440).

What was it that Potemkin dared not commit to paper? Although this question cannot be answered with certainty, it appears likely that Potemkin was particularly troubled by the Prussian court's increasing hostility toward him and its use of certain undisclosed "invisible means" to support such an attitude. The hidden weapon was none other than Catherine's own son, Grand Duke Paul. The pro-Prussian and anti-Potemkin sentiments of the grand duke were no secret, and Frederick William and a few of his key ministers decided to avail themselves of the grand duke in their struggle against Russia. Through a group of Russian Rosicrucians with links to Freemasons at the Prussian court, Paul entered into relations with the Prussian envoy in Petersburg and the Prussian king himself in a way that bordered on treason. Coded messages were exchanged that made mention of Paul's assuming power in Russia. Catherine and Potemkin became aware of this secret communication and of Prussia's efforts to woo Paul. Potemkin was naturally hesitant to discuss such a delicate issue in his correspondence, mindful as he was that his enemies, namely, Zubov and through him Nikolai Saltykov, who had close ties to the grand duke, had direct access to his letters.

There were other concerns as well. During his absence from the capital, Potemkin's authority over the War College had been gradually undermined by Saltykov, appointed its vice president in 1788. By returning to St. Petersburg, the prince clearly hoped to prevent any further damage. It is also possible Potemkin had grown anxious over the position Zubov and his supporters had managed to establish. The popular anecdote that Potemkin claimed to be returning to the capital in order "to pull out a tooth"—*zub* being the Russian for tooth—while most probably apocryphal no doubt expresses a real concern about the shifting balance of forces at court. Finally, the situation with Poland and the other powers required the kind of attention that could only come from Potemkin's presence in the capital. Catherine initially resisted his request, perhaps in response to subtle pressure from the Zubov faction, though in the end she consented (Letters 441, 442).

On 28 February 1791, Potemkin arrived in St. Petersburg. News that the prince was on his way had paralyzed the city for weeks. All important state affairs had been suspended until his arrival, and the Zubov faction practically trembled with nervous anticipation. Potemkin's return proved to be quite timely, for Russia was on the brink of one of the most dangerous moments in Catherine's reign. In March, Prime Minister William Pitt, intent on turning back the Russian advance into eastern Europe, drafted an ultimatum to Russia: Catherine had ten days to agree to peace with the Porte on the basis of the *status quo ante bellum,* or the Royal Navy would set sail for the Baltic and the Black seas, and Prussian ground forces would march into Livonia. On the 29th and 30th of March (n.s.), Parliament endorsed Pitt's request for a partial mobilization of the fleet. On 27 March (7 April), Frederick William ordered nearly 90,000 troops to the Livonian border in preparation for an attack on Russia. Word reached Catherine that the king's equipage was reportedly being readied in Berlin to convey him to the front.

Catherine was outraged by the naked attempt to blackmail her into renouncing Russia's war gains, and she dug in her heels, refusing to bargain with either Britain or Prussia. Catherine's intransigence, which Zubov had a hand in, was at odds with Potemkin's counsel that she negotiate with the Prussians and buy them off, and this difference of opinion led to harsh words, tears, and frightful rows between the two during the month of March and the first weeks of April. Potemkin raged at Catherine's stubbornness, fearing that it would surely lead to war. At times the strain became too much for Catherine to bear and she would remain in bed for days complaining of spasms and colic. Potemkin's advice to consult her doctor was rejected out of hand. Eventually Potemkin prevailed in pressuring Catherine to negotiate with Prussia. At the same time, however, the empress secretly ordered Potemkin to ready their forces for war.

While Catherine and Potemkin were arguing in St. Petersburg, back in London Pitt's gamble was crumbling. Parliament questioned how some remote scraps of land on the northern shores of the Black Sea warranted a war against Russia, with whom Britain still enjoyed considerable trade. Objections to the plan also arose from within the Royal Navy. On 5 (16) April, Pitt, fearing the collapse of his government, withdrew his ultimatum and sent a special envoy to Petersburg to seek a compromise. After two months of negotiations, Catherine got her way: Russia could keep Ochakov and the land between the Bug and Dniester rivers. By the end of July, the "Ochakov crisis" had been overcome.

Amid the saber-rattling and diplomatic maneuvering, Potemkin decided to throw a party. This was not to be any ordinary amusement, however. Rather, in keeping with its host's taste for the superlative, it was to be a night like nothing St. Petersburg had seen before. For weeks thousands of artisans and workmen labored on Potemkin's neo-classical palace (later known as the Tauride Palace) and its gardens, transforming them into a physical representation of their owner's unimaginable wealth and his unlimited devotion to the empress. Hundreds of thousands of rubles were spent on food, drink, musicians, and the most exquisite furnishings and ornaments. The massive main hall alone counted more than fifty chandeliers with some twenty thousand candles, the heat from which nearly melted the three thousand invited guests. The centerpiece of the palace's Winter Garden—the largest in all of Europe—was a temple with a statue of Catherine inside, for which Potemkin had composed an inscription: "To the Mother of the Fatherland and my Benefactress." In her hand, she held a cornucopia from which money and crosses of various knightly orders flowed.

The party began at seven o'clock on the evening of 28 April when Catherine's coach arrived at the palace, before which thousands of commoners helped themselves to free food and drink. She was met by Potemkin, sumptuously attired in a scarlet tail-coat and black cape adorned with diamonds. His hat was so heavily laden with gems it had to be carried about by a valet. Catherine and the other guests were treated to a ballet featuring the empress's grandsons, Alexander and Constantine, two French comedies, a ball, and a midnight supper. Catherine was so moved by Potemkin's overwhelming hospitality she did not leave until two in the morning, well past her normal bedtime.

Although Potemkin had long enjoyed putting on lavish entertainments, this particular event was chiefly intended as a political statement. First, it was meant to communicate to Russia's enemies—Britain, Prussia, and Sweden, too, who was being wooed at the time by Russia's foes—that even at the height of the war scare, St. Petersburg was not afraid and even found time and cause to celebrate on a grand scale. During the festivities Potemkin paraded out several pashas captured at Ismail as a reminder to his guests of what happened to those who attacked Russia. The audience for this political theater also included Potemkin's domestic enemies, namely the Zubov clan and its allies. The feast let them know in most dramatic fashion that Potemkin remained the richest, most powerful man in the empire and that no one could match, or hope to break, the bond he shared with the empress.

Another domestic political theme ran through the night's festivities, this one regarding plans for the succession after Catherine. The empress had long harbored doubts about her son Paul, and although no proof has survived, it is believed that Catherine drafted a succession plan expressing her wish that upon her death the throne pass not to her son, but to her grandson Alexander. Potemkin had highlighted Alexander during the evening of the party by casting him in a leading role in the ballet that greeted Catherine upon her arrival at the palace. The following day he wrote Catherine praising Alexander's talents and Catherine's own role in the boy's education. More importantly, he described the Russia that Alexander would find upon ascending the throne (Letter 444). Potemkin's letter lends credence to the idea that Catherine, quite possibly after consultations with the prince, had indeed decided to skip Paul in favor of Alexander. These plans, however, were subverted after Catherine's death.

Although they had narrowly averted war with the Triple Alliance, Catherine and Potemkin still faced the question of Poland, which became more acute with the proclamation of the Constitution of the Third of May (n.s.) making Poland a hereditary monarchy. Though it bore little in common with the revolutionary events then rocking France, to Catherine the new constitution smacked of Jacobinism. Throughout the spring and summer of 1791, Catherine and the prince worked on their plans for dealing with Poland. A strong Poland increasingly independent of Russia would not be tolerated, and various options for undoing the May Constitution—from Potemkin's earlier plan of inciting the Orthodox regions in the east against Warsaw, to a "reconfederation" led by aristocratic pro-Russian magnates, to a second partition—were considered. Nothing could be undertaken, however, until Russia had freed itself from its entanglements with the Turks. Poland was safe, for the moment. Complete dismemberment at the hands of Russia, Prussia, and Austria would come only a few years later.

As the English threat faded, Catherine wrote Potemkin in early May urging him to resume military operations against the Turks (Letter 445). She had barely survived perhaps the greatest threat to her reign, and the strain the past months had exerted on her and on her relations with Potemkin are evident in the letter's anguished pleading. Potemkin promptly complied. On 11 May, he sent orders to General Repnin, in charge of the ground forces in Potemkin's absence, and to Rear Admiral Ushakov to seek out and engage the enemy on land and sea. Russia's commanders responded accordingly: on 22 June, General Gudovich seized the fort of Anapa in the Kuban and Sudzhuk Kale soon thereafter; on 28 June, Repnin and his men routed the Turks south of the Danube at Machin; and on 31 July, Ushakov's fleet defeated the Turks near the cape of Kaliakra, forcing the Turkish vessels to retreat to Constantinople, where the Russian ships' guns could be heard (Letter 446). The Porte had finally had enough. That same day preliminary peace conditions were hurriedly signed by Prince Repnin and the vizier at Galatz.

At five o'clock on the morning of 24 July, Potemkin departed Tsarskoe Selo for the last time. He and Catherine were never to see each other again. Together they had achieved much during his tumultuous visit. They had withstood the Anglo-Prussian challenge, and on 11 July, the British and Prussian ambassadors officially accepted Russia's claim to Ochakov and the lands between the Bug and the Dniester. In addition, it was agreed that if the Turks did not sign a final peace agreement within four months, Russia would be free to resume hostilities. On the subject of Poland, Catherine issued Potemkin a rescript on 18 July granting him great authority to intervene in Polish affairs in order to undo the May Constitution once peace had been concluded with the Ottomans. Potemkin had also apparently been successful in defending himself against the machinations of Paul and his supporters. An unmistakable coldness inserted itself between Catherine and Paul around this time that may well have been a result of Potemkin's private words with the empress on her son's dangerous activities. While Potemkin had stymied Paul, he had less luck in countering Zubov and his party, whose place at court remained secure despite the prince's complaints of the new favorite's efforts to turn Catherine against him. Though they kept up a facade of cordiality for Catherine's sake, their mutual distrust lurked just beneath the surface.

Potemkin rode south with his usual great haste, traveling so fast, in fact, that his carriage repeatedly broke down under the strain. On 4 August Potemkin wrote Catherine from Olviopol that peace preliminaries had been signed by Repnin and the Turks on 31 July. After a mad dash to Jassy that left him weak and ill, Potemkin raced off to Galatz to take command from Repnin, arriving on 7 August (Letter 447). While pleased with the signing of the preliminaries, Potemkin and Catherine were upset that Repnin, ignorant of the latest agreement with Britain and Prussia, had signed an eight-month armistice (instead of only four) and also agreed not to arm the territory won from the Turks. In Galatz, Potemkin met with

Turkish representatives arriving from Sistova, where peace had been signed with the Austrians days earlier (24 July [4 August]). He called their bluff when they tried to wiggle out of the negotiations by letting them know that were they to do so, the previously agreed-upon conditions would become void and he would once again commence military operations. The Turks stayed at the table (Letters 448, 449). In a decision richly symbolic of the change in Russo-Turkish relations, Potemkin chose as the site for the upcoming talks the village of Gushcha outside Jassy where eighty years earlier Peter the Great had signed a humiliating peace following his defeat by the Turks.

Potemkin's burst of energy in August—he was simultaneously negotiating with the Turks, courting the pro-Russian opposition in Poland, overseeing the construction of his southern territories, building more ships, and even negotiating to bring Mozart to play for him in Jassy—belied his failing health. He was becoming ever weaker and suffering from spasms and fever. On 24 August, he wrote Catherine that although he was now better, for a time he had feared he would not survive. For several days he was unable to get out of bed, although he managed to keep working (Letter 450). While Catherine was still intent on being informed of matters with the Turks, her mind was increasingly occupied by Potemkin's illness. On 29 August, she attended vespers at St. Petersburg's Alexander Nevsky Monastery, where she made offerings of gold, silver, and diamonds, and prayed God to protect Potemkin against "this misfortune and that He spare me this blow which I cannot even contemplate without extreme affliction" (Letter 451). The day before Catherine had ordered Vasily Popov to write to her directly of Potemkin's health.

Throughout September the news from the south was by turns encouraging and discouraging. One day Potemkin seemed to be recovering, and the next he was racked by spasms, chills, and fever. All of this took its toll on Catherine, whose anxiety rose and fell with each letter. On the twenty-third, a particularly severe attack befell Potemkin. For days he lay moaning in bed drenched in sweat and bade farewell to those around him as he now despaired of living. The quinine prescribed by his doctors brought him some relief, and by the twenty-seventh Potemkin had revived. He took communion at noon and Popov wrote Catherine that thereafter the prince even became quite merry. That same night, however, his spasms returned, and he began vomiting heavily. Three days later, on his fifty-second birthday, Potemkin spoke of Catherine and wept bitterly, fearing that he might not see her again. He began slipping in and out of consciousness, and his hands and feet had become icy cold. The end was now near (Letters 452–464).

• • •

438. CATHERINE TO POTEMKIN

3 January 1791

My true friend, Prince Grigory Aleksandrovich. Valerian Aleksandrovich Zubov arrived early last Sunday and brought me your letters of 18 December. I immediately ordered that after Mass a service be held along with a large cannonade in honor of the taking of Ismail. I and our entire public have been extremely gladdened by this event. I congratulate you with all my heart on this fortunate success and the perfectly felicitous campaign, as you yourself write. The escalade of Ismail's town and fortress with a corps half the size of the opposing Turkish garrison located there is a feat almost never before seen in all of history, and it confers honor upon the fearless Russian army. I impatiently await Major-General Popov with the details. God grant that he arrive soon. I'm most sorry that the casualties were greater than at Ochakov. God grant that your successes compel the Turks to come to their senses and quickly sue for peace. When the opportunity arises, give the Turks a sense of how the Prussian King deceives them, now promising them to be a mediator, now to aid them by declaring war on us, as if both roles could be played simultaneously. All this was thought up solely to keep the Turks in the war as long as possible, and to give themselves a chance to grab some scrap of land for themselves. I suppose there will be a change of Vizier now, and this will present you with an opportunity to begin corresponding with the new Vizier, and perhaps to negotiate peace directly.[1] Both courts[2] here have already said that they would no longer insist on mediation.

Based on your testimonials and the others you sent, I have given Valerian Aleksandrovich Zubov the Cross of St. George 4th class. His most worthy brother is extremely glad that you gave his brother the opportunity to display his zeal. Please write me: did you commission Ferieri[3] to negotiate something in Vienna? He just sent me a courier along with a bill for 3,000 and just as many Chervontsi that he has spent, and he speaks of his negotiating with the Emperor himself, who is supposedly promising him cannons and arms and men. If you did not commission him with anything, then I shall order him stopped, otherwise he'll present us with a lot of chemist's bills, but will in fact spend all the money on food for himself.

Thanks, my true and dear friend, for all the fine and beneficial things you've done, and for the troops' good order and fearlessness. Tell them thanks from me, and I am taking it upon myself to discuss the decorations once I receive the details and your representations from Popov.

My health is improving, my pains aren't as frequent or as severe, but they haven't completely passed. Farewell, God be with you, I wish you every possible good and a Happy New Year.

1. Grand Vizier Sherif Hasan Pasha was executed in early February upon orders of the sultan and replaced by Koja Yusuf Pasha.

2. Berlin and London.

3. Peter Ferieri, the former Russian consul in Smyrna, was working to help supply the Greek flotilla operating in the Archipelago under Potemkin's command. Potemkin replied to Catherine that he knew nothing of Ferieri's talks with the emperor, but that he did know Ferieri was a "worthless fool."

439. POTEMKIN TO CATHERINE

11 January [1791]. Jassy

Beloved matushka, Your Most Gracious Majesty. After leaving Bender I fell terribly ill in Kishinyov, and had I not vomited a great deal I wouldn't have avoided a most severe illness.

A great and all pervasive fear has taken hold here ever since the subjugation of Ismail; nevertheless, the Sultan, an arrogant barbarian, still remains stubborn, having been completely blinded by the promises of the opposing powers.

I shall dispatch Popov with detailed reports soon after this, however, it's quite necessary, extremely necessary in fact, that I visit you for a short while, for it's impossible to describe everything. Allow me to look at you, even if only a little. Lucchesini is galloping from Sistova to Warsaw. It appears he feared falling into our hands.[1] Oh! Were I to get my hands on him I'd hang him from a lamppost, as you please.

Spring is here in all its glory, so much so that even without heating the rooms we sit with the windows open and complain how hot it is. A strong earthquake ought to be expected.

Farewell, my benefactress, I remain till death

your most loyal and most grateful subject

Prince Potemkin-Tavrichesky

1. Although the talks between the Turks and Austrians at Sistova were suspended for a time, they were later resumed, resulting in the Peace of Sistova on 4 August (n.s.).

440. POTEMKIN TO CATHERINE

Jassy. 13 January [1791]

Beloved matushka, Your Most Gracious Majesty. You are gladdened by the taking of Ismail and, the truth be told, there is reason to be. Their army of crack troops was routed in large numbers, something that's never happened before. In the Battle of Kagul not even three hundred Turks were

killed.¹ Thanks to God's mercy the campaign is a glory to us and a catastrophe for the Turks. They have lost at least 50 thousand men,² and as for
cannons, pray consult the register. In addition, this brave action has filled
them with terror. It's just and necessary that you deigned to mark this
with a cannonade, both for the sake of wounding my ill-wishers and for
the sake of the justice owed your brave army. The latter has nothing to do
with me, for I take no credit for either the knowledge or the stratagems
pertaining to this art, even though our operations were carried out me-
thodically, and with success and foresight everywhere, in a territory comprising almost a quarter of the globe. Moreover, our movements were so
well camouflaged that not only the foreigners, but even our own men
were deceived. I ought not to be proud, attributing our successes to God.
Pray thank Him alone, matushka. As for me, I produce nothing but errors,
which obligate me to be humble. Shunning arrogance and following your
motherly advice after the last campaign, I ought now to be humbler still
since this campaign is incomparably greater and is rare or, better said, unprecedented. The Eugenes, Prussian Kings³ and other crowned heroes
would loudly boast of such a victory, I, however, do not perceive in myself
the qualities of a hero and boast only of those that constitute my true
character: that is, my boundless zeal for you and the gratitude I feel for
your munificence, which you have not stopped showing me since my very
first youth and through which you have given me the right to call myself
your charge. If there is something good in me, then you have created it!
How could I prove my worthiness? You gave me the means to do this. I
shall boast of that which no one else can: given that I belong to you, so
do all of my fine successes belong to you personally. You deign to pity our
losses, but what do they represent? In the last war, Giurgevo,⁴ which is not
worth one of Ismail's bastions, cost us twice as much.

Regarding getting the Turks to see that they should not rely on the
Prussians' promises, I never stop trying to bring them to this realization.
But what is to be done? Nothing works. The Sultan's blindness, or perhaps
fate, leads him to this loss. A barbarian and an embittered tyrant, he will
heed nothing. The Vizier sent the Reis-Efendi⁵ to him to describe the bad
state of affairs so as to win him over to peace, but for this he almost lost his
head. Four couriers sent by the Vizier with news of Ismail were not permitted
to enter Tsar Grad, and their heads were cut off instead. Those around the
Sultan are now deceiving him by saying that England will send its fleet, and
all he wants is an occasion to be deceived, for this makes him happy. Believe
me that in general all the officials desire peace, but no one dares open his
mouth. And so it is imperative that I visit you, even if only for the shortest
while, so that the necessary measures can be taken and so that I may disclose
my zealous and useful ideas. This is now a slack period when nothing can be
undertaken, for no one dares to navigate along the Danube till February

given the danger of getting trapped in the ice somewhere, which can happen even as late as the end of February. Should the Turks send an armistice proposal, as I expect, there is no way at all I shall agree to it without confirmation of the borders they are demanding. It would be harmful for us to attend to them. And so we must wait for them to act first.

Beloved matushka, I directed Valerian Aleksandrovich to ask that should it be your will to allow me to come, I would rush there for a short while. But I still haven't an answer, which inhibits me greatly, and I need, need very much, to speak with you myself. It's impossible to describe everything, d'autant plus on il y a beaucoup et de pour et de contre.[6] I shall leave Prince Repnin here during my absence. Matters will suffer no loss for this short while. I have news that I cannot entrust to paper, and what's more, it would be difficult to explain things through letters.

The Prussians draw upon all visible and invisible means to damage me in your eyes. I have no doubt of your constant favor, however, they go to great lengths to make you vacillate and to make me lose my patience. I must survey the building of vessels on the Dnieper, and so am leaving here. I'll remain there so that once I receive your permission I shall already be that much farther along on the way to Petersburg, and shall thus shorten my journey.

Major-General Popov is leaving today. I have intentionally sent this courier so that he could request permission for me to come for the shortest while. For life I remain

your most loyal and most grateful subject
Prince Potemkin-Tavrichesky

1. On 21 July 1770, Rumiantsev's 25,000 troops defeated 150,000 Turks at the Battle of Kagul, which cleared the land between the Dniester and the Danube for the Russians. A young Lieutenant-General Potemkin had participated in the battle.

2. The actual number was closer to 30,000.

3. A reference to two great European military commanders: Prince Eugene of Savoy (1663–1736) and Frederick the Great.

4. Located on the northern bank of the Danube in Romania just across the river from Rushchuk, Giurgevo traded hands several times between Russia and the Porte during the First Russo-Turkish War.

5. The Ottoman foreign minister, Abdullah Birri Efendi.

6. "all the more so as there is much both for and against."

441. CATHERINE TO POTEMKIN

22 January 1791

My true friend, Prince Grigory Aleksandrovich. Bauer[1] arrived on the twentieth of this January and delivered your letters of the 11th and communiqués on the operations of the Kuban Corps that took place in September and October. It's a pity that that land is so far away it takes four months for news from there to reach us, for although these events truly are important, after so much time has passed one feels somehow less involved in them and they do not afford one the same pleasure. News arrives more quickly from America and Siberia than it does from there. I'm most sorry about the death of Lieutenant-General Rosen[2] and consider it a loss. I can easily imagine that the conquest of Ismail has filled the Turks with fear. However, I hunger to know what will follow from this fear, and I imagine that, first, there will be a change of Vizier and after that, perhaps, peace talks. I admit that it is with agitated blood that I impatiently await from Popov the details on the taking of Ismail that you promised six weeks ago, for I don't much care for the saying qu'il vaut mieux tard que jamais,[3] rather I love the freshest news about that which interests me.

Concerning your visit here, I shall tell you that personally I am always glad to see you, as you yourself well know. In addition, talking with each other and writing letters are, of course, quite different things, and agreements can be reached much quicker through conversations than through letters. But now, in this murky state, it is more important that precious minutes not be lost that you could use more effectively there, rather than here, to make peace with the Turks as we desire. And so I consider it most necessary that you stay there to await news about the impression the taking of Ismail is making in Tsar Grad. Should they be such, and you judge for yourself, that your visit here won't spoil matters, won't delay the peace talks, or should the earlier opening of the campaign not be stopped by this, then I permit you to come converse with us. However, should it appear to you that the Turks are inclined toward peace, which may well be, especially once they see that no matter how they may try to gather their troops, they are by no means moving nor want to; or should your visit here prevent an earlier opening of the campaign, then I find it necessary to implore you to favor the good of affairs and not to absent yourself. Yet once you've made peace, then return as a peacemaker, or come visit once you've arranged everything so that our operations will themselves force the Turks to agree to make peace.

You write me that Lucchesini is returning to Warsaw from Sistova. They feared nothing more there than that you might use the Cossacks to dispel the congress of Sistova. They thought this was a possibility; they were obviously mistaken, for you didn't send them. It would've been amusing if, having rounded up the entire congress, you'd sent the ambassadors here, to Petersburg, on their way home.

It's springtime where you are, while here we still haven't had any signs of winter. One day it was seven degrees below freezing, but the rest of the time it's been at or above freezing; just yesterday I saw with my own eyes from the Hermitage a carriage being pulled by two horses cause the ice on the river to crack open and the front wheels to fall into the water.

Your Cornet of the Chevalier-Gardes[4] continues to comport himself without fail in a praiseworthy and exemplary and judicious manner. I am extremely content with his honesty, goodness and his artless attachment to me. He is most grateful for your kind gestures toward him, and you will find him to be worthy of them. My health is improving, and I have already gone four and even five days without any pain, and since last Friday, to be exact, I no longer feel a thing. I'm most sorry you were ill. Farewell, my friend, God be with you, and may He exhort you.

---

1. An aide-de-camp to Potemkin, Colonel Karl Fyodorovich Bauer (1767–after 1811) was with the prince when he died later that year.

2. In an earlier report, Potemkin had notified Catherine of the death of Lieutenant-General Baron Vladimir von Rosen, head of the Kuban Corps.

3. "better late than never,"

4. Platon Zubov.

442. CATHERINE TO POTEMKIN

24 January 1791

My dear friend, Prince Grigory Aleksandrovich. Awaiting at any moment Major-General Popov with detailed information on the taking of Ismail, I still find it impossible to express to you and everyone my gratitude for this weighty affair. I received from yesterday's courier your letter of 15 January from Jassy. Though they are angry, even the ill-wishers themselves cannot dispute the great successes you have achieved, with which the Almighty has crowned your zealous and skillful labors and assiduity. I praise you for not priding yourself on them as I advised; in addition, more than pride, may you also be free of disparagement. For I want you to enjoy your successes and for your manner to be pleasing and kind. It won't be hard for you to carry out this task since in so doing your native wit will freely join with your good heart. Vos sentiments à mon égard me sont connus, et comme je suis persuadée qu'ils font partie de Votre existence, je suis persuadée aussi qu'ils ne sauroitent changer; je ne Vous en ai encore jamais connu d'autres.[1] Sir, my charge, you have justified my opinion of you, and I have attested and do attest to you that you are a most fair gentleman and the Prussians are malevolent fools. I wrote you in my previous letter that should affairs not suffer from your coming here, you should decide for yourself when to come. I now see from your letter you consider this to be a slack period. And so I suppose you're already on your way, and I'm writing this on the off chance, contrary to expectation, that you haven't left, and I grant you permission once again to come here once you see that your arrival won't spoil matters. When Valerian Aleksandrovich ar-

rived I thought that Major-General Popov would quickly follow right behind him, and I have been waiting for him everyday now to this very moment, but he still hasn't appeared. Farewell, my true friend, till we meet.

---

1. "Your feelings for me are known, and as I am convinced that they form part of your being, I
am also convinced that they will never change. I have never known you to have any others."

443. POTEMKIN TO CATHERINE

Jassy. 9 February [1791]

Your Most Gracious Majesty. Having received your permission to come visit, I
report that till now a chest pain and a cough have kept me from departing.
Although I've not yet fully recovered, nevertheless I'll depart today.

The Vizier sent the Reis-Efendi to Tsar Grad with a peace proposal, but
the Sultan nearly cut off his head. An envoy has been dispatched to Berlin
with questions. His return will determine what will be. After learning of Ismail, the capital[1] was in danger of rebelling, however, the taverns were
closed, all the wine was confiscated, gatherings were prohibited, and as a
result things quieted down. No one dares speak to the Sultan, and he's
been drinking.

In preparation for leaving I've entrusted command to Prince Repnin
and given him detailed instructions. I shall myself soon return, since I've
no other need than to see you and to report on affairs, after which I shall,
of course, hurry back.

I received a most gracious letter from the Emperor and congratulations
from many in Vienna. When the people in Galicia and Austria heard that
I was supposedly on my way to Vienna, they were well disposed to greet
me and to take the reins of my horses. For this too I am obliged to you,
Your Majesty. While alive I remain

> your most loyal and most grateful
> subject Prince Potemkin-Tavrichesky

---

1. Constantinople.

444. POTEMKIN TO CATHERINE

[29 April 1791][1]

Beloved matushka, Your Most Gracious Majesty!
Your children were the main adornment at yesterday's banquet, where
they charmed the hearts of everyone. The first-born[2] of the nestling eagles
is already fledged. Soon, after spreading his wings, he will soar over Russia,

and it will reveal itself to him as the most expansive of maps. He will see expanded borders, armies, fleets and cities that have multiplied, a populated steppe, peoples who have abandoned savagery, rivers filled with vessels. But he will no longer behold springs flowing with the blood of the guilty.

He will be presented with a family of countless fellow men, for you are a mother to your subjects, and to me most of all, for your blessings to me outnumber even the hours that comprise my life. Such will be the beautiful sight before him, and we shall have the pleasure of seeing in him a Prince who possesses the qualities of an angel, meekness, a pleasing appearance, a majestic bearing. He will awaken in everyone love for him and gratitude toward you for his education that has rendered nothing but gifts to Russia.

---

1. Although Lopatin dates this letter 22 April 1789, this date proposed by Eliseeva (*Perepiska,* 120–21) is more likely.

2. Grand Duke Alexander Pavlovich, the future Alexander I.

445. CATHERINE TO POTEMKIN

[Before 11 May 1791]

If you want to remove the stone from my heart, if you want to calm my spasms, quickly send a courier to the armies and permit the land and naval forces to begin operations as soon as possible, or else you'll drag out the war for much longer, which, of course, neither you nor I desire.

446. CATHERINE TO POTEMKIN

[12 July 1791]

Two celebrations in one day,[1] my friend, and some other marvelous developments as well: the allies have accepted our conditions,[2] il faut qu'ils ayent bien envie de finir puisqu'ils prennent pour prétexte la navigation sur la Rivière du Dnester, sur laquelle les vaisseaux marchands ne feront pas beaucoup de chemin n'y ayant pas d'eau.[3]

I'll arrive in town tomorrow for the celebration.[4] Farewell, my friend, God be with you. I'll await your representations on the men who've distinguished themselves.

---

1. Two couriers arrived on 11 July: the first brought news of Repnin's victory at Machin (28 June), and the second brought the keys to Anapa and word of the Turks having fled Sudzhuk Kale.

2. On 11 July the Prussian and British ambassadors agreed to Russian demands to keep Ochakov and the land between the Dniester and Bug rivers.

3. "it must be that they really want to finish matters, for they are using the navigation on the Dniester River as a pretext, upon which no merchant ships can travel due to the lack of water." The agreement on making the Dniester River Russia's new western border included a phrase establishing free navigation on the river. If the Turks refused to accept this, and the other terms, both Britain and Prussia would withdraw their mediation.

4. A celebratory public prayer service was held at St. Petersburg's Church of the Kazan Mother of God on 13 July.

447. POTEMKIN TO CATHERINE

4 August [1791]. Olviopol

Beloved matushka, Your Most Gracious Majesty! Thank God the preliminaries, which were signed before my departure, have been ratified.[1] I shall be in Galatz on the 7th and shall try to finish everything ahead of the agreed-upon schedule.

The declaration about the border along the Dniester was made according to the precise words of the Spanish minister, just as he explained it to me in Petersburg. I left Yelizavetgrad for Nikolaev to survey the ships being armed because the horses did not reach me in time on the other side of the Bug. But that I am just barely able to move, God is my witness. What heat—I've never before seen anything like it. I kiss your tender hands and remain till death

your most loyal and most grateful subject
Prince Potemkin-Tavrichesky

P.S. The fleet left again for the coast of Rumelia in search of the enemy before having received my order. I have sent the small vessel "Berezan" along with two Turks to announce the decreed armistice, and I hope they soon reach one of the fleets.[2]

---

1. The peace preliminaries were agreed to on 24 July and ratified by Prince Repnin and the grand vizier on 31 July.

2. Potemkin sent word to Admiral Ushakov, who had set out to sea on 29 July to engage the Turks and had defeated them two days later (which the prince did not know about at the time), that an armistice had been signed. He sent two Turks along in case they first came across Turkish ships.

448. CATHERINE TO POTEMKIN

From Tsarskoe Selo. 12 August 1791

My true friend, Prince Grigory Aleksandrovich. You gladdened me quite unexpectedly with the preliminary articles of peace, for which I thank you with all my heart and soul. God grant that this beneficial matter be brought to a quick end with the signing of the actual peace. An eight-month armistice is long. Do try to end matters soon, all the more so since the courts have been told, and they agreed, that if in four months the Turks do not desist, then they will abandon them, and we shall be quite free to make the conditions even more onerous. And so, the eight-month term contradicts that of four months. However, we could simply say that Repnin didn't know of the provisos with the courts aiding the Turks.[1] The courts were also told that every Sovereign has the right to build fortresses in his land, and so do try to make sure this is achieved by the treaty. The same goes for the article concerning the Treaty of Kainardji, which the Turks have already recognized as having been renewed.[2]

I do so hope that the intense heat and the difficulties of the journey have not injured your health, especially at the present time when every minute demands new labors. Adieu, mon Ami, may God help you. We here are all so terribly glad.

---

1. Unaware of the agreement signed by the British and Prussian ambassadors on 11 July in St. Petersburg (which granted Russia the right to resume hostilities should peace not be reached in four months), Repnin had agreed to an eight-month armistice with the Turks. Fearing this would grant the Turks an opportunity to rebuild their forces and desirous of beginning hostilities against a now weakened and abandoned enemy, Catherine sought to change the armistice with the Porte.

2. Catherine had successfully resisted Prussian and British demands that Ochakov be razed prior to their agreement of 11 July. One of the main terms for the armistice with the Turks was Turkish acceptance of the Treaty of Kuchuk Kainardji (which ended the First Russo-Turkish War) with the provision that the border be moved to the Dniester River.

449. POTEMKIN TO CATHERINE

15 August [1791]. Galatz

Beloved matushka, Your Most Gracious Majesty. I arrived in Galatz on the 7th and on the next day the Vizier sent his dragoman and Bin-chaush[1] to greet me. He didn't say anything in his letter, rather he merely entrusted the commission to speak to me. According to our conversation, the Sultan supposedly didn't approve of anything, and he is in trouble. I voiced my agreement, and then everything went smoothly.[2] Much was said, but I cannot describe it, I don't have the strength. I'm extremely ill, and should my fever turn into a bilious malady, as is common here, then I shan't be strong enough to endure.

Our fleet is out at sea, and I think things are going poorly for the Turks given that the Vizier requested that I order the fleet stopped. But it's beyond Varna by now, having driven off the Turkish fleet. I expect news soon.

The Prince of Württemberg has passed away, and I fell ill as they were carrying out his body.[3] As God is my witness, I'm all worn out; I'm suffering from a 2nd paroxysm which continues unabated.

Till death I remain

> your most loyal and most grateful subject
> Prince Potemkin-Tavrichesky

This place is so unhealthy that nearly everyone is ill.

My compliments to Platon Aleksandrovich, I can't write any more.

I'm enclosing the Vizier's letter and a report on his departure from Sevastopol.

---

1. The grand vizier's interpreter and adjutant.

2. As a negotiating tactic, the Turkish delegation informed Potemkin that the peace proposals accepted by the grand vizier had not been approved by Selim, and for this reason the vizier was in trouble. Potemkin simply informed them they were free to break off negotiations, but if they did, Russia would be free to ignore what had been agreed upon earlier.

3. Prince Karl of Württemberg died of fever on 13 August. According to legend, Potemkin accidentally mistook the prince's hearse for his own carriage and climbed upon it, which he took as a portent of his own approaching death.

450. POTEMKIN TO CATHERINE

24 August [1791]

Thanks to God the danger has passed, and I'm better. I remain very weak. The critical day was brutal. I had lost all hope of ever seeing you again, beloved matushka, Your Most Gracious Majesty. I'm on my way to Jassy, to Chardan.

Be assured that I shan't neglect your interests. It's true that eight months is a long term, I have, however, rectified this by letting the Vizier know that I wouldn't let him drag this out even a minute longer. I'll send a detailed record of everything that happened from Jassy.

I'm not well, farewell, my dear beloved and mother. Till my final breath I remain

> your most loyal and most grateful subject
> Prince Potemkin-Tavrichesky

My compliments to Platon Aleksandrovich

451. CATHERINE TO POTEMKIN

28 August 1791

My true friend, Prince Grigory Aleksandrovich. Your letters of 15 August have reached my hands, from which I learned of the dispatches exchanged by you and the Vizier, and that he ordered you be told that he is in trouble, and that you answered that you considered all of this an attempt to deceive.[1] However, what I most extremely regret and what cruelly torments me is your illness and that you write to me that you don't feel strong enough to endure. I beg God that He turns away from you this misfortune and that He spare me this blow which I cannot even contemplate without extreme affliction.

News of the driving off of the Turkish fleet was greeted here with great joy, however, all I can think about is your illness.

The Prince of Württemberg's death has caused the Grand Duchess considerable sorrow. Order someone there to write me more frequently about yourself. I learned from your letter of the appointment of the plenipotentiaries. All of this is good, and the only bad thing is that you're ill. I pray God for your recovery. Farewell, Christ be with you.

Platon Aleksandrovich begs his compliments to you and will write to you himself.

---

1. In a second letter written on 15 August, Potemkin informed Catherine that he was departing for Gushcha and had appointed Aleksandr Samoilov, José de Ribas, and Sergei Lashkarev as Russia's plenipotentiaries to the peace talks.

452. CATHERINE TO POTEMKIN

Saint-Petersburg. 4 September 1791

My true friend, Prince Grigory Aleksandrovich. Your letter of 24 August calmed my soul's worry over you, for I saw that you are better, though before that I had been extremely anxious. Nevertheless, I don't understand how you can move about from place to place while so extremely weak.

Rear Admiral Ushakov frightened Selim quite opportunely. Reports arriving from everywhere confirm the news that Mecca has been plundered by the Arabs, and that the Sherif of Mecca is being held prisoner and that Mecca has been seized.[1] I am quite curious to see the promised record. Kindly write me—through whom did you send the Order of St. George, the sword, and my letter to Duke Richelieu?[2] He still hasn't received anything as of yet.

Platon Aleksandrovich begs his compliments to you and will write to you himself. He was quite worried about your illness, and for an entire day he didn't know how or with what to ease my sorrow.

Farewell, God be with you. I am well. Till now the days here have been nice and warm.

---

1. Rumors that the Wahhabi sect had sacked Mecca and seized the sherif of Mecca, an Ottoman official, were false.

2. French volunteer Armand du Plessis, duc de Richelieu (1766–1822) was awarded for his participation in the siege of Ismail. He went on to become town governor of Odessa and governor of the province of New Russia.

453. POTEMKIN TO CATHERINE

6 September [1791]

I was feeling well, but have gotten worse. Four days of uninterrupted fever and headache and extreme weakness. I'm at God's mercy, however, your affairs will not suffer interruption till the last minute. Don't worry about me, matushka, and have faith in what God Himself knows, that till my final breath I shall remain with unlimited gratitude and true filial affection

your most loyal and most grateful subject
Prince Potemkin-Tavrichesky

My sweat's relieved me.

My sincere compliments to Platon Aleksandrovich. I truly couldn't write.

454. POTEMKIN TO CATHERINE

10 September [1791]

Thanks to God, I'm feeling better, my beloved matushka, Your Most Gracious Majesty. I'm anticipating the plenipotentiaries, and upon their arrival I'll begin to try to conclude matters with God's help.[1]

My benefactress, I remain till my last breath your

most loyal and most grateful subject
Prince Potemkin-Tavrichesky

---

1. Potemkin had just received news from the Turkish plenipotentiaries that they would soon be arriving in Jassy.

455. CATHERINE TO POTEMKIN

16 September 1791

My true friend, Prince Grigory Aleksandrovich. I have received your letters of 29 August[1] and 6 September. The first made me very happy, for I saw you were better, and the second only increased my worry, since I saw that for four days you had an uninterrupted fever and a pain in the head. I beg God to give you strength. I don't doubt that matters will be taken care of, but what attending to them does to one who's sick, this I know for myself.

I, thank God, am well, and my colic is completely gone, which I attribute to the waistband and the Hungarian wine you recommended. Farewell, my friend. Christ be with you.

Platon Aleksandrovich thanks you for your compliments and will write to you himself.

1. Potemkin sent Catherine several reports dated 29 August informing her of the fleet's return to Sevastopol and of some presents he had received from the grand vizier.

456. POTEMKIN TO CATHERINE

16 September [1791]. Jassy

Beloved matushka, Your Most Gracious Majesty. Thanks to God I'm beginning to get my strength back, although only bit by bit. However, a ringing in one ear torments me. There's never been a year like this one—everyone's ill. My house looks like an infirmary. In the army field hospitals there are 8 thousand sick, and 10 thousand more in the regiments. Thank God they're not dying.

I expect the Turks in four days. I anticipate a lot of trickery, but shall be on my guard. I'll send with the next courier a description of everything that was said with the dragoman and the others. Oh, God, I can't write any more my head's so weak.

I kiss your tender hands and remain till death

your most loyal and most grateful subject

Prince Potemkin-Tavrichesky

I sent everything to Richelieu with Prince Nassau. He was the only one who could do it. From his letter I thought he was leaving for the army, but have learned from Sombreuil that he hasn't departed.

457. POTEMKIN TO CATHERINE

21 September 1791. Jassy

Beloved matushka, Your Most Gracious Majesty!
My paroxysms continue for a third day. I've lost all strength and don't know when the end will be. I remain till death

your most loyal and most grateful subject

Prince Potemkin-Tavrichesky

My compliments to Platon Aleksandrovich.

458. POTEMKIN TO CATHERINE

21 September 1791. Jassy

Secret[1]
Should we, with God's help, soon agree on peace, then I must be allowed in advance a way from here, for should it not be via Poland there'll be no

chance to feed the horses anywhere, nor will there be any means to convey the sick across the steppe. I'm also most anxious about the oared fleet. I fear the Liman will freeze over before it can arrive.

Pr. P. T.

---

1. One of Potemkin's last official letters to Catherine.

459. POTEMKIN TO CATHERINE

26 September[1] 1791. Jassy

Your Most Gracious Majesty! Exhausted by my cruel sufferings, I cannot write myself. Popov will inform Your Majesty of my condition,[2] while I shall remain till my very last breath
your most grateful and most loyal subject
Prince Potemkin-Tavrichesky
My beloved matushka.

---

1. Though so dated, this letter was probably written on 25 September.

2. Popov included with Potemkin's brief note a description of the prince's suffering and his current condition as well as the journal of his illness compiled by Drs. Timan, Massot, and Sankovsky who were attending to the dying prince.

460. POTEMKIN TO CATHERINE

27 September 1791

Beloved matushka, my not seeing you makes it even harder for me to live.

461. CATHERINE TO POTEMKIN

30 September 1791

My true friend, Prince Grigory Aleksandrovich. I'm so extremely worried about your illness. For Christ's sake, if necessary, take what the doctors recommend might give you relief.[1] And I beg you, after taking it avoid all food and drink that might counteract the medicine. I beg God to hurry and give you back your strength and health. Farewell, my friend.

Platon Aleksandrovich thanks you for your compliments and grieves very much over your condition. I'm sending you my best wishes and a nice little fur coat on your name-day.[2]

1. Catherine's response to a worried letter from Popov of 21 September.

2. The tardiness with which Catherine sent her greetings and gift (the letter was apparently written on the prince's name-day and so would have arrived over a week late) suggests that given her agitated state Catherine may have dated the letter incorrectly. Indeed, Popov makes reference to Potemkin having received a fur coat and dressing-gown from Catherine on 27 September.

462. POTEMKIN TO CATHERINE

2 October 1791. Jassy

Your Most Gracious Majesty! In my present condition, exhausted by illness, I pray the Almighty to preserve your precious health and prostrate myself at your blessed feet.

Your Imperial Majesty's
most loyal and most grateful subject
Prince Potemkin-Tavrichesky

Matushka, oh how sick I am.

463. CATHERINE TO POTEMKIN

3 October 1791

My true friend, Prince Grigory Aleksandrovich. I received today your letters of the 25th and 27th a few hours apart and confess that they worry me extremely, although I see that your final three lines are written somewhat better. And your doctors assure me you are a bit better. I pray God to hurry and return you to health.

464. POTEMKIN TO CATHERINE

Jassy. 4 October 1791

Your Most Gracious Majesty. I've no more strength to endure my torments. My only remaining salvation is to abandon this town, and I have ordered myself conveyed to Nikolaev. I don't know what's to become of me.

Your most loyal and most grateful subject

My only salvation is to leave.

• • •

Potemkin, his body exhausted by months of intensifying illness and wracked by spasms, had to dictate this final brief letter to Vasily Popov. When Popov had finished, he placed the note in front of the dying prince for his signature, but in a trembling, barely legible hand, Potemkin scrawled a last plea for salvation instead.

Several days earlier Potemkin had decided to abandon disease-infested Jassy for his beloved Nikolaev and had set 4 October as the day of departure. Throughout the early morning hours of the fourth he repeatedly inquired what time it was and whether everything was ready for the journey. At 8 a.m., after scribbling his departing words to the empress, he set out in a dense fog on his final journey accompanied by his cherished niece, Aleksandra, his long-time quartermaster, Mikhail Faleev, his doctors Massot, Timan, and Sankovsky, and two of his trusted generals. The party traveled slowly and quietly, arriving around two o'clock in the afternoon at the village of Puncheshta, some thirty versts from Jassy, where they stopped for the night. The doctors noted that the prince had handled the trip surprisingly well; his color had improved and although he complained of feeling weak, his pulse was strong. They retired that evening full of hope that should the prince make it safely to Nikolaev, there was a good chance of recovery.

After a fitful night, the procession set out again early the following morning. They had traveled no more than ten versts when the carriages halted on a remote hillside in the Bessarabian steppe. Legend has it that Potemkin, sensing his time had come, called out: "That's enough now, there is no point in going any further. Take me out of the carriage, I want to die in the field." Just before noon on 5 October under a broad southern sky, Potemkin's ravaged body, covered in the silk dressing-gown he had received from Catherine just days before, was removed from the carriage and laid upon a Persian rug spread out over the grass. After a few anxious moments, Potemkin was dead.

The prince's body was returned to Jassy, where an autopsy was performed. There were rumors that Potemkin had been poisoned, although there is nothing to substantiate them. For years Potemkin had suffered off and on from fevers, probably malarial, and a lifetime of excessive food and drink and an exhausting schedule of work and travel had destroyed his health by the age of fifty-two. The final blow most likely came in the form of bronchial pneumonia. After embalming, Potemkin's body lay in state in Jassy before being conveyed to Kherson where it was placed in a specially constructed crypt in the Church of St. Catherine. Potemkin's entrails, removed during the embalming, remained behind and were apparently buried in Jassy's Golia Monastery. The precise fate of the prince's heart, also separated from the body at that time, remains a mystery.

News of Potemkin's death reverberated throughout Europe and the Ottoman Empire. In England, Parliament interrupted its meetings, and in Constantinople, Grand Vizier Yusuf Pasha, sensing that with the Porte's great vanquisher now gone their losses could be reversed, urged Selim to break off peace negotiations. In St. Petersburg, Catherine wept. She asked Khrapovitsky through her tears how she could ever replace Potemkin. "He was a true nobleman," she sobbed, "a smart man, he could not be bought. Nothing will ever be the same." Days later she wrote to Baron Grimm in desperation: "Every burden now falls upon me. Be so good as to pray for me." Her sense of isolation and abandonment increased with time. A few months later she wrote again: "It is impossible to replace him since another person like him would first have to be born, but the end of this century somehow hardly presages any heroes. I am not losing hope that at least some intelligent men will appear, but that requires time, effort, and experience." During the months following Potemkin's death, Catherine retreated from public life.

The Imperial Council met the night of the twelfth and decided that Aleksandr Bezborodko should be sent to Jassy to take Potemkin's place at the peace talks. Bezborodko arrived in Jassy in early November and quickly concluded a final peace agreement with the Turks. On 29 December 1791, the Treaty of Jassy was signed ending four and a half years of war. The Ottoman Porte recognized the Russian annexation of the Crimea and granted Russia the territory between the Dniester and Bug rivers and Ochakov as well. Potemkin's nephew, Aleksandr Samoilov, returned with the ratified treaty to St. Petersburg on 30 January 1792. Catherine admitted him, dismissed her company, and together they wept.

At home, the death of the most powerful man in the empire created an intense power vacuum that Platon Zubov and his kinsmen greedily sought to fill. Though he lacked the requisite skill and experience, Zubov, then a mere twenty-four years, quickly attained supreme authority in both domestic and foreign affairs. Over time he covered himself with enough titles and honors to rival—if not surpass—Potemkin. Unlike Potemkin, however, Zubov contented himself with the voluptuous pleasures of court and shared little of his rival's intelligence, immense capacity for hard work, and selfless devotion to Russia and the empress.

These final years of Catherine's life and reign with Zubov cannot be counted among her finest. While much of this can be attributed to the loss of Potemkin, other factors played a part. Catherine was now an old woman by the standards of the time, and age and declining health had done much to reduce her abilities. She felt alone, the great men who had served under her for decades were now all gone, and her thoughts were increasingly directed less toward the future and more toward the past. The growing chaos of the French Revolution, which threatened to spread its contagion to all the monarchies of Europe, presaged a new world more hostile to Catherine than anything she had seen before. She responded by trying to make the world safe for autocracy. She became obsessed with stamping out the hydra of revolution, at home and abroad, and used this to justify the final partitions of Poland in 1793 and 1795.

Although with time Catherine came to accept the loss of Potemkin, he remained a very real presence at her side. She surrounded herself with men like Popov and Samoilov, who shared her memories of Potemkin and in whose faces she saw his reflection. When discussing affairs with her advisors, Catherine would turn to Popov for guidance, seeking his opinion on what Potemkin might have recommended. Zubov himself found it impossible to get completely out from under Potemkin's immense shadow. Toward the end of his life he reminisced how, "Although I won a partial victory over him, there was simply no way I could entirely remove him from my path; and it was necessary to remove him because the empress herself always met his desires and quite simply feared him as if he were an exacting husband. Me, she only loved and frequently pointed to Potemkin as an example for me to follow."

Catherine's counsel was unfair, for as she herself knew better than anyone else, Potemkin and his life had been incomparable. It was this fact that had made their partnership so remarkable and, as a result, Catherine's reign one of the most celebrated in Russian history. Twenty-two years earlier, while off fighting the Turks in the previous war, Potemkin had written Catherine of his unshakeable devotion to her, affirming that death alone would end his service to her and the empire. He had kept his word.

Appendix I—*Maps*

Russian Territorial Gains

- First partition of Poland (1772)
- Treaty of Kuchuk Kainardji (1774)
- Annexation of the Crimea (1783)
- Treaty of Jassey (1792)
- Pre-partition boundary

White Sea

Arkhangelsk

Helsingfors

Stockholm

St. Petersburg

RUSSIAN

Novgorod

Kazan

BALTIC SEA

COURLAND Riga

Tver

Orenburg

Dvina R.

Moscow

Karlskrona

Danzig

Dubrovna   Smolensk   Tula

EMPIRE

Yaik R.

PRUSSIA

Mogilyov

BELORUSSIA (WHITE RUSSIA)

Thorn

Warsaw

Breslau   POLAND

UKRAINE

Chernigov

Reichenbach

Kiev   LITTLE RUSSIA

Volga R.

GALICIA   Dniester R

Dnieper R.

Yekaterinoslav

Don R.

Vienna

Bug R.

AUSTRIA

CASPIAN SEA

BANAT

TAURIDE   Kuban R.

Danube R.

BLACK SEA

CAUCASUS

OTTOMAN

PERSIAN

Constantinople (Tsar Grad)

EMPIRE

EMPIRE

| 0 | | 300 Mi. |
| 0 | | 500 Km. |

Russia and neighboring countries in Catherine's reign.

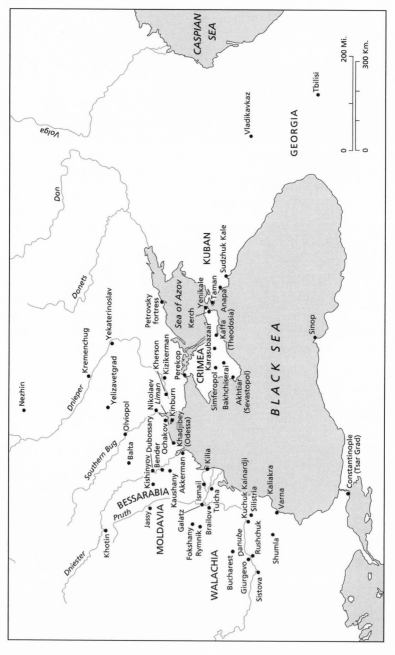

Southern Russia and the Black Sea.

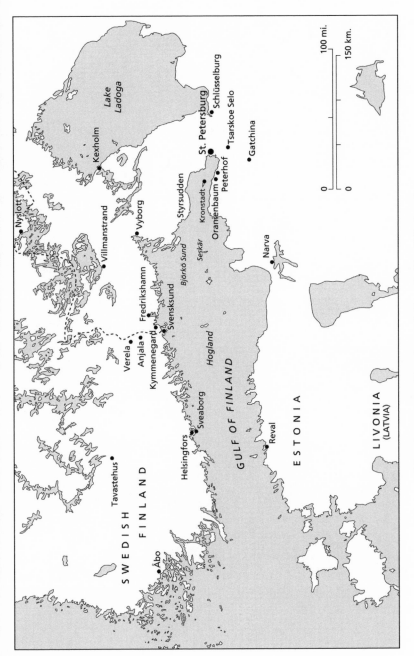

Northwestern Russia and the Gulf of Finland

Appendix II—*Chronology*

1729   Sophia Augusta Fredericka of Anhalt-Zerbst (future Catherine the Great) is born in Stettin on the Baltic Sea

1739   Grigory Aleksandrovich Potemkin is born in the village of Chizhevo near Smolensk

1740   Frederick II (the Great) of Prussia and Maria Theresa of Austria ascend the throne

1741   Elizabeth Petrovna, daughter of Peter the Great, overthrows the infant Ivan VI and seizes the Russian throne

1744   Sophia arrives in Russia, converts to Russian Orthodoxy, becomes Grand Duchess Catherine, and is officially engaged to Grand Duke Peter

1745   Potemkin moves to Moscow and begins his studies
       Grand Duchess Catherine and Grand Duke Peter are married

1752   Catherine begins liaison with Sergei Saltykov

1754   Catherine gives birth to Paul Petrovich, the future Paul I (1796–1801)

1755   Potemkin is enrolled in the Horse Guards
       Catherine begins liaison with Stanislaw Poniatowski

1757   Potemkin visits St. Petersburg and is presented to Empress Elizabeth in recognition of his academic success

1760   Potemkin is expelled from Moscow University for laziness
       George III of England ascends the throne

1761   Catherine begins affair with Grigory Orlov
       Potemkin leaves Moscow for St. Petersburg
       Empress Elizabeth dies; Peter III ascends the throne

1762   Catherine gives birth to Aleksei Bobrinsky, her son by Grigory Orlov
Peter III is overthrown and murdered; Catherine is proclaimed empress

1764   Stanislaw Poniatowski is elected king of Poland

1765   Emperor Francis I dies; Joseph II of Austria becomes emperor and
co-regent with his mother, Maria Theresa

1767   Legislative Commission opens in Moscow; Potemkin serves as
"Guardian of the Tatars and other Exotic Peoples"

1768   First Russo-Turkish War (1768–1774) begins

1769   Potemkin volunteers for duty and leaves capital for the front

1770   Potemkin awarded Orders of St. Anne and St. George for fighting
at Fokshany, Brailov, and Giurgevo; Russian navy defeats Turks
at Battle of Chesme

1772   Gustav III of Sweden carries out coup to restore powers of the crown
First Partition of Poland

1773   Grigory Orlov falls from grace; Aleksandr Vasilchikov becomes favorite
Pugachev Rebellion begins

1774   Potemkin returns to capital; replaces Vasilchikov as favorite, and
possibly marries Catherine
Louis XVI of France ascends the throne
Treaty of Kuchuk Kainardji ends First Russo-Turkish War

1775   Pugachev is executed in Moscow
Zaporozhian Cossack Host destroyed; territory incorporated into
Russian Empire
American War of Independence begins

1776   Potemkin's favor ends; Pyotr Zavadovsky becomes favorite
American Declaration of Independence is signed

1777   Semyon Zorich replaces Zavadovsky as favorite
Alexander Pavlovich, Catherine's grandson and the future
Alexander I (1801–1825), is born

1778   Prussia declares war on Austria beginning War of the Bavarian Suc
        cession (1778–1779)

1780   Aleksandr Lanskoy becomes favorite
        Catherine meets Joseph II in Mogilyov
        Maria Theresa dies

1781   Russo-Austrian treaty of alliance concluded
        Battle of Yorktown ends land combat in American War of
            Independence

1783   Russia annexes the Crimea; Treaty of Georgievsk makes Georgia
            a Russian protectorate
        Potemkin is stricken with malaria; Grigory Orlov dies
        Treaty of Versailles ends war of France and Spain with Great Britain

1784   Treaty of Constantinople is signed by which Ottoman Porte recognizes
            annexation of Crimea
        Potemkin officially founds city of Sevastopol
        Favorite Aleksandr Lanskoy dies

1785   Potemkin is appointed commander in chief of the Russian armed
            forces in case of war with the Porte
        Catherine issues charters to the nobility and towns

1786   Aleksandr Dmitriev-Mamonov becomes favorite
        Frederick the Great of Prussia dies; Frederick William II ascends
            the throne
        Potemkin founds Yekaterinoslav (Dnepropetrovsk)

1787   Catherine and Joseph II tour southern Russia and the Crimea with
            Potemkin
        The Porte declares war beginning Second Russo-Turkish War
            (1787–1791)
        Drafting of U.S. Constitution

1788   Joseph II declares war on the Porte
        Triple Alliance among Britain, Prussia, and Holland is formed
        Gustav III attacks Russia beginning Russo-Swedish War (1788–1790)
        Estates General are summoned in France
        Turkish fortress of Ochakov falls to Potemkin

1789   Sultan Abdul Hamid dies; succeeded by Selim III
        Fall of Mamonov; Platon Zubov becomes favorite
        Revolution begins in France; storming of the Bastille
        Russian victories over Turks at Fokshany, River Rymnik, Bender
        Russian naval victory over Swedes at First Battle of Svensksund
        Austrians take Belgrade and march into Bucharest
        George Washington is elected president of United States

1790   Alliance between Prussia and the Porte is signed
        Joseph II dies; Leopold II ascends the throne
        Defensive alliance signed by Prussia and Poland
        Convention of Reichenbach establishing armistice between Austria
            and the Porte is signed
        Treaty of Verela is signed ending Russo-Swedish War
        Russian victories over Turks at Tulcha and Ismail

1791   Ochakov Crisis: Britain and Prussia threaten Russia with war
        Potemkin visits St. Petersburg for last time
        Revolution in Poland: Constitution of the Third of May
        Louis XVI flees Paris and is caught at Varennes
        Peace of Sistova is signed ending war between Austria and the Porte
        Potemkin dies on the way to Nikolaev
        Treaty of Jassy is signed ending Second Russo-Turkish War

1792   Gustav III is murdered in Sweden
        Russia invades Poland
        Monarchy falls in France; France declares war on Austria

1793   Louis XVI is executed in Paris; Reign of Terror begins
        Second Partition of Poland

1794   Polish insurrection is crushed by Russia
        Robespierre is toppled in France

1795   Third Partition of Poland
        The Directory is put in power in France

1796   Nicholas Pavlovich, Catherine's third grandson and the future
            Nicholas I (1825–1855), is born
        Catherine the Great dies; Paul I ascends the throne

Appendix III—*The Table of Ranks*

In 1722, Tsar Peter I promulgated the Table of Ranks as part of his attempt to reform the Russian state apparatus. The table comprised fourteen classes (one being the highest) with corresponding ranks *(chiny)* in the three branches of state service: military (including the navy), civil, and court. In the eighteenth century, hereditary nobility was granted to those men who achieved a rank at the bottom of the table (class 14) in the military, and to those men in the civil service achieving class 8. The Table of Ranks, although frequently modified, remained the basis of the Russian bureaucracy until 1917. The chart below shows how the Table of Ranks looked (in simplified form) in the reign of Catherine the Great.

Class	Military	Naval	Civil	Court
1	Field Marshal	Admiral-General	Chancellor	——
2	General-in-Chief	Admiral	Vice Chancellor or Real Privy Counselor	Chief Chamberlain Chief Marshal Chief Steward Chief Equerry Chief Master of the Hunt Chief Cup-Bearer
3	Lieutenant-General	Vice Admiral	Procurator-General	Marshal Steward Equerry Master of the Hunt Chief Master of Ceremonies
4	Major-General	Rear Admiral	Privy Counselor	Chamberlain
5	Brigadier	Captain-Commander	Herald Master	Master of Ceremonies Gentleman-of-the-Bedchamber
6	Colonel	First Captain	Collegiate Counselor	Purveyor-of-the Bedchamber*

Class	Military	Naval	Civil	Court
7	Lieutenant-Colonel or Captain (Guards)	Second Captain	Court Counselor	——
8	Major	Third Captain	Collegiate Assessor	——
9	Captain	Lieutenant-Captain	Titular Counselor	Court Purveyor*
10	Lieutenant-Captain	Lieutenant	Collegiate Secretary	——
11	——	Ship's Secretary	——	——
12	Lieutenant or Cornet (Guards)	Second Lieutenant or Midshipman	Provincial Secretary	——
13	Second-Lieutenant	Ship's Commissioner	——	——
14	Standard-Bearer (*fendrik*)	——	Collegiate Registrar	——

Source: Based on L. E. Shepelev, *Chinovnyi mir Rossii: XVIII–nachalo XIX v.* (St. Petersburg, 1999).

* Although not officially included in the Table of Ranks at the time, the ranks of Purveyor-of-the-Bedchamber (*kamer-fur'era*) and Court Purveyor (*gof-fur'era*) were de facto positions. The rank of adjutant-general was included in the original Table of Ranks in 1722, but over time was removed from the official list. Like nearly all the other court ranks, it was bestowed at the personal discretion of the tsar or tsaritsa. Catherine the Great decreed that the rank of adjutant-general could not be lower than that of Lieutenant-General, thus placing it, along with nearly all the other court ranks, among the Generals' ranks (classes 2–3). Beginning in the reign of Tsar Peter III, the monarch's aides-de-camp were placed on par with army Colonels.

The original Table of Ranks did not list any positions for women, although six female court ranks or titles (*zvaniia*) were laid out in an addendum. In the reign of Catherine the Great, the following female ranks were recognized at court: Chief Stewardess of the Court, Stewardess of the Court, Lady-in-Waiting (of which there were twelve in 1796), and Maid-of-Honor (also twelve in 1796). The first two ranks were entrusted to those women in charge of the court's female staff and the empress's and the grand duchesses' private offices; the latter two were honorary positions at court and carried no court duties with them. Catherine also had several Maids-of-the-Bedchamber, although it is not entirely clear whether these were official ranks. They were not included in the list of court offices in 1796.

Bibliography

Not intended to be an exhaustive list of the scholarship on Catherine and Potemkin, this bibliography lists those works that were most helpful in editing their correspondence and that might be of the greatest interest to readers seeking to learn more. Several works were particularly useful in composing the chapter introductions. They are designated by asterisks.

Adamczyk, Theresia. *Fürst G. A. Potemkin. Untersuchungen zu seiner Lebensgeschichte.* Emsdetten, 1936.

Adamson, John, ed. *The Princely Courts of Europe, 1500–1750.* London, 1999.

Alekseeva, Tat'iana Vasil'evna. *Vladimir Lukich Borovikovskii i russkaia kul'tura na rubezhe vosemnadtsatogo-deviatnadtsatogo vekov.* Moscow, 1975.

*Alekseevskii, B. "Orlov, kniaz' Grigorii Grigor'evich." *Russkii biograficheskii slovar'.* Vol. 12. St. Petersburg, 1905.

*Alexander, John T. *Catherine the Great: Life and Legend.* New York, 1989.

———. "Favourites, Favouritism and Female Rule in Russia, 1725–1796." In *Russia in the Age of the Enlightenment: Essays for Isabel de Madariaga,* edited by Roger Bartlett and Janet M. Hartley. London, 1990.

———. "Politics, Passions, Patronage: Catherine II and Petr Zavadovskii." In *Russia and the World of the Eighteenth Century,* edited by R. P. Bartlett, A. G. Cross, and Karen Rasmussen. Columbus, OH, 1988.

Alpatov, M. A. *Russkaia istoricheskaia mysl' i zapadnaia Evropa (XVIII–pervaia polovina XIX v.).* Moscow, 1985.

Anderson, Howard, Philip B. Daghlian, and Irvin Ehrenpreis, eds. *The Familiar Letter in the Eighteenth Century.* Lawrence, KS, 1966.

Anderson, M. S. *The Eastern Question, 1774–1923.* New York, 1966.

*Anderson, R. C. *Naval Wars in the Baltic, 1522–1850.* 1910. Reprint. London, 1969.

———. *Naval Wars in the Levant, 1559–1853.* Princeton, NJ, 1952.

Andreevskii, I. "O meste pogrebeniia tela fel'dmarshala kniazia Potemkina-Tavrich-skogo." *Zapiski imperatorskogo Odesskogo obshchestva istorii i drevnostei* 5 (1863): 1006–10.

Anisimov, Evgenii. *Elizaveta Petrovna.* Moscow, 1999.

———. *Rossiia v seredine XVIII veka: Bor'ba za nasledie Petra.* Moscow, 1986.

Annenkov, Ivan Vasil'evich. *Istoriia leib-gvardii konnogo polka, 1731–1848.* 4 parts. St. Petersburg, 1849.

Arkhiv kniazia Vorontsova. Vol. 12. Moscow, 1877.

Babich, Marina Vilenovna, ed. "Pis'ma Ekateriny II k G. A. Potemkinu." *Voprosy istorii* 12 (1994): 151–62.

Bantysh-Kamenskii, Dmitrii Nikolaevich. *Biografii rossiiskikh generalissimusov i general-fel'dmarshalov.* 4 parts. St. Petersburg, 1840–41.

Barskov, Ia., ed. "Pis'ma Ekateriny II k Potemkinu." Manuscript Division, Russian State Library (Moscow), *fond* 369 (V. D. Bonch-Bruevich), *k.* 375, *n.* 29.

———. "Pis'ma imperatritsy Ekateriny II k gr. P. V. Zavadovskomu. (1775–1777)." *Russkii istoricheskii zhurnal* 5 (1918): 223–57.

Bartenev, P. B. "Dopolnenie k stat'e o brake Ekateriny Velikoi s Potemkinym." *Russkii arkhiv* 2 (1911): 105–8.

———. "Iz zapisnoi knizhki." *Russkii arkhiv* 3 (1906): 613–23.

*Barton, H. Arnold. *Scandinavia in the Revolutionary Era, 1760–1815.* Minneapolis, MN, 1986.

Beskrovnyi, L. G. *Russkaia armiia i flot v XVIII veke (ocherki).* Moscow, 1958.

Birzhakova, E. E. "Shchegoli i shchegol'skoi zhargon v russkoi komedii XVIII veka." In *Iazyk russkikh pisatelei XVIII veka,* edited by Iu. S. Sorokin. Leningrad, 1981.

Black, Jeremy. *The Rise of the European Powers, 1679–1793.* London, 1990.

Bode, Andreas. *Die Flottenpolitik Katharinas II und die Konflikte mit Schweden und der Türkei (1768–1792).* Wiesbaden, 1979.

Brückner, A. G. *Potemkin.* 1891. Reprint. Moscow, 1996.

Catherine II. *Correspondence of Catherine the Great, when Grand Duchess, with Sir Charles Hanbury-Williams and Letters from Count Poniatowski.* Translated and edited by the Earl of Ilchester and Mrs. Langford-Brooke. London, 1928.

———. "Liubovnye zapisochki vysokoi osoby XVIII veka." Edited by P. Bartenev. *Russkii arkhiv* 3 (1881): 390–403.

———. *The Memoirs of Catherine the Great.* Edited by Dominique Maroger, with an introduction by G. P. Gooch, and translated by Moura Budberg. New York, [1955].

———."Pis'ma imperatritsy Ekateriny II k Grimmu (1774–1796)." *Sbornik imperatorskogo russkogo istoricheskogo obshchestva.* Vol. 23. St. Petersburg, 1878.

Catherine the Great and Gustav III. Swedish Nationalmuseum Exhibition Catalogue No. 610. Helsingborg, 1999.

[Cérenville, Jeanne Éleonore de.] *Memoirs of the Life of Prince Potemkin, Field-Marshal and Commander-in-Chief of the Russian Army, Grand Admiral of the Fleets . . . .* London, 1812.

Cross, Anthony. *By the Banks of the Neva: Chapters from the Lives of the British in Eighteenth-Century Russia.* Cambridge, 1997.

Dashkova, Ekaterina Romanovna. *The Memoirs of Princess Dashkova.* Translated and edited by Kyril Fitzlyon, with an introduction by Jehanne M. Gheith and an afterword by A. Woronzoff-Dashkoff. Durham, NC, 1995.

Dixon, Simon. *Catherine the Great.* Harlow, England, 2001.

Dmitriev-Mamonov, A. M. "Pis'ma grafa A. M. Dmitrieva-Mamonova k Ekaterine II. 1790–1795." *Russkii arkhiv* (1865): 633–41.

Druzhinina, E. I. *Kiuchuk-Kainardzhiiskii mir 1774 goda (ego podgotovka i zakliuchenie).* Moscow, 1955.

———. *Severnoe prichernomore v 1775–1800.* Moscow, 1959.

Dumas, François Ribadeau. *Cagliostro.* Translated by Elisabeth Abbott. London, 1967.

Eidelman, N. Ia., comp. "Pis'ma Ekateriny II k G. A. Potemkinu." *Voprosy istorii* 7 (1989): 111–34; 8 (1989): 110–24; 9 (1989): 97–111; 10 (1989): 102–16; 12 (1989): 107–23.

———. *Tvoi vosemnadtsyi vek. Prekrasen nash soiuz . . . .* Moscow, 1991.

Eliseeva, O. I. "Au, sokol moi . . . " *Nauka i religiia* 3 (1994): 8–10.

———. *Geopoliticheskie proekty G. A. Potemkina.* Moscow, 2000.

———. "K voprosu o russkom iazyke Ekateriny II v ee perepiske s G. A. Potemkinym." In *Issledovaniia po istochnikovedeniiu istorii Rossii (do 1917 g.)*. *Sbornik statei*. Moscow, 1993.

———. "Opredelenie vremeni i mesta voznikoveniia zapisok Ekateriny II i G. A. Potemkina drug drugu za 1774–1776 gg." In *Arkheografiia i istochnikovedenie istorii Rossii perioda feodalizma. Tezisy nauchnoi konferentsii*. Sverdlovsk, 1991.

———. "Perepiska Ekateriny II i G. A. Potemkina 1774–1776 gg. kak istochnik dlia vossozdaniia ikh istoriko-psikhologicheskikh portretov (po materialam OR GPB)." In *Sorok let nauchnomu studencheskomu kruzhku istochnikovedeniia istorii SSSR*. Moscow, 1990.

*———. *Perepiska Ekateriny II i G. A. Potemkina perioda vtoroi russko-turetskoi voiny (istochnikovedcheskoe issledovanie)*. Moscow, 1997.

———. "Rekonstruktsiia zapisok G. A. Potemkina k Ekaterine II za 1774–1776 gg." In *Realizm istoricheskogo myshleniia. Problemy otechestvennoi istorii perioda feodalizma. Chteniia, posviashchennye pamiati A. L. Stanislavskogo. Tezisy dokladov i soobshchenii*. Moscow, 1991.

Elliott, J. H., and L. W. B. Brockliss, eds. *The World of the Favourite*. New Haven, CT, 1999.

Engelgardt, L. N. *Zapiski*. Moscow, 1997.

Esterhazy, Valentin, Comte de. *Nouvelles lettres du comte Valentin Esterhazy à sa femme, 1792–1795*. Edited by Ernest Daudet. Paris, 1909.

Fisher, Alan. *The Crimean Tatars*. Stanford, 1978.

*———. *The Russian Annexation of the Crimea*. Cambridge, 1970.

Fuller, William C., Jr. *Strategy and Power in Russia, 1600–1914*. New York, 1992.

Fursenko, V. "Zorich, Semen Gavrilovich." *Russkii biograficheskii slovar'*. Vol. 7. St. Petersburg, 1896.

Gardiner, Robert, ed. *The Line of Battle: The Sailing Warship, 1650–1840*. Conway's History of the Ship. London, 1992.

Garnovskii, Mikhail. "Zapiski Mikhaila Garnovskogo." *Russkaia starina* 15 (1876): 9–38, 237–65, 471–99; 16 (1876): 1–32, 207–38, 399–440.

Glete, Jan. "Sails and Oars. Warships and Navies in the Baltic during the 18th Century (1700–1815)." In *Les marines de guerre européenes XVII–XVIIIe siècles*, edited by Martine Acerra, José Merino, and Jean Meyer. Paris, 1985.

Golovina, Varvara Nikolaevna. *Memoirs of Countess Golovine, a Lady at the Court of Catherine II*. Translated by G. M. Fox-Davies. London, 1910.

Gooch, G. P. *Catherine the Great, and other Studies*. London, 1954.

*Goodwin, A., ed. *The American and French Revolutions, 1763–1793*. Vol. 8 of *The New Cambridge Modern History*. Cambridge, 1965.

Gordin, M. A., B. G. Kipnis, I. A. Murav'eva, Z. E. Zhuravleva, eds. *G. A. Potemkin. Ot vakhmistra do fel'dmarshala. Vospominaniia. Dnevniki. Pis'ma*. St. Petersburg, 2002.

Gribovskii, A. M. *Zapiski o imperatritse Ekaterine Vtoroi*. 1847. Reprint. Moscow, 1989.

Gvosdev, Nikolas K. *Imperial Policies and Perspectives towards Georgia, 1760–1819*. New York, 2000.

Helbig, Georg von. *Russische Günstlinge*. Munich, 1917.

Hughes, Lindsey. *Russia in the Age of Peter the Great*. New Haven, CT, 1998.

Inalcik, Halil. *The Ottoman Empire: The Classical Age, 1300–1600*. Translated by Norman Itzkowitz and Colin Imber. New York, 1973.

Ingrao, Charles W. *The Habsburg Monarchy, 1618–1815*. 2d ed. Cambridge, 2000.

Ivanov, O. A., V. S. Lopatin, and K. A. Pisarenko. *Zagadki russkoi istorii. XVIII vek.* Moscow, 2000.

Ivanova, O. A. "Zagadki pisem Alekseia Orlova iz Ropshi." *Moskovskii zhurnal* 9 (1995): 13–19; 11 (1995): 10–18; 12 (1995): 9–17; 1 (1996): 37–43; 2 (1996): 32–39; 3 (1996) 25–29.

Kamenskii, Aleksandr B. *Pod seniiu Ekateriny.* St. Petersburg, 1992.

———. *The Russian Empire in the Eighteenth Century.* Translated and edited by David Griffiths. Armonk, NY, 1997.

———. *Zhizn' i sud'ba imperatritsy Ekateriny Velikoi.* Moscow, 1997.

Karnovich, E. P. *Zamechatel'nye bogatstva chastnykh lits v Rossii.* 1885. Reprint. Moscow, 1992.

Kashina-Evreinova, Anna. "Velikaia v liubvi. Ekaterina II po tol'ko chto opublikovan-nym pis'mam k kniaziu Potemkinu." *Illiustrirovannaia Rossiia* 40 (29 September 1934): 1–4; 41 (6 October 1934): 2–4; 42 (13 October 1934): 6–7; 43 (20 October 1934): 8–10.

Keep, John L. H. *Soldiers of the Tsar: Army and Society in Russia, 1462–1874.* Oxford, 1985.

Khrapovitskii, A. V. *Pamiatnye zapiski A. V. Khrapovitskogo.* Edited by G. N. Gennadi. 1862. Reprint. Moscow, 1990.

Kudriashov, K. "Zubov, Platon Aleksandrovich." *Russkii biograficheskii slovar'.* Vol. 7. St. Petersburg, 1896.

[Kuznetsova, Elvira Fedorovna, ed.] *Znamenitye rossiiane XVIII–XIX vekov. Biografii i portrety.* St. Petersburg, 1995.

Lambert, Andrew. *War at Sea in the Age of Sail, 1650–1850.* London, 2000.

Lashkov, F. *Kniaz' G. A. Potemkin-Tavricheskii, kak deiatel' Kryma.* Simferopol, 1890.

Lebedev, Petr. *Grafy Nikita i Petr Paniny.* St. Petersburg, 1863.

LeDonne, John P. *Ruling Russia: Politics and Administration in the Age of Absolutism, 1762–1796.* Princeton, NJ, 1984.

Ligne, Charles-Joseph, Prince de. *The Prince de Ligne: His Memoirs, Letters, and Miscellaneous Papers.* Translated and edited by Katharine Prescott Wormeley. 2 vols. Boston, 1902.

Longinov, M. N. "Liubimtsy Ekateriny Vtoroi." *Russkii arkhiv* 2 (1911): 319–20.

*Lopatin, V. S. *Ekaterina II i G. A. Potemkin. Lichnaia perepiska, 1769–1791.* Moscow, 1997.

*———. *Potemkin i Suvorov.* Moscow, 1992.

Loviagin, A. "Potemkin, Grigorii Aleksandrovich." *Russkii biograficheskii slovar'.* Vol. 14. St. Petersburg, 1905.

*Lukowski, Jerzy. *Liberty's Folly: The Polish-Lithuanian Commonwealth in the Eighteenth Century, 1697–1795.* London and New York, 1991.

*Madariaga, Isabel de. *Catherine the Great: A Short History.* New Haven, CT, 1990.

*———. *Russia in the Age of Catherine the Great.* New Haven, CT, 1981.

Meehan-Waters, Brenda. *Autocracy and Aristocracy: The Russian Service Elite of 1730.* New Brunswick, NJ, 1982.

———. "Catherine the Great and the Problem of Female Rule." *Russian Review* 34, no. 3 (July 1975): 293–307.

Mitchell, Donald W. *A History of Russian and Soviet Sea Power.* New York, 1974.

*Montefiore, Simon Sebag. *Prince of Princes: The Life of Potemkin.* London, 2000.

O privatnoi zhizni kniazia Potemkina. Potemkinskii prazdnik. Moscow, 1991.

Oakely, Stewart P. *War and Peace in the Baltic, 1560–1790.* London and New York, 1992.

Orlovskii, Ivan Ivanovich. *Na rodine svetleishego*. Smolensk, 1906.

Oudard, Georges, ed. *Lettres d'amour de Catherine II à Potemkine. Correspondence inédite*. Paris, 1934.

Panchenko, A. M. "'Potemkinskie derevni' kak kul'turnyi mif." *Vosemnadtsatyi vek* 14 (1983): 93–104.

Panchulidzev, S. *Sbornik biografii kavalergardov, 1762–1801*. St. Petersburg, 1903.

*Petrov, A. N. *Vtoraia turetskaia voina v tsarstvovanie imperatritsy Ekateriny II, 1787–1791*. 2 vols. St. Petersburg, 1880.

Polevoi, Nikolai. *Russkie polkovodtsy, ili zhizn' i podvigi rossiiskikh polkovodtsev, ot vremen imperatora Petra velikogo do tsarstvovania imperatora Nikolaia I*. St. Petersburg, 1845.

Poniatowski, Stanislaw August. *Mémoires du roi Stanislas-Auguste Poniatowski*. Vol. 1. Edited by Sergei Goryanov. St. Petersburg, 1914.

Potemkin, Grigorii Aleksandrovich. "Bumagi kn. G. A. Potemkina-Tavricheskogo." Edited by N. F. Dubrovin. *Sbornik voenno-istoricheskikh materialov* 6 (1893); 7 (1894); 8 (1895).

———. "Ordera kniazia Potemkina praviteliu Tavrichskoi oblasti." Edited by G. K. Kireenko. *Izvestiia Tavrichskoi uchenoi arkhivnoi kommissii* 3, 2d ed. (1897); 4, 2d ed. (1897); 6 (1888); 7 (1889); 8 (1889); 10 (1890); 11 (1890); 12 (1891); 13 (1891).

———. "Ordera kniazia Potemkina-Tavricheskogo." *Zapiski imperatorskogo Odesskogo obshchestva istorii i drevnostei* 4 (1858): 363–77.

———. "Ordera svetleishego kniazia Grigoriia Aleksandrovicha Potemkina-Tavricheskogo Novorossiiskogo general-gubernatora." *Zapiski imperatorskogo Odesskogo obshchestva istorii i drevnostei* 11 (1879) 324–434.

———. "Pis'ma svetleishego kniazia Grigoriia Aleksandrovicha Potemkina-Tavricheskogo raznym litsam." *Zapiski imperatorskogo Odesskogo obshchestva istorii i drevnostei* 8 (1872): 191–256.

———. "Rasporiazheniia (ordera) svetleishego kniazia Grigoriia Aleksandrovicha Potemkina Tavricheskogo praviteliu Tavricheskoi oblasti V. V. Kakhovskomu za 1784 i 1785 gg." *Zapiski imperatorskogo Odesskogo obshchestva istorii i drevnostei* 15 (1889): 594–710.

———. "Rasporiazheniia svetleishego kniazia Grigoriia Aleksandrovicha Potemkina-Tavricheskogo kasatel'no ustroeniia Tavrichskoi oblasti s 1781 po 1786 god." *Zapiski imperatorskogo Odesskogo obshchestva istorii i drevnostei* 12 (1881): 249–329.

———. "Sobstvennoruchnye ordera svetleishego kniazia Potemkina-Tavrichskogo kontr-admiralu grafu Voinovichu." *Zapiski imperatorskogo Odesskogo obshchestva istorii i drevnostei* 7 (1868): 199–218.

Pushkin, A. S. *Sobranie sochinenii*. Edited by D. D. Blagoi. Vol. 7. Moscow, 1962.

Raeff, Marc. "In the Imperial Manner." In *Catherine the Great: A Profile*, edited by Marc Raeff. New York, 1972.

Raleigh, Donald J., ed., A. A. Iskenderov, comp. *The Emperors and Empresses of Russia: Rediscovering the Romanovs*. Armonk, NY, 1996.

Ransel, David L. *The Politics of Catherinian Russia: The Panin Party*. New Haven, CT, 1975.

Razumovsky, Maria. *Die Rasumovskys. Eine Familie am Zarenhof*. Köln, 1998.

Redford, Bruce. *The Converse of the Pen: Acts of Intimacy in the Eighteenth-Century Familiar Letter*. Chicago, IL, 1986.

Rice, Tamara Talbot. *Elizabeth, Empress of Russia*. London, 1970.

Roberts, Michael. *The Age of Liberty: Sweden, 1719–1772.* Cambridge, 1986.

Roider, Karl A. *Austria's Eastern Question, 1700–1790.* Princeton, NJ, 1982.

Rumiantseva, Ekaterina Mikhailovna. *Pis'ma grafini E. M. Rumiantsevoi k ee muzhu, fel'dmarshalu grafu P. A. Rumiantsovu-Zadunaiskomu, 1762–1799.* Edited by D. A. Tolstoi. St. Petersburg, 1888.

*Samoilov, A. N. "Zhizn' i deianiia generala-fel'dmarshala kniazia Grigoriia Aleksandrovicha Potemkina-Tavricheskogo." *Russkii arkhiv* 4 (1867): 575–606; 7 (1867): 993–1028; 10 (1867): 1203–62; 12 (1867): 1537–78.

Scott, H. M. "The Rise of the First Minister in Eighteenth-Century Europe." In *History and Biography: Essays in Honour of Derek Beales,* edited by T. C. W. Blanning and David Cannadine. Cambridge, 1996.

Ségur, Louis Philippe, Comte du. *Memoirs and Recollections of Count Segur, Ambassador from France to the Courts of Russia and Prussia, etc., written by Himself.* 3 vols. London, 1825–27.

Semevskii, M. I. "Kniaz' Grigorii Aleksandrovich Potemkin-Tavricheskii, 1739–1791." *Russkaia starina* 12 (1875): 481–522, 681–700; 13 (1875): 20–40, 161–74; 14 (1875): 217–67.

———. "Kn. Platon Aleksandrovich Zubov. Biograficheskii ocherk, 1767–1822." *Russkaia starina* 16 (1876): 591–606; 17 (1876): 39–52, 437–62, 691–726.

*Shaw, Stanford. *Between Old and New: The Ottoman Empire under Sultan Selim III, 1789–1807.* Cambridge, MA, 1971.

Shcherbatov, Prince M. M. *On the Corruption of Morals in Russia.* Edited by A. Lentin. Cambridge, 1969.

Shepelev, L. E. *Chinovnyi mir Rossii: XVIII–nachalo XX v.* St. Petersburg, 1999.

[Shigin, Vladimir Vilenovich, comp.] *Pod andreevskim flagom.* Moscow, 1994.

Shubinskii, S. N. *Sobranie anekdotov o kniaze G. A. Potemkine-Tavricheskom.* 2d ed. St. Petersburg, 1869.

Shugurov, M. "Grobnitsa kniazia Potemkina." *Russkii arkhiv* 2 (1867): 203–18.

Stedingk, Curt Bogislaus Christophe, Comte de. *Un Ambassadeur de Suède de Catherine II, feld-maréchal comte de Stedingk: choix de dépeches diplomatiques, rapports secrets et lettres particulières de 1790 à 1796.* Edited by La Comtesse Brevern de la Gardie. Stockholm, 1919.

Trevenen, James. *A Memoir of James Trevenen.* Edited by Christopher Lloyd and R. C. Anderson. London, 1959.

Turgenev, Aleksandr Ivanovich, ed. *La cour de Russie il y a cent ans, 1725–1783. Extraits des dépêches des ambassadeurs anglais et français.* Paris, 1858.

Vasil'chikov, A. A. *Semeistvo Razumovskikh.* 5 vols. St. Petersburg, 1880–94.

Waliszewski, K. *The Romance of an Empress: Catherine II of Russia.* 1894. Reprint. N.p., 1968.

———. *The Story of a Throne (Catherine II of Russia).* 2 vols. 1895. Reprint. Freeport, NY, 1971.

Wilson, Arthur M. *Diderot.* New York, 1972.

*Zamoyski, Adam. *The Last King of Poland.* London, 1992.

Zavadovskii, P. V. *Pis'ma grafa P. V. Zavadovskogo k fel'dmarshalu grafu P. A. Rumiantsevu, 1775–1791 godov.* Edited by P. Maikov. St. Petersburg, 1901.

Index

Saltykov, Sergei Vasilievich, xviii, xlv n.29, 9, *10*
Samoilov, Aleksandr Nikolaevich, xxxviii, *26,* 45, 54, 69, 85, 116, 263, 274, 299, 301, 312, 317, 386, 392, 393
Samoilov, Nikolai Borisovich, 31, *32*
Samoilova, Princess Yekaterina Sergeevna, 219
Sapieha, Prince Kazimierz Nestor, 361, *362*
Sarti, Giuseppe, 355, *356*
Saxe-Coburg-Saalfeld, Prince Frederick Joseph of, *233,* 281, 298, 301, 302, 307–9, 310, 315, 316, 321, 326, 354
Scheffer, Count Ulrik, *94*
Schultz, Baron Wilhelm von, 300
Ségur, Count Louis-Phillipe, xxxviii, *162* 194, 210, 212, 217
Selim III, Sultan, *279,* 282, 308, 325, 328, 340, 356, 358, 365, 376, 377, 381, 384, 385, 386, 391–92
Selunsky, I., Russian vice consul, 185, 192
Seniavin, Dmitry Nikolaevich, 256, *257*
Seskär, 346
Sevastopol. *See* Akhtiar
Shagin Girey, khan, *98,* 115–25, 133–37, 144–45, 151–53
Shakhmatov, Prince Nikolai, *132,* 133
Shcherbachev, Aleskei Longinovich, 61, *62*
Shcherbatov, Prince Mikhail Mikhailovich, xxxvi
Shcherbatova, Princess Daria Fyodorovna, 279–80, 291–*92,* 293, 296–97, 304
Sherif Hasan Pasha, Grand Vizier, 325, 328, 330, *331,* 332, 334, 340–42, 347, 348, 356, 376
Shkurina, Maria Vasilievna, 304

Shumla, 325
Shuvalov, Count Andrei Petrovich, 312, *313*
Shuvalov, Ivan Ivanovich, xvi, xxxiii, xxxv, xl
Shuvalov, Count Pyotr Ivanovich, xxxv
Silistria, 5, 8, 9, 28
Sinelnikov, Ivan Maksimovich, 258
Sistova, 328, 356, 365, 374, 376, 379
Skavronsky, Count Pavel Martynovich, 91, 113–*14*
Slizov, Pyotr Petrovich, 346, *347,* 348
Solms, Count V. F. von, 13
Spiridov, Aleksei Grigorievich, 266, *267*
Spiridov, Grigory Andreevich, 40, 41
Sprengtporten, Baron Göran Magnus, 285, *286*
Stackelberg, Count Otto Magnus von, *74,* 271, 319, 320, 330, 332, 336, 338, 339, 366
Stedingk, Baron Curt von, 358, *359,* 363
Stockholm, 234
Strekalov, Stepan Fyodorovich, *20*
Struensee, Count Johann Freidrich, xxxiii
Sukhotin, Aleksandr Nikolaevich, 343, *344*
Suvorov-Rymniksky, Count Aleksandr Vasilievich, xxxii, 119, *135,* 143, 152, 188, 189–90, 196–97, 200, 206, 208–10, 211, 212, 223, 240, 248, 251, 257–60, 281–82, 298, 302, 305–6, 307–11, 328, 354, 365
Sveaborg, 260
Svensksund, 303, 327, 351–53

~ T ~

Tamara, Vasily Stepanovich, *151*
Tauride. *See* Crimea

Yelizavetgrad, 139, 219–21, 229, 231
Yermolov, Aleksandr Petrovich, xlii,
155–56, *160*

~ Z ~

Zaborovsky, Ivan Aleksandrovich,
227, *228*
Zagriazhsky, Aleksandr Artemevich,
62
Zanovichi brothers (Mark and Hannibal), 138
Zavadovsky, Pyotr Vasilievich, xxv,
xxvi, xxxvi, xli, *69–70*, 72, 85,
90, 93, 107, 133, 190, 196, 237
Zolotukhin, Vasily Ivanovich, *310*
Zorich, Semyon Gavrilovich, xlii, 90,
93, *94*, 95, 96, 98, 99, 105, 106,
109, 110, 137, 138, 156, 227, 228

Zubov, Dmitry Aleksandrovich,
314, *315*
Zubov, Nikolai Aleksandrovich,
299, 301
Zubov, Platon Aleksandrovich,
xxvii, xxviii, xxxviii, xl, xli, xliii,
280–81, *292*, 294, 295, 297–300,
303, 306, 308, 310, 317, 321,
323, 329, 333, 343, 344, 347,
348, 349, 351, 354, 355, 356,
358, 359, 363, 364, 365, 370,
372, 373, 375, 380, 385–89, 392,
393
Zubov, Valerian Aleksandrovich,
xxviii, *299*, 301, 303, 306–8,
310–11, 314, 347, 348, 368, 375,
378, 380–81